Documents of Witness

A History of
the Episcopal Church,
1782-1985

Don S. Armentrout
Robert Boak Slocum

Church Hymnal Corporation
445 Fifth Avenue
New York, NY 10016

Contents

Dedication

Dedicated to The Right Reverend Girault McArthur Jones
(June 30, 1904–   ) seventh Bishop of Louisiana,
March 9, 1949–August 31, 1969, and sixteenth Chancellor
of the University of the South, June 5, 1967–May 28, 1973.
Leader, Pastor, Author, Friend, and a Man of God.

Foreword

Oliver Cromwell once observed, "what are all histories but God manifesting himself." Nowhere is this more evident than in church history, the manifestation of God in the world through the story of God's people. *Documents of Witness: A History of the Episcopal Church, 1782 to 1985* is a significant collection of seminal documents that makes manifest the story of the Episcopal Church. It is an invaluable historical account and a unique contribution in telling us who and whose we are as God's people.

With over one hundred sixty documents broadly covering the many aspects of the Episcopal Church, this volume represents a "tour de force" in terms of its breadth and inclusivity. The selections disclose different perspectives that are representative and aid in our understanding of the church's evolution since its beginning over two hundred years ago.

During this Decade of Evangelism we are called to share our stories with others. An obvious presupposition is that we know our story. Don Armentrout and Rob Slocum, in gathering the varied documents in this important volume, provide a clearer sense of our own identity and thereby enable us to tell our story with confidence and conviction. Furthermore, this important collection of primary documents will serve us well as we share our story with others in terms of ecumenical conversations and inter-faith dialogue.

Given the pluralism and secularism of our age, a clear rehearsal of our corporate memory as a church is needed in aiding our sense of identity and authority for contemporary ministry. I commend this volume as an important historical document, and as a book that will be meaningful for those who desire a clearer sense of their own identity and past to empower them for the challenging vocation of ministry in these times.

Craig B. Anderson, Ph.D.
VIII Bishop of the Diocese of South Dakota
President and Dean of The General Theological
Seminary of the Episcopal Church
Advent 1993

Acknowledgments

The writers acknowledge the kind assistance of the following persons and institutions: V. Nelle Bellamy, Mark J. Duffy, T. Matthew DeWaelsche, May D. Lofgreen, and Andrea Matlak of the Archives of the Episcopal Church USA; Thomas Edward Camp, former Associate Librarian, James Warren Dunkly, Associate Librarian, Sue E. Armentrout, Head of Interlibrary Loans, John Livingston Janeway IV, Assistant Librarian, and Anne Armour, Archivist, DuPont Library, the University of the South; Marion J. Hatchett, Professor of Liturgics and Music, the School of Theology; Dean Guy F. Lytle III, the School of Theology; James David Jones, managing editor of *Sewanee Theological Review*, who managed the typesetting of the manuscript; Charles Francis Edgar III, a student at the School of Theology, who proofread the manuscript; Thomas Keith Talbert, a student at the School of Theology, who assisted in the research; Susan Pullen Sloan, a student at the School of Theology, who prepared the index; Mitzi Garrett and Julia Randle of the Bishop Payne Library, Virginia Theological Seminary; Alvin O. Turner, Northwestern Oklahoma State University; John E. Booty, historiographer of the Episcopal Church; Byron D. Stuhlman, who read the manuscript and made many helpful suggestions; Owanah Anderson, Head of American Indian/Alaska Native Ministries of the Episcopal Church; Ann Elizabeth Proctor McElligott, associate rector of St. Paul's Church, Indianapolis; The Ven. Charles F. Rehkopf, historiographer of the Diocese of Missouri; The Rt. Rev. William C. Wantland; and the staffs of the DeKoven Center, Racine, Wisconsin, *The Living Church*, Milwaukee, the Library and Archives of Nashotah House, and the Wisconsin Historical Society.

Preface

This volume is a documentary history of the Episcopal Church from 1782 to 1985. It begins with 1782 because that is when the Church of England in the American colonies began to think and plan seriously for its formation and organization as a church in the United States.

The guiding principle in selecting the documents was two-fold: (1) to address the issue of Episcopal identity, and (2) to show the adaptation of the Episcopal Church to the American environment. The documents selected illustrate what the Episcopal Church believes and what it has done. They also show how the Episcopal Church has developed in the context of American culture, such as its response to the realties of the Civil War and a divided nation.

The documents are arranged chronologically in thematic chapters. Care has been taken to see that the documents are widely representative of various positions in the church. Official and non-official selections are included. Numerous authorities on the history of the Episcopal Church have been consulted for ideas and suggestions.

Many of the selections in the collection are excerpts. Ellipsis points are used to indicate the omission of a paragraph or paragraphs. An excerpt is identified at the end of the citation.

This book includes writings drawn from the history of the Episcopal Church from 1782 through 1985. Although there were many significant documents published subsequent to 1985, these now seem more like current news than history. Such documents have not been included. The one exception to this "rule of thumb" is the concluding chapter on "Identity," which includes documents from a variety of sources that are of general and timeless interest.

The editors hope that the reader can hear the history and drama of the Episcopal Church through the many voices assembled here. The goal has been to let these witnesses speak for themselves, with few editorial interruptions. These documents have much to say about the Episcopal Church: what it has been, what it is, and what it needs to be.

D.S.A. & R.B.S.
Sewanee, Tennessee

Permission to Publish

The Domestic and Foreign Missionary Society of the Episcopal Church granted permission to reprint the following: Absalom Jones, "A Thanksgiving Sermon," 2-7, and Nathan Wright, Jr., "Self-Development and Self-Respect," 52-56, in John M. Burgess, *Black Gospel/White Church* (New York: Seabury Press, 1982); Massey H. Shepherd, Jr., *The Worship of the Church*, 97-99, 102-106 (Greenwich, Conn.: Seabury Press, 1952); Charles P. Price and Louis Weil, *Liturgy for Living*, 18-19, 30-31 (New York: Seabury Press, 1979); Massey Shepherd, "Praying," 49-53, and Urban T. Holmes, "Education for Liturgy," 131-135, 137, in Malcolm C. Burson, ed., *Worship Points the Way: A Celebration of the Life and Work of Massey Hamilton Shepherd, Jr.* (New York: Seabury Press, 1981); Hughell E. W. Fosbroke, *God in the Heart of Things* (Greenwich, Conn.: Seabury Press, 1962), 50-56; *The Church Looks Ahead to the New Curriculum Specifications* (New York: National Council, Protestant Episcopal Church, 1948), 7-10, 40, 46-47; Theodore O. Wedel, *The Church's Teaching: An Introduction* (New York: National Council, Protestant Episcopal Church, 1949), 5-10, 16-19, 21-23; Lyman C. Ogilby, "The Church's Mission II," 246-248, 250-253, in John B. Coburn and W. Norman Pittenger, eds., *Viewpoint: Some Aspects of Anglican Thinking* (Greenwich, Conn.: Seabury Press, 1959); W. Norman Pittenger, *The Christian View of Sexual Behavior* (Greenwich, Conn.: Seabury Press, 1954), 61-65; Angus Dun, *Behold the City of God* (New York: Woman's Auxiliary to the National Council, 1946), 40-45; H. Boone Porter, *The Day of Light: The Biblical and Liturgical Meaning of Sunday* (Greenwich, Conn.: Seabury Press, 1960), 81-82; and John H. MacNaughton, *Stewardship: Myth and Method: A Program Guide for Ministers and Lay Leaders* (New York: Seabury Press, 1975), 42-43. All of the above are reprinted "Courtesy of the Archives of the Episcopal Church." George Washington Doane, "The Missionary Bishop," and James O. S. Huntington, "Beginnings of the Religious Life for Men in the American Church," are reprinted with permission from *Anglican and Episcopal History/The Historical Magazine of the Protestant Episcopal Church*, Vol. IV, No. 3 (September 1935): 180-194, and Vol. II, No. 1 (March 1933): 35-36. Winfred Douglas, *Church Music in History*

Background and Origins of the Episcopal Church (1782-1789)

Introduction

The Anglican Church in the American colonies was in disarray after the American Revolution. Many Anglicans fled the colonies during this time, and the Anglican Church itself was suspect because of its ties to English authority. The colonial church had been nurtured by English missionary societies such as the Society for the Propagation of the Gospel and the Society for Promoting Christian Knowledge. Support from these societies was unavailable after the war. In some colonies the Anglican Church was accustomed to economic benefits of establishment such as income from farm property dedicated to the church (glebes). These sources of income were lost, and the church was left in a depressed condition. Most importantly, the church's doctrine, discipline, and worship called for the presence of bishops in the church, and there were no bishops. Before the end of the war, William White proposed the temporary solution of a church without bishops. Samuel Seabury, bishop-elect of Connecticut, was refused ordination in England because the loyalty oath to the crown could not be dispensed at an ordination. Finally, Seabury was ordained bishop by the Scottish Episcopal Church, with no loyalty oath required. Not long afterwards, the loyalty oath was legally dispensed for bishops serving outside the British Empire, allowing William White of Pennsylvania and Samuel Provoost of New York to be ordained bishops at Lambeth. The two lines of the episcopacy in America were subsequently reconciled, and joined with the ordination of Thomas Claggett of Maryland in 1792. The episcopacy was passed to America. But the church still faced the challenge of organizing 13 independent state church bodies into a national church federation. The Episcopal Church was organized through

1

General Conventions in 1785, 1786, and 1789, with the Church Constitution completed at the 1789 General Convention in Philadelphia. The emergent constitution of the Episcopal Church paralleled in many ways the federal democracy of American civil government. The church was organized by states rather than "dioceses," and governed by a bicameral legislative body.

1.

William White, "The Case of the Episcopal Churches in the United States Considered," 1782

William White (April 4, 1748–July 17, 1836) was the rector of the United Parishes of St. Peter's and Christ Church, Philadelphia, from 1779 until his death. He was consecrated Bishop of Pennsylvania on February 4, 1787 in London's Lambeth Palace. He was Presiding Bishop, July 28, 1789-October 3, 1789, and September 8, 1795-July 17, 1836. White's ministry is commemorated in the Episcopal Calendar of the Church Year on July 17. "The Case" was published on August 6, 1782, when White thought there was little present likelihood in securing ordination for American bishops in England. He called for ordination by presbyters on a temporary basis.

The Case, &c.
Chapter I.

To form an idea of the situation of the Episcopal[1] Churches in the present crisis, we must observe the change their religious system has undergone in the late revolution.

On whatever principles the independence of the United States may be supposed to rest; whether merely on establishments which have very probable appearances of being permanent, or on withdrawing the protection of the former sovereign, or (as the author of these sheets believes) on the inherent right of the community to resist and effectually to exclude unconstitutionally and oppressive claims, there result from it the reciprocal duties of protection and allegiance, enforced by the most powerful sanctions of natural and revealed religion.

It may reasonably be presumed, that, in general, the members of the Episcopal Churches are friendly to the principles, on which the present governments were formed; a fact particularly obvious in the southern states, where the Episcopalians, who are a majority of the citizens, have engaged and persevered

---

[1]The general term "Episcopal" is usually applied, among us, to the churches professing the religious principles of the Church of England. It is thought by the author to be sufficiently descriptive, because the other Episcopal Churches in America are known by names peculiar to themselves.

in the war, with as much ardour and constancy as their neighbours. Many even of those whose sentiments were at first unfavourable to the revolution, now wish for its final establishment, as a most happy event; some from an earnest desire of peace, and others from the undistinguished oppressions and ravages of the British armies. Such persons accordingly acknowledge allegiance, and pay obedience to the sovereignty of the states.

Inconsistent with the duties resulting from this allegiance, would be their subjection to any spiritual jurisdiction connected with the temporal authority of a foreign state. Such a dependence is contrary to the fundamental principles of civil society, and therefore cannot be required by the Scriptures; which, being accommodated to the civil policy of the world at large, neither interfered with the constitution of states as found established at the time of their promulgation, nor handed down to succeeding ages any injunctions of such a tendency.

To apply these observations to the case of the Episcopal Churches in the United States. They have been heretofore subject to the ecclesiastical authority of the Bishop of London. This authority was derived under a commission from the crown; which, though destitute of legal operation, found a general acquiescence on the part of the churches; being exercised no farther than to the necessary purposes of ordaining and licensing ministers. Hereby a connection was formed, between the spiritual authority in England and the Episcopal Churches in America, the latter constituting a part of the Bishop of London's diocese.

But this connection is dissolved by the revolution. Had it been matter of right, it would have ceased with the authority of the crown; being founded on consent, and the ground changed, it cannot be allowed of in future, consistently with the duties resulting from our allegiance.[2] Even suppose the Bishop of London hereafter exempted, by act of Parliament, from the necessity of exacting the oaths, a dependence on his lordship and his successors in that See, would be liable to the reproach of foreign influence, and render Episcopalians less qualified than those of other communions, to be entrusted by their country; neither (as may be presumed) will it be claimed after the acknowledgement of the civil independence, being contrary to a principle clearly implied in many of the institutions of the Church of England, particularly in the 34th article of religion; which asserts, that "every particular or national church hath authority to ordain, change, and abolish ceremonies or rites of the church, ordained only by man's authority, so that all things be done to edifying." Though the Episcopal Churches in these states will not be national or legal establishments, the same principle applies, being the danger of foreign jurisdiction.

---

[2] Were the British colonies independent of their parent kingdom, the Episcopalians in this country would be a society independent of the national church.

3

The ecclesiastical power over the greater number of the churches, formerly subsisting in some legislative bodies on this continent, is also abrogated by the revolution. In the southern states, where the Episcopal Churches were maintained by law, the assemblies might well have been supposed empowered, in conjunction with the other branches of legislation, to regulate their external government; but now, when the establishments are overturned, it would ill become those bodies, composed of men of various denominations (however respectable collectively and as individuals) to enact laws for the Episcopal Churches, which will no doubt, in common with others, claim and exercise the privilege of governing themselves.

All former jurisdiction over the churches being thus withdrawn, and the chain which held them together broken, it would seem that their future continuance can be provided for only by voluntary associations for union and good government. It is therefore of the utmost consequence to discover and ascertain the principles, on which such associations should be framed.

Chapter III.

The author offers the following sketch of a frame of government, though he is far from thinking it complete; to make it so even according to his own ideas, would carry him beyond the compass intended in this essay.

As the churches in question extend over an immense space of country, it can never be expected, that representatives from each church should assemble in one place; it will be more convenient for them to associate in small districts, from which representatives may be sent to three different bodies, the continent being supposed divided into that number of larger districts. From these may be elected a body representing the whole.

In each small district, there should be elected a general vestry or convention, consisting of a convenient number (the minister to be one) from the vestry or congregation of each church, or of every two or more churches, according to their respective ability of supporting a minister. They should elect a clergyman their permanent president; who, in conjunction with other clergymen to be also appointed by the body, may exercise such powers as are purely spiritual, particularly that of admitting to the ministry; the presiding clergyman, and others to be liable to be deprived for just causes, by a fair process, and under reasonable laws; meetings to be held as often as occasion may require.

The assemblies in the three larger districts may consist of a convenient number of members, sent from each of the smaller districts severally within their bounds, equally composed of clergy and laity, and voted for by those orders promiscuously; the presiding clergyman to be always one, and these bodies to meet once in every year.

4

The continental representative body may consist of a convenient number from each of the larger districts, formed equally of clergy and laity, and among the clergy, formed equally of presiding ministers and others; to meet statedly once in three years. The use of this and the preceding representative bodies is to make such regulations, and receive appeals in such matters only, as shall be judged necessary for their continuing one religious communion.

These are (what was promised) no more than outlines; which it will not be proper to dismiss, without a few observations on the degree of power to be exercised, in matters of faith, worship, and government.

For the doctrinal part, it would perhaps be sufficient to demand of all admitted to the ministry, or engaged in ecclesiastical legislation, the questions contained in the book of ordination; which extend no farther than an acknowledgement of the scriptures, as a rule of faith and life; yet some general sanction may be given to the thirty-nine articles of religion, so as to adopt their leading sense;[3] which is here proposed rather as a chain of union, than for exacting entire uniformity of sentiment. If the last be considered as a desirable object, the articles have undeniably been found insufficient for the purpose; which is not here said from an opinion that such was the intention of the compilers, but rather with a conviction that they designedly left room for a considerable latitude of sentiment; if to the above there be objected the danger of a public opposition between ministers, this obvious answer may be made; that the strictest tests ever devised cannot be so effectual to prevent such conduct, as the regulation contained in the 53d canon; which considers it as indecent and punishable, independently of the merits of the doctrines litigated.

As to divine worship, there must no doubt be somewhere the power of making necessary and convenient alterations in the service of the church. But it ought to be used with great moderation; otherwise the communion will become divided into an infinite number of smaller ones, all differing from one another and from that in England; from whence we may expect considerable numbers to migrate hereafter to this country; who if they find too wide a deviation from the ancient practice, will probably form an independent communion of their own. Whatever may in other respects be determined on this head, it is presumed the

---

[3]Suppose, for instance, a form resembling that which Dr. Ferdinando Warner, a late ecclesiastical Historian of the Episcopal church, says (book 16) was proposed in the reign of Charles II. by the Lord Keeper Bridgman, Bishop Wilkins and Chief Justice Hale, "to serve instead of all former subscriptions." The form was this, "I do hereby profess and declare, that I approve the doctrine, worship and government established in the church of England as containing all things necessary to salvation, and that I will not endeavour by myself or any other, directly or indirectly, to being in any doctrine contrary to that which is so established; and I do hereby promise that I will continue in the church of England, and will not do anything to disturb the peace thereof."

Episcopalians are generally attached to that characteristic of their communion, which prescribes a settled form of prayer.

On the subject of government, whether civil or ecclesiastical, there is great truth and beauty in the following observation of the present Bishop of St Asaph, "the great art of governing consists in not governing too much." Perhaps it would be sufficient, if an immoral life were followed by exclusion from the sacrament and ecclesiastical employment; deprivation from church benefices following of course. The above is not to be understood as excluding the enforcing such rules, as are necessary to preserve decency and order. As to excommunication or an entire separation from the church, however necessary it was in the primitive ages, when christianity itself, being not generally known, and misrepresented as a sanction for lewdness, treason and clandestine murders, must have been essentially wounded by the immoralities of any of its professors; there is great room to doubt their being the same use in it at present, when the vices of a professing christian are universally known to be opposite to the precepts of his religion. Such are the tyranny and hypocrisy too frequently arising from the exercise of this power, that it may be thought safest to leave men to those great sanctions of duty, the will of God and a future retribution; attended as they will generally be with a sense of shame, dissuading from actions so notoriously scandalous, as to be a foundation for church censures.

In the preceding pages, the idea of superintending ministers has been introduced; but not a word has been said of the succession supposed necessary to constitute the Episcopal character; and this has been on purpose postponed, as demanding a more minute discussion.

Chapter IV.

On the subject of Episcopacy, the general opinion of the churches in question is of peculiar consequence; yet it can be collected only from circumstances; to assist in ascertaining it, the two following facts are stated.

Wherever these churches have been erected, the ecclesiastical government of the church of England has been adhered to; they have depended on the English bishops for ordination of their clergy, and on no occasion expressed a dissatisfaction with Episcopacy. This, considering the liberty they enjoyed in common with others, of forming their churches on whatever plan they liked best, is a presumptive proof of their preferring the Episcopal government; especially as it subjected them under the former connection to many inconveniences, such as sending to the distance of three thousand miles for ordination, the scandal sometimes brought on the church by the ordination of low and vicious persons,[4] the difficulty of getting rid of immoral ministers, and that several of the clergy formed attachments of which this country has been always jealous, and which have at last proved extremely prejudicial to her interests.

On the other hand, there cannot be produced an instance of laymen in America, unless in the very infancy of the settlements, soliciting the introduction of a bishop;[5] it was probably by a great majority of them thought an hazardous experiment. How far the prerogative of the king as head of the church might be construed to extend over the colonies, whether a bishop would bring with him that part of the law which respects ecclesiastical matters, and whether the civil powers vested in bishops in England would accompany that order to America, were questions which for aught they knew would include principles and produce consequences, dangerous and destructive to their civil rights.[6]

From these two facts it may fairly be inferred, that the Episcopalians on this continent will wish to institute among themselves an Episcopal government, as soon as it shall appear practicable, and that this government will not be attended with the danger of tyranny, either temporal or spiritual.

But it is generally understood, that the succession cannot at present be obtained. From the parent church most unquestionably it cannot; whether from any is presumed to be more than we can at present be informed. But the proposal to constitute a frame of government, the execution of which shall depend on the pleasure of persons unknown, differing from us in language, habits, and perhaps in religious principles, has too ludicrous an appearance to deserve consideration; the peculiar circumstances of the war in which our country is engaged preclude us from procuring the succession in those quarters to which alone application could consistently be made; the danger of offending the British government constraining (perhaps) a refusal of what it would of course be indelicate in us to ask.

---

[4]Generally by deceptions on the Bishop of London.

[5]If there has been any, it must have been from so few, as rather to corroborate than weaken the sentiment conveyed.

[6]Whether the above appendages would have accompanied an English bishop to America, the author is no judge. That they were generally feared by the Episcopalian laity, he thinks the only way of accounting for the cold reception they gave (a fact universally known) to every proposal for the introduction of a bishop. Those who pleaded for the measure on a plan purely spiritual, thought he would not be invested, by the laws of England, with such powers; but in case it had proved otherwise, they proposed the limiting him by act of parliament. What the people would have thought of measures, which must have required an act of that body to render them harmless, no person formerly acquainted with their temper and sentiments need be told; and whether they judged right or not, recent events have abundantly shown.

Now, on the other hand, to depart from Episcopacy, would be giving up a leading characteristic of the communion; which, however indifferently considered as to divine appointment, might be productive of all the evils generally attending changes of this sort. On the other hand, by delaying to adopt measures for the continuance of the ministry, the very existence of the churches is hazarded, and duties of positive and indispensable obligation are neglected.

The conduct meant to be recommended, as founded on the preceding sentiments, is to include in the proposed frame of government a general approbation of Episcopacy, and a declaration of an intention to procure the succession, as soon as conveniently may be; but in the mean time to carry the plan into effect without waiting for the succession.

The first part of this proposal is conceived to be founded on the plain dictates of propriety, prudence, and moderation; for if the undertaking proceed on acknowledged principles, there will be far less shock to ancient habits, and less cause of intestine divisions, than if new principles are to be sought for and established. To illustrate this by an allusion; had our old governments been so adjusted to the genius of the people and their present circumstances, as at the revolution to have required no farther change than what necessarily arose from the extinction of royal authority, it is obvious, that many pernicious controversies would have been prevented. Such, however, except in a few instances, was not the happiness of the colonies. But it is precisely the situation of the Episcopal churches in their religious concerns; none of their constituent principles being thereby changed, but what were founded on the authority of the king.

In the minds of some, the idea of Episcopacy will be connected with that of immoderate power; to which it may be answered, that power becomes dangerous, not from the precedency of one man, but from his being independent. Had Rome been governed by a presbytery instead of a bishop; and had that presbytery been invested with the independent riches and dominion of the papal see; it is easy to conceive, of their acquiring as much power over the christian world, as was ever known in a Gregory or a Paul.

It may be further objected, that Episcopacy is anti-republican; and therefore opposed to those ideas which all good citizens ought to promote, for securing the peace and happiness of the community. But this supposed relation between Episcopacy and monarchy arises from confounding English Episcopacy with the subject at large. In the early ages of the church, it was customary to debate and determine in a general concourse of all christians in the same city; among whom the Bishop was no more than president. Matters were indeed too often conducted tumultuously, and after a manner which no prudent and peaceable man would wish to see imitated; but the churches were not the less Episcopal on that account. Very few systems of religious discipline on this continent are equally

8

republican with that proposed in the preceding pages. The adage of King James I. "No Bishop no King," and "No King no bishop," ought only to be understood concerning that degree of Episcopal power, together with its civil appendages, of which he certainly meant it.

But it will be also said, that the very name of "Bishop" is offensive; if so, change it for another; let the superior clergymen be a president, a superintendent, or in plain English, and, according to the literal translation of the original, an overseer. However, if names are to be reprobated, because the powers annexed to them have been abused, there are few appropriated to either civil or ecclesiastical distinctions, which would retain their places in our catalogue.

The other part of the proposal was an immediate execution of the plan, without waiting for the Episcopal succession. This is founded on the presumption, that the worship of God and the instruction and reformation of the people are the principal objects of ecclesiastical discipline: if so, to relinquish them from a scrupulous adherence to Episcopacy, is sacrificing the substance to the ceremony.

It will be said, we ought to continue as we are, with the hope of obtaining it hereafter. But are the acknowledged ordinances of Christ's holy religion to be suspended for years, perhaps as long as the present generation shall continue, out of delicacy to a disputed point, and that relating only to externals? It is submitted, how far such ideas encourage the suspicion of want of attachment to any particular church, except so far as is subservient to some civil system. All the obligations of conformity to the divine ordinances, all the arguments which prove the connexion between public worship and the morals of a people, combine to urge the adopting some speedy measures, to provide for the public ministry in these churches; if such as have been above recommended should be adopted, and the Episcopal succession afterwards obtained, any supposed imperfections of the intermediate ordinations might, if it were judged proper, be supplied without acknowledging their nullity, by a *conditional* ordination resembling that of *conditional baptism* in the liturgy; the above was an expedient proposed by Archbishop Tillotson, Bishops Patrick, Stillingfleet, and others, at the revolution, and had been actually practised in Ireland by Archbishop Bramhall.[7]

But it will be said, the dropping the succession even for a time would be a departure from the principles of the Church of England. This prejudice is too common not to deserve particular attention.

---

[7]Nichol's Defence of the Church of England, Introduction.

9

Chapter VI.

It is to be expected, that the far greater number of writers in defence of Episcopal government, confine their observations to the ordinary state of the church, without giving their opinions on supposed cases of necessity. Yet, it if were required to multiply authorities, and writers were consulted with that view, it is probable that many more than the following might be produced. But, as the lawfulness of deviation, in cases of necessity, is a fair inference from the sentiments of expressly to the purpose (perhaps) all, it will be sufficient if those quoted rank among the most respectable for their authority.

The first mentioned shall be the venerable Hooker. His books on ecclesiastical polity are universally allowed to be a work of masterly judgment, and deep erudition; they are frequently spoken of as containing the most rational and complete defence of the Church of England; and were recommended by king Charles I. (whose attachment to Episcopacy will not be doubted) as the best for fixing the principles of his children, on those questions which had distracted the nation. This accomplished writer, after asserting with great zeal the authority of Episcopal government, makes the following exception; "when the *exigence of necessity* doth constrain to leave the usual ways of the church, which otherwise we would willingly keep; when the church must needs have some ordained and neither hath nor can have possibly a bishop to ordain; in case of *such necessity* the law of God hath oftentimes and may give place: and therefore we are not, simply and without exception, to urge a lineal descent of power from the apostles, by continued succession in every effectual ordination."[8]

The same great man, speaking in another place of some churches not Episcopal, says, "This their defect and imperfection, I had rather lament in such a case than exaggerate; considering that men oftentimes, without any fault of their own, may be driven to want that kind of polity or regiment, which is best; and to content themselves with that which either the irremediable error of former times, or the *necessity of the present* hath cast upon them."[9]

Had Mr. Hooker been asked to define "*the exigence of necessity*," could he have imagined any more urgent than the case in question? Or had he been enquired of concerning the "*necessities of present times*," could he have mentioned any in the cases to which he alludes (those of Scotland and Geneva,) so strongly pleading for the liberty he allows, as those now existing in America?

---

[8]Ecclesiastical Polity, Book 7, Section 14. *Hooker*
[9]Ibid, Book 3, Section 11.

10

The name of Bishop Hoadly will probably be as long remembered, as any on the list of British worthies; and will never be mentioned without veneration of the strength of his abilities, the liberality of his sentiments, and his enlightened zeal for civil liberty. He has written in defence of Episcopal government, with more argument and better temper than is commonly to be met with in controversial writings. This amiable prelate expresses himself as follows, "as to the credit of the reformed churches abroad we think it no presumption, as we censure them not, who *in a case of necessity* went out of the ordinary method, so to expect they will not censure us for not approving such irregularities, where there is *no such necessity* for them.[10] In another place he says, "for my own part I cannot argue that Episcopacy is *essential* to a christian church, because it is of apostolical institution; and on the other hand, I do argue, that we are obliged to the utmost of our knowledge, to conform ourselves to the apostolical model, unless in such where the imitation is *impracticable* or would manifestly do more hurt than good to the church of Christ; neither of which can possibly be affirmed in the *ordinary* state of the church."[11]

What necessity was there of the "reformed churches abroad" equal to ours? Is not an immediate imitation of the ancient usage *"impracticable?"* Would not such a plan as has been proposed be conforming (as far as circumstances allow) to our ideas of "the apostolic model?"

The character of Archbishop Ur[s]her for extensive learning and fervent piety is generally known; and is distinguished both by his great moderation on the subject of Episcopacy, and by the service it has received from his indefatigable researches. In a letter to Dr. Bernard he writes thus, "in places where bishops *cannot be had*, the ordination of presbyters stands valid."[12] What part of the christian world could the learned primate have named, of which it could have been so properly said as it may be of ours, that "ordination by bishops *cannot be had?*"

The great reformer and martyr Archbishop Cranmer was one of the first characters of the age in which he lived, for learning, piety, and virtue; and is supposed to have done more than any other towards compiling the liturgy of the Church of England; "His equal (says Dr. Warner) was never yet seen in the see of Canterbury, and I will take upon me to say, that his superior never will." In the reign of Henry VIII, according to Bishop Burnet, there were proposed by the

---

[10]Reasonableness of conformity, part I.
[11]Defence of Episcopal ordination, conclusion.
[12]Quoted from Neale's History.

King, to this great man, in conjunction with other learned divines, certain question, among which are the two following, with the Archbishop's answers annexed:

Question. Whether if it fortuned a Prince Christian, to conquer certain dominions of infidels, having none but the temporal learned men with him, it be defended by God's law, that he and they should preach the word of God there or no, and also make and constitute priests there or no?

Answer. It is not against God's law; but contrariwise they ought indeed so to do; and there be histories that witness, that some christian princes and other laymen have done the same.

Question. Whether it be defended by God's law, that if it so fortuned that all the bishops and priests of a region were dead; and that the word of God should remain there unpreached; and the sacrament of baptism and others unministered; that the King of that region should make bishops and priests to supply the same or no?

Answer. It is not forbidden by God's law.

The above may be offered as the opinions of not only Cranmer, but also of most of the eminent bishops and other clergy of that period; for whoever will attend to all the questions with the several answers as recorded by Burnet, will find, that although the Archbishop seems singular in his sentiments as to the original institution of bishops and priests, they generally agree with him on the supposed occasions of necessity. On the former subject, the learned historian believes, that Cranmer soon afterwards changed his opinion: but the reason assigned for that belief, if it be well founded, does not extend to the purpose for which his authority is here cited.

Now every circumstance in the cases supposed makes the principle apply, with the greater force, to that now under consideration. If a christian King may on an emergency constitute a bishop, much more may the whole body of the churches interested; especially when they interfere not thereby with the civil magistrate. If a Prince would be justifiable in taking such a step, rather than have recourse to the spiritual authority of some neighbouring and allied kingdom, much more would we, who labour under peculiar political difficulties. If it were commendable on the mere hope of converting infidels to the christian faith, it would be more so, for the purpose of maintaining the principles of christian knowledge and practice, among those who are already of the number of its professors. If a prince ought to do this from concern for the spiritual welfare of his subjects, much rather ought we, for that of ourselves and our children.

On the credit of the preceding names, the author rests this the last part of his subject; and if his sentiments should meet with an unfavorable reception, he will find no small consolation from being in a company so respectable.

12

Perhaps, however, there would be little room for difference of sentiment among the well informed, if the matter were generally taken up with seriousness and moderation, and were to rest on religious principles alone. But unhappily there are some, in whose ideas the existence of their church is so connected with that of the civil government of Britain, as to preclude their concurrence in any system, formed on a presumed final separation of the two countries. Prejudices of this sort will admit of no conviction but such as may arise from future events; and are therefore no farther considered in this performance, than with a sincere sorrow, that any persons, professing to be of the communion of the church of England, should so far mistake the principles of that church, as to imagine them widely different from what form the religion of the scriptures; which, as Bishop Sherlock observes, "stand clear of all disputes about the rights of princes and subjects; so that such disputes must be left to be decided by principles of natural equity and the constitution of the country."[13]

As for those who are convinced that the "United States," have risen to an independent rank among the nations or who even think that such may probably be the event of the war, they are loudly called on to adopt measures for the continuance of their churches, as they regard the public worship of God, the foundation of which is immutable; as they esteem the benefit of the sacraments, which were instituted by the supreme bishop of the church; and as they are bound to obey the scriptures, which enjoin us "not to forsake the assembling of ourselves together, as the manner of some is."

More especially is this their duty, if they entertain a peculiar preference for the principles and worship of their own communion, from a persuasion of their superior excellence. That the church of England is a creature of the state, an engine of civil policy, and not otherwise to be maintained than by human laws, has been said by some, as a reason for their dissenting from her. If the same prejudice has been with others a reason for conformity, it is to be hoped they are comparatively few, and that the great majority of Episcopalians, believing that their faith and worship are rational and scriptural, have no doubt of their being supported, independent of state establishments; nay, it is presumed there are many, who, while they sincerely love their fellow christians of every denomination, knowing (as one of their prayers expresses) that the "body of Christ" comprehends "the blessed company of all faithful people," are more especially attached to their own mode of worship, *perhaps* from education, but *as they conceive*, from its being most agreeable to reason and scripture, and its most nearly resembling the pattern of the purest ages of the church. On the consciences of

---

[13]Vol. 4. Discourse 13th.

such, above all others, may be pressed the obligation of adopting speedy and decisive measures, to prevent their being scattered "like sheep without a shepherd," and to continue the use of that form of divine service, which they believe to be "worshipping the Lord in the beauty of holiness."

THE END.

William Stevens Perry, ed., *Journals of General Conventions of the Protestant Episcopal Church in the United States.* Vol. III: *Historical Notes and Documents* (Claremont, N.H.: Claremont Manufacturing Co., 1874), 420-422, 424-428, 433-436.

2.

**Concordat of Bishop Seabury and the Nonjuring
Scottish Bishops, His Consecrators, 1784**

Samuel Seabury (November 30, 1729–February 25, 1796) was the first Bishop consecrated for the Episcopal Church in the United States. Connecticut Episcopalians, dissenters with a strong sense of self-identity in a state where the Congregational Church continued to be the legally established church into the first decades of the nineteenth century, were less willing than William White to organize on an emergency basis without bishops. Elected by the Connecticut clergy, Seabury applied to the bishops of the Scottish Episcopal Church for ordination as bishop when he was unsuccessful in his attempt to secure ordination from the English bishops. The Scottish Episcopal Church had been organized after 1688 out of the Episcopal remnant of the established Church of Scotland. After the Glorious Revolution of 1688, when James II had been overthrown as British king, the bishops of the Church of Scotland, like many of their English colleagues, had declined for conscience's sake to take the oath of allegiance to William and Mary—a refusal which earned them the name of "non-jurors." In the aftermath, the established Church of Scotland abolished the episcopacy in 1690 and returned to a presbyterian polity. Continuing Episcopalians in Scotland worshipped under severe restrictions, but their disestablished status gave them the freedom which English bishops did not have to ordain an American who could not take the oath of allegiance to the British crown. The concordat which Seabury signed with the Scottish bishops pledged him, among other things, to seek to secure the use of the Scottish communion office by American Episcopalians. Seabury's efforts, as well as those of others, resulted in adoption by the Episcopal Church of a eucharistic prayer whose structure

14

follows the Scottish tradition rather than that of the Church of England. Securing the episcopate and the consecration of Seabury are commemorated in the Episcopal Calendar on November 14.

CONCORDAT

In the name of the Holy and Undivided Trinity, Father, Son, and Holy Ghost, one God, Blessed for ever. Amen.

The wise and gracious providence of this merciful God having put it into the hearts of the Christians of the Episcopal persuasion in Connecticut, in North America, to desire that the blessings of a free, valid, and purely ecclesiastical Episcopacy might be communicated to them, and a Church regularly formed in that part of the western world, on the most ancient and primitive model; and application having been made for this purpose by the Rev. Doctor Samuel Seabury, Presbyter in Connecticut, to the Right Rev. the Bishops of the Church in Scotland, the said Bishops having taken this proposal into their serious consideration, most heartily concurred to promote and encourage the same as far as lay in their power, and, accordingly, began the pious and good work recommended to them, by complying with the request of the clergy in Connecticut, and advancing the same Dr. Samuel Seabury to the high order of the Episcopate, at the same time earnestly praying that this work of the Lord, thus happily begun, might prosper in his hand, till it should please the great and glorious Head of the Church to increase the number of Bishops in America, and send forth more such labourers into that part of His harvest. Animated with this pious hope, and earnestly desirous to establish a bond of peace and holy communion between the two Churches, the Bishops of the Church in Scotland, whose names are underwritten, having had full and free conference with Bishop Seabury, after his consecration and advancement as aforesaid, agreed with him on the following Articles which are to serve as a Concordate, or bond of union, between the Catholic remainder of the ancient Church of Scotland, and the now rising Church in Connecticut.

ARTICLE I. They agree in thankful receiving, and humbly and heartily embracing the whole doctrine of the Gospel as revealed and set forth in the Holy Scriptures, and it is their earnest and united desire to maintain the analogy of the common faith once delivered to the saints, and happily preserved in the Church of Christ through His Divine power and protection, Who promised that the gates of hell should never prevail against it.

ARTICLE II. They agree in believing this Church to be the mystical body of Christ, and of which He alone is the head and supreme Governor, and that under Him the chief ministers or managers of the affairs of this spiritual society are those called Bishops, whose exercise of their sacred office being independent of

15

all lay powers, it follows, of consequence, that their spiritual authority and jurisdiction cannot be affected by any lay deprivation.

ARTICLE III. They agree in declaring that the Episcopal Church in Connecticut is to be in full communion with the Episcopal Church in Scotland, it being their sincere resolution to put matters on such a footing as that the members of both Churches may with freedom and safety communicate with either, when their occasions call them from the one country to the other. Only taking care, when in Scotland, not to hold communion in sacred offices with those persons who, under the pretence of ordination by an English or Irish Bishop, do, or shall take upon them to officiate as clergymen in any part of the National Church of Scotland, and whom the Scottish Bishops cannot help looking upon as schismatical intruders, designed only to answer worldly purposes, and uncommissioned disturbers of the poor remains of that once flourishing Church, which both their predecessors and they have, under many difficulties, laboured to preserve pure and uncorrupted to future ages.

ARTICLE IV. With a view to this salutary purpose mentioned in the preceding article, they agree in desiring that there may be as near a conformity in worship and discipline established between the two churches, as is consistent with the different circumstances and customs of nations; and in order to avoid any bad effects that might otherwise arise from political differences, they hereby express their earnest wish and firm intention to observe such prudent generality in their public prayers, with respect to these points, as shall appear most agreeable to apostolic rules, and the practice of the Primitive Church.

ARTICLE V. As the celebration of the Holy Eucharist, or the administration of the Sacrament of the Body and Blood of Christ, is the principal bond of union among Christians, as well as the most solemn act of worship in the Christian Church, the Bishops aforesaid agree in desiring that there may be as little variance here as possible. And though the Scottish Bishops are very far from prescribing to their brethren in this matter, they cannot help ardently wishing that Bishop Seabury would endeavor all he can, consistently with peace and prudence, to make the celebration of this venerable mystery conformable to the most primitive doctrine and practice in that respect, which is the pattern the Church of Scotland has copied after in her Communion Office, and which it has been the wish of some of the most eminent divines of the Church of England, that she also had more closely followed than she seems to have done since she gave up her first reformed liturgy, used in the reign of King Edward VI., between which and the form used in the Church of Scotland, there is no difference in any point, which the Primitive Church reckoned essential to the right ministration of the Holy Eucharist. In this capital article, therefore, the Eucharistic service, in which the Scottish Bishops so earnestly wish for as much unity as possible, Bishop Seabury also agrees to take a serious view of the

16

Communion Office recommended by them and if found agreeable to the genuine standard of antiquity, to give his sanction to it, and by gentle methods of argument and persuasion, to endeavor, as they have done, to introduce it by degrees into practice, without the compulsion of authority on the one side or the prejudice of former custom on the other.

ARTICLE VI. It is also hereby agreed and resolved upon, for the better answering the purposes of this Concordate, that a brotherly fellowship be henceforth maintained between the Episcopal Churches in Scotland and Connecticut, and such a mutual intercourse of ecclesiastical correspondence carried on, when opportunity offers or necessity requires, as may tend to the support and edification of both Churches.

ARTICLE VII. The Bishops aforesaid do hereby jointly declare, in the most solemn manner, that in the whole of this transaction they have nothing else in view but the glory of God, and the good of His church; and being thus pure and upright in their intentions, they cannot but hope that all whom it may concern will put the most fair and candid construction on their conduct, and take no offence at their feeble but sincere endeavors to promote what they believe to be the cause of truth and the common salvation.

In testimony of their love to which, and in mutual good faith and confidence they have, for themselves and their successors in office, cheerfully put their names and seals to these presents, at Aberdeen, this 15th day of November, in the year of our Lord 1784.

> ROBERT KILGOUR, *Bishop and Primus, L.S.*
> JOHN SKINNER, *Bishop, L.S.*
> ARTHUR PETRIE, *Bishop, L.S.*
> SAMUEL SEABURY, *Bishop, L.S.*
> ARTHUR PETRIE, *Clerk.*

Francis L. Hawks and William Stevens Perry, eds., *Documentary History of the Protestant Episcopal Church in the United States of America: Connecticut.* Vol. II (New York: James Pott, Publisher, 1864), 249-251.

3.

Samuel Seabury to William Smith, August 15, 1785

On August 15, 1785, Samuel Seabury wrote to William Smith (September 7,

1727–May 14, 1803) then rector of Chestertown, Maryland, about the office of bishop. Smith presided over the meeting of Maryland clergy at Annapolis on August 13, 1783, that adopted the name "Protestant Episcopal Church." This convention elected Smith Bishop of Maryland, but he was never consecrated.

New London, Aug. 15th, 1785.

[The Rev. Wm. Smith (the elder)]

Revd and dear Sir,

The grand difficulty that defeated my application for Consecration in England, appeared to me to be the want of an application from the State of Connecticut. Other objections were made, viz: That there was no precise diocess marked out by the civil authority, nor a stated revenue appointed for the Bps support: But those were removed. The other remained—for the civil authority in Connecticut is Presbyterian, & therefore could not be supposed would petition for a Bp. And had this been removed, I am not sure another would not have started up: For, this happened to me several times. I waited, and procured a copy of an Act of the Legislature of Connecticut, which puts all denomination[s] of Christians on a footing of equality, (except the Roman Catholics, & to them it gives a free toleration) certified by the Secretary of the State: For to Connecticut all my negotiations were confined. The Abp. of Cant. wished it had been fuller, but thought it afforded ground on which to proceed. Yet he afterward said it would not do; & that the minister, without a formal requisition from the State, would not suffer the Bill, enabling the Bp. of London to ordain foreign Candidates without their taking the Oaths, to pass the Commons, if it contained a Clause for the Consecrating American Bps. And as his Grace did not choose to proceed without parliamentary authority—though if I understood him right, a majority of the Judges & Crown Lawyers were of opinion he might safely do it—I turned my attention to the remains of the old Scots Episcopal Church, whose Consecrations I knew were derived from England, & their authority in an ecclesiastical sense, fully equal to the English Bps. —No objection was ever made to me on account of the legacies left for American Bps. Some people had surmises of this kind, but I know not whence they arose.

I can see no good ground of apprehension concerning the titles of estates or emoluments belonging to the Chch in your State. Your Chch is still the Chch of England subsisting under a different civil government. We have in America the Chch of Holland, of Scotland, of Sweden, of Moravia, & why not of England[?] Our being of the Chch of England, no more implies dependence on, or subjection to England, than being of the Chch of Holland implies subjection to Holland.

The plea of the Methodists is something like impudence. Mr Wesley is only a Presbyter, & all his Ordinations Presbyterian, & in direct opposition to the Chch of England: And they can have no pretence for calling themselves Chchmen till they return to the unity of the Chch, which they have unreasonably, unnecessarily and wickedly broken, by their seperation & schism.

Your two cautions respecting recommendations & titles are certainly just. Till you are so happy as to have a Bp of your own, it will be a pleasure to me to do every thing I can, for the supply of your Chches: And I am confident the Clergy of Maryland, & the other States, will be very particular with regard to the qualifications & titles of persons to be admitted into their own Order. Should they think proper to send any Candidates hither, I could wish that it might be at the stated times of Ordination; because the Clergy here living so scattered, it is not easy on every emergency to get three of them together; & never without some expence which they cannot well afford. . . .

I thank you for your communications respecting Washington College, & the various Conventions you have had in your State, & neighbourhood. The Clergy & Laity have particular merit in making so great exertions to get our Chch into a settled & respectful State. But on objects of such magnitude & variety it is to be expected that sentiments will differ. All men do not always see the same object in the same light: And persons at a distance are not always masters of the precise reasons & circumstances which have occasioned particular modes of acting. Of some things therefore in your proceedings I cannot be a competent judge, without minute information; & I am very sorry that my present circumstances, & duty here, will not permit me to make so long a journey at this time; because by personal interview & conversation only can such information be had.

But, my dear Sir, there are some things which, if I do not much misapprehend, are really wrong. In giving my opinion of them, I must claim the same privilege of judging for myself which others claim; & also that right of fair & candid interpretation of my sentiments which is due to all men.

1. I think you have done wrong in establishing so many, & so precise, fundamental rules. You seem thereby to have precluded yourselves from the benefit of after consideration. And by having the power of altering fundamental rules diffused through so large a body, it appears to me next to impossible to have them altered, even in some reasonable cases, because cases really reasonable may not always appear so to two thirds of a large assembly. It should also be remembered that while human nature is, as it is, something of party, passion, or partiality, will ever be apt, in some degree, to influence the views & debates of a numerous & mixed assembly.

2. I think you have to[o] much circumscribed the power of your Bp. That *the Duty & Office of a Bishop, differs in nothing from that of the other* Priests, *except in the power of Ordination & Confirmation*, (Pamph. p. 16) & *the right of Precedency* &c is a position that carries Jeroms opinion to the highest pitch— *Quid facit Episcopus, quod Presbyter non faciat, excepta ordinatione?* But it

19

does not appear that Jerom had the support of the Chch, in this opinion, but rather the contrary. Government as essentially pertains to Bps as ordination; nay ordination is but the particular exercise of government. Whatever share of government Presbyters have in the Chch, thay have from the Bp, & must exercise it in conjunction with, or in subordination to him. And though a Congregation may have a right—& I am willing to allow it—to choose their minister, as they are to support him & live under his ministry, yet the Bps concurrence or licence is necessary, because they are part of his charge; he has the care of their souls, & is accountable for them; & therefore the ministers authority to take charge of that congregation must come through the Bp.

The choice of the Bp. is in the Presbyters, but the neighbouring Bps who are to consecrate him must have the right of judging whether he be a proper person or not. The Presbyters are the Bps council, without whom he ought to do nothing but matters of course. The Presbyters have always a check upon their Bp. because they can, neither Bp nor Presbyters, do any thing beyond the common course of duty without each other. I mean with regard to a particular diocess; for it does not appear that Presbyters had any seat in general Councils, but by particular indulgence.

The people being the patrons of the Chches in this country, & having the means of the Bps & Ministers support in their hands, have a sufficient restraint upon them. In cases that require it, they can apply to their Bp, who, with the assistance of his Presbyters, will proceed, as the case may require, to censure, suspension or deposition of the offending Clergyman. If a Bp behaves amiss the neighbouring Bps are his judges. —Men that are not to be trusted with these powers are not fit to be Bps or Presbyters at all.

This, I take it, is the constitution of the Christian Chch, in its pure & simple state. And it is a constitution which, if adhered to, will carry itself into full effect. This constitution we have adopted in Connecticut; & we do hope & trust that we shall, by Gods grace, exhibit to the world, in our government, discipline & order, a pure & perfect model of primitive simplicity.

Presbyters cannot be too careful in choosing their Bp; nor the People in choosing their Minister. Improper men may, however, sometimes succeed: And so they will, make as exact rules, & circumscribe their power, as you can. And an improper man in the Chch, is an improper man, however he came there, & however his power be limitted. The more you circumscribe him, the greater Temptation he is under to form a party to support him; & when his party is formed, all the power of your convention will not be able to displace him. In short if you get a bad man, your laws & regulations will not be effectual—if a good man the general laws of the Chch are sufficient.

Where civil States have made provision for ministers, it seems reasonable that they should define the qualification, & regulate the conduct of those who are to enjoy the emolument. But voluntary associations for the exercise of such powers as your Convention is to have, are always apt—such is the infirmity of human nature—to fall into parties; & when party enters, animosity & discord soon follow. —From what has been said you will suppose I shall object.

3. To the admission of Lay members into Synods &c: I must confess I do, especially in the degree your fundamental rules allow. I have as great a regard for the laity as any man can have. It is for their sake that Ministers are appointed in the Chch. I have no Idea of aggrandizing the Clergy at the expense of the laity: Nor indeed of aggrandizing them at all. Decent means of living is all they have a right to expect. But I cannot conceive that the Laity can with any propriety be admitted to sit in judgment on Bps & Presbyters, especially when deposition may be the event; because they cannot take away a character which they cannot confer. It is incongruous to every idea of Episcopal government. That authority which confers power can, for proper reasons, take it away: But where there is no authority to confer power, there can be none to disanul it. Wherever, therefore, the power of Ordination is lodged, the power of deprivation is lodged also.

Should it be thought necessary that the laity should have a share in the choice of their Bp—if it can be put on a proper footing, so as to avoid party & confusion—I see not but that it might [be] admitted. But I do not apprehend that this was the practice of the primitive Chch. In short, the rights of the Christian Chch arise not from nature or compact, but from the institution of Christ, & we ought not to alter them, but to receive & maintain them, as the holy Apostles left them. The government, sacraments, faith & doctrines of the Chch are fixed & settled. We have a right to examin[e] *what they are*, but we must take them *as they are*. If we new model the government, why not the sacraments, creeds & doctrines of the Chch; but then it would not be Christs Chch, but *our* Chch; & would remain so call it by what name we please.

I do therefore beseech the Clergy & Laity, who shall meet at Philadelphia, to reconsider the matter before a final step be taken: And to endeavour to bring their Chch government as near to the primitive pattern as may be. They will find it the simplest, & most easy to carry into effect; & if it be adhered to it will be in no danger of sinking or falling.

I do not think it necessary that the Chch in every State should be just as the Chch in Connecticut is; though I think that the best model. Particular circumstances, I know, will call for particular considerations. But in so essential a matter as Chch government is, no alterations should be made that affect its foundation. If a man be called a Bp who has not the Episcopal powers of government, he is called by a wrong name, even though he should have the power of Ordination & Confirmation.

William Stevens Perry, ed., *Journals of General Conventions of the Protestant Episcopal Church.* Vol. III: *Historical Notes and Documents* (Claremont, N.H.: Claremont Manufacturing Company, 1874), 76-81.

4.

To the Most Reverend and Right Reverend the Archbishops of Canterbury and York, and the Bishops of the Church of England, 1785

The first General Convention met at Christ Church, Philadelphia, September 27-October 7, 1785. The delegates from seven states wrote to England requesting consecration of persons elected bishops by the several states. On June 26, 1786, Parliament passed the necessary legislation empowering the Archbishops of Canterbury and York "to consecrate to the office of Bishop, Persons, being Subjects or Citizens of Countries out of His Majesty's Dominion." The following letter requests the Archbishops of Canterbury and York to consecrate bishops for the American Church.

We the Clerical and Lay deputies of the Protestant Episcopal Church in sundry of the United States of America, think it our duty to address your Lordships on a subject deeply interesting, not only to ourselves and those whom we represent, but, as we conceive, to the common cause of Christianity.

Our forefathers, when they left the land of their nativity, did not leave the bosom of that Church over which your Lordships now preside; but, as well from a veneration for Episcopal government, as from an attachment to the admirable services of our Liturgy, continued in willing connection with their ecclesiastical superiors in England, and were subjected to many local inconveniences, rather than break the unity of the Church to which they belonged.

When it pleased the Supreme Ruler of the universe, that this part of the British empire should be free, sovereign, and independent, it became the most important concern of the members of our Communion to provide for its continuance. And while, in accomplishing of this, they kept in view that wise and liberal part of the system of the Church of England which excludes as well the claiming as the acknowledging so such spiritual subjection as may be inconsistent with the civil duties of their children; it was nevertheless their earnest desire and resolution to retain the venerable form of Episcopal government handed down to them, as they conceive, from the time of the Apostles, and endeared to them by the remembrance of the holy Bishops of the primitive Church, of the blessed Martyrs who reformed the doctrine and worship of the Church of England, and of the many great and pious Prelates who have adorned that Church in every succeeding age. But however general the desire of compleating the Orders of our Ministry, so diffused and unconnected were the members of our Communion over this extensive country, that much time and negotiation were necessary for the forming a representative body of the greater number of Episcopalians in these States; and owing to the same causes, it was not until this Convention that sufficient powers could be procured for the addressing your Lordships on this subject.

The petition which we offer to your Venerable Body is, - that from a tender regard to the religious interests of thousands in this rising empire, professing the same religious principles with the Church of England, you will be pleased to confer the Episcopal character of such persons as shall be recommended by this Church, in the several States here represented - full satisfaction being given of the sufficiency of the persons recommended, and of its being the intention of the general body of the Episcopalians in the said States respectively, to receive them in the quality of Bishops.

Whether this our request will meet with insurmountable impediments from the political regulations of the kingdom in which your Lordships fill such distinguished stations, it is not for us to foresee. We have not been ascertained that any such will exist; and are humbly of opinion, that as citizens of these States, interested in their prosperity, and religiously regarding the allegiance which we owe them, it is to an ecclesiastical source only we can apply in the present exigency.

It may be of consequence to observe, that in these States there is a separation between the concerns of policy and those of religion; that; accordingly, our civil rulers cannot officially join in the present application; that, however, we are far from apprehending the opposition or even displeasure of any of those honorable personages; and finally, that in this business we are justified by the Constitutions of the States, which are the foundations and control of all our laws. . . .

SIGNED BY THE CLERICAL AND LAY DEPUTIES OF THE CONVENTION.

IN CONVENTION:
Christ Church, Philadelphia
October 5th, 1785

William Stevens Perry, ed., *Journals of the General Convention of the Protestant Episcopal Church in the United States, 1785-1835*, Vol. I: *1785-1821* (Claremont, N.H.: Claremont Manufacturing Company, 1874), 26-27. (Excerpt)

5.

The Constitution of the Protestant Episcopal Church in the United States of America, 1789

The third General Convention met at Christ Church, Philadelphia, in two sessions, July 28-August 8, and September 30-October 16, 1789. At the second session the convention met for the first time as the House of Bishops and the House of Deputies. This session adopted the constitution of nine articles and seventeen canons. The language of the constitution echoes the language of the federalism of the era: it generally speaks of "states" rather than "dioceses" and thinks of the national church as a federation of state churches.

Art. 1. There shall be a General Convention of the Protestant Episcopal Church in the United States of America on the second Tuesday of September, in the year of our Lord 1792, and on the second Tuesday of September in every third year afterwards, in such a place as shall be determined by the Convention; and special meetings may be called at other times, in the manner hereafter to be provided for; and this Church, in a majority of the States which shall have adopted this Constitution, shall be represented, before they shall proceed to business, except that the representation from two States shall be sufficient to adjourn; and in all business of the Convention, freedom of debate shall be allowed.

Art. 2. The Church in each State shall be entitled to a representation of both the Clergy and the Laity, which representation shall consist of one or more Deputies, not exceeding four of each Order, chosen by the Convention of the State: and in all questions, when required by the Clerical or Lay representation from any State, each Order shall have one vote; and the majority of suffrages by States shall be conclusive in each order, provided such majority comprehend a majority of the states represented in that Order. The concurrence of both Orders shall be necessary to constitute a vote of the Convention. If the Convention of any State should neglect or decline to appoint Clerical Deputies, or if any of those of either Order appointed should neglect to attend, or be prevented by sickness or any other accident, such State shall nevertheless be considered as duly represented by such Deputy or Deputies as may attend, whether lay or clerical. And if, through the neglect of the Convention of any of the Churches which shall have adopted, or may hereafter adopt this Constitution, no Deputies, either Lay or Clerical, should attend at any General Convention, the Church in such State shall nevertheless be bound by the acts of such convention.

Art. 3. The Bishops of this Church, when there shall be three or more, shall, whenever General Conventions are held, form a separate House, with a right to originate and propose acts for the concurrence of the House of Deputies, com-

24

posed of Clergy and Laity; and when any proposed act shall have passed the House of Deputies, the same shall be transmitted to the House of Bishops, who shall have a negative thereupon unless adhered to by four-fifths of the other Houses. And all acts of the Convention shall be authenticated by both Houses. And in all cases, the House of Bishops shall signify to the Convention their approbation or disapprobation, the latter with their reasons in writing, within three days after the proposed act shall have been reported to them for concurrence, and in failure thereof it shall have the operation of a law. But until there shall be three or more Bishops as aforesaid, any Bishop attending a General Convention shall be a member ex officio, and shall vote with the Clerical Deputies of the State to which he belongs; and a Bishop shall then preside.

Art. 4. The Bishop or Bishops in every State shall be chosen agreeably to such rules as shall be fixed by the Convention of that State. And every Bishop of this Church shall confine the exercise of his Episcopal office to his proper Diocese of District, unless requested to ordain or confirm, or perform any other act of the Episcopal office, by any Church destitute of a Bishop.

Art. 5. A Protestant Episcopal church in any of the United States not now represented, may, at any time hereafter, be admitted, on acceding to this constitution.

Art. 6. In every State, the mode of trying Clergymen shall be instituted by the Convention of the Church therein. At every trial of a Bishop there shall be one or more of the Episcopal Order present: and none but a Bishop shall pronounce sentence of deposition or degradation from the Ministry on any Clergyman, whether Bishop, or Presbyter, or deacon.

Art. 7. No person shall be admitted to Holy Orders, until he shall have been examined by the Bishop and by two Presbyters, and shall have exhibited such testimonials and other requisites as the Canons in that case provided may direct. Nor shall any person be ordained until he shall have subscribed the following declaration: "I do believe the Holy Scriptures of the Old and New Testament to be the word of God, and to contain all things necessary to salvation: and I do solemnly engage to conform to the doctrines and worship of the Protestant Episcopal Church in these United States." No person ordained by a foreign Bishop shall be permitted to officiate as a Minister of this Church, until he shall have compiled with the Canon or Canons in that case provided, and have also subscribed the aforesaid declaration.

Art. 8. A Book of Common Prayer, Administration of the Sacraments, and other Rites and Ceremonies of the Church, Articles of Religion, and a form and manner of making, ordaining, and consecrating Bishops, Priests, and Deacons, when established by this or a future General Convention, shall be used in the Protestant Episcopal Church in those States, which shall have adopted this Constitution.

Art. 9. This Constitution shall be unalterable, unless in General Convention by the Church in a majority of the States which may have adopted the same; and all alterations shall be first proposed in one General Convention, and made known to the several State Conventions, before they shall be finally agreed to, or ratified, in the ensuing General Convention.

Done in General Convention of the Bishops, Clergy, and Laity of the Church, the second day of October, 1789, . . .

William Stevens Perry, ed. *Journals of General Conventions of the Protestant Episcopal Church in the United States, 1785-1835.* Vol. I: *1785-1821* (Claremont, N.H.: Claremont Manufacturing Company, 1874), 99-100.

Chapter Two

The Episcopal Church: Post-War Recovery (1814-1834)

Introduction

The church's losses of property, glebe income, and overseas support required the Episcopal Church to seek a new independence. The church could no longer depend on the economic crutches that provided support during the colonial period. But these losses proved to be the seeds for new life and vitality in a church whose economic needs would be the responsibility of her members' stewardship. The Episcopal Church's own resources had to be summoned to function in a post-establishment era. New energy and leadership were evident in the Episcopal Church in 1811 when Alexander V. Griswold, an evangelical, was ordained bishop for the Eastern Diocese in New England, and John Henry Hobart, a high churchman, was ordained assistant bishop for New York. As the new church began to forge its identity, its hallmarks were (in the words of John Henry Hobart) evangelical truth and apostolic order. In the first years of the church's history, the emphasis on evangelical truth (which focused on personal religion) was characteristic of those in the church like Griswold, who thought of themselves as "Evangelicals." The emphasis on apostolic order and the corporate life of the church was characteristic of those who would be identified as "high church," like Samuel Seabury.

6.

John Henry Hobart, Sermon, 1814

John Henry Hobart (September 14, 1775–September 12, 1830) was consecrated Assistant Bishop of New York on May 29, 1811, and became the third bishop of New York when Bishop Benjamin Moore died on February 27, 1816. Bishop Hobart was the aggressive leader of the High Church Party. His life and ministry are commemorated in the Episcopal Calendar of the Church Year on

The present situation of our Church, and the duties thence resulting.

And here there will appear, cause both for sorrow and for congratulation.

The war of the revolution stripped our Church of a large proportion of her clergy, of many of her influential members, and of the nursing care and protection of the venerable society for propagating the Gospel in foreign parts. Her congregations, with diminished numbers and impoverished means, were left without clergy, and destitute for many years of the episcopacy, clergy were not to be obtained. The age of your preacher at this period does not enable him to speak from personal knowledge; but judging from information, he appears warranted in expressing the opinion, that our Church was placed in circumstances of so great depression and difficulty, that it became a serious question whether she would be able to preserve the characteristic of an apostolical Church, episcopal ordination. While, therefore, her present primitive organization claims for the patience, the prudence, and the persevering zeal of the agents in this most important work the highest praise (may their names ever be held in grateful remembrance) her preservation in all her characteristic features may be traced to the protecting presence of her divine head, and under him to her evangelical and apostolical character, and to her inestimable liturgy. But she still exhibits, in many places, the face of desolation. The clergy, who have been ordained since we obtained the episcopacy, have not in many states supplied the wants even of the old congregations. Our Church in many places mourns that none come to her solemn feasts, because there are no priests to make the celebration: while in the new and extensive districts filled by the increasing population of our country, the members of our Church are wandering as sheep having no shepherd, and either joining other folds, or mourning, desolate and solitary, their exile from their Zion.

Amidst these causes of sorrow, it is a subject for congratulation, that our people are awakening to a sense of the duties which they owe to their Church, to the necessity of making provision for a learned, a pious, and laborious ministry, of providing for their support in the vineyard, of sending missionaries to the destitute quarters of our Zion, of disseminating information in the truths of religion, and the distinctive principles of our Church. It is a subject of congratulation that correct views of her distinctive principles are becoming more prevalent; that her worship, overcoming the prejudices which may have subsisted against it, is gradually exerting its evangelical influence on the hearts of her members; that the preaching of the doctrines of the cross is the aim of her clergy, and more and more demanded by her people; and that all orders among us seem disposed and desirous to cherish the spirit of Christian love and unity, to know no other aim but the glory of God, the honour of the Redeemer, and the advancement of his kingdom; and to these glorious objects to devote their talents, their influence, their hearts.

It is incumbent on us, my clerical and lay brethren of this convention, standing as we do in the high and responsible station of the general council of our Church, pre-eminently to display these divine dispositions, these harmonious and pious views. Happily organized as our Church is in her doctrines, her worship, and her discipline, and entrusted, as her supreme officers are, with many of those concerns, which, under a different organization, would be a subject of popular discussion and determination; our principal duty at these ecclesiastical meetings consists in obtaining information concerning the state of our Zion; in watching over her principles, her purity, and her peace; in adapting, but with a cautious and a temperate hand, the provisions of our laws to the changing exigencies of affairs; and, above all, it should here be our object, as in the presence and under the influence of the spirit of our divine Lord, to excite, to cherish, and to strengthen our mutual zeal in his service, in the cause of his holy religion, and in the advancement of the prosperity of his spouse and body the Church.

Since your last meeting a change has taken place in our episcopal body by the removal of two venerable brothers from their duties on earth to their rest in the Paradise of God.[1] It is a subject of congratulation, however, on the present occasion, and an indication of a growing zeal for our Church that the present ecclesiastical assembly is more numerously attended than usual. The difficulties of a long journey have not prevented the attendance of the bishop and clerical deputies from the distant diocess of South Carolina; and our hearts are cheered by the presence, long earnestly desired, of a deputation from the Church in Virginia. And it is particularly a subject of thankfulness that this diocess, where our Zion has long been languishing, and seemed almost extinct, has made provision for filling the episcopate in the reverend person[2] whom having presented to us the testimonials required by the canons we shall now proceed to consecrate.

But little more than half a century has elapsed since our Church universally prevailed through the rich and flourishing dominion of Virginia. In every county there were churches and chapels, all of them decent and substantial, some of them even splendid in their decorations. In those temples were stately performed all the services of our primitive liturgy. The parishes, not much short of one hundred, were all supplied with clergy. What is the contrast? We have wept

---

[1] Right Reverend Bishop Jarvis of Connecticut, and the Right Reverend Bishop Madison of Virginia.
[2] The Rev. Richard Channing Moore, D.D. Rector of St. Stephen's Church, New York.

29

over it. Our hearts have been wrung with shame, with grief, that this contrast has been produced, not entirely (God forbid we should sink them under this tremendous guilt) but in no inconsiderable degree by many of the clergy themselves. What is the contrast? Few are the parishes in Virginia which enjoy the regular ministrations of a clergyman. In many places the liturgy is scarcely known, but as some antiquated book which was once used by their fathers. The edifices, where their fathers worshipped, now in a state of ruin, fix the astonished gaze and excite the mournful sigh of the passing traveller; and in those courts where the living God was once invoked and the messages of mercy through his Son proclaimed, no sounds are heard but the screams of the bird of night, or the lowings of the beasts of the field. It was not possible that this state of things could long continue. Man does not feel himself safe even with his fellow man loosened from the restraints of religion—He cannot live without its consolations—He cannot enter on futurity without its hopes—The night of adversity has passed, and the morning, I would fain hope, of a long and splendid day is dawning on the Church in Virginia. I think I see the pledge of this in the attachment to our Church and in the anxious desire to serve her manifested by laymen of the highest influence and talents, and by a few zealous clergy. They have combined, and they have resolved, under God, that the Church in Virginia shall not perish. From my soul I revere and love them for the holy resolve. My God! in this remember them for good.

The Origin, the General Character, and the Present Situation of the Protestant Episcopal Church in the United States of America—A Sermon Preached in St. James's Church, in the City of Philadelphia, on Wednesday, May 18th, A.D. 1814, On the Occasion of the Opening of the General Convention of the Said Church, and of the Consecration of the Right Rev. Bishop Moore, of Virginia. By John Henry Hobart, D.D. Assistant Bishop of the Protestant Episcopal Church in the State of New York, Published by Desire of the Convention, 1814, 32-38. (Excerpt)

7.

William White, The Past and the Future,
A Charge, on Events Connected With the Organization
of the Protestant Episcopal Church in the United States of
America, and the Lessons They Inculcate, 1834

William White lived through the American Revolution, the organization of the Episcopal Church, and its post-Revolutionary difficulties. He was Bishop of Pennsylvania from 1787 until his death in 1836. He also served as Presiding Bishop from 1795 to 1836. This "charge" of 1834 gives his reflections on this significant period in the life of the church.

AN EPISCOPAL CHARGE, &c.

Reverend Brethren, the clerical members of the Convention, and other clergymen of the diocese, present:

This is the fiftieth annual convention in which your bishop has been present and presiding in the representative body of the diocese. The circumstance that we are at the end of half of a century from the beginning of our organization, has seemed to him a suitable occasion to look back on what we were at the end of the revolutionary war; and to make it a ground of some counsels, which may have a salutary influence on the future concerns of the church. To this he is the more inclined, because of a period which cannot be remote, when his voice will be heard among you no more.

In the whole history of the christian church, it would probably be impossible to name an instance in which there was so great a portion of population, discharged from all authority for the taking of order, tending to the improvement of their condition. During our colonial state, the tie which connected our congregations was the superintendence of the bishops of London, under delegation from the crown. That being withdrawn, every congregation was independent of all exterior control, either in England or in America. There remained, however, the principles inherited by them from the mother church, in doctrine, in worship, and in ecclesiastical constitution. These were materials, giving reason to hope that there might be raised from them a religious communion, resembling that from which we were descended, as nearly as local circumstances should permit.

What aggravated the exigency, was the very small number to which our ministry was reduced; partly by death, and partly by the migration of some to Great Britain, and of others to the colonies on this continent, remaining subject to her jurisdiction. It will probably be new to the greater number present, to be informed that, for a short time, he who addresses you was the only Episcopal clergyman in the commonwealth of Pennsylvania; and that when he was elected to the episcopacy, there were only three of his brethren present and voting. They were all who could have given clerical voices in the measure, with the exception of two brethren who were absent and resided at distances, but afterwards signified their concurrence.

In addition to the privation, there was the withdrawing of much of the pecuniary supply for ministerial support. In all of the colonies to the north of

Maryland, with the exception of the larger cities, the clergy were missionaries, in the service of the Society for the Propagating of the Gospel in foreign parts. Their salaries ceased with the acknowledgment of our independence, and an addition to the migration of our clergy was the consequence. The withdrawing of the stipends ought not to attach blame to the venerable Society, whose charter limited their operations to the dependencies of the British crown: so that there remains the debt of gratitude for the fostering care extended to us in our infancy.

In the midst of these discouragements, measures were put into operation for the organizing of our church in the states individually, and in the United States. Some, with the best intentions as to the object, did not approve of this as an incipient step; but after a while the general opinion was in its favour; especially as it appeared, by information relied on from the quarter to which we looked for the completing of the orders of our ministry, that there was nothing to be expected in virtue of an application from our clergy in their individual characters, and without its carrying with it evidence of the concurrence of our episcopal population, who, as well as the clergy, possessed an interest in the favour to be solicited. The information received, gave great encouragement to the endeavours which had been begun.

Whatever might eventually be the disposition of the English prelacy towards us, for it was the source to which we naturally looked, there were perceived formidable discouragements to the making of an application. At different times, there had been discussed the question of an American episcopate; and in controversies engendered by the subject, episcopacy had been described as bringing in its train Baronial titles and authorities, the powers of certain temporal courts hitherto conducted under the laws of our colonial legislatures, and even the claim of tythes. These prejudices were not only cherished and propagated by persons differing from us in religious profession, but had their effect on the minds of no small proportion of the members of our church; who, although preferring it to every other, were jealous of a proposed innovation, which might be the beginning of changes, destructive of the principles on which the colonies had been settled, and on which they had remained in an intercourse with the mother country, advantageous to her and to themselves. What aggravated the fear of a reverse, were some measures of the British parliament, nearly coincident with the controversies referred to, indicative of new views to an incalculable extent.

It may be thought, that after the establishment of American independence, and, of course, the ceasing of the dangers supposed to result from an episcopacy subject to the English hierarchy, the dread of encroachments on the liberties of our citizens had ceased. It is true, that the grounds of the former fear of evils, whether real or imaginary, was done away: so that to have opposed exterior hindrances to what we were contemplating, would have been an avowed persecution, not likely to be countenanced by popular opinion. If this laid a restraint on any, we may hope that, among our fellow citizens generally, it was a christian spirit which caused them to refrain from all agency in our concerns. Notwithstanding this advantage, however, it had happened that in the heats of the foregoing controversies, Episcopacy, even in its general character, and independently on what might have rendered it unacceptable by incidental associations, had been exhibited as exceedingly adapted to alarm. It had been described as in itself hostile to civil liberty, as nourishing pride and arrogancy in those elevated to the station, as the means of acquiring more wealth than was salutary to the church, and as indulgent to idleness and expensive living. All these charges were contended to be verified in the persons of the English bishops; and it was often in vain to plead, in addition to the absence of proof, that in every age from that of the reformation, records had been left by many of them, not only of distinguished piety and of unblemished lives and conversation, but of prominence in every branch of learning, especially of the theological. Had the allegations been true, as certainly was not the case, they were evidently irrelative to the merits of the subject, and imputable to an indiscreet or else corrupt organization.

The prejudices gradually declined, under the weight of more correct statements, and especially under the irresistible conviction, that the obtaining of the episcopal order was essential to the keeping of us together, as a branch of the christian church; that a great proportion of our population would have adhered to a constitution which they know to have been from the beginning, had prevailed universally during fifteen hundred years, and had been transmitted to them by a church, considered in the character of a parent, although now severed from them by a revolution, which had turned on questions of civil policy and duties. The privilege of acting for themselves in this matter, was secured by the liberal constitution of these states; and if there should be any organized opposition to the design, there was no other alternative, than either conformity to the views of their more consistent brethren, or of their relinquishing of communion with them. It was easy to perceive that in the latter event, the dissentients must have become merged in the many societies marked by discrepant principles, and abounding within our civil union. . . .

. . . .

After determination on the measure of applying to the English bishops for consecration, there occurred a point of difficulty and delicacy in the consequent procedure. We were rendered uneasy by an opinion, confidently maintained and propagated, that the Right Reverend persons whom we had addressed could not but be offended, by its not merely being implied through the whole tenor of the application, but expressed in plain although in respectful language in the begin-

33

ning of it, that we were a church competent in the point of right to the government of ourselves, being now separated from that by which we had been fostered, and of which we had been so long a part. This may be classed as another difficulty: for although we were aware that it was founded on error, yet the tendency of it was to weaken our hands in the work before us. Accordingly, it was a great relief, when we found in the first letter from our former superiors, that they not only noticed as "christian" and "brotherly" the address which had been pronounced by some among ourselves to be contumacious, but avoided whatever might have seemed to dictate; or rather, they so expressed themselves as might be considered to admit our claim of independence in its extent.

There was another source of embarrassment generated among ourselves. It was the question of including the laity in our ecclesiastical legislatures. The first movements to the point were made in this state. Although the example was soon followed in several of the other states, yet there was strong repugnancy against it in certain respectable members of our ministry. This must have been owing to their not having duly considered the constitution of the church from which we are descended. In construing the canons of that church, a distinction is always taken in the courts of law between those which are binding *"proprio vigore,"* as being the ancient canon law of the realm, and so applying, like the canon law, on the footing of immemorial usage, and other canons, enacted by the convocation only. The latter are held to be binding on the clergy, but no further; not having had the sanction of the laity in parliament. It is not so, in regard to the liturgy and its rubrics. These possess the concurrence of the said authority, and it is held that the same is necessary to any alterations which may be thought expedient in future. This point is ably handled by the Rev. Richard Hooker, in his immortal work on Ecclesiastical Polity, in which he defends the sanction given by the parliament, as the only form in which the laity can consent to laws by which they are to be governed: a circumstance which that sagacious man contends for, as what ought to be attached to every provision intended to have the force of law. Certain it is that the English bishops never found fault with our lay representation, which met their eyes in our proceedings. It was probably owing to this, added to more mature consideration, that the prejudice gradually died away, until now it no longer shows its head, except as at present, in notice taken of it in the light of an historic fact.

There was the danger of a more important hindrance to our expectations in the right which we claimed, and which we exercised in the form of a "Proposed Book," recommended to our American churches; of the making of alterations in the articles and in the liturgy; not only accommodated to the change of our civil relations, but further, as in our judgments expediency had rendered eligible; there being still an adherence to the doctrines of the Gospel as held by the mother church. So far as the subject, either of the articles or of the liturgy was matter of human judgment and discretion, the English bishops did not manifest any disposition to interfere. But they were jealous for the integrity of their faith, our invasion of which had been affirmed to them by persons whom they could not but respect, but whose political attachments had betrayed them into unfounded suspicions and reports. The bishops, on receiving the details of our transactions, were satisfied of our orthodoxy; and although a few points were thought to require reconsideration, yet their suggestions to this effect were complied with, consistently with the not surrendering of any right on our side, and the not relaxing of christian vigilance on theirs.

. . . .

II. It is clearly deducible from the premises, that our church is pledged to the point of continuing to maintain the doctrines of the Gospel, as held by the church of England. If it should be asked why there should be such an adjunct to the requirement, the answer arises from the history already given of our origin. In our colonial state, the congregations then formed subjected themselves to her pastoral care, were under the government of her episcopacy, and in many instances were aided by her bounty. When, in consequence of a civil revolution, we had become severed from her, without its having of any bearing on the truth of our holy religion, we still professed to consent with her, in doctrine, in worship, and in discipline. All the churches which have since risen, have, in their origin, professed to stand on the same foundation. Charters have been solicited and granted, recognising the same principle; sundry other indulgences have been extended, and pecuniary gifts of individuals, to a great amount, have been contributed to the same effect. To consummate the obligation, we have applied to our venerable mother for the completion of the orders of our ministry; and the favour has been granted, in full faith of our continuance in the doctrines professed by her through many ages.

For those reasons, it will always be a duty lying on us, to "look to the rock from which we were hewn;" and in obeying the scriptural admonition of "asking for the old paths," to trace them in the institutions and in the history of the church from which we are descended. In our favoured country, every individual is vested with the privilege of manifesting his religious belief, in the form of profession the most agreeable to his judgment or to his fancy. He may depart from our communion but he ought not to remain in it to the disturbance of its peace. Even in the very improbable event of dissatisfaction with our doctrines, in the minds of the greater number of our members, however unquestionable their civil right of departure, there will remain the spiritual right of the minority to the means of public profession and worship, before common to both.

But it will be urged by some, that the church ought to deem it sufficient to affirm the obligation of the truths of the gospel generally, without reference to any standard in which they may be held to be correctly defined. It will not be denied, that taking shelter under the more general name, there are opinions which will not be endured by hearers accustomed and attached to what they conceive to be "the faith once delivered to the saints," for which they are instructed by scripture "earnestly to contend." What is essentially contrary to the word of God, will and ought to be repelled. The only alternative, is the providing that this be done with due advisement and by the public voice of the church, or the leaving of it to every pastor within the limits of his charge, to be ordered according to his judgment or to his humour. In this case it cannot but occasionally happen, that from the interference of private views, or from the excitement of passion, or from the not distinguishing of the different grades of error, he may make himself a pope within the small compass of his parish. Besides all this, there will be a scope given to endless diversities of determination. Even in the ecclesiastical counsels, there will always be the danger of an extreme in this matter, so as that there shall be an invading of the province of private opinion, without any benefit resulting from it to the church. But in the event of its being abandoned to individual judgment and caprice, the excess may be considered as certain, while for its consequences there will be no remedy.

It would be contrary to the sense of the deliverer of these sentiments, if they should be construed to extend to the denial of the right of our church in her independent character, to modify the terms in which her doctrines are presented as the standard of her profession, to any extent, that shall not be a departure from the substance of them. Whatever is human, must be susceptible of such change. There is proof of this, in the fluctuation of language. Some error also may be now so little encouraged, as that they may the most profitably pass unnoticed. Even such as deserved great severity of reprehension in one age, may have become so qualified by the maintainers of them, as to give occasion to more qualified censure. The first General Convention of our church, with their suit to the church of England for the episcopacy, presented a modification of her thirty-nine articles, which, although containing the substance of them, succeeding conventions thought it expedient to withdraw. But this was not on any requisition of the English bishops; who, in all their intercourse with us, punctiliously avoided interference with the independence of the American church: but still adhering to the requisition of agreement in essential doctrine. When, in the year 1801, the general convention adopted the thirty-nine articles, with the exception of certain provisions peculiar to the civil institutions of England, and even retaining the antiquated phraseology, it was not a renunciation of her formerly asserted power, but a delay of the exercise of it. When there shall arrive the day for this, may

God grant that there shall be regard to the distinction between temperate alteration, and such as is radical and ruinous.

III. The third inference deducible from the facts recorded under the other branch of this charge, is the duty of sustaining the episcopacy in whatever is appropriate to its character; and the propriety of defending it on the ground on which it has been transmitted to us by the church of England. When that church reformed from popery, it was with the purpose of altering no further than wherein the existing power had departed from scriptural and from immediately succeeding times. They found that in the origin of the ministry, it comprehended three orders, the highest of which were the apostles and others whom they associated with themselves in the same supereminent trust, to be transmitted by them in perpetual succession. Concerning ministerial acts, that of ordaining in particular, they found no instance of its having been performed by a minister of inferior grade. As to any organized body, with authority to perform this act, or indeed any other, independently on that higher grade, there is not even alleged evidence of a vestige of it. The course continued, without exception and without strife, for 1500 years, and until the era of the reformation. On the continent of Europe many respectable bodies of the reformed saw no way of accomplishing their work but by dispensing with episcopacy, partly because of there being no reforming bishops, and partly from the subjects being much interwoven with secular interests, over which the reformers had no control. Whatever may be the measure of allowance due to exterior necessity, there did not exist any such hindrance in England; and therefore her church availed itself of the advantage of combining ancient order with recently acquired liberty.

These facts are probably as familiar to the clerical hearers, as to the reciter of them. But this exercise being prospective, it was expedient briefly to lay the ground for the charge to be now given, with the hope of its being acted on by those who shall be associated with or succeed us in the ministry, that they consistently sustain this point of the divine institution of the episcopacy, not accommodating, in the least degree, to contrary opinion. When this characteristic of our communion is lost sight of, under any specious plea of temporary accommodation to popular prejudice, instead of being conciliatory, as is imagined, it brings conflicting opinions into view to the loss of christian charity; or, if this be not the consequence, to the sacrifice of a truth of scripture. As to our fellow christians of other denominations, when any of them obtrude on us men not episcopally ordained, however it may put on the face of liberality, and profess for its object the promoting of christian unity, it is too decisive a proof of a spirit which, if the character of the times permitted, would wrest from our church her present freedom of religious profession, and put her members under the restraint of partial laws.

With deep solicitude for the sustaining of the integrity of our system in this matter, there is not perceived the necessity of carrying it to the extreme of denouncing all communions destitute of the episcopacy, as departing from the essentials of the christian faith, and as alien from the covenants of promise. Let it be borne in mind, that the object is to inculcate the duty of continuing the subject in the institutions of our church, on the ground on which it has been transmitted to us by the church of England. While in her articles and in her ordinal, there has been regarded the precise medium here advocated, contemporary with the enactments of them, there are uncontradictory facts, which are their safe expositors, and undeniable evidence of the sense of the reformers. If there should be any among us who make larger conclusions from the same premises, it is matter of private opinion, and not to be obtruded as the determination of the church.

William White, *The Past and the Future, A Charge, on Events Connected With the Organization of the Protestant Episcopal Church in the United States of America, And the Lessons They Inculcate* (Philadelphia: Published by Order of the Convention, 1834), 3-6, 7-8, 11-15. (Excerpts)

Chapter Three

Church Parties (1793-1937)

Introduction

As the church grew stronger, like-minded Episcopalians identified themselves with church parties. The high church party developed under the leadership of John Henry Hobart. He insisted that the Episcopal Church is the one, holy, catholic, and apostolic church in America. Hobart also urged that the Episcopal Church is the continuation of the historic church, but free of the extremes of protestantism and papacy. The evangelical party also developed during this period under the leadership of Alexander V. Griswold, Richard Channing Moore, Charles P. McIlvaine, and William Meade. The evangelical McIlvaine was one of the sharpest critics of the high church Oxford Movement and its impact on the Episcopal Church. Baptismal regeneration was another controversial issue during this period. Evangelicals urged the necessity for an accompanying moral change and actual experience of conversion. They disputed the possibility of regeneration through the sacrament of Baptism alone, and some refused to use the word "regeneration" in the Baptismal rite. These tensions eventually led to schism, and the organization of the Reformed Episcopal Church. James DeKoven found himself in the middle of a controversy over church ritual during this period. His piety favored a strong emphasis on the real presence of Jesus in the Eucharist, which was the basis for Eucharistic adoration. Others in the church did not share DeKoven's views. However, DeKoven argued convincingly at General Convention for a comprehensive Episcopal Church that would be broad enough to include a variety of perspectives. In many ways, he anticipated the promise of a later generation that there should be "no outcasts" in the Episcopal Church.

8.

Samuel Seabury, On Christian Unity, 1793

Samuel Seabury, first Bishop of the Episcopal Church and second Presiding Bishop, October 5, 1789–September 8, 1792, presented his views on Christian unity in the following sermon. Seabury, like John Henry Hobart, considered the episcopacy as part of the apostolic order of the church and implicitly identified "the church" with the Episcopal Church, effectively "unchurching" other denominations. Evangelical Episcopalians, on the other hand, while affirming the apostolic order of the Episcopal Church, were generally unwilling to "unchurch" other denominations. Evidence for this "high-churchmanship" is the office for the Institution of a Minister, added to the 1789 Book of Common Prayer *in 1804 on the basis of forms adapted in Connecticut in 1799 and New York in 1802. (See introduction to I, 2.)*

On the oneness, or unity of Christ's Church stands the necessity of Christian unity. Could there be more Churches of Christ than one, the obligation and necessity of Christian unity would be at an end; and we might be either of them, and still be united to Christ. And, was it possible that all the discordant sects and denominations of Christians, differing in their government, doctrine, sacraments, were all parts of the one church of Christ, we might be either of them; if not with the same advantage, yet at least with a safe conscience. Let us then attend to the nature of Christ's Church according to the text; and we shall, I trust, be convinced that it can be only one.

I. Christ, the head of the Church is but one; and, therefore, the Church which is the body, can be but one. It is against nature for the same head to have more than one body; and, it is equally against nature, for the body belonging to that head to be divided into distinct and contending portions. For though the same body may have different members, it cannot have separate parts; because whatever is separated from the body ceases to be part of it. As therefore Christ is one—"one Lord;" so the Church, which is his body, can be only *one*.

II. The same consequence will follow from that "one faith" in the "one Lord" to which all Christians are called, and which they must all hold, that they may become living members of that "one body." This faith, though it consists of various articles, can be but *one*, because it stands on one ground, the truth, or word of God; and centres in one object. Therefore it is, that the Apostles speak of a "unity of the faith," as well as "of the knowledge of the Son of God"—of a "faith once delivered to the saints for which they must earnestly contend"—of "the faith of the gospel," for which they must strive together: "in *one* spirit with *one* mind"—of a like," that is, of the *same* "precious faith"—of "the *common* faith," which all Christians are supposed to hold. These expressions show evidently that this faith is but one, and that whoever wants it cannot be in the unity of Christ's Church.

III. The same conclusion will follow from that "one Baptism" by which we are admitted into the Church of Christ and made members of his "one body;" and for the due reception of which, the "one faith" is an indispensable requisite. We know of but one way of admitting men into the Church, and making them members of the "one body" of Christ, by uniting them to him the one head of that body, and that is by the *"One Baptism of water and of the Spirit"* which he himself hath appointed for that purpose. The Baptism being but one, the body of Christ, to which it unites us, can be but one.

IV. Another reason why the Church is, and can be, but one, is, that there is but "one God and Father of all," who, by his essence, "is above all," being the origin and fountain of the Divinity, and of every thing which exists; by the energy of his nature, is "through all," pervading and governing everything which he has made; and, by the operation of his Spirit, is "in you all" who are members of the Church of his beloved Son; for,

V. That there is but "one body" of Christ (the Holy Catholic Church) appears from the "one Spirit," the life-giving Spirit of God, which animates that "one body." Of this Spirit every member partakes, by virtue of his union with that "one body," which is animated by this "one Spirit." As all the members of the natural body are animated by that spirit which animates the whole body, in consequence of their being members of the body, and united to it; so it is with the members of the Church: The gifts and graces of the Holy Spirit which they receive, come to them in consequence of their relation to Christ, and union with him.

The Spirit, therefore, which animates the Church, being the Spirit of God, and but one; the Church, animated by it, must also be one.

VI. The text furnishes another reason why the Church of Christ is but one; namely, the "one hope of our calling"—the hope of eternal life through Jesus Christ. As this hope is but one, and common to all good Christians, so the Church which furnishes this hope, can be but one.

As, therefore, there is one Father, the fountain of the Deity; one Lord Jesus Christ, the eternal Son of God, who is "over all, God blessed for ever"—the *head* of the Church which he hath redeemed and purchased with his blood; one Holy Spirit, proceeding from the Father, by whom "the whole body of the Church is governed and sanctified;" one faith in this Father, Son, and Holy Spirit, to the profession and acknowledgment of which all Christians are called; one Baptism by which we profess this faith, are admitted into Christ's Church, and made partakers of that Spirit in whom our union with Christ subsists; one hope of our heavenly calling—the hope of seeing God in glory; so the Church,

41

distinguished by these blessings and characters, depending on this *one* Father, governed by this *one* head, sanctified by this *one* Spirit, cemented by this *one* faith, washed by this *one* baptism, supported by this *one* hope, can be only One.

On this ground, as I said before, stands the Unity of the Church; and from it arises the duty of every member to continue in it, and to serve God faithfully in the station to which his providence has called him, using devoutly all the means of grace and holy living, which his goodness has provided for him.

The Church, therefore, is not the institution of man, but of God—not a confused company, but a regular society, founded by divine authority. It is Christ's Church, because he purchased and redeemed it with his blood. He called it out of the world, and separated it from the world, that it might be holy unto himself, and the school of holiness to all, who, being admitted into it, would conform to its holy and divine nature. For this purpose, He appointed its government; He instituted its priesthood; He ordained its sacraments; He bestowed on it his Holy Spirit; He is the "author of its faith;" and He gave to it the promise of eternal life. Its design is to take men out from under the sin, folly, and vanity of this wicked world; to unite them to Christ, and to one another, by a new birth from the Holy Spirit of God; and to train them up, in holiness and obedience, for the heavenly kingdom of their creator, in whose "presence is the fulness of joy, and at whose right hand there is pleasure for evermore."

This being the nature and design of the Church of Christ, it must be a visible institution, and not hard to be distinguished; otherwise, it would fail of obtaining the end proposed by it. It is to be known by its government, doctrine, and sacraments; where these are, as Christ ordained them, there is the Church of Christ; where these, or any of them, are wanting, there the Church is not; at least, not in a sound and perfect state. What the government, faith, and sacraments are, which were appointed by Christ, the Scriptures of the New Testament inform us. But, that the Scriptures may have their proper and full effect, it is necessary that the reader be free from prejudice, and disposed to receive and obey the will of Christ; that is, to believe what he hath said, and to do what he hath commanded. Where difficulties arise, the practice of the Apostles, and of apostolic men in the next age after them, together with the customs of the first Churches, will be the best comment to guide our inquiries.

Another property of Christ's Church in this world is that it is Catholic or Universal; that is, it is not limited to any period of time, but is to continue to the end of the world; nor confined to one nation, as the Jewish Church was, but admits for its members people of all countries and nations, as well as of all ranks, and degrees, and sexes, and ages. The world is its scene: But, as members from the whole world cannot meet in one place, for the purpose of worship and communion the Church must necessarily be divided into different portions, each portion being a member of the one Church of Christ. Locally considered, these portions may be denominated particular Churches, and take their names from the city where the Bishop resides; as the Church of Jerusalem, of Antioch, of Alexandria, &c. The union of a number of these Churches, under a metropolitan or Archbishop, is denominated from the country as the Church of Egypt, of Syria, of France, of England, &c.

In the mode of their worship, in the particulars of their discipline, in their rites and ceremonies, they may differ; but, so long as they retain the government, faith, and sacraments instituted by Christ, they are parts or members of his Church; and their Bishops have the right, not only of communion, but of being considered as true and valid Bishops of Christ's Church, wherever they shall go.

These local Churches, each under its own Bishop, must again be divided into congregations, each under its proper Presbyter, all subject to the Bishop of the Diocese. The people of the several congregations keep up their unity with the Church, by submitting to its discipline, by communion with their Presbyter, and by their right of communion with every branch of the Catholic Church, wherever God's providence may cast them: the Clergy preserve the same unity, by their submission to their Bishop, by their communion with him, and with each other. In this way was the unity of the primitive Church preserved; its government, faith, and sacraments maintained in their integrity, and its discipline duly administered. The people preserved communion with their Presbyter, the Presbyters with their Bishop, the Bishops with each other, in government, doctrine, sacraments, and councils. So that all orders and degrees of Christians may, in this way, enjoy all the means of grace and holy living which the all gracious Head of the Church hath appointed for them; and each member of the same, in his vocation and ministry, may truly and acceptably serve God; and, "holding the faith in unity of spirit, in the bond of peace, and in righteousness of life," may finally obtain the hope of his calling, eternal life with God in heaven.

This view of the subject necessarily supposes an union of Christians with each other, and with Christ the head of the Church. The Church is the body of Christ; every Christian is a member of that body, and of course is united to every other member, and to Christ the head. This union is effected and kept up by the operation of the Holy Spirit, who was given to the Church in consequence of Christ's ascension into heaven—"By one Spirit we are all baptized into one body"—"and have all been made to drink into one Spirit." This Spirit being from Christ, and Christ being the head of the Church, it is evident that every Christian receives the Spirit of Christ, by his being a member of his Church. Hence appears the guilt and danger of departing from the unity of the Church. By so doing, we separate ourselves from the body of which Christ is the head, and whose animating principle is the Holy Spirit of God. For if we receive the

Spirit, in consequence of our being members of Christ's Church; to preserve his presence with us, we must preserve our union with the Church, through which we first received his heavenly influence.

Samuel Seabury, *On Christian Unity. A Sermon* (New York: Protestant Episcopal Tract Society, 1793), 2-5. (Excerpt)

9.

The Life of the Reverend Devereux Jarratt, 1806

Devereux Jarratt (January 17, 1733–January 29, 1801) was the rector of Bath Parish, Dinwiddie County, Virginia, 1763-1801. He was converted to evangelical Christianity under Presbyterian influences. But he preferred the catholicity of Anglicanism, and he was ordained a priest in the Church of England. He played a leading role in the Southern phase of the Great Awakening and led a revival among Southern Anglicans in North Carolina and Virginia. Jarratt was opposed by his fellow Anglicans who regarded him as a dissenter and fanatic. He hoped that the Methodists would be an instrument for continued revival in Anglicanism, and was disappointed when they separated from the colonial Church of England at the Christmas Conference, December 25, 1784. Francis Asbury preached his funeral sermon. Jarratt has been called the first Evangelical of the Church of England in the American colonies. The following excerpt from a letter to The Rev. John Coleman shows some of his theological concerns.

February 24, 1796.

Rev. and Dear Sir,

I understood there was to be a general convention of our church last fall, at Philadelphia; but whether there was, or not, I have never been able to learn; of consequence, I have neither seen, nor heard of any thing that was done, in case that there was a convention. Dr. Magaw, in a letter, informed me, a convention was expected, and probably a revision of the articles would make a part of the business. I have had some anxiety on this head, and should be glad to know whether there has been any revision of the articles of our church, and also to get a sight of the articles so revised.

I have had my fears, that, as our church has been distinguished by the loose lives and ungodly practices of her professed members, so will she be distinguished, shortly, by proportionable corruptions in doctrine. Indeed, most of the clergy, as far as I can learn, have preached, for a long time, what is little better than deism, notwithstanding our old articles were so pointed and clear on the peculiar doctrines of the christian religion: such as the Trinity—the Godhead or Divinity of the Redeemer—the incarnation of the son of God—the atonement made by his death, &c. But should *Unitarianism, Socinianism,* &c. once creep into *the articles,* and give a sanction to that useless kind of preaching, so long in vogue, we may anticipate worse times than ever we have yet seen. I say, *the articles,* for should any thing derogatory to the Divinity of the son of God—any thing to insinuate even a doubt respecting his incarnation, atoning sacrifice, and the merits of his blood and righteousness be introduced, I should not call such *our articles,* but would reject and renounce them in the most decided terms and public manner.

. . . .

Arians, Socinians, and *Unitarians,* in their mad attempts to support an hypothesis, greatly obscure the principal and distinguishing glory of the gospel, and sap the foundation of a poor sinner's comfort. For my part, I find I stand in need of an Almighty Saviour—an Almighty Helper—an Almighty Physician— an Almighty Shepherd. If I am one of his people, and of the sheep of his pasture, then I am an individual of a very numerous flock—a flock wide diffused and scattered on a thousand hills throughout the habitable world: And if my shepherd be not possessed of attributes unlimited and incommunicably divine, I should fear being overlooked amidst the multiplicity of objects and concerns which must engage his attention. But if Jesus, my shepherd, be the omnipotent, omniscient, and omnipresent Jehovah, as David's shepherd was, then my fears depart—suspicious glooms disperse, and cheerful hopes of safety and protection dawn and revive. I see in my shepherd every perfection requisite for the office he sustains, and every qualification necessary to enable him to take care of such needy, oppressed, frail creatures as we are. He is perfectly acquainted with every individual of his flock—he is intimately near them—his eye is upon them, and his ear is open to the prayers of all, equally as to the prayer of any particular one; his arm supports, leads, guides, and protects them at all times, in all ages, and in all places: their thoughts, their wants, their weaknesses, and complaints are all known to him; he is all-wise and all-mighty, and therefore he is able to penetrate the most secret devices and hidden machinations of their enemies, controul the infernal powers, and take the wise in their own craftiness: the government is upon his shoulders, and the administration of universal providence, over all nations, families, and persons, throughout the universe, is in his hand, and he can so effectually restrain, controul, and manage in every case and circumstance, as to cause all things to work together for the good of those, who have put themselves under his pastoral care, and trust him with their all. "He feeds his flock, as their shepherd, he carries the lambs in his arms, and gently leads those, that are with young."

45

Such, my friend, is our shepherd—and could I be induced to suppose, for a moment, that he is not possessed of every attribute of divinity, supreme, and incommunicable, my hopes would sink, my heart faint, and my soul despair. But the very nature of his office requires that he should be possessed of these divine perfections, and the holy scriptures assure us that he is possessed of them. And are we indeed under the care, management, and protection of such a shepherd? Can we, through grace, say, we are his people and the sheep of his pasture? Then, surely, we have as good a right as David, to say, *we shall lack nothing—* nothing essential to our supreme, and final God.—Like sheep, we are weak and prone to wander; but he restores the soul, reclaims from crooked ways, and leads in paths of righteousness for his *name's sake.* And what is his name, here referred to, but, the Lord, the *shepherd?* This is a name of office, which he will not forget; but in every punctilio, act in character, as the tenderest, the kindest, the best, and the most vigilant and careful shepherd. O how safe, and happy are his people! I am a poor, weak, wandering, and stupid creature; I know it—I feel it: I am oppressed, defenceless in myself, and surrounded with enemies and ravenous beasts of prey. You, I doubt not, are in the same predicament. Yet, why should we fear, seeing all is made up in the fullness, power, wisdom, faithfulness, care, and compassion of our divine shepherd. My trust is, that he will provide for us, heal, restore, protect, and guide us by his counsel, and, in spite of the combined powers of earth and hell, lead us safe to glory. Then shall we see him as he is, be transformed into his likeness, be seated near him, and dwell in his presence for ever.

Your sincere friend,
D. JARRATT.

The Life of the Reverend Devereux Jarratt, Rector of Bath Parish, Dinwiddie County, Virginia, Written by Himself, in a Series of Letters Addressed to the Rev. John Coleman (Baltimore: Warner & Hanna, 1806; repr., New York: Arno Press & The New York Times, 1969), 195-203. (Excerpt)

10.

John Henry Hobart, The Origin, the General Character, and the Present Situation of the Protestant Episcopal Church in the United States of America, 1814

John Henry Hobart, a high churchman, describes the origin, general character, and present situation of the Episcopal Church in 1814 in this sermon at the consecration of Richard Channing Moore. While Hobart's emphasis on apostolic order placed him, like Seabury, in the high church tradition, the two differed on eucharistic theology. Seabury espoused the dynamic virtualism of the

English Non-jurors and Scottish Episcopalians, while Hobart followed the receptionism of Daniel Waterland (1683-1740) and the English high church tradition.

The general character of our Church may be ascertained by a view of some prominent features in her *doctrine, order, and worship.*

1. Her whole system of *doctrine* is founded on the truth of the defection of man from original righteousness, so that without God's preventing grace he is disposed to evil and impotent to good: at the same time the Church no where declares the accountableness of man for any but actual transgressions committed against grace received; or the total absence of all good propensities in his nature; though she undoubtedly maintains that there can be no principle in man called into holy operation but by the preventing and sanctifying power of the Spirit of God.

On the corruption of human nature and the guilt of man, our Church founds the necessity of a Mediator—for through a Mediator it hath pleased God to conduct his dispensation of mercy—a Mediator, *man* indeed that he might obey the law, the violated authority of which was to be vindicated, and sustaining its penalties, ward them off from the guilty offenders—*man* indeed, that he might be touched with a feeling for our infirmities, and knowing how to pity and to succour us embolden us to come unto God through him—but also a mediator, the *Son of God*, whom the Almighty Father would view with complacency, whose atonement he would accept as of infinite value, and whose intercession would be all prevailing. The doctrine of a *Divine* Mediator our church sets forth most prominently in her Articles and Creeds, and explains and guards with every variety of expression—and it is his mediation, his merits, his intercession, which, animating all her prayers, her collects and services, make them the source of comfort, of peace, and of exultation to the penitent soul.

The redemption, effected by the sufferings and death of this Mediator, who, in the language of Scripture is "the Saviour of *all* men, especially of them that believe," our Church extends to all mankind; making salvation possible through his merits to those, who, destitute of Gospel light, follow the dictates of conscience and the secret monitions of the divine spirit, as well as to those actual believers, to whom the blessings of the atonement are visibly signed and sealed by the word, the ministry and ordinances. These are the explicit declarations of our Church—"The offering of Christ once made is that perfect redemption, propitiation and satisfaction for all the sins of the whole world, both original and actual." "By his one oblation of himself once offered, he made a full, perfect, and sufficient sacrifice, oblation and satisfaction for the sins of the whole world."

The principle, by the operation of which we obtain a vital interest in the merits of this great mediator, is *faith*. "Wholesome and very full of comfort," in the judgment of our Church, is the doctrine "that we are justified by faith only." For it is faith which sends us as guilty and perishing sinners, grieved with our sins and bowed down under their burden, to Christ for rest and deliverance. It is faith which places our hope of acceptance—not on our tears; they cannot wash away the stain of our sins—not on our repentance; it needs to be repented of—not on our works of righteousness; when we have done all, we are unprofitable servants—but on the all sufficient merits and all-perfect righteousness of the Lord Jesus Christ, through whom, whosoever cometh unto God shall in no wise be cast out. United by faith to Him, we have an anchor of the soul that will secure us against every assault of the adversary; we have an hope, that even in the day that shall burn as an oven, and consume every false dependence, will not make us ashamed, but will animate us with rejoicing in the Lord, with joy in the God of our salvation. "Wholesome and very full of comfort is the doctrine that we are justified by faith." Blessed Saviour, it is faith which leads us to thee!

But the Church knows no true and lively, no justifying faith which does not produce the fruit of good works. An inspired apostle knew no justifying faith which did not "work by love and purify the heart and overcome the world." And these works, which are the fruits of a true and lively faith, "are pleasing and acceptable unto God in Christ." For it is a truth essentially and vitally resulting from his perfections, from his government, from the relations of man to him, and from the nature of the happiness of Heaven, that "without holiness, no man shall see the Lord."

But in a creature so dependent, so weak, so corrupt, and so exposed to temptation as man, these works must be wrought by divine aid, and this holiness produced in the soul by the power of divine grace. "Wherefore," saith our Church, "we have no power to do good works pleasant and acceptable to God, without the grace of God by Christ preventing," going before "us that we may have a good will."—But our Church disclaiming the doctrine of the irresistibility of grace which destroys man's free agency, subverts the nature of virtue, and renders man an unfit subject of reward and punishment, declares that the grace of God works "with us when we have that good will." And our Church disclaiming the equally injurious and unfounded doctrine of the indefectibility of grace, declares, that "after we have received grace we may fall into sin, and by the grace of God may arise again and amend our lives."

By this agency of the divine spirit is produced the renovation and sanctification of the heart, which the most superficial observer must acknowledge is a doctrine prominently displayed in all the offices and services of our Church. Inconsistent indeed would she be with herself, as well as contradictory to

Scripture, if, while she maintains with emphasis that we are "born in sin," that "there is no health in us," that "the flesh lusteth against the spirit," that we are "far gone from original righteousness," she, at the same time, should fail to inculcate the necessity of the renewing of our corrupt natures by divine power, and of our restoration to a state of purity, of soundness, of evangelical righteousness.

On this subject there is a remarkable characteristic of our Church. The avowal, with clearness and with force, of a doctrine, which indeed pervades every part of her system, that baptism is the sacramental commencement of the spiritual life. Infants, who according to the terms of the covenant, to the declarations and practice of our Saviour and his apostles, are fit subjects of baptism are made in this sacrament members of Christ, children of God, and heirs of the kingdom of Heaven. To adults properly qualified by repentance and faith, baptism is the means and the pledge of the same blessings. And even adults destitute of the necessary qualifications, certainly so far receive in this ordinance a proffer on the part of God, of grace, pardon, and salvation, as to leave them without excuse, and to increase their guilt and their condemnation, if they do not by repentance and faith secure the spiritual blessings sacramentally offered them. This important change of situation whereby the subjects of baptism are called into a state of salvation, is denominated by our Church, in the language of scripture and antiquity, *regeneration*. But if any persons would hence assert that our Church enforces no spiritual change but what takes place in baptism, they are confuted not only by the spirit and the language of all her institutions, but by the most explicit declarations of the office of baptism, which prays for those who are baptised that "the old Adam may be so buried that the new man may be raised up in them," that "all sinful affections may die in them, and all things belonging to the spirit may live and grow in them," that "they may have power and strength to have victory and to triumph against the devil, the world, and the flesh;" and the same office enforces on the baptized person the duty of "dying unto sin and living unto righteousness, and of continually mortifying all his evil and corrupt affections, and daily proceeding in all virtue and Godliness of living." To promote and effect this sanctification of the soul, there are provided the ordinance of confirmation, the ministrations of the word, and of the sanctuary, and of the altar; all which as well as baptism will only be unprofitable and condemning to the soul without the exercise of deep and unfeigned repentance, of lively faith, of watchfulnes and prayer. The "washing of regeneration" will not avail to salvation without "the renewing of the Holy Ghost;" and, in the language of the Church in one of her Collects, they who are "regenerate and made God's children by adoption and grace, must daily be renewed by his holy spirit."

This succinct view of the prominent doctrines of our church will serve I trust to establish her claim to the title of evangelical, in the scriptural, the primitive, the sober and the highest sense of the term—evangelical as proclaiming to all mankind not a nominal but a real Saviour; offering to all the means of an interest in his salvation. The doctrines of the Church are truly the doctrines of grace, tracing man's redemption to the love of God, who appointed for him a divine mediator, his only begotten Son; exhibiting the merits of this Saviour received by faith as the only ground of the sinner's acceptance; directing man to the power of the divine spirit—operating not with resistless force, but in consistency with his free agency, and conveyed through the instrumentality of the sacraments, and the ordinances and ministrations of the sanctuary, received with humble penitence, faith and prayer—for deliverance from the bondage of sin, for the renovation of his affections, for strength to advance with increasing vigour in the divine life, and finally to attain in triumph the heavenly glories of his calling. . . .

2. It is a distinguishing excellence of the worship of our Church, to which, as another prominent feature in her *general character*, I now proceed to direct your attention, that it exhibits the whole system of evangelical doctrine with unrivaled clearness, simplicity, strength, and pathos.

That our Church in conducting her services according to a prescribed order, has conformed to the practice of the ancient Jewish Church, to the example and authority of our Lord and his Apostles, and has thus also adopted the most effectual method of securing a rational, an enlightened, a sober, impressive, and dignified devotion, constitutes without doubt one of her great excellencies.

But a still higher ground of boast is it, and on this alone your time will permit me to enlarge, that her services exhibit the whole system of evangelical doctrine with unrivaled simplicity, strength, and pathos. They unfold all the exercises of the penitent and believing soul.—They furnish her with language for uttering all her emotions in her communion with her God. Does she wish to give vent to the feelings of guilt?—"I am grieved, O my God, with the remembrance of my sins; I am bowed down with their intolerable burden." Does she seek to deprecate the wrath of her offended Maker?—"Enter not into judgment with thy servant, O Lord, who am vile earth and a miserable sinner." "Deal not with me according to my sins; reward me not according to my iniquities." Does she wish to supplicate his mercy?—"Spare me, Good Lord, spare me—have mercy upon me, have mercy upon me—for thy Son Jesus Christ's sake forgive me all that is past— After the multitude of thy mercies look upon me, through the merits and mediation of thy blessed Son." Does she seek to enjoy the consolations of pardon?— "Receive and comfort me, O God, who am grieved and wearied with the burden of my sins—Lamb of God that taketh away the sins of the world, grant me thy peace." "Almighty God—make me know and feel that there is, none other name under Heaven given to man, in whom and through whom I can receive health and salvation, but only the name of the Lord Jesus Christ." Does she earnestly desire the sanctifying and consoling power of the Holy Ghost? "Cleanse the thought of my heart, O God, by the inspiration of thy Holy Spirit: May he in all things direct and rule my heart; that by Him I may have a right judgment in all things, and evermore rejoice in his holy comfort." Does she wish to love, and fear, and serve her God?—"Make me to have a perpetual fear and love of thy holy name—nourish me with all goodness, that withstanding the temptations of the world, the flesh, and the devil, I may with a pure heart and mind follow thee, the only God." In this her state of exile, does she pant to be elevated to Heaven her eternal home?—"O God, the King of glory, may I in heart and mind ascend to the same place whither my Saviour Christ hath gone before, and there continually dwell where thou hast prepared unspeakable joys for them that love thee." Does she in the anxious view of the regions of the grave, lift her soul to him who holds the keys of death and Hell? "When my soul is departing the body, may it be precious, O my God, in thy sight. Delivered from its earthly prison, may it live with thee in joy and felicity; and passing through the grave and gate of death to a joyful resurrection, may I have my perfect consummation and bliss both in body and soul in thy eternal and everlasting glory."

Now, my brethren, imperfect as is this display, I ask you with confidence to pronounce is it possible for piety short of that which warms the adoring seraph, is it possible for language which is not dictated by that inspiration that touched the lips of the Prophet, to breathe devotion more ardent, more sublime, yet more chaste and tender; to express with more force more simplicity or more pathos, the precious truths and promises of the Gospel? In this form these truths and promises are daily presented to the people, and carried to their understanding, their hearts and affections. The liturgy then preaches with an eloquence and a power that breathes in no uninspired book, that animates no uninspired tongue. The liturgy like the ark of the covenant preserves the heavenly law. By the liturgy was the flame of divine truth kept burning amidst the darkness and the desolation of our Zion. It is an invaluable depositary of all those truths which constitute the gospel, the power of God unto salvation; and from thence the servants of the sanctuary may display them in primitive lustre and apostolic power.

If these things be so brethren, Clergy and Laity, a question occurs in the view of your preacher deeply important. Shall we directly or indirectly loosen the hold which this Liturgy ought to have on the affections of our people, and thus prepare the way for the gradual extinction of the purest sources next to the Bible of divine truth and celestial devotion?

Cold indeed must be that heart which advocates the liturgy merely because the Church has prescribed it, venerable as is her authority; which make it merely the Shibboleth of a sect; which while it denounces the least departure from its prescriptions, neither glows with its fires nor speaks with its tongue. The Liturgy commands our veneration, our devoted attachment, as the sacred relick of apostolic times, as the precious legacy which martyrs warmed with their spirit and wrote in their blood; as the prescription of the Church which in this case speaks with an authority that is ratified in Heaven—But, I repeat it, the Liturgy commands our veneration, our devoted attachment still more, as, next to the Bible, the purest source of divine truth and celestial devotion.

The question then, I repeat it also, is deeply important—Shall we directly or indirectly, weaken or limit the influence of this invaluable manual of truth and piety? It would be an insult to your judgment to attempt to prove, that aberrations from this Liturgy tend to this deplorable result. The question then concerning these aberrations is not solely a question concerning the obligation of rubrics and ordination vows; but a question whether we shall preserve to the Church this source of truth, this light of devotion. The evangelical excellence of our public service is not its security. Against its venerable and sober forms, the spirit of enthusiasm wages irreconcilable war, and it will be ultimately successful if the Clergy, the appointed guardians of this liturgy, voluntarily surrender any of its holy devotions. Where individual judgment is substituted for public authority, and where private fancy moulds the service at pleasure, all security is lost for its preservation. Who shall direct or who shall restrain where private judgment has wrested the reins from public law? What part of the service is secure, when the almost infinitely varying judgments of men are permitted to alter it? How long will it retain its place in the *temple*, if when the members of our Church meet for social worship, they substitute for the *daily* morning and evening prayer, extempore effusions, or even premeditated devotions, necessarily inferior in excellence and authority? If *one* should omit the law of God as proclaimed in its awful prescriptions and sanctions by Jehovah himself, on Sinai's mount, what shall prevent *another* from withholding those sacred services which exhibit the cheering consolations of Zion's hill? One part of the service may be omitted for one reason, and another part for another. The part omitted by one constitutes, in the judgment of another, the brightest feature in the liturgy. Omissions, alterations, additions in the public service, most certainly and naturally produce the impression that some parts of it are defective, others imperfect, others of little moment, and others wholly unnecessary. The inevitable result is, that where the liturgy is venerated and loved, that veneration and attachment are weakened; and where lukewarmness and enthusiasm have excited an aversion to the liturgy, that aversion is fortified by the authority even of its guardians. What more certain, than the fatal results of innovation. Friends then of evangelical truth! Honest advocates of vital piety—will you be accessory in depriving the people of the pure exhibition of this truth which the liturgy contains, and of the influence of the ardent spirit of piety which animates this liturgy? Friends of the Church—will ye extinguish her brightest glory?

To preserve then this liturgy, it is essential that both clergy and people adhere to it as prescribed by the wisdom, the piety, and the authority of the Church. But let both clergy and people remember that the possession of this invaluable blessing will only tend to their condemnation, if they do not unite in its holy devotions with unfeigned repentance; with lively faith and love; and if they do not display in their life and conversation the humble, the pure, and the heavenly tempers which, by God's blessing, it is calculated to form in the soul.

3. I pass from the worship to the exhibition of another prominent feature of our Church, her

Apostolic Order, under the strong impression, my brethren, that I have already trespassed on your patience, and that therefore I must be as brief as possible.

That an *external commission* as well as an internal call of the spirit, is necessary to authorise a person to minister in holy things; that his commission must be derived from the head of the Church the source of all power in it, through that order of men whom he appointed successively to convey it; that three orders of the ministry were appointed by Christ and his apostles, and the first order invested with the power of commissioning to the ministry, are truths founded on the word of God and supported by the strongest primitive testimony. Whatever variety of opinion there may be concerning the terms in which these truths may be stated, and the consequences which may be deduced from them, there is certainly one ground on which all churchmen may meet—the ground taken in her articles and offices by the venerable Church from which we are descended, and maintained by our own. Now these articles and offices declare that "it is not lawful for any man to take upon him the office of public preaching or ministering the sacraments in the congregation before he be lawfully called and sent to execute the same"—that "from the apostles' times there have been these orders of ministers in the Church, Bishops, Priests, and Deacons," that the bishop alone receives the power of "ordaining, sending, and laying hands on others," and that, therefore, "no man shall be accounted or taken to be a lawful bishop, priest, or deacon in this Church, or suffered to execute any of the said functions, except he hath had episcopal consecration or ordination." This, my brethren, is no new language—these are are not the effusions of sectarian bigotry—they are not the declarations of private individuals. They are the principles, the declarations, the language of the venerable Church from which we derive our immediate origin; principles which at the period of the reformation she restored to primitive shape and form and laid at the foundation of her polity; principles, in her attachment to which, a revolution that for a while subverted them, served more to confirm.

They are principles, which no difficulties, not even the apprehension of being unable to carry them into effect, could induce our Church to relinquish; and for which her wishes, her prayers, her exertions were at last crowned with success. They are principles which she has deliberately and solemnly laid at the foundation of her polity, and which, if assailed or shaken, the whole edifice will be endangered. Against these fundamental principles, sanctioned by the wisdom and preserved through the changes of ages, I fear not that any innovating hand will be lifted up.

These principles which pre-eminently entitle our Church to the character of an Apostolic Church, it is the obvious duty of both clergy and people to revere, to inculcate, to defend; and to carry into full effect as it respects the admission to the ministry, the exercise of discipline, and the preservation of the unity of the church.

But let no person be guilty of the gross inconsistency and criminality of insisting on the *means*, while he is indifferent to the *end*. The salvation of souls, the promotion of vital practical godliness is the *end* for which the order of the Church is the divinely appointed *means*. And there can be no character more inconsistent, or who does greater injury to the cause which he professes to advocate, than the churchman, whether clergyman or layman, who contends with zeal for the order and the other externals of the church, while he neglects or undervalues that vital godliness and evangelical piety which they are designed to cherish and to preserve.

The order of the church then as it respects the constitution of the ministry is apostolic and primitive. In respect to her *government* properly so called, the forms by which she exercises her legislative, executive and judiciary powers, there are a few pre-eminent characteristics which you must permit me merely to point out.

And here we first recognise the important principle involved indeed in the very nature of all good government, that all orders of men affected by the laws should have a voice in framing them. Accordingly, no act in our church, not necessarily involving a point of divine institution, has the force of law, until it has received the sanction, under the forms of the constitution, of her bishops, her clergy, and laity.

We notice also the conformity of our ecclesiastical to our civil constitutions, in the *division of power* in the exercise of legislation; the bishops of the church constituting one house, in general convention, and the clerical and lay deputies another, with co-ordinate and equal powers. All the advantages of deliberation, of experience, and of security to individual rights, of which by this arrangement, our civil constitutions boast, are secured in the organization of our church.

We notice a similar conformity and further excellence in the *unity* of her executive head; her bishops being vested by the very nature of their office with the executive authority—And thus are secured that vigour, that decision, that promptness, and at the same time that responsibility, and of course the fidelity, which it would be impossible to secure at least in an equal degree, were the executive power of our church entrusted to large and popular assemblies.

In like manner, though from the nature of his office, the bishop is the ultimate judiciary tribunal, yet he can inflict no public censure and no punishment but in the due course of law, by which a knowledge of the charges against him, the means of defence, and a trial by his peers, are enjoyed by every individual.

Apart then from the *divine institution of the ministry*, we have cause of boast respecting the ORDER of our church, that it exercises the *powers of government* agreeable to the principles of right and justice, and of those forms of civil polity, on which experience has impressed the stamp of wisdom.

The exhibition then of the *general* character of our Church, impresses the duty of the most devoted attachment to her. Let not this attachment, best expressed by fidelity to all her principles, be branded as narrow bigotry, and sectarian zeal. It is an enlarged, an elevated, a noble feeling excited by the evangelical spirit which animates all the public confessions and formularies of the church, and by the apostolic character which distinguishes her ministry and ordinances. It is an attachment therefore to a system which, exhibiting the faith once delivered to the saints and bearing the stamp of apostolic authority, must be the best calculated, if its advocates and professors are faithful to its principles, to extend in its purity the kingdom of the Redeemer, and to advance most effectually the salvation of man.—Let us then my brethren, with united hearts and voices and in the fulness of affection, offer for our Church the prayer—"Peace be within thy walls and prosperity within thy palaces."

John Henry Hobart, *The Origin, the General Character, and the Present Situation of the Protestant Episcopal Church in the United States—A Sermon Preached in St. James's Church, in the City of Philadelphia, on Wednesday, May 18th, A.D. 1814, On the Occasion of the Opening of the General Convention of the said Church, and of the Consecration of the Right Rev. Bishop Moore of Virginia* (Philadelphia: J. Maxwell, 1814), 14-20, 22-31. (Excerpts)

11.

Charles P. McIlvaine, Oxford Divinity Compared, 1841

Charles Pettit McIlvaine (January 18, 1799–March 13, 1873) was consecrated the second Bishop of Ohio on October 31, 1832. During his episcopate he was the leader of the Evangelical party and an opponent of the Oxford Movement. The publication of Tract 90 on January 25, 1841, was the catalyst which polarized theological opinion in the Episcopal Church and changed the character and tone of theological debate, so that Episcopalians now often defined themselves in terms set by agreement or disagreement with Tract 90's reconciliation of the 39 Articles to the decrees of the Council of Trent. This represented a considerable shift from the older high churchmanship and also led "low churchmen" to define themselves in negative terms, by what they opposed rather than by what they affirmed. McIlvaine started proceedings against one of his clergy for the use of a vested choir. His Oxford Divinity condemned the Oxford leaders as unscriptural, contrary to the Thirty-Nine Articles, leading Anglicans to Rome, and as obscuring justification by grace through faith.

Oxford Divinity is represented partly in the Tracts, but in other writings also of various authors, some of whom are known as leaders, others as followers, all disclaiming the name of being connected together as a school or a party, or in any way to be associated but as having been raised up, in the same age, under the same divine providence and teaching, to testify against the same departures from primitive truth, and in favour of the same restoration of the Church Catholic from the supposed disintegrating influences of what they have united in branding as *Ultra Protestantism*. In this concert of action and purpose, and real system, so long as there was not common symbol or confession marking our their common peculiarities, it would not unfrequently occur that an attempt to designate the doctrines of the class, by particulars from individuals, would be met by the answer, that Oxford Divinity was not responsible for whatever might appear in the writings of all who professed to coincide with that way.

This difficult diffusiveness of essence, without corporate tangibility, has been, in some wise, removed by the publication in England, and the reprint in this country, of "A Letter by the Rev. E. B. Pusey, D.D., Regius Professor of Hebrew, in the University of Oxford," addressed to the Bishop of Oxford;—a work of more than two hundred well-filled pages, and purporting to contain, in behalf of the author and his fellow labourers, a declaration of faith on the points whereon they have been accused, with a special view to a vindication of their doctrines from the charge of a tendency to Romanism. The object of the author of that Letter is, in his own words, to lay before the Bishop *"An explicit confession."*

How far the confession is explicit on all points, professedly exhibited, may hereafter appear. How far it tends to remove the imputation of a dangerous tendency to Romanism, need not yet be said. It certainly places the question of Oxford Divinity—*what it is, what it is responsible for, and where it is to be found*, in a much more satisfactory position for investigation than that in which it appeared before. Its distinct mention of other vouchers beside itself, particularly the Lectures of Mr. Newman on Justification, as containing an exhibition of Oxford Divinity equally authentic and responsible with itself, enables the inquirer to embrace a wider field of reference, without fear of depending upon authorities which might afterwards be called in question.

The present writer has devoted a long time and a great deal of pains to the study of the *system*, as exhibited in the several sources to which the Letter of Dr. Pusey has opened the way. With great truth he can say that he has diligently STUDIED the system, and that too with every effort to judge it fairly, kindly, conscientiously, and with frequent prayer to know the truth with regard to a movement which promises so much influence, good or evil, upon the state of Religion in the Protestant Churches.

He is constrained to say that every further step of insight into what is indeed a thoroughly wrought, highly complex, and deep-laid scheme or system of doctrine, (much as the name of system is rejected by its advocates) has produced but a deeper and deeper conviction on his mind, that, whatever may be the intention or supposition of those who maintain it,—it is a systematic abandonment of the vital and distinguishing principles of the Protestant faith, and a systematic adoption of that very root and heart of Romanism, whence has issued the life of all its ramified corruptions and deformities. In this declaration it is not meant that all the divers particulars—all the far-reaching extremities of error and corruption into which the system of Romanism has spread, and by which, far more than its deep-rooted principles, it is known in modern controversy, are manifested in the system under consideration. Far from it. Romanism did not grow into its present stature and wide extension of limb and shade in an age. But in the essential and characteristic life of its divinity it existed nevertheless, and was not less Romanism when modestly sending out its feelers, and quietly widening its under-ground roots and shooting forth its branches, as the *times* allowed,—than it is Romanism now, in all its maturity and boastfulness. And so may Oxford Divinity be essentially Romish Divinity, built on the same foundations, squared with reference to the same cardinal points, and by the law of its own nature, necessarily proceeding, in proportion as room is given, and the "Times" will bear, to make itself known in all those evils to the Gospel of Christ, by which the sway of Romanism has been so lamentably distinguished; while as yet, being truly a system "*for the times*," it may not be Romanism in such overt self-confession and unreserved manifestation, before an unprepared community, or even in the unprepared minds of its immature, but growing disciples, as to strike the common eye, or be generally recognized, as of the house and lineage of Popery.

The present writer is fully convinced that such is the precise character and such are the certain results of Oxford Divinity, in proportion as its tendencies shall have time and room to develop themselves. Every additional examination of the system, as additional documents have appeared from its advocates, or a closer dissection of those long in hand, has been made, has only rendered this conviction more and more immovable. Instead of this conviction being in any degree impaired by the consideration that sundry branches of Romanism have not been avowed, or have been really opposed by the advocates of this system; the fact only shows that, if their doctrine be Romanism, in essential character and influence, its imperfect ramification, by making the evil more invisible, only renders it the more dangerous. A more rapid development would be the better warning to the unwary, and would arouse a more vigorous effort for its extinction.

Charles P. McIlvaine, *Oxford Divinity Compared With That of the Romish and Anglican Churches; With a Special View of the Doctrine of Justification By Faith* (London: R. B. Seeley and W. Burnside, 1841), 5-9. (Excerpt)

12.

Evangelical Knowledge Society, 1847

Some of the Evangelical leaders became concerned that the General Protestant Episcopal Sunday School Union was favoring the Tractarian party. At the General Convention in New York, October 6-28, 1847, some of these Evangelicals decided to form a new organization, the Protestant Episcopal Society for the Promotion of Evangelical Knowledge, usually known by its shorter title, the Evangelical Knowledge Society. The experiential emphasis on pardon, justification, renovation, and sanctification is characteristically evangelical.

"EVANGELICAL"

We use the term in its well understood sense, as indicating the leading and fundamental doctrines of the glorious Reformation. Our system of doctrine will readily be recognized by a statement of a few of its particulars.

Scripture, the sole rule of faith; *not* Scripture and tradition its joint rule.

Man, an utterly lost and helpless sinner; and *Christ*, a most free and sufficient Saviour.

Pardon, the direct gift of Christ to every one that believeth with the heart; with no intervention other than that needed to bring him to faith; not dependent on a priestly act or any human intervention for the forgiveness of sin.

Justification, a gracious act of God, received by faith without works; not an inward character in man, consisting of faith as one of a catalogue of justifying graces.

Renovation, the work of the Holy Spirit in the regeneration of man, operating mainly through the Truth, and making us new creatures in Christ.

Sanctification, distinguished from justification, as the fruit from the seed; not blended with justification as making therewith one whole of inherent righteousness.

The Church, "the blessed company of all faithful people."

Episcopacy, as having existed "from the apostle's times."

The Sacraments, divine signs and seals, pledges and means of grace to faith; not standing miracles, whereby Christ is made incarnate in his members.

Jesus, the immediate High Priest and sole Intercessor in behalf of every individual believer; not approached through the necessary medium of any ministerial intervention.

Worship, according to our Liturgy, simple and scriptural; not loaded with human inventions and unauthorized ceremonies.

E. Clowes Chorley, *Men and Movements in the American Episcopal Church* (New York: Charles Scribner's Sons, 1946), 60-61.

13.

William Meade, The True Churchman, 1851

William Meade (November 11, 1789–March 14, 1862) was consecrated Assistant Bishop of Virginia on August 19, 1829, and became the third bishop of Virginia when Bishop Richard Channing Moore died on November 12, 1841. Meade was a leading Evangelical bishop. The True Churchman, *an address delivered to the Convention of the Diocese of Virginia on May 21, 1851, presents his position. Meade was unwilling to deny to other denominations the name of church.*

[L]et me now sum up in a few words the impression which prevails in my mind as the character of a true churchman in our branch of the christian church.

1st. He is one who is sincerely attached to the doctrines thereof, as seen in the prayer book, and confirmed by the contemporaneous writings of those who drew up the prayer book in England, or revised it in America; not as interpreted by the fathers or what is called catholic consent. Nevertheless according to the prayer book he acknowledges the bible as the only divine rule of faith, and esteems the doctrines of the church because he believes them to be according to that divine rule.

2dly. He loves the liturgy of the church because he believes it to be according to the doctrines of the bible and prayer book. As to her worship, he seeks to enter into its deep spirit of devotion, without which all his admiration and praise of it will be of no avail. If he be a minister, he will read it as one who feels its truth, and will seek to induce his congregation to unite audibly and heartily with him. If a parent, he will not only open his mouth and utter it as one not ashamed of it, but seek to lead his children and others to do the same. **3dly.** As to the ministry and government of the church, he will show his belief of its apostolic appointment and many excellences, by obeying, according to his station, those who are over him in the Lord. He will honor each order of that ministry which he believes to have come down from the apostles, according to its office and the authority given to it, not wishing to elevate or depress either of them. **4th.** As to those divisions of christendom which have, whether through unavoidable necessity or mistaken judgment, deviated from what he conceives to be the apostolic regimen, he will seek to judge of them and act towards them as God sets the example and our forefathers followed. He will see that God chose to use them as he did the reformers of our mother church, for restoring true faith and piety when they were almost vanished from among men, and that to the present day, he still continues to use them for the purpose of promoting his cause upon earth. While therefore he laments what he regards as a defect, through which great evils have entered their communion, he dares not reject from the church of Christ those whom Christ hath thus honored, but as he hopes to meet with them and be ever with them in his presence hereafter, so he delights to walk with them in love here below, and co-operate in all good works, so far as can be done without the sacrificing of conscience, and the engendering of discord and confusion. As a man may be a patriot and a philanthropist at the same time, may love his own country especially, and yet love the whole human race, so the churchman may love above all other his own particular church and seek its prosperity more diligently, and yet love all the people of God, by whatever name they be called. Thus while especially devoted to his own church, and even to some portion of the same, it may be truly said of him,

> "To sect or party his large soul
> "Disdains to be confined,
> "The good he loves of every name
> "And prays for all mankind."

His charity only begins at home; it knows no bounds but those set by God himself for his own benevolence.

"God loves from whole to parts, but human soul
"From individual to the whole."

I confess, my brethren, that I have always loved our own and mother church for this, as for many other reasons, that I think in her whole history, from the Reformation to the present day, there has been a due admixture of this liberal feeling towards others with a most ardent attachment to her own peculiarities. If in either of them there has been, whether in public acts or private opinions, any thing to the contrary, nor is this denied, it is believed that the great body of the members has not partaken of it. The high station they have occupied, and the intelligence belonging to them, have doubtless contributed not a little to such liberality, but the spirit breathing through all her devotions, and the character and example of her early reformers and martyrs, and the compilers of her prayer book have contributed much more. In her whole history there is much to interest, though not without that which we must all lament and condemn. Let the history of the English church be stricken from the annals of Christendom, let the memories of many of her bishops, other ministers and eminent laymen be consigned to oblivion, let all the volumes of sermons, theological treatises and devotional works be dismissed from the libraries of the divines of every denomination, and what a melancholy blank would be created. And may I not add, that if the history of her youthful daughter in America, as seen in the early efforts for her first establishment on the part of English friends, in the difficulties encountered in our own country, in the character of many of her leading advocates both among the clergy and laity, and in the success which, through God's blessing, has crowned their labors be considered, we have much to interest our minds and much to endear her to our hearts. And may I not further add, that as there is a church of England and America which we are allowed to love above all other great divisions of the church of Christ upon earth, so there is to us, my brethren and friends, a church in Virginia which we may love and care for with a yet more special affection. Is there nothing peculiarly interesting in her history to justify the historiographer of the church in the United States to choose it for his first effort? Is there nothing in her earliest history to excite even a romantic interest in her behalf, though there be much to mourn over in the progress thereof? Is there nothing to the same end in her struggles for existence itself at the close of the revolution, when thousands were crying out "down with her, down with her even to the ground?" Is there nothing to sustain our faith and excite our gratitude to God, in the most unexpected resuscitation of her from a state of apparent death? Is there nothing to endear her to the heart in the repaired temples, and even in the yet remaining ruins of some of the old temples of our fathers? Is there nothing to commend her to our choice in the character of those individuals and families who in times of desertion still adhered to her fallen fortunes, and whose descendants now constitute the great body of her communion? Is there nothing to commend it to our affection and confidence in that seminary which has not only supplied our own state with so many faithful ministers, but whose hundreds of alumni are to be seen in all parts of our own land, and yet more, who form so large a proportion, almost indeed the entire band, of those devoted missionaries who, in Europe, Asia and Africa, are seeking to spread the glorious gospel through the world?

Is it weakness, my friends, to love such a church, and speak of it sometimes even to boasting? Not, if at the same time we mourn over our unworthiness as members thereof, and do not withhold the candid acknowledgment of much error and sin pervading our portion, as well as all other portions of Zion. But with such a feeling and confession we may, and I trust all of us will, as to our church in its wide extension through the earth, and in her special location in our midst, take up the language of one of our sweet hymns.

> "Beyond my highest joys
> "I prize her heavenly ways,
> "Her sweet communion, solemn vows,
> "Her hymns of love and praise.
> "If e'er my heart forget
> "Her welfare or her woe,
> "Let every joy this heart forsake
> "And every grief o'erflow.
> "For her my tears shall fall,
> "For her my prayers ascend,
> "To her my cares and toils be given,
> "Till toils and cares shall end."

William Meade, *The True Churchman* (Charlottesville: James Alexander, 1851), 20-23. (Excerpt)

14.

Evangelical Education Society, 1862

Founded on November 3, 1862, the Evangelical Education Society is the oldest voluntary organization in the Episcopal Church. It was founded to provide scholarships for students preparing for ordination. Nearly a century later it was enlarged by its merger with "The Society for the Promotion of Christian

Knowledge," organized in 1848 as "The Protestant Episcopal Society for the Promotion of Christian Knowledge." In 1961 the Episcopal Evangelical Fellowship, also known as "Liberal Evangelicals," joined the Evangelical Education Society. The following document is a twentieth-century statement concerning the identity and principles of the Evangelical Education Society.

I. Who Are We?

The Evangelical Education Society is a voluntary association of the Protestant Episcopal Church of the United States of America. The E.E.S. exists to affirm and promote the Reformed and Protestant principles within the church, as these are expressed in the Prayer Book and the Thirty-nine Articles.

More particularly, the Society, in a variety of ways, works to further the theological education of evangelical Episcopalians for lay and ordained ministry in the church's accredited seminaries. The society advances reformed and evangelical Christianity within the Episcopal church, encourages communication and fellowship among evangelical Episcopalians, and fosters biblically based personal prayer and study for Christian nurture.

II. What Do We Stand For?
The Primacy of God's Word

As evangelicals and Episcopalians we affirm the importance of the Ministry of the Word. The proclamation of the Good News of God's redeeming Love in Jesus Christ within the church and to the whole world, we believe, is at the center of the church's identity and mission. We believe the church is renewed primarily through the preaching of the Gospel. Indeed, we seek a renewal of the great Anglican tradition of expository preaching. The proclamation of God's judgment, mercy and pardon to all people is a central concern of the Society.

The Meaning of the Word of God

Pre-eminently the meaning of God's Word is that in the person of Jesus Christ God speaks to us, that God also accomplishes in Christ his saving deeds for us, so that in both words and deeds the world might be reconciled to him. In the knowledge of this reconciliation we know that we are justified by God's graciousness, through faith alone, and not by any achieved goodness on our part.

The Primacy of God's Word Over Our Lives

For us, the importance of God's Word includes daily living out of the Holy Scriptures. This goes beyond mere lip-service to biblical authority or admiration for the Bible and quoting the Bible; it means submitting our understanding and behavior to the mind of Christ, as witnessed to in Scripture.

Scripture as the Word of God

We hold the Bible to be "God's Word written," to use the phrase of Article 20. The Word of God, authenticated by Christ, is in the meaning of the biblical passages, not simply in their form of words. That meaning is *reliable* when it tells us about God and his truth, *authoritative* when it calls men and women to trust, confidence and obedience. We affirm the use of critical methods of Bible study so that we may better understand the forms and meanings of the biblical text. We believe that truth is one and affirm the need, in each age, to find fresh ways to interpret and apply the biblical text.

The Cross of Christ

As Evangelicals we emphasize not only the Incarnation of the Word of God but also the Cross of Christ. In Christ's saving death, God was and is reconciling the world to Himself. In Christ's death on our behalf and in our place, sin and death are overcome. In Christ's birth, ministry, and especially passion, death and resurrection, God entered once for all our human predicament and emerged victorious over every form of sin and evil. With St. Paul, therefore, we desire that the church's preaching should be "Jesus Christ and him crucified." The goal of such evangelical preaching should be a response of trust, confidence in God, obedience to God in word and works, and baptism into Christ's body, the church.

The Worship of the Christian Community

We believe God makes himself known and present through the sacraments of baptism and eucharist. We also affirm the importance of other non-verbal aspects of worship: architecture, color, music, the other arts, and ceremonial. We affirm the Anglican tradition of beauty, decency and order in worship. We emphasize, however, the need to avoid letting the means of worship become the focus of attention, hindering God's Word speaking to people and evoking a personal response from them. True Christian worship is the work of Christian people gathered to receive God's Word in sermon and sacrament and to respond in prayer and song. True worship is not a spectacle to look at but a liturgy in which we take part.

Daily Disciplines of Grace

We seek to have church members committed to the daily reading and study of the Bible and the practice of personal prayer. These disciplines of grace remind us daily of God's claim on our lives, deepen our trust in his promises, and call us each day to a life of faithful witness.

The Ministry of All Christians

We affirm the ministry of all the laity. Following Luther and Calvin, we urge laypersons to regard their daily work as a vocation from God, as a most significant arena of Christian ministry. We also wish to promote the concept of mutual ministry, that lay and ordained persons together constitute the ministers of Christ's church.

An Ecumenical Commitment

We rejoice in our Anglican, Reformed and Protestant heritage. We seek union, consonant with this heritage, with non-Episcopal Protestants and with Orthodox and Roman Catholic churches. We rejoice in the ecumenical movement and believe evangelically minded Anglicans have fundamental truths to contribute to the dialogue.

God's Call to Serve Society

As Evangelicals of an older time led the way to prison reform, abolition of slavery, education based on ability not social class, to justice as a basis of peace, so the Society calls the church to be a servant to the world. We call the church to relate to all aspects of human culture, testing the spirit of cultural expressions and forms by the Spirit of Christ. We call the church to prophetic critique wherever culture debases human dignity and to support wherever culture expresses human wholeness as measured by Christ.

We affirm that Christians in America have the religious duty and constitutional right to let their beliefs inform their political views and decisions in matters of public policy. With the First Amendment we also affirm that the institutions of church and government should be separate. We urge the realistic recognition that civil legislation often protects and promotes basic moral principles. We also recognize the dangers involved when Christians attempt to impose their moral convictions by legislative means on those who strongly hold different positions.

God's Providence

The Society urges a reawakened trust in God's providential care for the world. The decay of civic virtue, the deterioration of our cities, the increasing rate of divorce, the wide disregard for the centrality of marriage and family for the health of society, the widespread neglect of young children and of the elderly, the poor and mentally ill can easily increase despair and moral resignation. As evangelicals, however, we affirm God's covenant fidelity with His creation, sealed in Christ's death and resurrection. Convinced of God's victory over every form of evil, we believe God will not forsake us.

A Statement to Further the Historic Evangelical Witness in the Protestant Episcopal Church (brochure), no pagination.

15.

Pastoral Letter on Baptismal Regeneration
and Eucharistic Adoration, 1871

The Ritual Controversy was especially divisive in the Episcopal Church from 1868 until 1874. At the General Convention in Baltimore, October 4-26, 1871, a "Canon on Ritual" was presented by the Joint Committee on Ritual Uniformity. It was defeated after considerable debate, but the Pastoral Letter of that year condemned auricular confession, warned against extreme veneration of the saints, and criticized eucharistic adoration.

The Bishops in council, with an extraordinary unanimity, have, during the present Convention, set forth a Declaration, touching our Offices for the Baptism of Infants, in the following words:

"We the subscribers, Bishops of the Protestant Episcopal Church in the United States, being asked, in order to the quieting of the consciences of sundry members of the said Church, to declare our conviction as to the meaning of the world 'regenerate' in the offices for the ministration of Baptism of Infants, do declare that in our opinion the world 'regenerate' is not there so used as to determine that a moral change in the subject of baptism is wrought in the Sacrament."

This declaration was made in the loving hope and confidence that many consciences might thus forever be freed from false impressions, which have been prevalent, concerning the teaching of the Church as respects spiritual religion and personal piety. We exhort you, brethren, to be ever mindful of the tender love of our Master Christ for little children, and to think highly of the privileges to which those are admitted whom, through the agency of His Church, He still takes into His arms and blesses. We entreat you to regard them as His own children by adoption and grace, as heirs of God to be brought up in the nurture and admonition of the Lord. Let them not suppose that the faith, and the prayers, and the obedience of little children, are lightly regarded by the Father of Mercies. But remember, also, that baptism does not supersede the necessity of repentance, of justifying faith in Christ, growth in grace, and that "holiness without which no man shall see the Lord." We exhort all the members of this Church fully to recognize and deeply to feel, therefore, the weight of responsibility which the baptismal covenant lays upon them and their children. It is still true that if the baptism of infants be not recognized as requiring such Godly training as may secure by the Divine blessing the submission of their whole nature, body, soul, and spirit, to the renewing and sanctifying influences of the Holy Ghost, then the mind of Christ and the purpose of the Church for the child are not fulfilled. If refraining, henceforth, from discussion of words in the acceptance of which there seems to be far less of real disagreement than has been imagined, we might now give ourselves with one heart to the rearing of our children in the fear of God, and to securing the great work of their salvation; then we shall have succeeded in rendering our formularies so practical and so fruitful in godliness as to elevate the whole sentiment of the Church to a lofty spirituality not likely to be disturbed by agitations to which, perhaps, we have subjected ourselves by manifold inconsistencies between our professions and our practices, in the relations we bear to God in covenant.

As we dwell on these things, dear brethren, our minds recur to others, of which we must not fail to speak.

We counsel you to bear in mind that while on the one hand we must not suffer ourselves to deny any real good by reason of mere popular outcries against ritual forms, so, on the other hand, we are never to allow professions of self-denying labour and service to blind us to the actual dangers of any movement in the Church. What is known as "ritualism" is mainly a question of taste, temperament, and constitution, until it becomes the expression of doctrine. The doctrine which chiefly attempts as yet to express itself by ritual, in questionable and dangerous ways, is connected with the Holy Eucharist. That doctrine is emphatically a novelty in theology. What is known as "Eucharistic adoration" is undoubtedly inculcated and encouraged by that ritual of posture lately introduced among us, which finds no warrant in our "Office for the Administration of the Holy Communion."

Although men may, by unlawful reasoning on Divine mysteries, argue themselves into an acceptance both of the practice, and the doctrine which it implies, these are most certainly unauthorized by Holy Scripture, entirely aside from the purposes for which the Holy Sacrament was instituted, and most dangerous in their tendencies. To argue that the spiritual presence of our dear Lord in the Holy Communion for the nurture of the faithful is such a presence as allows worship to Him, thus and there present, is, to say the very least, to be wise above that which is written in God's Holy Word. For the objects of this Holy Sacrament, as therein revealed, are first, the memorial before God of the One Sacrifice for sins forever; and secondly, the strengthening and refreshing of the souls of the faithful. Moreover, no one can fail to see that it is impossible for the common mind to draw the line between the worship of such an undefined and mysterious presence, and the awful error of adoring the elements themselves. Wherefore, if a teacher suggests this error by act or posture, he places himself in antagonism to the doctrine of this Church and the teachings of God's Word, and puts in peril the souls of men. In the presence, therefore, of this danger, we call upon the ministers and members of the Church to bear in mind that while they should always cherish and exhibit that true and genuine reverence which devoutly recognizes "the dignity of that holy mystery, and the great peril of the unworthy receiving thereof," yet it is the bounden duty of each one to deny himself the outward expression of what to him may be only reverence, if that expression even seems to inculcate and encourage superstition and idolatry.

Pastoral Letter of the House of Bishops, 1871, 5-8.

16.

John Johns, Reply of Bishop Johns to
Rev. J. A. Latané's Letter of Withdrawal, 1874

John Johns (July 10, 1796–April 5, 1876) was consecrated Assistant Bishop of Virginia on October 13, 1842, and became the fourth bishop of Virginia when Bishop William Meade died on March 14, 1862. James Allen Latané (January 15, 1831–February 21, 1902) left the Episcopal Church over the baptismal regeneration controversy and joined the Reformed Episcopal Church which was organized on December 2, 1873. Latané was Presiding Bishop of the Reformed Episcopal Church from 1883 to 1887 and 1900 to 1902.

You need not, my dear brother, apprehend any ungenerous construction of *your* motives in taking this serious step. For our brethren in Virginia, I can engage that one and all will render *you* full credit for conscientiousness however decidedly they may disallow the reasons you assign for leaving the Episcopal Church, and regard it as a causeless separation.

Your just testimony as to the unchanged Protestant and Scriptural teaching of the Articles and Offices of the Church is no more than was to have been expected from one of your intelligence and candor, though it is testimony which many persons must find difficult to reconcile with your "withdrawal."

Your testimony may be presented as follows: You, of course, regard the doctrines held by what you call the "Low-Church Party" to be sound and Scriptural. Now, on page thirteen you represent "the Thirty-nine Articles of the Church, which were designed to be the standard of doctrine for the Church," as sustaining the Low-Church Party in its teaching, and as proving "conclusively that it (the Low-Church Party) holds to-day the doctrines held by the framers of the Prayer Book."

The passage in its connection affords favorable testimony to the orthodoxy of the XXXIX Articles, and indirectly to the orthodoxy of the Prayer Book.

Again, page 4: "It is true that her standards of doctrine remain unchanged, and the XIX. and XXIII. Articles in the Prayer Book still testify to her original

Protestant stand on this question" (the question of the Ministry, which carries with it the whole question about Priest, Sacrifice, and Altar).

Once more, page 4: "I am satisfied that this doctrine (that Baptism invariably effects regeneration) was *not held* by the framers of the Prayer Book, *nor intended to be expressed* in the Service, and therefore *is not really* the doctrine of the Church."

I do not cite these passages as dissenting from them, for I think them accurately true; but as expressing your deliberate opinion as to the strict conformity of the teaching of the Church, in the Articles and Offices, with the Word of God as interpreted by the Reformers.

For separation from a Church justly entitled to such testimony, what reason can be assigned? Those alleged in your letter I cannot recite in full, nor is it necessary, being, as you say, "just those which have been for some years a burden and grief to many in the Church," and it might be added, which have been often and clamorously urged by adversaries without. They may be thus summarily stated:

There are in some of the Formularies provided in the Book of Common Prayer a few, very few, words or phrases which, though if rightly interpreted according to the intent of the framers, express true doctrine, yet are liable to be misunderstood, and, in *fact*, have been and are so misunderstood and perverted, as to subserve the cause of serious doctrinal errors. This statement is unhappily true, and furnishes a good and sufficient reason for such *alterations* as may be necessary to obviate the evil. But it is no valid reason for repudiating the Book or *withdrawing from the Church*. If *this* were admitted, consistency would require us to reject the Pauline Epistles, and withdraw from Christianity. St. Peter (2, iii. 16) writes, that in all those Epistles "are some things hard to be understood," and which "certain persons wrest, as they do also the other Scriptures, unto their own destruction." You would not expect me to allow the validity of a reason capable of an application so wide and so destructive, and which would make a clean sweep of all we both hold to be most precious.

The true lesson taught by the facts which are admitted is the importance of such alterations in the terms and phrases alluded to, or in the Rubrics relative to their use, as may most effectually guard against misunderstanding and perversion. Any such interference with the text of Sacred Scripture is out of the question; but for an uninspired document no such exemption can be claimed. Now this Church, after the example of the Church of England, has, in her Preface to the Book of Common Prayer, laid it down as a rule that: "The particular forms of Divine Worship, and the Rites and Ceremonies appointed to be used therein, being things in their own nature indifferent and *alterable* and so *acknowledged*, it is but *reasonable* that upon weighty and important considerations, according to the various emergencies of times and occasions, *such changes and alterations should be made therein* as to those who are in authority should, from time to time, seem either necessary or expedient."

Wise and ample provision is thus made to remedy just such evils as those of which you complain.

But you despair of relief in this way, pronounce it an "absolute impossibility;" represent the effort made in this direction by the nine Bishops, in a letter to their brethren, as a "signal failure," ending in a "mortifying discomfiture." Having been present in the House of Bishops during the entire proceeding to which you so slightingly refer, and having watched it with intense interest for those whom it was intended to relieve, and having carefully committed it to writing *at the time*, I feel at liberty to correct the erroneous impression you have received.

Before an opportunity offered for presenting the Letter of the nine Bishops, the whole subject was introduced in a promising form, and with a very appropriate statement by one of the majority. The discussion, which continued for several days, was conducted not only with exemplary courtesy, but in a fraternal spirit, which will not soon be forgotten by those who witnessed it with admiration and gratitude. Instead of widening the distance between those who differed, that distance diminished with every day's deliberations. The measure at first proposed was from time to time variously modified with most amazing concord, and at last adopted and signed as published, by the whole House, with only one exception. The names of forty-eight Bishops are affixed to the Declaration. This result you will scarcely characterize as "mortifying discomfiture." You, my dear brother, may think and say that "the Declaration" is not in "any sense" "a gain" to those for whose relief the nine Bishops were concerned. I can assure you that though what those Bishops sought was but partially attained, yet it was so much beyond what they hoped from a first move, and was yielded so handsomely, that they "thanked God and took courage." I will add, that when the Declaration as adopted was previously submitted to Bishop McIlvaine, with the inquiry, "How does this strike you?" he very emphatically replied, with a smile of unmistakable satisfaction. "The best thing yet!" But the circular addressed by the nine Bishops to those whom they sought to relieve, and which was prepared and sent to press after the Declaration was adopted, and to which I beg leave to refer you, may enforce my brief report, and perhaps modify your views of the transaction and its results.

It placed you, and others who agree with you, doctrinally, in an easier and more advantageous position, leaving you unchanged in your conviction that the great spiritual change, the new birth unto righteousness, is not inseparably connected with the administration of Baptism, and that the contrary view "was not held by the framers of the Prayer Book, nor intended to be expressed in the Service, and is not, therefore, the doctrine of the Church;" and, moreover, sustaining you in this your conviction, by this Declaration of forty-eight Bishops in Council, who state that, "being asked, in order to the quieting of the consciences of sundry members of the said Church (Protestant Episcopal Church in the United States), to declare our conviction as to the meaning of the word 'Regenerate,' in the Offices for the Ministration of Baptism of Infants, do declare that, in our opinion, the word 'Regenerate' is not there so used as to determine that a moral change in the subject of Baptism is wrought in that Sacrament."

That efforts would be made by some to explain away the meaning and force of this testimony was to be expected; but there it stands, to be understood and used agreeably to the express design of the signers and the proper import of its terms; and, as the nine Bishops and very many others thought, worth considerably more than "nothing," both in itself, for the excellent spirit in which it was done, and the hope thus given that, as it should become apparent that other measures were needed "for the preservation of the unity of the Church, and cutting off occasion from them that seek occasion of cavil or quarrel against her Liturgy," such measures would be adopted.

Another consideration which you urge with much feeling is the "attitude which the Protestant Episcopal Church has assumed towards the great bulk of Protestant Christians." Of course, you do not mean "the Church," for you say in the same immediate connection that her standards of doctrine remain unchanged, and the XIX. and XXIII. Articles in the Prayer Book still testify to her original Protestant stand on this question. I therefore understand you to mean what you indicate by "the prevailing opinion," the "current of public sentiment." Such "sentiment" and "opinion" you regard as imperious and unchurching in reference to all ministers not Episcopally ordained.

"Public opinion," when counter to our own, may be annoying, but it is of no authority. "Prevailing sentiment" is too variable and fallacious to be entitled to the consideration and influence which you seem to allow it, even when you denounce it as pernicious. Under such circumstances, it would be more like yourself to stand immovably witnessing for the truth, trusting to its power for triumph, and not to seek relief by getting away from opposition. Your known spirit authorized me to anticipate a calm but unflinching maintenance of a right position in a right cause. I confess I am disappointed.

When, in any matter involving conscience, be it in reference to faith or practice, public sentiment is erroneous, and becomes so prevalent and aggressive as to pass into law, *then*, indeed, the grievance is intolerable. This is precisely what you *fear* on the subject of the Ministry. You think the drift is decidedly towards the high latitudes, and the current so strong that the result is inevitable; that the bearing of legislation is increasingly in that direction, and has already progressed so far, that if we accept the current interpretation of certain canons, no minister of the Episcopal church can now, *by any one official act*, recognize any other Protestant Church, or the ministers of any other Church, as lawful ministers.

I am not aware of any such advance in legislation as you describe. The only action on this subject of recent date, was the adoption of Canon II, Tit. I, "Of persons not ministers of this Church officiating in any Congregation thereof." It simply prohibits the officiating in any one of *our Congregations* of any person, without sufficient evidence of his being duly *licensed or ordained to minister in this Church*. The language of this Canon is by no means as strong as that in the preface to "the Form and manner of Making, Ordaining, and Consecrating," established in General Convention, Sept. A.D. 1792. In both, the purport and scope are the same; to protect the congregations of this Church against the ministrations of persons who are not responsible to this Church for what they may teach and do. It does not declare that no persons are *Ministers* except those ordained to minister in this church, but simply that such only are allowed to officiate for our people. It is a prudential municipal regulation, that our congregations may not be exposed to disturbance by the insidious teaching of some one who might delight in the opportunity for creating confusion, especially as he was not liable to be dealt with for the evil he had caused. . . .

This, my dear brother, is my clear conclusion, after a careful consideration of the reasons you assign for your "withdrawal," not one of which, as far as I am capable of judging, furnishes any justification of your act.

You know how fully our Theological views harmonize. I also agree with you in reference to grievances of which you complain, though I think you over-estimate their extent and power. That I regard you as mistaken as to the duty which these grievances impose on the Clergy and Laity of the Church, and as to the proper mode of obtaining relief, the previous pages sufficiently disclose. You will believe me, when I assure you of the great reluctance with which I make to you this communication in *this mode*, but your letter in print and published left me no choice.

In what I have thus written there is, I hope, not a word discordant with the fraternal relations which have obtained since our intercourse began, or to impair them in the future.

The scriptural example, which you adduce to support your policy of withdrawal I readily accept, and fervently hope it will have your entire conformity. Paul and Barnabas had "sharp contention," and they "departed asunder one from the other;" sought separate spheres of service, *that was all;* neither of them *withdrew from the Church.* If, however, you think you must make the experiment, I trust you will only depart for a season, that we "may receive you forever a brother beloved." And if my already prolonged life is extended so far, you will find me ready at the entrance, or rather hastening as fast as my tottering steps will permit, to meet you, to accompany and welcome you to your early home.

Then may I say, as did the aged Simeon, "Lord, now lettest Thou Thy servant depart in peace, for mine eyes have seen Thy salvation."

Four Documents (Philadelphia: M'Calla & Stavely, n.d.), 32-39, 42-43.

17.

James DeKoven,
The Canon on Ritual, 1874

James DeKoven (September 19, 1831–March 19, 1879) was the most widely known and respected leader of the Anglo-Catholic movement of the nineteenth century. At the General Conventions of 1871 and 1874 he defended eucharistic adoration, and pleaded for comprehensiveness in doctrine and worship. DeKoven's life and witness are commemorated in the Episcopal Calendar of the Church Year on March 22. His famous speech on "The Canon on Ritual and the Holy Eucharist" was delivered at the General Convention on October 26, 1874.

Let me say that I believe this Church has the right, if it does it in a lawful way, to regulate its ceremonies as it pleases; and if it chooses to forbid the use of incense, I have nothing to say. I am a Presbyter of this Church of twenty years' standing, and I am accused of Ritualism. Allow me to say that, though I have attended Ritualistic services in England and this country—and I am well aware that incense is and has been used—I never was in any church in connection with the Protestant Episcopal Church at a time when incense was used. I remember upon one occasion having a gentlemen call to see me at my own chapel, and when he arrived in the chapel a very singular thing came over him. He commenced making a sort of snuffing as if he were smelling something; and finally he said to me, "My dear brother, is that incense that I smell?" [Laughter.] I was compelled to say to him that I never had used incense, and that I thought the smell was nothing but the smell of oakwood; and he was perfectly satisfied. [Laughter.]

Now let it be noticed; and in order to get the force of my argument you will have to follow the Canon, and I believe the argument to be one which, if I can set it forth, will convince the House that at least that specification, "the use of incense," is an utter piece of nonsense. Let us see. It says, "Ceremonies, or

73

practices during the celebration of the Holy Communion not ordained or authorized in the Book of Prayer, and setting forth or symbolizing erroneous or doubtful doctrines, have been introduced into a parish within his jurisdiction; and, as examples, the following are declared to be considered as such."

That is, it does not simply forbid the use of incense—I wish that were all. What it does is to say that the use of incense symbolizes erroneous or doubtful doctrines, which is a dreadful thing to commit this House to. For this House to forbid the use of incense is a very proper thing, perhaps; but for this House to say that the use of incense symbolizes false doctrines, is for this House to put itself in utter and total opposition to the Holy Scriptures; for, remember, what does David say? "Let my prayer be set forth in Thy sight as the incense, and let the lifting up of my hands be an evening sacrifice." In other words, David says that the use of incense, to which that holy prophet and king was accustomed—having not lived in our own day—symbolized prayer; and will this church say—is it prepared to say,—that the use of incense, which symbolizes prayer, symbolizes false doctrine?

Then again, I heard it read in St. Thomas' Church yesterday morning at the beginning of the services, "From the rising of the sun even unto the going down of the same, my name shall be great among the Gentiles, and in every place incense shall be offered unto my name, and a pure offering; for my name shall be great among the heathen, saith the Lord of Hosts." I am not going to enter into the question whether that was a prophecy of something that was literally to take place. Some people say it was, but I am afraid they are Ritualists. My only question is as to its symbolical meaning. The prophet Malachi holds that incense symbolizes the pure offering,—I suppose the Eucharistic offering; and for the sake of this argument I am willing for the moment to concede that that offering is nothing but an offering of prayer and thanksgiving; though I do not think so. Then we are to understand that incense, symbolizing the pure Eucharistic offering, symbolizes false doctrine! Or again—and this is something more awful—when Aaron stood between the dead and the living with the censer in his hands, and the smoke of the incense was wafted to heaven; the people were saved. What did he typify but that Eternal Son of God who alone stands between the dead and the living, and whose mediation for the souls of men forever ascends to the right hand of God? And what did the ascending incense symbolize but the atoning Sacrifice and the everlasting Mediation? And is this Church then, prepared to say that the eternal Mediation and the awful atoning sacrifice are false doctrines? Or, when the priest on the great day of atonement went before the mercy-seat, and clouds of incense covered it, typifying the ceaseless intercession of the Son of God, is this Church prepared to say that such a use of incense symbolized false doctrines? But this Canon, if it be passed as it stands, makes it so!

74

I pass over the second specification, although I must say that I do not think the iconoclasm goes quite far enough; for when, in St. Thomas' Church only yesterday morning, I witnessed the great statues of the Apostles standing all around, I am free to say that, had I not been as much of a Protestant as I am, as I bent and bowed, I might have been led into the Roman error of worshipping images or something of that kind. [Laughter.] I do not think that thing goes quite far enough. Cut out the crucifix from the stained windows, put it out of your prayer-books, forbid pictures as well as images, if it be necessary; but do not let us believe, in this day, that the mere looking at the image of the human nature of our Divine Redeemer, and exciting our emotions by his thorn-crowned brow and his bleeding head and pierced hands, can possibly be said to symbolize false doctrine!

Now I pass over "the Elevation of the Elements in the Holy Communion in such a manner as to expose them to the view of the people as objects towards which adoration is to be made," only with one remark for it will answer something that was said by the clerical Deputy from Maryland, and that is this: that if this is to be decided to be a thing which symbolizes false doctrine, I am free to say that we shall pronounce against every other true portion of the Christian Church that has ever been since the beginning of time. No one can read the ancient Liturgies without finding just this: "When the consecration is over, before priest or people have received, and the priest comes forward holding the holy things in his hands, turning towards the people he says, 'Holy things for holy persons,' and the people answer, 'To Thee, O Lord,' and burst forth into a hymn of adoration and of praise to the present Saviour." I say that after the consecration is over, according to the Liturgy of St. Mark, which writers on this subject date back to about the year 200, the priest comes forward with the holy things in his hands, and actually turns to the people and says, "Bow the knee to Jesus," and the people answer, "To Thee, O Lord." Again, I say, that in the Liturgy which the most careful Anglican writers declare to be that Liturgy that most represents the mind of the Apostles, the Clementine Liturgy, when the priest comes forward and says, 'Holy things for holy people,' the people break forth into this hymn, "There is one Holy, one Lord Jesus Christ. . . . Glory to God in the Highest, and on earth peace and good-will toward men; Hosanna to the son of David; blessed is he that cometh in the name of the Lord; God is the Lord, and He hath appeared unto us. Hosanna in the highest."

And let me call the attention of the Lay and Clerical Deputies from New Jersey to the fact that I am told that in the Diocese of New Jersey the bishop, when he consecrates, when he comes to that part of the service where he breaks the bread, turns around to the people, and breaks it in presence of the people; and again, in the apsidal chancel, when the priest stands behind the altar facing the people, he does exactly that self-same thing: and shall we say that this symbolizes false doctrine?

Now I come to another point: "Any act of adoration of or toward the Elements in the Holy Communion, such as bowings, prostrations, genuflexions, and all such like acts, not authorized or allowed by the Rubrics of the Book of Common Prayer." I am exceedingly pleased to find that this Canon makes a distinction which the public mind has not made before this session. I was delighted to hear the Clerical Deputy from Massachusetts (Rev. Dr. Huntington), who is always clear in whatsoever he says, state very carefully and distinctly the difference between outward adoration and inward adoration, between external acts of adoration and internal acts of love and honor. The distinction is a vital one. It is one which it behooves this Church carefully to remember, for I am free to say one thing, which, believe it, I say with the deepest humility; and yet I know when I say it there are a thousand hearts that will respond to me. You may take away from us, if you will, every external ceremony; you may take away altars, and super-altars, and lights, and incense, and vestments; you may take away, if you will, the eastward position; you may take away every possible ceremony; and you may command us to celebrate at the altar of God without any external symbolism whatsoever; you may give us the most barren of all observances, and we will submit to you. If this Church commands us to have no ceremonies, we will obey. But, gentlemen, the very moment any one says we shall not adore our Lord present in the Eucharist, then from a thousand hearts will come the answer, as of those bidden to go into exile, "Let me die in my own country and be buried by the grave of my father and my mother!" for to adore Christ's person in His Sacrament, is the inalienable privilege of every Christian and Catholic heart. How we do it, the way we do it, the ceremonies with which we do it, are utterly, utterly indifferent; the thing itself is what we plead for, and I know I should not plead to unkind or unfeeling hearts. . . .

Mr. President, we live in troublous times, and around us are all sorts of terrible questions. It does seem to me the need of the day is not now to legislate on nice points of doctrine, or to prescribe exactly the measure of a genuflexion, or the angle of inclination which can express an orthodox devotion. The answer to all this panic and all this outcry is one, and one only. It is *Work*; work for the cause of Christ; work for the souls of men; and a fuller, deeper, more noble sense of the obligation of the Church, developing its powers, and sending it forth to mould and form this mighty nation, and to give new life and vigor to every effort that is made for the salvation of men. I see the storm-cloud gathering. I see the lightnings flash. I hear the thunder roll afar. I hear the trumpet call. In my ears the bugle blast is ringing. And I call you, brethren, in a time like this, not to narrow-hearted legislation, but broad, Catholic, tolerant charity, and to work, as never men worked before, for the souls of those for whom the Saviour died.

James DeKoven, *The Canon on Ritual, and the Holy Eucharist; A Speech Delivered in the General Convention, October 26, 1874* (New York: T. Whittaker, 1874), 13-19, 42.

18.

James DeKoven, A Letter, 1875

James DeKoven was nominated for bishop five times and on February 4, 1875, was elected Bishop of Illinois. The election was not confirmed by a sufficient number of Diocesan Standing Committees because they believed he held "unsound doctrine as to the Holy Eucharist." In his letter of August 31, 1875, to the clergy and laity of the Diocese of Illinois "in Convention assembled," he states his position with regard to the presence of Christ in the Eucharist.

The Holy Eucharist is the doing in the sensible world, by God's appointment under material forms, what Christ our Head and Chief is ever doing in the spiritual world. There is an earthly altar, and a human priesthood, and bread and wine; but Christ is really present as priest, and offering, and the food of the faithful who feed upon the sacrifice. One would expect that since Christ is in the Eucharist as priest and offering, His human nature, by the presence of which in Heaven He ever pleads for us what once It endured, should also be in the Eucharist; and so we find that He said of the elements: "This is my blood which is being shed for you." And again: "He that eateth Me, even he shall live by Me."

The controversies of the times compel us to go further than this simple assertion of the presence of Christ, God and man in one person, in the Holy Eucharist, to declare that while we assert our belief in the presence, we refuse to define the mode or manner of the presence.

We do not affirm with the Roman Catholic, that it is by transubstantiation, or the annihilation of the substance of the bread and wine, and the substitution for it of the substance of Christ's body and blood.

We do not affirm (if there be any who do), that it is by consubstantiation or impanation; namely, that "the substance of the Lord's body and blood co-exists in union with the substance of bread and wine, as iron and fire are united in a bar of heated iron."

We do not affirm that it is by identity of substance, that is, that the substance of the Eucharist is at one and the same time the substance of bread and wine and the substance of Christ's body and blood.

We refuse to explain away the mystery by saying that the holy elements are *mere figures* or *images* or *symbols* of Christ's *absent* body and blood. In short, we accept no device or explanation of human reason, and where Christ and the church have refused to define, we refuse to define also.

The only word which the church has used to express, without defining the fact of the presence, is the word "SACRAMENTAL," and so I hold that Christ's human nature is in sacramental union with the consecrated elements. This presence is called REAL, to show that it is no mere figurative or symbolical presence. It is called SPIRITUAL, to show that it is no visible, carnal, material or local presence; "for that which is seen is not real; that which is material is dissoluble; that which is local is but partial." This presence is also called spiritual, because it is the especial work of God's Holy Spirit to make Christ's human nature present, for the third Person of the adorable Trinity has come "not to supply Christ's absence, but to accomplish His presence."

Thus whenever and wherever I have asserted that Christ is present "*in the elements*," "*under the form or species of bread and wine*," I mean thereby that He is there present sacramentally and spiritually, and thus really and truly. . . .

I do not believe, my brethren, that this doctrine has ever been rejected by our church. I do not believe that it is a doctrine which our church merely tolerates, but that it is the fair and reasonable interpretation of her liturgy and formularies, and when more fully understood will be accepted with loving hearts by all her faithful children. If it be said that the fact that the members of the church do not generally accept it is a proof that the church does not hold it; it is sufficient to reply that the history of the American church proves that she has steadily grown into a fuller and deeper appreciation of her Catholic heritage, and that every one who has been called to proclaim the forgotten truths has done so with the notes of reproach and suffering for Christ's sake. That it should be otherwise, as the great blessing of the Sacramental Presence of Christ in the Eucharist begins to be more fully realized, is not to be looked for.

A Letter from The Reverend James DeKoven, D.D., Warden of Racine College, to the Clergy and Laity of the Diocese of Illinois, in Convention Assembled, September 14, 15, 16, 17, A.D. 1875 (Chicago: Mitchell and Hatheway, 1875), 6-7, 10.

19.

Morgan Dix, The Oxford Movement, 1884

Morgan Dix (November 1, 1827–April 29, 1908) was the ninth rector of Trinity Parish from November 10, 1862 until his death. He was elected president of the House of Deputies five times, serving from October 6, 1886 until October 2, 1901. He wrote a four-volume History of the Parish of Trinity Church, *and was a leader of Catholic Churchmanship.*

The Oxford tracts began by teaching the Apostolic Succession.

That is the germ of the whole system: no wonder that it is so offensive to the liberalism and sectarianism of the day, that men rage as they do about the figment of a "tactual succession" and deny that the descent can be proved. All follows on that fact that the Episcopal Order succeeds to the office and work of the first Apostles, propagating and governing the Catholic Church under her Supreme Head, Jesus Christ. On that hang, logically, "the doctrine, the Fellowship, the Breaking of the Bread, and the prayer," in other words, the Theological, Sacerdotal, Sacramental and Liturgical departments in our Holy Religion. The Creed, the Ministry, the Sacraments, the Worship, these rest finally, on the sure word of Christ spoken to His Apostles and their successors, "Lo, I am with you always, even unto the end of the world."

Now this is no mere speculative system, no theory for the closet of the recluse; it comes right into human life; it is intensely practical. It reaches us men, this "Catholic system" as we rightly term it, where we feel most deeply, need most urgently, and see most distinctly; again it is true of us that our faith is in that which we have seen, which we have heard, which our very hands handle, of the Word of Life. Three things stand in a logical order, one right after the other, each in its place, the Birth into Christ, the Life in Christ; the Beauty of Holiness, the three controversies I have mentioned were about these things. The Gorham Controversy was, substantially, a battle on the question of Man's birth into Christ; the Eucharistic Controversy involved the question of Man's Life in Christ; the Ritualistic controversy touched the subject of the external order and beauty of the worship of Almighty God. The three go together. You are born into Christ; you must live in Christ; you must see, for your joy and refreshment, somewhat of the King in His beauty. The Church and the world have different utterances on each of these heads. The Church places God first, the world places Man first. The victory won in each of those great battles was plainly a victory of the supernatural over the natural, of faith over doubt.

The Oxford Movement based on faith in the Apostolic Succession, declared the doctrine of Baptismal Regeneration: that regeneration is the specific gift of that Sacrament. The adversary denied, declaring that man may be regenerated before or after Baptism, but never in and by that Sacrament. The battle was fought and won; the doctrine of the Book of Common Prayer is as clear as the sun in the heavens, and they who dispute it must fain rank among the dissenters from the standards of the Church.

The Oxford Movement brought to light the truth of the real Presence of Christ in the Sacrament of the Altar. The adversary denied, advancing either the Zuinglian notion of a memorial feast or the Calvinistic notion of a virtual presence, with symbols to help the faith; anything indeed might be held, except that our Lord spake literal truth when He said, "This is My Body, this is My Blood." That battle also was fought and won. It has been ruled that our Office cannot by any art be made to accord with the Zuinglian theory; that the highest sacramental doctrine may be taught without straining one word or changing one letter.

Finally, the Oxford Movement revived the lost idea of worship. The adversary resisted, and now with fury; he laid hold on carnal weapons, stirred up rioters, gathered mobs about church-doors, stopped not short of sacrilege, desecrating and defiling holy places, profaning the very Sacrament; he called in Parliament to help; he got his Act to regulate Public Worship; effected the deprivation of priests, threw them into prison; would have hanged, drawn and quartered them gladly as of old, to stop the advance. What boots it? To the enemy has been left the burning shame of having organized, in this nineteenth century, the "Church Persecution Company, Limited." With us remain the substantial fruits of victory. I speak not of extremes, of useless adjuncts, of matters indifferent; of the "fads" of queer people and the eccentricities of some foolish persons; but of what is grave, decorous, beautiful, essential. The vested choir and the choral service; the altar in its own place with its "ornaments;" the distinctive garb of the priest, simple though it be; the position of the celebrant as one who ministers before God and not unto man: the ritual appropriate to that "Memorial" before the Father Almighty; these now are ours and undisputed; and these are fruits of the battle for order, right and truth.

I have spoken of three great Controversies; besides these, of course, there have been innumerable actions of minor importance, yet each has helped to confirm some truth, to bring out some point of the faith, to maintain and secure some right of priest or people. Next in order is it to enumerate some of the results of the work begun fifty years ago. It seems like a dream; it is the realization of visions which once appeared fantastic; nay, we may exclaim to one another, "Many prophets and righteous men desired to see the things which we see and did not see them, and to hear the things which we hear and did not hear them."

First of all: we have seen the rebuilding of the altar. When Elijah faced the priest of Baal, intent on his death, he began by repairing the altar of the Lord which was broken down. We have seen its rebuilding in the literal and the spiritual sense; its restoration to its ancient glory and honour, and the recovery of the truth and the faith in its Gift; it is the centre of the Church's worship, it is the Holy Table at which her children are fed with Angels' food. We have seen as a result the revival of ecclesiastical architecture: noble churches, with frescoes, mosaic, pictures, carved work; stately services, with bannered procession, and choral song. The Creed is held by faithful men, without mental reservation, in the Catholic sense; they revere the ministry as a priesthood, they see in the bishop the successor of the apostles. To the penitent is freely opened the way to confession with the comfort of absolution; none need to be tormented with the secret burden of sin, nor thirst in vain to hear that the Lord hath put it away. Communions are multiplied beyond number. Congregations are organized for works of charity and mercy. Sisterhoods show us the life of the Religious, and its results in the care of the sick, the poor, the fallen, the ignorant; they have their large and stately houses, their broad acres; their endowments, by gift of the faithful. Church Missions have extended immensely, they grow ever more and more. We have our roll of martyrs, and confessors, of scholars and saintly men, our Keble, Pusey, Neale, Selwyn, Patterson, and here in America our Schuyler, DeKoven, Mahan and Ewer, born of this movement and illustrating what it was. The Oxford Movement has given the world a Literature, a school of Art, a school of Music, a school of Architecture. We owe to it the Libraries of the Fathers of the Holy Catholic Church, of the Anglican Divines; the paintings of a Holman Hunt and a Millais, the poetry of the Christian year, the Lyras and the flower of the Hymnals, the immense liturgical treasures now ready to every student's hand, the music of Barnby, Helmore, Cobb, Martin; the oratory of a Liddon, the enthusiasm of a Lowder, the inexhaustible learning of a Littledale, the deep foundations of Clewer and East Grinstead; the utilizing of the English Cathedrals, the extension of the Home and Colonial Episcopate. It may be said of the Movement that it has stirred English Society and English-speaking people all the earth round, as none ever stirred them before; that it has made itself felt through the largest part of the circle of man's life; that it has aroused, awakened, illuminated, blessed, vast numbers of souls; that it has made an impression on the Church which cannot be effaced. . . .

The Oxford Movement was on lines drawn, as on a map or chart, in the Book of Common Prayer. It began when men had either thrust that book away in contempt, or were trying to revise it in the interest of dissent, or were making it a dead letter by keeping the word but denying the meaning. The Movement was, actually, a rehabilitation of that Book in its Catholic sense, a defense of it against aggressors, a development, practically and in ritual, of the truth which it enshrines. Our work now is to hold men up squarely to the principles and doctrines of that Book. Rubbish has been cleared away, light has poured into every dark corner. It is our business to see that the dust does not gather again; that the cobwebs are brushed off as fast as our rationalists and philosophic speculators spin them from their own prolific interior; that the Book remains, henceforth, a living book, which a man shall be ashamed to use unless he believes in his soul what it contains. While our doctrinal standards remain unchanged, the Creeds, the Sacramental offices, the dogmatic articles of religion, and while the sense of honor resides in the human spirit, we have nothing to fear. The truth is ours, barricaded, defended, proof against assault. Stand we firm, and the work of the past half century cannot be undone. It shall proceed, in larger outcome, and a wider reach; it shall appear to be the preamble of a vaster movement preparing the nation for the Second Coming of the Lord; that is the *terminus ad quem*; our eyes may yet behold it, as we stand, unshaken, in our lot at the end of the days. Even so come, Lord Jesus!

Morgan Dix, *The Oxford Movement*, 3rd ed. (Chicago: The Living Church Company, 1884), 10-14, 20.

20.

Fred S. Jewell, The Special Beliefs and Objects of Catholic Churchmen: A Statement, 1886

Frederick Swarty Jewell (January 23, 1821–December 27, 1903) was a teacher and served parishes in Connecticut, Illinois, and Wisconsin. His The Special Beliefs and Objects of Catholic Churchmen: A Statement *is an assertion of Anglo-Catholic belief and practice.*

I. Catholic Doctrine

Under the head of Catholic Doctrine, the following nine points cover all that appear vital to the present purpose:

1. *One Holy Catholic Church.* In distinction from those opposite and uncatholic extremes, Protestant disintegration and Roman exclusiveness—*we believe in one visible, divinely instituted, and only authoritative, Holy Catholic and Apostolic Church.* Hence, the Church is no Jonah's gourd of yesterday, but rather an heir-loom—a cherished descent of the ages. No changing product of upstarting passions or exigencies; it is an abiding, historic structure, standing for all time, no less than for all place. It is no fair but frail device of human speculation and logic; but it is contrariwise, the one, sacred organic legacy to mankind of our Lord's providential wisdom and power. No proposed or permitted object of the presumptuous individual beliefs or fancies of men; it is, like the Divine Will from which it sprang, sole, absolute and imperative, standing by Divine Authority against religious self-will, as the Gospel stands against sin. It is no fanciful composite of sectarian shreds and patches—a *one* Church, only as conceived of under the guise and delusion of some fine-spun invisible unity; but is truly one, as visible and determinate throughout the world—the one Organic Body of Christ, as sensibly and truly as was His human Body in the Incarnation.

Other Christian bodies. Nevertheless, it is cheerfully conceded, that outside of the Church—as thus, according to ancient authority, defined—there may, and doubtless do, exist a sincere faith, an exemplary piety, manifold good works, and shrewdly devised combinations and agencies for the support of the same. But it is not seen that the last possess a proper organic, or institutional, validity; or that the former, as existing outside of an obedient recognition of the Church, are a Christian fulfilling of "*all* righteousness" (S. Matt. iii, 15). All righteousness, as seen in our Lord's example, is as distinctly inclusive of the organic, as of the personal, in obedience.

2. *National Branches of the Church.* As alike opposed to the multitudinous divisions of the sects, and the assumed universality of the Roman Church—anarchical errors on the one extreme, and imperious excess on the other—*we claim that there may rightfully exist,*—and without any rending of the Body of Christ— *diverse national branches of the One Catholic Church; with substantially the same divinely constituted Faith, Order, and Worship; but with each its own national uses, and its own distinct local autonomy under its own patriarchal or conciliar rule, always subject, however, to the decisions of the one undivided Church, and to the Royal Law of Charity, inter-communion and co-operation.*

Internal combinations and local designation. While, however, this forbids alike all sectional isolation and continental consolidation, it in no way militates against provincial union and organization; nor does it, while freely allowing the adoption and use of any proper national or patriarchal title consistent with the verity of the one Catholic name of the whole Church, allow or excuse that mischievous implication against its unity and the divine balance of truth in the Faith—the fastening upon any such branch or body, of some sectarian denomination, only descriptive of some peculiar tenet or assumption.

3. *Holy Orders and a Valid Ministry.* Rejoicing in all good done in the Name of the Lord Jesus (Phil. i, 18), but insisting upon obedience to the divinely constituted Order of the Church, as in itself a *righteousness*; we object alike to sectarian ordination as irregular and invalid, and to the exclusive claims of the Papacy, as in conflict with the rights and immunities of the Catholic Episcopate;

and *claim that there are three only rightful Orders of Sacred Ministers in the Church of Christ—Bishops, Priests, and Deacons; and that these rest for their perpetuation and exclusive validity, on their divine origin and the fixed law of the Apostolic Succession as inhering solely in the Catholic Church, or in its Episcopate and Presbytery.*

Really divine and providentially sure. This origin is divine, not as merely finding a verbal basis in Holy Scripture, but as having sprung directly from our Lord's instructions given to the Holy Apostles during the Great Forty Days (Acts i, 3); and the succession is fixed, not as merely theoretic or presumptive, but as founded on our Lord's Last Promise, (S. Matt. xxviii, 20); as sustained by the repeated acts and utterances of the Holy Apostles as set forth in their writings; as most carefully secured by the traditions and Canons of the ancient Church touching the consecration of Bishops; and as never, until since the so-called Reformation, impugned by even the heretical, the hostile and the profane.

Other officers or functionaries. Nevertheless, beyond these three fundamental Orders, the Church, in the exercise of her supreme authority and adaptive wisdom, may rightfully create and employ such minor orders or special functionaries, as do not conflict with the foregoing, and as best meet the economic needs of her power and usefulness.

4. *Baptism and the Holy Eucharist.* We revolt from every semblance of the common and painful ignorance and misbelief, which make the sacraments—Baptism and the Holy Eucharist—mere forms, or ceremonies—outward and visible signs with no inward spiritual grace or substance;—the one simply typifying a thing as needful, and foreshadowing it as sometime possible; the other as, through a sort of mnemonic symbolism, formally calling to mind certain past facts, assuredly of too august a character to need the aid of arbitrary signs as stimulants of memory and emotion; *and hold both these sacraments to be substantial ordinances, instituted by our Blessed Lord in person and by Him positively set forth in the Gospel Record, with the express intent that they should be at once solemn reminders of Catholic truth, holy signs of divine operations performed and gifts bestowed; and the Church's supreme means of communicating to His followers—each after its species—a real, supernatural grace, by virtue of which they become saving ordinances.*

The benefits of this Substantial Grace. The benefits constituting this inward substance, we understand to be respectively these:—*in Baptism the forgiveness of all past sin, both original and actual; regeneration, or the implanting of the germ of a new nature in the soul; and the incorporation of the baptized into the organic Body of Christ: in the Holy Eucharist, absolution from post-baptismal sin; the cleansing of both body and spirit (as specified in the "Prayer of Humble Access"); and the nourishing of the divine life within, by the communicated*

Body and Blood of Christ; the implanting and sustaining of the heavenly germ of the resurrection life; direct access to the blessed Communion of Saints; and the efficient union of the believer's prayers with the intercession of our Lord before the Throne.

Grace for those lacking them. While, however, the fullness of divine grace is attainable only through the orderly observance of these sacraments, as divinely appointed and regularly administered by the Catholic Church; we do not presume to doubt, that sincere believers under the Gospel, who through ignorance, misguidance, or any practical inability, fail to obtain access to them and their appointed blessings, may, and do, under the executive exercise of the Divine sovereignty, through the faithful use of such means as are according to their light, obtain grace, mercy and peace, and the crown of everlasting life; for which, thanks be to God, through Jesus Christ our Lord!

5. *The other five Sacraments.* As for the other "five, commonly called sacraments; that is to say, Confirmation, Penance, Orders, Matrimony and Extreme Unction;" while we cannot accord to them the same dignity and necessary saving grace which belong to the former; inasmuch as they were instituted under Divine direction, are in substance set forth in the Apostolic writings as in some sort sacramental, Christian ordinances, and were for ages accepted as such by the Holy Catholic Church:—*we take them to be possessed of valid authority, a more or less distinct sacramental character, and—when reverently so used—an unquestionable utility.*

Points in their utility. Their utility as religious acts and a means of grace, while different from that of the other two sacraments, in both the degree and the kind of the gifts conferred, is by no means so doubtful or obscure as to need particularization, and is of high importance, as offering a solemn check and rebuke to that common evil, growth of sectarianism—low and still lowering views of the Christian ordinances severally concerned. These are views which make the Episcopate a mere office, and Ordination little more than a fraternal recognition of some assumed, personal, "divine call" to the ministry; which confound Confirmation with a sectarian "profession of religion," and reduce the "Laying on of Hands" to the level of a mere official stamp affixed to the candidate's ratification of his Baptismal vows; which degrade Christian Marriage to the vulgarity and vice of a mere contract—often only a conditional sex-partnership, terminable at the pleasure of some "incompatibility of temper," or rather higher compatibility of other unlawful loves; and which utterly discard Penance and Holy Unction, as though they were not divinely appointed means of grace and comfort to sorrowing souls and suffering bodies.

6. *The Real Presence.* Recognizing no such gross material presence of our Blessed Lord in the Holy Eucharist, as Transubstantiation, according to the *pop-*

ular notion, implies; and revolting from the still more painful Protestant oppo-site—the miserable product of the memorial-supper theory—which admits only a material presence of the Bread and Wine, and an immaterial, subjective pres-ence of the original Sacrifice, as a mere thought in memory,—a mere notional presence, with a real absence; *we hold most firmly and devoutly, that there is a Real, Objective Presence of our Blessed Lord in the Holy Sacrament as an offer-ing of the Typical Sacrifice; and that, by virtue of this presence, the Faithful do truly commune with Him, and do verily, though after a sacramental manner, receive His Body and Blood under the sacred species of the Bread and Wine.*

The Manner of the Presence a Mystery. Nevertheless, as being "an exceeding great and sacred Mystery," the manner or mode of this Real Presence, is above human comprehension, and is, therefore, beyond the reach of any rational defini-tion in philosophy, on which account the Catholic Church has for the most part maintained on this point a discreet and reverent silence, and contented herself with accepting the fact as set forth, without solution, in the Holy Scriptures, and guarding it in her Liturgies, against injurious obscuration and irreverent handling.

Eucharistic Adoration. Wherefore it cannot but be meet and right, that the Ritual of the Altar, should be most carefully and reverently ordered, albeit with-out excess of mere form or ceremony; and that whosoever, in accordance with the Divine Liturgy, duly offers the Holy Sacrifice or receives the sacred Body and Blood, should, out of his inner discernment and reverence, render such out-ward adoration as both bespeaks and befits the Real Presence of his Divine Lord;—and this without being blameworthy, as superstitions, or as offering idol-atrous worship to the visible species themselves.

7. *The Holy Eucharist the one divine office of Holy Worship.* While we depre-cate the holding by any branch of the Church, of such extreme views of the supernatural virtue of the Mass, as result in the rise and practice of ceremonial abuses like those condemned by the Articles of Religion; we no less deplore the opposite and common evil of robbing the Holy Eucharist of its proper place and pre-eminence, by subordinating it in order of time, and degree of attention, to those derivative, monastic services, Matins, Litany, and Evensong. Hence, in accordance with the terms of Holy Scripture; the practice of the Early Church; the manifest intent and scope of all the Liturgies; and the inherent dignity of the Office itself; *we maintain, that in the Holy Eucharist, as at once a Memorial Feast, a Holy Communion, an offering of Holy Gifts, and a typical Presenting and Pleading of the One Sacrifice, there is to be found the Church's only supreme and divinely authorized act and form of Catholic Christian worship; and that as such, it rightly claims, not only the foremost and most favored place among our Services, but also whatever glory of order, enrichment, liberality and devotion, we are able to lavish upon it.*

8. *The Communion of Saints.* Rejecting utterly that most uncatholic and distressful doctrine so rife among the sects, that there is in death an absolute separation of the living from the Faithful Departed;—a separation which renders the beloved in Paradise as remote, inaccessible, and foreign to us and to all our sympathies and prayers, as though the death of the body were the end of life to the spirit; a separation which would be tantamount to a rent and division in the mystical Body of Christ, effected by the very foe over which He is assumed to have triumphed; we hold, that by virtue of our Lord's Real Presence in the Holy Eucharist; through our sacramental union and communion with Him; and through the spiritual union and communion with Him of the Spirits of the Faithful in Paradise; *there is in the Holy Eucharist, a living and sympathetic communion of all saints with each other.*

Its power and blessedness. This Communion of the Saints is so real and potential, that the prayers and supplications of the present and the absent, the living and the departed, spiritually converge and commingle in the Sacrifice; and united with the intercessions of our Blessed Lord Himself, are by Him presented before the throne of the Father for gracious acceptance, if not even for answers of mercy and blessing:—a "Communion of Saints" which, as immeasurably more than a mere synonym for the Church, and more and better than even a devout reception of the Holy Communion by the living in common, is, though a mystery of the Mystery, and like that, indefinable to our gross, finite apprehension, nevertheless to a true faith, at once assured and comforting and full of sympathetic blessing.

9. *The Discipline of the Intermediate State.* In opposition alike to the low, materialistic notion, that death is a "sleep that knows no waking," an absolute end of man's whole being; to the still more irrational doctrine—being, as it is, in flat contradiction with the laws of mind—that the repose of the soul in Paradise involves a suspension of all progressive spiritual activity—a sort of heavenly hibernation; and to the absurd and unscriptural fancy of the sects and denominations, that the soul of the departed believer, in utter violation of every law of man's mental, moral and religious life and progress, and of the teaching of Revelation concerning the Resurrection, is somehow, at the instant of death, immediately perfected in holiness, translated to Heaven, and, as though the Resurrection were already past (2 S. Tim., ii, 18), admitted to its final employments and delights; *we believe in the existence of a conscious spiritual life, discipline and development in the soul in the Intermediate State, anterior to the Resurrection, and in necessary preparation for it*; of which disciplinary state, the common notion of Purgatory as a place of positively inflicted pains and punishments, is simply a distortion and excess.

Its practical ground and need. A proper ground and need for such a discipline and development is to be found in the fact that the spiritual nature of believers departing this life is, confessedly, for the most part, in a state of painfully imperfect sanctification, still retaining the soiled memories and sinful habitudes of the old sense-life—the footprints of sin in the soil of the soul. From these evil reminiscences and remains of the earthly state, the spirits of the Departed must be delivered—the memory must be discharged of all that is unhallowed; the lingering obscurations of the reason and the understanding must be swept away; the movements of desire must be cleansed from all intrusion of unholy impulse; the yet feeble or fluctuating purposes of the will must be wrought up to a divine stability and power; and the half-lit fire of holy love must be fed and fanned into glowing fervor and undying flame—all this, before the redeemed spirit can be fit to be clothed upon by the resurrection body. This, however, under the fixed laws of mind and the divine idea of spiritual life and growth, can only be attained through a gradual and advancing process—a growth and progress under the clearer light, the purer influences, the quickened power, and the freer spiritual activity of the life in the Intermediate State, as one in which the soul is cut off from all contact with enslaving and contaminating sense, and is brought more directly under the revealing light and the transforming impact of the Holy Spirit. Under these conditions, it is not possible that it should not awake to new and startling discoveries of the shame of sin and the beauty of holiness, and that it should not pass through vivid and profound experiences of alternating penitence and forgiveness, self-abasement and heavenly exultation, until, growing, gaining, rising, triumphing, through each succeeding stage of this grave though gracious discipline, it attains at length the glorious landing-place and level of a complete and final sanctification, and stands ready for the coming of its Lord and the glory and blessedness of the First Resurrection.

On these cardinal points of the Catholic Faith, thus we believe and hold.

Fred S. Jewell, *The Special Beliefs and Objects of Catholic Churchmen: A Statement* (Milwaukee: The Young Churchman Company, 1886), 7-14.

21.

Charles C. Grafton, The Catholic Movement, 1914

Charles Chapman Grafton (April 12, 1847–August 30, 1912) was one of the leaders of the Anglo-Catholic party. He was rector of the Church of the Advent, Boston, and he was the second Bishop of Fond Du Lac from April 25, 1889, until his death. The following statement presents some of the main ideals of the Anglo-Catholic movement.

As the Church grew, early in the nineteenth century there was a development here, under the guidance of God's Holy Spirit, of that same movement for the recovery of the Church's full heritage of doctrine and worship as had begun in England. The teachings of Hobart and Seabury laid the foundation for this recovery. Indeed, it has been thought by some that, as it was no imitation or echo of English teaching, they had led the way.

They taught the doctrines of the Church, the Apostolic Succession, Baptismal Regeneration, and the Prayer Book, as the Church's Rule of Faith. The teaching of some High Churchmen on the subject of the Holy Eucharist was very strong. In a note to his famous sermon preached by the Rev. Samuel Farmer Jarvis, before the Bishops, clergy, and laity, constituting the Board of Missions in 1834, by the title, " Christian Unity Necessary for the Converting of the World," he said: "We have no right to banish from our Communion those whose notions of the Real Presence of Christ in the Sacraments rise to a *mysterious change* by which the *very Elements* themselves, though they retain their original properties, are corporeally united with, or transformed into, Christ."

The revival of Church teaching began here, as in England, to be opposed. The slightest revival of enrichment in the services was condemned. Many of the churches then had the old three-decker arrangement, consisting of a pulpit beneath which was a reading desk, and beneath that a place for the clerk, who said responses. A recessed chancel was looked upon with abhorrence. Bishops insisted there should be nothing looking like an altar in the chancel. It must be an honest table with four visible legs. The introduction of flowers was sternly forbidden,[1] as was also a cross on the Holy Table. A cross having been placed on the wall over the altar in the Church of the Advent, Boston, the Bishop assigned it as a reason why he would not visit the Church for Confirmation.[2] A cross having been found in the chapel of the General Theological Seminary, on the front railing of the chancel, it was declared to be improper by the dean, and ordered to be removed.[3] Where there was a reading desk, where the prayers were said, it faced the people. On one occasion, when the venerable Dr. Edson of Lowell was saying the office stall-wise, Bishop Eastman, who was present, rose and took him by the shoulders, and made him turn round facing the congregation. There were no lights on the altar, no vested choristers, no cross borne in procession. The clergyman preached, and sometimes said the whole service, in the black Geneva gown, and the Holy Communion was but seldom administered.

---

[1]Appendix Gen. Conven., fol. 249.
[2]Life of William Croswell.
[3]Journal Gen. Convention, 1844, Appendix.

It is to be remembered that Miss Seton, a devout person, besought the rector of Trinity Church, New York, for more frequent celebrations. She was refused, and subsequently joined the Roman Communion, where she founded an order of the Sisters of Charity. In the forties, a meeting of some High Church clergy took place in New York, among whom were Dr. Muhlenberg and William Croswell of Boston, who discussed the possibility of having on every Sunday a celebration of the Holy Eucharist. There was much party spirit at this time. The Low Churchmen had many holy men among them, but some took here, as in England, to the tactics of persecution.

There was a young man at the General Theological Seminary by the name of Arthur Carey. He was a young man noted for his piety, and of considerable intellectual ability. He had adopted the opinion afterwards put forth by Dr. Pusey, that the decrees of Trent and our Thirty-nine Articles were capable, by explanation, of a reconciliation.

In 1843, at the time of his ordination by Bishop Onderdonk, the Rev. Dr. Smith and the Rev. Dr. Anthon rose and read a long protest, grounded on Carey's alleged doctrinal errors. Bishop Onderdonk, however, stated that the accusation had already been investigated, that there would be no changes in the service of the day, and that all the candidates present would be ordained. This brought Bishop Onderdonk into great disfavor with the Low Churchmen. He was himself the next object of their attack. They charged him with acts evincing a "prevalent impurity of mind." The evidence was imperfect,[4] and as the great Bishop Whittingham said in his written opinion, "The probabilities were strong against it." But the Low Church Bishops voted for his condemnation. It was obviously a mere party judgment. Bishop Onderdonk was suspended. Subsequently, in the same spirit, the great Bishop Doane of New Jersey was attacked. One charge related to money matters. His diocesan convention, clergy and laity, rallied to his support, and his masterful mind was able to defeat the attack.

In Massachusetts, the Rev. Oliver S. Prescott, at one time an assistant at the Church of the Advent, Boston, was presented for trial for erroneous teaching. Three trials took place. It was not proved that he had heard confessions, but that he had taught the right of every layman to resort to the Sacrament of Penance if he felt the need, and the priest, if he judged him penitent, to give him absolution. Prescott was condemned and suspended from exercising his priestly office until he should renounce his teaching. He was urged by counsel to appeal to the civil courts, being assured that they would grant relief in such an unjust sentence.

---

[4]Trial of Bp. Onderdonk, published by the Court.

But, unwilling to bring such matters before civil tribunals, he declined doing so. Eventually Bishop Whittingham of Maryland, saying, "What a Bishop could do, another Bishop could undo," invited him into his diocese, where he would be free from the sentence in which he had acquiesced. A few years previous, 1844, a fierce attack had been stirred up against the General Theological Seminary. A series of some forty-three inquisitorial questions was addressed to its dean and professors. "What had been taught there concerning the errors of Rome? the authority of General Councils? whether the works of Pusey, Newman, Keble, and Palmer were privately recommended, or the Oxford Tracts? whether the errors of the Romish Church were duly exposed? What superstitious practices of the Romish Church, such as the use of the crucifix, etc., were adopted?" It appeared that, as a matter of Christmas decoration, a cross, ornamented in part by artificial flowers, was placed on the front railing of the chancel. This occasioned a comment by the dean. A great effort was made at General Convention to obtain from the Bishops a public condemnation of these errors in doctrine and practice, "having their origin, it was said, in certain writings emanating chiefly from members of the University of Oxford in England."

The effort, however, which took the form of a resolution, was voted down. The House of clerical and lay deputies, as giving a quietus to the agitation, resolved that the liturgy, "offices and articles of the Church were sufficient exponents of her sense of the essential doctrine of Holy Scripture, and that the canons of the Church afforded ample means of discipline and correction for all who might depart from her standard. And further," they declared, " the General Convention was not a suitable tribunal for the trial and censure of, and that the Church is not responsible for, the errors of individuals, whether they are members of this Church or otherwise."

THE ATTACK ON THE PRAYER BOOK

Thus defeated, the Low Churchmen turned next to an attack upon the Prayer Book. It contained, they said, "Roman germs. It taught the doctrine of Apostolic Succession, Baptismal Regeneration, the priest's right to give absolution in private. It called the Holy Table an Altar, it upheld the doctrine of the Eucharistic Sacrifice." Now the basis of the sacramental system lies in the doctrine of baptism, as the effective instrument of regeneration. So clearly is the teaching of the Church expressed in her baptismal office, that it is a wonder any should not have admitted it to be so. Some had, however, invented an ingenious theory that regeneration was promised prospectively to a baptized infant, in virtue of the faith of the sponsors. But one, who was subsequently a Bishop of the Reformed Episcopal body, declared that in administering on one occasion baptism privately to a sick child, he perceived that no sponsors were required, but the Church went on to say that, "seeing this child is regenerated." His theory, he said, thus fell to the ground. The effort, however, to get the Prayer Book changed at the General Convention signally failed.

Upon this, a number of Low Churchmen, led by Dr. Cummins, Assistant Bishop of Kentucky, left the Church. Dr. Cummins said he had "lost all hope that the system now prevailing so extensively in England, and in the Protestant Episcopal Church, can or will be eradicated by any acts of the Church, legislative or executive." He left the Church, and was deposed by the House of Bishops.

THE HOLY EUCHARIST CONTROVERSY

Next arose the controversy over the Holy Eucharist. Dr. de Koven had defended the doctrine of the Objective Real Presence as taught in the Prayer Book and Catechism. Chosen to be Bishop of Illinois, his election was not confirmed. The movement, however, was not checked, but began rapidly to grow. A more developed ritual took place in certain churches, like that of St. Alban's, New York. Lights and vestments began to be introduced. The Cowley Fathers, coming from England in 1872, gave a great impulse to the Church spirit in Boston.

It was about 1874 that a further attack was made on ritual. It was sought to put it down by legislation. It was like the last fatal charge of the Old Guard at Waterloo. The fears of many Churchmen had been excited by the cry of Romanism. Under the pressure of the excitement a canon was forced through General Convention which forbade any acts of reverence by genuflection or otherwise towards the Elements. Here, we may reverently say, God took part in the struggle. The Low Churchmen were victorious in getting their canon passed, but God had struck its authors with judicial blindness, for the way in which they defeated themselves can be explained in no other manner. The canon which was to forbid all acts of reverence and adoration only forbade them as offered to the *elements.* The canon omitted to state the *consecrated elements.* The canon never was put in operation and finally was repealed in Boston thirty years later. One misunderstanding may here rightly be removed. As the Jewish priest waved the offering before the Lord, so the Christian priest elevates the sacred elements, doing this as *offering them to God,* not, as is sometimes supposed, for the adoration of the people.

It is also necessary to notice that there arose some of the Broad Churchmen here, as in England, who denied the Virgin Birth of our Blessed Lord. The Rev. Howard MacQueary and Dr. Crapsey were tried and condemned.[5] The effort made to liberalize the Church and make it more like the Unitarian, while popular with the worldly minded, is not being well received by the orthodox and devout.

---

[5]Christian and Catholic, Dr. Grafton.

Thus we see how the great movement on behalf of the recovery of our Catholic heritage in doctrine and worship has progressed, under God's good guidance, in our American Church.

THE CHANGES IN THE PRAYER BOOK

One further matter must be touched upon. After the separation from England, it became necessary that some changes should be made in the Book of Common Prayer. Our American Preface states that "when in the course of Divine Providence, these American States became independent with respect to civil government, their ecclesiastical independence was necessarily included." Alteration in the Liturgy became necessary in prayers for our civil rulers, and some other alterations were made. But it is declared that "the Church was far from intending to depart from the Church of England in any essential points of doctrine, discipline, and worship, further than local discipline should require."

It is important to note that this expressed intention gives us the rule by which all the changes are to be interpreted. It shows that mere omission would not mean rejection of either doctrine or practice. Thus, the Athanasian Creed was omitted from recitation, but remained as a true exposition of the Faith. The form of private absolution of the sick was omitted, but allowed to be given privately in a new office, the Visitation of Prisoners. The frequent repetition of the Lord's Prayer, to which some had objected, was obviated. Selections of Psalms were introduced, which allowed of the omission of the recitation of the imprecatory ones. The sign of the cross in baptism was made optional. The evangelical canticles of the *Benedictus, Magnificat,* and *Nunc Dimittis* were omitted. Even an Article in the Apostles' Creed, "He descended into hell," was bracketed. These concessions were made according to the request of sectarians, when union was sought in England between themselves and the Church. But they had no effect in America in diminishing the sectarian feeling of opposition. It only showed that concessions do not lead to union, but rather intensify sectarian pride and opposition. Our great Bishop Seabury allowed these changes, especially those in Morning and Evening Prayer. He left it, he said, " to a wiser generation to have them reinstated." In respect to the evangelical canticles, this has now been done. Seabury was willing to allow of these changes in the minor offices, provided that he could have the revision of the great office of the Holy Eucharist. He had been consecrated a Bishop in Scotland, and the Scotch Liturgy was far richer and more Catholic than the English one. The Scotch Bishops had requested Seabury to adopt their Communion office, and Bishop Seabury promised to do his best to induce the American Church to adopt it. The result has been that the American office is the most glorious Liturgy of all the Churches belonging to the Anglican Communion. We find, for instance, in the Institution Office the term "Altar." This term, save in the Coronation Service in England, was omitted in the English Book. The Holy Communion is also called in the Consecration office of a church, "the Blessed Sacrament of the Body and Blood of Christ." This it is well to remember, as there are those who have raised objections to the title "Blessed," being given to this Sacrament. It is, however, a Prayer Book definition and terminology. In the Institution office, we find the Holy Communion called by its ancient name, "the Holy Eucharist." In this office also, in its prayer, we find it asserted that Christ has purchased to himself an universal Church, and "has promised to be with the ministry of Apostolic Succession to the end of the world." The relation of the instituted priest and his people is called in the same office a "sacerdotal connection," and in the Visitation of the Sick, the minister, on behalf of all who are present, prays that "we may be gathered unto our fathers,—in the communion of the catholic Church."

More important, however, were the additions made to the Holy Communion consecration prayer or canon, as it is called. The English book is deficient, herein, in an explicit invocation of the Holy Ghost. This, which is held as so important in the Eastern Church, is fully stated in our own Liturgy. In it we pray "Thee, O merciful Father, to hear us; and, of thy almighty goodness, vouchsafe to bless and sanctify, with thy Word and Holy Spirit, these thy gifts and creatures of bread and wine; that we, receiving them according to thy Son our Saviour Jesus Christ's holy institution, in remembrance of his death and passion, may be partakers of his most blessed Body and Blood." It is to be noted here that the elements are not only called creatures, but, having been endowed with the sacramental gift by virtue of the Institution, are called "Holy Gifts," as well as creatures, having received the inward thing or gift of Christ's Body and Blood.

More liturgically important is the explicit statement and action that shows the Holy Eucharist is not only a Communion, but it is also a Sacrifice. It is one, we know, with that ever being presented on the Heavenly Altar, and a memorial re-presentation of the offering on Calvary. We make the oblation of the Sacrament, and offer it to God. So "we, Thy humble servants, do celebrate and make here before Thy Divine Majesty, with these Thy Holy gifts, which we *now offer unto Thee,* the memorial Thy Son hath commanded us to make." And this offering which we make and plead is stated to be for the "whole Church." We ask God to accept this our Sacrifice, that "we, and all Thy *whole Church,* may obtain remission of our sins, and all other benefits of His Passion." As previously, the priest had asked for prayers for the Church Militant, that is, the Church on earth; here, as the priest presents the great Memorial Sacrifice, he pleads it on behalf of the *whole Church.* Now the whole Church must include, not only those on earth, as the Church Militant does, but the faithful departed. So we profess in the hymn,

"Living Saints and dead, but one communion make." We may not know what the latter need, and so our Mother Church prays in general terms for all, "for forgiveness of sins, and all other benefits of Christ's Passion." This has been a great comfort and support to all who have lost dear ones who have gone before.

The special liturgical glory of the Anglican Church is her placing the *Gloria in Excelsis* after the Communion of the people. In the early liturgies, it stood at the beginning. The Liturgy which set forth the drama of the Incarnation and Christ's death, began then with the Song of the Angels at Bethlehem. But our Church placed it after the communicants had received. We were to sing it, as an act of worship and devotion, in the sacramental presence of our Blessed Lord. By this act she reserves the Blessed Sacrament, not for the purpose of Communion, but after Communion, for the purposes of devotion.

In respect to the attitude of the priest, the Bishops at the General Convention of 1832 declared that "as the Holy Communion is of a 'spiritually sacrificial' character, the standing posture should be observed by him, wherever that of kneeling is not expressly prescribed."[6] He should therefore stand, not kneel, while saying his preparatory prayers. He should stand also while receiving his Communion. He should kneel, as bidden by the rubric, when saying the Confession, in union with our Lord's kneeling in Gethsemane, as our Lord, being our representative Penitent, then knelt. He would kneel at the prayer, "We do not presume," etc., in memory of our Lord's falling under the Cross on the way to Calvary. He covers the elements after the consecration with a fair linen cloth, symbolical of our Blessed Lord's Body when taken down from the Cross being wrapped in a clean linen cloth and so laid in the tomb.

CEREMONIAL

In the American Prayer Book, the Ornaments Rubric of England, which referred to the second year of the reign of King Edward VI., was naturally omitted. As we have seen, the omission would not mean any legalized change of ceremonial. What was legal in England would still be allowable in America. This is our authority for the use of the surplice, and if of the surplice, of the other clerical vestments. Thus the deacons at their ordination are to be "decently habited," the term "habit" being here used in its Liturgical sense, "Let all things be done decently and in order." The retention by the Bishops of cope and mitre was declared to be legal by an official report to the House of Bishops concerning the Episcopal costume. The committee said, "the first Bishop of the American Church, Bishop Seabury, was accustomed to wear the mitre in certain Offices, and the first of our Bishops ever consecrated in America, Bishop Claggett of

---

[6]Journal of the General Convention, 1832, p. 451.

95

Maryland, continued to do so." In connection with Bishop Seabury's wearing the mitre, the following anecdote may be interesting: Bishop Coxe wrote, learning that the mitre of Bishop Seabury, used in his Episcopal ministrations, was still in existence: "I had the curiosity to obtain it through the Rev. Dr. Seabury of New York, and placed it in the library of Trinity College. An aged priest, the Rev. Isaac Jones, came into the library, and on his betraying some emotion at the sight, I said to him, 'You have probably seen that mitre on Seabury's head.' He answered, 'Yes; in 1785, at the first ordination in this country, I saw him wearing a scarlet hood and that mitre.' " In the opinion of the committee above referred to, this historical fact justifies any Bishop in resuming it. This report was signed by the Rt. Rev. William C. Doane, Bishop of Albany; Rt. Rev. Arthur Cleveland Coxe, Bishop of Western New York; Rt. Rev. Henry C. Potter, Bishop of New York.[7]

Neither the use of the Eucharistic vestments nor the cope and mitre should be made a matter of party strife. Both High and Low Churchmen believe in the Apostolic character of our Church, and the vestments and other ornaments only bear witness to the continuity of our Church from Apostolic times. They are not introduced in the way of imitation of Rome, but as a protest against her exclusive claims. Whether their introduction is desirable was answered lately by a body of clergy in England in this wise: "The question whether the vestments should or should not be restored depends on whether it is desirable to exhibit or conceal the continuity which they express." In America, surrounded as we are by Romans and sectarians, is it not wise that we should declare, not by word only, but to the eyes of our people, that our Church is the same as that founded by the Apostles, and has come down to us through the ages?

THE CHURCH'S TITLE

We come now to the *title of our Church.*

In 1785 the Church in America took for its legal title that of "Protestant Episcopal," but did not mean by that to deny that she was Catholic. The term Protestant has two significations. It may be used by those who, as members of a society, prefer not to leave but to remain in it under protest. In this way, our Church is a protestant Church. It protests against the additions made to the faith by Rome, and the subtractions made from it by sectarians. But it is not Protestant in the modern sense and use of the word, which involves a rejection of all Church authority and the sacramental system, and which has resulted in hundreds of sects. The Church in her government is "Episcopal." This distinguishes her from the Congregational, Presbyterian, and Papal systems. She

---

[7]Journal of Gen. Convention, 1886. p. 795.

believes that the government of the Church is vested in the Bishops and those under them. No one Bishop is independent of the others. His authority lies in his being a true exponent of the whole body of the Episcopate. We believe thus in the solidarity of the Episcopate. The authority that lies behind the individual Bishop is the corporate knowledge and consciousness of the whole undivided Church. The term "American Catholic" would now be more explicit in our attitude towards sectarians, and would discriminate us from the Roman Church. Our heritage in faith and worship, as expressed in our Book of Common Prayer, is a very grand and noble one. In these days, when Protestantism is disintegrating, and divisions are discernible in the Roman Communion, our Church, Apostolic and Orthodox, is being found a city of refuge. She has never placed herself, and does not now, in opposition to discovered facts of modern science. She does not repress reverent and scientific investigation of the construction of God's Word. She allows a certain amount of comprehensiveness by permitted diversities of ceremonial. We believe there is a growing spirit of union springing up within her. Men are outgrowing the little narrow prejudices which divided them into parties over trifling matters of ritual or speculative questions of doctrine.

We may, in conclusion, venture the criticism that the Church has been heretofore too much on the defensive. Now no cause that is chiefly defensive will ever succeed. It must be constructive and aggressive in order to do so. There should therefore be an earnest and united effort made to gain a more appropriate title for our Church.

It belongs, moreover, to all her members to be true to the great trust they have received from their spiritual forefathers, and not allow it to be impaired, for the sake of popularity with the world, by compromise. As we have all received a great treasure which has come down to us through the sacrifices made by doctors, confessors, and martyrs, it becomes us to hand it on unimpaired to others. As our spiritual forebears made tremendous sacrifices of life and fortune that we might receive this inheritance of the Faith, we must in like manner make sacrifices for the benefit of coming generations. What our members especially need is to be more fully instructed in the history, doctrine, and worship of the Church, to be more and more united together in the bonds of Christian fellowship, to work for the Church as the greatest cause life can present to us, to use all its means of grace, and to love it with all their hearts.

"The Catholic Movement," in *The Works of the Rt. Rev. Charles C. Grafton, S.T.D., LL.D., Second Bishop of Fond du Lac*, ed. by B. Talbot Rogers, Volume II (New York: Longmans, Green, and Co., 1914), 207-224.

22.

American Church Union, 1937

The American Church Union was one of the major Anglo-Catholic organiza-
tions of the twentieth century. It was organized on February 16, 1937, and was
patterned on the English Church Union, founded in 1859 to defend High Church
principles and practices. The American Church Union went out of existence in
the 1970s when its leadership joined several Episcopal splinter groups. This
statement describes the purposes of the ACU.

The Purposes of the Union: 1. To uphold the doctrine, discipline and worship of the Episcopal Church; to extend the knowledge of the Catholic Faith and Practice of the Church; to seek to bring everyone to worship and serve our Lord Jesus, Saviour and King. 2. To maintain unimpaired the position of the Episcopal Church as an integral part of the whole Catholic Church of Christ. 3. To disseminate religious knowledge, and to promote study and research and the dissemination of literature in all branches of theology and morals, and in all departments of learning related to religion. 4. To give counsel, assistance and encouragement to all seeking to further the Catholic Faith and sacramental worship. 5. To promote and encourage the practical application of Christian principles in all social relationships.

The Living Church Annual: The Year Book of the Episcopal Church (New York and Milwaukee: Morehouse Publishing Company, 1937), 114.

Membership Application

Any baptized person is eligible for enrollment as a CRUSADER FOR THE FAITH who states his or her belief that the Episcopal Church is a part of the Historic, Catholic Church of Christ and that the Orders of the Ministry are valid Catholic Orders; recognizes Baptism, Confirmation, Holy Eucharist, Penance, Holy Orders, Matrimony and Holy Unction as Catholic Sacraments, and expresses a desire to promote the objects of the Union.

The American Church News 27 (March 1960), 14.

CHAPTER FOUR

The Spirit of Missions (1820-1897)

Introduction

The Episcopal Church lacked an effective missionary strategy during the western expansion of the early decades of the nineteenth century. If a sufficient number of Episcopalians were gathered in one place on the frontier, a priest might be called and a parish formed. If a sufficient number of parishes were formed in a frontier territory or state, a bishop might be called. This did not prove to be a dynamic missionary strategy. A new approach to mission work began at the General Convention of 1835 when all members of the Episcopal Church were recognized as missionaries with a missionary calling. The General Convention agreed that missionary bishops should be sent, not called, to the frontiers of American expansion in the northwest and southwest. The Episcopal Church made the commitment to take the initiative in evangelizing the settlements of the West. Jackson Kemper was elected to be the first missionary bishop of the Episcopal Church, with jurisdiction and evangelical responsibility for the northwest. Throughout the nineteenth century the Episcopal Church continued the work of mission in both the domestic and foreign mission fields.

23.

Philander Chase, Sermon, June 7, 1820

Philander Chase (December 14, 1775–September 20, 1852) was the first Bishop of Ohio, February 11, 1819–September 9, 1831, and the first Bishop of Illinois (Chicago), March, 9, 1835–September 20, 1852. He was an energetic missionary in the West, and he traveled to New Orleans in 1805 to establish an Episcopal parish which was the first Protestant Church there. Chase was also deeply committed to education, especially of clergy for the West. He founded Kenyon College and the Theological Seminary of the Protestant Episcopal Church in the Diocese of Ohio (Bexley Hall) at Gambier. Later, while Bishop of Illinois, he founded Jubilee College at Peoria, which closed after the Civil War. The following excerpt from his sermon at the 1820 Ohio diocesan convention states his views about educating clergy.

It is written in

II. Cor. 2, 16, *Who is sufficient for these things?*

. . . If all men, in their natural state, are corrupt; and so insufficient to do the will of God, that they can do no good thing, without "God's special grace preventing;" how much more conspicuous is this deficiency, in the Clergy, when doing the great work of the gospel ministry?

The Apostle was speaking of the discharge of his duty, in preaching the gospel, in general; and especially in censuring the wicked, and encouraging the good. In these and all other official duties, he maintains that the ministers of Christ, in their *proper* characters, are accepted of God, through Jesus Christ. "We are, unto God, a sweet savour of Christ; in them that are saved and in them that perish. To the one, we are a savour of death unto death; and to the other, a savour of life unto life." Then the Apostle asks, in the words of the text, *"and who is sufficient for these things?"* You see, then, my Brethren of the Clergy, that the Holy Apostle, in all the duties of the ministry, would direct us to the knowledge of our deficiencies and dangers; and thro' this, he would prompt us to a constant dependence on Divine grace; and to an unremitting use of the means of attaining it.

"Who is sufficient for these things?" For the discharge of the manifold duties involving the fate of immortal souls, alas! who is sufficient? None;—*none are sufficient of themselves to think any thing, as of themselves*, much less to do what is acceptable; *"but* (as he a little further on adds) *our sufficiency is of God."*

Let us then pursue the method pointed out by the Apostle; showing how difficult and dangerous the priestly office is; and, from this difficulty and danger, argue the bounden duty, in every Clergyman, to seek aid from God, in all the means of grace. What, then, does God require in his ministers? That sufficiency, which is of God. What is that? The sufficiency which every minister is bound to attain, by the manifold means of grace, which to that end, God has bestowed on him, viz: *extensive knowledge, great prudence*; and *an undeviating holiness of life.*

My first item is *extensive knowledge*—Why? Because the Holy Scriptures have declared, that *"The Priest's lips should keep,* (or preserve) *knowledge."*— He is to be, as it were a *Treasurer*, to have always in possession, not only what will serve his own personal use, but that of all under his care. His repository of divine knowledge must be such; so ample, so well preserved; and so well arranged; that the people, when obeying the injunction, which immediately follows, may never be disappointed. *"The Priest's lips should keep knowledge*; and THEY (i.e. the people committed to his charge) SHOULD SEEK THIS LAW AT HIS MOUTH, (Mal: II, 7.) Can this be consistent with that scantiness of learning; that sterility of mind; that ignorance of divine things; too often observable in those, who have thrust themselves into the priestly office? Can this *treasury* of divine knowledge be compared with those empty heads, and vacant shelves, whose possessors, when they have preached a few sermons, have nothing further to supply the exigencies of immortal souls? We think not: for, our blessed Saviour says, that *"every scribe, that is instructed in the kingdom of Heaven, is like unto a man that is an householder, which bringeth forth, out of his treasure, things new and old."*

The *Kingdom of Heaven* is the characteristick name, which our Saviour gave to his church; and by the *scribe*, he means the ministers of that church; by *being instructed*, he must mean the attainment of that degree of learning, of which we are speaking, and the learning itself is called *thesauros*, a *treasure*. This is denominated *his treasure*; to denote that the learning must be *his own*, and *in plenty*.

I could add many other proofs in point; but these, joined with common sense, must be sufficient. Surely, if all other arts and callings demand knowledge, that of DIVINITY, the greatest of all, cannot be proferred without *knowledge*, and that in an extensive degree.

From speaking of *knowledge* in general; as requisite in a minister of Jesus Christ, I might descend unto particulars: and thereby demonstrate the great necessity of a constant application to the many means, which are afforded us to obtain the godly sufficiency spoken of by the Apostle. But, I fear our time will not allow us to be minute. This much, however, I cannot omit observing: that knowledge of divinity in *general*, is not the only requisite: it must be particular and well divided.

From a deficiency in these particulars, many Clergymen have made but a bad use of their *general* knowledge of divinity. Knowledge is like the materials for building: it may be *good* and *in plenty*; and yet, if the several parts thereof be not well selected and arranged; so that each *order* may be distinctly seen, and each *compartiment* as to beauty and use, clearly perceived, great confusion will ensue; and the effect of the whole will be disgusting. By the help of this simile, contemplate a Clergyman deficient in these particulars, attempting to discharge the several duties of his office, the *mode* of which is left to his discretion. Hear his discourses in publick: and in private. Of *Positive Theology*, or those necessary parts of our speculative Faith revealed in Holy Scriptures, how often is he so inadequate a teacher, that he leaves the minds of his hearers quite in the dark, for want of due distinction in the statement of them.

Of *Polemical divinity*, for that kind of knowledge, in divine subjects, which enables us to defend the faith once delivered to the saints, how often does such an one, from want of proper distinctions, expose, rather than aid, the cause of truth?

It being the character of a shepherd, not only to *feed*, but to *defend*, the sheep; *he*, who stands in the place of the Great Shepherd of souls, should always be found armed, with the proper weapons of the gospel of truth, to *defend* the lambs committed to his charge. And what can *he* do to this purpose, who knows not the avenues, thro' which the enemies, the Wolves and Tygers that devour the flock, make their approach? Many a Clergyman has weakened the cause of truth, and exposed the christian souls, under his care, to heresy and infidelity, by not knowing the true points in debate, or by not managing it with that skill and distinction, which are characteristic of digested knowledge and a well disciplined mind.

If you hear him on subjects embracing that all-important branch of a minister's duty, denominated *casuistical divinity*, how apparent is his deficiency and inability to do justice to his calling? How can *he* resolve difficulties in *cases of conscience*, who, perhaps, never stated them to his own mind; or if he *did*, never so digested them, as to be able to give a prompt answer according to truth? Shall the ministers of Christ, the spiritual Physicians, be less attentive to the exigencies of the soul, than natural Physicians, to those of the body? And does not the skill of the latter materially depend on a knowledge how to act, and how to advise, in the difficult cases, which occur? Is not this the chief part of their study? Even so, it is the duty of every minister of Christ to give his mind, constantly and ardently, to the study of this part of his profession; lest he fall under the dreadful crime of being an *Empirick* in Divinity.

But, my Brethren, we have dwelt long enough, perhaps too long, on this part of our subject; especially when we consider the importance of the next head, in the division of our discourse; which is the absolute necessity of GREAT PRUDENCE, to form that godly sufficiency mentioned by the Apostle.

By *prudence*, I mean that, which not only knows *what* to do; but *how*, and *when*, to do it, to the best effect.

By *prudence*, I understand that, which is, sometimes termed *wisdom*; and which is alluded to by our Blessed Saviour, when sending forth his disciples into a wicked world, and directing them how to contend with sinful man, and how to convert sinners to holiness. "*Behold I send you forth as sheep in the midst of wolves; be ye therefore, wise as serpents and harmless as doves.*"

This prudence, or wisdom, relates to ourselves, to our individual families, to the particular flocks committed to our charge, and to the Church at large. To be deficient in this quality of a Clergyman, in these respects, is to mar the whole face of our characters, and to render our very profession useless. A Clergyman's personal, is intimately connected with his official, character, if the former be liable, thro' lack of prudence, to misinterpretation; the latter, even in cases, where the heart is right, and the intention good, must suffer. We owe it, therefore, to ourselves, so to behave, that *"our good be not evil spoken of."* We owe it to ourselves, to open no door, whereby, false brethren within, or wicked enemies from without, can, thro' our sides, wound the peace of the Church, and hinder the progress of the gospel. God requires this at our hands. It is no inferior part of that sufficiency, which is from him, and to his glory. Again: we must manifest our wisdom in all things relating to our own individual families; teaching and governing them, in the ways of piety and virtue. A Clergyman's usefulness, in a very great measure, depends on this part of his ministerial sufficiency; and, as such, it is insisted on, as an indispensible qualification, in every christian shepherd, by the inspired Apostle. He must be "one," saith he, "that ruleth his own house; having his children in subjection, with all gravity: for, if a man know not how to rule his own house, how shall he take care of the Church of God." I. Tim. 3. 4.

What can be the reason, then, that many Clergymen (I speak now of the whole order as such) are so egregiously deficient, in this particular?—They have much to say to their parishes, (and the more, if well said, the better,) about a holy, sober, and a godly, life; but little, of this sort, to say to their own families. They can teach other women to be *"discreet, chaste, keepers at home, good, obedient to their own husbands, that the word of God be not blasphemed,"* while their own wives are, perhaps, the greatest *gossips, busy-bodies*, and *tattlers*, in the parish. They can preach an excellent sermon to young men, and young women; exhorting them *to obey their parents,* to be *sober minded; in all things, shewing themselves a pattern of good works*; while, their own children are left at loose ends: their sons ignorant, impudent, and disobedient: foul in their language, dishonest in their dealings, and regardless of the truth;—their daughters vain, idle, and disrespectful in their manners; neglecting every useful branch of female education; and mindful only of those frivolous accomplishments, praised only, in the almost only books they read, *Novels and Romances.*

When the world sees, yea, when their parishes see, that this is the effect of their Religion at *home,* what good will their public teaching compass? We fear very little.

Let it, then, be one important point, to manifest our wisdom and prudent sufficiency, as gospel ministers, by ruling well our own families; and by "training our children up in the nurture and admonition of the Lord."

Again: our sufficiency, in *wisdom* and *prudence*, must be manifested, in all that relates to our parishes, and the people committed to our charge.

And here, at every step, we discover the great importance of this part of our subject. We should be wise in our general deportment to all. Mindful of the dignity of our station, as embassadors of God towards man, we should be careful, that we dishonour not our calling, by mixing with low and vicious company; and tamely listening to their vile discourse, thro' any hope of *popularity*. This is but to degrade ourselves, without exalting them. And yet, we should never forget, that these very persons are the objects of our mission into a wicked world. To approach them, and converse with them, is our duty; but it should always be as Moses approached the children of Israel, from the mount of God; with a heavenly radiancy about our characters, at once commanding respect and love.

To the faithful and obedient disciples of the Blessed Jesus, we should endeavour to imitate the conduct of our adored Master to St. John. We should cultivate their love, and gain their confidence; that to us, they may resort for advice and comfort, in all the difficulties and troubles of life; and, when reposing on us, they should ever find faithful friends, able and willing advisers.

In relation to the poor of our parishes; we must not forget their spiritual, while we sedulously relieve their temporal, wants. If the latter cannot be done by ourselves, we should always prove their able advocates with those that *are* able; ever sensible, that it matters little, by *whom* the charity is done, if done it is: God's glory is the same. But, we should remember to keep a watchful eye over ourselves, that a pharisaical ostentation have no part in our charities. To let them be known, more than is absolutely necessary, is no less than to *sound a trumpet*, and thus to deprive us of our heavenly reward.

To the *rich* and *honourable*, in our parishes, we should be doubly prudent. While we respect them for their stations in life, and cultivate their friendship, for the noble purpose of exciting them to good works, in the support of the Church of God; we are never to forget, that we are their spiritual fathers, endowed with authority from on high; yea, most strictly commanded, to reprove them for their vices, to exhort them unto repentance; and to demand of them a strict conformity to the salutary discipline of the Church of Christ.

In our public discourses, being addressed to all, we should take care, that all have their portion of gospel instruction, in due season; ever remembering that we are placed as *stewards* of the manifold grace of God. To this end, their characters, their wants, dangers and temptations, should be well studied. To whatever sins they are inclined, so far from giving way to them, because they are popular; we should "set our face like a flint" against them; at the same time, taking

104

pains to manifest, that *we*, in reproving them, are governed more by a sense of duty to God, and a regard to their salvation, than by a love of satire in ourselves.

Should the blasphemies of Atheism, or the vapid arguments of Deism, be in circulation among our flocks, our Master commands us to put on the whole armour of God, and fight the good fight of faith. Like David, we are to go forth to *slay both the Lion and the Bear*; But, like him, we also, are to give all the glory to God; who will never fail to save those, who put their trust in him.

In short, we bear such a manifold relation to the souls committed to our charge, that, to be unmindful of the dictates of prudence and wisdom, in the discharge of our several duties resulting from those relations, would involve the highest crime. We are Embassadors of God to themward; and *they* are the *"people ready,"* by nature, *"to perish,"* to be saved by our ministration. We are their Teachers; and they our scholars, seeking the saving knowledge of the gospel at our mouth. We are their shepherds; and *they* our flocks, looking to us, for spiritual food and protection. *Who then is sufficient for these things?* What prudence, what wisdom, is required of us, in the duties hence resulting!

But, a Clergyman's prudence, or wisdom, does not end with his duty to his particular parish; it extends unto the Church at large.

An important duty, by our Canons, devolves upon every parish minister, and especially on such as are members of the standing Committee, in recommending Candidates for *Holy Orders*; and few things deserve more prudence than this. I have now been in the ministry twenty-two years; and most of the disturbances, which have arisen, in consequence of admitting improper characters to orders, might have been prevented, had those Clergymen, who recommended them, exercised that prudence, of which we are now speaking; for, bad Clergymen are generally found to have been bad, from the beginning. O, what a weight of sorrow must hang on the mind of a conscientious minister, for having been imprudently the means of introducing, to the sanctuary of God, a wicked and unsanctified man! What agony must pierce his breast, when he sees the wolf, which *he* had been the means of admitting into the fold, tearing the lambs and scattering the sheep upon the mountains! Be prudent, therefore, in this particular, that you may avoid such pangs as these.

Again: prudence, or wisdom, should be exercised by every Clergyman, in relation to the Church at large, by avoiding every thing, that may look like party, or party names. Against the sin of SCHISM, we supplicate the divine grace, in our prayers. May we therefore—may the Apostolic Church in this, our dear country never admit this deadly sin, in this shape—*Names*, we know, are innocent things; but if they stir up feuds, and produce rancour, they change their nature and become sinful.

The grand Enemy of the Church never did much harm, in his own proper character. To effect his designs, he changes his native dress; and assumes that of an angel of light. Shall we, therefore, be ignorant of his devices? And shall we, when knowing his devices, become a prey to them? May God, in his mercy to the Church of America, forbid it! May it always be a governing principle of our lives, to preserve *Charity*, the very bond of perfectness, that which holds the Church, the body of Christ, together, by love to God and man; by unity of design and harmony of effort.

This leads us to the third general head of our discourse; which was to shew, that an undeviating, exemplary holiness of heart and life, is absolutely necessary to form that sufficiency, mentioned in the text.

Every holy man is not, therefore, a minister of Christ; but every minister of Christ must be a holy man; or he is a wolf in sheep's clothing; the worst of traitors to his master; and the basest of Hypocrites.

By a holy man, I mean a good man; good at heart; and good in his life and dealings with mankind: upright and just; faithful to his word and promise; honest, honourable, and candid; above the mean arts and low maxims of policy, by which the world is governed; obliging to his friends; forgiving to his enemies; and merciful to the poor and needy: submissive to his superiors, in Church and state: and all this from the best of motives; from a principle of faith, which worketh by love; love to God and man; love which leadeth him to his prayers; prayers in public and in private; and, when there, makes his devotions arise to God, as the morning and evening incense, love which manifests the grace of God shed abroad in his heart, constituting him a new man, formed and fashioned after the pattern of his heavenly Master, in dealing justly, loving mercy, and walking humbly. This is the *good man*, whom we call a *holy man*; and, if without this holiness, the Scriptures affirm *no man can see the Lord*, above, how should he, who is deficient therein, be permitted to serve at God's altar, here below? There is, to every pious mind, something so disgustingly incongruous in a bad minister, that all other qualifications are in him, as nothing. Suppose him to speak with the tongues of men and angels; to possess all knowledge; and have prudence to set off his gifts to the best advantage; and, at the same time, known to be a bad man; to be deficient in holiness of heart and life, what will all his eloquence and learning avail, to the conversion of souls to God, or to the edification of his Church? They will be as sounding brass, and a tinkling Cymbal. What will his prudence avail, in recommending the cause of Religion? It will be justly regarded as the contemptible arts and manœuverings of a hypocrite, to accomplish, under the veil of a sanctimonious exterior, some base and sinister purpose.

It is, then, an exemplary and undeviating holiness of heart and life, that is to be the crown & perfection of a minister's sufficiency. Without this, all is as a dead body; a putrid carcass, offensive to God and man.

In common with the rest of mankind, the minister of Christ, is concerned to be a good and holy man, for his *own sake*, i.e. to save his own soul. He, as well as they, by living an unholy life, must, at the last judgement, be doomed to everlasting punishments, where the worm dieth not, and the fire is not quenched. Besides this, he has the additional motive to be a good man, for the sake of others; for the sake of the souls, whom he may be the instrument of introducing to the kingdom of Heaven. If he fail in this, the express design of his profession, and that, thro' the effect of his bad example, what a weight of guilt must hang upon his head! How deep will it sink his conscious soul in misery, when, to the just Judge of men and angels, he giveth in his account, it then be seen, that those, whom he was sent to save, were lost, thro' the influence of his unholy conversation!—With this view of the subject, how dangerous a profession is that of a clergyman; and how detestable a character is that of a *bad one*! To link his soul to the souls of thousands, and then betray, both himself and them, to the Enemy; and, together sink into eternal flames!

My Brethren; the words of our *ordination service* are so appropriate, to this part of our subject, that it would be criminal in me, in closing it, to omit them. "Have always, therefore, in remembrance, how great a treasure is committed to your charge. For they are the Sheep of Christ, which he bought with his death, and for whom he shed his blood. The Church and congregation, whom ye serve, is his spouse and body. And if it shall happen that the same Church, or any member thereof, take any hurt or hinderance by reason of your negligence, you know the greatness of the fault, and also the horrible punishment that will ensue."

This is the language of our pious Church, to all her ministers: and what shall we say; what shall we do, after such awful considerations, and such awakening exhortations as these? Where shall we find our sufficiency for these things? Where, but at the footstool of our all-powerful, meritorious, and gracious, Saviour? *There* bewailing our sins and acknowledging our weakness, let us implore his forgiveness and heavenly strength. *There* let us weep tears of blood, if it were possible, that the blood of souls, the guilt of dooming them to eternal misery, cleave not to our priestly garments. *There*, and *thence* alone, let us seek for that assemblage of pious, zealous, and effectual graces, which can arm us for the important warfare, into which we have enlisted. And then, with Jesus for our Leader, and the aid of his spirit for our comfort, we shall be sufficient, in, and thro', the day of trial, and, finally crowned with eternal life.

Journal of the Diocese of Ohio, 1820, pp. 5-16. (Excerpt)

24.

George Washington Doane,
The Missionary Bishop, September 25, 1835

George Washington Doane (May 27, 1799–April 27, 1859) was consecrated the second Bishop of New Jersey on October 31, 1832. At the eighteenth General Convention, August 19-September 1, 1835, Jackson Kemper (December 24, 1789-May 24, 1870) was elected Missionary Bishop of Missouri and Indiana, the first Missionary Bishop of the Episcopal Church. At Kemper's consecration, September 25, 1835, Bishop Doane preached this sermon on "A Missionary Bishop."

Romans X. 15.— How shall they preach except they be sent?

Brethren, we are assembled, under the protection of Almighty God, to partake in, or to witness, the consecration of A Missionary Bishop. It is a new office in this Church. The event has not occurred before. What we are now to do will go on record, as a precedent. Is it right that it should be done? Is it wise in us to do it? Is the Church prepared for the transaction?—Favor me, brethren, with your attention, while, according to the grace of God which is given unto me, I answer these plain questions. And Thou, divine and holy Saviour, who hadst compassion on the multitudes, "because they fainted and were scattered abroad, as sheep having no shepherd," imbue us with Thy tender love for all the flock,—accept and sanctify our present effort to extend Thy sacred fold,—and make of him, who waits before us to receive Thy warrant, a pastor according to Thine own heart, to feed Thy people with knowledge and discretion!

The Missionary Bishop

    I.   What is *the nature of his office?*

    II. Has it *divine or apostolic sanction?*

    III. Is there a *present call for its provision?*

    IV. Is it *consistent with the order and the genius of this Church?*

    I. In strictness, as every minister of Jesus is a *Missionary*,[1] so are the Bishops, as His chief ministers, *eminently* Missionaries—*sent out* by Christ Himself to preach the Gospel—*sent* to preach it in a wider field—*sent* to preach it under a higher responsibility—*sent* to preach it at greater hazards of self-denial and self-sacrifice, and under circumstances more appalling of arduous labour and of anxious care,—to fulfil, in a single word, that humbling, but most wholesome precept of the Saviour, "whosoever of you shall be the chiefest, let him be servant of

---

[1]Literally, one sent out,—synonymous with the scriptural words, Messenger, and Apostle.

108

all." But, though the "divers orders of ministers" which God, by His Holy Spirit, has appointed in the Church, have been, from the Apostles' time, and will forever be the same,—and though it is the chief glory of the highest as of the lowest, that, like the blessed Son of God Himself, they are all Missionaries, sent out to preach the Gospel of salvation to a ruined world,—the different circumstances of the Church, in different countries, and at different times, lead to a difference of relation in the ministry, which may apply alike to each of its three orders. In places where the Church has long been settled, there will be a settled ministry. The people will supply themselves, or be supplied, through means which are substantially their own, with the word and ordinances of God—in other terms, they have *diocesan* Episcopacy and a *parochial* Clergy. In places where the Church has not been introduced, or has but partial and precarious lodgment, it, of course, cannot be so. To them emphatically applies the argument of the Apostle, of which the text is part. True it is indeed so written in the Holy Scripture, "Whosoever shall call upon the name of the Lord shall be saved. But how"—the question is as true and pertinent at this day as when urged by fervent Paul—"how shall they call on him in whom they have not believed? And how shall they believe in him of whom they have not heard? And how shall they hear without a preacher? And how shall they preach, except they be sent?" In other words, if they have ministers of Christ to admit them to the Christian fold by baptism, to preach in their ears the word of reconciliation, break among them the bread of everlasting life, and help them to train up their children "in the nurture and admonition of the Lord," they must be *Missionaries*. If they have Bishops to oversee the flock, to lay hands upon them "after the example of the holy Apostles," "to ordain elders in every city, and set in order the things which are wanting," they must be *Missionary Bishops*. And precisely, as the Church, obeying the mandate of her divine Head, sends Presbyters and Deacons, to go "into all the world, and preach the Gospel to every creature," so may she, and so should she, emulating that divine compassion, which yearned over the fainting multitudes, that roamed, untended and unfed, among the mountains of Judea, send Bishops to them, to seek the wandering flocks, to lead them to the sacred fold, to appoint them under-shepherds, to oversee and govern them with due authority and godly discipline, and, "warning every man and teaching every man in all wisdom," to do what in them lies to "present every man perfect in Christ Jesus." And this is what is meant by A Missionary Bishop—a Bishop *sent forth by* the Church, *not sought for of* the Church—going *before* to organize the Church, not waiting till the Church has partially been organized,—a leader, not a follower, in the march of the Redeemer's conquering and triumphant Gospel— sustained by their alms whom God has blessed both with power and will to offer to Him of their substance, for their benefit who are not blessed with both or either of them—sent by the Church, even as the Church is sent by Christ; not to such only as have knowledge of His truth, and desire Him for their king, but to the ignorant and the rebellious, to them who know not of His name, or who will not have Him to reign over them, to the ungodly, the heathen, the idolatrous—to all who ignorantly are in unbelief, or wilfully "His enemies, by wicked works."

II. But, *is there sanction for this office of a Missionary Bishop in the instructions of the Saviour, or in the practice of the Apostles?* It is abundantly supplied in both. Take, for example, St. Matthew's record of the Saviour's first appointment of the ministry. "And Jesus went about all the cities and villages, teaching in their synagogues, and preaching the gospel of the kingdom, and healing every sickness and every disease among the people. But when He saw the multitudes He was moved with compassion on them because they fainted, and were scattered abroad as sheep having no shepherd."[2] "And when He had called unto Him His twelve disciples," He "sent" them "forth, and commanded them, saying," "as ye go, preach,—the kingdom of heaven is at hand."[3] Here surely is a most unquestionable exhibition of *the Missionary principle.*—The Saviour died, and rose again. But neither death nor life, the bleeding agony of the Cross, nor the triumphant glory of the Resurrection, could turn aside His steadfast heart from its benevolent and holy purpose. "Then the same day at evening," says the Evangelist St. John, "being the first day of the week," the same on which He rose, "when the doors were shut, where the disciples were assembled for fear of the Jews, came Jesus, and stood in the midst of them and said, "Peace be unto you"; "as my Father hath sent me, even so send I you."[4] And once again, when He was just about to rise to heaven, Jesus came and spake to the eleven, saying, "All power is given unto me in heaven and in earth. Go ye, therefore, and teach all nations, baptizing them in the name of the Father, and of the Son, and of the Holy Ghost; teaching them to observe all things whatsoever I have commanded you: and lo, I am with you alway, even unto the end of the world." Here was consummated and confirmed, by Jesus Christ Himself, with perpetuity of succession to the end of time, *the office* of Apostle, or—the inspiration and the power of miracles ceasing with the necessity for them—*of Missionary Bishop.*

If there be desired still farther precedent, what clearer instance, and what nobler model, of a Missionary Bishop than Paul, the Apostle of the Gentiles, traversing sea and land,—at Antioch, at Damascus, at Ephesus, at Jerusalem, at Corinth, at Athens, in Italy, in Spain,—not knowing the things that may befall

---

[2]St. Matthew ix. 35, 36.
[3]St. Matthew x. 1, 5, 7.
[4]St. John xx. 19, 21.

him there, nor counting his life dear unto himself, so that he may finish his course with joy, and the ministry which he had received of the Lord Jesus. Brethren, is there triumphal march recorded, of conqueror or king, that shines out through the mist of ages with a track so luminous? What limit shall we set to the transforming power of religion which could make the heart of a proud, persecuting Pharisee so overflow with self-denying love? Who would turn back from a career like this, though afflictions, bonds and death were multiplied a thousand fold along the way, to dream the longest life out in inglorious ease, or wear, even in its proudest and most palmy state, the purple of imperial Rome? And what poor dastards must we be, how utterly unfit to bear the name of Christ, if with such aids, such motives, such examples as we have, we still permit the ignoble thralls of time and sense to bind our spirits down to earth; and grovel in the mire of selfishness and sensuality, when we are called to tread the starry path by which not only Paul, but Polycarp, and Latimer, and Heber and Middleton, and Henry Martyn, and many more, whom time would fail us but to name, who "loved their lives not to the death," followed their Saviour into heaven!

III. But, *do the times require such efforts and such sacrifices?* Does Providence make plain before us the path of Christian duty? Is there a present call for the revival of what certainly received in the first ages the highest sanctions, that even heaven itself can lend—the office of a Missionary Bishop? Look for a moment out upon the world. Glance with a rapid eye at the strange signs which mark the times. Look Eastward, and behold how throughout Asia ancient superstitions seem worn out and tottering to their fall. The sway of the false Prophet is now the shadow of what once it was. The mystic spell which shut out China from the world is fast dissolving, and the light of Gospel truth begins to break on her benighted and degraded millions. And even in Africa, which, for so many centuries, has lain in awful silence, like some old forgotten grave, grown over with long grass and weeds, faint signs of renovated life are seen, or seem to be, and challenge, by the holiest and most powerful sympathy, our pity, our exertions, and our prayers. Do we look homeward? Through the regions of our own unbounded West see how the stream of life sets onward. Behold, in arts, in wealth, in power, a progress such as earth has never seen, outrunning even fancy's wildest dreams; but with no provision that at all keeps pace with it, for the securing of man's nobler and immortal interest. Observe with what a keen and shrewd regard the Church of Rome has marked that region for her own, and with what steadiness of purpose she pursues her aim; and seeks to lay the deep foundations of a power which is to grow as it grows, and to strengthen as it gathers strength.

Whence, in this crisis of the world, whence is the succour to be sought, that is to come up to the help of God against the mighty? To what source does the finger of His providence turn every eye that looks for rescue and relief? The Church of England, long by God's protecting favor, the stay and hope of Christendom, now needs her utmost succours for her own defence against the impious combination that attempts her overthrow. The Christian brethren, not of our communion, who have seemed to grow and multiply about us with a vigour so prolific, now begin to feel, and in some instances to own, the want of those inherent principles of union which alone can bind in one, large masses of mankind; and, destitute of ancient landmarks, stray insensibly from "the old paths," in which alone God's promise gives assurance of protection and of peace. Meanwhile, they turn instinctively to us. They recognize the doctrines which we hold, as the old faith which once was given to the Saints. They yield to us, with one accord, however they may differ from each other, the possession of a ministry with due authority from God to preach the Gospel of salvation, and set to its seals. They acknowledge the existence, in our institutions, of that tendency to fixed and certain centres, of those principles of unity, subordination and stability, which tend so powerfully to self-preservation, while they are so entirely indispensable to vigorous and enduring influence with others. They own that in the faithful use of our most scriptural and primitive service God may be worshipped, "in spirit and in truth," while man's infirmity is wisely guarded against much that tends to mar "the beauty of holiness," and to endanger the integrity of faith.

Brethren, these are no grounds of boasting on our part. There is nothing here that should be suffered to tempt us to glory over others, or to rely upon ourselves. No, God forbid! We have nothing, that we did not first receive. We have nothing for which we must not at the last account. We have nothing, which we ought not, in the spirit of true Christian meekness, to beseech our brethren, whom we love for Jesus' sake, to come and share with us. But, brethren, though we may not glory in our privileges, should we not be faithful in improving them? Though we may not boast of what the Lord has done for us, should we not be prompt and fervent in owning and proclaiming it? Though we may not triumph over others, who fall behind in any gift, should we not be earnest and untiring in commending our advantages to them, and urging their adoption, not by the force of argument alone, but by the persuasive and prevailing eloquence of our meek, humble, holy, charitable, Christian conversation? If we believe that God has done more for us, than for some others of His children, the proper evidence of our sincerity is our endeavour to make up to them, from our abundance, their "lack of opportunity." If we are conscious that His presence is among us, and His blessing is upon us, the proof of our sincerity in that conviction is in "unfeigned love of the brethren," and in untiring efforts to make our light—the light reflected in us from the face of Jesus Christ—"so shine before men," that they may glorify with us our Father who is in heaven. If we believe that our principles as Protestant Episcopalians are most in accordance with the divine will, and therefore most for the promotion of human happiness, it is our duty to demonstrate it in action, to carry them out before the world in vigorous and efficient practice, and to make visible to every eye, and palpable to every heart, the great things which the Lord has done for us.

Brethren, I believe, before God, that next to the possession of the pure and undefiled religion of the Gospel of His Son,—and, in the degree so close and intimate that human penetration never can discriminate between them,—we are most indebted, for all that we are and all that we have that is most precious to us, here of Christian privilege, or hereafter of Christian hope, to the maintenance, in integrity and purity, of the order of His holy apostolic Church. I believe that it is to us, as faithful in the maintenance of both, that God continues, and, so long as we are faithful, will continue, to us His presence and protection—blessing, as He has promised that He will, the ministry of His appointment; accompanying, as He has pledged Himself to do, the glorious Church which He purchased to Himself with the blood of His dear Son, "alway, even unto the end of the world." I believe that, as the truth of the blessed and glorious Gospel is attested, not only by the outward evidence of its divine original, but by its quickening and transforming power in the conversion and renewal unto righteousness of every heart that faithfully receives it; so the identity of the one, holy apostolic Church is and will ever be established, not only by the verifiable succession of its orders and sacraments, but by its effective and unquestionable agency as "the pillar and ground of the truth,"—as the conservator of God's pure and spiritual worship,—as the promoter in all human institutions, civil as well as religious, of order, strength and permanence,—as God's minister on earth of peace and good-will to man: the very purpose for which apostles, prophets, evangelists, pastors, teachers—in a word, the whole structure of the Church was given—being, as St. Paul declares, "for the perfecting of the saints, for the work of the ministry, for the edifying of the body of Christ, till we all come in the unity of the faith and of the knowledge of the Son of God, unto a perfect man, unto the measure of the stature of the fullness of Christ."[5]

Believing these things, professing myself, as most assuredly I do, to be entirely conscientious in my belief of them, my principles as a Churchman, my attachment to the Church cannot be charged upon me as bigotry—may not, in Christian candour or in Christian charity, be denounced as blind and arbitrary

---

[5]Ephesians iv. 11-13.

attachment. No, it is part and parcel of my Christianity. I am protected against censure or reproach for that profession, by my Christian birthright to that glorious "liberty wherewith Christ has made us free." Infinitely more and more important even than this—I am bound, bound most solemnly, bound by all my hopes of heaven, to offer, so far as in me lies, the same advantages, to commend and urge, so far as is consistent with that same glorious liberty, to the adoption of all others who have them not, the same inestimable privileges. Esteeming, as we do, beloved brethren, "the office of a Bishop," enjoying, as we profess to do, with grateful hearts, the rich blessings which God has showered upon the Church in which it is our happiness to worship, how is it that we can, how is it that we dare, keep back from others the means of that enjoyment? If due perpetuation of the Church, and chief authority, and the protection of God's promise, appertain to Bishops, as successors to the Apostles of the Lord, how can we encourage, so far as we have rightful influence, the extension or even the existence of the Church without a Bishop? If it be "evident," as we declare, "to all men diligently reading holy Scripture and ancient authors, that from the Apostles' time there have been these orders of ministers in Christ's Church, Bishops, Priests and Deacons," by what warrant can we withhold from any portion of the Saviour's family the chiefest of the three? If it be sound and true in practice, as it is certainly of primitive authority, "not to do anything without the Bishop,"[6] upon what principle is it that we permit the organization of dioceses—nay, that we invite the organization of dioceses, and yet until they have a certain number of duly organized parishes, and of duly settled presbyters, compel them to remain—without a bishop?[7] And if there be, in Indiana or Missouri, in

---

[6]See the Epistles of Ignatius, the disciple of St. John.

[7]Prudential reasons have been thought to require that no diocese in our communion should be allowed to proceed to the election of a Bishop until there have been duly settled in it six presbyters in charge of parishes for one year, and until there should also be six parishes duly organized. Such is the provision of the second Canon. Thanks be to God, it was provided at the last General Convention—which must be known hereafter as the Missionary Convention—that, on the request of any diocese, however few its parishes or presbyters, the House of Bishops may proceed to nominate a Bishop, who, if duly confirmed by the House of Clerical and Lay Deputies, or in the recess of the General Convention, by the several Standing Committees, may be consecrated the Bishop of that diocese. This provision, with the Canon for Missionary Bishops, completes the organization of the Church for the great ends of permanence and increase. The work will now begin at the right end. The Bishop may go out, as Titus went to Crete, "to ordain elders in every city." Dioceses will not be tempted to unseemly efforts to make apparent the canonical quota of parishes and presbyters. Bishops in new dioceses will not of necessity be elected under circumstances the most unfavorable to the best result of that most important transaction. The united wisdom of the fathers of the Church will be exerted for the protection of its infant members. The incipient measures in each diocese, on which so much depends, may be taken under the best auspices. The Clergy in distant and unsettled regions will enjoy episcopal oversight.

Louisiana, Florida or Arkansas, some scattered handfuls here and there of Churchmen—or if, obedient to the Saviour's mandate, to preach the Gospel unto every creature, we send our heralds of the Cross to China, Texas, Persia, Georgia, or Armenia—upon what principle can we neglect, or on what ground can we refuse,—since from their feebleness and poverty they cannot have a Bishop of their own, or in their ignorant blindness, they do not desire it,—to send to them at our own cost and charge, and in the Saviour's name, a Missionary Bishop?

Brethren, The Field is the Whole World. To every soul of man, in every part of it, the Gospel is to be preached. Everywhere, the Gospel is to be preached *by, through,* and *in* the Church. To Bishops, as successors of the Apostles, the promise of the Lord was given to be with His Church, "alway, to the end of the world." Upon Bishops, as successors of the Apostles, the perpetuation of the Christian ministry depends. With Bishops, as successors of the Apostles, the government of the Church, the preaching of the word, the administration of the sacraments, the care of souls, has been entrusted. Without Bishops, as successors of the Apostles, there is no warrant, and for fifteen hundred years from Christ there was no precedent, for the establishment of the extension of the Church. Professing these things, act accordingly. "Freely ye have received, freely give." Open your eyes to the wants, open your ears to the cry, open your hands for the relief, of a perishing world. Send *the Gospel.* Send it, as you have received it, *in the Church.* Send out, to preach the Gospel, and to build the Church,—to every portion of your own broad land, to every stronghold of the Prince of Hell, to every den and nook and lurking place of heathendom, a Missionary Bishop!

IV. But loud as is the call for this provision, imperative as is our duty to respond to it, *is it consistent with the order, and the genius of this Church to do so?* Yes, my beloved brethren, yes! And if it were not so, it were no Church for us. If it were not so, it were no Church of Christ. That could not be the Saviour's awful and beloved spouse, which had no heart to feel for, or no hand to feed, the hungry souls for whom He died. That could not be the Saviour's body which did not bear to each remotest limb, the care, the consolation, and the saving grace of its ascended and triumphant Head. Thank God, it is not, and it never has been, so with us! As from the first, so in all after ages, it has still been competent for the Church of Christ to emulate her Saviour's holy love, in sending out Apostles to the multitudes that wander and are faint, as sheep who have no shepherd. It is of the nature of a *trust,* that there be always given with it authority and power for the due execution of all its proper uses. It is still farther of the nature of a trust, that, on its acceptance, there devolves on the *trustee* the bounden duty to secure, so far as in him lies, its full and faithful execution. Now The Gospel is *God's gift, in trust,* for the conversion and salvation of lost man. The Church is

His *Trustee.*—Admirably indeed is she prepared and fitted for her trust. She is *divinely instituted.* Were she of *human* origin, she would be, like man, uncertain and capricious. She is of God, and like Him cannot fail, and never will betray. Were she a *voluntary* institution, she might cease without a miracle, for want of members. But God is wiser than men; and membership in His Church is thus made part of the plan of salvation. "Go ye therefore, and make disciples of all nations, baptizing them in the name of the Father and of the Son and of the Holy Ghost."[8] "He that believeth and is baptized shall be saved."[9]—To discharge the duties of a *continual* trust, the trustee of necessity must have continuance. The Church is, by divine appointment, *perpetual by succession* in the highest order of her ministry. "All power is given unto me in heaven and in earth."[10] "As my Father hath sent me, even so send I you."[11] "Lo, I am with you alway, even unto the end of the world."[12]—The Gospel is to be preached *to every creature;* and co-extensive with this trust is the intended influence of the trustee. "Go ye therefore into all the world, and make disciples of all nations, baptizing them." The kingdoms of this world shall all become the kingdoms of our Lord and of His Christ.[13] In other words, the Church of Christ is to become *universal.* And thus, in the capacities and powers essential to the execution of her trust, is God's trustee, the Church, shown to be "perfect and entire, wanting nothing."

Thence of necessity,—in strict agreement with that wise and equitable rule, "unto whomsoever much is given, of him shall be much required,"[14]—flow out *resulting trusts,* immense in value, and of infinite responsibility. She is to be a *Missionary Church*—"to the intent that now," not only to all men, but "unto the principalities and powers in heavenly places might be known by the Church the manifold wisdom of God."[15] Her *Bishops* are *Apostles,* each, in his proper sphere, sent out to "feed the Church of God." Jointly, and in agreement with established principles of order in the Church, they have the power which Christ imparted to the twelve—"as my Father sent me, even so send I you"—to send Apostles in His name. Her *Ministers* are all *Evangelists,* or preachers of glad tidings,—to go wherever God shall call them, through His Church, to bear the blessed tidings of salvation, through the blood of Jesus for a ruined world. Her *members,* baptized into the death of Jesus, and so purchased by His blood, are

---

[8]St. Matthew xxviii. 19.
[9]St. Mark xvi. 16.
[10]St. Matthew xxviii. 18.
[11]St. John xx. 21.
[12]St. Matthew xxviii. 20.
[13]Revelation xi. 15.
[14]St. Luke xii. 48.
[15]Ephesians iii. 10.

Missionaries all, in spirit and intent; to go, or—if themselves go not—to see that others go; and to contribute faithfully and freely of the ability which God shall give them, to sustain them while they go, and "preach the Gospel unto every creature."

Such, beloved brethren, as the Scripture teaches, and as reason,—justified in all the works of God, and not least clearly in His Church,—most fully and abundantly confirms, is the original, the permanent, the immutable constitution of the Christian Church. Such, by the solemn act of this highest legislative council, is declared to be the Constitution of this Church. Baptized into her, in the name of the eternal Three in One, you become *a party to the trust* with which she is honored by her heavenly Head, to preach the everlasting Gospel. It is a trust which *no man is free to decline*—for, "unless a man be born of water and of the Spirit, he cannot enter into the kingdom of God."[16] It is a trust which *no man who has once assumed it can put off*—for his baptismal vow is registered in heaven, and will go with him, in its consequences of unmingled bliss or woe, throughout all eternity. It is a trust which *no man who is permitted to assume it, can, without eternal ruin to his soul, neglect*—for if "any man love not his brother,"—and surely he can never claim to love him, who takes no care for his immortal soul,—"if any man love not his brother whom he hath seen, how can he love God, whom he hath not seen."[17] "Verily I say unto you, inasmuch as ye did it not unto one of the least of these ye did it not unto me. And these shall go away into everlasting punishment, but the righteous into life eternal."[18]

Brethren beloved, think upon these things. It has pleased the Lord to make you partakers of salvation, through the Gospel of His Son. Its law of universal love should be engraven on your hearts. "Whatsoever ye would that men should do to you, do ye even so to them."[19] "Look not every man on his own things, but every man also upon the things of others."[20] "Bear ye one another's burdens, and so fulfil the law of Christ."[21] "Love," my brethren, "is the fulfilling of the law."[22] The mark and measure of the love of Jesus Christ for us was shown upon the Cross, in the outpouring of His precious blood. How shall we bear to stand before that bleeding Saviour, when He cometh in the glory of His Father, with the holy angels, if, from our neglect to go, if we are ministers,—if, from our

---

[16]St. John iii. 5.
[17]St. John iv. 20.
[18]St. Matthew xxv. 45, 46.
[19]St. Matthew vii. 12.
[20]Philippians ii. 4.
[21]Galatians. vi. 2.
[22]Romans xiii. 10.

neglect to give, and strive, and pray, if we are members of His Church,—there be one to say, in that dread hour, whom our ministry, our bounty, or our prayers, might have redeemed, through Christ, from death, "No man cared for my soul."[23]

Beloved brethren, it is recorded of the holy Saviour, as He went about among the cities and villages of Judea, preaching the Gospel of the kingdom, that when He saw the multitudes, He was moved with compassion on them, "because they fainted and were scattered abroad, as sheep having no shepherd. Then saith He unto His disciples, the harvest truly is plenteous, but the laborers are few; pray ye therefore the Lord of the harvest, that He will send forth laborers into his harvest."[24] "And when He had called unto Him His twelve disciples," he sent them "to the lost sheep of the house of Israel," to go and preach, saying, "the kingdom of heaven is at hand."[25] Behold, dear brethren, in the service which assembles us this day, the result of God's especial blessing on the Church's holy emulation of her Saviour's love. Like Him, and in the pathway which His blessed footsteps traced with tears and blood, the Church has gone about among the villages and cities of this broad and sinful land. Everywhere she has found ignorant to instruct, mourners to comfort, rebels to reclaim, sinners to save. Everywhere she has had need for all the means with which her Saviour has entrusted her, to spread abroad His everlasting Gospel. But the West, the vast and distant and unsettled West, has fixed her eye, and agonized her heart. There indeed has she beheld great multitudes that fainted with the burden of the weary way, and wandered, cheerless and uncared for, as "sheep that have no shepherd." There indeed has she beheld the wily serpent and the prowling wolf, and wept with bitter tears that she could do no more to guard her Saviour's lambs. Moved with compassion, she bethought her of her Saviour's precept. "The harvest truly is plenteous but the laborers are few: pray ye therefore the Lord of the harvest, that He will send forth laborers into His harvest."

Encouraged thus by the divine assurance, she betook herself to prayer. She besought the Lord to have compassion, as He once had in the days of His suffering flesh, upon His erring sheep. She besought Him by His "agony and bloody sweat," His "cross and passion," His "precious death and burial," not to give up His heritage to the heathen, nor His people to reproach. With strong crying and tears, she supplicated the gracious Lord of that abundant harvest, white and bending to the sickle, that He would "send forth laborers into His harvest." He

---

[23]Psalm cxlii. 4.
[24]St. Matthew ix. 36-38.
[25]St. Matthew x. 1, 6, 7.

graciously inclined His ear and heard her prayer. He poured upon her members the abundance of His grace, and shed His love abroad in the hearts of His believing people. He was present by His divine and Holy Spirit, in the council of His Church, as He had been in the councils of the Apostles. He harmonized all hearts. He opened and illuminated, with the light from heaven, the eyes of all their minds. He lifted up the hands that hung down, and gave energy and vigour to the feeble knees. He suggested wisdom, He imparted courage, He communicated strength. Above all, He sent His Holy Ghost, and poured into their hearts "that most excellent gift of charity, the very bond of peace and of all virtues"; and so enabled them, *as but one man,* to contrive, digest, mature, propose, accomplish, and carry into practice the great Missionary work, that here, this day, with the whole Church to applaud, and God from heaven, by the clear shining of that glorious sun, smiling consent, we have come up before His altar, to present the first fruit of the Saviour's answer to His Church's agonizing prayer for her lost sheep in the vast West,—her first—God grant that it need not long be said!—her only, Missionary Bishop.

Brethren, it is the pledge of God that He will hear, that He will bless, that He will save His Church, placed thus upon the vantage ground of Christendom, and made—I speak it without the fear of contradiction—the Missionary Church of the whole world. It is, your pledge, my brethren, that you will go on, as you have now begun, in the benign and blessed impulse of that Missionary spirit which God has poured upon His Church. Brethren in the Episcopate, it is our pledge, laid up in heaven, that we will go, as Jesus went, to seek and save the lost and dying sheep. Brethren of the parochial Clergy, it is your pledge, that you will do your utmost, "praying with all supplication of the Spirit," to bring your people, one and all, to sustain us in the work which God has given us to do. Brethren of the Laity, shall it not be your pledge, that from this time forward, true as the day returns, to bring you rest from all your toil, and spiritual comfort in God's holy house, you will "lay by in store" such portion of His blessing as you shall justly think you owe to Him who saved your souls, and consecrate it, as a *Missionary offering*, to save, through Christ, the souls of other men? God of our salvation, be Thou witness, on Thy throne in heaven, to the sincerity of our united pledge! Write it in Thy book! Write it in our hearts! And send Thy Holy Ghost, to make us perfect in every good word and work, to do in all things Thy most blessed will!

Beloved brother, from the work to which the Lord, we trust, has called you, I may keep you back no longer. You are to go out, in the Saviour's name, *the first Missionary Bishop* of this Church. Going with the office, go in the spirit, of an Apostle! You are to preach the gospel of salvation to a ruined world. You are to bear "the ministry of reconciliation" to sinful men, the enemies of God, and of

119

their own souls, by wicked works. Like the Apostle Paul, preach to them "Christ crucified." Like the Apostle Paul, beseech them in Christ's stead, "be ye reconciled to God." Like the Apostle Paul, remind them that without holiness, no man shall see the Lord; and implore them, "by the mercies of God," that they present their bodies, "a living sacrifice, holy, acceptable to Him, which is their reasonable service."—Fear not, dear brother, though the load be heavy, and the way be long. He who hath called you, will give you strength to run the noble race which He has set before you; and, if you are but faithful unto death, will crown you with eternal life.—Fear not, dear brother, though there be many that oppose themselves, and set their battle in array to turn you back from the thrice glorious onset. They that are with you are more than they that are with them; and he who fighteth upon God's side bears victory and triumph on his banner.—Fear not, dear brother, though the fainting flesh and sinking spirit admonish you how frail the earthen vessel is in which you bear this precious burthen. The God you serve is greater than your heart; and, like the Apostle Paul, with Christ to strengthen you, you can do all things.—Fear not, dear brother, though fatigue and care and sickness may molest, and death, too early for the Church, cut off your work of love. It was through suffering and toil and shame that Jesus went to purchase for us pardon and eternal peace, and on the Cross He poured His soul out for us, with His blood. Remember, "it is a faithful saying," if we suffer, we shall also reign, and if we die, we shall forever live with Him. Blessed, glorious assurance! Welcome, in Jesus' name, the tears, the toil, the blood! Welcome, for Jesus' sake, the shame, the agony, the death! If we suffer, we shall also reign—if we die, it is to live with Him!—Beloved brother, go!

Go, bear, before a ruined world, the Saviour's bleeding Cross.

Go, feed, with bread from heaven, the Saviour's hungering Church.

Go, thrice beloved, go, and God the Lord go with you!

Historical Magazine of the Protestant Episcopal Church 4 (September 1935): 180-194.

25.

Jackson Kemper, The Duty of the Church With Respect to Missions, 1841

Jackson Kemper served as a Missionary Bishop for twenty-four years. In 1859 he resigned his missionary jurisdiction and accepted election as the first Bishop of Wisconsin. He was the greatest missionary bishop of the Episcopal Church and was largely responsible for the evangelization of the west. His life and work are commemorated in the Episcopal Calendar of the Church Year on May 24. Bishop Kemper preached this triennial sermon before the Board of Missions of the Protestant Episcopal Church gathered in St. Paul's Chapel, New York, on October 7, 1841.

ROMANS, X. 13, 14 and part of 15.

WHOSOEVER SHALL CALL UPON THE NAME OF THE LORD SHALL BE SAVED, HOW THEN SHALL THEY CALL ON HIM IN WHOM THEY HAVE NOT BELIEVED? AND HOW SHALL THEY BELIEVE IN HIM OF WHOM THEY HAVE NOT HEARD? AND HOW SHALL THEY HEAR WITHOUT A PREACHER? AND HOW SHALL THEY PREACH, EXCEPT THEY BE SENT?

There are many yet living who have witnessed the rise and growth of the sacred cause of missions within the boundaries of the American Church. It was very feeble at its commencement, and had but few friends to sustain it. They watched its progress with deep and anxious solicitude. Sometimes it was deemed inexpedient, if not wrong—sometimes it was contemned or treated with cold indifference—again every measure was thoroughly canvassed—and every false or unsuccessful effort was ridiculed. The ordeal was severe, but highly salutary; for, in the process of time, the doubting were satisfied, and objections, once formidable, were removed. At last, we acknowledged it to be the work of the Lord—we ranked ourselves as a Missionary Church—we openly confessed that the Field was the World.

Have we entered upon the work in a proper spirit? Do we realize the extent of our privileges, our responsibilities and our duties? If enabled at the present moment to remove one obstacle, to encourage one friend, or to interest one more heart in the cause, I shall not have preached in vain.

May the spirit of the living God grant us a right judgment in all things; and enable us to the extent of our abilities, to do our duty in the vineyard of the Lord!

The text, like many of the other declarations of the scriptures, presents us with an epitome of the gospel, and develops the unutterable importance of the subject. God, says our adorable Master, so loved the world, that he gave his only begotten Son, that whosoever believeth in him should not perish, but have everlasting life. For God sent not his Son into the world, to condemn the world, but that the world through him might be saved. And in the passage now before us, we learn from the apostle who was so wonderfully commissioned to preach the gospel, and who through toils and sufferings, often cast down but never despairing, carried the cross and its rich consolations to the remotest regions—we learn from him that salvation is pledged to those who call upon, invoke, or worship the Lord Jesus; and that to obtain this most precious of gifts, this gift that is

121

really everlasting,—to be partakers of eternal life,—they must believe through the preaching of those who are sent forth for that purpose. To whom then is the conversion of the world committed? As my Father hath sent me, even so send I you, said the Saviour to his apostles. To that spiritual society or fellowship, The Church, whose officers they were and for whom its great Head uttered the solemn prayer, "As thou, Father, art in me, and I in thee, that they also may be one in us: that the world may know that thou hast sent me,"—to the Church then, the spiritual spouse of the Redeemer, with her authorized ministers, and all her children—to her is committed the sacred trust of bringing Jew and Gentile into the fold—of making known the glad tidings to all who are living without God and without hope. Has the command been fulfilled—the command given to the apostles and their successors, "Go ye into the world, and preach the gospel to every creature?" And are we all—all the baptized members of the flock of Christ, striving mightily to obey the sacred injunction, "Do good unto all men, especially unto them who are of the household of faith?"

I submit the following propositions to your consideration:

I. The duty enjoined upon the Church is exceedingly arduous, and demands the utmost exertions and every sacrifice.

II. The Almighty has so far blest our efforts, that we have abundant reason to be thankful, and take courage.

Having illustrated these propositions in as brief a manner as possible, I will close with the inquiry, What is incumbent upon us at the present time, judging from our ability and the demands and opportunities pressing upon us and opening to our view?

I. The first proposition is this: That the duty enjoined upon the Church by her great and glorious Head is exceedingly arduous, and can only be accomplished by untiring efforts and a cheerful readiness to make every sacrifice that the cause demands. And what is this sacred and most imperative duty? It is to proclaim glad tidings—the glad tidings of mercy, pardon and eternal life to the guilty, the ruined and the lost. And as all have sinned—as there is none that doeth good, no, not one,—the Gospel is to be preached to Every Creature. This is the clear, the express requirement,—an injunction given under the most impressive circumstances, and given to those who were the representatives of the whole Church upon earth, if not the Church itself; and who, in the language of Scripture, went "every where" for its accomplishment.

Constrained by the love of Christ, that love which induced him to humble himself even to the agonies and the death of the cross to rescue us from unutterable wo[e], we are to prove our faithfulness by a deep and abiding interest for the spiritual welfare of our fellow beings. God has commanded—and he who has tasted and knows that the Lord is gracious, will delight to fulfil his will.

Actuated by the high and lofty views, and the sacred and endearing motives which the scriptures continually inculcuate, we cannot but feel, intensely feel for the degraded state of all who are aliens from the hopes and the consolations of the gospel. Sympathy must sway our bosoms when we behold those who were destined to immortality, selfish, wicked and hardened. Daily do we pray thy kingdom come—to come with power and peace to every heart, as well as to our own. And who is not anxiously solicitous for the honor of his Lord,—who does not cherish an intense desire to enlarge his Master's kingdom—who is not ready to make some sacrifices for Him who died that we might live?

This high commission—this magnificent effort the Church HAS assumed. Christ loved the Church, and gave himself for it. By gratitude and love then, and every motive that can sway the human breast, is every member thereof bound to seek for the mind that was in Christ Jesus; and, as he imbibes that spirit, to watch and pray, and strive with increasing earnestness, that there may be one fold and one shepherd. Our daily public worship opens with the sublime declaration: "From the rising of the sun, even unto the going down of the same, my name shall be great among the Gentiles; and in every place incense shall be offered unto my name, and a pure offering; for my name shall be great among the heathen, saith the Lord of hosts." In that inspired prayer which is used in every service, we beseech our heavenly Father not only to hasten the growth of his Church, but that his will may be done on earth,—with the same delight, the same universality,—as it is done in heaven. When humbly beseeching him for all sorts and conditions of men, we pray that he will be pleased to make his ways known unto them, his saving health unto all nations. And where could we find a more beautiful and appropriate missionary hymn than one of the daily chants in the Evening Prayer, when, after imploring God to be merciful unto us and bless us, we are taught to say: "That thy way may be known upon earth, thy saving health among all nations." And then we burst out in the glowing strains: "Let the people praise thee, O God; yea, let all the nations praise thee." In the Litany we supplicate for mercy upon all men; and on Good Friday, for mercy upon all Jews, Turks, infidels and heretics—that all ignorance, hardness of heart, and contempt of God's word may be taken from them, and that they may be brought home to the flock of our blessed Lord. In the ordinal the ministry is alluded to as appointed for the salvation of mankind; and in reference to a newly consecrated Bishop, we pray for such grace, that he may ever more be ready to spread abroad the Gospel, the glad tidings of reconciliation. The highest council of our Church, erred not then when she openly declared that the field before her is the world; and that every baptized person is pledged to support the sacred cause of missions. . . .

III. And *are we* blest? And is this work really of God? And is the vine, once so tender, spreading her brances to the north, the south, and the farthest west? Let us up then and be doing—let us tarry no longer in our indolence—let us ascertain, before the great Searcher of hearts—let us ascertain our actual position. I inquire not whether this is the destined period in the councils of the Most High for the conversion of the world—the path of duty should be found out—found out in all sincerity—and anxiously and earnestly pursued. How remarkably peculiar, how vastly important is the position of our Church! Possessing as we fully believe all those characteristics which distinguished the primitive folds:—A scriptural Liturgy—evangelical doctrines—and the apostolic successions—having the form of godliness *and* the power thereof—free from the false and worldly scruples and the time-serving policy of civil governments—independent—respected, and influential—in the midst of an intelligent, enterprising and commercial people—Brethren! may it not be *our* duty to convert the world—may not this high, this inestimable privilege be offered to *us!* And are we prepared—are we doing at the present moment *even one tenth* part of what we are capable? Our means and our power are extensive—and under the blessing of Him, without whom nothing is strong, nothing is holy, our aim—our constant undeviating, untiring aim should be great and lofty. "Glorious things are spoken of thee, O city of God."

With the talents we possess, (and for which, as good stewards, we must finally account, at that hour when no secrets can be hid,) with the talents committed to our trust and the privileges we enjoy, cannot our faith, our liberality and our self denial, *greatly* increase? Cannot our supplications be more fervent, our economy more strict, our love of souls more ardent? Have we, as individuals, or a Church, a deep and abiding interest in the success of missions?

Not a brother would I accuse of indifference or cowardice. But I would stir up, with God's permission, the pure mind of each one, by way of remembrance. It is the spirit of missions I earnestly and most affectionately advocate—the improvement of those opportunities of which the apostle speaks when he exhorts us to do good unto all men, and especially unto them who are of the household of faith. In well-doing we are never to be weary; for in due season we shall reap if we faint not. I say not that we are all required to contribute to the Foreign or even the Domestic Department—it is the improvement of opportunities I advocate—being steadfast and unmoveable in the work of the Lord. Thus the mother limiting all her efforts to her little ones, may exercise *her* commission to the full, while she really brings them up, with an ever-watchful spirit, in the true nurture and admonition, and leads them on in the footsteps of our adorable Saviour.

The division into Foreign and Domestic is often arbitrary, and might, without detriment, be abolished; for no one, I presume, would wish to withdraw our heralds of the cross from Africa, suspend our incipient efforts for Texas, or abandon the much injured aborigines to all the degrading vices they have learnt from unprincipled men who pretend to be civilized. Let us go where duty calls—where Providence points the way—and let us rejoice in the privilege, for we assuredly ought—O, let us rejoice in the privilege of sending forth in the name of the Lord and under the guidance of *his* Spirit *all* those, who, thoroughly instructed in sacred truths, hear the cry, Come over and help us—and *cannot* resist the deep, the abiding conviction concerning their sphere of duty—whose hearts burn within them when they hear of people or nations wholly given to idolatry, or licentiousness, or worldly-mindedness. Cultivate, dear brethren of the clergy, cultivate with the utmost assiduity your own vineyard—love with the strongest affection your own spiritual children,—but close not your hearts to the sufferings and the wants of your neighbors, those whom the events of life and the inquiries and efforts of our beloved Zion have made such—and wish, in the true spirit of the Gospel, wish God speed to those who are thrust out by their own absorbing and irrepressible convictions into new and hazardous fields. Many who now surround me, and whose difficulties and labors have far exceeded my own, can tell, how innumerable are the calls—how fervent, how heart-rending the appeals of those, our fellow citizens and fellow Churchmen, who once worshipped with us in the same sanctuary and participated of the same holy ordinances, but are now debarred from spiritual consolations, the church-going bell, the assembly of the saints,—and are exposed, perhaps fatally exposed, to the delusions of error, and the degradations of infidelity.

To theological students, in whose welfare I am most truly interested, I can speak with plainess; for at the present day if amid the prodigious efforts of Popery—the beautiful example set us by various denominations in this country—and the delightful, the noble stand which our highly honored mother, the Church of England, has at last taken in reference to missions, there is even one, looking to the ministry, who has not in all sincerity and from his heart said to his Saviour, Speak Lord, for thy servant heareth—and is not ready to say to the Church, Here am I, send me—he has mistaken his calling. The spirit to be cultivated at the schools of the prophets, is the spirit of unreserved and entire devotion to the cause of Christ Jesus and Him crucified. The heart, the whole heart is required. Self control should be rigorously exercised from the first day we look to the plough—mortification and fasting should often be practiced as beneficial, if not necessary duties—and martyrdom, the honor of losing our lives for the Saviour's sake,—should it not be considered the highest object of our attainment? For it, should we not daily prepare—daily be ready? Amid the convulsions of the world, and the interesting events which are constantly developing, we may be called to the hardest duties and the severest trials. But we see and know enough at the present hour to convince us, that a self-sacrificing spirit is necessary if we would win Christ, and be acknowledged by Him at the day of retribution. I advocate not austerities, or fanatical reveries, or solitary retirement—all I would ask is a diligent study of the Scriptures, and a readiness to receive, without gainsaying, their calm and holy influences, with a childlike disposition.

Brethren of the Society on whose concerns we are now assembled! Sustain, I beseech you, our missions, and increase the laborers. Put forth every effort, so that at least the Valley of the Mississippi, the country on our south-western Atlantic coast, and likewise that on the borders of the Upper Lakes, may blossom as the rose. A trust, a sacred trust is committed to us—let us not be *unfaithful*. There is that scattereth and yet increaseth. You are aware of the promises of God. Your hearts have often glowed when meditating upon the declarations of prophecy. Can we not hasten the time when the Saviour's kingdom shall come— when peace and good will shall reign triumphant? Remember the early labors of the primitive Church, and her wonderful success. We are now co-workers with the Most High—co-workers in his great and glorious designs. If much good can be accomplished—if a strict economy in all things, and an increased interest in the work will enable us to command more time and more money—withhold not your exertions, lest haply ye be found fighting against God. Be entreated by the love of Christ—more sacrifices can yet be made—more, more, many more fields can yet be possessed in our day. Let us up and be doing, for the Lord is with us. Send forth missionary bishops to Africa and Texas. Let the leaven spread—the grain of mustard grow—the net be cast into the deepest waters. *God will give the increase*. It is for us to plant and water.

Constrained by the undying love of Christ to love the immortal souls of our fellow beings—let us be ready for the privilege, if it is ever conferred, to scatter the precious seed on every field—to erect the banner of the cross on every mountain. Let us at least hasten the time—by our prayers, our exertions, and our sacrifices—when the joyous sound shall burst from every heart, "How beautiful are the feet of them that preach the Gospel of peace, and bring glad tidings of good things."

The Spirit of Missions 6 (December 1841): 353-356, 359-361. (Excerpts)

26.

James Lloyd Breck,
Indian Mission—Minnesota, 1854

James Lloyd Breck (June 27, 1818–March 30, 1876) was one of the founders of Nashotah House. He worked for the revival of a disciplined religious commu-

nity life and was a great western missionary. The "apostle of the wilderness" worked among the Oneida, Chippewa and Ojibwa Indians. One of his converts, Enmegahbowh, was the first Ojibwa Indian ordained to the diaconate. Breck's life and ministry are commemorated in the Episcopal Calendar of the Church Year on April 2. He describes life in an Indian mission.

What little, as a church, we have at any time done for the regeneration of the red man, has been abundantly blessed to encourage us to do more. The father of the young Ottawa Indian who is with us, preparing for the ministry, sent his son thither from the heart of Michigan, where he is the principal chief of the tribe, to procure for him an education in the Christian religion, so as to enable him to teach his own people or the Chippeways the better way of life. Whence this desire and this sacrifice of an old Indian for a son of the sweetest disposition? Once he had learned the white man's vice and was an habitual drunkard. He has now been a sober man for fifteen years, and for a long time a devoted Christian, whilst the *Grand Medicine* has been abandoned altogether, and the religion of the Cross adopted by his people. Whence this? The quiet and faithful labors of Selkrig, now an old man, tottering into the grave, will tell. And as a last bequest, which the faithful servant of the Cross would make to the cause of the Indian, he sends his youngest son to us, and asks us to take him and train him for the ministry of the Word amongst the Pagan of this land. From what I have now written you, you will learn, Christian brethren, that plants are ripening here for the harvest that comes on apace, before the reapers can be prepared to enter in. But you will like to know something further, viz., in what have the two years promised fruit, where we have been laboring? Seeds of glorious light have been sown, and they are even now shooting forth branches which promise, in due time, an abundant harvest.

Enter with me now, please, the neat squared-log church. It is the very picture of simplicity and solemnity. Ever kept sacred to the *Divine homage*, it is always in that perfect order which becometh his sanctuaries. These Indians call Christians the "praying people," and the church building the "Wigwam of Prayer." About eighteen months since we began connecting a simple form of religious worship, with the daily instruction of an advanced class of native youth. This attracted a few adults into the Mission House, which continuing through the winter, grew into a habit, and when the church was ready for consecration, we transferred the prayers to it and built a distinct house for the school; so that now every day, at half past 4 P.M., the bell rings and tolls for an Ojibwa service, whereupon the laboring Indians and others come up in their native dress (where they have not adopted our own habit,) and here they conduct themselves with the utmost propriety, for the most part observing all the usages of the

127

Liturgical worship. I have before informed you that the English Prayer-Book has been translated and published in Ojibwa by an English Society. This book is to us of the greatest possible assistance in conveying a knowledge of Christianity.

I have asked you, Christian friends, to enter the church. It is a week-day; fifty-six natives are present. The average number of daily attendants is over forty—quite frequently there are fifty; as large a number as you would see at their *medicine dance*, which occurs but twice in the year! Pagan is well translated into Ojibwa by one word, which signifies *the people who do not pray!* The small handful of whites you observe in the church, are my fellow missionaries in the Lord, who have, male and female, come thither to instruct the heathen in the better way of things, both temporal and spiritual. There are none other whites living hereabouts. The Indian that you hear interpreting is the same concerning whom I wrote you at the beginning, and who came to this place with us in the spring of 1852. He was once of the *Grand Medicine*, but born amongst the Canada Chippeways, he has had superior advantages to those living in the United States, and has received a fair English education, and is well versed in the English and Ojibwa New Testament. I am thankful to say I am able to read the liturgy in their own tongue, and thus appear before them in the true light of a clergyman. The interpreter gives the sermon and other instructions by word of mouth to the people, and also leads in the Ojibwa responses, which the people commit to memory and say orally, as our black congregations do in the South. Two Sundays since I baptized him, he is now ready, with our approbation, to prepare for the diaconate, according to the new canon. That young man of sixteen years of age, whom you observed entering the church late, and kneeling down for silent prayer, although the congregation was standing at the time, was also baptized a fortnight since. That mild and self-possessed countenance has ever distinguished him, although his great change in personal habits and attire could scarcely identify him with the same youth that had, two years before, stepped forward from amongst his Pagan comrades, the first of these people to help us to plant our frail tent of canvass cloth upon the ground were the mission houses are now standing. This willing conduct of a youth dressed in *blanket, leggings and braided hair,* falling down upon the back of each shoulder, according to the male costume of these people, was in truth his first *abrenunciation* of Paganism, for he was shortly after received into the mission family—and we now regard him as one that will soon be prepared to become a catechist to the younger children and eventually, we hope, a native clergyman. Amongst the children who occupy the chancel steps, please observe the largest of those boys. He was also baptized at the same time, and has been a member of the mission house for upwards of a year. These, my friends, do not stand alone as "people of prayer" with the Chippeway mission; *eighteen* others have been enrolled within the fold of the *redeemed*, so that our faith has not been tested to the degree that our brethren's to the north was, for they waited till the *third* year before they witnessed the first native baptism! How exceedingly thankful then, should we be, in this remote corner of the wilderness, to see not only a Christian temple built, but a body of *daily* worshippers in it, to the number that I have stated; nor only so, but amongst them three Indians and one white young man actually going through a course of preparation for the ministry; whilst from the white mission in Minnesota we have already sent three young men to Nashotah to prepare for holy orders! How thankful, I say, should we be for all this evidence of *life* in the use of all those divers helps which the Lord hath appointed in his church on earth.

The Southern Episcopalian 1 (November 1854): 351-353.

27.

Address to Their Brethren of the Laity of the Protestant Episcopal Church, By the Committee Appointed by the Session of the General Convention, 1859

At the twenty-sixth General Convention, October 5-22, 1859, Richmond, Virginia, a committee of twenty-eight laymen was appointed to write an address to the laity about their missionary responsibilities. The address makes clear that the extension of Christ's Church upon earth is the paramount duty of all its members.

As heads of households, and baptized members of Christ, we have no ordinary measure of responsibility in so leading the lambs of his fold committed to our trust, that none of them be lost through our neglect or carelessness. It is in the sacred precincts of home that the parent, having brought his children to Christian baptism, should labor most assiduously to instil into their young minds those holy desires and good counsels which will, in due time, qualify them, with the aid of the Holy Spirit, and in accordance with the requirements of the Church, to take upon themselves those sacred vows which will make them fellow-workers with us in Christ's visible kingdom. Careful Christian nurture, the inculcation of their responsibilities as baptized members of the Church, teaching, by precept and example, the duty and privilege of free offerings to God, are duties eminently incumbent upon the Christian layman; and he may justly hope that his children, accustomed to family-worship at home, taught to be regular and devout attendants in the house of prayer, and rightly instructed in their religious duties, will steadily continue in the christian course so faithfully commenced. The home is God's own institution for the nurture of the young. Through every change of earth, the Christian household will remain the work of heaven and the bulwark of the Church.

Again: The Christian layman has other duties and responsibilities, as a member of a parish. As part of an organized body, he owes it special and constant allegiance.

As the clergy alone are not the Church, so the rector alone is not the parish. The vital idea of a "parish" is presented in its etymology, denoting a "dwelling together," a working together, a brotherhood.

The layman does not discharge his duty, merely by attending the public ministrations of the Church, nor yet by money contributions, however liberal. He owes his parish as he owes the universal Church, something higher, something better. He owes it his time, his thought, his constant and cordial affection. Nor will he as an honest "co-worker," ever shrink from his fair and proper portion of the labor, or seek to impose it upon his spiritual pastor.

In training the youth of the parish, in giving religious instruction in the Sunday-school and Bible-classes, and in duly fostering and encouraging the parish-school, every layman is bound, to the best of his ability, to aid the rector.

The Bible-class instruction, of a more advanced kind, wherever possible, should follow the Sunday-school. There often may be laymen of our Church, perhaps one or more in the most secluded parishes, fitted for this work, which cannot all be done by the clergyman of the parish. Where the necessity exists, and under the proper diocesan sanction, the devout and worthy layman may, in the lay ministration of the sanctuary, do a good work, and keep up the services of the church, when the house of God would otherwise be closed, and the flock scattered; or he may collect the nucleus of a parish, in advance of regular ministrations.

In going among the poor and needy, in gathering the outcasts, and in bringing into the Church the indifferent, the uncared-for, and the degraded, the layman may ever be most properly and beneficially employed. This active charity, blessing alike him who gives and him who receives, is a duty no Christian has a right to neglect; and in this sense every Christian layman may become a missionary.

In the temporal matters of the parish, providing a proper support for the rector, and its prompt payment,—in the building and care of the church-edifice, the parsonage and the school-house,—the laity should assume the whole burden, and should each, individually, feel it his duty to see that none of these important matters are neglected. The pastor should never, as is too often the case, be required, by the neglect of his laity, to suffer from the want of an adequate support, or be expected exclusively or actively to assume in any parish the care and management of its temporal interest. How often have we seen the prosperity of a parish promoted and the heart of its rector cheered, by the prompt and efficient aid even of a single layman ready and willing to work for his Church! And, on the other hand, in how many parishes have neglect and indifference disheartened or driven away good and faithful ministers, unequal to the burden thoughtlessly imposed upon them! We assert, emphatically, that in all such secular and pecuniary affairs, the rector should not be required to assume any burden whatever, which may avert his thoughts from the higher duties of his sacred office; and that the laity, by promptly attending to all these matters, should relieve him from any necessity of doing so.

It is surely no unkindness or disrespect to our clergy, to affirm that neither by education nor habit are they specially qualified, as a class, to deal with pecuniary affairs. Their heads and their hearts are devoted, under God's blessing, to higher and nobler objects; and yet their best and holiest efforts may often be greatly aided by the kind and cordial co-operation of the laity within their proper sphere, and pre-eminently if the laity shall themselves exhibit in the "daily beauty" of their Christian lives, the true value of their Christian teaching.

But, further, the laymen of the Church are members of a much larger organization.

They are required to look beyond the local limits and narrow sphere of their parish boundaries, and recognize their responsibilities as connected with the diocese within which they are placed. The diocese, as such, besides its parishes as component parts, has many objects connected with its general well-being, in which all its laity are directly interested.

The bishop of the diocese, its chief pastor, requires a due support; and this very frequently depends on assessments upon the parishes, the faithful collection of which devolves upon the laity.

There are few of the dioceses where the support of their bishop is secured by the certain avails of an endowment or fund; but, in some cases, it is even left to the annual contribution of the members of the Church, paid by each in small sums. In many dioceses, these contributions are sadly deficient; and numerous parishes are yearly reported to the various diocesan Conventions as largely in arrear.

Brethren, we are pained to state this discreditable fact; and in all brotherly-kindness we appeal to you to exert yourselves at once to correct the evil, and to lend all your efforts to provide these, our honored diocesans, with the funds necessary for their proper support, and their travelling-expenses in visiting their various churches.

Annual assessments, either on parishes or individuals, are, evidently, objectionable in many respects, and always difficult of collection; and we firmly believe that it would greatly conduce not only to the general prosperity of the Church, but to the true dignity of the laity themselves, if, in every diocese, provision could be made by a permanent fund for the support of its bishop.

The earnest efforts of a few laymen in any diocese could readily lay at least the foundation of such an endowment, which would rapidly ripen to maturity.

The diocesan missionary operations, the building of churches in new and feeble parishes, aiding in the erection of parsonages, founding of training-schools and theological seminaries, with a view to the increase of the clergy and Church institutions of learning, all devolve upon the laity, and call upon them, individually, for assistance in their management and vigorous support. Where this support is cheerfully and generally given, the diocese prospers; otherwise, it languishes or remains stationary.

Again: We should never forget that the laity of the Protestant Episcopal Church in the United States are united, by their general Constitution, in one unbroken body; that every individual layman from the Atlantic to the Pacific forms an integral part of one vast, but harmonious, living organism; that, as such, he has a direct relation to the Church at large, and a sympathetic interest not only in her general welfare, but in prosperity of all her portions, however humble or remote. In view of her Book of *Common* Prayer, our American Republic, in all its wide extent, both present and prospective, is a religious unit.

The occupation of so vast a field requires our attention to be especially directed to the supply of laborers adequate to its rapidly increasing demands; and no subject should press upon our minds and hearts with greater force, than the means by which that supply shall be obtained. We earnestly maintain, that the laity should never rest content until every village or considerable settlement in our whole country shall possess, if not a regularly settled clergyman, at least the nucleus of an Episcopal Church, with missionary services whenever possible. . . .

The Church in this country is peculiarly a missionary body. Planted over an immense field, it occupies nowhere a tithe of the ground, but is ever increasing, ever building, ever planting anew, ever aiming, more and more widely, to preach the gospel to those who lie in darkness.

Our part in this vast work is threefold, as considered in reference to our immediate vicinity; to our country at large; and to the far-off regions covered with superstition and heathenism.

We have all a work to do near home. We have all a circle of influence around us in which, as laymen, we should actively employ both our time and means, to reach those who are living in neglect, indifference, or gross sin and shame. To go personally and kindly and frequently among them, to visit the abodes of wretchedness and sorrow, to carry them the Holy Scriptures, to procure their attendance at the services of the Church, to provide places of worship free to them all, this is the work which the layman is called upon to do among the heathen at his very door, and which, in the rural parish or city mission, he should zealously and untiringly labor to carry out.

But the Church also asks the co-operation of her laity, in diffusing her blessed influences among the distant and destitute masses of our ever-expanding population. The gospel must go forward, and the Cross be planted, by the free gifts of the laity; and we must fully recognize the claims of all our brethren, in the day of their weakness, to receive cheerful and constant aid. So far from being discouraged or annoyed, we should be positively encouraged and gratified, to find these appeals for aid daily becoming more numerous and urgent, so distinctly showing us, how widely the desire for the services of the Church is planted in the hearts of our countrymen, needing only our timely aid to carry it forward. From our rich abundance, and unexampled increase in material wealth, we are amply able to afford this aid; and we are surely called on, by every consideration of gratitude, to wake to our responsibility, in fostering and aiding the work of extending the Church, throughout the length and breadth of our favored land. We would not depreciate her high religious office, by unduly adverting to the increased security, moral and political, of person and property, to be afforded by the greater prevalence of her example and authority; but we will and do affirm, that the temporal happiness of ourselves and our descendants in this American Republic, necessarily embracing so many jarring elements, very materially depends on the wide diffusion of her tolerant and truly Christian doctrines.

The preaching of the gospel in the dark abodes of heathenism in other lands, is also a part of the blessed work committed by Christ to his Church, and upon which we have entered with strong faith and an assured hope, that God's blessing will always attend our efforts to christianize those who are now, as our ancestors once were, Gentiles and strangers to Israel's God. To the performance of this most interesting portion of our duty, and the support and maintenance of those faithful bishops and brethren who have been sent by the Church to remote and heathen lands, we urge you most affectionately.

We desire, brethren, most earnestly to appeal to you to bear in mind the missionary character of our Church, and to urge you, in the name and spirit of Him who commanded his apostles to go and preach the gospel to all creatures, to make the cause of missions one of constant prayer, and, above all, to sustain it periodically by systematic and regular contributions, however small your ability may be. Greater efficiency may be given to the work by union of effort and associated action, by regular missionary meetings, by auxiliary associations, and by the voluntary pledge of any sums, however small, to be paid at stated periods. Every member of the Church, as such, is a member of its missionary organizations; and we feel that we cannot too earnestly impress upon you the necessity for increased effort, to sustain and carry forward all the missionary work in which the Church is now engaged.

Journal of General Convention, 1862, 6-10, 12-14 (printed at back of journal).

28.

Henry Champlin Lay, The Missionary in the Field, 1869

Henry Champlin Lay (6 December 1823-17 September 1885) was consecrated Missionary Bishop of Arkansas and the Indian Territory on October 23, 1859. On November 20, 1868, he was elected the first Bishop of Easton. He draws from his experience to make some suggestions about how to conduct a missionary service.

How to Conduct a Missionary Service

Our young Missionary (let it be understood we write to one confessedly inexperienced) should make up his mind to give the people a service distinctively Churchly, and not strive, through the fear of adverse criticism, to tone it down after the fashion of an extempore worship. If you attempt other people's ways and methods, you will make a failure, and your effort will be tame and vapid. Besides, the people have come to hear "an Episcopal Service": anything less will disappoint them. Moreover, it ought to be a comfort to you to consider that thus far, at least, yours is a partial responsibility, you are about to let the dear old Mother speak for herself; your care is to express devoutly the words which she fashions for you. And wonderful is it to see how she can win her way in the face of ignorance and prejudice, if we are content to give her a chance, and to let people see her as she is.

We once knew the Service to be said by a Theological Student, in a loft, to a few sailors and fisherman, the Divinity Professor preaching a sermon. One of the congregation was overheard expressing his judgment thus:—"The old gentleman with the specs," said he, "did very well; but that short sermon the little man began with, was about as good a thing as I ever heard."

So it is; the Liturgy vindicates itself, if only we give it an opportunity.

It is a school-house, perhaps, filled with a buzzing crowd; young men about the door; girls with bare heads as if at a concert; a child or two straying about the floor, and older ones coming up now and then to the table for a drink of water. The time is night, and you have been at pains to ask your acquaintances to bring a candle or a lamp. Shall I wear my surplice? By all means. You can slip it on out of doors, and some friend perchance will relieve you of your bag and hat.

Clad in your surplice, you enter quietly, and, going to your desk, kneel down reverently. As you enter, there is, perhaps, a stir, a sensation, it may be a titter. But, as you bow in private devotion, stillness falls on the people. That official dress, and that silent recognition of the presence of the awful One, are more effectual to teach reverence than any sermon you could preach about it.

Your piles of "Mission Services" are on the table, hard-by that inevitable water-pail. You engage some friends to distribute them, or you distribute them yourself.

And now you make a speech, on this wise or "other like."

"We are about, my Friends, to engage in a religious service somewhat different from that to which you are accustomed, and I would detain you awhile with some words of explanation.

"The Church of which I am a Minister, has a prescribed service. You have often heard that we say prayers out of a book. I know that some excellent people think that this is very strange; they imagine we cannot pray with the heart, and at the same time say the prayer out of a printed book.

"Now there is one thing about which we are all of one mind. We can all *praise* out of a book. When you are singing, "Come Holy Spirit," or, "Come ye that love the Lord," it would not do for any one to say: 'All that is a mere form; you are not praising God from the heart.' Those are old hymns printed in all the books. You know better than that, and when your hearts are warm, you choose the old words and the old tunes by preference. Now if we can praise God acceptably and profitably by a form of words, may it not be that we can worship and pray to Him out of a book?

"Let me remind you, too, that Almighty God Himself is the author of the first Prayer-book. He inspired David and other holy men to write forms of prayer and praise. The Book of Psalms was the Prayer-book of the Jewish Church. They used it in public and in private. Our Lord Himself joined in this service and approved of it.

"I have read somewhere that pious Jews were accustomed to utter aloud the first verse of a psalm, and then say the rest to themselves. Now, our Lord upon the Cross uttered aloud the first verse of the twenty-second psalm—'My God! my God! why hast Thou forsaken me?' Did he not say the rest? If you will read it all, you must see that it was written for this very occasion. It seems as if our Lord Himself in His last hour, prayed to the Father out of the Book of Psalms.

"We are obliged to use forms. It is the only way in which we can teach our children to pray. I suppose not one of you ever came to God, in true penitence, that He did not borrow a form from the Publican and cry: 'God be merciful to me a sinner!'

"The Service we are about to use is mostly taken from the Bible. You will find it solemn and earnest. It strikes no jangling string of controversy, but breathes such accents as all faithful people can utter. There is not a single prayer to which the pious Presbyterian or Methodist cannot say Amen.

"One thing I must admit. Our Service will probably be without meaning or interest to you if you merely look on. Surely it must be irksome to Christian people to see others engaged in a worship wherein they have no share. But if you will follow along with our Service, printed for such occasions as this in the pamphlet which has been distributed among you, if you will join with me and answer back to me, I can promise you that you will find it most edifying and useful. And now the congregation will please rise."

The preamble may be varied according to circumstances; only care should be taken to cast no reflections on other people; to draw no comparisons between our own system and that of others. No offense is likely to be taken if the Missionary confines himself to that which all reasonable persons must deem legitimate—a temperate and uncontroversial explanation of the Church's teaching and worship. And now that you are to lead the congregation through a strange Service, try to be quiet and self-possessed. The great secret of self-possession, we need scarcely say, is to forget ourselves; to lay aside anxiety about results, and to realize that we are, in the exercise of a sacred function, teaching the people that which it is our business to understand and to impart.

You have asked the people to rise. Now, mention that the order for Evening Prayer may be found on the twenty-ninth page of the pamphlet. You proceed reverently with the Sentences and Exhortation; then say distinctly that: "We will all kneel down and say the Confession, Minister and people together." Before you get through the Lord's Prayer, the leaf must be turned and you will be encouraged by the rustle all over the house, showing that the people are following you. Now say: "The congregation will please rise." Sensitive people are much annoyed at being left on their knees, when others have risen around them. You announce the Selection on the same page, and tell the people: "I will read one verse, and you the other." There is apt to be a pause of uncertainty at the end of the first psalm. Say quietly: "Go on with the next verse," and when the Psalter is done, tell them to sit down again. So, after the first Lesson, say: "Page thirty-fifth. Please rise," and again: "Resume your seats." At every change announce the page, and remember that most of the awkwardness of a novel Service will be avoided, if you are careful to mention every change of posture. When they see that you know what you are doing, and can be trusted, they will almost invariably do just what they are told.

If it is a Morning Service, and you use the Litany, it is best, after the Prayer for the President, simply to say: "Page eighteenth," and pause a moment until they turn to it. The Collect for the day is best omitted; its introduction is very confusing at first. After the people have become familiar with the course of the Service, then it is easy to introduce that, and to vary the Psalter by using one of the selections found at page forty-three.

As for the singing, there are several hymns in the Mission Service which every one knows; such as, "When I survey the wondrous Cross," "Come, Holy Spirit, Heavenly Dove, "A charge to keep I have." Let these be preferred. If you have no chorister, and must set your own tunes, Old Hundred, Hebron, Ballerma, Ortonville and Boylston will never fail you. The whole American people sing them, although with slurs and variations not found in the books.

At last we reach the sermon. Preach something different from what they are used to. They are accustomed to a violent, denunciatory style; it is a relief to them when one comes whose harp is strung with gentler chords. They seldom hear a sermon on Christian experience. Speak to them of the inner conflict in the breasts of saintly people, or of the comforts which God ministers to his people in their troubles. You will surely interest them and win their sympathy. Again, they are not much accustomed to expository preaching. Instead of spinning a cob-web-sermon out of your own head, take up an incident, a parable, a miracle, which you have studied thoroughly. Begin with it, come back to it, unfold it; show them dear truths not patent to the casual reader; draw simple conclusions; make brief and pointed applications. Oh, that our Missionaries would not preach essays or orations, but get their sermons out of the Bible! Tell the people something they did not know; give them some noble, loving thought to carry home with them, and you will not preach in vain.

The Spirit of Missions 34 (October, 1869): 583-586.

29.

Samuel Isaac Joseph Schereschewsky, Appeal for Funds to Establish a Missionary College in China, 1877

Samuel Isaac Joseph Schereschewsky (May 6, 1831–October 15, 1906) was consecrated the third Missionary Bishop of Shanghai on October 31, 1877. He translated the Book of Common Prayer *into Mandarin, the vernacular language used by the majority of the Chinese, and after he resigned as bishop on*

September 30, 1883, he translated the Bible into Mandarin and into what is known as "easy Wenli," a form of the Chinese language. Because of paralysis he could only write painfully by pressing the keys of a typewriter with one finger of his hand. Bishop Schereschewsky's life and work are commemorated in the Episcopal Calendar of the Church Year on October 15. The following selection is an appeal for funds to establish a college in China. In 1878 he established what became St. John's University in Shanghai, one of the leading institutions of higher education in China.

From the earliest days of the Church, education has been an important agent in the propagation of Christianity. During the Middle Ages education was one of the chief instrumentalities by which Christianity was introduced among European nations. Rome has always availed herself of this power, both to extend her dominion and to regain lost ground. And if education has been an element of such importance in establishing Christianity in the West, have we any reason to believe that it will be a less powerful agent in establishing Christianity in the East? Not only so, but it seems to me that our endeavor to propagate the Christian religion *among* such a people as the Chinese (without it), would be most identified with the national life. It is only necessary as a proof of this to refer to the vastness of their literature, and the profound respect that is accorded to the pursuit of learning and literary men. A "literary degree" is the "open sesame" to all avenues of distinction in China, and in that land above all others the influence of such an institution as the one proposed could hardly fail to produce results exceeding perhaps our most sanguine expectations.

Again, the better one is acquainted with the state of things in China, and the more one studies the Chinese people with an heartfelt desire for their speedy conversion to Christianity, the more strongly one is convinced that the most effective agency that can be employed in carrying on the great work of evangelizing that nation, must be thoroughly-trained native Ministers, who shall go forth to proclaim the Gospel with a might and power which only a native Ministry can possess. A college such as the one proposed would be undoubtedly the most efficient means of attracting Chinese young men from all parts of the Empire, and bringing them under the influences of our Christian religion and Christian civilization.

And from these young men, with GOD's Blessing, we might look for constant accessions to the ranks of a native Ministry, and for hearty and efficient co-workers in carrying on the work of the Church in China.

Having thus briefly stated the pressing need of a Missionary College in China, and having indicated the importance of such an institution in carrying on our Missionary work there, it remains to be considered whether the establishment of such a college as the one proposed is a practicable undertaking. Certainly so if the Church can only be aroused to the importance of the enterprise, and provide the means to carry it out. China, long hermetically sealed from intercourse with Christian nations, is now thrown open to Missionary enterprise, and there is nothing to hinder the establishment of such a college in any part of China where Missionaries have found free scope for carrying on their work.

To begin this institution, I have appealed to the Church for a sum of money not less than one hundred thousand dollars. In the city of Philadelphia and elsewhere I have obtained promises for an amount equal to about one-third of that sum, and I pray that GOD may put it into the hearts of our Church people to complete the desired amount wherewith to commence the proposed institution, the need and value of which I have very imperfectly placed before them.

That our Church may be willing to give to China a Missionary College as an enduring testimony of our love to our LORD and Master is my earnest prayer.

SAMUEL I. J. SCHERESCHEWSKY.
PHILADELPHIA, *March* 17, 1877.

"The Rev. Dr. Schereschewsky's Appeal for Funds to Establish a Missionary College in China," *The Spirit of Missions* 42 (June 1877): 307-308.

30.

Thomas Gallaudet, Church Work Among Deaf Mutes, Past, Present and Future, 1881

Ministry to the deaf in the Episcopal Church began with Thomas Gallaudet (June 3, 1822–August 27, 1902), "the Apostle to the Deaf." In 1851 he established a Bible class for deaf people at St. Stephen's Church, New York City, and in 1852 in the same city founded St. Ann's Church for Deaf-Mutes. This parish became the center of missionary work to the hearing impaired, and as a result of Gallaudet's work mission congregations were established in other cities.

Henry Winter Syle (1846–January 6, 1890), who had lost his hearing as the result of scarlet fever, was encouraged by Gallaudet to seek ordination. Syle was ordained to the diaconate on October 8, 1876, by Bishop William Bacon Stevens of Pennsylvania at St. Stephen's Church, Philadelphia, the first deaf person to receive Holy Orders in the Episcopal Church. Gallaudet reviews his work in the following excerpt from the First Conference of Church Workers among Deaf-Mutes. He and Syle are commemorated in the Episcopal Calendar on August 27.

At the First Conference of Church Workers among Deaf-Mutes, it seems proper to put upon record a few facts in relation to the history of the movement with which we are connected.

As it fell to my lot to take the initiative, I desire to express my sincere gratitude for the providential circumstances which took me out of Congregationalism and brought me into membership with the Protestant Episcopal Church in the United States of America; for I am sure that in the system laid down by its Book of Common Prayer all educated deaf-mutes, not connected with the Roman Catholic Church, will find greater advantages than in any other religious body. They can readily join in all its liturgical forms, and find the Lessons of Holy Scripture which are regularly arranged according to a Calendar for the year. If all deaf-mutes would lay aside prejudice, and carefully examine the Book of Common Prayer, they would soon find it a rich treasury of devotions, to be used not only in public but in private worship.

After my ordination as a deacon in June, 1850, I was so impressed with the importance of doing something to promote the spiritual welfare of the adult, educated deaf-mutes of New York City, that I began a week-night Bible-class for them in the following September. It was first held in the vestry-room of old St. Stephen's Church, at the corner of Broome and Chrystie streets, under the Rectorship of the Rev. Joseph H. Price, D.D. The class rapidly increased and we soon removed to a room in Bond street, near the Bowery. Quite a number of deaf-mutes were baptized, confirmed and received to the Holy Communion in St. Stephen's Church.

I was led more and more intimately into pastoral relations with them, and at length conceived the idea of beginning a new parish in this city, in which the deaf-mutes should find a spiritual home.

Its first services were held on the first Sunday of October, 1852, in the small chapel of the New York University on Washington Square. It was called St. Ann's Church, and I became its first rector. It comprised not only deaf-mutes, but also their hearing and speaking friends, and its services were arranged so as to suit each class. Both came together at the Holy Communion. Services were continued in this chapel till the fall of 1857, when we removed to the lecture-room of the new Historical Society building at the S.E. corner of 2nd Ave. and 11th street. In July 1859, we purchased our present church property in 18th street, west of Fifth Avenue. It was originally Christ Church; in the summer of 1858 it was exchanged for property owned by a Baptist congregation at the corner of 5th

Avenue and 35th St.; we bought of the Baptists and thus restored the property to the Church. The seats in St. Ann's have always been free to all who would come to its services.

Soon I had the privilege of an assistant who could conduct services at St. Ann's during my occasional visits to other cities. These resulted in regular services for deaf-mutes in St. Stephen's Church, Philadelphia; Grace Church, Baltimore; and St. Paul's Church, Albany; with occasional services in Boston and other large places. The work in Philadelphia passed through several phases in connection with St. Stephen's Church, St. Chrysostom's Church and Calvary Church, finally returning to St. Stephen's, where it has been for several years under the Rev. H. W. Syle.

This Church-work among deaf-mutes grew so steadily through different parts of the country, that it was at length deemed best to have a society which should sustain and foster it more effectually; and so in October 1872, a meeting held at St. Ann's Church, resulted in forming such a society, which was incorporated under the name of "The Church Mission to Deaf-Mutes," having for its object to promote the temporal and spiritual welfare of adult deaf-mutes. It had a board of twenty-five trustees, of which the Right Rev. Bishop Potter was chosen the president.

As this Church-work among deaf-mutes extended, it attracted the attention of various Bishops and clergy. Four clergymen beside myself were able to conduct services in the sign-language,—the Rev. Drs. Clerc and Pennell, and the Rev. Messrs. Chamberlain and Berry. At length three deaf gentlemen were admitted to Holy Orders: Mr. H. W. Syle by the Rt. Rev. Bishop Stevens, in Philadelphia, Oct., 1876; Mr. A. W. Mann by the Rt. Rev. Bishop Bedell, in Cleveland, O., Jan. 1877; and Mr. Job Turner by the Rt. Rev. Bishop Whittle in Richmond, Va., Jan., 1880. Several lay-readers and Bible-class teachers were added to the number of workers from time to time, so that a large number of deaf-mutes in different parts of the country were reached in their ministrations.

. . . .

The peculiar field needs a larger income and more well-qualified laborers.

A common sign language and a common manual alphabet are used throughout the whole country. These are instrumental in conveying and receiving ideas with great rapidity. Deaf-mutes enjoy signs as those who hear enjoy sounds. But, as deaf-mutes are led by their education to understand the English language, they can also derive great profit by using Prayer Books and Bibles at the services of any Episcopal Church in the land. It is hoped they will find friends in every congregation who will assist them to find the places. We hope to see large numbers of them becoming communicants of the Church.

We are happy to observe that Protestants, no matter to what denomination their friends may belong, generally come into our Church. There are a few who do not like some of our peculiarities, but they usually do not understand the reasons for them; the surplice, for example, besides its historical associations, has many practical advantages, such as its producing uniformity in the attire of ministers. And as to baptism by immersion, our Church distinctly allows it, and anyone who prefers it to pouring, may be baptized in that manner.

A few thoughts as to the future must suffice for this brief paper. As soon as the proper time comes it will be well to have other local Boards of Trustees or Diocesan Commissions for different portions of the country, who will assume the responsibility of supporting those engaged in the work. I trust that the Twelfth Sunday after Trinity, on which the Gospel recites the miracle of our Lord's healing the deaf and dumb man, will every year bring larger offerings from the faithful, to the various departments referred to above and to others which may yet be formed. I trust that with love to all who profess and call themselves Christians, the workers who are represented in this conference will so earnestly and gracefully present the principles laid down in the Book of Common Prayer, so wonderfully in harmony with the Gospel system, that with GOD'S blessing, our deaf-mute brethren may generally come to understand and accept them.

I trust that more and more serious attention will be given to the Church-work among deaf-mutes, which, beginning with a small Bible-Class in September, 1850, has spread through the length and breadth of the land. Those who look upon it will acknowledge it is of GOD and cannot fail.

Thomas Gallaudet, "Church Work Among Deaf Mutes, Past, Present and Future," in *Proceedings of the First American Conference on Church Work Among the Deaf, Held at New York, October 4-5, 1888*, 5-8. (Excerpt)

31.

Thomas March Clark, The Mission of the Church: A Sermon Preached at the Opening of the General Convention of the Protestant Episcopal Church, in Christ Church, Philadelphia, Wednesday, October 3, A.D. 1883

Thomas March Clark (July 4, 1812–September 7, 1903) was consecrated the fifth Bishop of Rhode Island on December 6, 1854. He was the twelfth Presiding

Bishop, February 7, 1899-September 7, 1903. This sermon was preached at the thirty-fourth General Convention, October 3-26, 1883, in Philadelphia. He urges that the mission work of the church is in the world.

Nothing is foreign to the Church that pertains to humanity. Christ did not pray that His disciples might be taken out of the world, but only that they should be delivered from the evil. He Himself lived in the world preeminently, and made Himself familiar with men in all the relations of life. He visited their homes, attended their weddings, sat at their feasts, walked about their market places, talked with men on the highway, watched them at their fishing and planting, drew His illustrations, for the most part, from what He saw going on around Him, and He tells His people that they are to be in the world as a salt to purify it and as a light to illuminate it.

The strongest argument that can be urged in behalf of the kingdom of Christ is the benefit that it is to the world.

Of late years, our own Church has begun to recognize the fact that the sphere in which it is called to work is bounded by nothing but the necessities of the race to which we belong. In the establishment of hospitals, and homes of all sorts for the destitute, reading-rooms and places of wholesome resort for the floating population, and free Churches for all classes and conditions of men, I think it may be said, without vain boasting, that the Episcopal Church has taken the lead. There are individual parishes which are doing more to-day, in a great variety of practical ways, for the direct elevation of the humbler classes of society than was done by the whole Church half a century ago. A great deal of secular work, which becomes sacred by the spirit which prompts it, is now required of both priest and people, that was never dreamed of in former days. And this is only the beginning of an extension of Christian influence in other quarters where it is much needed. Simultaneously with this work of general charity there has been enkindled an interest in the cause of Christian missions, which, though it is by no means universal, has been steadily increasing during the last few years. At the General Convention, held half a century ago, the Domestic and Foreign Missionary Society reported their expenditures as follows: "On account of the Greek Mission, $3975; Green Bay Mission, $5000; Domestic Missionaries, $1275; other domestic objects, $1500; total, $11,750." That was the day of small things, and it is still the day of small things, as compared with what we hope to do in the future.

Nothing has done so much to quiet dissensions in the Church as the hearty enlistment of ministers and people in charitable and missionary work. The blotting out of party lines has not been effected by argument; we have "shot our arrows, even bitter words," and they have returned to us void. But when the cry is heard on the wind from a perishing world, "Come to our help!" we forget our disputes and vain janglings, and every faithful servant of Jesus asks, "What can I do to rescue those who are perishing for lack of knowledge?"

Standing in the presence of great realities, and in immediate view of the solemn charge that has been given us to "preach the Word, and be instant in season and out of season," our interest in all visionary schemes of doctrine, and in all minute details of form and ceremony, of necessity ceases: in matters of life and death, eternal life and eternal death, we have no time left to expend upon trifles. In the heat of battle the commander cares very little about the ornaments of his dress or the jewels on his scabbard; as a matter of course he wears the uniform prescribed by those whom he serves, and that is all which concerns him. He marshals his troops according to the manual, but in an emergency the rigid rules of military etiquette have to give way.

When the Apostles went forth on their errand of mercy, the burden of their mission was the story of Christ. They told the people how the Son of God had come into the world and died for their redemption. They never perplexed their hearers with subtle questions of theology, or with metaphysical theories of depravity, with discussions of prevenient grace and the grace of congruity, of moral and physical inability, of imputed righteousness as distinct from actual righteousness, of the philosophy of the atonement, of the nature and limits of Divine inspiration. They did not undertake to solve the mystery of Christ's double nature, or to explain the mutual relations of the three Persons in the Godhead, but they made men feel that they were sinners and uncovered the awful depths of corruption in which their souls were sunk; they declared in terms that could not be misunderstood the stern and impartial justice of God, and the absolute certainty of punishment for every unforgiven sin; they published abroad the inexhaustible love and mercy of God, and how He is always waiting for them with open arms whenever they come back as the prodigal did, sorrowing and repenting. They proclaimed the grace which bringeth salvation, and led men to the cross, and showed them the Saviour bleeding there in expiation of their transgressions; then they taught their converts plainly and explicitly what were the duties which they owed to God, and just how those duties must be discharged. They enforced a Gospel of righteousness and temperance, and chastity, and charity, and honest and honorable dealing. They told parents and children, and masters and servants and governors and employers and laboring men, how they should conduct themselves, and what were the motives by which they should be guided; they spoke blessed words of comfort to the weary and heavy-laden, the weak and the suffering, the down-trodden and oppressed. They told men how in Christ Jesus death had lost its sting and the grave its victory, and pointed to a world where the tears are wiped from every eye, and where there is no more sin, or sorrow, or dimness of vision, and it was thus that men were lifted heavenward and brought into the fold of Jesus. And when the ambassador of Christ is in earnest, whether he ministers to the refined and cultivated citizen of the metropolis, or the rougher and more enterprising emigrant on the outer borders of civilization, or to the oppressed and persecuted Indian, or to the unenlightened freedman, or the besotted and ignorant heathen, it is the same story of a loving Saviour which inspires his heart and gives efficacy to His Word.

If the little band of faithful men who met together in this consecrated place nearly a century ago could look in upon our Convention to-day, representing as it does a great Church, thoroughly consolidated and fully equipped for the work which it is called to do, with its sixty-six living Bishops, and its clerical and lay representatives from regions which, at the time of their assembling, were an unbroken wilderness, and are now teeming with a refined and enterprising people: if they could have foreseen in 1785, that they were legislating for a Church which, in the course of a century would cover a territory more than double the size of the Roman Empire, when it was said to rule the world, how impressive and eventful would the work have seemed to be, which, in all humility and lowliness of heart they had assembled to do!

A very solemn responsibility rests upon the Convention, which is assembled to carry on the work which they so well inaugurated. By excess of legislation, or by defect of legislation, the progress of the Church may be seriously hindered, and while we must always be true to the doctrine and spirit of our one only Lord and Sovereign, and to every usage and doctrine which is essential to the integrity of the Church, we should carefully consider the circumstances which surround us, and conform ourselves to the peculiar condition and necessities of the people among whom we live, remembering that arrangements which might have suited precisely the state of society as it existed in England two or three hundred years ago, may not be in every particular adapted to the wants of our heterogeneous and shifting community. There is other work for us to do beside fortifying and defending our citadel. Constitutions and canons are of value, so far as they aid in discharging the mission entrusted to us, and no farther. Rubrics are only the regulating power of the machine—indispensable parts of the mechanism, but without any inspiring force. And while we continue to walk in the old paths, let it be with an accelerated pace, and with our eyes looking forward and not backward.

This Church may become the rallying point and centre of unity for those who are weary of sectarian divisions, and are content to accept the simple faith, as we have received it from Christ and His Apostles. It was once the home of the English-speaking race, and if it had been as wise in its generation as it should have been, it might possibly have continued to be their home to the present day.

May the Spirit of God preside over the deliberations of this Convention and give to you a far-seeing and comprehensive vision, a generous and discriminating charity, an earnest and self-forgetting desire to set forward the work of Christ in this great Republic, so that His Name may be honored, and precious souls brought into the Kingdom of our blessed Lord.

Thomas M. Clark, *The Mission of the Episcopal Church: A Sermon Preached at the Opening of the General Convention of the Protestant Episcopal Church, in Christ Church, Philadelphia, Wednesday, October 3, A.D., 1883*, 20-27. (Excerpt)

32.

Sister Constance, Letter to Mother Superior, August 31, 1878

The Sisterhood of St. Mary was founded on February 2, 1865, at St. Michael's Church, New York, when five women made their professions before Bishop Horatio Potter. Harriett Starr Cannon (May 7, 1823–April 7, 1896), a former member of the Sisterhood of the Holy Communion, was the leader and Mother Superior until her death. In 1873 Bishop Charles Todd Quintard invited some of the members to Memphis to found a school and to establish a home for the sick and needy. The Sisters ministered to the ill when an epidemic of yellow fever developed. In 1878 the plague struck again, and the Sisters and others minis-tered to the sick and dying. Sister Constance, who was the Sister Superior in Memphis, died of the fever on September 9; Sister Thecla died on September 12, Sister Ruth on September 17, and Sister Francis on October 4, 1878. Constance's letter to the Mother Superior describes the horror of the situation, and the willingness of many to offer their lives in sacrifice to help others in need. Constance and her companions, commonly called "The Martyrs of Memphis," are remembered on September 9 in the Episcopal Calendar.

MY DEAREST MOTHER:

Your telegram brought me a kind of brightness, but I cannot help a great deal of anxiety for Sister Helen and Sister Ruth, my sense of duty in the matter is so divided between the feeling that I ought to secure all the help I can for these poor suffering people, and the fear for those who come. I will guard them to the utmost; but they know and you know that they are offering their lives. I am glad to have the East Grimstead Sister. They are trained nurses, and she will be invaluable. I will not send for the Clewer Sisters if I can help it. Dr. Houghton telegraphed to know if I wanted them. But on Monday if the fever spreads I must send, for we shall want all the help we can get. Cases that are nursed seldom die. Most of the dead have died of neglect or utter ignorance on the part of their attendants. The panic is fearful to-day. Eighty deaths reported, and half of the doctors refuse to report at all. We found one of our nurses lying on the floor in her patient's room down with the fever, another is sickening. Our ward visitor was here just now to give me some directions about to-morrow, "For I am down," he said. When I said something cheering he put a hand that fairly burned me on my wrist and asked me to feel his pulse if I could. He is a bright, brave young man, our opposite neighbor; his father is dying, his two poor sisters are here asleep, and I am sitting up waiting till Dr. Harris calls me to go to the old man with these two poor girls. There is little hope that the change which must come to-night will be for life, but I suppose it will not come before twelve. Mr. Parsons had a chill this evening; I shall know before twelve whether it was *the* chill. I really believe that Dr. Harris and I and the two negro nurses are the only well persons anywhere near. Mr. Brinkley's gardener and his son are ill. Dr. Armstrong has shut himself up for the night declaring himself "worn out." Sister Thecla and Miss Murdock are in bed worn out with last night's nursing and watching. We like Miss M., who came to us from Ohio (she has had the fever), so much. Sister H. is well; Sister F. much better; no more cases at Church Home, none at the Canfield Asylum, where there are thirty-two children gathered from the infected houses. This is the dreariest night we have had. If anything happens to Mrs. Bullock and to me, will you take care of little Bessie? Mrs. Bullock has helped us bravely, working like one of ourselves, and never shrinking. She was with me in the most pestilential room I have yet had to enter, and I never saw her hesitate. The calls for food and wine are incessant. I have been on my feet almost the whole day, for our old cook would not do a thing if one of us did not stay with her, whenever we could be spared from the sick. A nurse has just been here to say that he will not stay another night with his two patients—a father and daughter—if the dead mother is not buried. The body has been there for nearly two days, and no undertaker can be found who has time to bring a coffin. We are absolutely forbidden to touch the dead even if a coffin could be found. Dr. Harris is all that earthly strength can be to us, but he is far from strong. I do not think he even hopes to get through. Pray *doubly* for us now, dear mother. I think of the Sisters who are coming and of those who are praying at home so constantly.

Your loving
CONSTANCE, S.S.M.
August 31.

147

Sister Constance to Mother Superior, August 31, 1878, in Morgan Dix, "The Sisters of St. Mary at Memphis," *Church Work* 2 (October 1887): 314-315.

33.

Channing Moore Williams, Annual Report of the Missionary Bishop of Yedo, 1889

Channing Moore Williams (July 18, 1829–December 2, 1910) was consecrated the second Missionary Bishop of China with jurisdiction over Japan on October 3, 1866. He was the fourth Foreign Missionary Bishop, the first being William Jones Boone, the first Missionary Bishop of China. On October 23, 1874, the House of Bishops constituted Japan a missionary district, and named it the Missionary District of Yedo (Tokyo). Williams relinquished China and became the first Missionary Bishop of Yedo. Bishop Williams resigned on October 18, 1889. He translated portions of the Book of Common Prayer *into Japanese. His life and ministry are commemorated in the Episcopal Calendar of the Church Year on December 2. In this report to the Domestic and Foreign Missionary Society, Bishop Williams discusses the new constitution that gave Japanese citizens freedom of religious belief, and the challenge this new freedom presented to Episcopal missionaries.*

The New Constitution

Since the last report, an event unique in the history of the world has occurred, which is fraught with far-reaching consequences to Japan. On the 11th of February last, the Emperor, in fulfilment of the promise made several years ago, gave a liberal constitution to the country. This promise was made not through compulsion forced upon him in any way through fear, but simply at the instigation of certain ministers, some of whom had visited America and England, and imbibed liberal opinions. By this constitution Japan has, in a day, been changed from a despotism into a constitutional monarchy with a parliament which will meet annually to make laws which shall bind alike prince and peasant throughout the land.

One article of the constitution materially affects us, as a Church having a mission in the country. The 27th article declares that "Japanese subjects . . . shall enjoy freedom of religious belief." This is but another way of stating that Christianity is henceforward tolerated. For there has been no question of the toleration of Buddhism and Shintoism—the only other religions which can possibly make any efforts at propagation here. This may be considered almost as an invitation to Christians to put forth their strength to spread the religion of Christ in this "Land of the Rising Sun," and Christians of many names and divers beliefs—from Greek and Roman on the one side to Quakers and Unitarians on the other—are crowding into the country. There were at the end of last year 443 Protestant missionaries, of whom 150 were married men, twenty-seven unmarried, and 124 unmarried women. The Roman Church had two Bishops, eighty Priests, and forty sisters. The Greek Church was represented by one Bishop and two Priests. Our Church had only nine married men, two unmarried, and nine unmarried women—in all only twenty-nine missionaries.

Our Church must settle what part she is to take in the great work of bringing the people of this interesting country to the knowledge of and faith in the Lord Jesus; and what she determines to do must be done without delay. She cannot think that she has, in any sense, come up to the measure of her responsibility. For the truth is the mission has been sadly undermanned from its commencement to the present; and the fact is especially apparent at this time when, by the new treaties, the whole country is to be thrown open to our missionaries to travel and reside where they may please, without restrictions of any kind.

And now when, in view of the new and wider openings, the request for more men is made, the sickening response comes back that the receipts for last year will not justify an appropriation for new men. No blame in the matter is thought to rest on the Board of Managers. They are but acting as the whole Board of Missions directed. There seems no way out of the difficulty at present but to ask that some friends of the mission, to whom God has entrusted large means, or certain churches, would undertake the support of a few men in Japan for a term of years. This plan has been tried and should now be extended. This or some other method must be used to meet the present pressing need. And, as a last request, I earnestly beg that the means may be provided, and the men be sent out to help us with as little delay as possible, and that prayer may be offered for God's rich blessing on the work and the laborers in this land, and that numbers now without God and without hope may be brought by the power of the Holy Spirit to know and love Christ, the Light and Life of the world.

Respectfully submitted,
C. M. Williams,
Missionary Bishop of Yedo.
Tokio, Japan, August 8th, 1889.

Channing Moore Williams, "Annual Report of the Missionary Bishop of Yedo," *The Spirit of Missions* 54 (October 1889): 392-393. (Excerpt)

34.

J. A. Ingle, The Work at Hankow, China, 1897

James Addison Ingle (March 11, 1867–December 7, 1903) served all his brief ministry at Hankow, China. On February 24, 1902, he was consecrated the first Missionary Bishop of Hankow. He describes the challenges of mission work in China.

You ask me to write you a description of our methods of work in Hankow, and as there is much to say and I must not be prolix, I will waste no time in introduction, but proceed at once to my subject.

The backbone of our work is our native Deacons. You cannot imagine how powerless, even after years of experience, a foreigner is among the Chinese, unless he has faithful native assistants. The language, social and business customs, and modes of reasoning, of the Chinese are so different from our own and so intricate that both merchant and missionary must depend largely on natives. So the Deacons are more than backbone; they are eyes, ears, mouth, hands, and feet to the work. There are four of them connected with this place; three in Hankow, and one in the country at Hanchuan. Each has his congregation and chapel. The chapel is in most cases simply a rented Chinese house, always unprotected from heat and cold, and sometimes even from rain and snow. The Deacon's residence is usually in the same building.

In our Hankow work no public preaching for the heathen is done in the chapels, though this is the method in use among most missionaries here. The chapels are reserved for services for Christians, though, of course, heathen visitors are admitted if they wish to come. As a substitute for public preaching to the heathen we employ conversation in the guest-rooms. One of these rooms is fitted up, wherever we have a worker, with Chinese furniture, teacups, and a water-pipe. A sign is hung outside the door inviting all well behaved people to enter. When a visitor comes, tea is poured for him, the water-pipe offered, and the usual questions asked as to his "honorable name," "palatial residence," "exalted age," etc. To treat a man thus is to put him on his best behavior, and then it is easy to lead him into conversation on the subject of religion. When he leaves, he is invited to call again, and if he has seemed to be interested and sincere, he is looked up in his home. When he decides to apply for Baptism, he attends instruction classes, and commits to memory the Creed, the Lord's Prayer, and the Ten Commandments, and is taught the chief truths of religion. The time consumed ranges from three to eighteen months according to the man's ability. Often he has to be taught one word at a time with infinite labor. Meanwhile, his character and antecedents are looked up, and if they are satisfactory, he is admitted as a catechumen. After this he spends three months in further preparation. At the end of this time I examine him, and, if approved, baptize him.

As a matter of fact, the majority of our members do not casually stumble upon the guests' room, but are brought by friends and relatives. They are thus bound together more closely than if they were merely so many unconnected units.

The Deacon's duties are manifold. Inquirers are liable to call at any hour; the sick and poor have to be looked after; members who fail to attend service must be visited, and a general oversight kept over everything, for many of our people are as unsophisticated as children. For all these and yet other duties one man is insufficient. So each Deacon has two or three assistants to help him in these matters.

We have, besides, eight free day-schools in Hankow, where poor boys can get the rudiments of a Chinese education and at the same time learn something about Christianity. Of course, the latter is the main aim; but boys are not baptized unless their parents are Christians. These schools, also, are in the care of the Deacons.

Of course, in a large and extended work like this, embracing in all five stations, one sixty and one more than a hundred miles from Hankow, one foreigner can be little more than overseer, and cannot do even this work satisfactorily. The great need of foreigners is for teaching both those who are workers and the ordinary Church Members. There must be classes held for the Deacons, the assistants, the school-teachers, and the scholars. The first approach to the heathen can best be made by the native; but he must be taught and led and his spiritual life fostered by the foreigner. We are so short-handed that it is impossible to do this properly. By the welcome arrival of the Rev. Mr. Huntington we have now two men; but we need at least one more. Men can do no work among women; and for years we have had no lady worker stationed here. This is our greatest and most urgent need.

You ask for my general impressions of the work of the Church. I hesitate to touch the subject, for I feel very keenly the neglect of our work by the Church at home, and I cannot speak of results and methods here without touching on causes at home. Our work in China is small, though perhaps as large as could be expected under the circumstances. Almost from the beginning of the mission we have been undermanned and neglected. Under such circumstances no policy can be carried out and little lasting work accomplished. Our workers are above the average in ability, but pitifully few. We feel that we are barely tolerated by a rich and growing Church, which could easily quadruple our force if it chose, but prefers the very unbusiness-like plan of employing one man to do the work of three or four, and then actually expects to see growth, whereas there are not enough workers properly to supervise already existing work, much less extend it. Do you wonder that we on the outposts think our lot hard, and blush for our Church's indifference? It would be better if she were to renounce the profession of work among the heathen, and leave us to seek help and sympathy from, perhaps, the English Church, than to trifle thus with so solemn a commission as our Lord's parting mandate to her.

It is hard to predict accurately the "prospects of Christianity" in the Chinese Church. We have, I think, a great advantage in our liturgical service. The Chinese is an extreme conservative, and if once properly taught the doctrine and polity of the church, is likely to hold fast to them, because they have existed from of old. He is naturally practical, and not speculative like the Japanese, and I think it will be long before he demands the novelties in religion which seem to be prevailing in Japan. Ultimately, of course, the forms of service will be modified to suit the peculiar needs and tastes of the people; but that is only natural and healthy. It will, I think, be a long time yet before we can have a native Bishop and a self-supporting Church. In fact, unless the church radically changes her method of conducting the work, the day of this long prayed for consummation is indefinitely postponed. Pray for us and our people.

The Spirit of Missions 62 (March 1897): 128-130.

35.

Alexander Crummell, Modifications of Methods of Work Among the Colored People, 1897

Alexander Crummell (1819–September 12, 1898) was a black priest who served as a missionary in West Africa and as rector of St. Luke's Church, Washington, D.C. He was a leader in the organization of the Conference of Church Workers Among the Colored People in 1883, and formed the American Negro Academy in 1897. He urges new approaches for mission work among black people. The phrase "the class system" refers to organizing members of the congregation in small groups along the lines customary in early Methodism.

All work for God should be done with wisdom and discretion. At times, however, a duty arises which calls for unusual carefulness. Such a work, perchance, is so beset with difficulties, is so inherently critical, has so many side issues, and makes withal such large demands, that the greatest painstaking and the wisest management are needed for its carrying on. Such is, without doubt, the nature of the Church work among Colored people in our country. The further it is pushed the more evident becomes the fact of some past mistakes in its working, and of hesitating doubt as to its future development. The work, then, from its very nature, calls now and then for revision, for the rectification of imperfect plans, and the creation of new and more popular modes of operation.

1. One of the most harassing questions in our work is the lack of clergymen. The work is narrowed and limited from the want of ordained men to supply the calls for preachers and teachers. This deficiency of laborers, moreover, suggests the temptation of ordaining unfit or defective men. In this case the unfit man becomes too often either a hindrance to the work, or a burden on the hands of his Bishop. Yet, not seldom, it is a disastrous thing to leave a field uncared for, where worthy people are left in ignorance, or perchance will fall into the hands of deluded teachers who sow more tares than wheat.

Cannot this difficulty be obviated? It has been obviated in other lands, it would seem the part of wisdom to apply the remedy in ours. The remedy is the use of a large agency of catechists. This has been the recourse of the Church of England in similar circumstances, where there has been a lack of duly ordained clergymen. The Bishops of that Church in India, in West Africa, and in the West Indies, have, for well nigh a century, thus used its lay agents, in the endeavor to meet the needs of destitute peoples.

Why cannot something be done in our southern states amid the Black population? It will take a long time to prepare well trained men for the Ministry; and none but well trained men should be put in Orders. But wise, intelligent, and pious men can be found among the rising, instructed men of the race, willing to serve the Church and their people in the office of reader or catechist; attending, meanwhile, their ordinary secular callings, or teaching school. Moreover, from this class of catechists there might be found, now and then, a man of unusual spiritual and intellectual finesse who might, while thus ministering to the needs of his people, be moved by the Spirit to seek the Ministry of the Church.

2. Next, is there not the need of more elasticity in our system of spiritual culture, in order to meet the varied wants and novel conditions of the people? This race, *i.e.,* as a race, has been brought up under religious customs and routines widely divergent from ours. Their training has been largely that of the "class system" and the "prayer meeting." Is not the sudden change from such a system a violent wrench? Is it wise thus to repudiate entirely the spiritual habits of any people? Does not wisdom, does not experience suggest that we take the Negro as he is; striving indeed to make him what he should be, and making use of the very best material in him and in his habits? And this, not by divorcing him suddenly from all the customs of his fathers and his old religion, and throwing him into the routines of a system alien to his nature. This would be a non-natural procedure. When boys first learn to swim they do not generally plunge into deep water. They wade into it gradually, and gradually learn to swim; and is not some analogous adjustment to the habits and customs of this people desirable? Accustomed to free prayer and free speech, is not the change to absolutely fixed services at first likely to chill or perhaps repel them?

Moreover, the superintendence and the direction of the class system have their value. Rightly used, with the restraints of the Prayer Book and pastoral guidance, they may prove of special value to a new people, just now in a transitional state; and it is well to remember that this system, in its original, is a Church system, formulated and carried out by the Fletchers and Wesleys long before Methodism assumed its full form.

3. One other modification of our system seems desirable. The Romans of old when they entered upon a campaign or were on the eve of joining battle with an enemy, were always careful to free themselves of *impedimenta*. They had learned from experience the evil of carrying useless baggage on long journeys or into hazardous conflicts. They coveted as much freedom as possible in their movements, and strove to avoid a useless expenditure of force. Just such prudence is needed in this department of our Church work, for without doubt it has been the intrusion of *impedimenta* which has proved a hindrance in our efforts among the Colored people.

For instance, has not our vestry system proved in many cases a serious difficulty? Have not simple men been often saddled with the offices of wardens and vestrymen who were unfitted for those positions? Have there not been numerous instances where these offices served to exaggerate the self-importance of men and led to sad disturbances of churches? Where pious and thoughtful men have been accustomed to public functions, vestries are a necessary provision; but are not the cases exceptional in the South where competent men can be found for official positions? Ofttimes in our missions not a half-dozen men can be found who can read and write. Not seldom a mission is begun without a single confirmed or pious man interested in the work. One can easily divine the trouble and vexation which may arise by making ignorant and godless men guardians of our churches in their infant state. We hear often of clergymen who are called "failures"; but people forget that not infrequently it is the vestries who are the real failures.

The suggested changes are not serious: (a) Let our missions be organized simply as missions, under the care and guidance of the clergyman in charge. (b) As a mission advances and the clergyman feels the need of advice, let him "choose" two or more laymen, not as an organized board, but as occasional counselors. (c) At a later and more advanced stage, let him select a certain

154

number of men as a committee of counselors, avoiding resolutions at their meetings, but the clergymen keeping a record of their judgments. (d) At a still later period, when a goodly number of men have been confirmed, with the church built, a congregation secured, and the work established, let the regular organization obtain, and a vestry be elected as usual, but not until the Bishop considers this advisable.

The Spirit of Missions 62 (May 1897): 237-238.

CHAPTER FIVE

The Episcopal Church and the Civil War (1861-1865)

Introduction

The Episcopal Church was separated in body but not in spirit during the Civil War. The Episcopal Church in the Confederate States of America essentially continued the same doctrine, discipline, and worship of the Episcopal Church in the United States. The failure of the Episcopal Church to address slavery as a major moral and religious issue was one reason that there was no lasting division in the church between North and South. Although there were some harsh words, for the most part church leaders in the North and South continued to emphasize the bond of affection and prayer that they shared with their Episcopalian friends on the other side of the battle lines. The 1862 General Convention refused to recognize the division of the church, and Southern bishops were simply marked absent at the roll call for Convention. After the end of the Civil War, the Southern delegations were graciously welcomed back to the General Convention in 1865. Presiding Bishop John Henry Hopkins of Vermont played a leading role of conciliation in drawing the church together at this time. The Episcopal Church opened the door for reunion by accepting the consecration of Richard Hooker Wilmer, who was ordained bishop of Alabama by the Episcopal Church in the Confederate States during the Civil War. Consents were also given for the ordination of Charles T. Quintard, bishop-elect of Tennessee, despite his prior service as a chaplain in the Confederate Army during the Civil War. The Episcopal Church in the United States was once again a house united.

36.

Pastoral Letter of Bishop Leonidas Polk, January 30, 1861

Leonidas Polk (April 10, 1806–June 14, 1864) was consecrated Missionary Bishop of Arkansas and the Indian Territory on December 9, 1838. On October

16, 1841, he was elected the first Bishop of Louisiana. Polk supported the right of the Southern states to secede, and "buckled the sword over the gown" by accepting his commission as a major general in the Confederate Army in June 1861. He was killed in battle at Pine Mountain, Georgia. In this pastoral letter Bishop Polk explains the consequences of secession, and describes the continuity of faith of the Episcopal Church in the southern states with the rest of the church.

To the Clergy and Laity of the Protestant Episcopal Church in the Diocese of Louisiana:

MY BELOVED BRETHREN—The State of Louisiana having, by a formal ordinance, through her Delegates in Convention assembled, withdrawn herself from all further connections with the United States of America, and constituted herself a separate Sovereignty, has, by that act, removed our Diocese from within the pale of "The Protestant Episcopal Church in the United States." We have, therefore, an Independent Diocesan existence.

Of the circumstances which have occasioned this act, it may not be necessary now to speak. They are familiar to you all. It is, however, our happiness to know that in canvassing the sum of the political grievances of which we have complained, we find no contribution made to it by brethren of our own household. Our Church in the non-slaveholding States, as everywhere, has been loyal to the Constitution and the laws. Her sound conservative teaching and her well-ordered organization, have held her steadily to her proper work, and she has confined herself simply to preaching and teaching the Gospel of Christ. Surrounded by a strong pressure on every side, she has successfully resisted its power, and has refused to lend the aid of her Convention, her pulpits, and her presses to the radical and unscriptural propagandism which has so degraded Christianity and plunged our country into its unhappy condition.

In withdrawing ourselves, therefore, from all political connection with the Union to which our brethren belong, we do so with hearts filled with sorrow at the prospect of its forcing a termination of our ecclesiastical connection with them also, and that we shall be separated from those, whose intelligence, patriotism, christian integrity and piety, we have long known, and for whom we entertain sincere respect and affection. Unfortunately, the class they represent was numerically too small to control their section. They have been overborne, and silenced, and a different description of mind and character is in the ascendant. The principles and purposes of this party have long been the subject of careful observation by the people of the Southern States, and they have watched its rise and progress with anxious solicitude. They thought they saw in it, the seeds of all the evil from which our country is now suffering, and have not failed to employ all the resources at their command to avert it. Their efforts have been fruitless, and they have seen no way of escape from the consequences to themselves and their posterity, other than that they have taken. Of the justice of our cause, we have no doubt. Of the wisdom of the measures we have adopted to maintain it, we may judge from the character of the men who are engaged in supporting them. With here and there an exception, they represent the intelligence, the character, and the wealth of the State. We have taken our stand we humbly trust, in the fear of God, and under a sense of the duty we owe to mankind.

Our separation from our brethren of "The Protestant Episcopal Church in the United States" has been effected, because we must follow our Nationality. Not because there has been any difference of opinion as to Christian Doctrine or Catholic usage. Upon these points we are still one. With us, it is a separation, not division, certainly not alienation. And there is no reason why, if we should find the union of our Dioceses under one National Church impracticable, we should cease to feel for each other the respect and regard with which purity of manners, high principle, and a manly devotion to truth, never fail to inspire generous minds. Our relations to each other hereafter will be the relations we both now hold to the men of our Mother Church of England.

"Pastoral Letter of Bishop Leonidas Polk, January 30, 1861," *Historical Magazine of the Protestant Episcipal Church* 31 (September 1962): 296-298.

37.

Pastoral Letter of the House of Bishops, Protestant Episcopal Church, 1862

The twenty-seventh General Convention met at New York, October 7-17, 1862. By this time the War between the States was raging, but the General Convention refused to recognize the separation of the Southern dioceses. Charles P. McIlvaine, Bishop of Ohio and Presiding Bishop pro tem, wrote the Pastoral Letter, condemning the secession of the southern states.

BRETHREN:

We have been assembled together in the Triennial Convention of our Church under most afflicting circumstances. Hitherto, whatever our Church had to contend with from the fallen nature of man, from the power of this evil world, or the enmity of that mighty adversary who is called by St. Paul "the god of this world," her Chief Council has been permitted to meet amidst the blessings of peace within our national boundaries, and as representing a household of faith at unity in itself. Our last meeting was in the metropolis of a State which has long held a high place and influence in the affairs of our Church and Country. Long shall we remember the affectionate hospitality which was then lavished upon us, and the delightful harmony and brotherly love which seemed to reign, almost without alloy, in a Convention composed of representatives of all our Dioceses! Never did the promise of a long continuance of brotherly union, among all parts and sections of our whole Church, appear more assuring. But, alas! what is man? How unstable our surest reliances, based on man's wisdom or will! How unsearchable the counsels of Him who "hath his way in the sea, and his path in the mighty waters, and whose footsteps are not known"! What is now the change? We look in vain for the occupants of seats in the Convention, belonging to the representatives of no less than ten of our Dioceses, and to ten of our Bishops. And whence such painful and injurious absence? The cause stands as a great cloud of darkness before us, of which, as we cannot help seeing it, and thinking of it, and that most sorrowfully, wherever we go and whatever we do, it is impossible not to speak when we address you in regard to the condition and wants of our Church. That cause is all concentrated in a stupendous rebellion against the organic law and the constituted Government of the Country, for the dismemberment of our national Union—under which, confessedly, all parts of the land have been signally prospered and blessed; a rebellion which is already too well known to you, brethren, in the vast armies it has compelled our Government to maintain, and in the fearful expense of life and treasure, of suffering and sorrow, which it has cost on both sides, to need any further description here.

We are deeply grieved to think how many of our brethren, clergy and laity, in the regions over which that dark tide has spread, have been carried away by its flood; not only yielding to it, so as to place themselves, as far as in them lay, in severance from our ecclesiastical Union, which has so long and so happily joined us together in one visible communion and fellowship; but, to a sad extent, sympathizing with the movement, and giving it their active co-operation.

In this part of our address, we do not attempt to estimate the moral character of such doings. At present we confine ourselves to the statement of notorious facts, except as to one matter, of which this is the convenient place to speak.

When the ordained Ministers of the Gospel of Christ, whose mission is so emphatically one of peace and good-will, of tenderness and consolation, do so depart from their sacred calling as to take the sword and engage in the fierce and bloody conflicts of war; when in so doing they are fighting against authorities which, as *the powers that be*," the Scriptures declare "are ordained of God," so that in resisting them they resist the ordinance of God; when especially one comes out from the exalted spiritual duties of an Overseer of the flock of Christ, to exercise high command in such awful work,—we cannot, as ourselves Overseers of the same flock, consistently with duty to Christ's Church, His Ministry and people, refrain from placing on such examples our strong condemnation. We remember the words of our blessed Lord, uttered among His last words, and for the special admonition of His Ministers—"They that take the sword shall perish with the sword."

Returning to this great rebellion, with all its retinue of cost and sacrifice, of tribulation and anguish, of darkness and death, there are two aspects in which we must contemplate it, *namely:* as it comes *by the agency of man*, and as it comes *from the Providence of God*.

We desire, *first*, to call your attention to it as it proceeds from *the Providence of God*. So comprehensive is that Providence that it embraces all worlds and all nations; while so minute is it that not a sparrow falleth without the knowledge and will of our Father in Heaven. In its vast counsels, this deep affliction has its place. God's hand is in it. His power rules it. It is His visitation and chastening for the sins of this nation. Who can doubt it? Just as the personal affliction of any of you is God's visitation to turn him from the world and sin, unto Himself; so is this national calamity most certainly His judgment upon this nation for its good. And we trust, dear brethren, we are in no danger of seeming, by such interpretation of our distresses, to excuse, in any degree, such agency as men have had in bringing them upon us. God's Providence has no interference with man's responsibility. He works by man, but so that it is still man that wills and works. The captivities of God's chosen people were, as His Word declares, His judgments upon them for their sins; while the nations that carried them captive were visited of God for heinous guilt in so doing. St. Peter declares that our Lord was "delivered" unto death "by the determinate counsel and foreknowledge of God;" and that, nevertheless, it was "*by wicked hands*" that He was "crucified and slain." Thus we need be under no temptation to diminish our estimate of the present dispensation of sorrow, as coming from the hand of God, for the punishment of our sins, whatever the agency of men therein. It is our duty, as Christians and as patriots, so to consider it, that it may do us the good for which it is sent, and may the sooner be taken away.

It is not possible for us, in this address, to set before you, in detail, or in their true proportions, all the national and other sins which make us, as a people, deserve, and need, the chastisements of a holy God. It needs no Daniel, inspired from on high, to discover them. Surely you must all be painfully familiar with many of them, in the profaneness of speech with which God's name and majesty are assailed; in the neglect of public worship which so dishonors His holy day;

in the ungodliness of life which erects its example so conspicuously; and especially in that one great sin for which Jerusalem was given over to be trodden down by the heathen, and the people of Israel have ever since been wanderers and a by-word among the nations, *namely*, the rejection, whether in positive infidelity, or only in practical unbelief, of God's great gift of grace and mercy, His beloved Son, our Lord Jesus Christ, to be a sacrifice of propitiation for our sins, and an all-sufficient and all-glorious Saviour of our souls.

. . . .

Let us turn now to the other aspect of our great trial; namely, *as it comes from the agency of man.* We deeply feel, dear brethren, how momentous is this portion of our subject, and with what carefulness and charity, and at the same time with what decision and plainness of speech, with what faithfulness to Church and Country, and to those arrayed against us, as well as to ourselves, it becomes us to speak. Gladly would your Bishops avoid a subject so painful. But there is no possibility of avoiding it. Should we keep silence, we should not avoid it. Our silence would speak far and wide, and with a meaning by which we are not willing that our minds should be interpreted. At such an alarming crisis of our national and ecclesiastical union, as well as of our whole welfare, when a voice from such a body, occupying such intimate relations to a wide-spread communion, may be of such importance to the strength of the public counsels, through the guidance of the people of that communion,—should we address you on other topics of less prominence at the present time, and yet keep silence on that one which banishes almost every other from the thoughts of the nation, we should not only neglect an opportunity of usefulness which ought to be improved, and subject ourselves to imputations which we are not willing to bear, but we should inflict a serious injury upon a cause we are bound to aid.

It is the first time this Convention has met since these troubles began. God grant they may be ended long before it shall meet again! Ever since our Church had her Litany, we have been praying for deliverance "from sedition, privy conspiracy, and rebellion." And now that all the three are upon us, and in a depth of scheme, a force of action, a strength of purpose, and an extensiveness of sway such as the world never before saw united for the dismemberment of any government, shall we refuse to tell you in what light we regard that gigantic evil?

We are moved the more to speak, because we believe that you, brethren, desire it of us. You feel bound, by your views of duty, to take a position and manifest principles, too decided to be mistaken, in support of the national Constitution and Government in this day of their peril. Our communion is nobly represented wherever the nation's cause has dangers to brave, difficulties to be surmounted, sacrifices to be made, or sufferings to be borne. In the ranks, and through all the grades of command, our Church testifies her loyalty by the devotion of her sons. Many of them are her choice young men, whom it is hard to spare from works of Christian well-doing at home. Many of them are her Sunday-school teachers. They have gone to her armies, not in any bitterness of feeling toward those who have brought on us this war, but in a ready mind to love their enemies and to do good to those who hate them, as well as out of a well-considered and conscientious conviction of duty to their Country, to their Government, and to God. They look to us, their chief Pastors, especially as we are now gathered together here, to give them the support and comfort of our approbation, if we think they have rightly judged the great question of duty to the Government in the present struggle. Amidst the perils of battle, in hospitals and prisons, under privations and wounds, they feel the preciousness of such comfort. Acknowledging the reasonableness of such desires, we have pleasure in complying with them; not apprehending that in touching on this subject it can with reason be objected that we enter amidst questions with which, as Ministers of Him whose "kingdom is not of this world," we have nothing to do. Whatever the Apostles of Christ were inspired by the Holy Ghost to teach the Church; the Ministers and Stewards of that Church are bound to illustrate and enforce, for instruction of her members. "All Scripture is profitable for doctrine, reproof, correction, and instruction in righteousness." Whatever is contained therein is part of what has thus been "written for our learning"—part of that spiritual provision which you, brethren, are to "read, mark, learn, and inwardly digest;" and which, therefore, God's Stewards must distribute, as varying circumstances shall make it "a word in season."

Then what say the Scriptures touching the subject before us? We have no need to go beyond the words of St. Paul, in the thirteenth chapter of the Epistle to the Romans—"Let every soul be subject to the higher powers. For there is no power but of God. The powers that be are ordained of God. Whosoever, therefore, resisteth the power, resisteth the ordinance of God; and they that resist shall receive to themselves damnation."

Now, it is the application of these words to our duties, under present circumstances, of which we have need to inquire, if we would use this portion of Scripture as "a light to our feet." Where, then, do we find those powers and ordinances to which, as "ordained of God," we, recognizing the great truth that "there is no power but of God," are bound, for His Sake, to be subject? We answer, IN THE CONSTITUTION AND GOVERNMENT OF THE UNITED STATES. Under them, the people of all the States, now resisting them, were just as much bound to render obedience, when such resistance began, as we, whose allegiance is still unbroken. According to the Scriptures, that resistance, so far from making null and void those powers, is a resistance to ordinances of

162

God still in force; and, therefore, brings His condemnation on those so engaged.

. . . .

The reasons which make this so great a crime are the same which make the constituted authority so indispensable to the very existence of human society. God has invested the magistrate with power, and given him the sword to be borne, "not in vain," because he is His Minister *"for good;"* because, without him, all the floods of ungodliness would be set free; and the only remedy remaining for all social disorders would be that of force overcoming force, and of cunning overreaching cunning.

We have now, brethren, in strict confinement to the testimony of the Scriptures, ascertained a basis of principle and duty on which we may heartily rejoice in all the active and energetic loyalty with which the members of our Churches in union with their fellow-citizens, of all classes and conditions, are sustaining the Government in its vast efforts to reinstate the rightful control of its laws, wherever they have been disowned. We bid them never to be weary of that well-doing; and particularly would we say to those who, out of love to their country, and not out of any vindictive exasperation towards her enemies, have gone in our armies, *be of good cheer!* Whatever the dangers you may have to meet, or sufferings to endure, let it be your consolation that you have gone to sustain the power, ordained of God, and which rightfully claims your most devoted loyalty.

And now, we can ask your further attention only to a few concluding words, touching great spiritual interests, which the absorbing claims and the strong excitements of these times endanger. No doubt, dear brethren, you have all been painfully conscious of the powerful tendency of the present anxieties and excitements to draw down your thoughts and affections from daily communion with God; to elevate earthly interests and duties into injurious rivalry with those of the soul and eternity; to carry your minds away on this powerful flood of feeling and active concern for your beloved country, till they become, in a great degree, separated from all earnest engagedness in God's service. With some minds, under divine grace, the tendency of these troubles is to lead them nearer to God; while with others it is to take them away from God, to make His Word less precious, His holy day less sacredly kept, secret prayer less faithfully observed, and less their refuge and consolation; Christian example less decided and exalted.

We desire affectionately to exhort you to increased watchfulness and prayer in consequence of such danger. Let not love of Country make your love to God and your gracious Saviour the less fervent. Immense as is this present earthly interest, it is only earthly. The infinitely greater interests of the soul and of the kingdom of God remain as paramount as ever. We counsel, not that you feel less concern for the former, but that you seek God's grace so to sanctify all its anxieties that it may constantly lead you to Him for refuge, and rest, and peace; making you only the more earnest to secure, in exchange for this sinful and troublesome world, that inheritance which is incorruptible, that better country where "sorrow and sighing flee away."

And we also charge you, brethren, that you watch and pray, lest during this unhappy strife you should allow any bitterness of spirit to dwell in you toward those who, from whatever cause, have brought on us this war, with its great injuries and calamities, or who are now waging it against us. To hate rebellion, so uncaused, is duty; but to hate those engaged therein, is the opposite of Christian duty. Nothing can release us from the charge of our blessed Lord to love even our greatest enemies; do good to them that hate us, and pray for such as despitefully use us and persecute us. In this temper of mind let us be followers of Him who, when *we* were enemies, died for us.

House of Bishops, *Pastoral Letter, 1862*, 3-5, 7-9, 10-12. (Bound with other pamphlets in the Archives of the University of the South). (Excerpt)

38.

Pastoral Letter of House of Bishops, Protestant Episcopal Church in the Confederate States of America, November 22, 1862

The first preliminary meeting of the dioceses of the Confederate States was at Montgomery, Alabama, July 3-6, 1861. The second preliminary meeting was held at Columbia, South Carolina, October 16-24, 1861, and the constitution of the Protestant Episcopal Church in the Confederate States of America was adopted. The First General Council of the PECCSA met November 12-22, 1862, at Augusta, Georgia. Stephen Elliott of Georgia was the Presiding Bishop. This pastoral letter describes the missionary challenge facing the Episcopal Church in the Confederacy.

At your request, brethren of the Clergy and Laity, we conclude the session of our First General Council by presenting to you and reading in your presence a Pastoral Letter, addressed to the members of the Protestant Episcopal Church scattered throughout the Confederate States. By the mighty power of the Holy Ghost we have been permitted to bring our deliberations to a close in a spirit of harmony and peace which augurs well for the future welfare of our branch of the Church Catholic; and our first duty is to thank Him who has promised to be with His Church to the end of the world, for His presence with us during our consultations, and for the happy conclusion to which He has brought our sacred labors.

Seldom has any Council assembled in the Church of Christ under circumstances needing His presence more urgently than this which is now about to submit its conclusions to the judgment of the Universal Church. Forced by the providence of God to separate ourselves from the Protestant Episcopal Church in the United States,—a Church with whose doctrine, discipline and worship we are in entire harmony, and with whose action, up to the time of that separation, we were abundantly satisfied—at a moment when civil strife had dipped its foot in blood, and cruel war was desolating our homes and firesides, we required a double measure of grace to preserve the accustomed moderation of the Church in the arrangement of our organic law, in the adjustment of our code of canons, but above all, in the preservation, without change, of those rich treasures of doctrine and worship which have come to us enshrined in our Book of Common Prayer. Cut off likewise from all communication with our sister Churches of the world, we have been compelled to act without any interchange of opinion even with our Mother Church, and alone and unaided to arrange for ourselves the organization under which we should do our part in carrying on to their consummation the purposes of God in Christ Jesus. We trust that the Spirit of Christ has indeed so directed, sanctified and governed us in our work, that we shall be approved by all those who love our Lord Jesus Christ in sincerity and in truth, and who are earnest in preparing the world for His coming in glorious majesty to judge both the quick and the dead.

The Constitution of the Protestant Episcopal Church in the Confederate States, under which we have been exercising our legislative functions, is the same as that of the Church from which we have been providentially separated, save that we have introduced into it a germ of expansion which was wanting in the old constitution. This is found in the permission which is granted to existing Dioceses to form themselves by subdivision into Provinces, and by this process gradually to reduce our immense Dioceses into Episcopal Sees, more like those which, in primitive times, covered the territories of the Roman Empire. It is at present but a germ, and may lie, for many years, without expansion, but being there, it gives promise, in the future, of a more close and constant Episcopal supervision than is possible under our present arrangement.

The Canon law, which has been adopted during our present session, is altogether in its spirit, and almost in its letter, identical with that under which we have hitherto prospered. We have simplified it in some respects, and have made it more clear and plain in many of its requirements; but no changes have been introduced which have altered either its tone or character. It is the same moderate, just and equal body of Ecclesiastical Law by which the Church has been governed on this continent since her reception from the Church of England of the treasures of an apostolic ministry and a liturgical form of worship.

The Prayer Book we have left untouched in every particular save where a change of our civil government and the formation of a new nation have made alteration essentially requisite. Three words comprise all the amendment which has been deemed necessary in the present emergency, for we have felt unwilling, in the existing confusion of affairs, to lay rash hands upon a Book, consecrated by the use of ages, and hallowed by associations the most sacred and precious. We give you back your Book of Common Prayer the same as you have entrusted it to us, believing that if it has slight defects, their removal had better be the gradual work of experience than the hasty action of a body convened almost upon the outskirts of a camp.

Besides this actual legislation which we now submit to you, our assembling together has given us a view of the condition of the Church throughout the Confederate States which renders it our duty to speak to you as Chief Pastors over the flock of Christ, reminding you of the peculiar encouragements which surround us, specifying the points towards which our efforts, as a Christian Church, should be directed, and pointing out the deficiencies which require instant correction and amendment. No moment seems so propitious for the performance of this duty, as that in which we are beginning a new life in the Church, and are preparing to stamp ourselves upon the world for good or for evil.

Our highest encouragement is derived from the fact that we hold the sacred trust of the Faith once delivered to the saints, and that we hold it in connexion with a ministry whose succession from Christ and His Apostles is undoubted, and with a form of worship simple and pure yet sublime and scriptural. These are not gifts to make a boast of, but to use for the glory of God and the advancement of Christ's kingdom. Far from filling us with vain glory, their possession should humble us to the dust, unless we approve ourselves faithful stewards of such inestimable treasures. To whom much has been committed, from him will much be required, and it remains for us to prove whether we have deserved so spiritual an inheritance. But possessing them, we may rightfully feel that we enter upon our warfare with the world, the flesh and the devil, having all the strength that Divine Truth and a Divine Commission can give us. We can press on without any doubts resting upon our hearts as to the truth which we are teaching, as to the validity of the sacraments which we are administering, or as to the authority of the orders which we are transmitting. Upon all these points we are secure, and we can go forward offering to all men, with boldness and confidence, the gospel of our Lord Jesus Christ and the fellowship of the saints. Whatever hindrances we may meet, or whatever contradiction of men we may encounter, we can rest assured that truth will finally prevail, and that God will set His Son upon His holy hill of Zion.

Our next next source of encouragement is that we enter upon our work with our Dioceses fully organized, and with the means which Christ has instituted in His Church well distributed throughout the Confederate States. When we remember the very different auspices under which the venerated Fathers of the American Church began their work, and mark how It has grown and prospered, we should indeed take courage and feel no fear for the future. In their case all their ecclesiastical arrangements had to be organized; in our case we find these arrangements all ready to our hand, and with the seal of a happy experience stamped upon them. In their case every prejudice of the land was strong against them. In our case we go forward with the leading minds of our new Republic cheering us on by their communion with us, and with no prejudications to overcome, save those which arise from a lack of acquaintance with our doctrine and worship. In their case they were indeed few and separated far from one another in their work upon the walls of Zion. In our case we are comparatively well compacted, extending in an unbroken chain of Dioceses from the Potomac to the confines of the Republic. Despite all these disadvantages, "the little one became a thousand and the small one a strong nation," and shall we despond? If we be watchful, and strengthen the things that remain, our God will not forsake us, but will "lengthen our cords and stretch forth the curtains of our habitations." In visible token of this fact, we have already, since our organization, added to the House of Bishops the Rt. Rev. Dr. Wilmer as Bishop of Alabama, and received into communion with the Church the Diocese of Arkansas.

Another source of encouragement is that there has been no division in the Church in the Confederate States. Believing, with a wonderful unanimity, that the providence of God had guided our footsteps, and for His own inscrutable purposes, had forced us into a separate organization, there has been nothing to embarrass us in the preliminary movements which have conducted us to our present position. With one mind and with one heart we have entered upon this blessed work, and we stand together this day a band of brothers, one in faith, one in hope, one in charity. There may be among us, as there always must be, minute differences of opinion and feeling, but there is nothing to hinder our keeping the unity of the spirit in the bond of peace. We are all satisfied that we are walking in the path of duty, and, that the light of God's countenance has been wonderfully lifted up upon us. He has comforted us in our darkest hours, and has not permitted our hearts to faint in the day of adversity.

These striking encouragements vouchsafed to us from the Father of our Lord

Jesus Christ, should lead us even now to inquire, "Lord, what wilt thou have us to do?" And the answer to this question will lead us, your Chief Pastors, to specify the points towards which our efforts, as a Christian Church, should be especially directed.

Christ has founded His Church upon love—for God is Love. It is the highest of all Christian graces. "And now abideth Faith, Hope, Charity, these three, but the greatest of these is Charity." Charity! not mere alms-giving, which is only one of its manifestations, but Love! Christian Love! As Christ our Lord loved the world so divinely that he was satisfied to suffer all things for its redemption, so does He command us to love one another and to be ready to do all things for each other's salvation. This was His especial commandment: "A new commandment give I unto you, that ye love one another." And this is truly not only the new commandment, but the summary of all the commandments. The whole Gospel is redolent with it, with a broad, comprehensive, all-embracing love, appointed, like Aaron's rod, to swallow up all the other Christian graces, and to manifest the spiritual glory of God in Christ. A Church without love! What could you augur of a Church of God without Faith, or a Church of Christ without Hope? But Love is a higher grace than either Faith or Hope, and its absence from a Church is just the absence of the very life-blood from the body.

Our first duty, therefore, as the children of God, is to send forth from this Council our greetings of love to the Churches of God all the world over. We greet them in Christ, and rejoice that they are partakers with us of all the grace which is treasured up in Him. We lay down to-day before the altar of the Crucified all our burdens of sin, and offer our prayers for the Church Militant upon earth. Whatever may be their aspect towards us politically, we cannot forget that they rejoice with us "in the one Lord, the one Faith, the one Baptism, the one God, and Father of all," and we wish them Godspeed in all the sacred ministries of the Church. Nothing but love is consonant with the exhibition of Christ's love which is manifested in His Church, and any note of man's bitterness, except against sin, would be a sound of discord mingling with the sweet harmonies of earth and heaven. We rejoice in this golden chord which binds us together in Christ our Redeemer, and like the ladder which Jacob saw in vision, with the angels of God ascending and descending upon it, may it ever be the channel along which shall flash the Christian greetings of the children of God.

But while we send forth this love to the whole Church militant upon earth, let us not forget that special love is due by us towards those of our own household. To us have been committed the treasures of the Church, and those of our own kindred and lineage, who have sprung from our loins both naturally and spiritually, who are now united with us in a sacred conflict for the dearest rights of man, ask us for the bread of life. They pray us for that which we are commanded to give, the Gospel of the grace of God. They put in no claim for any thing worldly—for any thing alien from the mission of the Church. Their petition is that we will fulfil the very purpose of our institution, and give them the means of grace. Every claim which man can have upon his fellow-man they have upon us, and having these claims they ask only for the Church. They pray us not to let them perish in the wilderness; not to permit them to be cut off from the sweet communion of the Church. "If," says the Apostle, speaking of christian professors, and alluding to mere earthly things, "any provide not for his own, and especially for them of his own House, he hath denied the faith, and is worse than an infidel;" what shall we say of that Church which shall not provide for its own children? How can it hope to be watered itself with gracious rain from Heaven, when it hoards up for itself the river of life, which is ordained to flow through its channels of grace?

Many States of this Confederacy are Missionary ground. The population is sparse and scattered; the children of the Church are few and far between; the Priests of the Lord can reach them only after great labor and privation. Hitherto has their scanty subsistence been eked out from the common treasury of our united Church. Cut off from that recourse by our political action, in which they have heartily acquiesced, they turn to us and pray us to do at least as much for them, as we have been accustomed to do for the Church from which they have been separated by a civil necessity. We can do what they ask, and we ought cheerfully to do it. Unless we take care that the Gospel is sent to these isolated children of the Church, who will heed their cry? They have no Church to cry to, but the Church which we now represent, and they cast themselves upon us in full faith, that we will do our whole duty towards them. They are one with us in faith, in care, in suffering; they are bearing like evils with those which disturb us, and they have no worship to cheer and support them, no Gospel to preach to them patience and long-suffering. For Christ's sake they pray that they may be given at least a Mother's bosom to die upon.

Voices of supplication come to us also from the distant shores of Africa and the East, but only their echo reaches us from the throne of grace. The policy of man has shut out those utterances from us. How it can help their cause to separate the children of God from one another, He only knows, but we can hear them when we kneel in prayer, and commune with their Spirits through the Spirit of Christ. But God is perchance intending, through these inscrutable measures, to shut us up to that great work which He has placed at our very doors, and which is, next to her own expansion, the Church's greatest work in these Confederate States. The religious instruction of the negroes has been thrust upon us in such a wonderful manner that we must be blind not to perceive that not only our spiritual but our national life is wrapped up in their welfare. With them we stand or fall, and God will not permit us to be separated in interest or in fortune.

The time has come when the Church should press more urgently than she has hitherto done upon her laity, the solemn fact, that the slaves of the South are not merely so much property, but are a sacred trust committed to us, as a people, to be prepared for the work which God may have for them to do, in the future. While under this tutelage He freely gives to us their labor, but expects us to give back to them that religious and moral instruction which is to elevate them in the scale of Being. And while inculcating this truth, the Church must offer more freely her ministrations for their benefit and improvement. Her laity must set the example of readiness to fulfil their duty towards these people, and her clergy must strip themselves of pride and fastidiousness and indolence, and rush, with the zeal of martyrs, to this labor of love. The teachings of the Church are those which best suit a people passing from ignorance to civilization, because while it represses all fanaticism, it fastens upon the memory the great facts of our religion, and through its objective worship attracts and enchains them. So far from relaxing, in their case, the forms of the Church, good will be permanently done to them just in proportion as we teach them through their senses and their affections. If subjected to the teachings of a bald spiritualism, they will find food for their senses and their child-like fancies in superstitious observances of their own, leading too often to crime and licentiousness.

It is likewise the duty of the Church to press upon the masters of the country their obligation, as Christian men, so to arrange this institution as not to necessitate the violation of those sacred relations which God has created and which man cannot, consistently with Christian duty, annul. The systems of labor which prevail in Europe and which are, in many respects, more severe than ours, are so arranged as to prevent all necessity for the separation of parents and children and of husbands and wives, and a very little care upon our part, would rid the system upon which we are about to plant our national life, of these unchristian features. It belongs, especially, to the Episcopal Church to urge a proper teaching upon this subject, for in her fold and in her congregations are found a very large proportion of the great slaveholders of the country. We rejoice to be enabled to say that the public sentiment is rapidly becoming sound upon this subject, and that the Legislatures of several of the Confederate States have already taken steps towards this consummation. Hitherto have we been hindered by the pressure of abolitionism; now that we have thrown off from us that hateful and infidel pestilence, we should prove to the world that we are faithful to our trust and the Church should lead the hosts of the Lord in this work of justice and of mercy.

Another duty, which, for the present, devolves upon the Church, is an oversight of the children of God, as they lie without religion and without Christian care in the camps and hospitals of our Government. Far be it from us to say that there has been no Christian supervision of our soldiers, and we cheerfully concede all praise and thanks to those who have done their duty through danger and privation; but we must affirm that there is still a great lack of service on the Church's part in this connexion. From whatever cause it has arisen, whether from the scarcity of clergymen, or from unwillingness to bear the hardships of the soldiers' life, we are obliged to acknowledge that we have been unable to find men who were willing to answer this call and to take their places, not as soldiers fighting for their country, but as soldiers fighting for the victory of Christ over sin and death. In the opinion of the House of Bishops, no position is more suited, at this moment, to the true spirit of Christ and His Church, than that of a faithful minister of the grace of God and of the Sacraments of the Church to the soldiers in the field, or in the hospital; and we would urge it upon those ministers who have been exiled from their parishes, to enter upon this work as their present duty, trusting for support to Him who has said, "I will never leave thee nor forsake thee."

The most striking deficiency in the Church's work which we perceive in looking at the Church's life, is a lack of zeal in spreading the influences of the Church through her services and Sacraments. Our ministry has become too local and sedentary, too well satisfied to sit down and do the work which it has undertaken to do, and overlooking the fields white for the harvest which are spread out all around them, and which cannot be cultivated save through their agency. Every well established congregation should consider itself as a centre of Missionary work, and should encourage its pastor to extend his usefulness beyond its own limits, and while he is a Priest to them, to be, in some measure a Missionary to all about him. As long as the selfish idea is indulged, that a minister is tied down to a local congregation and has no business to work around him, the Church must languish or increase but slowly. Missionaries cannot be furnished for every village and neighborhood, and they must remain uncared for by the Church, unless the settled clergy will make up their minds to extend the sphere of their operations beyond the narrow limits of their own immediate cures.

Another deficiency which requires amendment, is the little spiritual intercourse which takes place among the Clergy in their work for the Church. Each man works in his sphere, but for the most part he gives nothing to his brother clergyman, and receives nothing from him in return. When our Lord sent forth his Apostles, He sent them two by two for the evident purpose that they should support, strengthen and comfort each other. The spirit of this action is very much overlooked in the Church, and the Clergy are weakened by it. While the House of Bishops would not specify any mode by which this defect should be remedied, it would recommend to the Clergy a more free, spiritual intercourse, a more frequent interchange of clerical services, greater communion in prayer and in counsel. Many a despondent heart would thus be cheered, and many a weak brother would be comforted and strengthened.

Another deficiency which requires amendment, is the little spiritual help which is given to the Clergy by the Laity. We have no reference now to the temporal support of the Clergy, although we might well dwell upon that, but to the spiritual help which a Christian Laity might give to the Clergy. In reading the Acts of the Apostles, we find many illustrations of this truth, and we perceive how the greatest of the Apostles was not above the help of his yoke-fellows in the Gospel. There are many ways in which spiritual and earnest Laymen can help their Clergy in the work of the Church, and under their guidance and direction, can become valuable Missionaries of Christ, even while unordained. It requires sacrifice and self-denial, but we must all remember that we are not our own, but are bought with a price, and belong to Christ, body, soul and spirit.

But over and above all these special deficiencies, looms up that greatest of all deficiencies, the lack of the Holy Spirit in and with our Churches. Because of the degree to which spiritual influences have been abused in our land, we have been tempted to run into the other extreme, and to forget that we are living under what the Apostle calls the dispensation of the Spirit, and that the Church's work must derive all its power from His presence. Our danger is to merge the Holy Ghost into the means of grace, and overlook the important fact that He is a personal agent, acting indeed through those means, but not necessarily tied to them. Our Saviour said: "The wind bloweth where it listeth, and thou hearest the sound thereof, but canst not tell whence it cometh or whither it goeth, so is every one that is born of the Spirit." And as with the individual, so with the Church. The Holy Spirit will be in the Church, if His presence is kept there by an acknowledgement of His power, by a sense of His necessity, by a constant prayer for His presence; but the addresses to the Churches in Asia Minor instruct us to be watchful over ourselves, and to hold fast by Him, who is the representative of Christ upon earth, while He is interceding and advocating for us in Heaven. Let the Church and her Ministers always bear in mind, that the growth of the Church, and the vitality of the Church are "not by might, nor by power, but by my Spirit," saith the Lord.

And now it only remains for us to bid you, one and all, an affectionate farewell. We cannot but remember that when we last separated from you, there stood among us two venerated brethren, dearly beloved in the Lord, who have since entered into their rest. When we parted we knew it must be so, but we could not foresee where the hand of Death would fall. And now again we know, that separating once more for the like space of time, we shall not all meet again. Whose shall be the summons? Well for us that the curtain of God's providence hides this knowledge from us, teaching us the lesson of Christian truth, that we must all watch and be sober, because we know neither the day nor the hour when the Son of Man cometh. May God's gracious Providence guide you in safety to your homes, and preserve them from the desolations of war. And should we not be permitted to battle together any more for Christ in the Church militant, may we be deemed worthy to be members of the Church triumphant, where with prophets, apostles, martyrs, saints and angels, we may ascribe honor and glory, dominion and praise to Him that sitteth upon the Throne, and to the Lamb, forever!

William A. Clebsch, ed., *Journals of the Protestant Episcopal Church in the Confederate States of America: Centenary Edition in Facsimile* (Austin, Texas: Church Historical Society, 1962): III-219–III-231.

39.

William Porcher DuBose,
"War Experiences"

William Porcher DuBose (April 11, 1836–August 18, 1918) graduated from the Military College of South Carolina in 1855, and was an officer and chaplain in the Confederate Army, 1861-1865. Later he became the first chaplain at The University of the South, Sewanee, Tennessee, and the second dean of its School of Theology. DuBose's ministry and theological contributions are commemorated in the Episcopal Calendar of the Church Year on August 18. This narrative provides a personal account of the experience of defeat by a Confederate Army officer.

FOUR years of my educational life—from sixteen to twenty—had been spent in military training. In the Military College I had held the highest offices in my class, and had had some experience in discipline and drill. Soon after the breaking out of the war in 1861 the Governor of South Carolina called for the organization, for State defence, the protection of our coast line and railroad connections, of a command to which he gave the name of the Holcombe Legion. It was to consist of a regiment of infantry and a battalion each of cavalry and artillery; the superintendent of the State Military College was to organize and command it, and I was appointed his adjutant. The appointment found me in the middle year of my seminary course; I accepted it and spent the following fall and winter in hard drill and discipline, in skirmishing with gunboats, and in the occasional more romantic experiences of camp life. We were soon mustered out of State into Confederate service, and the battles around Richmond necessitating a general concentration in Virginia, the legion as such was dismembered, and the infantry regiment, still under the same name, was incorporated into the Army of Northern Virginia, under General Lee. General McClellan's advance upon Richmond having been effectually disposed of, we began moving, about the middle of August, to meet the new army advancing from Washington under General Pope. After several preliminary engagements, in one of which I was painfully hurt, though not disabled, by a fragment from a shrapnel shell, the terrible battle of Second Manassas, or Second Bull Run, was fought on August 30. It was a great victory, but a bloody one, and our own brigade was wellnigh destroyed. My horse was shot, I was twice wounded, and I was the only field officer of the legion who was left or able to fight through the battle. It devolved upon me to reorganize the shattered regiment and to command it in the first Maryland invasion, which immediately ensued.

Two weeks after the great battle we made a forced march back from Hagerstown to Boonesboro Gap, to delay the passage across South Mountain of the third great Federal Army of that year, 1862, now again under General McClellan. General Lee needed the time to unite his two army corps for the approaching great battle of Sharpsburg or Antietam. On the fourteenth of September we barely succeeded in preventing the crossing that day. Our own command had had a fatiguing march of sixteen miles, had climbed the mountain on the north side, had fought and been forced back into the gap, and at about 9 P.M. had sunk dead with sleep in their tracks upon the turnpike. Out of this condition I was aroused by the command to take my most available men and to connect with and extend the picket line on the side of the mountain on which we had fought. This was no easy task on a dark night in the primeval forest, and it must have been toward midnight before it was accomplished. I had just spread my oil-cloth at the centre of the line and was wondering how I, or any of us, could manage to keep awake, when another order came: it was thought that the mountain above us was abandoned and the enemy withdrawn, and it was necessary to ascertain his movements. I was to ascend to the spot of the afternoon's engagement, discover, and report. It was a heavy and, unavoidably, a noisy as well as dangerous climb; and at the steepest point near the summit I left the men in position to obey any summons and proceeded alone. Upon the plateau on top I lightly and swiftly pushed my reconnoissance to the farthest limit, and seeing and hearing nothing, was in the act of returning satisfied that there was no one there, when it came to me that, to be perfectly certain, I ought to make a detour around the plateau. In this way it came about that I quite encircled a division of troops and walked straight into their lines. Walking back, in half security but very quietly and cautiously, with pistol in hand, I was suddenly brought up with a "Halt!" I could not be sure that it was not some of my own men come to meet me, nor they that I was not one of theirs,—and so it was that we were actually upon each other before we mutually recognized each other as enemies: I had come upon a sentry of two men in the midst of a bivouac, and the woods were as sunk in sleep and stillness as if there were no life in them. A man stood before me with the butt of his gun upon the ground. As he jerked up his gun I stepped quite up to him and drew the pistol which I had held cocked under a light cloak. In the act of both doing this and protecting myself from him, my pistol was discharged prematurely, and he, thinking himself shot, cried aloud and precipitated himself upon me. In an instant the mountain top was awake and alive, and I was upon the ground in the midst, in a desperate struggle for escape. The odds were against me, and I landed not many days later a prisoner in Fort Delaware.

Many years later a reference to that night's adventure and excitement appeared in the history of some Northern troops. The friends of a faithful and deserving old soldier from Pennsylvania made my capture the ground for an application for pension, and I was requested to further his claim. After getting from him his side of the story of our momentous encounter, I gave him my testimony and he got his pension. From that time on I occasionally received letters from Cronin expressing the desire to meet me again, and saying that he could not die happy without doing so. To my utter surprise, thirty-five years at least after our first meeting, our second took place at Sewanee. He suddenly appeared there, ill and travel-worn, having made the journey across several States to see me again before he died. He said I had come near killing him, and he had come nearer killing me; for when I had twice almost got away, he had at last, being of twice my strength, got me down, and then, with my own pistol, was in the act of shooting, when some mysterious force had held his hand and prevented him. He made me sit down and write for him an account of our two encounters in war and in peace, and then as mysteriously made his disappearance.

. . . .

It is said that life is lived only in our supreme moments. What of final impress or character I was to receive from the stern and unsparing discipline of war, was to be focussed and fixed in one such supreme experience. The brigade to which I was attached toward the close of the war was one which had been in every battle of the Army of Northern Virginia, and whose boast it was that it had never slept behind a field of battle. A time came at last when, through no fault of its own, a glorious victory of the morning was converted into a disgraceful rout in the afternoon, and that night the brigade slept some ten or fifteen miles behind its field of battle. When we finally rested about midnight, I could not sleep; the end of the world was upon me as completely as upon the Romans when the barbarians had overrun them. Never once before had dawned upon me the possibility of final defeat for the Confederate cause. That night it came over me like a shock of death that the Confederacy was beginning to break: the strain even of unbroken victory had been too long and too heavy: it would be impossible much longer to resist the force of the ever-renewed and ever-increasing pressure of new armies and inexhaustible resources. To represent the true spirit of our ranks I must add that there was quick reaction from that depression, and that when the real end did come some months later, I was almost as much surprised and shocked as I had been in that presentiment or prevision of it. But not really as much,—the actual issue was all upon me that fateful night in which, under the stars, alone upon the planet, without home or country or any earthly interest or object before me, my very world at an end, I redevoted myself wholly and only to God, and to the work and life of His Kingdom, whatever and wherever that might be.

William Porcher DuBose, *Turning Points in my Life* (New York: Longmans, Green, and Company, 1912), 33-38, 48-50. (Excerpts)

40.

Morgan Dix, A Sermon Preached in St. Paul's Chapel, Trinity Parish, New York, October 29, 1865

On April 9, 1865, General Robert E. Lee surrendered to General Ulysses S. Grant at Appomattox Courthouse, Virginia. The twenty-eighth General Convention met at Philadelphia, October 4-24, 1865. Presiding Bishop John Henry Hopkins wrote the Southern bishops to assure them of a cordial welcome. Richard Hooker Wilmer's consecration as Bishop of Alabama on March 6, 1862, by three Southern bishops was ratified, and the testimonials of Charles Todd Quintard, who had been elected Bishop of Tennessee on September 7, 1865, were accepted. This sermon by Morgan Dix celebrates the reunification of the church.

Psalm 46:5.—"God is in the midst of her: therefore shall she not be removed."
THESE words were uttered through the influence of that spirit of prophecy

which dwelt in holy men of old; so that, although they seemed, to those who first sang them or heard them sung, to apply to the ancient Church in the land of Judah, they referred, with equal clearness and directness, albeit so distantly, to the Catholic Church which was to succeed it. When we say them, or sing them, we think of her, the great Mother of many nations; and since every greater contains the lesser, we may apply them to any family of that Universal House of the Faithful, and express, in doing so, our gratitude for mercies shown to it, and our faith in the purpose and the promise of the Lord, as special providences seem to make them clear.

It will probably cause no surprise, if I speak to you to-day upon a subject on which, for three or four weeks past, our hearts and minds have felt much and thought much. The Triennial Council of our branch of the Church has closed its sessions since we last looked each other in the face. The work is completed, the task is done; the duty has been fulfilled, and the record is closed. Its acts have passed into history; and time shall show us whether they were wisely wrought. But this is, happily, a case in which a man may so far anticipate the verdict, as to allow himself to rejoice greatly in the things which he has seen, and thank Almighty GOD, and take courage. There are certain great principles of the doctrine of Christ, about which we can entertain no doubt, certain truths concerning the Kingdom of GOD, as to which we feel assurance; and when we hear those truths asserted, and observe those principles in active development as vital and energetic forces, we feel that GOD is in the midst of us, and are sure that greater glory is coming to Him, and that new salvation and deliverance are visiting His people. Among those truths and principles the following may be enumerated: that the Church should be one; that her law is the law of love; that her creed must be sound, and her ministry duly commissioned; that her light must be held up to the nations a clear, a warm, a steady flame; that her people must be reverent, humble, devout, zealous of good works. It is not premature to bless the Lord, when, having passed through a very trying crisis, we find no one of those principles impaired or weakened, but on the contrary every one, in a marvellous order, declared, enforced, and illustrated anew, as has been the case, thank GOD, during the sessions of that Council, henceforth to rank as one of the most memorable in the history of our beloved branch of Christ's Church, the General Convention of 1865.

Men looked forward to the assembling of that convention with great anxiety; they accompanied it with prayers that never ceased. The Reverend President of the House of Deputies said, in his address on the morning of the 5th day, "Most of us came in fear and apprehension." There was cause. The storm of war is over, but the great waves have not yet subsided; no one could tell what damage they might do. The leading religious denominations of this country had failed to resume their interrupted relations; political bitterness had proved more powerful that sectarian affinity, and Discord, still wearing the bloody garments of the past, and uttering the cries of party, ran between the divided ranks and drove them further and wider asunder. Were the scenes, the sounds, presented in and heard from those completely secularized bodies, to be reproduced among us? Could the North and the South meet together in peace? the North without offensive condescension, the South without the consciousness of humiliation? Could every thing be forgotten save this, that we are all one in Christ Jesus? Could subjects foreign to the Church be excluded from her Councils? Could men come together, and, still retaining their self-respect, say, in their official acts, not one word of the past? Could that spirit, which glories in the triumph of the warrior, and courts popularity by deliverances of themes extraneous to the Catholic Creeds and cognate to the order of the State, be quieted and stilled, if it should once arise in the midst? Could the temper of individualism, which plunges all things into confusion, be made to submit to that moral and intellectual habit by which the man is lost in the society which has formed him? Such were the questions which arose in many minds, which, unanswered, were referred to GOD in many a holy prayer. "I have looked," says the same Reverend person who was mentioned before, "to the present session of this Convention with intense anxiety." What he said of himself, was not less true of multitudes besides; they thought that the time had come in which many points would be settled, and among them this: whether the Protestant Episcopal Church in the United States is merely one of the loose denominations of the day, driven of the wind like them and tossed, or whether she is henceforth to wear, as hers beyond dispute, the venerable garments of a true and real member of the Catholic Church, whose voice is not as the voices of this world, and whose business is with men only so far as their citizenship is in heaven. Did ever questions more momentous hang in the balance of uncertainty?

They began to be answered the first day. When the Convention assembled in St. Luke's Church, for the opening service, one of the southern Bishops was there. He came alone, and took a seat among the congregation: he looked like a stranger. That was a sight which his brethren in the Apostolic Episcopate could not bear. They saw him; they became uneasy. At last they sent a dignified messenger to tell him that he must come to them. Then he hesitated no longer; he arose, and just as he was, with no vestment or robe of office, passed up to the chancel and went to his brethren. I was told that there was not a dry eye in that august company at that moment. Men felt that GOD was giving answer to the question whether this Church could be one again.

When the Convention assembled for business, the diocese of Texas, with a representation of both orders, answered to the roll-call. Before it adjourned, several other dioceses of the South had their delegates there.

Thus the breach, as the world of the ungodly called it, was fast closing up. Then came two of those test questions, which in the mode of their answer, sweep off at once a hundred side-issues and settle a thousand minor difficulties forever. The first was the question about the Bishopric of Tennessee. That Diocese had sent a priest to Philadelphia as its Bishop Elect; a godly and learned man, but one who had been most intimately connected with the revolted States, and with their military operations, as a chaplain in their army. How many points would be settled in his acceptance, or his rejection? Rejected he could not be, he was not. Accepted, and welcomed as few have ever been, he was consecrated on the 6th day of the session, in presence of an overwhelming congregation of clergy and laity, and with circumstances designed to show the significance of the act. Then, the next day, when the hearts of men were softened as by the dew of Hermon which fell upon the hill of Zion, came the second question and the last; that of the reception of the Bishop of Alabama. He was consecrated some two years ago, in the midst of the war, by Southern Bishops, by men who thought the disruption of the Nation a final one, and the rebellion a success. He was consecrated a Bishop of the Protestant Episcopal Church in the "Confederate States;" he belonged to us no more than a Bishop of the Church of England, or Scotland. Should he be received? If so, on what terms? Must not this man be required to make some act of abjuration, to sign some pledge of allegiance to the Government, to speak some confession of penitence acknowledging the error of his ways? Must he not, in the popular phrase of the day, "give evidence that he had repented him of his sins"? Not so thought the Council of the Church. Their idea was, "Let Cæsar look to the things that are Cæsar's; we legislate only for the Church of God." It was my privilege to be at the place where that tremendous question was brought up, and present when it was answered. The scene can never be forgotten by any who viewed it. After two days of earnest debate, they knelt in silent prayer; the stillness seemed almost supernatural. Then they arose, and, by their vote, said: "Let the Bishop of Alabama send full evidence that he has been duly consecrated into the office which we doubt not that he possesses; and let him send, in writing, and properly certified, that promise of conformity to the doctrine, discipline, and worship of the Church, which every Bishop takes among us, and we ask no more." It seemed as though the Lord had arisen and said, "Peace be to this house and to all that are therein." If any man had previously doubted concerning the reunion of the Church, he cast, at that moment, every doubt away.

Brethren, our Church has never been divided. Our enemies said that it was, but they were wrong. The storm of war deranged for a time our means of intercourse, and thereby necessarily suspended our rules of canonical action; but the life and the heart were one. If it had been GOD'S will that the rebellion had passed into a successful revolution, and that the Confederate States had become a nation, the Church would still have been one; no human power could have kept us apart. We should have been more closely allied with each other than we are with the Church of England: somehow we should have come together. How much more must it be so now? The Confederate States have ceased to exist; the causes of interruption to our intercourse are removed; we are one again. After what has occurred, no one can with truth affirm that the Episcopal Church has known a schism. We trust in the Lord for the future, as we trusted in Him in the past. The Church has never been divided. Let those who long for Catholic Unity bear that in mind.

Morgan Dix, *A Sermon Preached in St. Paul's Chapel, Trinity Parish, New York, on the Twentieth Sunday After Trinity, October 29, 1865* (New York: James Pott, 1865), 3-7. (Excerpt)

CHAPTER SIX

The Episcopal Church and
the Issues of Emancipation (1808-1907)

Introduction

There were Southern Episcopalians (including bishops) who were slave owners. Some offered a biblical justification for this practice, and were committed to christianizing the slaves. Some Episcopalians in the North, such as Phillips Brooks, were outspoken advocates for emancipation of the slaves. Other Episcopalians did not take a stand on the issue of slavery. After the end of the Civil War, the Episcopal Church faced the question how to minister to the newly emancipated blacks in the United States. The possibilities of separate jurisdictions or black suffragan bishops for work with blacks were considered and ultimately rejected. The Episcopal Church's official policy called for full integration of blacks into the life of the church. Unfortunately, the policy was far from reality.

41.

Absalom Jones, A Thanksgiving Sermon, January 1, 1808

Absalom Jones (November 6, 1746–February 13, 1818) was born in slavery in Sussex, Delaware, and was taken to Philadelphia in 1762, where he worked and purchased his freedom and that of his wife. He and the Rev. Richard Allen organized the Free African Society, which later organized the "African Church of Philadelphia." In October 1794 it was admitted into the Diocese of Pennsylvania as St. Thomas African Episcopal Church. Bishop William White ordained Jones a deacon on August 23, 1795, and a priest on September 21,

1802, the first Black ordained to these ministries. Jones is remembered on the Episcopal Calendar on February 13. This sermon was preached at St. Thomas Church on January 1, 1808, in thanksgiving for the abolition of the African slave trade.

> And the Lord said, I have surely seen the affliction of my peo-
> ple which are in Egypt, and have heard their cry by reason of
> their taskmasters; for I know their sorrows, and I am come
> down to deliver them out of the hand of the Egyptians. . . .
>
> (Ex. 3:7-8)

These words, my brethren, contain a short account of some of the circumstances which preceded the deliverance of the children of Israel from their captivity and bondage in Egypt.

They mention, in the first place, their *affliction*. This consisted in their privation of liberty; they were slaves to the kings of Egypt, in common with their other subjects, and they were slaves to their fellow slaves. They were compelled to work in the open air, in one of the hottest climates in the world, and probably, without a covering from the burning rays of the sun. Their work was of a laborious kind; it consisted of making bricks, and travelling, perhaps to a great distance, for the straw, or stubble, that was a component part of them. Their work was dealt out to them in tasks, and performed under the eye of vigilant and rigorous masters, who constantly upbraided them with idleness. The least deficiency, in the produce of their labour, was punished by beating. Nor was this all. Their food was of the cheapest kind, and contained but little nourishment; it consisted only of leeks and onions, which grew almost spontaneously in the land of Egypt. Painful and distressing as these sufferings were, they constituted the smallest part of their misery. While the fields resounded with their cries in the day, their huts and hamlets were vocal at night with their lamentations over their sons, who were dragged from the arms of their mothers, and put to death by drowning, in order to prevent such an increase in their population, as to endanger the safety of the state by an insurrection. In this condition, thus degraded and oppressed, they passed nearly four hundred years. Who can conceive of the measure of their sufferings during that time? What tongue, or pen, can compute the number of their sorrows? To them no morning or evening sun ever disclosed a single charm; to them, the beauties of spring, and the plenty of autumn had no attractions; even domestic endearments were scarcely known to them; all was misery, all was grief, all was despair.

Our text mentions, in the second place, that in this situation, they were not forgotten by the God of their fathers, and the Father of the human race. Though, for wise reasons, he delayed to appear in their behalf for several hundred years;

yet he was not indifferent to their sufferings. Our text tells us, that he saw their affliction, and heard their cry; his eye and his ear were constantly open to their complaint; every tear they shed was preserved, and every groan they uttered was recorded, in order to testify, at a future day, against the authors of their oppression. But our text goes further. It describes the Judge of the world to be so much moved, with what he saw and what he heard, that he rises from his throne—not to issue a command to the armies of angels that surrounded him to fly to the relief of his suffering children—but to come down from heaven, in his own person, in order to deliver them out of the hands of the Egyptians. Glory to God for this precious record of his power and goodness; let all the nations of the earth praise him. *Clouds and darkness are round about him, but righteousness and judgement are the habitation of his throne. O sing unto the Lord a new song, for he hath done marvellous things; his right hand and his holy arm hath gotten him the victory. He hath remembered his mercy and truth toward the house of Israel, and all the ends of the earth shall see the salvation of God*

The history of the world shows us, that the deliverance of the children of Israel from their bondage, is not the only instance in which it has pleased God to appear in behalf of oppressed and distressed nations, as the deliverer of the innocent, and of those who call upon his name. He is as unchangeable in his nature and character, as he is in his wisdom and power. The great and blessed event, which we have this day met to celebrate, is a striking proof that the God of heaven and earth is the *same, yesterday, and to-day, and for ever.* Yes, my brethren, the nations from which most of us have descended, and the country in which some of us were born, have been visited by the tender mercy of the Common Father of the human race. He has seen the affliction of our countrymen, with an eye of pity. He has seen the wicked arts, by which wars have been fomented among the different tribes of the Africans, in order to procure captives, for the purpose of selling them for slaves. He has seen ships fitted out from different ports in Europe and America, and freighted with trinkets to be exchanged for the bodies and souls of men. He has seen the anguish which has taken place, when parents have been torn from their children, and children from their parents, and conveyed, with their hands and feet bound in fetters, on board of ships prepared to receive them. He has seen them thrust in crowds into the holds of those ships, where many of them have perished from want of air. He has seen such of them as have escaped from that noxious place of confinement, leap into the ocean, with a faint hope of swimming back to their native shore, or a determination to seek an early retreat from their impending misery, in a watery grave. He has seen them exposed for sale, like horses and cattle, upon the wharves; or, like bales of goods, in warehouses of West Indian and American sea ports. He has seen the pangs of separation between members of the same family. He has seen them driven into the sugar, the rice, and the tobacco fields, and compelled to work—in spite of the habits of ease which they derived from the natural fertility of their own country in the open air, beneath a burning sun, with scarcely as much clothing upon them as modesty required. He has seen them faint beneath the pressure of their labours. He has seen them return to their smoky huts in the evening, with nothing to satisfy their hunger but a scanty allowance of roots, and these, cultivated for themselves, on that day only, which God ordained as a day of rest for man and beast. He has seen the neglect with which their masters have treated their immortal souls; not only in withholding religious instruction from them but, in some instances, depriving them of access to the means of obtaining it. He has seen all the different modes of torture, by means of the ship, the screw, the pincers, and the red-hot iron, which have been executed upon their bodies by inhuman overseers.

Overseers, did I say? Yes, but not by these only. Our God has seen masters and mistresses, educated in fashionable life, sometimes take the instruments of torture into their own hands, and deaf to the cries and shrieks of their agonizing slaves, exceed even their overseers in cruelty. Inhuman wretches! though you have been deaf to their cries and shrieks, they have been heard in Heaven. The ears of Jehovah have been constantly open to them; he has heard the prayers that have ascended from the hearts of his people, and he has, as in the case of his ancient and chosen people the Jews, *come down to deliver* our suffering countrymen from the hands of their oppressors. He *came down* into the United States, when they declared, in the constitution which they framed in 1788, that the trade in our African fellow-men would cease in the year 1808; *he came down* into the British Parliament when they passed a law to put an end to the same iniquitous trade in May, 1807; *he came down* into the Congress of the United States, the last winter, when they passed a similar law, the operation of which commences on this happy day. Dear land of our ancestors! thou shalt no more be stained with the blood of thy children, shed by British and American hands; the ocean shall no more afford a refuge to their bodies, from impending slavery; nor shall the shores of the British West India island, and of the United States, any more witness the anguish of families, parted forever by a public sale. For this signal interposition of the God of mercies, in behalf of our brethren, it becomes us this day to offer up our united thanks. Let the song of angels, which was first heard in the air at the birth of our Saviour, be heard this day in our assembly. *Glory to God in the highest, for these first fruits of peace upon earth, and good will to man.* O! let us give thanks unto the Lord, let us call upon his name, and make known his deeds among the people. Let us sing psalms unto him and talk of all his wondrous works.

Having enumerated the mercies of God to our nation, it becomes us to ask,

What shall we render unto the Lord for them? Sacrifice and burnt offerings are no longer pleasing to him; the pomp of public worship, and the ceremonies of a festive day, will find no acceptance with him unless they are accompanied with actions that correspond with them. The duties which are inculcated upon us, by the event we are now celebrating, divide themselves into five heads.

In the first place, let not our expressions of gratitude to God for his late goodness and mercy to our countrymen be confined to this day, nor to this house; let us carry grateful hearts with us to our places of abode, and to our daily occupations, and let praise and thanksgiving ascend daily to the throne of grace, in our families, and in our closets for what God has done for our African brethren. Let us not forget to praise him for his mercies to such of our colour as are inhabitants of this country, particularly for disposing the hearts of the rulers of many of the states to pass laws for the abolition of slavery, for the number and zeal of the friends he has raised up to plead our cause, and for the privileges we enjoy, of worshipping God, agreeable to our consciences, in churches of our own. This comely building, erected chiefly by the generosity of our friends, is a monument of God's goodness to us, and calls for our gratitude with all the other blessings that have been mentioned.

Secondly, let us unite, with our thanksgiving, prayer to Almighty God, for the completion of his begun goodness to our brethren in Africa. Let us beseech him to extend to all the nations in Europe, the same humane and just spirit towards them which he has imparted to the British and American nations. Let us, further, implore the influence of his divine and holy Spirit, to dispose the hearts of our legislatures to pass laws, to ameliorate the condition of our brethren who are still in bondage; also, to dispose their masters to treat them with kindness and humanity; and, above all things, to favour them with the means of acquiring such parts of human knowledge, as will enable them to read the holy scriptures, and understand the doctrine of the Christian religion, whereby they may become, even while they are the slaves of men, the freemen of the Lord.

Thirdly, let us conduct ourselves in such a manner as to furnish no cause of regret to the deliverers of our nation, for their kindness to us. Let us constantly *remember the rock whence we were hewn, and the pit whence we were digged. Pride was not made for man,* in any situation, and, still less, for persons who have recently emerged from bondage. The Jews, after they entered the promised land, were commanded, when they offered sacrifices to the Lord, never to forget their humble origin, and hence, part of the worship that accompanied their sacrifices consisted in acknowledging that *a Syrian, ready to perish, was their father;* in a like manner, it becomes us, publicly and privately, to acknowledge that an African slave, ready to perish, was our father or our grandfather. Let our conduct be regulated by the precepts of the gospel; let us be sober minded, humble, peaceable, temperate in our meats and drinks, frugal in our apparel and in the furniture of our houses, industrious in our occupations, just in all our dealings, and ever-ready to honour all men. Let us teach our children the rudiments of the English language, in order to enable them to acquire a knowledge of useful trades, and above all things, let us instruct them in the principles of the gospel of Jesus Christ, whereby they may become *wise unto salvation.* It has always been a mystery, why the impartial Father of the human race should have permitted the transportation of so many millions of our fellow creatures to this country, to endure all the miseries of slavery. Perhaps his design was that a knowledge of the gospel might be acquired by some of their descendants, in order that they might become qualified to be the messengers of it, to the land of their fathers. *Let* this thought animate us, when we are teaching our children to love and adore the name of our Redeemer. Who knows but that a Joseph may rise up among them, who shall be the instrument of feeding the African nations with the bread of life, and of saving them, not from earthly bondage, but from the more galling yoke of sin and Satan.

Fourthly, let us be grateful to our benefactors, who, by enlightening the minds of the rulers of the earth, by means of their publications and remonstrances against the trade in our countrymen, have produced the great event we are this day celebrating. Abolition societies and individuals have equal claims to our gratitude. It would be difficult to mention the names of any of our benefactors, without offending many whom we do not know. Some of them are gone to heaven, to receive the reward of their labours of love toward us; and the kindness and benevolence of the survivors, we hope, are recorded in the book of life, to be mentioned with honour when our *Lord* shall come to reward his faithful servants before an assembled world.

Fifthly, and lastly, let the first of January, the day of the abolition of the slave trade in our country, be set apart in every year, as a day of public thanksgiving for that mercy. Let the history of the sufferings of our brethren, and of their deliverance, descend by this means to our children, to the remotest generations; and when they shall ask, in time to come, saying, What mean the lessons, the psalms, the prayers and the praises in the worship of this day? Let us answer them by saying, the Lord, on the day of which this is the anniversary, abolished the trade which dragged your fathers from their native country, and sold them as bondmen in the United States of America.

Absalom Jones, "A Thanksgiving Sermon," in John M. Burgess, *Black Gospel/White Church* (New York: Seabury Press, 1982), 2-7.

42.

George W. Freeman, The Rights and Duties of Slave Holders, November 27, 1836

A number of Southern Episcopalians were slave owners. Many of them were committed to the evangelization of their Negro slaves. George Washington Freeman (June 13, 1789–April 29, 1858) was Missionary Bishop of Arkansas and the Indian Territory from October 26, 1844, until his death. He describes the rights and duties of slave owners.

[T]he class of duties towards our slaves, on which I would lay the greatest stress—and that the more especially, because there is reason to think them most frequently neglected, are those which have reference, not merely to their present well-being, but *to their future and everlasting happiness.*

And here, brethren, I have approached a subject, the contemplation of which, fills me with feelings of solemnity and awe—nay, almost overwhelms me with apprehension and dismay. When I look at it in all its bearings, I tremble for my countrymen, I tremble for Christian masters and mistresses throughout the land, I tremble for you, my hearers. Nay, looking into my own domestic relations, and beholding the fearful amount of responsibilities which there rests upon me, I tremble for myself. Have you, have I, have *any of us* "given"—to the full extent and meaning of the Apostle's precept, in respect to this, the most important of all their interests—*have we "given unto our servants that which is just and equal?"* Alas, alas! where is the man or woman? where is even the *Christian master* or the *Christian mistress*, who can say 'I have a conscience void of offence in this matter?' or, with the Apostle, *"I am pure from the blood of all men."*[1]

Brethren, let us seriously consider what *are* our responsibilities in reference to this subject. And first, let me ask, what is the relation in which we stand to our slaves, in respect to their condition as immortal and accountable beings, and our obligation to attend to their religious and spiritual culture, their training for the kingdom of heaven? Is it not a closer tie than that which binds us to our fellow-men in general? Undoubtedly it is. As Providence has placed them in a situation in which they are more immediately dependant upon us, so are we made *more directly responsible for their moral and religious improvement.* Our *children*, we all feel and acknowledge, have *decided claims* of this sort upon us. And in what respect, brethren, does the relation which we bear in this matter to our *children*, differ from that in which we stand to our *slaves*? They are both

---

[1] Acts, xx.26.

187

providentially placed under our protection. They are equally dependant upon us—equally subject to our authority—and they alike stand in need of our help and guidance in the all important concern of working out their salvation. If *we* coldly turn away from them, and sternly refuse them our help, *to whom can they go?* Who else on earth, holds in trust for them *"the words of eternal life?"* Our slaves, like our own offspring, are weak and helpless in themselves, and must, in the first instance at least, obtain support and direction from *us*, or be liable to wander in darkness, and to perish for lack of knowledge.

The conclusion, then, is obvious—*it cannot be avoided*. If we are in any measure responsible, as we are taught to believe we are, for the souls of our *children*, we must be, in at least an equal degree, *responsible for the souls of our slaves*. But we are actually *more* responsible for the latter. Our children, when they come to man's estate, leave the paternal roof, become their own masters, and take their station as independent members of society. We have no further actual authority or control over them, and our responsibility for them is, in a measure, at an end. But as for our *slaves*, their state of pupilage *never ceases*; they are *always* with us; they are *always* members of our families; they are *always* subject to our authority and control: and what is further and more to the point, though ever so far advanced in years, they are, from the very nature of their condition, *always children*; they are but children *in intellect*, children *in wisdom*, children *in understanding and judgement!*

Now then, if we consider what are our *acknowledged duties* in regard to the religious condition of our *children*, we shall at once understand what those are, which we owe to our *slaves*.

1. The first duty, brethren, which you as Christian parents feel yourselves called on to perform towards your children is, *to bring them into the Christian covenant by Baptism*. This you believe, and justly, to be *the very first step* towards a compliance with the Apostolic injunction to *"bring them up in the nurture and admonition of the Lord"*[2]—a step too, the omission of which, would involve you in no inconsiderable degree of criminality in the sight of God. Instructed by the reproving language of the Saviour, *"Suffer the little children to come unto me, and forbid them not,"* and his significant declaration, that *"of such is the kingdom of Heaven,"*[3] you are persuaded that your little ones *have a right* to be admitted to the privileges and blessings of the Christian covenant, and you cannot but strongly feel, *that what it is thus their privilege to enjoy, it is your bounden duty to help them to obtain.*

---

[2]Ephesians, vi.4.
[3]Mark, x.14.

188

But why, beloved brethren, are you bound to give this help to your own children, and not generally to the children of others? Is it not because you are their natural guardians, on whom they are wholly dependant, and to whom alone they have a right to look for help? Should an orphan child be providentially thrown upon you for protection, would not its claims and your obligation in this respect, be the same as in the case of your own offspring? Doubtless, you would so decide. And shall you not feel a similar obligation towards your slaves—especially their children? Is it *"just and equal,"* that you should claim the disposal of all their time, their labours, and their scanty talents here on earth, and yet, withhold the benefit of those blessed spiritual privileges, which they must, ordinarily acquire through you alone? If *you* are not bound to do that for them, which they (your slave *children* particularly) cannot do for themselves—to introduce them, as you take care to do your own offspring, to the blessings of the Christian covenant, and thus, to pave the way for their being *"brought up in the nurture and admonition of the Lord"*—*if you, their masters and mistresses are not under obligation to do this, who is?* Will you refer me to their natural parents as the persons on whom this duty rests? Alas, they are themselves, as we have seen, but *grown children*, needing to be guided at every step. And are they generally capable of comprehending and fulfilling the duties of sponsors? And if they had *the capacity*, are they responsible? Are they free agents? Have they the power or the means to dispose of, and to regulate, the time of their children, and to take care that they "be virtuously brought up to lead a godly and Christian life?" and especially, that having been duly "taught the creed, the Lord's prayer and the ten Commandments, and sufficiently instructed in the other parts of the Church Catechism," they "be brought at length to the Bishop to be confirmed by him?" And yet the obligation to do all this, *must*, according to the teachings of the Church, *rest somewhere.* Brethren, there can be but one answer to these questions; and God grant that the responses ready to burst from your lips may be echoed back upon your hearts and consciences, and produce such an impression there, as shall issue in the speedy commencement, and the faithful and persevering prosecution, of these your Christian duties!

But am I not urging upon you a new and hitherto unheard of course of duty? No, my brethren, I am but bringing again to light, that which was once well understood and uniformly practiced, both under the old and new dispensations; but which has, I regret to say, been greatly obscured, and, indeed, almost lost sight of, in this our day. When God laid the foundation of the Jewish Church, into which Circumcision was made the rite of initiation, as Baptism was, afterwards, that into the Christian Church, he commanded Abraham to administer the rite not only to his children and other dependants, but to his *slaves*; and accordingly, we read that *"all the men of his house, those born in this house, and those bought with money of the stranger were circumcised.*"[4] And this became, thenceforward, a law to the whole house of Israel—this continued to be the uniform practice of that people down to the end of their polity. So also, under the Gospel dispensation, the same rule was observed. When the heads of family were converted to the Christian Faith, we learn that both they and their *whole households* were invariably Baptised. And that many of these households consisted partly of *slaves*, is extremely probable, if not altogether certain. Such, we may well believe, were those of *Cornelius of Cesarea, of the Jailor at Phillippi, and of Lydia of Thyatira.* Indeed, that it was the ancient practice of the Christian Church, and that it was regarded as a high Christian duty to extend the privilege of Baptism, to *all the members of a family without distinction*, the heads of which were believers, may be fairly inferred from the fact, which we learn from history, that at an early period after Christianity became the Religion of the Empire, "there were laws of state, obliging *all masters* to take care of their families, so far as to see that *every individual person, slaves, as well as children were made Christians.*" "In default of this," it is added by the author whom I quote, "some penalties were annexed, depriving masters of certain privileges in the commonwealth, if they were found either remiss, or acting by collusion, in this part of their duty. So that all imaginable obligation was laid upon masters, both in point of interest, duty and charity, *to take care of the instruction of their slaves, and bring them with their own testimonials to Christian Baptism.*"[5]

2. But in addition to this *first step* in your duty to your children—*the bringing of them within the gracious covenant of the Gospel, by Baptism*—as Christian parents, you are bound *to instruct them also in the doctrines, principles and duties of Religion*; to endeavor to bring them up under its benign influences, and in such a manner as may lead them to be mindful of the "profession" represented unto them by their Baptism, and ready to "follow the example of their Saviour Christ, and to be made like unto him." That such *is* your duty, there is, I trust, no need that I should go in search of proof. You all, with one accord, admit the obligation. And if you have any proper sense of the value of your children's souls, when you think of your responsibility for them, you feel that your willful neglect of this duty, would bring down upon you a weight of guilt and condemnation, too heavy to be borne.

But here again, let me ask you to consider, whether this obligation does not, in like manner, extend to the *religious instruction of your slaves. Have they* not

---

[4]Genesis, xvii.27.
[5]Bingham's Antiquities, b. xi. ch. v. §. 4.

immortal souls as well as your *children?*—souls which must be saved or lost forever? Partaking of the corruption and sinfulness common to our nature, are they not as liable to perish for lack of religious culture, as your own offspring? And if *they should* thus perish, *through your neglect*, where, I ask, will the guilt of their blood lie?

George W. Freeman, *The Rights and Duties of Slave Holders: Two Discourses Delivered on Sunday, November 27, 1836, in Christ Church, Raleigh, North Carolina* (Charleston: The Protestant Episcopal Society for the Advancement of Christianity in South Carolina, 1837), 29-35. (Excerpt)

43.

John Henry Hopkins, Bible View of Slavery, January 1861

John Henry Hopkins (January 30, 1792–January 9, 1868) was consecrated the first Bishop of Vermont on October 31, 1832. He was the eighth Presiding Bishop from January 13, 1865, until his death. This essay expresses his opposition to the abolitionist movement. He believed that the Scriptures and tradition did not condemn slavery.

The word "slave" occurs but twice in our English Bible, but the term "servant," commonly employed by our translators, has the meaning of *slave* in the Hebrew and the Greek originals, as a general rule, where it stands alone. We read, however, in many places, of "hired servants," and of "bondmen and bondmaids." The first were not slaves, but the others were; the distinction being precisely the same which exists in our own day. Slavery, therefore, may be defined as *servitude for life, descending to the offspring.* And this kind of bondage appears to have existed as an established institution in all the ages of our world, by the universal evidence of history, whether sacred or profane.

Thus understood, I shall not oppose the prevalent idea that slavery is an evil in itself. A *physical* evil it may be, but this does not satisfy the judgment of its more zealous adversaries, since they contend that it is a *moral* evil—a positive *sin* to hold a human being in bondage, under any circumstances whatever, unless as a punishment inflicted on crimes, for the safety of the community.

Here, therefore, lies the true aspect of the controversy, and it is evident that it can openly be settled by the Bible. For every Christian is bound to assent to the rule of the inspired Apostle, that "sin is the transgression of the law," namely,

191

the law laid down in the Scriptures by the authority of God—the supreme "Lawgiver, who is able to save and to destroy." From his Word there can be no appeal. No rebellion can be so atrocious in his sight as that which dares to rise against his government. No blasphemy can be more unpardonable than that which imputes sin or moral evil to the decrees of the eternal Judge, who is alone perfect in wisdom, in knowledge, and in love.

. . . .

The first appearance of slavery in the Bible is the wonderful prediction of the patriarch Noah: "Cursed be Canaan, a *servant of servants* shall he be to his brethren. Blessed be the Lord God of Shem, and Canaan *shall be his servant.* God shall enlarge Japheth, and he shall dwell in the tents of Shem, and Canaan *shall be his servant.*" (Gen. 9:25.)

The heartless irreverence which Ham, the father of Canaan, displayed toward his eminent parent, whose piety had just saved him from the deluge, presented the immediate *occasion* for this remarkable prophesy; but the actual *fulfillment* was reserved for his posterity, after they had lost the knowledge of God, and become utterly polluted by the abominations of heathen idolatry. The Almighty, foreseeing this total degradation of the race, ordained them to servitude or slavery under the descendants of Shem and Japheth, doubtless because *he judged it to be their fittest condition.* And all history proves how accurately the prediction has been accomplished, even to the present day.

We come next to the proof that slavery was sanctioned by the Deity in the case of Abraham, whose three hundred and eighteen bond-servants, born in his own house, (Gen. 14:14), are mentioned along with those who were *bought with his money*, as proper subjects for circumcision. (Gen. 17:12.) His wife Sarah had also an Egyptian slave, named Hagar, who fled from her severity. And "the angel of the Lord" commanded the fugitive to *return to her mistress and submit herself.* (Gen. 16:9.) If the philanthropists of our age, who profess to believe the Bible, had been willing to take the counsel of that angel for their guide, it would have preserved the peace and welfare of the Union.

The third proof that slavery was authorized by the Almighty occurs in the last of the Ten Commandments, delivered from Mount Sinai, and universally acknowledged by Jews and Christians as THE MORAL LAW: "Thou shalt not covet thy neighbor's wife, nor his *man-servant, nor his maid-servant*, nor his ox, nor his ass, nor any thing that is thy neighbor's." (Exod. 20:17.) Here it is evident that the principle of *property*—"any thing that is thy neighbor's"—runs through the whole. I am quite aware, indeed, of the prejudice which many good people entertain against the idea of *property* in a human being, and shall consider it, in due time, amongst the objections. I am equally aware that the wives of

192

our day may take umbrage at the law which places them in the same sentence with the slave, and even with the house and the cattle. But the truth is nonetheless certain. The husband has a real *property* in the wife, because she is bound, for life, to serve and to obey him. The wife has a real *property* in her husband, because he is bound, for life, to cherish and maintain her. The *character* of property is doubtless modified by its design. But whatever, whether person or thing, the law *appropriates* to an individual, becomes of necessity his *property*.

The fourth proof, however, is yet more express, as it is derived from the direct rule established by the wisdom of God for his chosen people, Israel, on the very point in question, viz.:

"If thou buy a Hebrew servant, six years shall he serve and in the seventh year he shall go out free for nothing. If he came in by himself, he shall go out by himself. If he were married, then his wife shall go out with him. If his master have given him a wife, and she have borne him sons or daughters, *the wife and the children shall be her master's, and he shall go out by himself.*" (Exod. 21:2-4.) Here we see that the separation of husband and wife is positively directed by the divine command, in order to secure the property of the master in his bondmaid and her offspring. But the husband had an alternative, if he preferred slavery to separation. For thus the law of God proceeds: "if the servant shall plainly say, I love my master, my wife, and my children; I will not go out free; then his master shall bring him unto the judges; he shall also bring him to the door or unto the door post; and his master shall bore his ear through with an awl, and *he shall serve him forever.*" (Exod. 21:5, 6.) With this law before his eyes, what Christian can believe that the Almighty attached immorality or sin to the condition of slavery?

John Henry Hopkins, *A Scriptural, Ecclesiastical, and Historical View Of Slavery, from the Days of the Patriarch Abraham to the Nineteenth Century* (New York: W. I. Pooley & Co., 1864), 5-9. (Excerpt)

44.

Phillips Brooks, "Abraham Lincoln," April 23, 1865

Phillips Brooks (December 13, 1835–January 23, 1893) was an opponent of slavery and a great admirer of President Abraham Lincoln. He preached this sermon to praise Lincoln and condemn slavery. Brooks was rector of the Church of the Holy Trinity, Philadelphia, when he preached this sermon. It is one of his great sermons. He is commemorated in the Episcopal Calendar of the Church Year on January 23.

Abraham Lincoln was the type-man of the country, but not of the whole country. This character which we have been trying to describe was the character of an American under the discipline of freedom. There was another American character which had been developed under the influence of slavery. There was no one American character embracing the land. There were two characters, with impulses of irrepressible and deadly conflict. This citizen whom we have been honoring and praising represented one. The whole great scheme with which he was ultimately brought in conflict, and which has finally killed him, represented the other. Beside this nature, true and fresh and new, there was another nature, false and effete and old. The one nature found itself in a new world, and set itself to discover the new ways for the new duties that were given it. The other nature, full of the false pride of blood, set itself to reproduce in a new world the institutions and the spirit of the old, to build anew the structure of the feudalism which had been corrupt in its own day, and which had been left far behind by the advancing conscience and needs of the progressing race. The one nature magnified labor, the other nature depreciated and despised it. The one honored the laborer, and the other scorned him. The one was simple and direct; the other, complex, full of sophistries and self-excuses. The one was free to look all that claimed to be truth in the face, and separate the error from the truth that might be in it; the other did not dare to investigate, because its own established prides and systems were dearer to it than the truth itself, and so even truth went about in it doing the work of error. The one was ready to state broad principles, of the brotherhood of man, the universal fatherhood and justice of God, however imperfectly it might realize them in practice; the other denied even the principles, and so dug deep and laid below its special sins the broad foundation of a consistent, acknowledged sinfulness. In a word, one nature was full of the influences of Freedom, the other nature was full of the influences of Slavery.

In general, these two regions of our national life were separated by a geographical boundary. One was the spirit of the North, the other was the spirit of the South. But the Southern nature was by no means all a Southern thing. There it had an organized, established form, a certain definite, established institution about which it clustered. Here, lacking advantage, it lived in less expressive ways and so lived more weakly. There, there was the horrible sacrament of slavery, the outward and visible sign round which the inward and spiritual temper gathered and kept itself alive. But who doubts that among us the spirit of slavery lived and thrived? Its formal existence had been swept away from one State after another, partly on conscientious, partly on economical grounds, but its spirit was here, in every sympathy that Northern winds carried to the listening ear of the Southern slaveholder, and in every oppression of the weak by the strong, every proud assumption of idleness over labor which echoed the music of Southern life back to us. Here in our midst lived that worse and false nature, side by side with the true and better nature which God meant should be the nature of Americans, and of which he was shaping out the type and champion in his chosen David of the sheepfold.

Here then we have the two. The history of our country for many years is the history of how these two elements of American life approached collision. They wrought their separate reactions on each other. Men debate and quarrel even now about the rise of Northern Abolitionism, about whether the Northern Abolitionists were right or wrong, whether they did harm or good. How vain the quarrel is! It was inevitable. It was inevitable in the nature of things that two such natures living here together should be set violently against each other. It is inevitable, till man be far more unfeeling and untrue to his convictions than he has always been, that a great wrong asserting itself vehemently should arouse to no less vehement assertion the opposing right. The only wonder is that so few were swept away to take by an impulse they could not resist their stand of hatred to the wicked institution. The only wonder is, that only one brave, reckless man came forth to cast himself, almost single-handed, with a hopeless hope, against the proud power that he hated, and trust to the influence of a soul marching on into the history of his countrymen to stir them to a vindication of the truth he loved. At any rate, whether the Abolitionists were wrong or right, there grew up about their violence, as there always will about the extremism of extreme reformers, a great mass of feeling, catching their spirit and asserting it firmly, though in more moderate degrees and methods. About the nucleus of Abolitionists grew up a great American Anti-Slavery determination, which at last gathered strength enough to take its stand to insist upon the checking and limiting the extension of the power of slavery, and to put the type-man, whom God had been preparing for the task, before the world, to do the work on which it had resolved. Then came discontent, secession, treason. The two American natures, long advancing to encounter, met at last, and a whole country, yet trembling with the shock, bears witness how terrible the meeting was.

Thus I have tried briefly to trace out the gradual course by which God brought the character which he designed to be the controlling character of this new world into distinct collision with the hostile character which it was to destroy and absorb, and set it in the person of its type-man in the seat of highest power. The character formed under the discipline of Freedom and the character formed under the discipline of Slavery developed all their difference and met in hostile conflict when this war began. Notice, it was not only in what he did and was towards the slave, it was in all he did and was everywhere that we accept Mr. Lincoln's character as the true result of our free life and institutions. Nowhere else could have come forth that genuine love of the people, which in him no one could suspect of being either the cheap flattery of the demagogue or the abstract philanthropy of the philosopher, which made our President, while he lived, the centre of a great household land, and when he died so cruelly, made every humblest household thrill with a sense of personal bereavement which the death of rulers is not apt to bring. Nowhere else than out of the life of freedom could have come that personal unselfishness and generosity which made so gracious a part of this good man's character. How many soldiers feel yet the pressure of a strong hand that clasped theirs once as they lay sick and weak in the dreary hospital! How many ears will never lose the thrill of some kind word he spoke—he who could speak so kindly to promise a kindness that always matched his word! How often he surprised the land with a clemency which made even those who questioned his policy love him the more for what they called his weakness,—seeing how the man in whom God had most embodied the discipline of Freedom not only could not be a slave, but could not be a tyrant! In the heartiness of his mirth and his enjoyment of simple joys; in the directness and shrewdness of perception which constituted his wit; in the untired, undiscouraged faith in human nature which he always kept; and perhaps above all in the plainness and quiet, unostentatious earnestness and independence of his religious life, in his humble love and trust of God—in all, it was a character such as only Freedom knows how to make.

Phillips Brooks, *Addresses* (Philadelphia: Henry Altemus, n.d.), 147-153. (Excerpt)

45.

An Account of a Conference Held at Sewanee, Tenn., July 25 to 28, 1883, on the Relation of the Church to the Coloured People

William Mercer Green (May 2, 1798–February 13, 1887) was the first Bishop of Mississippi. He was Chancellor of the University of the South from December 21, 1866, until February 13, 1887. On April 2, 1883, he invited the bishops and others of the southern dioceses to meet at Sewanee to discuss "the relation of the Church to the coloured people." The Sewanee Conference drafted a proposed canon to separate black Episcopalians into nongeographical racial dioceses. An account of the conference follows.

On the second day of April, 1883, the Right Rev. the Bishop of Mississippi addressed the following communication to all the Bishops of the Southern States:—

RIGHT REV. BISHOP OF————.

My Dear Brother,—Among the many subjects that may justly claim the consideration of our approaching General Convention will, doubtless, be that of the relations of our Church to the late slave population of our States, and the best means that can be adopted for their religious benefit.

As this subject seems to be awakening the serious attention of both the patriot and the Christian, North as well as South, it has been suggested to me, by several of our Bishops, that it would be well if all the Bishops of the late Slave States would meet in council, and after due consultation, agree upon some plan to be laid before our General Convention for the accomplishment of that purpose.

In accordance, therefore, with that wise and timely suggestion, I hereby invite and urge your attendance at the University of the South on the last Thursday in July (being the week preceding the Commencement), for the purpose of conferring with your brother Bishops on a matter of such vital importance to the welfare of our country and the salvation of a race perishing in the midst of us for the want of right instruction.

Let me hope that nothing may prevent you from being present; and that you will bring with you some one of your Clergy who, either from much experience in instructing the negro, or from a becoming interest in his behalf, may be qualified to aid us by his counsel.

Affectionately your brother in Christ,
W. M. GREEN, *Bishop of Mississippi*

On the 28th of May following, the Bishop of Mississippi addressed a further note to his brethren of the Episcopate in the Southern States, asking them to bring with them each one Layman, in addition to the Clergymen, as above proposed. . . .

On the night of the fourth day of the Conference, the committee submitted their report as follows—

REPORT OF THE COMMITTEE

The Committee to which were referred sundry resolutions and suggestions, bearing upon the work of the Church among the coloured people of the South, would respectfully report to the Conference, that after most careful consideration, it has with great unanimity arrived at the following conclusions, viz.:—

1. The Committee is profoundly impressed by the difficulties surrounding this subject of the work of the Church among the coloured people of the South, and would begin the report by this acknowledgment, that there are grave embarrassments attending each and all of the proposed methods for the accomplishment of the work which is undoubtedly imposed by the commandment of the Lord.

2. Your Committee believes that because of the Apostolic character of the Episcopal office, which has been received "always and everywhere and by all men;" because of the Ecclesiastical unity thereby maintained and exhibited, which may not be broken; and because of the truest welfare of all mankind,—there can be but one fold and one Chief Shepherd for all the people in any field of Ecclesiastical designation. But your Committee is of the opinion that because of the peculiarity of the relations of the two races, one to the other, in our country, because of their history in the past and the hopes of the future, there is needed special legislation, appointing special agency and method for the ingathering of these wandering sheep into the fold of Christ.

Therefore your Committee would report, that in its judgment it is entirely inexpedient, both on the grounds of Ecclesiastical polity, and also of a due consideration of the interests of all concerned, to establish any separate, independent Ecclesiastical organization for the coloured people dwelling within the territory of our constituted Jurisdictions. Yet your Committee would not be understood to determine the success of this meeting by the number of resolutions and proposals for amendments of Canons which it may adopt. Your Committee does not measure the success of this deeply interesting Conference so much by the change of the method of constitutional or canonical procedure, as by the deepening of religious fervour, by the more effective stirring up the grace that is in us, by more entire personal and parochial consecration to the work which the Providence of God has laid upon us, by the demonstration of sympathy and of our real belief in the brotherhood of all men in Christ.

Your Committee, therefore, begs leave to submit the following draught of a Canon to be presented to the approaching General Convention, and also a series of resolutions to be offered to the same body.

CANON
OF MISSIONARY ORGANIZATIONS WITH CONSTITUTED EPISCOPAL JURISDICTIONS

§ **i.** In any Diocese containing a large number of persons of colour, it shall be lawful for the Bishop and the Convention of the same to constitute such population into a special Missionary Organization under the charge of the Bishop.

§ **ii.** When such special Missionary Organization shall have been constituted in any Diocese, the Bishop shall annually appoint two or more Presbyters, and two or more Laymen, Communicants of this Church and members of the Diocese, as an Executive Committee to act as an advisory council to the Bishop in all matters pertaining to the interests of said Missionary Organization; and specially it shall be the duty of said Executive Committee to aid the Bishop in the establishment of Missions and schools, by seeking out suitable candidates for the Ministry, and providing for their maintenance during candidateship, and by the performance of such other duties as the Bishop shall assign. Such Committee shall continue in office until their successors are appointed.

§ iii. The Bishop, to aid him in the superintendence of such Missionary Organizations may, as expediency shall suggest, appoint one or more Presbyters as Archdeacons, who shall perform such duties as the Bishop may assign, and by authority of the Bishop may convene the Clergy and Laity of said Missionary Organization in Convocation for the purpose of furthering its work.

§ iv. Every Bishop within whose Diocese the aforesaid Missionary Organization may be constituted, if assisted or supported by the Board of Missions of the Church in the United States, shall report to each General Convention his proceedings, and the state of the Church in said Missionary Organization, and also shall make a report of the same once a year to the Board of Managers.

§ v. Congregations organized under the provisions of this Canon, and Ministers exercising their functions within such special Missionary Organizations, may be received into union with the Convention of the Diocese on such terms and by such process as are provided by the said Diocesan Convention. Until such reception into union with the Convention shall have been accomplished, it shall suffice if the names of the Clergy in such Missionary Organizations shall appear on a separate list to be delivered to the Secretary of the House of Deputies, as containing all the names of the Ministry of this Church in the special Missionary Organization, and that they be not placed on the Diocesan list as the basis of determining the Diocesan ratio of contingent expenses. . . .

Lastly, your Committee suggests that a committee, consisting of two Bishops, two Presbyters, and two Laymen, be appointed by the Chair, to lay the proceedings of this Conference before the coming General Convention, and to urge such action as is herein suggested.

(Signed)
WM. M. GREEN, *Bishop of Mississippi.*
ALEXANDER GREGG, *Bishop of Texas.*
C. F. ROBERTSON, *Bishop of Missouri.*

T. B. LYMAN, *Bishop of North Carolina.*

T. U. DUDLEY, *Assistant Bishop of Kentucky.*

HUGH MILLER THOMPSON, *Assistant Bishop of Mississippi.*

W. C. WILLIAMS, D.D., *Georgia.*

A. TOOMER PORTER, D.D., *South Carolina.*

GEO. C. HARRIS, D.D., *Mississippi.*

W. C. GRAY, D.D., *Tennessee.*

PIKE POWERS, D.D., *Virginia.*

L. N. WHITTLE, D.D., *Georgia.*

R. H. FOOTMAN, *Georgia.*

ALBERT T. McNEAL, *Tennessee.*

E. D. FARRAR, *Mississippi*

C. RICHARDSON MILES, *Mississippi.*

Committee.

The report was adopted. almost without debate, the Bishop of Alabama dissenting.

The following was ordered to be spread upon the minutes:—

"The Bishop of Alabama, whilst in cordial sympathy with the object of the above proposed canon, could not vote for it, because, in his opinion, it involves the idea of class legislation." . . .

WM. M. GREEN, *Bishop of Mississippi, Chairman.*

F. A. SHOUP, D.D., *Secretary*

Journal of General Convention, 1883, 595-600, passim.

46.

Richard Hooker Wilmer,
Contrary to the Mind of Christ, 1883

Richard Hooker Wilmer (March 15, 1816–June 14, 1900) was consecrated the second Bishop of Alabama on March 6, 1862, the only bishop consecrated by the Protestant Episcopal Church in the Confederate States. He was the only bishop at the Sewanee conference who did not support the proposed canon for a separate jurisdiction for black Episcopalians. This statement expresses his dissent from the conclusions of the Sewanee conference.

It introduced, needlessly, as I thought, the objectionable feature of class legislation. It is proposed to set off missionary organizations for the colored people, not on the ground of their incapacity and ignorance, but upon the ground of *color*. I say 'not on the ground of incapacity or ignorance,' for it is notorious that there are multitudes of white people in some of our States who, as it regards intelligence, education and manners, are not superior to the colored population and are *quite inferior* to that class of colored people who are prepared to enter the communion of this Church. If then a separate missionary organization be desirable for any of our people on the ground of their incapacity and ignorance—and that point is the one now to be determined—why is it not equally desirable for people of *all* colors?

Why then introduce the word 'colored,' except to draw in Church legislation the color-line and thus bring into operation a caste and class legislation—a hitherto unknown feature in Church legislation? This was, as I thought, the un-Catholic feature in the canon. For my own part, I saw no sufficient reason for any special legislation, and proposed to the Conference a resolution which embodies the sentiments of this present address. The resolution was as follows:

'Resolved, That in the judgment of the Bishops and other clergy and of the laity assembled to consider the relation of the Church to the colored population, it would be contrary to the mind of Christ, inconsistent with true Catholicity and detrimental to the best interest of all concerned, to provide any separate and independent organization or legislation for the peoples embraced within the communion of the Church.'

'Contrary to the mind of Christ, because containing the element of 'partiality' and 'respect of persons' in His Church which He purchased with His most precious blood. Christ was, when 'made man,' the manifestation to Universal Humanity of the Divine Fatherhood. In His body, the Church, there was no recognition of race, color, condition or estate. Barbarian, Scythian, bond or free, were one in him through His Incarnation. Thus, through Him, Our Lord, there was one faith, one baptism, one God and Father of all, above all through all and in them all.

'Inconsistent with true Catholicity,' because it legislated invidiously for a class, and thus introduced the element of caste into a 'Kingdom which is not of this world.'

'Detrimental to the interests of all concerned,' because it tends to throw off the one part, the least wise and capable, to themselves, thus depriving them of the fullness of privileges granted to others, and also depriving the other part of the body of the benefits which flow from the exercise of the graces of condescension and sympathy which can only find full scope in integral unity and union.

George F. Bragg, *History of the Afro-American Group of the Episcopal Church* (Baltimore: Church Advocate Press, 1922), 305-307.

47.

Report of Joint Committee on Memorial From Conference of Workers Among the Colored People, 1907

The Conference of Church Workers Among Colored People was organized at St. Philip's Church, New York, in reaction to the Sewanee Conference proposal to have nongeographical racial dioceses. It opposed the segregation of black Episcopalians and wanted them integrated into the Episcopal Church. This report to the General Convention of 1907 expresses the recommendations of the Joint Committee.

The Joint Committee, consisting of five Bishops, five Presbyters and five Laymen, appointed in 1904 to consider and report upon "A memorial to the General Convention of the Protestant Episcopal Church in the United States of America" from the Conference of Church Workers among the Colored People, have endeavored to fulfil the letter and spirit of the duty with which they were charged, and with the aid of the information which they have sought, have addressed themselves to the subject with labor and earnest deliberation.

They have likewise had before them the memorial from the Twenty-third Conference of Church Workers among the Colored People, assembled at Asbury Park, N.J., September 17-20, 1907, and the presentation made in person by the Committee from the last named Conference, together with a Memorial from the Diocese of Arkansas.

From our consideration of these memorials from the workers among the Colored People, and from the personal conference which we have had with their representatives, we would first recognize and bear testimony to the solicitude and anxiety manifested by them for the evangelization of their race, and we would further testify to the earnestness with which they have declared their loyalty and devotion to the Church's faith and order, and to the insistence with which they have urged their belief that the proposed plan will not lead to schism, but to "mutual good-will and hearty co-operation."

We regard it as important to recall attention to the fact that, while the adoption of the proposed canon on Special Missionary Bishops would enable Dioceses to seek the establishment of Special Missionary Districts and the appointment of Negro Bishops for the Negro race, and while the petitioners would necessarily expect the provisions of the Canon to be applicable to their race, still the Canon itself as proposed does not specifically name the Negro race,—and the view of the petitioners is to be interpreted as seeking to include other races in the benefits which they believe to be connected with the plan presented.

Approaching the memorial with this realization of the loyal spirit and the Missionary enthusiasm of the memorialists, and fully conscious both of the essential duty of the Church to press forward the work of evangelization and of the special conditions and problems which exist in connection with the Negro race, the Committee find themselves unable to recommend the adoption of the proposed Canon. Amongst the objections to be urged against its adoption is the fact that it traverses the prevailing usage and tradition of the Church which have associated jurisdiction with territory, and have held to an undivided Diocesan administration in the territorial jurisdiction over all the races which constitute the population.

Again, in relation to the Council of Advice to the Missionary Bishop which it is suggested shall be constituted of the Diocesan Bishops within the bounds of the contemplated Missionary District, it appears to our judgment that such a Council would be superfluous if it possessed no authoritative control, or that, if it did possess such authority, the Missionary Bishop so appointed would lack the independence which pertains to other Missionary Bishops. A dependent administration of this kind could only be a tentative plan, and bring segregation and racial cleavage without the satisfaction of thorough liberty and initiative.

Again, if the rights of a Missionary Bishop so appointed were actually to be identical with those of a Domestic Missionary Bishop, he would necessarily become eligible to election as a Diocesan Bishop; and there would arise the further complicating prospect of not only a Missionary District but a Diocese on lines of racial instead of territorial jurisdiction.

In view of the possibility that changing needs and conditions, or unsatisfactory results from the tentative plan itself, might justify and require the termination of such a Missionary District, it does not appear that the provisions of the proposed Canon touching a termination adequately protect the free action of the Church in the case of so radical a departure from its prevailing usage and tradition.

But beyond this consideration, in part, of the context of the measure presented, the Committee must emphasize other and most fundamental matters: The action which the petitioners earnestly request includes not only the subject of special Episcopal ministrations for a particular race, but also the subject of race segregation and race representation in ecclesiastical legislative assemblies separate from the Diocesan Convention and race representation in the General Convention, and they seek this action because they are dissatisfied with the representation now accorded their race in the Diocesan Conventions and because they believe that their proposed measure will meet their needs for representation, make for concord between the White and the Negro, supply incentive to the Negro to membership in the Episcopal Church, and promote the evangelization of their race. Over against this subdivision on race lines we place the ancient ideal of the Church for an ecclesiastical order in which men as Christians, and not as members of particular races, may co-operate for their moral and spiritual welfare, and for the advancement of the Kingdom of God amongst all mankind, and without sacrificing their essential political or social convictions; and whatever may be the present strain and problem in connection with the franchise in the legislative assemblies of the Church, we cannot counsel the abandonment of that ideal.

Legislation to establish race Missionary Districts would be a step farther in asserting that the races cannot co-operate in moral and spiritual matters, and race representation in the General Convention would tend to increase the demand for special race legislation and the concentration upon racial instead of general interests.

In view of the fact that changes of population may modify Diocesan conditions, and conduce towards the solution of the problem of representation, it is wiser to leave to Dioceses the provisions for special needs rather than for the General Convention to attempt to meet them by general laws in the direction of a new type of Missionary Districts.

Besides the foregoing considerations, the grave question arises as to whether, when the momentum towards ecclesiastical segregation is started, the impulse to separate self-government will not accumulate, and without any aim or desire of schism on the part of the originators of the plan work on to that result through racial pressure, or through new leaders whose realization of Churchly unity may be weakened in the school of partial autonomy.

The Committee having thus expressed their inability to recommend the adoption of the Canon, and without entering into the history of the successive demands and plans which have been presented in relation to the extension of the Church's work amongst the negroes—and which are matters of public knowledge—would ask whether, after all, the results of the Church's work amongst this race truly deserve to be called a failure, and whether these results in reality demonstrate the need of such radical experiments in organization. In raising this question we are thoroughly conscious of the obligation upon the Church to preach the Gospel to every creature; we realize that, when sufficient time has been allowed to the work, numerical results must enter into the judgment by which success or failure is to be estimated; and we know, as all Churchmen know, that the Church has activities and resources which must be consecrated in far vaster measure to this cause and the general missionary cause before its duty shall have been fulfilled.

But when the disparity between the total of the Negro population and the statistics of their membership in the Episcopal Church is pressed as a ground of discouragement, it is to be remembered that the Episcopal Church has consistently striven to fulfil a task of tremendous difficulty—the task of maintaining an undivided Church, the task of holding in an ecclesiastical unity two races in a time when social problems and political strife and change have made antagonism between the races, and when the Negroes have developed autonomous religious organizations in entire separation from the White race. The measure of its success in that task is to be weighed as a great achievement, whatever be the numerical results; and if the Christian men of both races can keep that Church bond unbroken, whatever be the problems of ecclesiastical franchise, the Christianity of the future, and probably also the country, will be the better for the allegiance and wisdom, the patience and self-control with which they have maintained a great truth. Without tabulating statistics and without seeking to minimize short-comings in this department of the Church's work, yet seeking that it be not underestimated, we submit that actual results indicate that further organization is not necessary save in the form of auxiliary Episcopal ministrations in those Dioceses which may need and wish to secure them.

If the expenditure of money is to be considered in the judgment as to whether results signify success or failure, attention is called to the fact that the appropriation for work amongst the colored people, which was originally $55,000, was increased to $75,000, and that for Cape Palmas, with 250,000 people, the appropriation is $52,000. In view of this disparity between the money expended and the magnitude of the Negro population in this country, the results do not point to inadequacy in our present organization, but to inadequacy of expenditure.

Returning to the hopeful outlook which the memorialists believe to exist in the establishment of a race Missionary District, it appears to us that there is peril lest the immediate need and benefit of ecclesiastical franchise be unduly magnified, lest emphasis grow upon it till the election by the race of their race Bishop be logically the final desire, and the problem of race jurisdiction instead of territorial jurisdiction be still further accentuated.

To seek a race Missionary District in order to escape from Diocesan disfranchisement would be to surrender, as far as the Diocese is concerned, the effort toward the ideal of an ecclesiastical unity and co-operation in which Church members stand on another basis than that of race; and surely the time has not come to abandon hope that the Church will be guided to some consummation in which these problems of franchise will be settled without division, and yet in which this legislative coordination will not signify that the Church is seeking to establish social equality or embroil itself in partisan politics. We point to the fact that representation in some Diocesan Conventions now stands on the basis of missions and parishes, and in others on a convocational basis; and remembering that Anglo-Saxon Churchmen have earned by centuries of toil and suffering the right to leadership in teaching and guarding the faith and order of the Church, we cannot but think that our Negro brethren will accept that leadership in the working out of the problem of Diocesan representation, which is beset with so many perplexing conditions. Cherishing true sympathy with their aspirations for the best development of their racial capacities, sharing with them the profound desire for the extension of the Church amongst their people, we yet press the need of making essential religion and education paramount to the possession of numerical equality in the ecclesiastical franchise.

Patience and wisdom and service are demanded alike of white and black in the process of solving this problem, and with minds and hearts fixed on preserving the unity of the Church, and in the spirit of service and even at the cost of sacrifice, let the Churchmen of both races steadfastly endeavor to avoid experiments in organization which may wreck that ideal, but go forward with a new fidelity to that ideal and a new obedience to the call of Him who is Saviour of the world, and genuinely make trial of our present organization, together with such auxiliary Episcopal ministrations as can be provided without separation into race jurisdiction.

To the Memorial from the Diocese of Arkansas, which has been referred to this Committee, we have given respectful attention. While we recognize the zeal which animates the memorialists for the welfare of the Negro race, and the careful study which they have given to the subject of ecclesiastical organization for the benefit of that race, we are unable to recommend the adoption of the resolution proposed. The grounds of objection to the plan there presented are stated in the general principles set forth in the body of this report. We believe that it would be contrary to the genius and tradition of the Church to segregate the African race in this country into a distinct and self-governing ecclesiastical system, and that such action would be the abandonment of our missionary responsibility and relation to that race, and would create division which would tend to schism.

We appeal for a more earnest, active and practical sympathy and support for the Church's work amongst the Colored People on the part of those who have heretofore expended their beneficence upon institutions not connected with the Church. We call upon the Church at large to sustain the Bishops and others responsible for this work, and we urge Churchmen to adopt such Diocesan methods, and if possible with some measure of uniformity, as may be found needful to preserve a proper oversight and yet adjust the problem of Diocesan representation on a just, peaceful and safe basis. We recommend in the direction of organization an auxiliary Episcopate in the Dioceses which may need this help for special racial conditions, and which may apply this agency, when secured on their initiative and request, to the service of any race which may require particular provision. In making this recommendation we beg to record our conviction and counsel that, in case this auxiliary Episcopate is instituted, both the Diocesan Bishop and the auxiliary Bishop should be protected with all due safeguards, and we further record our conviction of the fundamental importance of securing to the auxiliary Bishops seats in the House of Bishops. We present the following resolution:

Resolved, the House of Bishops concurring, That the following change be made in the Constitution, and that the proposed alteration be made known to several Diocese, in order that the same may be adopted in the next General Convention in accordance with Article XI. of the Constitution, as follows:

Insert in Article II. as Section 4 the following, and renumber the present Section 4:

It shall be lawful for a Diocese, with consent of the Bishop of that Diocese, to elect one or more Suffragan Bishops, without right of succession, and with seat and without vote in the House of Bishops. A Suffragan Bishop shall be consecrated and hold office under such conditions and limitations other than those provided in this Article as may be provided by Canons of the General Convention. He shall be eligible as Bishop or Bishop Coadjutor of a Diocese, or as a Suffragan in another Diocese, or he may be elected by the House of Bishops as a Missionary Bishop.

Respectfully submitted,

DAVIS SESSUMS,* *Chairman.*
THOMAS F. GAILOR,*
WM. N. McVICKAR.*
EDWIN S. LINES·*
J. R. WINCHESTER.
WM. R. HUNTINGTON.
LEWIS BROWN.
JOSEPH BRYAN.
B. L. WIGGINS.
G. A. ROCKWELL.
W. W. OLD.
JAMES McCONNELL.

*Consent to the general principles of the report, but would prefer another title than Suffragan, with vote in the House of Bishops.

Journal of General Convention, 1907, 518-522.

CHAPTER SEVEN
Building Bridges (1853-1895)

Introduction

William Muhlenberg's Memorial represented the beginning of significant ecumenical activity by the Episcopal Church. The memorial called for greater flexibility by the Episcopal Church in adapting the shape of ministry to the needs of local situations. William Reed Huntington's book *The Church Idea* provided the basis for ecumenical unity with other religious denominations. Four essentials for ecumenical unity were identified: the Old and New Testaments, the Nicene Creed, the sacraments of Baptism and Eucharist, and the historic episcopate. The Quadrilateral was approved at the 1886 General Convention in Chicago, and subsequently approved with minor modifications at the 1888 Lambeth Conference. Commitment to the historical episcopate has shaped the nature and scope of the Episcopal Church's ecumenical relationships.

48.

Muhlenburg Memorial, 1853

William Augustus Muhlenburg (September 16, 1796–April 8, 1877) was a great presbyter of the Episcopal Church. His life and ministry are commemorated in the Episcopal Calendar of the Church Year on April 8. This memorial, which he and others presented to the twenty-fourth General Convention at New York, October 5-26, 1853, suggested to the bishops that they make liturgical and canonical changes to work with clergy of other denominations to present the Gospel in an American context. He was a proponent of evangelical Catholicism, founder of a hospital, a school, a sisterhood for social work, a significant contributor to the hymnals of the era, a leader in the movement for free pews and other means of supporting the church than pew rents, a thoughtful but not uncritical advocate of the Gothic revival, and an advocate of the increased use of music, art, and ceremony.

To the Bishops of the Protestant Episcopal Church, in Council assembled.
RIGHT REVEREND FATHERS:

The undersigned, presbyters of the Church of which you have the oversight, venture to approach your venerable body with an expression of sentiment, which their estimate of your office in relation to the times does not permit them to withhold. In doing so, they have confidence in your readiness to appreciate their motives and their aims. The actual posture of our Church with reference to the great moral and social necessities of the day, presents to the minds of the undersigned a subject for grave and anxious thought. Did they suppose that this was confined to themselves, they would not feel warranted in submitting it to your attention; but they believe it to be participated in by many of their brethren, who may not have seen the expediency of declaring their views, or at least a mature season for such a course.

The divided and distracted state of our American Protestant Christianity, the new and subtle forms of unbelief adapting themselves with fatal success to the spirit of the age, the consolidated forces of Romanism bearing with renewed skill and activity against the Protestant faith, and as more or less the consequence of these, the utter ignorance of the Gospel among so large a portion of the low classes of our population, making a heathen world in our midst, are among the considerations which induce your memorialists to present the inquiry whether the period has not arrived for the adoption of measures, to meet these exigencies of the times, more comprehensive than any yet provided for by our present ecclesiastical system: in other words, whether the Protestant Episcopal Church, with only her present canonical means and appliances, her fixed and invariable modes of public worship and her traditional customs and usages, is competent to the work of preaching and dispensing the Gospel to all sorts and conditions of men, and so adequate to do the work of the Lord in this land and in this age? This question, your petitioners, for their own part, and in consonance with many thoughtful minds among us, believe must be answered in the negative. Their memorial proceeds on the assumption that our Church, confined to the exercise of her present system, is not sufficient to the great purposes above mentioned—that a wider door must be opened for admission to the Gospel ministry than that through which her candidates for holy orders are now obliged to enter. Besides such candidates among her own members, it is believed that men can be found among the other bodies of Christians around us, who would gladly receive ordination at your hands, could they obtain it, without that

209

entire surrender which would now be required of them, of all the liberty in public worship to which they have been accustomed—men, who could not bring themselves to conform in all particulars to our prescriptions and customs, but yet sound in the faith, and who, having the gifts of preachers and pastors, would be able ministers of the New Testament. With deference it is asked, ought such an accession to your means in executing your high commission, "Go into all the world and preach the Gospel to every creature," be refused, for the sake of conformity in matters recognized in the preface to the Book of Common Prayer, as unessentials? Dare we pray the Lord of the harvest to send forth laborers into the harvest, while we reject all laborers but those of one peculiar type? The extension of orders to the class of men contemplated (with whatever safeguards, not infringing on evangelical freedom, which your wisdom might deem expedient), appears to your petitioners to be a subject supremely worthy of your deliberations.

In addition to the prospect of the immediate good which would thus be opened, an important step would be taken towards the effecting of a Church unity in the Protestant Christendom of our land. To become a central bond of union among Christians, who, though differing in name, yet hold to the one Faith, the one Lord, and the one Baptism, and who need only such a bond to be drawn together in closer and more primitive fellowship, is here believed to be the peculiar province and high privilege of your venerable body as a College of CATHOLIC AND APOSTOLIC BISHOPS *as such.*

This leads your petitioners to declare the ultimate design of their memorial—which is to submit the practicability under your auspices, of some ecclesiastical system, broader and more comprehensive than that which you now administer, surrounding and including the Protestant Episcopal Church as it now is, leaving that Church untouched, identical with that Church in all its great principles, yet providing for as much freedom in opinion, discipline and worship as is compatible with the essential faith and order of the Gospel. To define and act upon such a system, it is believed, must sooner or later be the work of an American Catholic Episcopate.

In justice to themselves on this occasion, your memorialists beg leave to remark that, although aware that the foregoing views are not confined to their own small number, they have no reason to suppose that any other parties contemplate a public expression of them, like the present. Having therefore undertaken it, they trust that they have not laid themselves open to the charge of unwarranted intrusion. They find their warrant in the prayer now offered up by all our congregations, "that the comfortable Gospel of Christ may be truly preached, truly received, and truly followed, in all places to the breaking down of the kingdom of Sin, Satan, and Death." Convinced that, for the attainment of these blessed ends, there must be some greater concert of action among Protestant Christians, than nay which yet exists, and believing that with you, Rt. Rev'd Fathers, it rests to take the first measures tending thereto, your petitioners could not do less than humbly submit their memorial to such consideration as in your wisdom you may see to give it—Praying that it may not be dismissed without reference to a Commission, and assuring you, Right Reverend Fathers, of our dutiful veneration and esteem,

    We are

    Most Respectfully,

    Your Brethren and Servants
        in the Gospel of Christ,
        W. A. MUHLENBERG,
        C. F. CRUSE,
        PHILIP BERRY,
        EDWIN HARWOOD,
        G. T. BEDELL,
        HENRY GREGORY,
        ALEX H. VINTON,
        M. A. DE WOLFE HOWE,
        S. H. TURNER,
        S. R. JOHNSON,
        C. W. ANDREWS,
        and others.

New York, October 14th, 1853.

Concurring in the main purport of the above memorial, and believing that the necessities of the times call for some special efforts to promote unity among Christians, and to enlarge for that and other great ends the efficiency of the Protestant Episcopal Church, but not being able to adopt certain suggestions of this memorial, the undersigned most heartily join in the prayer that the subject may be referred to a Commission of your venerable Body.

        JOHN HENRY HOBART,
        A. CLEVELAND COXE,
        ED. Y. HIGBEE,
        FRANCIS VINTON,
        ISAAC G. HUBBARD,
        and others.

Journal of the General Convention, 1853, 181-183.

49.

Preliminary Report on the Memorial, 1856

The General Convention of 1853 appointed a commission of five bishops to study the Muhlenburg Memorial and make a report at the General Convention of 1856. This report of the commission was critical of the rigid organization and missionary failures of the Episcopal Church. It urged greater variety in liturgical services as well as the re-establishment of the office of Evangelist, and the diaconate as a vocation. The most concrete result of this report was to change the pattern of Sunday worship in Episcopal parishes. Up until this date, the Book of Common Prayer *had been understood to require Morning Prayer, the Litany, and the first part of the Eucharist through the sermon. After this report, the permission to separate these services resulted in the pattern familiar until recent decades of an early communion, and a later service on most Sundays of Morning Prayer and Sermon, except in Oxford Movement parishes. The memorial had goals which encompassed mission and ecumenium as well as liturgy, but the principal result at the time was liturgical.*

Report of Commission on Memorial of Rev. Dr. Muhlenburg and Others.

In considering the means and measures necessary for giving increased efficiency to the Church as the Divinely appointed instrument for reforming and saving mankind, we must never forget, that no organization will be of avail without an animating, internal principle imparting health, vigor and activity to the entire system, controlling and directing all its movements: while on the other hand, an imperfect, or even a defective organization invigorated by an active spiritual life, will exhibit energies and accomplish results in the moral transformation of human nature as marvelous as they are glorious. Still, as life is effectual to the accomplishment of useful ends, in proportion to the perfection of the organs through which it acts—as structure and adaptation are conditions of the greatest efficiency, so it behoves us as "co-workers with God," in the recovery of this world from the dominion of sin and the Devil, not only to use the appointed weapons of our warfare, but to use them in the way best adapted to ensure success. Our weapons may not be carnal, still they will not be found "mighty to the pulling down of strongholds," unless they be adapted to the objects to be effected. Wisdom and skill, combined with use and experience, are necessary to the successful employment of the most perfect instruments.

Our Liturgical services, be it remembered, were framed with a special view to the wants of a worshipping people. They were provided with a direct reference to organized parish Churches. They were intended to furnish two or more daily services to a population already won to the Church. But our actual mission is to many, in truth, to a large majority not yet conciliated to the Church, and for the most part strangers to her forms of worship. We have to seek those who have not been gathered into organized Parishes—who do not recognize in us any claim to spiritual oversight over them. We have to labor in places where very much of our work is outside of that contemplated in the plans of our offices, and in the prevalent methods of our preaching.

The Church was originally composed of converts gathered, by the labors of the Apostles, from the ranks of Judaism and Paganism. We have to deal with men who are generally not ignorant of our doctrine, but who are hardly more conversant with the system of worship to which we wish to conciliate them, than were the Jews and Gentiles, in the days of the Apostles, with the religion of our Saviour.

In seeking to modify or adapt our forms of worship to the actual wants and condition of a very large portion of our population, we do but act upon a principle distinctly recognized in our own and our Mother Church. In the preface to the Book of Common Prayer it is declared "that in every Church, whatever cannot be clearly determined to belong to the doctrine may be referred to discipline; and therefore by common consent and authority may be altered, abridged, enlarged, amended, or otherwise disposed of, as may seem most convenient for the edification of the people, according to the various exigencies of times and occasions." It is also affirmed in the same preface, that the Church of England having made various reviews and changes—her aim hath been "to do that which according to her best understanding, might most tend to the preservation of peace and unity in the Church; the procuring of reverence, and the exciting of piety and devotion in the worship of God; and finally the cutting off occasion from them that seek occasion of cavil or quarrel against her Liturgy."

In no country in the world, perhaps, will there be found united under the same form of government, so great a variety of people and so much diversity in intellectual, moral, social, and religious character as in this land. Immigration annually brings in its vast contribution to the elements of division in the religious sentiment and practice of our countrymen. There are found here men of all grades of intellectual development, from the most improved condition of mind, enlarged and elevated by the best advantages of education, to the grossest and most stupid ignorance growing out of poverty, and absolute neglect. There are seen all complexions of social character diversified by the physical and moral differences which exist among the people of the old world, and which fix a lasting, if not an indelible impression upon the habits of human thought and action. In the population of the same State and not unfrequently in the same Town, will be found all these varieties in national origin, in social, intellectual and religious character, at which we have barely glanced, and which present most serious obstacles, as painful experience most clearly proves, to the exercise of any wholesome and abiding influence on the part of the Gospel Ministry. Out of this anomalous condition of things arises the necessity of that diversity in our modes of operation which has not been, heretofore, sufficiently appreciated, and the need of that versatility of talents in the ministry, which in our case is more or less indispensable, and which is always found to be eminently useful.

It is not the purpose of this report to supply a treatise on the gifts of the ministry or to direct specifically how they may be most usefully employed. This is not the time, nor does it fall within our province to enter upon such a discussion. We can do no more, at present, than indicate, from an extended field of observation, and from the earnest representations made from every part of the Church, what seems to be most needed in order to the more vigorous prosecution of the great work with which we, in common with others, feel ourselves charged. That work looks almost exclusively to the inculcation of religious truth as the basis of a healthy moral sentiment securing national and individual prosperity, and as the foundation of that faith in God which leads to holiness of life, and the hope of salvation.

The sentiment of the Church is every where the same and emphatic in its expression as to the necessity of more force and directness in our preaching, and more special adaptation to the varying circumstances of the Congregations which we are called to address. The habits of our people moulded in a considerable degree by the nature of our civil and social institutions, and the constitution of the human mind, which impels us in most cases to prefer fervour to coldness, and that which is simple to that which is abstruse, are considerations which plainly indicate that our methods of dealing with men should be more direct and more manifold. They explain the reasons for that partiality with which extempore preaching is regarded—the superior influence which ministers accustomed so to preach possess in gathering together large congregations, and they account, in good part at least for the numerical superiority of most denominations of Christians over the Protestant Episcopal Church in almost all the states, towns and cities in the Union.

An examination into the relative increase of the various bodies of Christians in the United States within the last thirty years will exhibit some startling facts, which may well rouse us to serious consideration, and lead us to ask ourselves the questions, "what have we been doing? and what shall we do?" We have been in the habit of looking merely at the increase of our ministers and members within given periods, as the proper exponent of our growth without considering how that increase compares with the rate of increase in the population at large. Making our estimate in this way, and it is the only accurate method to ascertain the ratio of our growth or increase as a Church, it will be found that we are by no means keeping pace with the population of the country in the provision we make for their religious instruction—to say nothing of our duty to heathen and foreign lands—that we are consequently falling very far below the measure of our responsibility, and that our growth in the last half century, which has been dwelt upon with complacency if not with a spirit of vain glory, furnishes matter of deep humiliation and shame, rather than of boasting.

It is submitted to the serious and candid consideration of this House, whether with all the lights of past observation and experience before us, it be not wise to recommend to our ministers as an important means of enhancing their usefulness and efficiency, the cultivation of a habit of extemporaneous address and of expository preaching, at least during one portion of the Lord's Day. It is not designed to favor the idea of cultivating a habit of declamation or fervid exhortation at the expense of persevering and severe study. It is humbly conceived that previous and careful preparation is entirely consistent with the practice of extempore preaching, as here contemplated. With brief notes or heads of discourse, suggestive of topics and the preservation of a lucid arrangement, the fruits of much laborious research and reflection may be made available with their utmost effect. We see no reason why a minister should not in this way, present to the consideration of his congregation, the high and concerning truths of the gospel and enforce them by its awful sanctions as effectively, as persuasively, and as convincingly as a lawyer states and argues his case from his brief, at the bar. The plan suggested would have this further advantage. It would enable the preacher to avail himself of all suitable opportunities for proclaiming "the truth as it is in Jesus," which the diversities of time, place and circumstance might present. He need not always wait till a congregation can be gathered in some fixed place of worship furnished with the conveniences of lectern and pulpit, but after apostolic example, let him preach, if it be expedient, in an upper chamber, or in the market place, by the sea shore, or in the courts of the prison, by night or day, in storm and tempest, or in the sunshine of bright and cloudless skies. Every where, in season and out of season, he is to exercise his vocation, as need may require, and like a beacon on the stormy ocean of life, point the voyager to the way of safety and the haven of rest. He need not be bound by any rules or restrictions which custom may have established as to the length of his discourses. This should vary with emergencies, and especially with the state of those who hear. His quick and discerning glance will easily detect any restlessness or listlessness on the part of his hearers and furnish him the best chronometer to graduate his sermons. Thus too he will be enabled to suit his subject to the character of his congregation; and bringing out of his treasures—the accumulated stores of reading and study—of observation and reflection—things both new and old; he may use a written discourse or speak from notes, he may furnish food for the thoughtful mind, by unfolding some great doctrine of Christianity, or by animating exhortation rouse the desponding to renewed exertion for the prize of eternal life; he may enforce the high and commanding morality of the Gospel, or he may attract, edify and charm, by portraying the example of Christ doing good to the souls and bodies of men and may exhort them to its imitation. In a word, the vast range of the Gospel takes in all the interests of man as a rational and accountable creature, it comprehends all his relations to God and his fellow men, it embraces all his hopes for time and eternity, and from them all, the preacher may choose his theme, and—from the boundless field of nature, in the rich exuberance of her productions—the endless variety of objects which garnish the heavens above, or beautify the earth beneath, or replenish the waters under the earth—he may draw from them all, illustrations to enforce and adorn his subject.

These remarks point to the expediency, not to say necessity, of a corresponding variety, to some extent, in our Liturgical services. It is the general voice of our Communion, that in adjusting the length of our public services, more regard should be had to the physical ability of both minister and people; and this is especially important in those parts of our country where the heats of summer are long continued and debilitating, rendering mental exertion burdensome, and even perilous to health. More attention also seems to be demanded to the degree of Liturgical culture among the people, and a more economical use of our Clerical force. By the arrangements which the Commission would recommend, it is believed that in most of our established congregations, three services may be had on Sunday, and several during the week, without over-burdening the strength and ability of the Minister.

We read that, in the primitive Church, "gifts" were bestowed by our blessed Lord upon his members, "differing according to the measure of grace given unto them." These gifts were intended to supply every thing that was needful for carrying on the work our Lord had appointed to his Church. However they manifested their influence by "diversities of operations and differences of administrations" in the work of Apostles, or Prophets, or Evangelists, or Pastors, or Teachers, they were all given "for the perfecting of the Saints, for the work of the Ministry, for the edifying of the body of Christ." But that such varieties of gifts were bestowed "for the edifying of the Church," seems in a great measure to be overlooked or forgotten. It would appear that all Ministers are now expected to be Priests, whether they have "the gift of ministering" or not: all to be Rectors of Parishes, whether they have the gift of ruling or not: all to be Teachers, whether they show aptitude for instruction or not: and very many ("who name the name of Christ,") seem to have reached the conclusion that there is no such gift as that mentioned by the Apostle, when he enjoins it as a duty to give "with simplicity."

The consequences of this ignorance or forgetfulness have been exhibited in the history of the Church, even within the memory of some now living, with startling effect, and melancholy frequency. Ministers are found who yet do not minister: Rectors who cannot govern: Pastors who do not feed the flock: Teachers send forth theological essays for the instruction of the Church, who might find better employment in studying the Bible and Catechism: while the necessary means for maintaining religious services, too often have to be wrung from those who appear reluctant to recognize it as a Christian obligation to give of their ability, as God has prospered them, with liberality, with cheerfulness, and with simplicity. On every side the complaint is heard, that the work of the Church languishes, or is not done. That we have refused or neglected to use many gifts which Christ has bestowed on his Church, is apparent from our not providing employment for those members of the body which are fitted for special duties. We see, for example, persons who have a fondness or peculiar aptitude for searching out the poor and helpless. No cellars are too low and dark, no garrets too high and comfortless, to deter them in their efforts to find and relieve the hunger-bitten children of poverty. Vice and filth do not offend them, but excite their compassion and their tears. Degradation and infamy do not repel them, but inspire their charity, and give fervency to their prayers.

There are those, on the other hand, who have no inclination to engage in this humble and merciful work, or whose qualities of mind and body unfit them for such employments. They may not have the tact, wisdom, or resources necessary to guide them in the selection of means adequate to ensure success to such schemes of benevolence. Still they wish to do good, and the Minister of a Parish, if he be prudent and judicious, will find them employment. Some of them may be used in reading Prayers and the Holy Scriptures to the people, whose situation or opportunities do not allow them to attend the regular and stated services of the sanctuary. In the almost infinite variety of conditions in which our population is now found there can be no lack of opportunity for the employment of every talent which the Church can command.

Again there are men whose temperaments incline them to be constantly moving from place to place. Connected with this constitutional peculiarity, there is generally a frankness and cordiality of manner which render such persons favorites wherever they go. They may not possess any great breadth or variety of learning; nor any great powers of thought; but they have a faculty of correct and close observation, a knowledge of men as individuals and in masses, and perhaps extraordinary skill and tact in controlling them.

Again we see men who have that peculiar power or gift which is necessary for organizing and ruling bodies of men; who seem by intuition to know just when this quality is to be stimulated and that to be laid under restraint—when this particular trait can be neutralized by the development of another: when it is proper to rebuke one and when to encourage another. They have a ready perception of the thought that will touch the common sense of mankind and harmonize the mass. It is impossible to describe all the qualities which go to make up the character of such men: we perceive them when we say that such men were born to be rulers.

In this class will be found those best calculated of all, perhaps, in the Church to fill the office of Evangelists. Men, whose chief, if not their sole employment, it shall be to preach the Gospel in remote and morally destitute parts of the country, or in the neglected districts of our large cities, where the Pastors of established Congregations never come and the Preachers at Missionary Stations but rarely. Men who shall be under the special direction of the Bishop or the Diocese, laboring where he shall appoint, distributing books and tracts where opportunity shall serve, and reporting to the Bishop as often as he shall require.

Such a corps of active laborers seems almost indispensable to the complete organization of the Church according to the primitive model and unquestionably necessary to its extension in our land. It may be supposed and the idea has been sometimes advanced that the Bishops can and ought to do all the work contemplated by the creation of this class of preachers. With Dioceses of the present extent it is, in most cases, simply impossible. Many of our Bishops spend much the greater portion of their time in travelling and preaching. Almost the only increase made to the Church in many parts of the country is attributable to the labors of the Episcopate. But observation and experience have demonstrated that the utmost exertions of the Bishops cannot meet the growing demands of our population.

And here we are constrained to call attention to the wasted energy and unemployed power of the women of the Church. The Sisters of Charity in the Romish communion are worth, perhaps, more to their cause than the combined wealth of their Hierarchy—the learning of their priesthood—and the self-sacrificing zeal of their Missionaries. The providential government of the world leaves every where a large number of unmarried and unemployed females, and thus appears to point the Church to a wise appropriation of their peculiar talents or gifts, in the cause of Christ and of humanity. The associated charity and benevolence of Christian Sisterhoods which we have in mind, is the very opposite of the hermitage and the nunnery. Instead of a criminal and cowardly withdrawal from the world and the duties which the wants and distresses of humanity may claim, it is the voluntary consecration to Christ of all the powers of body and soul in the active performance of the most tender, the most endearing, and yet the most neglected offices of charity. Many have seen and many lament our loss in this respect: but individual zeal and effort can effect but little in the way of providing a remedy. The constituted authorities of the Church must take hold of the subject—deal with it without reserve—combine effort in the cause, and give direction to it without the fear of man.

With such instrumentalities as are now in use, the Commission is constrained to report further, that in their judgment the debt of the Ministry and members of the Church to the young is not sufficiently felt and adequately discharged. In families acknowledging the obligations of a Christian profession there is too little positive and regular religious instruction and too little of pious, paternal training or discipline. By Pastors there is want of attention to catechising—to the Sunday School—and to such preaching and services as are best calculated to reach, impress, and influence those who have arrived at the period of juvenescence.

It is also very certain that the full effect of our ministrations cannot be obtained and the reasonable expectations of the Church at large be met and fulfilled in this behalf, until our Candidates for Orders and our Ministers be trained to more robust, intellectual habits by a more thorough and severe mental discipline: and to this very necessary preparation must be added a clear apprehension of the moral wants of the times, and the precise intellectual wants of the people. Next to this, and hardly of less importance, there is need of more practical common sense, in dealing with men upon the subject of religion, and recommending it to their attention. In this country almost every man and woman feel competent to discuss questions of theology and give instruction on the doctrines of the Gospel. These pretensions have to be met by the Ministry, and to be met in a spirit of meekness and of deep compassion for the erring and deceived. Hence we have found in very many of the communications made to us by Clergymen and Laymen, the opinion or rather the conviction very earnestly expressed, that in preparing candidates for the work of the Ministry, more attention should be paid to practical training for its duties—that there should be also more cultivation of the powers of thought, and taste for investigation—more rhetorical culture—more rigid and searching examinations and better established habits of systematic study after ordination.

But among the many wants of the Church in order to her energetic and effective influence—that fulness and completeness which we desire for her—few perhaps are more obvious, and none more generally deplored, than the want of an impressive and devotional manner of reading the Liturgy. This is a great and crying evil, and to its existence is to be attributed, no doubt, much of the complaint which is urged against the length and formality of our services. The evil is the more inexcusable and intolerable, for the simple reason that it might be remedied, in a vast majority of cases, by due care and persevering efforts on the part of those whose bounden duty it is, and pleasure it ought to be, to qualify themselves for the becoming and decent performance of this, the most sacred part of their holy functions. He who leads the devotions of a congregation, in their approaches to the mercy-seat, with the offerings of praise and prayer to the Divine Majesty, can make no acceptable apology to his people, and no excuse to his own conscience, for carelessness and irreverence. An experienced Clergyman, in a communication to the Commission, complains of this evil as very prevalent, and proposes the following remedy:

"Let all candidates be taught to read English. The only certain method of correcting vicious modes of reading is, to employ the services of some one who can give the student an *accurate rehearsal* of his own performances. After many repetitions of this discipline, the young man will begin to detect the similar vice in his own tones, and then only will it be possible for him to correct it."

In this connection we cannot but allude to important duty devolving on the members of our congregations, to take their part earnestly and effectively in our public services. Were this done in the responses, in the chants, in the metrical Psalmody—done in the way in which the Church, in her wisdom, has prescribed, and with a hearty observance of her decent rules and usages—much of the complaint now made, of the wearisome length of the services, would be hushed. What is not done as it should be is usually wearisome. It is a duty imperative on the clergy, to see to it that any failure in this important matter shall not be justly chargeable to the want of proper instruction and urgency on their part.

The Commission is of opinion that every Minister having Parochial charge, should be diligent in the use of means for interesting and retaining under wholesome religious influences boys and young men.

1st. By giving them employment in the Church and the Sunday School.

2d. By frequently meeting with them and manifesting interest in their welfare.

3d. By directing their choice in reading—recommending proper books, &c.

4th. By cultivating among them a love for Sacred music.

It is deemed of vital importance that the Ministry should with every class, but particularly with the young, insist earnestly upon their responsibility as stewards of the grace of the Gospel—employing them as helpers to the Ministry, not only in the Sunday School and Bible Classes, but when found apt and prudent, in district visiting—in Lay-reading and Catechising in destitute places, on the principle that they are bound to labor, as well as to give of their substance for the promotion and increase of true religion—that they cannot be faithful to God, unless they improve the talents committed to them, and, that they must begin this work when young, if they would be efficient in manhood, and happy when old.

And here we are reminded of one of the most mournful of our deficiencies, and which ought to move us all to deep humiliation and earnest prayer. We refer to the small number of our Clergy compared with our existing wants, and the inadequate provision made for their support. Few are found pressing towards that which ought to be regarded as the happiest, the most useful and the most honorable of human pursuits; and of those who engage in it, few receive more than a meagre recompense for their services. Does not this indicate on the part of young men, a sad want of zeal and devotion in the cause of Christ, and on their part also, who as parents, Pastors and friends ought to move the young to aspire to this holy office? And, does it not show on the part of Christians whom God has made the stewards of his bounty, a deplorable insensibility to their duty and their privilege, when they suffer Ministers and Missionaries to languish in want, while they pay without stint for the services of men of all other professions and occupations in life? For this sore evil, it becomes us to seek earnestly a proper remedy. A more abundant measure of God's grace is doubtless the first and most important requisite, and for this the Church should call upon her children to pray importunately and continually. But it cannot be denied that were more careful and general consideration given to the subject, means would be devised to elicit much more ample gifts from the Laity, and to draw to the ranks of the Clergy many an earnest spirit now destined to other callings. Almsgiving and other acts of Christian beneficence require to be cultivated as habits; and no Pastor should be satisfied unless his methods of proceeding are sufficiently varied and steady to enlist the interest and engage the active and continued cooperation of all his people. Most congregations need on this subject, it is feared, more instruction than they receive, and this instruction needs to be followed by more active superintendence from the Clergymen, and more extended sympathy and aid from individuals of the congregation.

The Commission have also taken counsel with each other, and earnestly sought to devise some plan which might contribute to heal the divisions which so unhappily distract the Christian world. We cannot but rejoice in the interest which the members of our own household of faith, have manifested in common with all good men of other denominations of Christians upon this subject; and we doubt not that all will rejoice, if measures can be taken to restore the unity of the Church, and promote God's blessing, an increase of charity among all "who name the name of Christ." We must all, however, be well aware that the first step towards this happy and greatly desired result must be sought in unity of spirit, rather than unity of doctrine and discipline; and therefore mutual allowances, and a large toleration are indispensable requisites for which we should fervently and devoutly pray. The action which the Commission recommends upon this subject will be stated in the form of a Resolution, and of a Prayer at the conclusion of this Report.

We cannot but earnestly and affectionately recommend to our brethren and friends every where, in view of the momentous interests involved in the final disposition of this question, to strive to keep the unity of the Spirit in the bond of peace.

1st. By doing justice to the merits of other systems as readily as they expose their demerits.

2dly. By repressing a spirit of self-complacency and self-laudation.

3dly. By infusing into our worship, preaching, and general policy more of the ancient and historical element on one side, and of the popular and practical on the other.

4thly. By a more cordial manner towards Ministers of other religious bodies who are inquiring into the claims of our communion.

5thly. By considering whether we cannot safely lessen Canonical impediments in the way of Ministers, Licentiates, and others desirous of our Orders, with sufficient guarantees for soundness in doctrine, discipline, and worship.

6thly. By fruitfulness in all good works. If our Ministers were more fervid, self-denying, and laborious; our people more charitable, exemplary, and devout—if, in a word, we were all that we ought to be, and might be from the alleged superiority of our gifts and privileges, the attraction to the Church would be universal and irresistible.

In conclusion, the Commission place before the House the positive results which they have reached. In a large proportion—indeed, it may be said that (with a few exceptions), in all of the communications made to us by members of our Church, the opinion has been expressed that the Morning service might sometimes be shortened with advantage, and that greater variety ought to obtain in services which are beside the regular offices of Morning and Evening Prayer in established congregations. These are ends to which the efforts of many in the Anglican Church are now anxiously directed. Earnest expression has also been given to the wish in many quarters, that the calendar of lessons should be revised, that additional hymns, anthems, and canticles should be provided, with other emendations, which would affect no doctrine of the Church and might materially aid in the edification of her people. It has been the purpose of the Commission, however, so far as their present labors go, to leave the Prayer Book untouched: they have also doubted how far the consideration of such proposed alterations would fall within the duty assigned to them; and at all events, they felt that if any alterations of the Prayer Book were proposed, the House of Deputies would be entitled to take part in the preliminary discussions connected with them, and that much more time ought to be devoted to the work than they have been able to command. They have concluded, therefore, to commend this subject to the General Convention, to be disposed of as in its wisdom it may judge to be most expedient. They have many valuable papers embodying the results of much labor and learning and of a very extended experience, which will be at the service of a committee should the Convention decide to appoint one.

After much reflection, the Commission have come to the unanimous conclusion that some of the most material of the improvements, which are loudly called for and which commend themselves to our own judgment, might be attained without legislation. There is nothing in the Rubrics or Canons which requires that, when the Holy Communion is administered it should be preceded immediately or otherwise by the office for Daily Prayer. The practice rests merely on usage, and there are occasions, when for want of physical ability on the part of the Minister or from the very large number of persons communicating, or for other reasons, it would be right that the liberty which the laws do not withhold of omitting the Daily Prayer should be exercised. To secure this, nothing more would be needed it is thought, than a declarative resolution of this House. The same discretion seems allowable in respect to the time of using the Litany and the Ante-Communion Office. Canon XLVII., of 1832, already provides for special services to be set forth by Bishops in their own Dioceses, and the Commission have concluded that by exercising the power thus given, provision could be made for those local necessities which result from peculiarities in the character of the population, or in the circumstances under which the Church is to be extended.

They therefore recommend unanimously, that the following *Preamble* and *Resolutions* be adopted by the House of Bishops.

WHEREAS, the order of worship as prescribed by the Book of Common Prayer, or as settled by usage, has been framed with special reference to established Parish Churches and to a population already incorporated with the Church; and

WHEREAS, our actual work is or should be among many not yet connected with our congregations, or where there are no established parishes, or where said parishes, are yet in their infancy: and

WHEREAS, there are or may be in different dioceses, peculiar emergencies arising out of the character or condition of certain portions of the population, which demand some special services. And

WHEREAS, it is desirable that the use of the Book of Common Prayer as the vehicle of the Church's devotions, should be such as to cultivate an enlightened love for the Liturgy, and enable the Clergy and people to make their labors for Christ most effective, therefore,

Resolved, as the sense of the House of Bishops,

I. That Ministers may at their discretion, use separately the office for

Morning Prayer, and that where a third service is to be held, the Litany, or the Ante-Communion office or both may be used in the afternoon: the order for Evening Prayer being reserved for said third service.

II. That the order for the Holy Communion, in its entirety, may, with a sermon, be used separately, provided, nevertheless, that on the greater Festivals it should in their judgment be preceded by the office of Morning or Evening Prayer.

III. That on occasions or services other than regular Morning and Evening Prayer, in established congregations, Ministers may at their discretion use such parts of the Book of Common Prayer and such Lessons as shall in their judgment tend most to edification.

IV. That the Bishops of the several Dioceses may provide such special services as in their judgment shall be required by the peculiar spiritual necessities of any class or portion of the population within said Dioceses.

V. That to indicate the desire of this Church to promote union amongst Christians, and as an organ of communication with different Christian bodies or individuals who may desire information or conference on the subject, it is expedient that five Bishops be appointed by ballot at each General Convention, as Commissioners for the foregoing purpose, to be entitled the Commissions on Church unity. . . .

> JAS. H. OTEY, *Chairman*
> G. W. DOANE,   ALONZO POTTER,
> GEORGE BURGESS,   JNO. WILLIAMS.

Journal of General Convention, 1856, 342-352.

50.

Chicago Quadrilateral, 1886

William Reed Huntington (September 20, 1838–July 26, 1909) was committed to the reconciliation of Christians in the United States. In his book, The Church Idea: An Essay Toward Unity *(1870) he set forth the basis for this reunification. On October 20, 1886, the House of Bishops at the thirty-fifth General Convention at Chicago adopted this report of the Committee on Christian Unity which included Huntington's four principles for the doctrinal basis of a national church.*

The Bishop of Long Island presented the following report of the Committee on Christian Unity, viz.:

The Committee to whom were referred sundry memorials addressed to the Bishops in Council and to the House of Bishops, praying that some plan may be devised which, in a practical way, will promote the restoration of Christian unity, all which memorials emanated from certain of the clergy and of the laity of the Church, the former numbering about one thousand, and the latter nearly two thousand, beg to report that they have given to the same the full and earnest consideration which the gravity of the subject and the fervent prayer of the petitioners demanded. The conclusions of your Committee are set forth in the following preamble and declarations:

WHEREAS, In the year 1853, in response to a Memorial signed by many Presbyters of this Church, praying that steps might be taken to heal the unhappy divisions of Christendom, and to more fully develop the Catholic idea of the Church of Christ, the Bishops of this Church in Council assembled did appoint a Commission of Bishops empowered to confer with the several Christian Bodies in our land who were desirous of promoting godly union and concord among all who loved the Lord Jesus Christ in sincerity and truth;

AND WHEREAS, This Commission, in conformity with the terms of its appointment, did formally set forth and advocate sundry suggestions and recommendations intended to accomplish the great end in view;

AND WHEREAS, In the year 1880, the Bishops of the American Church, assembled in Council, moved by the appeals from Christians in foreign countries who were struggling to free themselves from the usurpations of the Bishop of Rome, set forth a declaration to the effect that, in virtue of the solidarity of the Catholic Episcopate, in which we have part, it was the right and duty of the Episcopates of all National Churches holding the primitive Faith and Order, and of the several Bishops of the same, to protect in the holding of that Faith, and the recovering of that Order, those who have been wrongfully deprived of both; and this without demanding a rigid uniformity, or the sacrifice of the national traditions of worship and discipline, or of their rightful autonomy;

AND WHEREAS, Many of the faithful in Christ Jesus among us are praying with renewed and increasing earnestness that some measures may be adopted at this time for the re-union of the sundered parts of Christendom:

Now, therefore, in pursuance of the action taken in 1853 for the healing of the divisions among Christians in our own land, and in 1880 for the protection and encouragement of those who had withdrawn from the Roman Obedience, we, Bishops of the Protestant-Episcopal Church in the United States of America, in Council assembled as Bishops in the Church of God, do hereby solemnly declare to all whom it may concern, and especially to our fellow-Christians of the different Communions in this land, who, in their several spheres, have contended for the religion of Christ:

225

1. Our earnest desire that the Saviour's prayer, "That we all may be one," may, in its deepest and truest sense, be speedily fulfilled;

2. That we believe that all who have been duly baptized with water, in the name of the Father, and of the Son, and of the Holy Ghost, are members of the Holy Catholic Church;

3. That in all things of human ordering or human choice, relating to modes of worship and discipline, or to traditional customs, this Church is ready in the spirit of love and humility to forego all preferences of her own;

4. That this Church does not seek to absorb other Communions, but rather, co-operating with them on the basis of a common Faith and Order, to discountenance schism, to heal the wounds of the Body of Christ, and to promote the charity which is the chief of Christian graces and the visible manifestation of Christ to the world;

But furthermore, we do hereby affirm that the Christian unity now so earnestly desired by the memorialists can be restored only by the return of all Christian communions to the principles of unity exemplified by the undivided Catholic Church during the first ages of its existence; which principles we believe to be the substantial deposit of Christian Faith and Order committed by Christ and his Apostles to the Church unto the end of the world, and therefore incapable of compromise or surrender by those who have been ordained to be its stewards and trustees for the common and equal benefit of all men.

As inherent parts of this sacred deposit, and therefore as essential to the restoration of unity among the divided branches of Christendom, we account the following, to wit:

1. The Holy Scriptures of the Old and New Testament as the revealed Word of God.

2. The Nicene Creed as the sufficient statement of the Christian Faith.

3. The two Sacraments,—Baptism and the Supper of the Lord,—ministered with unfailing use of Christ's words of institution and of the elements ordained by Him.

4. The Historic Episcopate, locally adapted in the methods of its administration to the varying needs of the nations and peoples called of God into the unity of His Church.

Furthermore, Deeply grieved by the sad divisions which affect the Christian Church in our own land, we hereby declare our desire and readiness, so soon as there shall be any authorized response to this Declaration, to enter into brotherly conference with all or any Christian Bodies seeking the restoration of the organic unity of the Church, with a view to the earnest study of the conditions under which so priceless a blessing might happily be brought to pass.

A. N. LITTLEJOHN.
G. T. BEDELL.
M. A. DE WOLFE HOWE.
SAMUEL S. HARRIS.
J. N. GALLEHER.

Journal of General Convention, 1886, 79-80.

51.

Chicago-Lambeth Quadrilateral, 1888

The four points of the report of the Committee on Christian Unity, the "Chicago form" of the quadrilateral, was presented to the third Lambeth Conference, July 3-27, 1888. Some revisions were made, and it is now known as the Chicago-Lambeth Quadrilateral. The principal modifications were that the Scriptures were described as "containing all things necessary to salvation," and the addition of the Apostles' Creed as "the sufficient statement of the Christian faith." It is the minimum Anglican basis for discussions that might lead to church unity.

Resolution 11.

That, in the opinion of this Conference, the following Articles supply a basis on which approach may be by God's blessing made towards Home Reunion:—

(A) The Holy Scriptures of the Old and New Testaments, as "containing all things necessary to salvation," and as being the rule and ultimate standard of faith.

(B) The Apostles' Creed, as the Baptismal Symbol; and the Nicene Creed, as the sufficient statement of the Christian faith.

(C) The two Sacraments ordained by Christ Himself—Baptism and the Supper of the Lord—ministered with unfailing use of Christ's words of Institution, and of the elements ordained by Him.

(D) The Historic Episcopate, locally adapted in the methods of its administration to the varying needs of the nations and peoples called of God into the Unity of His Church.

Randall T. Davidson, comp., *The Six Lambeth Conferences, 1867-1920* (London: S.P.C.K., 1929), 122.

52.

Francis J. Hall, The Historic Episcopate, 1895

Francis Joseph Hall (December 24, 1857–March 12, 1932) was professor of dogmatic theology at Western Theological Seminary, 1886-1913, and at the General Theological Seminary, 1913-1928. One of his major works was the ten-volume Dogmatic Theology. *Hall's statement on the historic episcopate is in response to the Bishops' Declaration of Unity, which came to be known as the Quadrilateral.*

It is my privilege to address you concerning the Historic Episcopate.

I need not labor to convince you of the importance of the subject. The air is full of it. Christians of every name are wrestling with the problem of Church Unity; and the sectarian world about us considers our insistence upon the Historic Episcopate to be the chief barrier to unity, while our own Bishops have asserted that Ministry to be "incapable of compromise or surrender." It is clear that no unity is possible between parties thus opposed to each other, until the claims of the Historic Episcopate have been duly examined and an agreement has been reached as to their validity.

Other issues are involved in this controversy, and of vital nature. It is a fact that the rejection of the Episcopate has been followed sooner or later by heresy, decay of faith in the doctrine of supernatural grace, disintegration and unbelief. To one who believes in the doctrine of Apostolic Succession this seems perfectly natural; for what is more logical and inevitable than that such results should follow upon a loss of the Ministry—and the only Ministry—which God has ordained and empowered to guard the Faith, dispense the means of grace, and hold the faithful together in unity until the end of days?

The subject of the Historic Episcopate necessarily has peculiar interest for us. The Protestant world invites us to justify the attitude assumed by our Bishops in their Declaration of Unity, wherein they insist upon the Episcopate as upon an *ultimatum*, refusing to compromise or surrender it even when called upon to do so for the sake of unity and charity. This invitation is a natural one; and, if we would avoid appearance of evil, we must give a sufficient reason for our position, and one equivalent to religious necessity. Nothing short of this will justify the setting forth of an *ultimatum* as to the course to be pursued in restoring visible unity to the Church of God.

In order to exhibit such a reason we may be obliged to display truths and convictions which are not acceptable to those who question us. But in such case, the interests of honor as well as of charity will require that we should lay bare the true nature of the hindrances in this direction which must be removed before unity can be secured.

It is my purpose to exhibit as well as I can (*a*) the meaning of our fourth term of unity; (*b*) an outline of the historical argument which justifies that term; (*c*) its practical bearing on the problem of Church Unity.

I.

The fourth term of unity, set forth in 1886, reads: *The Historic Episcopate, locally adapted in the methods of its administration to the varying needs of the nations and peoples called of God into the unity of His Church.*[1]

(*a*) This language is not fairly charged with ambiguity, especially if the nature of the Declaration in which it occurs is considered. Its leading phrase, "the Historic Episcopate," was surely intended, and has been taken by many, to be simply "the polite equivalent of a controversial term [Apostolic Succession] which had long been in use," as one of our Bishops[2] expresses it.

But this, the natural interpretation, has been explained away by certain eminent Churchmen, and their explanations have misled certain Protestants and have disturbed many among ourselves who look to the chief Pastors of the Church to give forth no uncertain sound.

Our Bishops are said to have "fastened on certain words, the characteristic of which is, that they express a fact without at all insisting upon any theory of the fact. . . . That government by oversight, which is what "episcopacy," when translated, means, has been historically the prevailing method of polity in Christendom, certainly from the second century onwards, is beyond dispute. . . . That if we are to have organic unity at all, it is more reasonable to expect that it should be brought about under this method of pilotage than any other." In short we are told that "it is a simple falling back on fact. Think as you please, the Bishops seem to say, about the nature and sanction of the Christian Ministry."[3]

We have no quarrel with the amiable spirit which lies behind such an interpretation; but we cannot accept its reasonableness, nor can we discover how the Episcopate will be made more acceptable to Protestant denominations by our refusing to give any more adequate reason for insisting upon it than the fact that it has existed for a long time. Does mere antiquity make a thing necessary? Can the phrase "incapable of compromise or surrender," employed by our Bishops, be rightly applied to anything which is not necessary in itself? Does an opinion on our part that "it is more reasonable to expect that" unity "should be brought about under this method of pilotage than any other" make the

---

[1] Journal Gen. Conv. 1886, p. 80.
[2] Bishop McLaren, in the New York Independent, Mch. 8, 1894.
[3] Dr. Huntington's Peace of the Church, pp. 204, 205.

Episcopate incapable of compromise or surrender? It is thought, I know, that, if we claim Divine sanction for the Episcopate, we shall be considered presumptuous. But shall we be thought less so in requiring the religious world to yield to us with reference to what we refuse to say is of more than human sanction? Is not humility with those who magnify their office on the ground that it is of Divine institution and held in trust, rather than with those who do the same thing on grounds purely human? Are our Protestant brethren incapable of answering such questions with common sense?

It is indeed true, as even so staunch a Churchman as the late Canon Liddon could say, that, in asserting Apostolic Succession, "we are not formulating a theory, but stating a fact of history."[4] But, as that saintly Priest would readily have agreed, there are facts, of which Apostolic Succession is one, which cannot be stated without immediate implications of doctrinal nature, which we cannot escape without evasion of the facts themselves. Thus, the doubting Thomas found himself obliged, the instant in which he realized the fact that his Master had risen in very flesh and bones from the dead, to acknowledge His Godhead and adore Him; and those who lose their hold upon the reality of the physical resurrection of our Lord come ultimately, if they live long enough, to a denial of His Person. The phrase "Historic Episcopate" stands for a fact of such nature; and the fact signified is that the Episcopate was instituted by Christ to be the earthly source of spiritual jurisdiction and the bond of visible unity in the Church to the end of days.

We cannot accept such a fact without treating the Episcopate as of Divine requirement, and believing that its maintenance is inseparably bound up with the maintenance of true religion. It is as absurd to speak of believing in the Historic Episcopate as a fact merely, as it is to speak of believing in God as a fact merely. God is a Being Whose very Nature requires our loyalty, so that the fact of His existence cannot be duly stated without doctrines and consequences appearing which should modify our lives. In like manner, the Historic Episcopate is by nature or, if you prefer to put it so, historically, a fact with implications as to authority which we cannot evade without ignoring the contents of the fact itself. The fact includes Christ's mission, and a Divinely sanctioned government in the Church, from which there can be no earthly appeal, as well as a permanent stewardship of grace and truth.

In view of such considerations, we hold that our Bishops were not likely to have submitted the Historic Episcopate "simply as a question of polity," as a brilliant and amiable Presbyterian professor expresses it.[5] Nor can we assent to

---

4Clerical Life and Work, pp. 291, 292.
5Prof. Shields's United Church of the United States, p. 157.

his assertion that "it is of prime importance that such dogmas [as Apostolic Succession] . . . should sink out of view while we are considering its claims and merits as a Christian institution."[6] To require "the Historic Episcopate, as neither enjoining nor forbidding any doctrine of Apostolic Succession"[7] would be mere trifling, whatever our convictions might be. If we look upon the Episcopate as essential to the maintenance of true religion, what right have we to enter into an arrangement which will sooner or later place it in the power of those who regard it as of human origin and subject to human modification? If, on the other hand, we believe, as we do not, that the Episcopate is merely desirable and not essential, how can we answer satisfactorily the question of the Secretary of the Evangelical Alliance, who asks, "Why make that essential to the organization of all Churches into one, which is conceded to be unessential to the legitimate organization of any?"[8] Truly "such a position cannot be successfully defended as a *sine qua non* to Church union."[9] And the light in which thoughtful sectarians usually regard it is truly expressed by a well-known editor, when he says, it "is arrogance, and arrogance is not the road to Christian union."[10]

It is, in fact, just such interpretations as I have been reviewing which occasion and justify the charge so frequently made that our insistence upon the Episcopate is the chief barrier to unity. We cannot refute such a charge on any other than the highest doctrinal ground, viz., that the Episcopate is of Divine institution and requirement, and for that reason "is incapable of compromise or surrender" by its stewards and trustees.

(*b*) To proceed: if our fourth term cannot be cleared from the charge of absurdity except on high doctrinal grounds, neither should it be regarded as committing this Church in the slightest degree, unless it is consistent with her formularies. Our Bishops, as they themselves have said recently, speak "not as truth-seekers, but as truth receivers, 'ambassadors in bonds,'" and their "sole inquiry is: What does this Church teach? What is the declaration of God's Holy Word?"[11] Their elevation to the Episcopate did not nullify their priestly obligation and vow "always so to minister the Doctrine and Sacraments, and the Discipline of Christ, as the Lord hath commanded, and as this Church hath received the same." They may indeed say and do much in their episcopal capacity simply, making use of methods not provided for in the Constitution and Canons

---

[6]Ibid.
[7]Ibid. p. 182.
[8]Dr Josiah Strong, in The Question of Unity, edited by Dr. Bradford, p. 25.
[9]Ibid. p. 26.
[10]Ibid. p. 38.
[11]Pastoral Letter of 1894, p. 9.

of our General Convention. They have often done so—"in Council" and in the Lambeth Conferences. But they cannot alter the Constitution and Canons, nor can they lawfully commit the General Convention to the necessity of such alterations, except by methods constitutionally provided.

In view of these elementary principles, we are unwilling to read into the Declaration touching the Historic Episcopate any meaning which would require an alteration in the doctrines of this Church or a change in its polity. No doubt our Bishops will always be ready to do what in them lies toward locally adapting our episcopal polity to the peoples with whom they have to do; but we have too much confidence in them to believe that they will attempt this by unconstitutional methods, inconsistent with the terms on which they have received their Office.[12] It is hardly necessary to add, that to interpret any part of their Declaration on Unity, issued as it was without legislative action, as intended to commit this Church, under conditions of their own naming, to doctrinal and ecclesiastical changes of radical nature, is to deal somewhat severely with reputations for loyalty. Surely we are warranted in denying that their language pointed to any "structural surrender";[13] and in treating their fourth term as intended to be in harmony with the existing formularies and principles of this Church.

Her principles are clear enough in this matter. She has not, indeed, treated her doctrine of the Ministry, or any other portion of her Faith, as requiring legislative enactment, or as affected in the slightest degree as to its binding force by its being inscribed in the Constitution of her General Convention.[14] It is also true that she has nowhere set forth her doctrine of the Ministry in connected order and detail in her formularies. But we can discover sufficient indications of her mind none the less.

She has said in the Preface of her Ordinal that "from the Apostles' time there have been these Orders of Ministers in Christ's Church, Bishops, Priests and Deacons. Which Offices were evermore had in such reverend estimation, that no man might presume to execute any of them, except he were first called, . . . and also by public Prayer, with Imposition of Hands, were approved and admitted thereunto by lawful Authority. And therefore to the intent that these Orders may be continued, and reverently used and esteemed in this Church, no man shall be

---

[12]When they were consecrated they vowed to "exercise such discipline as by the authority of God's Word, and by the order of this Church, is committed unto" them. See Ordinal.

[13]Bishop McLaren, in New York Independent, March 8, 1894.

[14]The General Convention is not "this Church," but a legal corporation employed by and subject to this Church. Its Constitution is mutable and deals with changeable things. The Church's own Constitution, including her Faith and polity, is divine and immutable. The General Convention legislates for its maintenance, not for its enactment, definition, or revision.

accounted or taken to be a lawful Bishop, Priest or Deacon, in this Church, or suffered to execute any of the said functions, except he be called, tried, examined and admitted thereunto, according to the Form hereafter following, or hath had Episcopal Consecration or Ordination." In her prayers the Church assumes that God has appointed "divers Orders" in His Church, by His "Divine Providence,"[15] and by His "Holy Spirit";[16] and that the Apostolic Commission is a proper reason for consecrating Bishops to be the "Pastors" of Christ's Church and to "administer the godly discipline thereof."[17] She interprets the Scriptural injunction "to lay hands suddenly on no man" as properly applicable to the Consecration of Bishops;[18] and connects those gifts of the Holy Ghost whereby He makes "some Apostles, some Prophets," etc., with the same action.[19] She professes "by the imposition of the hands" of her Bishops to confer the Holy Ghost "for the Office and work of a Bishop in the Church of God."

In her Office of Institution she testifies that Christ hath "promised to be with the Ministers of Apostolic Succession to the end of the world."[20] She receives into her Ministry those who have received Episcopal ordination in other Communions,[21] and treats all other so-called ordinations as null and void, in the Constitution and Canons of her General Convention.[22] In brief, if she has not defined the doctrine of Apostolic Succession in set terms, she has at least tied herself to modes of address to God and man, and to rules of action, which are inscrutable on the supposition that that doctrine does not express her mind.

There has been no reason for formal definitions. This Church is a daughter of the Church of England, being under the Episcopal oversight of the Bishop of London before the Revolution, and asserting her origin and structure by the name Episcopal when the division of national jurisdiction took place. She declares in the Preface of her Prayer Book that she "is far from intending to depart from the Church of England in any essential point of doctrine, discipline or worship." In acting and praying on the basis of the doctrine of Apostolic Succession, therefore, she but retains her ancient constitution and Faith; for, in spite of the vagaries of individual writers and schools and in spite of laxity of individual ecclesiastics in the exercise of discipline, the *corporate position* of

---

[15]Collect in the Ordinal of Deacons.
[16]Collect in the Ordinal of Priests. Also the prayer before the examination of Bishops-elect.
[17]Collect in the Ordinal of Bishops.
[18]Address to the Bishop-elect before his examination.
[19]Prayer before the laying-on of hands. Cf. Ephes. iv.11; I. Cor. xii. 28.
[20]Second prayer before the benediction.
[21]Title I., Canon 15, Digest of 1892.
[22]Title I., Canon 3 § vi.; cf. Canon 17.

the English Church, as embodied in her formularies and displayed in her elaborate care for the preservation of the Historic Episcopate and succession, has been unmistakable, and in agreement with Catholic doctrine.

(c) Having shown to the best of my ability that our fourth term is absurd, presumptuous and disloyal, unless submitted from a high doctrinal point of view, I only need to give explicit proof, by quotations from their own language, that our Bishops were neither unreasonable nor disloyal, but assumed in their fourth term a defensible and Catholic position.

The Declaration consists, as you are aware, of preamble and body. The body of the Declaration includes not only the so-called "terms" of unity (an inaccurate phrase), but also some explanatory matter and an express statement of the *doctrinal reason* for insisting upon the Episcopate and other "terms" of unity. Permit me to quote from it.

We do hereby affirm, our Bishops say, *that the Christian unity now so earnestly desired . . . can be restored only by the return of all Christian Communions to the principles of unity exemplified by the undivided Catholic Church during the first ages of its existence; which principles we believe to be the substantial deposit of Faith and Order committed by Christ and His Apostles to the Church unto the end of the world, and therefore incapable of compromise or surrender by those who have been ordained to be its stewards and trustees for the common and equal benefit of all men.*

As inherent parts of this sacred deposit, and therefore as essential to the restoration of unity among the divided branches of Christendom, we account the following, to wit:

4. The Historic Episcopate,[23] *etc.*

I have spoken at considerable length on the interpretation of our fourth term of unity, because I am convinced that the novelties which have been imputed to our Bishops will do more harm to the cause of genuine Church Unity, if allowed to pass, than can be repaired for a long time to come. I think, however, that I need not say more in connection with this, except to give a brief outline of the sense in which our fourth term appears to be submitted.

1. That term, so far as it may be called a term, is an *ultimatum,* for our Bishops declare that the Episcopate is "incapable of compromise or surrender."

2. The reason advanced for thus insisting upon the Episcopate is that it is an "inherent part" of a "sacred deposit," "the substantial deposit of Faith and Order committed by Christ and His Apostles to the Church unto the end of the world."

3. The Catholic doctrine of the Episcopate is not expressly mentioned among

---

[23]Gen. Conv. Journal, 1886, p. 80.

our terms of unity; but the reason given for offering the terms which are mentioned, and, therefore, the *sense* in which the Historic Episcopate is insisted upon, make it impossible to accept the fourth term in good faith without accepting that doctrine.

4. No action has been contemplated by this Church which would be likely, at any future time, to render the maintenance of the traditional position and doctrine of the Episcopate an open question.

Francis J. Hall, "The Historic Episcopate," in *Christian Unity and the Bishops' Declaration, Lectures Delivered in 1895 Under the Auspices of the Church Club of New York* (New York: E. & J. B. Young & Co., 1895), 149-164.

CHAPTER EIGHT

Liturgy, Music, and Prayer Book Revision (1786-1985)

Introduction

The organization of the Episcopal Church was accompanied by a newly revised Prayer Book for the church in America. An initial revision of the Prayer Book was proposed in 1786, but it was not accepted. The first Episcopal Prayer Book was published in 1789, and it included elements of the Scottish rite (reflecting Bishop Seabury's Concordat with the Episcopal Church of Scotland) and material from the English Prayer Book with necessary alterations due to American independence. The process and commitment for Prayer Book revision continued in following generations, with revisions published in 1892, 1928, and 1979. The process of Prayer Book revision has at times prompted strong emotions for members of the Episcopal Church. Change has been resisted. Although the colonial church made extensive use of the metrical psalter for its hymnody, hymns eventually replaced metrical psalmody in the Episcopal Church after it established its independence from the Church of England. Music and texts for both hymns and service music were separately and privately printed for the first century of the life of the Episcopal Church. The church officially adopted a musical edition of the Hymnal after that time. Periodic revision of the Prayer Book and Hymnal have become characteristic of the Episcopal Church's life and witness. Recent Prayer Book and Hymnal revisions have emphasized the importance of the ministry and participation of all baptized members in the life of the church community. Modern church architecture has likewise encouraged the full participation of the whole community gathered for worship. In some parishes, architectural change has been needed to express the community life shaped by the revisions of the Prayer Book and Hymnal.

53.

William Smith, The Preface, Proposed
Book of Common Prayer, 1786

William Smith (September 7, 1727–May 14, 1803) was one of the major revisers of the first Book of Common Prayer. *He prepared the preface for the Proposed Book of 1786. The Proposed Book of 1786 was not accepted, but Smith's preface has been used in later Prayer Books in a condensed form.*

It is a most invaluable part of that blessed *"liberty wherewith CHRIST hath made us free"*—that, in his worship, different *forms* and *usages* may without offence be allowed, provided the *substance of the faith* be kept entire; and that, in every church, what cannot be clearly determined to belong to *doctrine* must be referred to *discipline*; and, therefore, by common consent and authority may be altered, abridged, enlarged, amended, or otherwise disposed of, as may seem most convenient for the edification of the people, "according to the various exigencies of times and occasions."

The CHURCH OF ENGLAND, to which the Protestant Episcopal Church in these States is indebted, under GOD, for her first foundation and a long continuance of nursing care and protection, hath in the preface of her book of common prayer laid it down as a rule, that — "The particular forms of divine worship, and the rites and ceremonies appointed to be used therein, being things in their own nature indifferent and alterable, and so acknowledged, it is but reasonable that upon weighty and important considerations, according to the various exigencies of times and occasions, such changes and alterations should be made therein, as to those who are in place of authority should, from time to time, seem either necessary or expedient."

. . . .

If, therefore, from the reasons above set forth (namely, the change of times and circumstances, and the fluctuation of our language itself), so many different reviews, alterations, and amendments were found necessary in the first *hundred and twelve* years after the *reformation*; it could not be expected, but (the same causes and reasons still operating) some subsequent *reviews*, alterations and amendments would not only be found necessary, but be earnestly desired by many true members of the Church, in the course of at least *one hundred* and *twenty* years more. And we accordingly find that in less than *thirty* years after the last review in 1661 (viz. on the 13th of September 1689) a commission for a further review of the liturgy and canons, &c, was issued out to a number of bishops and other divines; "than whom (it hath been truly acknowledged) the Church of

England was never, at any one time, blessed with either wiser or better, since it was a Church."

The chief matters proposed for a *review* at that time, and which have been since repeatedly *proposed* and stated under the decent and modest form of *queries*, are included under the following heads.

1st. Whether the *public service* on Sunday mornings be not of too *great length*, and tends rather to diminish than encrease devotion, especially among the lukewarm and negligent?

2d. Whether it might not be conveniently *contracted*, by omitting all unnecessary *repetitions* of the same prayers or subject matter; and whether a better adjustment of the necessary parts of the three different services, usually read every Sunday morning in the Church, would not render the whole frame of the service more uniform, animated, and compleat?

3d. Whether the old and new translations of the psalms ought not to be compared, in order to render both more agreeable to each other and to their divine original; so as to have but one translation, and that as compleat as possible?

4th. Whether *all the* PSALMS of David are applicable to the state and condition of *christian societies*, and ought to be read *promiscuously* as they now are; and whether some other method of reading them might not be appointed, including a *choice* of psalms and hymns, as well for ordinary use, as for the *festivals* and *fasts*, and other special occasions of public worship?

5th Whether the subject matter of our *psalmody* or *singing* psalms should not be extended beyond those of David, which include but a few heads of *christian worship*, and whether much excellent matter might not be taken from the New Testament, as well as some parts of the Old Testament, especially the prophets; so as to introduce a greater variety of *anthems* and *hymns*, suited to the different festivals and other occasions of daily worship, private as well as public?

6th. Whether, in particular, a psalm or anthem should not be adapted to and sung at the celebration of the *Eucharist*, as was the primitive practice, and that recommended in our first liturgy?

7th. Whether all the lessons which are appointed to be read in the ordinary course are well chosen; and whether many of them may not be subject to one or more of the following objections, viz.—1. Either inexpedient to be read in mixt assemblies; or 2. Containing genealogies and passages either obscure, or of little benefit to be read, in our congregations; or 3. Improperly divided; sometimes abrupt and unconnected in their beginning, as having respect to something that hath gone before; and sometimes either too *short* or too *long*, and *apocryphal lessons* included among the number?

8th. Whether our epistles and gospels are all of them well selected; and whether after so many other portions of scripture they are necessary, especially unless the first design of inserting them, viz. as introductory to the communion, should be more regarded, and the communion be again made a daily part of the service of the Church?

9th. Whether our *collects*, which in the main are excellent, are always suited to the epistles and gospels; and whether too many of them are not of one sort, consisting of the same kind of substance? and whether there is any occasion of using the collect for the day twice in the same service?

10th. Whether the Athanasian creed may not, consistently with *piety, faith* and *charity*, be either wholly omitted, or left indifferent in itself?

11th. Whether our catechism may not require illustration in some points and enlargement in others; so that it may not only be rendered fit for children, but a help to those who become candidates for confirmation? And whether all the other offices, viz. the litany, the communion office, the offices of confirmation, matrimony, visitation of the sick, churching of women, and more especially those of baptism, burial and communion, do not call for a review and amendment in sundry particulars?

12th. Whether the calendars and rubrics do not demand a review and better adjustment; and whether any *words* and *phrases* in our common prayer, which are now less intelligible or common, or any way changed in their present acceptation from their original sense, should be retained? And whether others should not be substituted which are more modern, intelligible, and less liable to any misapprehension or construction?

13th. Whether the *articles of religion* may not deserve a *review*; and the subscription to them and the common prayer be contrived after some other manner, less exceptionable than at present?

These are the principal matters which have been long held up for public consideration, as still requiring a review in the book of common prayer; and altho' in the judgement of the Church, there be nothing in it "contrary to the word of God, or to sound doctrine, or which a godly man may not submit unto, or which is not fairly defensible, if allowed such just and favourable construction as in common equity ought to be allowed to all human compositions; yet, upon the principles already laid down, (namely "the promoting of *peace* and *unity* in the Church, the exciting of *piety* and *devotion*, and the removing, as far as possible, of all occasion of cavil or quarrel against the liturgy,") the pious and excellent divines who were commissioned in 1689, proceeded to the execution of the great work assigned them. They had before them all the exceptions which had, since the act of uniformity, been at any time made against any parts of the church service, which are chiefly set forth in the foregoing *queries*. They had likewise many propositions and advices, which had been offered at several times by some of the most eminent Bishops and Divines upon the different heads in question. Matters were well considered, freely and calmly debated; and all was digested into *one entire correction* of every thing that seemed liable to any just objection. But this great and good work miscarried at that time, and the civil authority in Great Britain hath not since thought it proper to revive it by any new commission.

But when, in the course of divine providence, these American States became *independent* with respect to civil government, their *ecclesiastical independence* was necessarily included; and the different religious denominations of christians in these states were left at full and equal liberty to model and organize their respective Churches and forms of worship and discipline, in such manner as they might judge most convenient for their future prosperity, consistently with the constitution and laws of their country.

The attention of this Church was, in the first place, drawn to those alterations in the liturgy which became necessary in the *prayers* for our civil rulers, in consequence of the revolution; and the principal care herein was to make them conformable to what ought to be the proper end of all such prayers, namely, that "*rulers* may have grace, wisdom and understanding to execute justice and to maintain truth; and that the *people* may lead quiet and peaceable lives, in all godliness and honesty."

But while these alterations were in *review* before the late CONVENTION, they could not but, with gratitude to God, embrace the happy occasion which was offered to them (uninfluenced and unrestrained by any worldly authority whatsoever) to take a further review of the *public service*, and to propose to the *church* at large such other alterations and amendments therein as might be deemed expedient; whether consisting of those which have been heretofore so long desired by many, or those which the late change of our circumstances might require, in our religious as well as civil capacity.

By comparing the following book, as now *offered* to the Church, with this *preface* and the *notes* annexed, it will appear that most of the amendments or alterations which had the sanction of the *great Divines* of 1689, have been adopted, with such others as are thought reasonable and expedient.

The service is arranged so as to stand as nearly as possible in the *order* in which it is to be read. A *selection* is made both of the *reading* and *singing* psalms, commonly so called. Wherever the Bible-translation of the former appeared preferable to the old translation, it hath been adopted; and in consequence of the new selection, a new division and considerable abridgement of the daily portions to be read became necessary; and as the "Glory be to the Father," &c. is once said or sung before the reading of the psalms in Morning and Evening prayer, it was conceived that, in order to avoid repetition, the solemnity would be encreased by allowing the minister to conclude the portion of the psalms which is at any time read, with that excellent doxology somewhat shortened, "Glory to God on high," &c. especially when it can be properly sung. With respect to the *psalmody* or *singing psalms*, for the greater ease of chusing such as are suited to particular subjects and occasions, they are disposed under the several *metres* and the *few* general heads to which they can be referred; and a *collection of hymns* are added, upon those *evangelical* subjects and other heads of christian worship, to which the psalms of *David* are less adapted, or do not generally extend.

It seems unnecessary to enumerate particularly all the different alterations and amendments which are proposed. They will readily appear, and it is hoped the reason of them also, upon a comparison of this with the former book. The *Calendar* and *Rubricks* have been altered where it appeared necessary, and the same reasons which occasioned a table of *first lessons* for Sundays and other Holy days, seemed to require the making of a table of *second lessons* also, which is accordingly done. Those for the morning are intended to suit the several seasons, without any material repetition of the epistles and gospels for the same seasons; and those for the evening are selected in the order of the sacred books. Besides this, the table of first lessons has been reviewed; and some new chapters are introduced on the supposition of their being more edifying; and some transpositions of lessons have been made, the better to suit the seasons.

And whereas it hath been the practice of the church of England to set apart certain days of thanksgiving to Almighty God for signal mercies vouchsafed to that church and nation, it hath here also been considered as conducive to godliness that there should be two *annual* solemn days of prayer and thanksgiving to Almighty God set apart; viz. the fourth DAY OF JULY, commemorative of the blessings of *civil and religious* liberty in the land wherein we live; and the *first Thursday* of November for the *fruits of the earth*; in order that we may be thereby stirred up to a more particular remembrance of the signal mercies of God towards us; the neglect of which might otherwise be the occasion of licentiousness, civil miseries and punishments.

The case of such unhappy persons as may be imprisoned for debt or crimes claimed the attention of this church; which hath accordingly adopted into her liturgy the form for the visitation of prisons in use in the church of Ireland.

In the creed commonly called the *Apostles creed*, one clause[1] is omitted, as being of uncertain meaning; and the *articles* of *religion* have been reduced in

---

[1]*The clause meant is, "Christ's descent into hell," which as Bishop Burnet, Bishop Pearson, and other writers inform us, is found in no creed, nor mentioned by any writer, until about the beginning of the 5th century; . . .*

number; yet it is humbly conceived that the doctrines of the Church of England are preserved entire, as being judged perfectly agreeable to the gospel.

It is far from the intention of this Church to depart from the Church of England any farther than local circumstances require, or to deviate in any thing essential to the true meaning of the thirty-nine articles; although the number of them be abridged by some variations in the mode of expression, and the omission of such articles as were more evidently adapted to the times when they were first framed and to the political constitution of England.

And now, this important work being brought to a conclusion, it is hoped the whole will be received and examined, by every true member of our church and every sincere christian, with a meek, candid, and charitable frame of mind; without prejudice or prepossessions; seriously considering what *christianity* is, and what the truths of the gospel are; and earnestly beseeching Almighty God to accompany with his blessing every endeavour for promulgating them to mankind in the clearest, plainest, most affecting, and majestic manner, for the sake of Jesus Christ, our blessed Lord and Saviour.

William Smith, *The Book of Common Prayer* (Philadelphia, 1780), no pagination.

54.

Vestry Minutes of St. Michael's Church, Charleston, South Carolina, 1803

Henry Purcell (1742–March 24, 1802), the fourth rector (1782-1802) of St. Michael's Church, Charleston, and the organist, Samuel Rodgers, 1789-1809, were both trained in the English cathedral tradition. A boy choir was organized at St. Michael's some time after 1791. Under Rodgers and the fifth rector, Thomas Gates (1748–August 23, 1833), St. Michael's had one of the finest musical programs in the country. The vestry minutes of February 27, 1803, provide an interesting picture of early musical customs.

THE ORGANIST Shall perform the Duties of his Office, which Shall from Time to Time be directed by the Ministers, in the Mornings & Evenings of every Sabbath Day in the year; also on Such Festivals or Holy days, as now are, or shall hereafter be appointed by Authority:—He shall perform on the Organ, at all Times preceding the Services of the Day, the time usually adapted to the 36th. Hymn, or any other Solemn piece of Music; to begin at the exact Time the

Clergyman enters the Desk, & to continue the Music for one Verse only, or for a reasonable Time.—He shall chant the *Venite exultemus* & the *te Deum*, on alternate Sundays; & shall play a solemn & well adapted Voluntary, preceding the first Lesson; & Shall receive from the Clerk such Psalms or Hymns as the Ministers shall appoint for the Day, in Order to adapt them to suitable Tunes.— He shall not only accompany the Clerk with the Organ, in such Psalms and Hymns as may be appropriated by the Ministers; but shall join the Clerk in the Gloria Patri, which shall invariably be sung after every Sermon; He shall also perform at all Funerals, to which he may be invited, accompanying the Clerk with the Organ in the Gloria Patri, which shall always be sung at the Conclusions of Funerals, Psalms, or Hymns: He shall, in Conjunction with the Clerk, instruct such Youth as chuse to attend (who shall be particularly placed under his charge) in the Rules & Practice of Psalmody; & he shall command and require of them, a serious and decent Deportment, during the Time of divine Service: And at the Conclusion of Morning & Evening Service, the voluntary, which he shall play shall be some Piece of *sacred Musick*, of rather *slow Time*, such as will tend to cherish the solemn Impressions made by the pious Exercises of Prayer & Exortation. And lastly, it is fully understood and required that he shall be under the Direction of the Clergymen of the said church for the Time being, in all such things appertaining to its religious Services—

Leonard Ellinwood, *The History of American Church Music* (New York: Morehouse-Gorham Company, 1953), 43-44.

55.

William White, An Episcopal Charge, 1834

William White (April 4, 1748–July 17, 1836) was one of the revisers of the first Book of Common Prayer *(1789). In the charge that follows he discusses the principles of Prayer Book revision.*

Our origin in the church of England directs our view to our adherence, in substance, to those services and those forms which have come down to us from her reformers, in the book of common prayer. In this department, there is more room for the exercise of a discretion accommodating to times and circumstances, than under the head of doctrine. But it should be a sound discretion of our ecclesiastical councils, not acting often or in haste, or in any manner unfavourable to stability.

The liberty now presumed, is recognised in the preface to the English book. The extent in which it was put into operation, coincidently with our suit for the episcopacy, caused no hindrance to the meeting of our wishes. Our right to this effect was brought into requisition in the General Convention of the year 1789: the different services and offices, as then established, continuing in authority to the present day.

Should the book be brought again under review, there will unquestionably be manifested discordant opinions concerning different particulars of proposed change, and concerning the extent to which it should be carried: not affecting essentials, as may be hoped, but according to diversities of judgment and even of taste. The only security against consequent discord and its attendant ills, must be the spirit of mutual concession, in all points not interfering with the leading attributes of the church, manifested in the general mass of her devotions. In the meantime, there shall be taken the liberty of disclosing an apprehension for some time felt, in reference to the important subject. It is well known that a portion of our clergy indulge themselves, in various instances, of departure from the use of the liturgy, as prescribed by the rubrics. It is a great impediment to the correcting of the irregularity, that they are possessed of the plea of there being combined services intended by the compilers to be kept distinct, and to be read at different hours: which has the effect of causing repetitions, besides the lengthening of the time of the public service, at least when the communion is to be administered, beyond what is convenient, and certainly beyond what the compilers could have contemplated. The fear is, that the deviations will become of such an extent and of such continuance, as to cover themselves under the positions so much set up in the concerns of civil life, that laws, remaining for a long time unregarded, and this without authoritative censure, may be construed as having fallen under a tacit permission of neglect, and cease to have a binding operation. If there be any among us who cherish the less dangerous error of abiding, in every particular, by what long practice has endeared to them, however expedient and useful, in general opinion, may be submission to moderate change; it is in the opposite extreme to that which affects changes without improvements, and like extremes on all subjects, they here tend to issues in contrariety to what was in the minds of the conceivers of them.

Your bishop, at this late period of his ministry is not likely to witness the result of a review, so as to endanger the excitement either of his passions or of his prejudices by the circumstances which will be attendant on it. But as the question is already agitated within the church, he thinks it will not be inconsistent with the determination declared by him of not endeavouring to dictate for future times, when he takes occasion to record his opinion concerning the form in which the measure should be conducted, if it should be resolved on.

Let a committee of bishops be chosen by the house of bishops, and another of presbyters, by the house of clerical and lay deputies. Let this combined committee assemble at some place convenient for the consultation of books. Let them maturely, and not without continued prayer, devote themselves to the work. And when it is prepared, let there be a call of the General Convention: the revised liturgy to be received or rejected by them, without debate. This plan will resemble, as nearly as difference of circumstances permits, the form in which the English book of Common Prayer was prepared and adopted; and we know the duration of it. As to conventional reviews, they will be always liable to so much haste, to so much heat and pertinacity of opinion, generated by opposition; and added to all, defect of theological learning in no small a proportion of the reviewers, that in the estimation of your bishop there is little likelihood of their being either judicious or stable.

On this subject of the book of Common Prayer, he is desirous of impressing on the mind of his reverend brethren the guarding against even the appearance of a fault, with which some of our ministry have been untruly charged—the elevating of the book to a level with the holy Bible, by making the acceptance of the former a condition for the bestowing of the latter. The charge has been publicly made and publicly denied, and has been continued without proof; contrary, in some instances, to better knowledge. For the avoiding of the appearance of so great a fault, the best experiment will be, that each of us, within his sphere of action, and in the line the most agreeable to his judgment, should give his aid to the zeal which has been brought into action for a general dissemination of the Word of Truth: accordance with which is the greatest glory of that other book which we are accused of holding in extravagant esteem.

Let not our esteem for it be lessened by a charge so injuriously made. Besides its usefulness as a form of public worship, we have abundant evidence of its being blessed to the exciting of devotion in families and in individuals. When, during the revolutionary war, very many districts of our country had become deprived of the means of grace; in some of them, devotion was kept alive in domestic circles, by their possession of books of Common Prayer; so that when, after the lapse of many years, a christian ministry became restored to them, the intervening privation had not obliterated the instruction of preceding times. Neither ought we to be regardless of the fact, that in many a case of a life spent in utter forgetfulness of God, and perhaps in gross sin, the recollection of the devotions of the book in question, has been the means of repentance and reformation.

For these reasons the book of Common Prayer ought to be considered as an important adjunct in our missionary efforts, both foreign and domestic. By its incitements to devotion, and by its helps in it, the cause may be aided in places in which the itineracy of the missionary will not permit him to remain. Even in the cases of a reasonable proportion of settled pastors, their flocks are generally so extended in their several places of residence, as that it is difficult to command personal aid at the times of unexpected sickness, or of the happening of any extraordinary calamity, when there would be peculiar propriety in the application for religious counsel. Far from the present intention be the dispensing with ministerial aid, in the extent to which it can be carried by the zeal and by the active labours of the minister. But there being physical limits, beyond which his agency cannot be extended, it is no small relief of the wants to which he should be ever ready to contribute his succour, that they may at least in some degree be met by the compilation, which comprehends counsels suited to all states of mind, and devotions expressive of any desires, of which present circumstances ought to be the mean of excitement.

William White, *The Past and the Future, A Charge on Events Connected with the Organization of the Protestant Episcopal Church in the United States of America, and the Lessons They Inculcate* (Philadelphia: By Order of the Convention, 1834), 15-18. (Excerpt)

56.

Thomas C. Brownell, Of the Advantages of Forms of Prayer for Public Worship, 1868

Thomas Church Brownell (October 19, 1779–January 13, 1865) was consecrated the third Bishop of Connecticut on October 27, 1819. He was the seventh Presiding Bishop, September 20, 1852, until his death. He notes that a distinctive element of the Episcopal Church is the use of written forms and prayers.

Forms of prayer possess many *important advantages*. When public worship is conducted according to a prescribed form, the people are previously acquainted with the prayers in which they are to join, and are thus enabled to render unto God a *reasonable and enlightened* service. In forms of prayer, that *dignity and propriety of language*, so necessary in supplications addressed to the infinite Majesty of Heaven, may be preserved. They prevent the *particular opinions and dispositions* of the *minister* from *influencing* the devotions of the *congregation*. They serve as a *standard of faith and practice*, impressing on both minister and people, at every performance of public worship, the important doctrines and duties of the Gospel. And they render the service more *animating*, by *uniting* the *people* with the *minister* in the performance of public worship. . . .

Thus, then, we see how excellent and superior in all respects is the liturgy of our Church; and how admirably she has provided for the two important objects of the public service, *instruction* and *devotion*. The *lessons*, the *creeds*, the *commandments*, the *epistles* and *gospels*, contain the most important and impressive instruction on the doctrines and duties of religion: While the *confession*, the *collects* and *prayers*, the *litany* and *thanksgivings*, lead the understanding and the heart through all the sublime and affecting exercises of devotion. In this truly evangelical and excellent liturgy, the supreme Lord of the universe is invoked by the most appropriate, affecting and sublime epithets: all the wants to which man, as a dependant and sinful being, is subject, are expressed in language at once simple, concise, and comprehensive; these wants are urged by *confessions* the most *humble*, and *supplications* the most *reverential* and *ardent*; the *all sufficient merits* of Jesus Christ, the Saviour of the world, are uniformly urged as the only *effectual plea*, the only *certain pledge* of divine *mercy* and *grace*; and with the most *instructive lessons* from the sacred oracles, and the most profound *confessions* and *supplications*, is mingled the sublime *chorus* of *praise* begun by the Minister, and responded with one heart and voice from the assembled congregation. The mind, continually passing from one exercise of worship to another, and, instead of one continued and uniform prayer, sending up its wishes and aspirations in short and varied collects of supplications, is never suffered to grow languid and weary. The affections of the worshipper ever kept alive by the tenor and animating fervor which breathes through the service; he worships his God and Redeemer in spirit and in truth, with reverence and awe, with lively gratitude and love; the exalted joys of devotion are poured upon his soul; he feels that it is *good for him to draw near unto God, and that a day spent in his courts, is better than a thousand passed in the tents of the ungodly.*

Thus delightful and edifying will every person find the service who joins in it with sincerity; who unites his heart with his voice, in the parts of the service assigned to the people; and who accompanies the minister in thought and affection through the supplications and prayers, lifting up his heart in secret ejaculations corresponding to the public addresses of the minister to the throne of God. A person who thus sincerely offers his devotions according to the liturgy of the Church may be satisfied that he is worshipping God "with the spirit and with the understanding also." The more frequently and seriously he joins in the service, the more will he be impressed with its exquisite beauties, which tend at once to gratify his taste and to quicken his devotion. That *continued change of language* in prayer which some persons appear to consider as essential to spiritual devotion, it would be impossible to attain, even were every minister left to his own

247

discretion in public worship. The same expressions would necessarily recur frequently in his prayers. They would soon sink into a form, destitute of that propriety and dignity of sentiment and language, of that variety; that simplicity, and affecting fervor which characterize the liturgy of the Church.

If the charge of dull uniformity may with propriety be urged against the prayers of the Church, it may with equal justice be urged against that exalted and inspired composition the Lord's prayer. And yet we can surely offer no prayer more acceptable to God than the one prescribed by his blessed Son. A lively glow of the fancy and animal spirits may be excited where there is little of the spirit of true devotion, where the understanding and feelings are not deeply and permanently interested. The *novelty* that is sought for in extempore effusions tends to occupy the imagination with the words that are employed, and thus diverts the mind from the proper business of devotion. He who with sincerity and humility makes it his regular business to worship God according to the solemn forms of the liturgy, may be assured that he renders unto God an acceptable service, even if he should not always feel those lively and ardent emotions which depend in no inconsiderable degree upon constitutional temperament, upon the state of health, and various external circumstances. . . .

The *length* of the service has been sometimes a subject of complaint. Yet so excellent and appropriate is every part of it, that it would be difficult to determine where with propriety it could be curtailed. On this subject there would certainly be a great diversity of opinion, and the Church would therefore probably lose much more than she would gain by any alteration of the service. In its present state it has become venerable from time, and has always served as an animating guide to the devotions of the pious. Let every person who objects to the length of the service seriously consider, whether this objection does not arise in a considerable degree from an indisposition to discharge the duties of public worship, and from laying too much stress on *preaching*, which, though an appointed means of grace, ought certainly ever to be subordinate to the more important duty of worshipping God. It is worthy of remark also, that the service is not entirely occupied with prayer. The reading of portions of the Holy Scriptures and the reciting of the psalms constitute no inconsiderable part of it. The blending of instruction and devotion; the transition from prayer to praise, and from one short supplication to another; the mingling of the responses of the people with the addresses of the minister, afford an interesting variety in the service, which is one of its most excellent and valuable characteristics.

Long then may the Church preserve inviolate a form of service, which is calculated to cherish in her members a spirit of devotion equally remote from dull and unprofitable lukewarmness on the one hand, and from blind, extravagant, and indecent enthusiasm on the other—a form of service which has ever served to brighten the pious graces of her members; and in the season of declension and error, to preserve the pure flame of truth and the genuine spirit of evangelical piety. With such sacred and commendable caution, does the Episcopal Church in America guard this service, that she exacts from all her ministers, at their ordination, a solemn promise of conformity to it; and, in one of her canons, forbids the use of any other prayers than those contained in the liturgy.

Where indeed a form of prayer is provided, the introduction of extempore prayers, would appear liable to the charges of being unnecessary and presumptuous—unnecessary, because it is to be supposed that the Church has fully provided in her service for every subject of prayer; and presumptuous, because it carries the idea, that it is in the power of an individual to compose prayers for the congregation superior to those prepared by the united wisdom and piety of the Church. Equally presumptuous would be any attempt in an individual minister to alter the language of prayers universally admired for their correctness, and their simplicity—prayers in the language of which, the most eminent divines, and the first scholars in every age have esteemed it a privilege to express their devotions.

Were these wholesome restraints which confine the clergy to the prescribed form removed; were every minister allowed at pleasure to alter *the service*, to depart from the rubrics, and to introduce prayers not approved by the Church; that *uniformity* of worship which constitutes one peculiar excellence of the Episcopal Church would be destroyed. No limits could be set to a liberty peculiarly liable to abuse. There would be reason to apprehend, that the spirit of irregular enthusiasm, which experience proves is seldom satisfied with its encroachments, or soothed by indulgence, would fundamentally change, and perhaps finally subvert that liturgy, which is now at once the glory and safeguard of the Church, the nurse of evangelical truth, and of spiritual and sober devotion.

Thomas Church Brownell, *The Family Prayer Book, or The Book of Common Prayer, and Administration of the Sacraments, and other Rites and Ceremonies of the Church, According to the Use of the Protestant Episcopal Church in the United States of America; Accompanied by a General Commentary, Historical, Explanatory, Doctrinal, and Practical* (Philadelphia: Claxton, Remsen & Haffelfinger, 1868), 1, 8-10. (Excerpt)

57

William Reed Huntington, Revision of the
American Common Prayer, 1881

William Reed Huntington (September 20, 1838–July 26, 1909) was for many years the most influential member of the House of Deputies. Not only were his writings the source of the Quadrilateral, but he had a major influence on the 1892 revision of the Book of Common Prayer. *Huntington's contributions are commemorated in the Episcopal Calendar of the Church Year on July 27. In this essay he describes the need for continuing Prayer Book revision.*

[. . .] Shrewd and far-seeing as were William White and his coadjutors in their forecast of nineteenth century needs made from the standpoint of the Peace of Versailles, they would have been more than human had they succeeded in anticipating all the civil and ecclesiastical consequences destined to flow from that memorable event. Certainly it ought not to be held strange that this "new America" of ours, with its enormously multiplied territory, its conglomerate of races, its novel forms of association, its multiplicity of industries not dreamed of a generation ago, should have demands to make in respect to a better adaptation of ancient formularies to present wants, such as thoughtful people count both reasonable and cogent. That a Prayer-Book revised primarily for the use of a half-proscribed Church planted here and there along a sparsely inhabited sea-coast, should serve as amply as it does the purposes of a population now swollen from four millions to fifty, and covering the whole breadth of the continent, is marvel enough; to assert for the book entire adequacy to meet these altered circumstances is a mistake. "New time, new favors and new joys," so a familiar hymn affirms, "do a new song require." We have conceded the principle so far as psalmody is concerned, why not apply it to the service of prayer as well as to that of praise, and in addition to our new hymns secure also such new intercessions and new thanksgivings as the needs of to-day suggest.

The reference in the resolution to the approaching completion of the century has since been playfully characterized as a bit of "sentimentalism."[2] The criticism would be entirely just if the mere recurrence of the centennial anniversary were the point chiefly emphasized. But when a century closes as this one of ours has done with a great social revolution whereby "all estates of men" have been more or less affected, the proposal to signalize entrance upon a fresh stretch of national life by making devotional preparation for it is something better than a

---

[2]Church Eclectic for Nov., 1880.

pretty conceit; there is a serious reasonableness in it.

Every revision of the Common Prayer of the Church of England, and there have been four of them since Edward's first book was put in print, has taken place at some important era of transition in the national life: and conversely it may be said that every civil crisis, with a single exception, has left its mark upon the formularies.

To one who argues that because we in this country are evidently entering upon a new phase of the national life we ought similarly to re-enforce and re-adjust our service-book, it is no sufficient reply to urge the severance effected here between Church and State. The fact that ours is a non-established Church does not make her wholly unresponsive to the shocks of change that touch the civil fabric. In so far as a political renewal alters the social grading of society, bringing in education, for instance, where before it was not, or suddenly developing new forms of industrial activity, the Church, whether established or not, is in duty bound to take cognizance of the fresh field of duty thus suddenly thrust upon her, and to prepare herself accordingly.

William Reed Huntington, "Revision of the American Common Prayer," *American Church Review* 33 (April 1881): 15-17. (Excerpt)

58.

William J. Gold, The Continuity of the Principles of Divine Worship, Contained in the Book of Common Prayer, 1894

William Jason Gold (June 17, 1845–January 11, 1903) taught at Seabury Hall (Divinity School), Racine College, and Western Theological Seminary. His major area of teaching was New Testament Exegesis and Liturgics. He attended the General Conventions of 1886, 1889, and 1892, where he exercised a significant influence on the 1892 Book of Common Prayer. This statement describes the values that guided the 1892 revision of the Prayer Book.

The long period of revision through which the Prayer Book has recently passed has given a fresh impetus to the study of its principles and history. It is safe to say that in our theological schools and elsewhere this study will hereafter be more thorough than it has been hitherto, and that it will be conducted upon broader and more philosophic lines.

All along it has been instinctively perceived that the offices of worship contained in this Book are distinguished in some peculiar manner from other books of devotion or directories of worship which religious men or societies have produced. This has been tacitly acknowledged far beyond the boundaries of the Church herself, and this precious treasury of worship has furnished much of the material for numerous liturgical experiments among various denominations of Christians. But at the same time the reason for this preëminence has been very dimly apprehended. Churchmen have been fond of speaking of "our incomparable liturgy," but they have often known as little as others what made it incomparable.

It will be the purpose of the present paper to offer some contribution towards an answer to this question, to justify on rational and historical grounds that conservative instinct which has so carefully guarded the Prayer Book ever since the reign of Elizabeth and which has more than once saved it from radical alteration.

During the progress of the recent revision, now, it is to be hoped, closed for a long time to come, this conservative feeling throughout the Church opposed an effectual barrier to all serious innovations. People were not, in the long run, led away by the enticing character of certain proposals which would have introduced elements of a more or less sentimental cast, foreign to the gravity which is so marked a feature of the Book as a whole. Even when it was urged that by certain alterations this or that unpopular or perhaps questionable development of the present day might be "put down," although these were matters about which men felt strongly, such propositions were not finally adopted. It was felt that practical difficulties of this nature were nothing new. They are inseparable from the character of a living Church, a Church instinct with earnest desire to fulfil in every possible way the work committed to its care. Practical experiments and adaptations of various kinds may safely be left to the test of time and use. There was a possibility that in the attempt to provide against present abuses or excesses, real or supposed, some vital principle might be violated, or some new principle be inadvertently introduced which would be found, in the end, inconsistent with deeper and essential considerations. Nothing could better illustrate the extraordinary value placed upon the Prayer Book by American Churchmen, than the jealousy with which the work of revision was watched during the entire twelve years of its progress and the comparatively small amount of change which resulted from so much labour.

Some devout and eloquent writers have supposed that the distinguishing merit of the Prayer Book consists in its eminently scriptural character, and they have very justly enlarged upon the admirable system by which the Holy Scriptures have been applied to the instruction of the faithful; the use of the Book of Psalms; and the scriptural truths which form the themes of many a prayer and collect. But it must not be forgotten that instruction is not the primary purpose of the Prayer Book, and it is far from being a mere cento of Biblical texts and passages. It has a distinct spirit and purpose of its own, and its employment of Holy Scripture is subsidiary to this purpose. It is a Book of Worship and its constant features are, Praise, Thanksgiving and Prayer.

. . . .

Our recent revision has affected the Communion Office very slightly. It has been rightly treated as the "ark of the Lord," too sacred to be handled with impunity. The changes elsewhere have chiefly served to restore those beautiful features of the English Book which are among the characteristic marks of the morning and evening Prayer, but which were not appreciated at their true value at the close of the last century. This revision has taken place at a period when religious changes are in the air. Christian societies are agitating the revision of the very articles of faith upon which they have hitherto taken their stand, men of repute are declaring that those points upon which they insisted in times past as necessary to salvation are not necessary. Others are urging the abolition of the discipline which was formerly their chief pride and the main source of their usefulness. Liberal religion, that is, religion without a positive revelation, is advancing with great strides. As in 1786-9, the "Proposed Book" preceded the Prayer Book as finally settled, so, in our latest revision, the "Book Annexed" received the favourable vote of one convention,—a production, which, though it did not, after all, invade the sphere of doctrine in any direct or intentional way, was far from exhibiting correctness in liturgical principles. But, in spite of these influences from without and within, this work has been brought to completion, without a single departure from the sound principles of Christian worship and the standards of our ancient faith, and with some improvement in liturgical detail. Indeed, in one respect, the requirement that the Catholic Creed of the Church shall be said upon the greater festivals, it has profoundly strengthened the cause of belief, and thus a marked and encouraging contrast is presented to movements going on elsewhere in the religious world.

I have spoken at the beginning of this paper of the fascination which the Prayer Book and its system of worship have had for religious minds, and I have endeavoured to bring to light some of the grounds upon which this power rests. And now there are many indications that this power so far from showing any signs of diminution, is destined to become yet stronger in coming days, not only among Churchmen who are coming to understand more fully the value of the treasure they possess, but also among those who by training and religious association have been strangers to the privileges we enjoy in our ancestral institutions.

The great revival of the essential principles of divine worship under the leadership of the Anglican Communion, has impressed itself upon devout and thoughtful souls far beyond her boundaries. This movement, indeed, on account of its very practical and educating character, has in itself the promise and the earnest of a force stronger than argument and controversy or all theoretical apologetics, to make the minds and hearts of Christians, tasting here the heavenly gift and the powers of the world to come, invulnerable to the anti-Christian movements of the day, which often seem so formidable. The realm of instinct and intuition where the primary principles of religion have their seat, lies deeper than that of mere intellect; and when the intellect has expended its utmost labour and skill to undermine the Christian faith, the voice which issues from this deeper seat, still demands that wants which lie in the very constitution of human nature itself shall have their realization and that system in which such realization is to be attained, will still prevail.

William J. Gold, "The Continuity of the Principles of Divine Worship, Contained in the Book of Common Prayer," *The Church Eclectic* 22 (May 1894): 97-98; (June 1894): 201-202. (Excerpts)

59.

Winfred Douglas, Music Expresses Human Life, 1935

Charles Winfred Douglas (February 15, 1867-January 18, 1944) was a leading Episcopal musicologist and served on the Joint Commission on the Revision of the Hymnal which produced The Hymnal 1940. *Among Douglas's achievements was his role as the major adapter of plainsong to English prose. In 1935 he delivered the Hale Lectures at Seabury-Western Theological Seminary entitled "The Praise of God." In 1962 these lectures were revised by Leonard Ellinwood (February 13, 1965–   ) and republished. Ellinwood was another Episcopal musicologist, and editor of* The Hymnal 1940 Companion. *The Hale Lectures were endowed by Charles Reuben Hale (March 14, 1837–December 25, 1900), who was consecrated Assistant Bishop of Springfield on July 26, 1892. This passage concerns the role of music in moving, expressing, and forming the heart's devotions.*

Music is an art of human expression which directly voices the human soul in tone governed by rhythm. It can really utter the voice of the spirit through the flesh; and make the spoken word more intensely vital, more sincere, truer. In its combination of the sensible and the spiritual, it corresponds to the nature of man, and to the sacramental idea characteristic of the religion of Jesus. Both religion and art are *qualitative* expressions of the nature of being, and therefore allied. Science, on the other hand, is *quantitative* in its approach to reality.

What are the sources of the unique art of music?

Music has a double source in man's very existence, springing from the co-ordination of two quite diverse human impulses. The first is the impulse of emotional self-expression, the external manifestation of life as personal feeling. It is this which produces *tone,* sustained sound, the material out of which music is made. The high wandering sounds of a baby's voice communicate directly the baby's inner mood, long before speech. We may call this the *song* impulse. The second is an impulse of ordered law which corresponds to his own individual life processes, but is also significant because it relates them to the universe outside of himself. The beat of the baby's heart, the steady rise and fall of his breath, correspond in kind with the sequence of day and night, with the ordered swing of planets and suns. The baby will very early yield to this impulse by making rhythmic movements which express his delight in corresponding to something outside of himself. We therefore call it the *dance* impulse. The rattle, the drum, will take the baby's rhythmical expression into the realm of sound. A little later in life, when sustained tone is wedded to ordered rhythm, *music is* created—music, which is the most human of all the arts, because it can *directly* express personality in action or life. It is necessary to lay stress on this unique characteristic of music itself before we can rightly estimate the nature of Christian music.

A widespread belief, not always wholly conscious, exists in America that music, far from being an essential art of life, is merely a surface decoration. People think of music as an escape from silence of which they are unconsciously afraid, as an excitant whose exaggerated mechanical rhythms take the place of a calm which they cannot attain, as a sensuous pleasure which they can buy, paying the highest prices to the best purveyors of it, and estimating its excellence merely by the objective delight which it gives, as an emotional intoxicant, a spiritual drug whose emotion leads to no action and therefore leaves the spirit weakened as by an opiate, as a superior sort of circus which astonishes them by a display of mechanical or of intellectual dexterity. We have heard every one of these misuses of music in churches in this country. This is perhaps not strange in a civilization but recently out of the pioneer stage, and still in the commercial stage, intensely preoccupied with material things. But as life becomes more deeply conscious of spiritual values, so the expression of life in religious music must become more real, more sincere; it must become true *worship* music, in which the ordered tone, whether sung or only heard, will be the veritable voice of the worshipper's prayer. No valid church music was ever made merely to be listened to as a sensuous pleasure.

It is a grave impoverishment of our culture that so many classify music as an amusement, and not as a collective voice of mankind that unites men on a higher level of spiritual sensitiveness than they could otherwise attain. Music is not merely a succession of pleasing sound-patterns formed of sensuous tone; but is essentially an utterance, an elemental utterance of the whole man. Its message is not primarily addressed either to the intellect or to the emotions, but to the complete personality of the listener; and that message, to be valid, must spring from the complete personalities of both composer and performer. In it, heart speaks directly to heart, mind to mind, life to life. To singer or to listener, the message becomes as his own voice speaking within, not only an external revelation of beauty but also the vital utterance of his own soul, so that he adores with the voice of Palestrina, prays with that of Bach, rejoices in the mighty tones of Beethoven, loves and suffers in the surging crescendos of Wagner.

Music is thus not only closely related to life by its power of personal utterance, but still more by its essential character as rhythmic flow; for our life is a continuous movement, of which we are conscious through periodic recurrences of experience. Life is never a state, but always a process; never a being, but always a becoming. Of music alone among the arts is this wholly true. The drama and the dance possess rhythmic flow in varying degree, but they remain external to all but the participants. Other arts are static in their relation to the life of man. Architecture permanently shelters and expresses the various manifestations of his social activity; painting records his interpretation of the world which he sees; jewelry and clothing adorn his body; sculpture perpetuates the forms of that body in its more perfect or passionate states; poetry delineates particular aspects of his thought and feeling. Only music moves and changes as his whole being moves and changes, lives parallel with his life, agonizes with his struggle, mourns with his grief, exults with his joy, prays with his adoration. From the far dim dawn in barbarism of that "Light which lighteth every man that cometh into the world," the sense of divine vision has evoked the mysterious power of music to express man's reaction to the numinous, to vitalize and supplement speech in the utterance of worship.

Winfred Douglas, *Church Music in History and Practice: Studies in the Praise of God. Revised with Additional Material by Leonard Ellinwood* (New York: Charles Scribner's Sons, 1962), 6-9. (Excerpt)

60.

Walden Pell and Powell M. Dawley, The Worship of the Church, 1943

Walden Pell II (July 3, 1902–March 23, 1983) was headmaster of St. Andrew's School, Middletown, Delaware, and Powell Mills Dawley (March 1, 1907–July 10, 1985) was dean of the Cathedral Church of St. Luke, Portland, Maine, at the time they wrote The Religion of the Prayer Book. *Dawley was later professor of ecclesiastical history at the General Theological Seminary, 1945-1971. This statement describes the centrality of worship and the need for liturgy.*

Most people find the center of their religious life in a parish church. Many of them take part there in some active work. They may be members of a men's club, a servers' guild, a brotherhood, or a young people's fellowship. Possibly they are associated with the work of a missionary society like the Women's Auxiliary, a sewing guild, or some other service organization. Bible study classes, the Church School, and confirmation classes provide activities in Christian education; altar societies and acolytes' guilds present opportunities for the service of the sanctuary. Together these activities of the parish appeal to a wide variety of interests. Some exist for the benefit of the parish church itself; some are charitable works for the poor and the afflicted; others help to support the missionary program of the whole Church. All these things are good. Most of them are important. Some are necessary, but not one of these activities is the chief function of the parish church.

The supreme activity of the Church is the worship of God. The first activity of any parish church, therefore, is to set forth for its people the worship of God. The essential work of the parish does not center in its organizations and clubs, but in the administration of the Sacraments, the Sunday services, and the daily worship of God. All other activities of fellowship and service draw their strength from this primary duty of prayer. If worship stopped, then all other works would gradually die out. If, on the other hand, all organizations were disbanded, public worship could still continue, and were it the right kind of whole-hearted offering of ourselves to God, new ways of expressing service and fellowship would quickly grow up again.

Clearly, worship is the chief function of the Church. For that reason the Office of Instruction says that the *first* duty of a Christian is "to worship God every Sunday in his Church." It is his second duty "to work and pray and give for the spread of the kingdom." What does this mean? Simply that all the activities of the *parish house* are the result of the worship which is offered day after day, Sunday after Sunday, before the *parish altar*. A man who truly worships God will love and serve both God and his fellowmen. A man who never worships God will most likely love and serve himself only. A parish church which is not first a body of worshipers will soon cease to have any Christian activity in service, fellowship, or missionary effort. The worship of God is that which keeps our membership of His Family alive.

But why should the Church's highest activity be the worship of God? It is because man's highest activity is the worship of God. The life of men and women starts and finishes with God. He is the Alpha and the Omega, the beginning and end of all things. He created us. He guides our destinies with His loving hand. He died on the Cross that our sins might be forgiven us. He gives us the gift of eternal life through Jesus Christ. These are stupendous facts, yet they are the only facts by which we can make sense out of our lives. As soon as a man clearly recognizes the truth of these facts and what they mean to him, he has only one response—to worship God. That means to devote his entire being, body, mind, and soul, to love God whose love for us passes all human understanding. Our highest pursuit cannot be other than to worship Him through whose Providence we were brought into this world, and under whose protecting arms we shall one day pass from this world to a better one.

The Church's worship is necessarily public or common worship, that is, worship in which people participate together as one group. Men worship God privately, but that satisfies neither their natural instincts, nor their Christian obligation. The Family of God worships as a Family, just as a human family engages in its activities together as one group. Common worship is frequently called *corporate worship*, which means simply the worship of a whole body of people.

Since the very earliest days of the Church corporate worship has been the chief means of offering prayer. In the beginning the Disciples met to pray. The important thing to remember is not that they prayed, but that they met to pray together. So today we still meet to pray together in the church. There we express in our outward worship all the inward movement of our souls toward God. We concentrate all our thoughts and prayers upon His goodness and love and great glory; we consecrate ourselves anew to His service among our fellows.

Men and women cannot pray and worship together without some formal order. Without an orderly worship God's glory would not be much advanced, nor would we derive any of the strength which comes to the united body of worshipers. Imagine what would happen if we met together to worship exactly as we liked. We might come to church on Sunday and find some people singing hymns, and not necessarily the same hymn; some reading Psalms; others in silent prayer; still others celebrating the Holy Communion, and so on. To worship God properly the Church must have orderly ways and methods. Thus we use regular forms of service, and these forms we call the liturgy of the Church. We find them in the *Book of Common Prayer*. Many people, especially those who belong to Protestant denominations, object to what they call "set forms" of public worship on the grounds that the worship of God should be spontaneous, that one's devotional aspirations should be allowed to have free play. The Catholic Church, however, from her ages of wisdom, has realized the value of orderly liturgies to guide the common corporate worship. Five important reasons why we use liturgical forms in our public services are these:

A liturgy saves us from disorderliness. When we meet together to worship we are all united in the same prayers, the same reverence, the same adoration, and the same praise of God. It is in this unity that the strength of God's Family lies.

A liturgy saves us from being dependent upon our own feelings. People are very much dependent upon their feelings. If they are sad or worried or tired, they do not *feel* much joy or trust or strength. If left alone to worship God their worship would be seriously affected by their feelings at the moment. This should not be, for good prayer does not depend on feeling. Yet as long as men and women allow their feelings to affect them, a liturgy is necessary to provide the power to lift us above our own feelings. Without it we should be unable to rise above thoughts about ourselves to concentrate upon God.

A liturgy saves us from being dependent upon a Minister. Without forms of prayer the congregation of worshipers is dependent upon the prayers and order of service made up by the minister or clergyman. The excellence of the worship will depend upon his training and knowledge, his personality, and the depth of his spirituality. But ministers are, after all, human beings, subject to human imperfections. With a liturgy, however, we depend not upon the abilities of men but upon the prayers of the whole historic Church.

A liturgy saves us from the loss of perspective. Without a liturgy the danger is that we shall concentrate too much upon the problems of our own time, and not upon those fundamental truths of God and man which are timeless. One can imagine that in time of war people's worship would be seriously affected by their inability to shake off the war-temper which surrounded them. Or, in times of great prosperity and success people would forget their utter dependence upon Almighty God. A liturgy prevents this loss of the due proportion of things because it keeps always before us the basic truths about God and about man and about Christ which are necessary to our salvation.

A liturgy preserves for us all that is best from past ages. In some ages the devotion of men and women is deeper than in others. The prayers and orders of service which grow up in an age of great piety and clear knowledge of God's ways are preserved by means of fixed forms for all subsequent ages. In our Prayer Book, for example, many of the collects have been in constant use since

600 A.D. Parts of the service of Holy Communion date back even to the first century. By using the same forms of worship which have been passed down through the history of the Church we are the inheritors of the rich devotion of the past.

We not only preserve our continuity with the Church of the Apostles, the Fathers, and the Saints; we also maintain our unity in worship with all those who have gone before us to the Church in Paradise. It is only in a great liturgical heritage that we are able to discern the full meaning of "Therefore with Angels and Archangels, and with all the company of heaven, we laud and magnify thy glorious Name; evermore praising thee, and saying, Holy, Holy, Holy, Lord God of hosts."

Sometimes one hears the criticism that set forms of prayer and worship are rigid and tend to become meaningless repetitions. This criticism generally comes from persons who have had no experience of liturgical worship. A liturgy is a *live* and *flexible* thing, it is not a set of dead or meaningless prayers. Its life comes from the life of the Church, for forms of worship grow along with the growth of devotion in the Church. Its flexibility is seen in its many forms and services suitable to express the worship of all people in all times and places.

The worship of the Church is not only "liturgical," it is also "sacramental." This means that our highest forms of worship are expressed in the Sacrament— for example, in Baptism, in the Holy Communion, and others. Sacramental worship differs from other kinds of worship because it is the whole of the whole man, body, mind, and spirit. In non-sacramental worship we bring into play our minds and spirits. In sacramental worship something is done which is bodily or physical, and by means of this outward physical act an inward spiritual truth is perceived, and an inward spiritual benefit is received. This is what is meant by the definition of a sacrament in the Office of Instruction as "an outward and visible sign of an inward and spiritual grace." In other words, the sacramental principle is this: *spiritual effects come through material means.*

This sounds difficult, but actually it is quite simple. It happens to us all the time. A handclasp or a kiss is a sacrament. First, it is an outward and visible sign that we are friendly or in love with the person who joins in it with us. Second, it is the means whereby we help to strengthen that love or friendship. This is its inward and spiritual effect. We might call the handclasp or kiss the Sacrament of Friendship.

The Sacraments given to us by our Lord work in precisely the same way. God knows that while we live in physical bodies our souls cannot be separated from those bodies. So He has given us certain Sacraments which unite us to Him in perfect love and worship by the effect upon the soul of some outward and material act. The best example of this is, of course, the Holy Communion. Here, in receiving the consecrated Bread and Wine (the outward and visible physical act), we receive also the very life of Jesus whose Body and Blood they have spiritually become (the inward and spiritual strength).

One last word about worship. True worship of God is always associated with right conduct in our everyday life. There are many people who worship God every Sunday in His Church and who then spend the next six days ignoring Him. Even worse are the people who seem to worship God and yet do not try to lead decent, wholesome, and honest lives. The trouble with all these people is not with their lives but with their worship. If they were to worship God truly with all their hearts and minds and strength, they would discover that good Christian living is the result of that worship. In other words, prayer is not important because it helps us to live right. God is all important. Prayer brings us to Him. Right conduct is the result.

Walden Pell and Powell M. Dawley, *The Religion of the Prayer Book* (New York: Morehouse-Gorham Co., 1943), 58-62. (Excerpt)

61.

Prayer Book Studies I, 1950

During the 1940s the Standing Liturgical Commission received many suggestions for Prayer Book revision. At the fifty-sixth General Convention at San Francisco, September 26–October 7, 1949, the Standing Liturgical Commission reported that "the accumulated number of these requests and suggestions has now become so great and comes from such a variety of sources, that we are forced to believe that a general revision of the Prayer Book is not far away." This convention authorized the Standing Liturgical Commission to produce a series of Prayer Book studies. The objective was the same as that expressed by the Commission for the Revision of 1892: "Resolved, That this Committee, in all its suggestions and acts, be guided by those principles of liturgical construction and ritual use which have guided the compilation and amendments of the Book of Common Prayer, *and have made it what it is."*

. . . It is not possible to avoid every matter which may be thought by some to be controversial. Ideas which seem to be constructively valuable will be brought to the attention of the Church, without too much regard as to whether they may ultimately be judged to be expedient. We cannot undertake to eliminate every proposal to which anyone might conceivably object: to do so would be to admit that any constructive progress is impossible. What we can do is to be alert not to alter the present *balance* of expressed or implied doctrine of the Church. We can seek to counterbalance every proposal which might seem to favor some one party of opinion by some other change in the opposite direction. The goal we have constantly had in mind—however imperfectly we may have succeeded in attaining it—is the shaping of a future Prayer Book which *every* party might embrace with the well-founded conviction that therein its own position had been strengthened, its witness enhanced, and its devotions enriched.

The Standing Liturgical Commission of the Protestant Episcopal Church in the United States of America, *Prayer Book Studies I: Baptism and Confirmation* (New York: Church Pension Fund, 1950), vi-vii. (Excerpt)

62.

Massey H. Shepherd, Jr., The Christian Year, 1952

Massey Hamilton Shepherd, Jr. (March 14, 1913–February 18, 1990) was one of the great liturgical scholars of the Episcopal Church. He was professor of church history at the Episcopal Theological Seminary, 1940-1954, and of liturgy at the Church Divinity School of the Pacific. This writing concerns the meanings of the different seasons of the church year.

It comes as a surprise to many people, upon opening the Book of Common Prayer for the first time, to discover that it begins with an almanac. The introductory portion contains some fifty pages filled with calendar notes, time tables and schedules. Again, in the very heart of the Book almost one-third of its contents are given over to specific prayers and lessons assigned to every Sunday and other stated days of the year. Closer scrutiny of the Prayer Book will reveal that its entire contents are laid out according to an ordered time-sequence of rites and observances.

The initial services in the Book provide our corporate morning and evening devotions, day by day, year in and year out. Each service, every day, has its own appointed psalms and Bible lessons, as set forth in the tables of the introduction. In addition, a series of occasional Prayers and Thanksgivings, the Litany, and A Penitential Office, present us with appropriate forms for various and special occasions and the needs that recur from time to time in the daily round of our common life as Churchmen and as citizens.

The middle section of the Prayer Book—the heart of its contents—includes the Order for the Holy Communion, with the Collects, Epistles and Gospels for the specified Sundays and Holy Days. There is no rule, of course, that limits the celebration of Holy Communion to these days. In many places it is celebrated daily. When our Lord instituted the sacrament and commanded His disciples to repeat it in thankful remembrance of Him, He did not say how often they should observe it. Yet from its earliest days the Church has deemed it fitting to celebrate the Holy Communion on Sundays and other festal anniversaries when faithful disciples come together for their corporate worship. Thus week by week and year by year the Body of His faithful servants throughout the world and throughout all generations has been sustained and nourished by continual communion in Him.

There follows a third section in the Prayer Book, containing Occasional Offices that mark successive stages of our growth in life's ongoing way from birth to death. The spiritual rebirth of Baptism follows upon our natural birth in time. Confirmation comes at the maturing time, when we reach years of discretion and personal responsibility. Then at the momentous decisions and crises of marriage, childbirth, sickness and death, the liturgy seals the event with the blessing of God. It relates these significant times to His ultimate redeeming and sanctifying purposes, both for our own selves and for the living fellowship of all His people.

The liturgy of the Church takes time seriously. Just as our ordinary daily tasks and activities are regulated by clocks and calendars, so also our spiritual life and growth are ordered by "times and seasons." By means of the prayers and praises of the daily offices, the recurring cycle of the Christian Year, and the occasional rites of dedication and of blessing, the liturgy helps us to "redeem the time." And the things that are temporal become sacraments of the things that are eternal.

THE LITURGY AND TIME

The time pattern of the liturgy continually confronts us with ever new moments of decision. This is obvious with respect to the occasional offices. Baptism is a once-for-all renunciation of evil, a profession of allegiance, and a promise of obedience. Its gift of spiritual birth can never be repeated. In Confirmation a definite acceptance of Jesus Christ as Lord and Saviour is promised. A once-for-all gift of the Spirit is imparted for our daily increase in His manifold gifts of grace. A life-long pledge of fidelity and love is exchanged by the parties to Holy Matrimony—a decision that is binding until death.

The day-to-day and week-by-week worship of the Church makes the same decisive demands upon us for response to God here and now. They are no meaningless cycle, any more than history itself, of vain repetitions. Unless we make a mockery of them our lives must of necessity be different after every act of participation in them. In the daily offices of Morning and Evening Prayer we confess our past sins and pray for God's forgiveness, "that we may *hereafter* live a godly, righteous, and sober life." And the priest, in the Absolution, exhorts us to prayer for true repentance and the gift of the Holy Spirit, "that those things may please him which we do *at this present*; and that the rest of our life *hereafter* may be pure and holy."

Similarly in the penitential portions of the Holy Communion, past, present, and future are incisively distinguished. In the Invitation we are called to repent of our sins past, to be "in love and charity with our neighbours" now, and to "intend to lead a new life" in the future. The General Confession repeats these resolves: "Forgive us all that is past; and grant that we may ever hereafter serve and please thee in newness of life." Again, the Absolution asks God to "pardon and deliver" us from all our sins past, to "confirm and strengthen [us] in all goodness" now in this present, and to bring us finally "to everlasting life."

The annually recurring seasons of the Christian Year also afford us ever new opportunities for a fresh start. This is stated with special emphasis in the Sunday Epistles read at the beginning of our preparatory seasons for the two great festivals of Christmas and Easter:

> And that, knowing the time, that now it is high time to awake out of sleep: for now is our salvation nearer than when we believed. The night is far spent, the day is at hand: let us therefore cast off the works of darkness, and let us put on the armour of light. (Prayer Book, pp. 90-91.)

> For he saith, I have heard thee in a time accepted, and in the day of salvation have I succoured thee: behold, now is the accepted time; behold, now is the day of salvation. (Prayer Book, p. 126.)

The late Dean William Palmer Ladd of the Berkeley Divinity School often reminded his students of the cogent force of the word *now* in our Advent Collect—this word makes vividly real to us in the present time both the first coming of our Lord in His Incarnation and His second coming in Judgment.[3] In a similar way this opening Collect of the Christian Year is matched by the Collect for St. Andrew's Day, which stands at the head of the calendar of saint's days in the Prayer Book. As the apostle "readily obeyed the calling" of Christ

---

[3]Prayer Book p. 90. See W. P. Ladd, Prayer Book Interleaves, New York: Seabury Press, 1957, p. 28.

and "followed him without delay," so we pray that "we, being called by thy holy Word, may *forthwith* give up ourselves obediently to fulfil thy holy commandments" (Prayer Book, p. 226).

Every season and every holy day of the Christian Year is for us an advent, a coming in the present time of God's mighty acts of old in His Christ and in His saints. When we "make memorial" of them we relive them as though we ourselves were the very historic participants in the drama, the very ones who were summoned to make choice and take a stand for God and for His Christ. God's revelation of Himself, His redeeming mercies given to His people in past ages, the witness of His saints and martyrs to His truth—all these wondrous events of history are made present to us here and now, that we may appropriate them for our very own.

The Jewish rabbis used to say of the Passover observance that "in every generation a man must so regard himself as if he came forth himself out of Egypt." The same principle holds good of our Christian Year. In Advent we look forward to the coming of Messiah in company with the prophets and heralds of the Old Testament. At Christmas we join the shepherds in worship and adoration of the new-born Babe. At Epiphany we bring to Him our treasures in company with the Magi. In the fast of Lent we join our Lord for "forty days and forty nights" in His retreat in the wilderness. Through Passiontide and Eastertide we take with Him "joyfully the sufferings of the present time, in full assurance of the glory that shall be revealed" (Prayer Book, p. 144). And at His Ascension to the Father we pray that we "may also in heart and mind thither ascend, and with him continually dwell" (Prayer Book, p. 177). Note, too, how the brief phrase "as at this time," in the Collect for Whitsunday, makes the outpouring of the Spirit on the apostles at Pentecost almost two thousand years ago an ever renewed and renewing experience of our own.

We owe to the genius of the Jews this distinctive character of our sacred feasts and fasts. Originally the Hebrew people, like their pagan neighbours, built their religious observances about the seasonal courses of nature or of the heavenly bodies. But the insight of the prophets into God's workings in history led the Jewish leaders who codified the Law after the Exile to reinterpret the calendar as days of historical commemoration. Passover, for example, was in origin a spring moon festival combined with an ingathering of the first-fruits of spring harvest. It became the celebration of the deliverance of Israel from the bondage of Egypt. Yet it was always more than a recalling of this supreme act of God's redemption of His people. The Passover was also the promise of a future deliverance from present oppressors when God should establish His Kingdom. From the moral viewpoint Passover was deliverance from the bondage of sin, by putting away of "old leaven," the sour dough from a past baking, and the eating of unleavened bread as a sign of a new, fresh start in life wholly consecrated to God.

The link between the Jewish calendar of the Old Testament and the Christian calendar of the New Testament is that Passover celebration when Jesus of Nazareth was slain, as it were a Paschal lamb, and rose again the third day, "the firstfruits" of them that sleep in sin and death. From the beginning Christian faith has seen in this event the end of one era of history and the dawn of another. More than that, the Passion and Resurrection of Christ were the very opening of the age to come, when history itself shall have an end and God's triumph over sin and death shall be manifestly complete. The Christian Passover is the celebration of the final deliverance by God of His people, the formation of the New Israel of God, the Church, and the foretaste of His everlasting and eternal Kingdom. Thus in the Christian festival the past event is commemorated and the future consummation is anticipated. But the feast is neither mere remembrance nor unfulfilled hope. It is a present reality in the hearts of faithful believers.

Massey H. Shepherd, Jr., *The Worship of the Church* (New York: Seabury Press, 1952), 97-99, 102-106. (Excerpts)

63.

The Problem and Method of Prayer Book Revision, 1961

In Prayer Book Studies XV, *the Standing Liturgical Commission articulates its method of prayer book revision. This volume indicated two major changes in liturgical revision: (1) the return to the early church rather than the Reformation Prayer Book as the norm; and (2) the proposal of trial use as a means of revision. This process reached its conclusion with the publication of the 1979* Book of Common Prayer.

There is one advantage to trial use that possibly outweighs all objections. It removes the task of liturgical revision from the realm of purely theoretical discussion and provides a basis of judgment on proposed forms from concrete experience. It has been aptly said that when the disciples asked the Lord to teach them to pray, He did not give them a lecture or a pamphlet to study, but He gave them a prayer to be said. One learns to worship and pray by doing it far more than by considering and discussing it. For the Spirit helps our infirmities in and through the act of worship itself. The whole purpose of trial use is summed up in the consideration that we cannot really tell what we ought to say and to do until we try it out under the provident assistance of the Spirit of God working in us.

. . . .

Trial use has one inestimable advantage in the Church today, considering its present size and complexity and diversity of membership. It allows every member an opportunity to voice his or her reaction to proposed changes in the liturgy on the basis of actual experience. It would thus make the decisions of the General Convention more truly representative and responsive to broad sentiment within the Church. There would be less likelihood that a relatively small number of revising "experts" on the one hand or of powerful committee leaders on the other would dominate the course and results of revision. Of course, there would not be unanimity on every point and issue. Nor is there any way of predicting whether the opportunity afforded for a wider participation by the rank and file of church membership in the task of revision would lead to conservative, moderate, or radical changes. But this is not of great moment, compared to the prospect of creating a liturgical reformation that could witness to an informed and responsible public opinion throughout the Church based upon the broadest possible experience of actual participation in the task.

We must bear ever in mind today, in any process of liturgical revision, certain insights provided by the modern science of liturgical research and study with regard to the way in which the great rites of the historic Church have come into existence and exercise a living and creative influence upon the spiritual growth of the Church. As the late Dom Gregory Dix said so pointedly, "The good liturgies were not written; they grew." That is to say, a great liturgy is not merely an external, imposed law. It is a process welling up in continually fresh streams of devotion from the inner life of believing, practicing Christians. Law plays a very necessary part in liturgical revision, in that it preserves standards recognized and approved by the whole Church. But liturgies also develop through the emergence of unwritten customs responsive to needs of actual worshipping congregations. The recognition of this fact was a significant factor in the modern revisions of our Prayer Book in their ideals of "enrichment and flexibility" that modify in some degree the principle of a rigid uniformity.

The Standing Liturgical Commission of the Protestant Episcopal Church in the United States of America, *Prayer Book Studies XV: The Problem and Method of Prayer Book Revision* (New York: Church Pension Fund, 1961), 11-14. (Excerpt)

64.

Report of the Joint Commission on Church Music, 1961

The Joint Commission on Church Music was established by the forty-sixth General Convention, October 8-24, 1919. Its task was to stimulate discussion among clergy and church musicians concerning church music. This report discussed the role of music in liturgy.

Congregational Participation

During the past twenty years there has been a marked increase in congregational participation in the services of the Church. This has been in a large measure due to the Liturgical Movement which has stressed the importance of this aspect of a service of worship of Almighty God. The stress has been on the *whole* Christian family in church uniting in the praise and worship of its Creator. Advancement in Christian Education also has brought into being the Family Service—a service designed for Church families to meet and to participate in an offering to God through the Holy Communion.

This corporate activity has been strengthened in many ways through the activity of church musicians and a deepening understanding of church music. The hymnal revision of 1937-40 brought into use a book with music within the range of most singers; it also produced four settings of the ordinary of the Holy Communion for use in churches of various degrees of musical skill. Its recognition of plainsong as universal music and not that which bore the stamp of a "particular" Christian body added a new opportunity for congregational music. Chanting came to be recognized as "speaking on a musical tone or tones" and not a series of rapidly uttered phrases, unintelligible and confused; to be followed by a slow cadence and emphasis upon unimportant syllables and words. The employment of hymns as anthems by choirs not prepared to sing more elaborate settings has supplied a long felt need and helped greatly to eliminate much of the "easy" but cheap trash which formerly was to be found in every choir library.

During the forty years since the first Report our public and private schools have developed fine programs of musical instruction. Through this source many of our congregations today find little difficulty in reading music and are aware of the high standards that should be sought both in composition and performance. The former emphasis on unison singing as the best method for obtaining congregational participation is no longer as valid and the day may not be far distant when our congregations will be singing the parts of hymns and service music provided they are supplied with copies of the latter. There will still be need for choir leadership and there must always be an opportunity for choirs to make their distinctive contributions to the service by means of anthems or large settings of service music.

The great value of congregational participation lies in the fact that worship becomes what it should be—a corporate act in which the whole family of the church united together offer their hearts and minds and bodies to God to be "a reasonable, holy and living sacrifice."

MUSIC AND WORSHIP

The music performed in the church must always be considered as secondary to liturgy; it does not exist for itself alone, nor must it draw undue attention to itself. It must be judged from the standpoint of its fitness to accompany the liturgy. That in itself indicates a very high standard, for nothing but the best can be offered to God in His house.

It must be recognized that all music used in divine worship must pass the rigid tests of musical excellence; a badly written hymn tune has no more place in the church than the music of the popular music hall. An anthem whose workmanship is shoddy should not be set beside the works of the great masters of music which are and always will be models.

On the other hand, the music heard in church must differ from the type that is heard in other places. Secular influences, whatever their form, should not be allowed place in the sanctuary. Music which has a secular origin or connection should not be permitted entry, except in the few instances where the origins are so ancient or obscure that they have long since been forgotten. (Actually, some of the best known and best loved chorale melodies can be traced back to a popular source.) One must also remember that the music does not automatically become sacred just because it is set to a sacred text.

What, essentially, makes a piece of music churchly? First of all, there should be evidence of very great care in the setting of the words. The supreme model is Gregorian chant in which the text is set to unmetrical music which flows evenly and smoothly. If a setting does not enhance the text and make its message even more telling the primary purpose of the music has not been served. It is quite obvious that if the lilt or thump of meter in the music is obtrusive one is more apt to associate it with the dance than with the Church.

Secondly, the music will have the dignity and yet the warmth, that has characterized the greatest music written for the Church throughout the ages. If it be of the proper standard it will avoid the commonplaces and cliches which are the stock in trade of the hack composer, be he connected with the Church or with some secular endeavor. It may be brilliant, but not merely showy; expressive, but not merely sentimental; solemn, but not merely dull. It may even evidence its measure of excitement, but there must be no taint of the sensual in it. In short, it must carry the conviction that it is addressed to God, as praise, adoration or prayer.

Music of all periods, if it conform to these high standards, has its place in the Church; in fact, the literature of church music is the oldest, noblest and most extensive of all. In one style or another, commencing with the ancient plainsong, there has always been an outpouring of music for the Church, much of it great. Until fairly recent times the bulk of it which did not meet the strictest standards of excellence has disappeared into oblivion. It is in regard to the music of the nineteenth and twentieth centuries that we must exercise careful selectivity, for much that has been found unworthy has gained a foothold, and it is difficult for many reasons to root it out.

In regard to our own time, it is important to realize that the composer of today has the right—nay, the obligation—to be heard in the idiom of today. The thing to remember here is that the really good work cannot always be immediately distinguished from the inferior imitations. Time puts this matter to rights; history teaches us that the true is eventually but invariably recognized—and so is the counterfeit. It is important to consider that music which is sanctimonious or merely "respectable" can never be thought of as meeting the standards of the music one could think fitting to present to the Almighty.

There have been periods in the history of music when composers wrote music for the Church which was of precisely the same style and character as the secular music of the time. This music has its place, of course, in the Concert hall, for, as music, it may be of excellent quality; but to allow or encourage its use in church simply hinders the appreciation of the true standards of music for the Church. Much music of this sort has been frequently heard and has endeared itself to many precisely because of its familiarity, as well as its superficial charm or brilliance. But those who have the responsibility for choosing the music to be used in the church are derelict in their duty if they make the attractiveness of the music to the worshippers the principal criterion; the congregation does not—or should not—come to the church to be entertained. Essentially, the music is not addressed to the congregation, but to God.

It must be pointed out that it is not necessary that difficult music be presented in the service; music within the capacity of the organist, the choir and the congregation (when the congregation takes an active part in the service) should always be selected. The music performed by a choir in a metropolitan church will certainly not be the same as that done in a parish church in a small town or in the country, but both types of church can present music of the same excellence, each in its own sphere, if it is wisely chosen. We will know that the music of the Church can not only bring us closer to God but will help to bring the realization of God into our lives.

CHURCH MUSIC

The primary purpose of Church music is worship, and worship only. This may be an obvious truism, but it is very necessary to be born in mind, as, being so plain, it is most easy to forget. The simple idea of worship is not so difficult to grasp but what does it mean put into actual practice? How can we worship through music?

Music in worship has a twofold aspect—offering and edification. The offering to God, and the edification of the faithful. The first thought suggests that we must offer the best and highest that is possible to produce with the material at hand: the best kind rendered in the best way; the second that, though it may be granted, that there is an absolute duty independent of the feelings of people, yet for practical purposes we should use that form of it which is felt to be beautiful by the majority of the best authorities.

We offer to God a thing of beauty upon which all our talents and energies should be expended. The quality should be such that it may carry with itself a further offering, by inspiring the faithful with higher motives and nobler resolves for which purpose no power on earth is more potent than music.

Bearing in mind the secondary object of Church music, edification, our work should be built upon a foundation of its primary object, the Offering to God. Music is active and living, its message can be conveyed to the word only by living agents interpreting it at a given time. The composer of the music directs the performers but the music proper does not exist until they obey those directions. Here is at once the weakness and strength of music.

In most parishes and missions those to whom the development of church music is committed, we find a tremendous lack of simple technical knowledge of tone production; the simple rules of enunciation, and the knowledge of choral technique. The above are primary and necessary for the rendition of even the simplest service. A great common fault resides in the choosing of material beyond the ability of not only the singers but also the ability of the choirmaster to guide them in its performance.

Church music involves the composer, the choirmaster, and the singers. We must, therefore, first decide what music to use, and then next how it shall be performed. It may be a comparatively easy task to select suitable music; it is far more difficult to assure its adequate rendition. How to acquire the techniques, how to keep them, and how to use them, is the constant care of the true guardian of Church music. The primary objectives should always be in the foreground of the thinking of those responsible for the music of the Church—that it is ever an offering to God and the edification of the faithful.

THE HYMNAL

The Hymnal is a third tool with the Book of Common Prayer and the Bible for the work of worship. In the service it offers an opportunity for an approach to Almighty God in all of the aspects of worship. In the home and in the church both it offers unlimited aid for private devotion.

It is essential to remember that a hymn is a literary work either of prosedy in rhythmic or metrical form capable of being set to music. From this follows the fact that a hymnal is a book of words. This is something that too often escapes the vast majority of our laity and of which many of our choirmasters and organists seem equally ignorant. This is due to the fact that most people are familiar with a hymnal only as a *tune book* even as they think of a hymn in terms of its tune. The classical example today is "Materna," the familiar tune to "O Mother Dear, Jerusalem," which is becoming known as "America the Beautiful." A musical edition of a Hymnal can only be published after the *hymnal* (a collection of poetry) has been compiled.

The Report of 1922 made this important statement: "The first requisite of a hymnal must be that its contents, in the main, are suitable for congregational use." Such a requisite demands that the content of a hymnal be theologically sound; of good literary quality; of such character as can be sung by all people without "hypocricy." Many find devotional poems which are eminently suited to private devotions cannot be sung truthfully by everyone. An older generation may sing sincerely "O Paradise, O Paradise, who doth not crave for rest"; but to put these words into the mouths of "teen-agers" causes them to sing something which they deny was a real aspiration or hope.

The Hymnal 1940 was in part a response to the demand of the Church for a hymnal that would meet the needs of a changing world. In its development these matters were given consideration. While the vast majority of the hymns may be sung with sincerity by everyone some hymns were included for the sole purpose of providing expression of personal devotion and prayer. Because these are set to tunes does not mean that they need to be sung or used in the usual services; yet on some occasion of a special nature; a mission service, perhaps at the time of a burial or a national disaster, their use might become most appropriate and supply a real need.

It also must be born in mind that before the Hymnal 1940 had reached the Church in 1943 new hymns of varying degrees of value were being written and that since that time we have seen vast changes in world conditions. These have called for new expressions of faith; and poetry frequently has been the medium for giving voice to such expression. No matter how fine any hymnal may be at the time of its publication there will come a day when the needs of the Church require the elimination of works which met the needs of an earlier day but which must give way to newer works that speak to man in terms with which he is familiar.

THE ORGANIST

The well-equipped church organist should possess, to a satisfactory degree, each of the following qualifications:

(a) Sound musicianship. Under this designation are included familiarity with the fundamental principles of harmony, musical form and composition; practical experience in chorus conducting; knowledge of the history and evolution of church music, from which proceed naturally the appreciation of values in church music, be it hymn-tunes, services, or anthems; some knowledge of voice production, in the care of boy-choirs extended specialized skill.

(b) Good organ-playing. Not necessarily that of the virtuoso, or even ability as a giver of recitals; but the capacity to accompany well, both choir and congregation; to lead them both with sound judgment in matters of tempo, rhythm, and nuance of expression; and so to fuse the various musical elements into the service itself as to enhance its continuity and ensure its unity.

(c) Character and personality. The relationship of the organist to the members of his choir is an intimate one, carrying with it limitless possibilities of moral influence, with the practical certainty that some influence will be exercised, consciously or not, in one direction or the other. Especially upon choir boys is such an influence potent, and as lasting as is that of the secular school teacher. As the organist, who should be a communicant of the Church, demonstrates in himself qualities of Christian manliness, reverence, respect for superior authority, punctuality, consciousness of duty and grasp of opportunity, so will he influence his choristers. And to these qualities must be added that sympathy of association which will attract and hold the interest and loyalty of the singers.

The rector is, under Canon Law, the authority over the music in his parish, but it is upon the organist that he must depend for its successful administration. Between them must exist the fullest sympathy and understanding.

One of the recommendations of the Report of 1922 concerned the establishment of instruction in Church music in the seminaries of the church. Every seminary of the church today is making some provision for such instruction but the degree and the thoroughness are not in any sense equal. There is need for drafting a basic curriculum that can serve as the foundation for the development of a music department. The Commission feels that such a curriculum should include both the study and practice of chanting; a knowledge of the various schools of church music and what constitutes music suitable for the worship of the Church; a course in hymnody and certainly a study of the duties laid upon the priest by the canons in his relation to the music of the parish. He should, further, have instruction in the musical portions of the service assigned to the priest. Despite the progress made much more can be achieved.

The Commission is encouraged by the action of the instructors in church music in a number of our seminaries, of meeting together to discuss the nature of their work.

Likewise the organists and choirmasters needed a broader education than that of technical skill. They need to know the nature of worship; the function of music in the services of the Church; the place of the organist in relation to the priest. Such knowledge would make it possible for them to avoid any indulgence in hazardous or ill-advised innovations based neither upon liturgical principles nor sound musical appreciation.

Many of the unfortunate situations which have developed in the past could have been obviated by education—education of clergy and organists.

As a step towards bettering relations between the organist and the rector the Commission recommends that the Code of Ethics adopted by the National Council of the American Guild of Organists be adopted in each parish where professional musicians are employed. This code provides the following rules:

I. No organist or choirmaster shall apply for a position, nor shall any teacher or School of Music, seek to place anyone in a position, unless a present or prospective vacancy definitely is determined.

II. When requested, churches should give organists and choirmasters a yearly contract, which may be terminated upon expiration, at ninety days notice. (Such a contract would have to be given with the full approval of the Rector to conform to canonical requirements.)

III. None but the regular organist of a church shall play at weddings or funerals, except by arrangement with said organist. . . .

Journal of General Convention, 1961, 569-573, 581-582. (Excerpts)

65.

Standing Liturgical Commission, On Baptism and Confirmation, 1970

The fifty-sixth General Convention at San Francisco, September 26-October 7, 1949, authorized the Standing Liturgical Commission to produce a series of prayer book studies. These prayer book studies led to the 1979 revision of the Book of Common Prayer. Prayer Book Studies XVIII: On Baptism and Confirmation *was at the heart of the 1979 revision and contributed to the renewed emphasis on the ministry of all baptized members of the Church. The debate on Christian initiation focused on the original unity of baptism, confirmation, and communion as an integrated rite of initiation. PBS XVIII sought to restore this unity by eliminating confirmation as a rite separate from baptism and reintegrating it into the baptismal rite. The eventual solution was somewhat different: a reintegration of the original sacramental components of confirmation into the baptismal rite, so that "Holy Baptism is full initiation by water and the Spirit into Christ's Body the Church" (BCP, page 298), while retaining a non-initiatory rite known as Confirmation as an affirmation of the baptismal covenant with the laying on of hands by the bishop.*

1. Baptism

BAPTISM is the sacrament in which we accept salvation from sin and reconciliation with God by participation in the death and resurrection of Jesus Christ. By the Holy Spirit a person is born anew into the fellowship which, because it is responsive in faith, is used by Christ as his Body through which he continues to work and serve in the world. In Baptism, as in all the sacraments, the principal action is God's. He accepts the candidate as his own child by incorporating him into the Son, and raises him to newness of life. He gives him the power of the Holy Spirit to fulfill his vocation in this world and to reign with Christ in his eternal kingdom.

But because God is love and always seeks with man a relationship of love, our free and willing acceptance of his benefits is necessary. Acceptance involves faith in what God has done in Christ to achieve our salvation, and commitment to follow him in the way of worship and service.

The necessity for the response of faith has given rise to the controversy whether infants are fit subjects for Baptism. For several centuries there have been those who have maintained that since the infant is unable to make an act of faith, he is incapable of being baptized. Today some members of Churches that have always advocated infant Baptism are expressing misgivings about this practice. A baptismal liturgy, therefore, which may be used for infants must confront this problem of faith.

The problem has been particularly acute in the past four centuries because of a prevailing individualism. Faith has been conceived of by many as exclusively an individual act. In this sense an infant cannot make an act of faith. But to what extent can an adult? The difference between infant Baptism and believers' Baptism is easily exaggerated. Although in the latter the candidate can declare his faith, it may or may not reflect a true commitment. Far more important is the response of faith of the Church into which one is sacramentally incorporated by Baptism. This is true both for an adult and for an infant.

Faith and commitment remain voluntary throughout a Christian's life. The capacity for them, as well as the willingness to exercise them, varies considerably. They do not always increase with age. Indeed, open and childlike acceptance is often succeeded by a period of doubt. Even the committed adult finds from time to time difficulty in reconciling his knowledge of the universe, of human nature, and of society, with Christianity as he understands it. Today many earnest seekers after God and dedicated servants of humanity cannot in conscience follow Christ as he was portrayed to them in their childhood.

The likelihood of fluctuations in faith and commitment underlines the need for continuous instruction geared to a person's intellectual growth and experience, and for continuous emphasis on the call to commitment. It is possible that continuity in both these areas has been seriously disrupted by the practice of Confirmation as the Episcopal Church has received it in the western tradition of Christianity.

Before we turn to Confirmation, however, we should take note of another argument for infant Baptism. Psychologists have helped us to see that there is a level of human understanding—vital for growth into maturity—that is non-verbal and non-rational. We now know that this unconscious level responds to reality as it is conveyed by means of symbolic forms and actions. We know that such an unconscious response begins at birth, if not earlier.

The truth about God and his relation to man is received by our unconscious mental processes through many channels. Long before a child can be reached in verbal and rational ways, his life-style is already being permanently shaped.

In the liturgy, the symbols, figures, and actions awaken the depths of the human psyche to genuine relationship with God. The Baptism of infants, followed by participation in the Eucharist, corresponds to the natural basic patterns of human growth. Sacramental living beginning in infancy, is a solid witness to the psychological and religious fact that explicit verbal communication and conscious individual decisions, important though they are, do not by any means constitute the whole of life.

But this corporate and liturgical influence on the growing child presupposes not only that he is a regular participant in the worship of the local congregation (instead of being relegated to a Sunday School "worship service"), but also that the local congregation is a loving fellowship in the Body of Christ. It has the obligation of being a true family of God, with a personal concern on the part of all its members for the nurture of its children and the full development of their individual characters. It will, therefore, include the children in terms of their growing capacities both in its eucharistic worship and in its mission to the community, and will give them the best possible instruction in the foundation, significance, and responsibilities of the life of Christ.

2. Confirmation

IN THE EARLY CHURCH the Bishop was the normal president at Baptism as he was at the Eucharist. When it became impossible for him to be present at every Baptism in person, one of two adjustments was made. Almost everywhere the parish priest replaced the Bishop as the minister of the entire rite, as he had earlier replaced him as the usual celebrant of the Eucharist. However, in Rome and those parts of Italy under the direct supervision of the Pope, the final anointing and Laying-on-of-hands were reserved to the Bishop alone, and so became separated from the rest of the rite on those occasions when no Bishop was present at the administration of Baptism. During the Middle Ages, this local Roman usage spread throughout Western Europe.

This separated episcopal action has developed into what we know as Confirmation. In the course of the centuries, three other practices have become associated with it: before Confirmation the candidate is instructed in the Christian Faith and practice; he commits himself to it by a renewal of his baptismal vows; and Confirmation is normally required as a preliminary to the reception of Holy Communion. It should be emphasized that these three practices associated with Confirmation as we know it are medieval or Reformation additions.

People today commonly deplore the alleged inadequacy of confirmation instruction. As a matter of fact, many priests work hard at the preparation of children for Confirmation. That the result is less than satisfactory is due not so much to their lack of effort, as to other factors inherent in the situation. One of the reasons for the endless dispute about the right age for Confirmation is that none of the usual ages is suitable for the instruction. From ages six to eleven, children are too young for the conceptual form of teaching in which the Faith and much of the practice are expressed. At about age twelve there begins a process of questioning the religion they have accepted as children. This is a necessary part of their thinking things through for themselves, but it makes a difficult time to review the Faith and practice.

Great damage, moreover, is done to the normal pattern of Christian education. The confirmation instructor, faced with the urgency of ensuring that the child knows all that is thought necessary to be known before he is confirmed, and recognizing that some of the children (because of faulty teaching, poor attention, or irregular attendance), have learned little in their previous instruction, is tempted to try to get the whole Christian religion into a single brief course. To the extent that he yields to this temptation, he breaks the continuity of Christian education. It is not surprising that many confirmands, after a condensed survey of the whole Faith and practice, feel that their education is complete and that they have now "graduated from Sunday School," if not from the Church itself.

In the same way, the continuity of Christian commitment is broken by the once-for-all renewal of baptismal vows which is demanded in Confirmation. On the one hand, a child, as soon as he is able to make self-determined choices, should strive to carry out his baptismal commitment to follow Christ. On the other hand, even in the mid-teens, a young person living at home, or in a Church school, is still under pressures that hinder his making a fully independent commitment. Although he may at the time be entirely sincere, he is likely to repudiate it a few years later, if for any reason, good or bad, he is unable or unwilling to participate in the Church's life.

One who in infancy has been incorporated into the household of faith needs, of course, to affirm personally his baptismal commitment. But affirmation best takes the form of commitment *now*, regularly renewed at frequent intervals. The intent of the liturgy here proposed is that it shall be celebrated as the main Sunday service several times a year, with the whole congregation joining in the baptismal promises. It is designed to express the corporate faith with which the candidates for Baptism are being united, and to allow every person present, explicitly to renew his own commitment, and to enable the fellowship to recognize its responsibility to the candidates. And since Baptism is here associated directly with the Holy Communion, that sacrament will come to be understood, even on other occasions, as an opportunity for personal and corporate commitment, self-oblation, and re-consecration to Christ.

Finally, Confirmation as currently practiced disrupts the connection between Baptism and the Holy Communion. Those who have been made members of the family of God have the right to be fed at the Lord's table. Those who have been incorporated into Christ should be able to complete their eucharistic self-oblation in worship and love by receiving him. Those who are admitted by Baptism into the Communion of Saints should be allowed to partake of the Holy Communion.

Instead, at present we exclude baptized Christians from Communion until they reach the age at which their parish custom permits them to be confirmed. It is not surprising that some of them think of Communion as a reward for having attended the confirmation instructions and for renewing their baptismal vows, rather than as an offering of themselves to Christ in worship and love.

3. Unifying the Rite

THE BASIC PRINCIPLE of this proposal is the reunion of Baptism, Confirmation, and Communion into one single continuous service, as it was in the primitive Church. Thus, the entire liturgy will be recognized as the full reception of the candidate into the family of God by the power of the Holy Spirit: beginning with the acceptance, through faith, of forgiveness of sins and redemption in Christ—of burial with Christ in the water in order that we may rise in him to newness of life; followed by the conferring of the gifts of the Spirit by the Laying-on-of-hands; and ending with participation in the holy meal at which the entire family is united, nourished, and sanctified.

This proposed rite avoids both the practical disadvantages of delaying Confirmation, and the theological problem of attributing to Confirmation separately, some necessary aspects of Christian initiation that belong to the very beginning of our Christian life. It will make possible a proper understanding of the priesthood of all believers, which the baptized are to exercise in the worship of God and the service of man.

The proposed liturgy will also strengthen the personal contact between the Bishop and his flock. It is intended that when the Bishop visits a parish, he will officiate at the administration of Baptism, the Laying-on-of-hands and the Eucharist. This will demonstrate that he is the chief sacramental minister of the Diocese, the clergy of the parish joining with him as fellow ministers. By making provision for the Bishop to take the leading role in the whole sequence of initiatory rites, this proposed liturgy expresses more clearly the true relationships among the Bishop, the priest, the deacon, and the people, than the present practice of reserving to the Bishop only one small section of the action of Christian initiation. This might help to correct the impression of many laymen today that the only function a Bishop performs, apart from administrative duties, is to confirm. When, because of unavoidable circumstances, the Bishop cannot be present, the unified rite provides that the priest be empowered to act as his deputy and to perform the Laying-on-of-hands. There are ample historical precedents for the delegation to the priest of the complete sequence of initiatory rites. This will, of course, mean that personal contact with the Bishop will not be required at every service of initiation. But far from eliminating the Bishop from the life and thought of the average layman, the intention of this proposed liturgy, as indicated above, is quite the contrary.

Baptism with the Laying-on-of-hands followed by regular Communion from an early age should strengthen the continuity and effectiveness of Christian education. The child can be led step by step to a deeper understanding of the Faith and practice, each year's teaching being geared to his capacities, and all against the background of full sacramental participation in the Church's life.

The age at which a child is admitted to Communion on a regular basis is a pastoral problem which will require sensitive handling. There will, of course, be those who object to a young child's receiving Communion on the grounds that he does not understand what he is doing. Again, the question might be asked, How much does an adult understand? A small child often has a natural recognition of the Sacrament; but even when there is little evidence of such recognition, early admission to the Altar has this great value: Communion becomes an integral part of the child's Christian experience from the beginning. He can never remember when he was not fed at the table of the Lord.

But in the course of history we have made admission to the Lord's table conditional upon one portion of the rite isolated from its context. We have made of it a separate rite, called Confirmation, and have thereby obscured the intimate relationship between the two sacraments ordained by Christ himself.

Those who were baptized as infants, and therefore have no conscious memory of the event, think of Confirmation as the great moment of Christian initiation, the time when one "joins the Church" or when one "becomes an Episcopalian." The result of giving such importance to Confirmation is to depreciate the full significance of Baptism and to make Confirmation alone, rather than Baptism, the sacrament that leads to the Altar. This, in turn, may be the reason why many of us regard ourselves primarily as having joined a denomination, rather than as being "members incorporate in the mystical Body of Christ."

To emphasize the essential unity of Christian initiation, the Standing Liturgical Commission proposes to bring together the separated acts of the sacramental drama of salvation, by placing Baptism with the Laying-on-of-hands within the context of a celebration of the Holy Communion.

Standing Liturgical Commission, *Prayer Book Studies 18: On Baptism and Confirmation* (New York: Church Pension Fund, 1970), 13-22. (Excerpt)

66.

Marion J. Hatchett,
Sanctifying Life, Time and Space, 1976

Marion Josiah Hatchett (July 19, 1927–) is professor of liturgy and church music at the School of Theology, the University of the South. He has written the Commentary on the American Prayer Book *(1980), along with other works concerning the worship of the church. In this passage he discusses sanctification through the liturgical rites.*

In these days when liturgical changes and revisions seem to be inevitable, liturgical study cannot be approached as a how-to course or as an exposition or examination of a fixed rite. Its goals must include the ability to bring intelligent criticism to bear upon both the old and the new; ability to distinguish between that which is basic to a liturgy and that which is peripheral, inconsistent, or antithetical; an awareness of relationships between liturgy and theology, Bible,

280

church history, and pastoralia; an ability to distinguish between responsible experimentation and eccentricity or gimmickry; an ability to assess ceremonial expressions; an awareness of ecumenical and missionary implications; an ability to recognize and label the liturgies of secular life; and an awareness of liturgical voids in community life which are filled by neither churchly nor secular liturgies....

The Ritual Pattern: The Sanctification of Life

Any society shapes and is shaped by certain rites which enact the myth of the community. To function within the society a person needs these rites (contrast the Englishman and the half-breed in the movie *A Man Called Horse*). Traditionally these rites center around certain crisis points in the life of the individual and the community.

Initiation—The community rite par excellence is initiation. When a child reaches an appropriate age, he passes ritually from childhood to adulthood. He is instructed in the myth of the community. He is tested for readiness. The rites are designed to make an indelible impression. Such liturgies are almost universally spoken of as new birth and as death and resurrection. Those who have been through the same rites are blood brothers, people who can be counted on to the death, people who bear their weight within the adult community.

Penance—Certain offenses which seriously endanger or disrupt the community bring excommunication, separation from the community. After appropriate penalties, self-examination, testing, and re-education an excommunicate may be reinstated, reincorporated into the community.

Marriage—When persons approach marriage a series of rites separates them from their parents and from among the bachelors and spinsters of the community, prepares them for marriage, and integrates them into the life and responsibilities of the married couples of the community.

Pregnancy—At some point an expectant mother is formally relieved of certain of her family and community responsibilities. After the birth of the child, regardless of whether the child lives or dies, she is reincorporated into the life of the community, resuming her normal responsibilities within the family and the community, or, if it is a first child and it lives, assuming a different place within the life of the community from that which she had occupied hitherto.

Childbirth—Within a period of days or weeks after a birth, the child is presented publicly to the community and recognized as a member of its family and of its community. Certain persons, in addition to the parents, are publicly recognized as having certain special responsibilities for that child.

Vocation—For certain vocations persons are separated from among the laity, instructed, tested, and finally integrated among those of the vocation and recognized publicly as belonging to this vocation.

Sickness—In certain types of sickness a person is separated from the normal life and responsibilities of the community, and the community brings to this crisis appropriate rites which provide help and support.

Death and burial—Tightly scheduled days of texts and actions are made use of in connection with a death and burial. The rites are designed to make certain that the dead stay dead and to carry the members of the community through the grief process, re-align the family structure, and redistribute the property and the community responsibilities of the deceased, so that the family and the community can move on.

The Sanctification of Time

In almost every society, certain components which are a normal part of these crisis rites (repetitions of the myth, sacrifices, and meals) are periodically repeated, normally in some relationship to the cycles of nature. Through these cyclic rites the members of the community immerse themselves in the myth of the community, offer to the gods, receive strength from the gods, and thus bind themselves to the other members of the community and celebrate with them. Through these the community is re-created, reinforced, brought under the judgment of its myth.

The Liturgical "Day" and Liturgies of the Word—Liturgies of the word develop from the repetitions of the myth by the old seers of the community and by the singing of songs and dancing of dances within which the myth is proclaimed or acted out.

The Liturgical "Week" and Sacrifices and Meals—At certain intervals the community offers sacrifices and participates in community meals. The sacrifices and meals provide for differentiation and cohesion. Those who eat together tend to think alike, act alike, profess the same faith, share the same values, and be loyal to one another. Sacrifices and meals tend to center about three elements: *meat, bread,* and *alcohol.* To eat *meat* is to gain the vitality of that from which the meat comes. It is related to sacrifice. We identify with animals killed. Blood binds together. *Bread* is basic to existence. It is related to slaughter. Man puts something of himself into producing bread. It is a symbol of fellowship (a *"companion"* is one with whom one shares bread). *Alcohol* is associated with vitality, fellowship, joy, celebration, the numbing of pain, the overcoming of fatigue, the liberating of inhibitions, the opening up of communication, the swearing of loyalty (the toast).

The Liturgical "Year" and Creation, Manifestation, and Initiation—The community is typically re-created or resurrected and members of the community recall their initiation into the community in rites which are repeated annually which recall the principal manifestations of the god. These rites are typically

282

related to the agricultural cycle and to the initiation of new members into the community.

Most societies justify their crisis rites and their cyclic rites not in terms of producing "invisible grace" but by pointing to concrete results. The rites do not function as signs of what they are supposed to do; they *do* what they are supposed to do. Their liturgies are functional.

The Sanctification of Space

Sacred space is a point from which to acquire orientation, a "position." It is the "center of the world." It is the threshold, the place of passage, "the gate of heaven." It is the whole of creation on a microcosmic scale. It is a place of pilgrimage, the heavenly home. The sacred space speaks of the world, the community, the eschaton.

Every community marks such events, times, and places. For example, "the American way of life" involves initiation consisting of naturalization for immigrants or such mile-stones as graduation, the attaining of a driver's license, and/or service in the armed forces for the native. Criminal offenses bring excommunication, and the whole process is replete with rites and ceremonies. Certain rites and ceremonies are expected in connection with marriage, childbirth, entering upon certain vocations, sickness, and death. The rhythm of the year (the school year, the fiscal year, the calendar year) is marked by certain ceremonies. Certain days (Thanksgiving Day, Independence Day, Washington's Birthday, Labor Day) reinforce the myth. Certain activities, foods, and manners of dress are associated with certain periods of the day, of the week, or of the year. Certain places (Mount Vernon, the Capitol, the Statue of Liberty, state parks) partake of the nature of sacred space, reinforcing the myth; they are places of pilgrimage.

Marion J. Hatchett, *Sanctifying Life, Time and Space: An Introduction to Liturgical Study* (New York: Seabury Press, 1976), 3, 7-11. (Excerpts)

67.

Parish Eucharist, 1977

In 1946 a number of Episcopal priests organized the Associated Parishes, now known as the Associated Parishes for Liturgy and Mission. It is a group of persons committed to the renewal of Christian life and worship. Associated Parishes promotes the centrality of the Eucharist as the norm for public worship on the Lord's Day, and stresses the essential unification of "The Proclamation of the Word of God" and "The Celebration of the Sacrament." Associated Parishes first published The Parish Eucharist *in 1951.*

Foreword

The words in our title help define one another. A parish (or mission, or any regular congregation of Christians) is a community of the baptized—a local, specific manifestation of the Body of Christ. As a community, it is not meant to be simply an aggregate of individuals but a living, identifiable unity of people who understand themselves as belonging to Christ and, in Christ, belonging to one another.

The most characteristic activity of the parish is the worship of God; and the supreme expression of that worship is the Holy Eucharist. The word Eucharist derives from a Greek word meaning Thanksgiving, and in this case it signifies more than an attitude; it is a manner of living. Thus, the Eucharist is more than an expression of gratitude (although it certainly is an act of thanksgiving), it is our fullest response to the mighty, saving work of God—a response that includes proclamation and communion, mission and prayer, claiming and offering, sharing with and caring for one another. It is our Liturgy—another word derived from the Greek and meaning common work. The Eucharist is the paradigm of our life as the Body of Christ.

Eucharist, then, is what the parish does—in response to what God has done for all humankind. Liturgy involves all our physical, intellectual, and emotional senses; it includes words and movements and feelings; it is experienced by the whole person. The purpose of this booklet is to set forth briefly WHAT we do, what we intend by what we do, and HOW we do the Liturgy of the Holy Eucharist.

The Holy Eucharist
The Liturgy for the Proclamation of the Word of God
and Celebration of the Holy Communion

The Episcopal Church provides a variety of prayers and other materials for use in the celebration of the Holy Eucharist, and a great deal of flexibility in the use of those materials, in order to make the Liturgy appropriate for a variety of situations. Even so, the Liturgy of the Eucharist is not simply a matter of each community of Christians "doing their own thing." It is God's thing we do. It is the Church's thing—belonging to the Body of Christ. It is our thing in that we are made members of His Body and claim His life as our own. In the Liturgy we do what the Church has always done to worship God. With all our variety, options, and flexibility, we follow a common Order for the eucharistic celebration—an outline which makes it quite clear that whatever the particular rite used or options exercised, we are doing the same Liturgy, and that Liturgy is the same one which the Church has done since apostolic times.

. . . Although the *action* of the Liturgy conveniently divides itself into two portions, these are to be seen as two acts of a single, unified drama. The Celebration begins when the community gathers. Communion takes place from the first greeting between friends and in the prayers and readings of the Christian story. The Word of God continues to be proclaimed in the sharing of the Body and Blood of Jesus Christ.

Parish Eucharist (Alexandria, Virginia: Associated Parishes, Inc., 1977), 1-2. (Excerpt)

68.

Charles P. Price and Louis Weil, Liturgy for Living, 1979

Liturgy for Living is volume five of "The Church's Teaching Series." This series of seven volumes was prepared in the 1970s at the request of the Executive Council of the General Convention of the Episcopal Church as part of the church's educational materials for adults. Charles Philip Price (October 4, 1920–) is William Meade Professor of Systematic Theology Emeritus at Virginia Theological Seminary. Louis Weil (May 10, 1935–) is Professor of Liturgics at the Church Divinity School of the Pacific. He taught at Nashotah House Seminary for many years. This selection discusses liturgy in the context of the entirety of life.

Worship and the Holy

Worship is our human response to the *holy* God. It is our ascribing of ultimate value to what we know to be worthy of such a response. "Love so amazing, so divine, Demands my soul, my life, my all," as Isaac Watts' hymn puts it. For consider all the especially human capacities which flow from this encounter with the holy, when we learn to see the holy as the absolute, the fixed point to which we are able to refer our decisions. In the encounter with the holy, when the absolute gives itself to us, we become able to make decisions, we are free enough from our environment to compare one thing with another, and to choose one thing in preference to another. In that freedom we are able to worship in the original sense of the word. We are able to assign proper values to the whole range of things which we encounter in our daily lives.

Christians worship God as he has given himself to us in his Son, Jesus Christ. We believe that he is of absolute worth for us, for he has shown us, through the church and the sacraments, through the lives of other persons, and in the many other ways in which he communicates himself, his life-changing power to forgive sins and his power over death itself. In Christian worship, we commit ourselves ultimately to Christ, for in him we perceive the ultimate meaning of existence.

At this point, we can begin to address our attention to one of the most important contentions of this book—that worship has implications for the whole of life. Worship and ethics are intimately related. After we have responded to God in Christ as the ultimate or absolute in an act of worship, we go on to ascribe or assign value, to the persons and things we encounter in the ordinary course of life, using the criterion provided by our meeting with the holy. For Christians, that criterion is the love of God revealed in Jesus Christ, the love which "bears all things, believes all things, hopes all things, endures all things" (1 Cor. 13:7). The application of this criterion to the decisions which Christians make is the content of Christian ethics, the subject of the next volume in this series. Here we must content ourselves with emphasizing the close relationship between worship and ethics. Worship undergirds ethical activity. In fact, ethics is a form of worship.

Worship and Ritual

The English word *worship* has led us to a study of worship as a valuing activity. In the Bible the Hebrew and Greek words for worship point in quite a different direction. The most frequent Hebrew word, for example, is *shachach*. It denotes a physical activity—falling prostrate. Like the word genuflect, which also denotes a physical activity, *shachach* is used only in a religious context. It is a ritual word. The connection between falling prostrate and the worship of the holy God is expressed in the line of the Venite,

> O come, let us worship and fall down,
> and kneel before the Lord our Maker.
>> as well as in Psalm 99:5,
> Proclaim the greatness of the Lord our God
>> and fall down before his footstool;
>> he is the Holy One.

Similarly, one of the Greek words for worship, *proskyn\O(e,⁻)\O(o,⁻)*, is used to designate the custom of prostrating oneself before another and kissing the other's foot. Persians did this in the presence of their kings, Greeks in the presence of their gods. It is obvious that prostration is not a characteristic Anglican response to the holy God. Nevertheless, these words serve to remind us that worship has physical components. When we stand in the presence of God, we not only engage in the moral and intellectual activity of assigning values. More immediately and dramatically, we do something with our bodies. Ritual action, as well as decision making, is an inalienable part of worship. Worship is an activity of human beings in their complete selfhood, flesh in inextricable unity with spirit. The holy God demands of us a total response.

Liturgy and Community

[The] response of faith to the actions of God on our behalf must not, and indeed for Christians *cannot*, be conceived in narrowly individualistic terms. The response of faith is a personal response within the community of faith, the church. At the very beginning of the Christian life, at baptism itself, our relation to God through Christ is set in the context of the Christian community. The faith we profess at baptism and reaffirm at every Eucharist is the faith of the church, the faith of the one people of God gathered in the unity of the Spirit.

The unity of the church is thus not an organizational option; it is a divine imperative. The faith proclaimed and made manifest in the Eucharist is the basis for our unity in Christ, a unity forged by his presence through the Spirit: "Christ has died, Christ is risen, Christ will come again." This is no mere social unity, as in a club of like-minded members. It is a unity of identity in the Spirit. "We are one in the Spirit, we are one in the Lord," as a familiar hymn runs. Baptism has made us one with Christ. Our common memory is the source of our common identity and at the same time the imperative for our unity, locally within the congregation and universally as a worldwide fellowship of love. This spiritual unity in Christ will be a sign to the world, for the goal of the incarnation is not merely the unity of the congregation or even of the whole church. It is the unity of humanity itself.

From all this it is manifest that the liturgical celebration of the church is no narrowly religious activity. It finds its meaning in the total extent of Christian life and witness in the world. Our parochial liturgies are often lifeless because their rooting in this wider framework has not been perceived, and thus the authentic sources of liturgical vitality become dry and withered. True liturgy, on the other hand, is the expression of an authentic Christian community. It springs from the common life of the church and becomes a sign of the existence of that common life and a source of nourishment for it.

The scandal of our present liturgical situation is not its diversity of style. Most of us, often to our surprise, discover that we can adjust to new styles of worship rather easily, if they are celebrated with integrity and express a true community of faith. Diversity is not the problem. The problem is the separation of liturgy from the life of the Christian person and from the life of the Christian community. Liturgy then becomes objectified and depersonalized, a printed text, rather than the expression in action of a community of faith.

Is the church a static reality? Its worship, doctrine, and organization fixed once for all time? Or is it an unfolding life, a community confident of the abiding presence of Christ with his people in the Spirit, leading us into all truth? We make no claim to infallibility, but we insist that God is with the church today, through the Spirit, and always has been. Authentic liturgy is the expression of that presence.

Charles P. Price and Louis Weil, *Liturgy for Living* (New York: Seabury Press, 1979), 18-19, 30-31. (Excerpts)

69.

Marion J. Hatchett, The Musical Ministry of the People, 1980

Marion Josiah Hatchett (July 19, 1927–) prepared this manual for the Standing Commission on Church Music. This manual provides guidance to encourage the musical participation of the congregation in worship.

The songs of the people. The rubrics of the new BOOK OF COMMON PRAYER are true to tradition in reserving for the people the responses to the Opening Acclamation, the Salutation, the acclamations at the beginnings and endings of Lessons, responses in the Prayers of the People, the response to the Peace, responses in the introductory dialogue of the Eucharistic Prayer, and the response to the Dismissal. The Amen, wherever it occurs, belongs to the people. The Kyrie and the Trisagion are songs of the people. The Sanctus and Benedictus qui venit, the Memorial Acclamation, and the Lord's Prayer are songs which the people sing along with the celebrant. The word *hymn* is used in the rubrics to indicate a metrical song of the people. In other rites, as well as in the Eucharist, certain portions are reserved for the people as, for example, the responses to the Opening Preces and the Suffrages in the Daily Office. The Apostles' Creed and the Lord's Prayer are songs which the people and celebrant sing together. It is highly inappropriate for these portions of the rite to be pre-empted by a choir. These portions belong to the people; unless the congregation can sing them easily, they should say them. Music too complicated for the congregation should not be used for these portions of the rites. A church music director desiring to perform a more complicated setting of one of these texts (for example, the Sanctus) should do so either at a time within the service appropriate for an anthem or at a concert. In early Anglicanism the more elaborate settings of the Sanctus were used, not within the Eucharistic Prayer, but rather as an introit for the rite. Often the Sanctus within the Prayer was said or sung to a simple setting, so important was congregational participation in the historic songs of the people.

In addition to those portions of the rites reserved to the people, traditionally the congregation sings hymns or canticles as a part of the entrance rite; the response in the Gradual Psalm (or the Psalm itself); the Alleluia, Psalm or Sequence hymn prior to the announcement of the Gospel; the Nicene Creed; the Fraction Anthem; and possibly hymns or psalms during the preparation of the Table, during the Communion of the People, and before or after the postcommunion prayer. In the Daily Office it is traditional for the people to sing the Invitatory Psalm, the Psalmody of the Day, and the Canticles, or to sing antiphons when a cantor or choir sings the aforementioned portions of the rite.

The function of the songs of the people. The aim of the songs of the people is that "full, conscious, and active participation . . . demanded by the very nature of the liturgy" (*The Constitution on the Sacred Liturgy*, 14).

Though music may add solemnity, effectiveness, beauty, enjoyment, and unity to a celebration, that is not always true. It is not always better to sing than to say; silence is to be preferred at times to sound. It is essential to consider the particular gathering of people, the size of the group, their traditions, their musical abilities, the available musical leadership, the architectural setting, and the relative importance of the day or occasion. Also important are the predominant age group, the degree of experience with a particular service, and the musical interest of the particular gathering. The music must not dominate the rite but instead highlight its basic structure.

Marion J. Hatchett, *A Manual for Clergy and Church Musicians* (New York: Church Hymnal Corporation, 1980), 23-24. (Excerpt)

70.

Urban T. Holmes, Education for Liturgy, 1981

Urban Tigner Holmes III (June 12, 1930–August 6, 1981) was the ninth dean of the School of Theology, the University of the South, August 1, 1973, until his death. Holmes argues in this essay that liturgical revision was intended to change the theology of the Episcopal Church.

It is unfortunate in one sense—although strategically understandable—that we were not clear to ourselves and to others that a real theological crisis lay behind the liturgical movement. This explication of the theological crisis would have served to make what was happening in the new rites not just a pastoral concern or a question of literary taste, but a theological response to our age. It would probably have also made revision even that much more controversial.

The freedom, if not license, that the awakening to change in Western religious consciousness begot, not only stimulated superficiality in theology, but also had its liturgical component. An unbelievable sentimentality pervaded some liturgy—what Talley once called "balloons and grabass." I well remember processing to the grave of James DeKoven one spring day in the course of a Eucharist of giving thanks for his life and witness. Each one of us was carrying a helium-filled balloon. My partner was the Bishop of Milwaukee. At one point our eyes met and he said to me, "Terry, don't you ever tell anyone what we're doing." (Ten years later I trust Donald Hallock will forgive me for relating our mutual discomfort.)

There was a great deal of negative learning in these "pop" liturgies and, if nothing else had countered them, we would probably have returned to Cranmer with relief. But there were more sophisticated agents of education. The diocesan liturgical commissions which were formed in the late 1960s became valuable forums, depending upon the commitment of the bishop, for reflection, education, and agitation. (It was possible to tell how serious a bishop was in having a diocesan liturgical commission by whether he appointed a rector or a second curate to be chairman.) When the chairmen of diocesan liturgical commissions began meeting nationally every year in 1971—the first two times under the sponsorship of AP [Associated Parishes]—further education was generated. In the 1973 meeting at St. Louis, where I was a speaker, the chairmen of the diocesan liturgical commissions gathered on their own, apart from AP, because they did not want to be identified with AP. From 1975 the Chilton Powell Institutes, which were designed for musicians and liturgists together and were sponsored by the SLC [Standing Liturgical Commission], were another means to broaden the informed base for liturgical revision. These occasions for short conferences, educating the clergy and lay leaders, had behind them the publication of solid liturgical scholarship as well as the leadership of a learned cadre of scholars.

The Liturgy of the Lord's Supper, made available through a nationally distributed pamphlet as well as in some diocesan editions, became very familiar to many church-going Episcopalians—just about the time it was beginning to pall and the SLC became aware that they must try again. But it gave a large number of church people a taste of what might be, and there was encouragement to continue. (There is, incidently, no evidence that *PBS* [*Prayer Book Studies*] *XVII* was the "brainchild" of Bayard Hale Jones, despite what I have been told. He had died long before the SLC or anyone else thought of it.)

1970 was an important year. Probably the bravest and most consistent with scholarship of all of the *Prayer Book Studies* was *18: On Baptism and Confirmation*. It was written by a subcommittee of the SLC with E.C. Whitaker's *Documents of the Baptismal Liturgy* (London: SPCK, 1960) in one hand and Marion Hatchett's STM thesis, *Thomas Cranmer and the Rites of Christian Initiation*, in the other. [Bonnell] Spencer was the chairman of that remarkable committee, which I had the privilege to join only in its later days. Margaret Mead and Lee Mitchell were some of the other leading lights. Its recommendations were more than the bishops of the Episcopal Church could fathom. They had been out of seminary too long and were too threatened; so it never came to be. Here was an educational failure.

Also in 1970 the General Convention gave permission for the communion of unconfirmed children with permission of the bishop of the diocese. Together with trial use this was one of the two most significant events in educating the rank-and-file Episcopalian to liturgical change. It opened the person in the pew to the possibility of an understanding of sacramental theology. My own little book, *Young Children and the Eucharist* (New York: Seabury Press, 1973), continues to sell widely today. It sought to develop a theological understanding built upon the interaction between sacramental theology and developmental psychology.

Then in 1970 we also received *Prayer Book Studies 19-24*, including the new church year, an entirely revised eucharistic rite, the Daily Offices, the first part of the new translation of the Psalter, an ordinal, and the pastoral offices. All of this went in to make up *Services for Trial Use* (STU) or the "Green Book." Something very much like a new *Book of Common Prayer* was now appearing in the pews of many Episcopal churches. All the educational advantages and disadvantages of trial use were operating widely.

With the publication of STU and the pressure for prayer book revision building, it was inevitable and right that a counter pressure build. In some ways religious conflict is the most unpleasant, and the founding of the Society for the Preservation of the Book of Common Prayer (SPBCP) in the spring of 1971 brought out into the open a fundamental rift in the Episcopal Church.

The idea for the SPBCP was formed at Sewanee, in the living room of William Ralston, associate editor of the *Sewanee Review* and a member of the faculty of the English Department in the College of Arts and Sciences. (It is ironic, to say the least, that Sewanee was the center for both liturgical renewal and the resistance to the product of that renewal.) A recent graduate of the College and a medical student at Vanderbilt, Jimmy Sullivan, was the spark that set it going. Three members of the English faculty at Vanderbilt were present as well at the initial conversation. The SPBCP formed a lobby to the General Conventions of 1973 and 1976. But they were more than a lobby. They were in the business of theological education, and grew almost spontaneously to over 100,000 members. Clearly liturgy has power in people's lives.

Often the SPBCP is caricatured as a group of dilettantes with an inordinate fondness for sixteenth-century English—although at least one of their tracts insisted that it was really fourteenth-century English. The caricature is unfair. Their interest was in the rhetoric of the trial services, true; but even more they were concerned for the theology. They were correct when they said, as they did repeatedly and sometimes abrasively, that the theologies of the 1928 Book of Common Prayer and STU were different. The SLC probably was strategically wise in not affirming this too loudly, but its members knew that the SPBCP was correct. There is a clear theological change.

The issue is the one I have already outlined. The members of the SPBCP clearly hold to a classical—I might say "precritical"—theology. This is particularly evident in reading their criticisms in *Draft Book Critiques*, published prior to the 1976 General Convention. My personal disagreement with their position is theological. I disagree with the viability of a sixteenth-century theology. Sometimes their criticisms were picayune, if not simply inept. But they are to be commended for clarifying the issues of prayer book revision to the church, even though no one seemed to be willing to take them on in a way that the people in the pew understood.

My impression is that the SPBCP leadership reflected more than anything else that element of the Catholic revival in Anglicanism untouched by the spirit of Vatican II and consistent with a late nineteenth-century Anglo-Catholic theology and piety that drew principally from a seventeenth-century French Roman Catholic model. This was compatible with the theology of the Tractarians who had much in common with the Evangelicals of their day in regard to the doctrines of humanity, sin, and individual salvation. Those priests in the American Church Union who were impervious to contemporary Catholic theology certainly worked with the SPBCP, even those who had never had a 1928 Book of Common Prayer on their altars. . . .

Discovering the New Prayer Book (1976–present)

As I reflect upon the educational process that has brought the Episcopal Church to the 1979 Book of Common Prayer, it seems clear that it is a symbol of a theological revolution, which is a victory for none of the old "parties" that those of us over forty remember so vividly from our youth. The new prayer book has, consciously or unconsciously, come to emphasize that understanding of the Christian experience which one might describe as a postcritical apprehension of symbolic reality and life in the community. It is consonant with

Ricoeur's "second naiveté" and is more expressive of Husserl, Heidegger, Otto, and Rahner than Barth or Brunner. It embraces a Logos Christology. This viewpoint was shaped liturgically at Maria Laach, transmitted to Anglicanism by Hebert, Ladd, and Shepherd, and reenforced by Vatican II and a cluster of theologians and teachers who are, directly or indirectly, part of the theological movement reflected in that most significant gathering of the church in the twentieth century.

It is evident that Episcopalians as a whole are not clear about what has happened. The renewal movement in the 1970s, apart from the liturgical renewal, often reflects a nostalgia for a classical theology which many theologians know has not been viable for almost two hundred years. The 1979 Book of Common Prayer is a product of a corporate, differentiated theological mind, which is not totally congruent with many of the inherited formularies of the last few centuries. This reality must soon "come home to roost" in one way or another.

In other words, the revision was itself the product of an awakening, a newly educated theological consciousness. Now it becomes a *source* for a much broader awakening through participation and reflection upon the meaning of the participation. For those of us that believe that the theological emphases of the 1979 book are appropriate for people in the late twentieth and early twenty-first centuries this is a splendid opportunity. It is why we do not see the choice between 1928 and 1979 as a matter of taste. It is more a question of truth for our time. Two standard Books of Common Prayer would be theologically naive, to put it kindly. The task that lies before us is to show how in fact *lex orandi* is *lex credendi* and to rewrite our theology books in the light of our liturgy. This can be a tricky process.

Urban T. Holmes, "Education for Liturgy: An Unfinished Symphony in Four Movements," in *Worship Points the Way: A Celebration of the Life and Work of Massey Hamilton Shepherd, Jr.*, ed. by Malcolm C. Burson (New York: Seabury Press, 1981), 131-135, 137. (Excerpts)

71.

Introducing the Hymnal, 1982

The 1976 General Convention requested the Standing Commission on Church Music to begin considering the revision of The Hymnal 1940. *The 1982 General Convention approved 600 texts for a new* Hymnal. Hymnal Studies Two: Introducing the Hymnal 1982 *was written to introduce the organization and content of the new* Hymnal. The Hymnal 1942 *was officially dedicated at a service at the Cathedral of Saint Peter and Saint Paul, Washington, D.C., on January 16, 1986. This statement presents the ten precepts for the work of revising the* Hymnal.

Foreword from the Proposed Texts for the Hymnal 1982

As Episcopalians we have been deeply affected by the "far-reaching liturgical changes" manifested in the *Book of Common Prayer* (1979). It is therefore crucial that a new edition of the *Hymnal* be authorized to provide this Prayer Book with complementary music and to satisfy the pressing need for new and revised hymn texts that reflect our time. In response, the General Convention of 1979 adopted the resolution directing "the Standing Commission on Church Music to present to the 1982 General Convention a collection of hymn texts for an enriched and updated *Hymnal*."

Early in 1981 the Standing Commission adopted a philosophy for hymnal revision establishing ten precepts for its work.

The first principle states:

1. *The* Hymnal *should be a companion for use with the* Book of Common Prayer. *A new edition of the* Hymnal *should support the* Book of Common Prayer *(1979) with its expanded lectionary, its revised calendar (which includes additional feasts and new emphases), its renewed emphasis upon Holy Baptism as a public rite, its enrichment of the Daily Office, the Proper Liturgies for Special Days, the rites for Holy Eucharist, the Pastoral Offices, and the Episcopal Services.*

. . . .

2. *As the Church itself is constantly being made new, so the music of the Church has reflected the life of its many generations. The* Hymnal *has been and will be an essential part of the record of this life and growth. It should retain classic texts and music which have been honored by history and are staples for singing congregations. At the same time it should present a prophetic vision that will speak to the Church of the future as well as to the Church of today.*

. . . .

3. *Hymn texts serve as a practical book of theology for the people of God and should present the Church's teaching authentically and fully.*

. . . .

4. *In both words and music, the* Hymnal *should be comprehensive in its coverage of all the major historic periods, without stressing any particular period. The* Hymnal *must reflect and speak to people of many races and cultures.*

5. The texts of the Hymnal *should wherever possible use inclusive language which affirms the participation of all in the Body of Christ, the Church, while recognizing our diverse natures as children of God.*

. . . .

6. Language *that is obscure or so changed in contemporary usage as to have a different meaning should be clarified. Exceptions to this will be those classic texts which are firmly established in the worship of the Church and are deeply rooted in the spiritual life of its people.*

. . . .

7. Although *prepared specifically for use in the Episcopal Church, the* Hymnal *by its nature should be ecumenical, drawing upon the entire Christian heritage. It is hoped that it will be valuable to other Churches and congregations including those with whom the Episcopal Church shares a common lectionary.*

. . . .

8. The Hymnal *is not primarily a choir book, although it is usable by a choir for anthem materials. The collection should be practical. Keyboard settings should be playable by the performer with average skills and, where appropriate, guitar chords may be included. Metrical forms of many canticles and often-used Psalms should be included.*

. . . .

9. The Hymnal *should present various musical possibilities when tunes are used more than once. The repeated versions could be presented in different arrangements, or transposed.*

. . . .

10. Although *the* Hymnal *should be musically accessible, there should be settings in a variety of styles which represent the best expressive artistic creativity of musicians.*

Hymnal Studies Two: Introducing the Hymnal 1982 (New York: Church Hymnal
  Corporation, 1982), 9-15, *passim.*

72.

Robert A. Bennett, The Power and the Promise of Language in Worship: Inclusive Language Guidelines for the Church, 1984

One of the major issues facing the church and much of society today is that of inclusive language, language that includes both males and females. This issue is particularly significant for Episcopalians with regard to liturgy. Robert Avon Bennett, Professor of Old Testament at the Episcopal Divinity School, addressed this issue in The Occasional Papers of the Standing Liturgical Commission. *The paper was first published in March 1984.*

Language in the Liturgy

The male bias of patriarchal assumptions—male as superordinate and female as subordinate, male as representative of the species and female as a sub-species—has been under attack by linguists, educators, child psychologists and book publishers for many years now. The National Council of Teachers of English, for example, published in 1975 its own set of *Guidelines for Nonsexist Use of Language* in NCTE Publications. These groups have recognized that male nouns and pronouns no longer carry a generic force within the English language for a growing number of people and should no longer be used to include female as well as male referents.

The churches have also begun to respond to this situation by establishing guidelines for helping the language of worship to express the joy of the inclusion of all persons in Christ. Inclusive language guidelines have been produced, for example, by the Roman Catholic, Lutheran and Presbyterian Churches. The Revised Standard Version of the Bible, as well, is being revised so as to limit the bias of translation in which male terms have been used for feminine or neutral terms in the original Hebrew and Greek. The National Council of Churches has produced an experimental *Inclusive Language Lectionary*. Here the Sunday lessons have been recast—it is not a new translation—into more inclusive terms. Indeed, some of these very issues were already addressed in the language of Rite Two in the 1979 Book of Common Prayer and in its Psalter.

Despite its own culturally conditioned patriarchal bias, the Bible proclaims the equality of male and female before God and the gift of redemption as open to all. The Old Testament acknowledges that both male and female have been created in the image of God (Genesis 1:27). The New Testament witness of Paul, even though he was very much a child of his culture, is that our baptism in Christ means that our redeemed humanity can no longer recognize any form of superordination or subordination. He writes,

"There is Neither Jew nor Greek, there is neither slave nor free, there is neither male nor female; for you are all one in Jesus Christ." (Galatians 3:28)

Some examples point to the Church's recognition of the language problem within worship. Recently, Roman Catholic bishops voted to change one of the English texts for the Mass prepared by the International Committee on English in the Liturgy (ICEL) to avoid exclusionary language. At the Words of Institution, instead of the Blood of Christ being "shed for you and for all men so that sins may be forgiven," it will now read "for you and for all so that. . ." The Book of Common Prayer, Morning Prayer, Rite Two, also recognizes this type of problem when it reads, in the General Thanksgiving (p. 101), "to us and to all whom you have made," in place of Morning Prayer, Rite One (p. 58), "to us and to all men." Similarly, the Gloria in Excelsis, Rite Two (p. 356), reads "and peace to his people on earth" in place of the Rite One (p. 324) "on earth peace, good will towards men."

As many young people hear "men" language, not as generic, but as male-specific and excluding females, so increasing numbers of adults acknowledge that they too hear such language as exclusionary, and in the context of worship are pained that the community of faith should countenance it. Not only females, but males as well, long for language which more precisely addresses them in worship as equal parts of humanity, and not as if one were superordinate and the other subordinate, or, as linguists point out, as if male is taken as the species and female as the subspecies. Such usage is not conducive to worshipful praise of the God who created male and female equal in the image of God, nor of the way we should view and relate to one another. Language shapes who we are as much as it expresses what we think of ourselves. The liturgy, as the prime arena in which we encounter the living God and engage one another as the household of the redeemed, must be faithful to the liberating word that emerges even out of the patriarchal language of the Bible and tradition.

Since we acknowledge our being made in the image of God, our anthropology informs our theology; our view of humanity informs our view of God. Change in language usage forces upon us, therefore, a corresponding change in expressing who we are as human beings and how we relate to one another, as well as in expressing who we believe God to be. The power and the problem of language today is that the Word made flesh in Christ demands that we be responsible in our use of language both about one another and about God. If we are open to such a demand, then we can talk instead about one another and about God. If we are open to such a demand, then we can talk instead about the power and the promise of language. The humanity of Jesus, which Christians believe to be a sign of what God intends for redeemed humanity, redefines how we are to treat one another.

Jesus calls us to move beyond cultural patterns of dominance and powerlessness as the key to defining relationships. These social configurations have been used as a theological justification for making God a dominant male master over subservient human subjects. Yet this caricature does not correspond to the biblical revelation nor to the resurrection witness of the Church. Women (no less than men, for example) followed Jesus, learned from him, and were the first to witness to the resurrected Christ. They too, therefore, bear the marks of discipleship. This reality, no less than the obvious fact that females as well as males share fully in God's redemption, needs to be expressed more clearly, precisely, and lovingly in contemporary liturgical speech. The liturgy celebrates that in Christ we are all truly brothers and sisters and no longer servants but children and heirs of divine promise.

Robert A. Bennett, "The Power and the Promise of Language in Worship: Inclusive Language Guidelines for the Church," in *The Occasional Papers of the Standing Liturgical Commission: Collections Number One* (New York: Church Hymnal Corporation, 1987), 41-43. (Excerpt)

73.

Marion J. Hatchett, Architectural Implications of The Book of Common Prayer, 1985

Changes in church architecture must often accompany revision of the Book of Common Prayer. *This was especially true of the 1979 revision. Marion Josiah Hatchett, Professor of Liturgics and Church Music at the School of Theology, the University of the South has considered these architectural implications of the 1979 revision in* The Occasional Papers for the Standing Liturgical Commission.

Different houses dictate differences in lifestyle; changes in lifestyle often dictate a move or remodeling. Through most of Church history, worship patterns have determined architectural settings. Changes in worship patterns, such as those which occurred in the fourth, the eleventh, or the sixteenth centuries, have sparked rethinking of architectural settings. In the mid-nineteenth century, however, the medieval Gothic church came to be accepted as the ideal, and the building began to determine the worship rather than the worship determining the setting. This model fostered worship in which the members of the congregation were more or less passive spectators rather than active participants.

The Book of Common Prayer 1979 seriously challenges the suitability of this architectural model. It sets forth clearly a pattern which calls for Daily Morning and Evening Prayer as regular services and the Holy Eucharist as the principal service on Sundays and Holy Days. The Liturgy of the Word has its own integrity. The congregational nature of Baptism and Confirmation is stressed. All rites involve congregational participation, and many involve processions or other movements. The book provides for Reconciliation of a Penitent, for reservation of the eucharistic elements, and for use of chrism (oil of baptism) and of oil for the sick. Many provisions and new or recovered emphases of the Book of Common Prayer have architectural implications.

What follows, then, may be of real help to a congregation planning a new building or extensive remodeling within an existing building. We hope that others also will find this paper of interest and helpful.

The Three Liturgical Centers

The rite for the Consecration of a Church makes clear that the church contains not one but three liturgical centers: the place of Baptism (font), the place of the Word (ambo, pulpit, lectern), and the place of the Eucharist (altar-table). These should stand out, and should have approximately equal dignity and prominence. They might be set off from other furnishings by use of rich or contrasting materials, vivid colors, or elaboration of decoration.

The Font—The font should be in a prominent place, so that baptisms are visible, and to be a constant reminder of baptism. It might be at the back of the nave near a principal door, in the chancel, on the floor at the front of the nave, or at the center of a large entrance hall.

Since the Book of Common Prayer gives precedence to immersion as the mode of baptism, the font might well be large enough for immersion; at the very least it should be of significant size. The font, or the area around it, might be decorated with biblical types or symbols of baptism. A convenient table or shelf should be provided for books, towels, baptismal candles, and the chrism. An aumbry (a locked case) for the chrism might be located near the font, and the Paschal Candle should normally stand at the font, except during the Great Fifty Days.

The Pulpit—The pulpit symbolizes Christ's presence in his Word as the altar symbolizes his presence in the eucharistic sacrament. Ideally, one pulpit should be used for the lessons, the gradual psalm, the Gospel, and the sermon; and also for the *Exsultet* at the Easter Vigil. It should be a prominent piece of furniture, that can accommodate a large Bible, and with a shelf for other books or items. Its construction and placement should allow torchbearers to stand near the reader. It should be accessible, so that lectors, the cantor, the reader of the Gospel, and the preacher (and possibly the leader of the Prayers of the People) can make their way to and from it easily and with dignity. The pulpit and the area around it might be decorated with symbols of the Scriptures, or of the Scriptures being read, translated, or preached.

The Altar-Table—Until the very late medieval period, when eucharistic piety centered on the elevation of the host, altars were normally rather small, typically about as wide and as deep as they were high, symbolizing an altar of sacrifice and a table of fellowship. Larger altars tend to dwarf the other liturgical centers and to create a barrier between clergy and people, rather than serving as a table around which clergy and people gather. The altar should be far enough from any wall or other furniture for movement around it to be dignified and easy. The altar and the area around it might be decorated with biblical types and symbols of the Eucharist. It is not necessary that the altar be in the center of the chancel; in fact, an off-center location may be a good solution in many cases, for the focus moves with the movement of the rite. There should only be one altar in the room.

Marion J. Hatchett, "Architectural Implications of The Book of Common Prayer," in *The Occasional Papers of the Standing Liturgical Commission: Collection Number One* (New York: Church Hymnal Corporation, 1987), 57-59. (Excerpt)

74.

Leonel L. Mitchell, Praying Shapes Believing, 1985

A characteristic of Anglicanism is that the law of prayer determines the law of belief, or that praying shapes believing. The Book of Common Prayer *is the primary theology textbook for the Episcopal Church. The liturgies of the* Book of Common Prayer *are the theological sources for what Episcopalians believe. Leonel Lake Mitchell (July 23, 1930–   ), Professor of Liturgics at the Seabury-Western Theological Seminary, explains this in the following selection.*

The Religion of the Prayer Book
Probably more than any other contemporary religious group, Episcopalians are people of a prayer book. Not only do we use the *Book of Common Prayer* for the conduct of our public services; it is the guide for our private prayer and the source of most of our theology. The recent revision of the Prayer Book was more for us Episcopalians than simply the alteration of a service book. It called for a readjustment of the language of our relationship with God, and therefore

affected that relationship itself. Traditionally this dependence of theology upon worship has been expressed in the Latin maxim *lex orandi lex credendi,* or more accurately *legem credendi lex statuat supplicandi,* which means that the way we pray determines the way we believe. Anthropologists say, "Creed follows cult." Worship, religious activity in all of its aspects—what we do and how we do it, as well as what we say and how we say it—underlies religious belief.

Although these principles are equally true for all religions in the broadest possible sense, most religions (certainly most Christian churches) do not equate their worship with a liturgical book, nor do they see their identity bound up in their service book. The Orthodox Churches, for example, clearly see the liturgy as an experience in which they participate, rather than as a book. In this they are certainly correct. Episcopalians really believe this too, but we tend to express our beliefs in terms of the Prayer Book. Ceremonial changes, for example, which were mentioned in neither the 1928 nor the 1979 Prayer Book, were frequently cited by churchgoers as objections to the revised Prayer Book. Clearly it was the total experience of the liturgy, not simply the text of the Prayer Book, to which they were reacting.

In a real sense, then, we Episcopalians are liturgical theologians. We read our theology out of the *Book of Common Prayer* and the manner in which we celebrate its services. Formally, the theology of the liturgy is called primary theology, or *theologia prima.* Theology is "God-talk," and primary theology is the language we use when we talk *with* God, not simply the words we speak, but the entire liturgical act. Secondary theology, which is often simply called theology, is the body of statements or propositions based upon or derived from reflection upon our interchange with God. It is talk *about* God. The "Outline of the Faith" in the Prayer Book is this kind of theology. It spells out the beliefs which are proclaimed in the worship. In a sense, this distinction between primary and secondary theology is technical and academic, but the primary nature of the language of worship is real and important. For example, it is not necessary for every Christian to understand the doctrine of the Trinity as it is spelled out in the Athanasian creed. However, it is necessary for every Christian to offer prayer and praise to the Father and Creator of all through Jesus Christ in the fellowship of the Holy Spirit, for such is at the heart of our faith.

Leonel L. Mitchell, *Praying Shapes Believing: A Theological Commentary on the "Book of Common Prayer"* (Minneapolis: Winston Press, 1985), 1-2. (Excerpt)

CHAPTER NINE

The Church and the World (1874-1934)

Introduction

The Episcopal Church provided leadership in a variety of ways during the social gospel era of the late nineteenth and early twentieth centuries. Church members were actively involved in issues of capital and labor through organizations such as the Church Association for the Advancement of the Interest of Labor. General Convention resolutions expressed the church's concern. Some monastic communities were deeply involved in social issues through feeding programs, health care, educational work, and advocacy for social reform. James O. S. Huntington, founder of the Order of the Holy Cross, was a pioneer of social reform in the late nineteenth century. Another issue of concern during this era was world peace. Although one Episcopal bishop was forced to resign due to his opposition to American participation in World War I, the Episcopal Church began to address the issue of world peace in the years following the first World War.

75.

William D. Wilson, The Mutual Obligations of Capital and Labor, October 1874

William DeLancey Wilson (May 21, 1851–January 13, 1926) was a professor at Hobart College and Cornell University for thirty-six years, and later was dean of St. Andrew's Divinity School, Syracuse. This address was given at the first Church Congress held in New York, October 6-7, 1874. These congresses met until 1934 to discuss social and religious issues. This address describes Christian social responsibility concerning the issues of capital and labor.

The relation of labor to capital is one of the great problems of the age—of all ages. In the lowest stage of human society, capital does not exist. The labor, such as it is, is performed by each one, man and woman alike, for himself or for herself. But soon, at a stage above, this ceases. The strongest party shirk the work, devolving it on the women, and take to themselves the more lordly occupation of war and hunting. At the next stage we find the institution of slavery, and a servile class, without rights, without so much as the ownership of themselves, doomed to do the work, while the masters live at ease, and enjoy themselves on the proceeds of the labor.

But as society advances, slavery is found to be both inhuman and uneconomical, and anti-slavery sentiment arises. But, without this, it is much preferable in many respects that the master should cease to be a master and man-owner and become only the capitalist, dealing with those who do the work, not as slaves, but rather as equals, laborers employed by contract and consent. And we have now society divided into capitalists and laborers—both free, both equal before the law—but very unequal in respect to culture, social position, and the means and opportunities for enjoyment. And even this state of society, which is usually regarded as civilization, as the two preceding stages have been respectively regarded as savagery and barbarism, tends and looks forward to another in which all shall be capitalists, and all be laborers; every man shall work for the living he has, and every one shall own the capital he needs wherewith to do his work, and culture will be universal, if not equal. Means and leisure for all reasonable enjoyment will be within the reach of all; and moral purity, a high state of integrity, and a benevolent regard by all persons for the welfare of all others will be the prevailing sentiment. Shall we call this the Christian stage—the millennium—the divine ideal fully realized?

Doubtless our blessed Lord saw these great problems, as he saw all others that have oppressed and embarrassed humanity. But in this, as in all other things, he gave no scientific or philosophic solution. He came not to teach a philosophy, but a religion. Not, as has been quaintly said, to teach us how the heavens go, but how we may go to heaven. Instead of solving the problem for the intellects of his disciples, he solved it practically for all those who, adhering to his method, would believe in order to know, and obey in order to understand.

There are two precepts of Christianity which seem to me likely to work out a solution of this problem.

When the forerunner of our Lord said to the soldiers who had inquired of him what they would do, "Be content with your wages," he uttered a precept which, I think, we may take to be universal in its character, and applicable alike in all time for those who work for wages. This is, then, the first of the two precepts to which I have referred.

And for the second, I turn to St. Paul, whom I take to have been uttering the mind of his divine Master, his Lord and ours, when he said, "We beseech you, brethren, that ye study to be quiet, and to do your own business, and to work with your own hands, as we commanded you." (1st Thessalonians 4:10,11.) There may, indeed, arise some doubt whether this is to be taken as a general or universal precept, when we consider the fact that most of the early Christians were poor people, belonging to the laboring classes, as they are called. But when we call to mind the many things that are said in the Bible about the danger of rich men trusting in their riches, and the impossibility of those who do so entering into the kingdom of heaven, and the many warnings and denunciations against oppressing the hireling in his wages, I think we shall be reconciled to regarding it as the inculcation of a universal precept of Christianity.

Now, I am aware that here is no attempt to determine the amount of wages which the poor should receive or the rich ought to give. I use the words rich and poor as well as capitalist and laborer, for in the popular sense of the words, and in the discussions of science on this subject, the laborers are the poor, and the poor are the laborers; while for all practical purposes, the rich and the capitalists are one and the same class. I say then our Lord makes no attempt to determine the amount of wages that should be given. He recognizes the fact that there are two classes. He doubtless knew, though he did not expressly admit, that the wages of the poor, or the laborers, as modern science prefers to call them, are often grossly and most unjustly inadequate. But he was no agitator. He was no violent revolutionist. He did not even state all the elements of the problem. He told, as was his manner of teaching, what we should do, not what we should say. To the poor he said, "Be content with your wages," and to the rich, "Work with your own hands."

This, you may say, was no solution of the problem. And so it was not. But herein is illustrated the contrast between our Lord's method of dealing with the great problem of humanity, and that of the modern men of science, who look to themselves and their own vision rather than to God for their wisdom. Our Lord told men what to do; informed them that knowledge and wisdom—the solution of problems, nay, the comprehension of mysteries—would come in time, as the result of the faith working by love. It would come as a result. Modern scientists would, on the other hand, stand and wait, and teach their followers to wait, until the problem is solved and the mystery comprehended, before they begin to work, before they take the first step toward doing what lies before them.

And history justifies this method. I have not time to illustrate; but all the ages from that day to this are a proof and illustration of the many problems in philosophy and science which have been solved in this way. All the fundamental principles of modern life and civilization have been reached by this method. The

Greeks, who pursued the other method, speculated and philosophized, and did every thing but believe and obey, and yet they solved none of these great problems. Faith and obedience brought the solutions; and so it will ever be. Political economists have labored long and faithfully—though faithlessly—to determine how much the laborer ought to receive, and how much the capitalist ought to give. But this has hitherto been in vain, and it must be forever in vain if they adopt no other method than the one they have been accustomed to pursue. They may stand, wait, and speculate forever, but no solution will come in their day. Meanwhile the evil thickens upon them; the atmosphere is dark with the coming storm; its winds howl and its thunders roar, but they cry in vain for some one to show them any good. Our Lord's solution they will not accept. One of their own they can not hope to find.

But let us preach the Gospel. To the poor say, with our Lord, "Be content with your wages; work for what you can get, but work; go to work now; work always and constantly; accept what you can get; deserve more, and in the Lord's good time you will get more if you deserve it. Doubtless your wages, in some cases, at least, are not what they ought to be. But you know, as Christians—if not, it is our pleasure and privilege to teach you—that what you suffer here from the injustices of others will turn to your account hereafter. Be quiet. Whatsoever your hands find to do, do it, and be content with your wages. God will take care of the rest." To the rich we should say, "Study to be quiet, to do your own business, and work with your own hands." The former precept—that addressed to the poor—has been proclaimed and applauded with hurrahs and amens until the world is sick of hearing it. Its echo, which meets us everywhere, has too much of the tone of self-interest and grasping greed to be altogether pleasing to human ears. The latter—the message to the rich—I fear, is seldom heard anywhere in these days. The prevalent doctrine seems to be that, if a man is able to live without work of any kind, he may do so, and be none the worse Christian for his idleness and self-indulgence.

In reference to the purely secular aspect of the problem, however, it may be well enough for us to say that while science has not yet determined, and never can determine, precisely how much of the income of the combined influence of capital and labor should be given to the laborer in order that justice may be done, it does treat of, and has taught us one important element of the solution, which, however, is like our Lord's, a practical precept—a direction for action, and not a theoretical solution that gives a precise result.

What science has done for us is to teach us that in our country, where the laborers are all free, and are, moreover, the equals, both civilly and politically, with the rich, we are to leave the matter to free competition, under the law of supply and demand, and the result will work itself out. It will come by work and not by philosophy, by doing what is before us rather, and not by any *a priori* speculations on assumed premises. In other countries, it may be otherwise; but here the laborers are the equals of the employers. They are duly impressed with the dignity and importance of that equality, and they have sufficient self-assertion and independence to demand all they can get. They can hire capital if they can not get the wages they demand for their labor, and the path is open for them, as they well know, to the greatest wealth, the highest office, and the most coveted social positions. They can not be oppressed here. The ballot is their defense against all evils that can come from that source. The rate of wages can not be long kept below what is fair and just as between the laborer and the capitalist, if it is now or ever has been below that point. In this way experience will work out the result. Science accepts our Lord's method, and says to both parties, Go to work with things as they are; and science adds something which He did not, with regard to the way in which the method is to work out the solution, and confirms the assurance He gave that it will come.

But no solution can come in the speculative or *a priori* way. It sets the parties to work in a wrong spirit, or rather it recognizes as right their position and aims while there is an element that is radically wrong in them. The poor are seeking to find how much they may demand with the prospect of getting it, and trying to get as much as they can for the work they do. And the rich are seeking to give us as little as they can for the amount of work they need to have done. And the secular efforts to solve the problem go upon the assumption or admission that this is right. But if there is any one thing that the Gospel teaches with more of plainness and emphasis than another—a teaching which confirmed by all the experience of life and all the teaching of history—it is that in all cases, of doubt and uncertainty it is better to err, if err we must, on the side of generosity rather than on that of selfishness; on the side of self-denial rather than on that of self-indulgence. It is better, if either must be, that we suffer wrong than do wrong, even to the humblest and poorest of God's creatures. Let men see and accept this fundamental truth, and they will find no difficulty in accepting and being satisfied with Christ's method of solving the question of capital and labor. I have no doubt this solution of the problem will be unwelcome to the rich. But let us consider their case a little more in detail.

In the first place, let us say emphatically that there is nothing wrong or sinful in the mere fact of one's being rich. Neither the laws of man nor the laws of God set any limits to the amount of wealth one may honestly possess, so far as I know or believe. If one has come honestly by what he has, he may be honest in the possession of it. There may have been dishonesty in the acquisition of it; there may be wrong and sin in the use that is made of it; but there is not, necessarily, any wrong or sin in the act of ownership or possession.

In the second place, we must define exactly what we mean by work and labor. Labor does not always imply the use of hands or feet. It is not always, nor is all of it, occupied with the manual operation so often called work. Work may be of the mind as well as of the body. And I would define work to be any exertion of mind or body or both, which is undertaken for the creation of value, or for the promotion of human good. But in order to be work, it must be exertion; it must imply thought and direction. It implies self-denial and self-control, and it must be carried to the point, sometimes, at least, of weariness and of fatigue. It must sometimes bring the sweat to the brow, the aching limbs, and the weary heart. Nothing short of this can answer the meaning of the word labor, as used in our discussion of the problem. It must be exertion for a purpose, and it should be undertaken with a conscious desire of promoting and advancing the welfare of others as well as our own. Doubtless there is much of the exertion that is made by the rich, which they call labor—which, at all events, fatigues and worries and exhausts them—that does not come under this definition. Much of what they do by way of taking care of what they have, and most of what they do by way of devising and executing plans for enjoying it, must, I fear, fail to be passed to their credit as labor or work performed in accordance with our Lord's require-ment, as stated by St. Paul. Labor, in the Christian view of it, must be exertion for the good of others, for something that increases the grand aggregate of means to supply human wants; something that alleviates human suffering, that educates or helps to educate the ignorant, to instruct and convert the erring and perverse; something that does good to men and promotes the glory of God. Nothing less than this is the labor we speak of. There is nothing contrary to God's law in man's being rich. But there is much that is contrary to this law in the way in which rich men, for the most part, live. This may be shown in many ways.

All wealth is created by labor, and is limited in quantity. Objects in nature have, indeed, some intrinsic value or capacity to satisfy human wants, but most of them are useless as they are, and derive much of their intrinsic and all of their exchangeable value from human labor. It is labor that gives them their value and makes them wealth. Now, the man, whether rich or poor, who lives without labor is all the while consuming the products of labor without doing anything to create them. No matter how rich he is, he is living upon other people, consuming what has cost them the sweat of the brow and the weariness of heart, the product of exertions that he does not make. Living would be easier for other men, or they would have something more to enjoy in life, if he would but take hold and do a part of what needs to be done, and bear the share of the burdens that must be borne by somebody, instead of leaving them all, or as much of them as he can, to others.

307

Again, it is an obvious fact everywhere, that not the sons and daughters of the wealthy are the most enterprising, the most efficient for good, or the most useful members of society. If the community were made up of them alone, sad indeed would be its case. The very idea which prevails in their childhood's home, that they have enough to live upon, and that, since they have enough to live upon without labor, they might live as they please, enervates them. They are apt to be as little given to self-control as to self-exertion. Law, and order, and right, and duty are less cared for than ease and mere æsthetic enjoyment. Hence, novels are preferred to science, fiction to fact, and every kind of sentimentalism takes the place of moral earnestness—ritualism takes the place of religion, and we find either a vague pantheistic mysticism, or a still more vague and senseless rationalism, according to the temperament of the individual, instead of that substantial faith in realities unseen which nerves the souls of men and women for great deeds, for endurance, and for martyrdom.

But again, the rich, as such, are a short-lived race. I believe it was the great Niebuhr that first called attention to this fact, and all of the more recent investigations have confirmed his statement. It can best, perhaps, be expressed in some such way as the following: The rich families—the capitalists who can live without labor—in a community consist to-day, we will say, of so many thousands. Doubtless they are, in the aggregate, more in number than they were fifty years ago, and they will be more fifty years hence than they are now. But this increase comes entirely from accessions from without. It is not a development from within. New men and new families rise up to join their ranks and be counted in the number of the rich. But if we take note of those who are regarded as the rich people or the rich families to-day, it is morally certain that their descendants will be less numerous in the next generation than they are themselves now. The succeeding generation will witness a still further diminution, and so on until in a few generations scarcely any of them will remain. Their name and their posterity are clean cut off from the earth. Infertility shrinking from the pains and perils of child-birth and child-rearing inefficiency, nervous diseases leading to debility of body and mind, announce the coming doom of family extinction. Such is the fact. Such is God's way of proclaiming in the life of men, in the destiny of families, and in the history of nations, his law that "if any will not work, neither should they eat."

Of course, there are exceptions to this rule, but they are comparatively few. And I think it will be found that all the exceptions, and the only exceptions, are really no exceptions at all. They are those who, although rich and powerful, do nevertheless work and labor in the cause of humanity. For it is not wealth but laziness that eats out the manhood of humanity. It is not the possession of much riches, but the indolence and self-indulgence for which wealth furnishes the opportunity and the means, that brings into families the invincible leprosy of decay.

If we look into the history of some of the great families whose lineage has lasted long and occupied a conspicuous place in the page of history, we shall see abundant reason to believe that the cares, anxieties, and labors of their respective stations do as effectually exclude all thought of ease, idleness, or the indulgence of effeminate luxuries as the stern necessities of labor and poverty drive these pests of humanity from the dwelling of the humble poor.

Thus God in his word and in his work calls us to labor, to labor with the hand or with the head, either or both, according to the endowment he has given us. Let men and women too realize this great law, and set themselves to do the duty to which it points, and the problem of the relation of capital and labor is resolved, or rather disappears. The honest poor do not pine or complain because they are poor. It is rather because that while there is enough and to spare in the world, and within the very sight of their eyes, they and their families have not the means of culture and education, of social enjoyment and religious worship. And they complain of the rich not because they are rich, but rather because they consume their riches on their lusts, in idleness, self-indulgence, and are a fraud and cheat—as they, from their point of view, are apt to regard them—a fraud and a cheat upon humanity. But let the rich recognize the Christian doctrine of self-denial, and the sacred obligation to labor—an obligation binding equally, though perhaps for different reasons, upon all, whether rich or poor—and show themselves, as Christians ought, to be more ready to sacrifice than to indulge themselves, for the good of men and the glory of God, and envy and jealousies on the part of the poor will disappear.

I believe the greatest, most fundamental, and the most pernicious error of our age is the doctrine that persons, if they are only able to live without work, may do so. In my view, the materialism of scientific men, the rationalism of compromisers, nay, the doctrine of the Immaculate Conception, and of the Papal infallibility itself, are harmless in comparison with this great, wide-spread, and deeply-rooted error. These may be refuted by reasoning; they are all repugnant to the instincts of the human heart in all the hours of its most intense earnestness; but this takes from the heart all instincts but the one it creates and fosters.

I think, then, we may clearly infer and confidently teach mankind that God has clearly foretold, has taught the way to, and in his providence is working to usher in, that brighter age of humanity—that stage which, according to our enunciation at the beginning of this essay, is forthcoming—when all shall be capitalists and all shall be laborers; none shall have enough to feel at liberty to live without labor, and no honest laborer shall be so poor that he shall need to be ignorant, boorish, unrefined, and unchristianized. Men will not, of course, be equal in intellect, in station, or in wealth; but they will be equal in the common lot of humanity, its sin and fall, its redemption and restoration, the labor that secures the one and the sorrows that are inseparable from the other. And when we all shall feel that to serve God and glorify the name of the Redeemer is more than all else, is so important that all other distinctions and all other considerations sink in comparison into utter insignificance, the great problem of capital and labor will have been solved to the satisfaction of all parties, and not, I fear, before that time.

I have written earnestly upon this subject, and I have used strong language. I have done it intentionally and designedly, for I believe that, next after the Atonement made on Calvary, to work, and the necessity for it—not works—is the most efficient means of human welfare, whether we regard the condition of the body in this world or the salvation of the soul in the next.

W. D. Wilson, "The Mutual Obligations of Capital and Labor," in *Authorized Report of the Proceedings of the First Church Congress of the Protestant Episcopal Church in the United States, Held in the City of New York, Oct. 6th and 7th, 1874.* (New York: T. Whittaker, 1875), 52-57.

76.

Constitution of the Church Association for the Advancement of the Interest of Labor, 1887

The Church Association for the Advancement of the Interest of Labor (CAIL) was organized on May 18, 1887, by William Dwight Porter Bliss (August 20, 1856–October 8, 1926) and others. It disbanded in May 1926.

C.A.I.L.

The Church Association for the Advancement of the Interests of Labor, believing that the clergy and laity of the Church should become personally interested in the social questions now being agitated, should inform themselves of the nature of the issues presented and should be prepared to act as the necessities of the day may demand, sets forth the following principles and methods of work for its members:

Principles

1. It is the essence of the teaching of Jesus Christ that God is the Father of all men and that all men are brothers.

2. God is sole possessor of the Earth and its fulness; man is but the steward of God's bounties.

3. Labor being the exercise of the body, mind and spirit in the broadening and elevating of human life, it is the duty of every man to labor diligently.

4. Labor, as thus defined, should be the standard of social worth.

5. When the divinely-intended opportunity to labor is given to all men, one great cause of the present widespread suffering and destitution will be removed.

Methods

1. Prayer.

2. Sermons, setting forth the teachings of the gospel as the guide to the solution of every question involved in the interests of Labor.

3. The proper use of the press and the circulation of tracts as occasion may require.

4. Lectures and addresses on occasions when the interests of Labor may be advanced.

5. The encouragement by precept and example of a conscientious use of the ballot.

Special Duties

It shall be the duty of each member to take, or read at least one journal devoted to the interests of Labor.

It shall be the duty of each member to devote a certain portion of his time to study of the social questions in the light of the Incarnation.

Collect

O Lord Jesus Christ, who didst glorify labor by Thy life of toil, bless, we beseech Thee, the efforts of our Society, that we may both rejoice to work with Thee, and may also strive to open to all our brothers and sisters the way to honest labor, and secure to them the fruits of their toil; who with the Father and the Holy Ghost, livest and reignest one God, world without end. Amen.

Brochure of the Church Association for the Advancement of the Interest of Labor, undated.

77.

William Reed Huntington, Popular Misconceptions of the Episcopal Church, That It Is Given Over to Worldliness, 1891

William Reed Huntington (September 20, 1838–July 26, 1909) was an ecumenical leader and the main force behind the 1892 revision of the Book of Common Prayer. *He was also a social reformer. In this writing he counters the accusation that the Episcopal Church "is given over to worldliness."*

Nothing is more necessary in discussing "worldliness" than to be careful in our choice of words, lest before we know it we do ourselves an injury by doing others an injustice. There is a way of loving the world which is not only innocent, but actually Godlike; again, there is another way of loving the world which drags the soul down to its ruin. We emulate the divine love of the world whenever we let the heart go out in honest pity and compassion toward the sinning, sorrowing, toiling people, God's creatures and our fellow-creatures, of whom the world is full. We fall, on the other hand, into the bad way of loving the world whenever we let things win the precedence of persons in our heart's affections, whenever we allow getting to absorb our thoughts to the forgetfulness of being; whenever, in short, we suffer the lust of the flesh and the lust of the eyes and the pride of life to enter like a murky cloud at the windows of the soul and fill with their bad presence every nook and corner of the room within. Always, and by all means, we are to shun "worldliness" as we would the plague; only let us know what we shun.

Every one of us has a pretty definite notion of what is meant by the expression, "the things the world can give a man." Well then, does not the essence of worldliness lie just here, namely, in caring more for these "things" which the world can give a man, than for truth, for righteousness, for purity of heart, or for the peace of God?

"Worldliness" may take on various forms and fashions; the inordinate love may be a love of popularity, or it may be a love of money, or a love of dress, or a love of pleasure, or a love of power: the thing that makes it worldliness is the fact that it is a love which has overridden and usurped the place of the love of God. And here we touch a point of real moment. How many people there are who, in judging of this question of worldliness, carelessly confound symptom and disease, forgetting how very untrustworthy outward appearances often are. They see one neighbor well dressed; they see another a general favorite in society; they see a third rapidly accumulating a fortune; they see a fourth who, endowed with a keen sense of enjoyment, appears just now to be getting a great deal of happiness out of life, and though perhaps they know absolutely nothing of what is actually going on in the hearts and consciences of the persons observed, the charge which rises instinctively to the lips is this sweeping one of "worldliness." Because the man is well dressed, because popular, because prosperous, because light-hearted, therefore he must be "worldly." It is a quick and decisive sort of reasoning, but is it the logic of the Sermon on the Mount? Did Christ bid us judge the tree after any such fashion? Indeed, did He not indirectly warn us against this very thing? A thousand accidental circumstances may affect the look of the leaves; the real questions are: What of the root? and, What of the fruit? No doubt the man you criticise may be worldly, he may be verily eaten up with worldliness; only do not assume such to be the fact, do not make his unproved worldliness the basis of all your interpretations of his character and his doings, until you have some better evidence than is afforded by the mere looks. "Judge not according to the appearance, but judge righteous judgment." The question is: Where are the affections really set, and on what? Worldly men in tatters on the curb-stone may sometimes fling the envious curse after the carriage wheels of holy and humble men of heart.

This blunder of confounding the symptom with the sickness has been common in all ages. Among the anchorites and ascetics of the early Church, for instance, it seems to have been generally considered that personal cleanliness was a form of worldliness. This, to our modern eyes, looks extraordinary, but it admits of an easy and natural explanation. The public baths were a prominent feature of the machinery of luxury in the polite society of those days. They corresponded in a measure to the casino of modern Europe. To frequent the bath was to be brought into continual contact with heathen usages, and out of this wise avoidance of what was bad, grew an unwise avoidance of what was good. Esteeming it a dictate of piety to differ from the heathen as widely as possible, these well-meaning but misguided enthusiasts came to the conclusion that to be ragged and uncleanly would be to establish sanctity.

Again, it is a mistake to suppose that we can avoid falling into worldliness by running away from people, and away from the places which people frequent.
"What exile from himself can flee?"
It is in the self that the real worldliness resides, and self we carry with us whether we tread city streets or country roads. "He hath set the world in their hearts;" that is where the real taint of worldliness lurks; would you kill it in yourself, trace it to that source. A Londoner or a Parisian, looking in upon the daily life of some quiet, well-ordered little provincial town, might ask with a smile: What can be the possible temptations to, or opportunities for worldliness here? Again, one of the people of this very town visiting some out-of-way village in a secluded corner of the country might in the same spirit ask the same question. And yet who that has given the matter any serious thought will doubt

that the certainty of finding worldliness somewhere in the village is equal to the certainty of finding unworldliness somewhere in the city, or that both certainties are real certainties? No, it does not matter whether a community be made up of many families or few, whether the building in which it is housed be of stone or of brick or of wood, whether the people meet together frequently or rarely, whether they dress expensively or cheaply—given one single human heart and you have a soil in which the lust of the flesh and the lust of the eyes and the pride of life may thrive, blossom, and bear fruit.

Let us consider, then, what would be the symptoms, the outward and visible tokens of this sickness in case a Church were really infected with it. What sort of evidence, that is to say, would justify us in fastening the charge of "worldliness" upon any large body of Christians as a whole? Well, let us begin with the ministry. The priests of a religion are supposed to be the exponents of it. If their standard of right living be low, we cannot reasonably expect that of their flocks to be much higher. It is fair, then, to make the ministry of any Church, to some extent, at least, a criterion by which to judge the Church itself. If the ministry of any Church can be shown to be idle, luxurious, given to trifling pursuits, greedy of gain, more bent on making a living than on making a life out of the work of shepherding the flock of Christ, why, then, it may fairly be inferred that into such a Church worldliness has crept. There have been times in the life of the Church of England, for example, to go no further afield, especially in that dismal period of her history covered by the reigns of the four Georges, when such a charge might with justice have been brought. Had English bishops in the last half of the last century been caring more about the souls of their people and less about the revenues of their sees; had English rectors and vicars kept better in mind that fair ideal of what a priest should be which the first of English poets sketched in the Canterbury Tales, the followers of John Wesley would, in all likelihood, be to-day within the Anglican Communion instead of without it. Take the clergy of the Church of England now, and we may proudly challenge for it collectively, and as a body, comparison with any clergy in Christendom, whether as regards learning, faithfulness in the cure of souls, or general elevation of character; but the heritage of ill-repute handed down from the generation before the last has proved a sad burden this many a year. And probably there are not a few worthy people who at the present moment are firmly persuaded that in the established Church of England there is not a bishop who is not arrogant and purse-proud, not a country parson who does not habitually drink with the squire and follow the hounds across the farmers' fields, not a curate who is not coveting by day and dreaming by night of possible preferment. Such force has the old tradition of bad times to mar the good report of present excellence! I have taken this illustration of a way in which the worldliness of a Church may betray itself through the lives of its clergy from the history of the Anglican Communion, not because I might not have found instances elsewhere, but because of a strong desire to avoid any, even the slightest, appearance of trying to make out a case.

Suppose, now, we go on to consider some of the ways in which the worldliness of the Church may find expression in the lives of the people who make up its congregations and are enrolled on its lists. One such indication would certainly be the general prevalence of a low standard of honor, of integrity, and of social purity. When we see people habitually giving themselves up to the gratification of their appetites, bending their whole energy, or such flabby semblance of energy as they have, to the attainment of comfort, incapable of any conversation above the level of gossip and scandal, showing no sign of lofty aspiration, of earnest purpose, of unselfish motive, we may fairly and without breach of charity set them down as worldly. And this sort of thing, if it could be proved to be characteristic of a Church as a whole, would certainly stamp such a Church as worldly. But is it a sort of thing which exclusively characterizes any one denomination of Christians in this republic of ours? I think not. Faithful inquiry would probably bring out the fact that whenever wealth abounds in any given community, and more especially newly-acquired wealth, the vices of luxury, indolence, selfishness, and the fondness for display will also abound, and that, too, quite, or almost quite, independently of the circumstance that this or that form of Christianity happens to be dominant there. That the Episcopal Church is wholly free from the low breeding and vulgarity which force themselves noisily and showily upon ears and eyes of men, God forbid that I should assert. Only this I say : "Let that Church which is without sin among you cast the first stone at her." Instead of mutual recriminations, what we want is that all good Christian people everywhere should join hearts and hands in the effort to frown down, to laugh down, and to make disreputable all violations of that standard of modesty, quietness, and self-restraint which ought to be reckoned the common law of Christendom.

Another way in which a Church may show itself involved in the sin of worldliness is by turning a cold shoulder upon the poor. Happily, we have in this country, as yet, no such thing as a peasant class. "The poor" as a fixed and recognized body do not exist among us, simply because under the working of our social system the poor of to-day may be the rich of to-morrow, and the rich of this year the poor of the next. Still, it remains true that the poor in one sense we have always with us, and still it remains true that the Church of Christ owes to the poor precisely the same amount of care, watchfulness, and consideration that it owes to the rich. But the great danger of society, Christian society I mean, in its relations to the poor, is not so much that it will deliberately trample on their feelings, wantonly insult them, or purposely injure them—not so much as this, as that it will simply forget them. And this is what I meant by saying that a Church betrays worldliness when it turns a cold shoulder on the poor. It is so easy to forget those who are not conspicuous. The Psalmist in a moment of despondency seems to have felt as if even Jehovah Himself were in danger of this lapse: "Forget not," he cries, fervently, "the congregation of thy poor."

The ways in which a Church has it in its power to bless and help the poor are numerous. The most obvious one is that of making the House of God as accessible as possible. The Church is bound to see to it that the excuse, "I cannot worship God in public because I have no money," be taken out of the mouth of every man that breathes. Whether what is known as the "free-church system" be or be not the best method of bringing this end to pass is an open question. I merely note in passing that a bad sort of worldliness in a Church is that which forgets all about asking whether the poor have or have not the Gospel preached to them.

But not merely floor room for the poor on Sundays: the unworldly Church will be bound in conscience to furnish more that that. Hospitals, orphanages, homes, refuges—these are things that the Church ought to build and endow and look after, if it would do its whole duty to society. A Church which is a praying and preaching Church only, will with great difficulty save itself from becoming a worldly Church. "Lord, Lord, did we not prophesy in thy name?" is a plea that sounds religious as well as plausible, but we have good authority for believing that alone by itself it will not be accepted at that day. The "Come ye blessed of My Father" is reserved for those who have remembered the hungry and thirsty, the stranger, the prisoner, and the sick. The Church which, in a quiet, unostentatious way, shall succeed here in America in doing the most of this sort of thing will best deserve the title of unworldly.

Another way in which the laity have it in their power to defile a Church with worldliness is in the management of its financial affairs. I speak, of course, of those Churches in which the control of the revenues is, as it should be, in the hands of the laity. Illegitimate methods of raising money for sacred purposes, criminal recklessness in the contraction of debts, and almost criminal tardiness in paying them—these also are among the tokens of worldliness which, in making up our judgments, we shall do well to take note. The reason why these things indicate worldliness is because they show that the hearts of the people are not in the object for which the Church exists. Men who are in earnest about accomplishing a purpose seldom go to work circuitously to raise the needed means. If a mill is to be built, no elaborate scheme is first contrived for indirectly getting the necessary funds from other people without their knowing that they have contributed. And yet how much wheedling and coaxing and indirect taxation and mitigated gaming is carried on in the name and for the supposed advantage of the Church and Jesus Christ! It is all wrong. The treasury of God is not really replenished by any such remittances as these. Only so much money as is given from the heart and at the dictate of the conscience is ever really given to God. Churches built to glorify the builder, and churches built to enhance the value of landed property in the neighborhood, remain private houses, though you consecrate them ten times over and plaster them from floor to ceiling with polychromatic emblems of Faith. And what applies to the building of church edifices applies to the use and maintenance of them when built. An unworldly management of the temporal affairs of a Church does not mean an unbusiness-like management of them. Far from it! On the contrary, an unworldly administration of church affairs means such an administration that the keenest man of business you can find, looking on with a critical, nay, even with an unfriendly eye, shall not be able to put his finger anywhere and say scornfully, There is a blot. No; give us stainless honor in the management of all that pertains to the temporal interests of the Church of God, and unworldliness is so far forth secured.

And now, does the reader expect me to maintain that the Protestant Episcopal Church in the United States is wholly and entirely above reproach as respects all these points which have been touched? Even if I thought so, it would be most unseemly and ill-judged of me to make the boast. But honestly I do not think so, and, therefore, while fully appreciating the power which reckless and unlimited assertion gives to the champion of a Church, I cannot say so. Personally, I entertain no doubt that the Episcopal Church is open to serious censure on the score of worldliness. That many of her members are living selfish, luxurious, aimless lives is true. That her clergy, all of them, fall far short of what the ministers of Jesus Christ ought to be in diligence, in devoutness, in sympathetic ministration to the needs of men, is true. That her temporal interests are in many instances administered from worldly motives and in worldly ways is true.

But when it comes to singling out the Episcopal Church for especial blame in these respects; when, for example, it is alleged of the Church that it is "notorious for worldliness;" then its friends are thrown into the attitude of defence, and words which might otherwise seem boastful become natural. Yet even from such natural boasting, if we may call it such, I would rather refrain, although the precedent of an apostle might be claimed for indulging in it. There was a pleasant mixture of satire and of compliment in the text with which a minister of another communion once prefaced a sermon eulogistic of the Episcopal Church: "Let another man praise thee and not thine own mouth; a stranger and not thine own lips." But some things which may not be said in boastfulness may rightly be said in thankfulness. Churchmen have reason to feel profoundly thankful that all over the land there seems to be a general waking up to the fact that the Church is nothing unless it be a working Church; that it can not be in any real sense the "Body of Christ," unless, like Him, it be going about doing good. In the providence of God it has come to pass that this Church has within its fold a very large proportion of poor. With the exception of the Roman Catholics, there is, I suppose, not one among the larger Christian denominations which, in the proportion to its size, numbers so many of the very poor. In doing our duty by those whom God has given into our charge, we shall, as a people, find the best possible antidote to worldliness. In addition to our poverty, we have also, as a Church, more especially in the larger cities, a great deal of wealth. Behold, then, the opportunity! Wealth is often, not always, the indication of intelligence. That wealth is found in a church is, therefore, no reproach to it, provided the wealth represents intelligence. Poverty, on the other hand, is often an inherited misfortune; often, not always, the fruit of undeserved calamity. That poverty is found in a church is a call for sympathy. That the intelligence of the land should be taught to be sympathetic with the poverty of the land, is confessedly our greatest need. Alarm about the stability of social order would largely abate if only between classes there lived a better understanding, if only there were more sympathy in the air. Forgetting, then, and casting away that love of the world which kills the soul, be it the Church's aim to catch that higher love of the world which moves to sacrifice, the love wherewith God loved it when He gave his Son.

William Reed Huntington, *Popular Misconceptions of the Episcopal Church.* (New York: Thomas Whittaker, 1891), 31-42. (Excerpt)

78.

Charles D. Williams, The Value of a Man, 1909

Charles David Williams (July 30, 1860–February 14, 1923) was consecrated the fourth Bishop of Michigan on February 7, 1906. He was a social reformer and argues in this essay that labor is not a commodity.

Isaiah xiii. 12. "I will make a man more precious than fine gold; even a man than the golden wedge of Ophir."

During the terrible disaster in New York harbor, when the ships of the North German Lloyd line were burning at their wharves, certain tug captains are said to have coolly passed by, or even ruthlessly ridden down, struggling, drowning men, who had flung themselves into the water to escape fiery death; and given chase instead to the floating bales of cotton which had been thrown from the burning deck and dock. The reason was this: the rescued cotton would be worth forty dollars a bale on the market. The rescued man would fetch nothing. And therefore, in the eyes of these creatures, a bale of cotton was more precious than a man.

We shudder at the story. Its calculating inhumanity sets our hearts aflame with indignation. And yet are we altogether guiltless of the very same thing? May not some prophet of God lay his hands upon you or me and say, "Thou art the man"? For, after all, this incident is but an unusually crude and frank expression of a spirit quite prevalent in our modern world, though it generally appears under less crass and shocking forms. It is the spirit of commercialism. It is the mind or the habit of thought which in its estimate of values invariably puts things above men, merchandise above manhood.

It was this spirit which our prophet found incarnate in ancient Babylon,—that Babylon which afterward, in the language of the New Testament Apostle and seer, became the mystic symbol and type of the kingdom of this world as over against the kingdom of God. Isaiah looked yearningly forward to the time when in the coming of the Kingdom of Heaven to this earth, in the setting up of the celestial civilization in the world, the Lord "should make a man more precious than fine gold; yea, a man than the golden wedge of Ophir." But that time has not yet fully come, and the prophetic vision and promise still await fulfilment. Our modern civilization still has lingering about it a strong Babylonish flavor, and the name of the ancient city is not an unfitting symbol of what to-day we call *the world*—that is, human society as organized apart from the will of God, and as distinguished from that ideal state when human society shall be organized quite according to the will of God, when the will of the Father-king shall be done on earth even as it is done in Heaven. We may have—we surely have— made great advances in the Christian ages toward the goal of the prophetic vision. But we are a long way off from it still. Thank God, we no longer openly sell men on the slave block for gold. And in our theories of humanity, our ideals of society, even in our common law, we put men above things. But in our practice—industrial, social, national, and individual—we still value things above men, and especially do we value merchandise above manhood.

Indeed, commercialism may be said to be *the* characteristic sin of the land and age in which we live. This is, or has been (for, thank God, there are some signs of the mitigation of our materialism), a most materialistic age, and we are essentially a commercial people. And the Babylonian standard, the Babylonian estimate,—in a word, if I may coin one, *Babylonianism*,—affords the constant temptation of the modern world and of the American people in particular.

Naturally, the most vivid illustrations and most direct expressions of the Babylonian temper are to be found in our industrial world. The most striking, to me the most appalling, thing about the business world is, not its inhumanity, but its prevailing and persistent dehumanity, if I may use the word the way human beings are depersonalized and dehumanized in its speech, its thought, its practice. Labor, for instance, is habitually thought and spoken of, not as the toil of human hands, the sweat—sometimes the bloody sweat—of human brows, the thought and skill of human brains; ay, the daring risk, the courage, the heroic self-sacrifice of human souls as it is in all dangerous occupations; nay, but this strangely vital and personal composite of sweat and blood and tears, of brains and heart and soul, becomes, in the language and practice of the business world, simply a commodity, so much stuff to be bought in the cheapest market and sold in the dearest. We discuss its price as dispassionately, we bull and bear its markets as coolly, as we do the market in pig-lead or fertilizers. Laborers are commonly termed "hands"; they are the instruments, the tools of industry; they are to the economic eye like the steam in the boiler, the electricity in the dynamo, or the power in the waterfall, simply so much capacity for production; in the estimation of the industrial and commercial world, men become things, and generally about the cheapest things, with which that world has to deal. If a machine breaks down in a great factory, this is a calamity. Repairs must be made, and they cost money; a delay ensues and that costs money. But if a man is maimed or crushed, if he loses limb or life, it may cost a small doctor's bill, or possibly—provided the ignorance and weakness of the poor sufferer or his friends are able to cope at the game of law with the legal cunning and the influence of a great corporation—a suit for damages: but the grind of production goes on unhindered, because another man stands eager to take the place of the toiler who has fallen out of the ranks. Men are cheaper than machines. If the price of nails sinks below the figure the greed of commerce demands, a trust is formed, factories are closed, and thousands are thrown out of employment. Misery ensues, families fall upon public charity or starve, multitudes are shorn of the means of warding off sickness and death. But what of that? The price of nails is enhanced, and nails are worth more than men.

The Napoleon of finance must turn his millions. The bargain counter must be baited for the feminine soul. Our luxurious dames must be able to boast of their marvellous cheap purses. And therefore the sweat shop must reek with its physical and moral filth, and the shop-girl must be forced (sometimes under her employer's deliberate advice) to sell her body into shame that she may eke out her pitiful wage to living proportions. What if souls are damned thereby? Bargains are worth more than souls.

With the tremendous and unprecedented organization of our industrial and commercial world, all personal relation between employer and employee has been practically destroyed, and consequently personal consideration rendered nearly impossible. The other day a new consolidation of railroad interests was effected. Immediately a man was sent out on the road to reduce forces in all offices of the system. Fewer clerks must do the work. It is a notorious fact that railroad offices are very frequently undermanned. But nevertheless, an increase must be had of one per cent in the annual dividend on the preferred stock of the corporation, and that one per cent increase was of more worth than the welfare of thousands of faithful employees and their dependent families. The increase of work due to the reduction of the clerical force might grind and use men up faster, but what of that? Men are the cheapest things on the market.

Every pastor knows what this absorption of men in the industrial mill signifies to spiritual life and religious work. Let me give you a typical leaf out of my own pastoral history. It tells a tale that has been repeated again and again in my own experience. A young man comes into the parish. He is regular in his attendance of church and devout in worship. He is earnest and eager for work. He is put into some position in the church's activities and devotes himself faithfully and efficiently to the work assigned him. But by and by (alack the day), he gets a "good position," as it is called, with some prominent firm. Business increases. But instead of increasing their office force, they begin to work him overtime. They claim and absorb his evenings. He gives up his church work in consequence. He has no mind, no energy, no interest, no time, even, left for it. Business claims him wholly, body, mind, and soul. By and by he drops off in his church attendance. You ask him why? He answers that he is so exhausted by his week's work, night and day, that he is too tired to turn out on Sunday. Or even worse, the firm must have him at the office for extra work one or two Sundays out of every three. And so the man's religious work ceases, and his spiritual life is absorbed in the rush and grind of commercialism. He ceases to be a man in the highest sense of the word; he becomes a mere calculating machine for the corporation that employs him, to be used until worn out and then cast aside for a new one. That man's manhood, his spiritual manhood, has been sacrificed for gold; and even *he* does not get the gold. Such is the story of many a clerk's and bookkeeper's life.

But it is not only the poor or the dependent whose manhood is held cheaper than merchandise; the rich themselves often estimate their own manhood as of less worth than their gold. Take one illustration from our educational world. The son of a wealthy family is sent off to college to get an education, as the phrase runs. Look at the course marked out for the boy, and in many a case you will find it something like this: the classics are eliminated altogether, because they will never sell in the money market. The humanities are generally rigorously restricted for the same reason. Philosophy and history are ignored, for they have no speculative value. Only the modern commercial languages are taught, tongues that will sell in trade. The educational is made strictly practical and technical. It is a wholly business training; that is, everything that ministers primarily to general culture, everything that would make of the boy a well-rounded, well-developed, well-disciplined man, a man of the fullest and richest manhood possible,—all that is sacrificed to the immediately practical and technical. This is as it is because the father wants the son to be, not the best sort of a man, but the best sort of a money-maker, a machine such as you may find in any of our mints for stamping out bright coin from the raw bullion. That influence of commercialism is being felt everywhere throughout our educational system. Our colleges and schools are largely yielding to it. Many of them are sinking into mere technical schools, training for trade and business instead of giving the most generous culture and developing the richest and largest manhood.

Again that squint of commercialism affects our vision and judgment in estimating our national strength and well-being. Do we ask, "Is the national life sound and healthy? Is the country strong and safe? Are we a prosperous people? Are we developing the true ideal of our national life and character?" Ask such questions, and nine times out of ten the answer comes in terms material rather than vital, moral, or spiritual. You are pointed to the smoke belching from the factory chimney, to the full dinner pail of the workman, to the large dividends upon invested capital, to the clearing-house reports and savings-bank accounts, to the estimate of per capita wealth, to the excess of exports over imports, to the extension of commerce and the acquisition of new markets, to anything and in fact everything, except that which alone constitutes the strength of a State; namely, the patriotism of her sons, the manhood of her citizens, their intelligent devotion to national principles, their love of justice, righteousness, and freedom, and the courage and self-sacrifice with which they will stand for these principles. I sometimes think that our government is fast being made a machine for promoting commercial schemes for privileged parties rather than an institution for protecting the common rights of the common people and developing the patriotism of the average citizen. I hold no brief for any political party. I stand here for no particular policy, for expansion or anti-expansion, for imperialism or anti-imperialism. All these are more or less external matters and surface questions. The question that probes to the heart of our American civilization, the question that tests the essential quality of our national life is this: What are the prevailing temper and mind of our people? Do we, in estimating our national prosperity and well-being, count things above men or men above things? Merchandise above manhood, or manhood above merchandise? Principle above self, or self above principle? That civilization and national life which count the gold more precious than the man, however fat and luxuriant and even phosphorescently brilliant on the surface, are rotten at the heart. It is its human wealth and not its material wealth which measures the prosperity of a nation; that is, the well-being of its citizens and not its accumulation of substance.

It is also far too frequently so with our personal lives. Ask what a man is worth, and the answer comes almost invariably, not in terms of character, of manhood, or mental, moral, or spiritual values, but in terms of the market, stocks and bonds and lands and houses, in values measurable by gold. That shows the standard prevailing in the popular mind; it is the standard that makes gold more precious than the man. And men are living by that standard every day. They are daily trading off the spiritual for the material, because according to this accepted standard of values, the material is of more worth than the spiritual. For instance, why is faith so weak among men? Why does religion, particularly the religion of Jesus Christ, have so small a part in their thoughts, and still less in their lives? I do not believe that it is intellectual difficulties, the difficulties raised by the discoveries of our modern science, the higher criticism, and other learning. I do not believe that it is these things that keep most of the men who stand aloof from Christ away from Him. Nay, most of them do not even know these things, and if they do know of them, they do not stop to think of them twice. Nay, it is moral difficulties, it is spiritual obstacles, that keep men away from Christ. It is because they know that the convenient conventional codes of respectability and honesty and honor prevailing in the business and commercial world will not stand in the searching light of Christ, because they know that the precepts, laws, and ideals of Christ are impracticable in the business world as it is at present organized; because of such knowledge as this, be it consciously or only half consciously held, they stand aloof from Christ. They cannot make money as easily in the ways they are now making it and in such masses as they are now making it, if they consistently follow Christ; and they care more for money than they do for Christ; gold is more precious than man, than the Son of Man. And therefore they will have none of Him. And I honor them more than I do the hypocrite of the church, who, while loudly professing to reverence Christ and even serve him, yet daily uses business methods which stultify and profane the very name of Christian. The spirit of commercialism, the spirit which puts things above men and merchandise above manhood, rapidly dulls all spiritual sensibility, destroys all capacity for faith in the unseen and spiritual, all ability to respond to Christ, which is, after all, the truest description of faith. Let me illustrate: Here is a boy still within the sacred walls of home, a boy with clean-cut features, with frank, fearless eyes that look straight and steady at you without shrinking; soulful eyes are they, for in their depths you discern the beauty of a transparent and unsullied soul. He is religious in the deepest sense of the word. He is responsive and loyal to Christ. He is full of generous ideals, high enthusiasms, spiritual aspirations. It is an inspiration to be with him. He has noble ideas about honor and truth and principle. Perhaps, in our worldly wisdom, we smile and call them quixotic. He will not swerve a hair's-breadth from the right line of honesty and justice,—no, not for anybody or anything. He will not compromise his standards of conscience or trail his banners in the dust,—no, not for the world. He realizes the poet's ideal of the youth who, "by the vision splendid is on his way attended . . . trailing clouds of glory do we come from God who is our home."

But after a while your boy goes out of the home life into the business world; you come across him by and by grown into middle age, and you see a change. Perhaps there is nothing overtly bad or positively immoral about him. He has been too prudent and parsimonious to spend his substance extravagantly upon low indulgences and sins of the flesh. But you find the cold, calculating eye and the shrewd, practical temper of the accomplished and successful money-maker. Everything is measured by money standards now. He smiles indulgently at his youthful notions of sensitive honor and transparent sincerity and absolute justice and all that. They are impractical ideals, if one would get along in the world; too fragile ware for human nature's daily use; well enough for bric-a-brac to be kept under glass cases on parlor mantelpieces, but by no means to be trusted in the kitchens of life, where the food is to be cooked. One needs tougher ware there. He has no more visions. He would call them dreams, illusions, delusions, now. Conventional respectability is now to him a sufficient standard of conduct, and the commercial code—what is legitimate or even legal, what is allowed by the trade rather than what is essentially and inherently true and honest and righteous and just—is a high enough law of conscience. The man has become no longer a man in the best sense of the word, but a mere sordid and shrivelled money-bag. He has sold his soul, his spiritual capacity, for gold. And yet you cannot put your finger on any single definite bargain like Faust's, wherein the sale was consummated. No, it was here and there, gradually and imperceptibly, that he lost to himself, his best self, that noble, beautiful, ideal manhood, whose rudimentary possibilities showed so fair in the face of his youth. For souls are lost, not so much by the sudden damnations of great crimes as by the shrinkage and shrivelling of an insidious worldliness.

Is not this sin of commercialism, of Babylonianism, this sin that puts the thing above the man and merchandise above manhood, the representative sin of our age and of our land? Does it not threaten to sap the higher life and manhood of our civilization, our nation, our religion, and our individual souls? By it we are getting things just upside down in our industrial and commercial world. We have exactly reversed all right relations. Industries were meant to feed men, but we are turning men into the food of our industries. We are making of trade a huge Minotaur to which we deliberately sacrifice the freshness and beauty of our choicest youth, the culture and full-rounded development of our manhood and the lives of our poor. We are making wealth not simply the material basis upon which a higher, nobler life is to be builded, but we are making it the whole of life. We are putting things above men and men beneath things. We are making men the servants and things the masters. There are many reforms proposed for remedying the evils of our industrial and social world; some wise, some otherwise. But not one will avail aught permanently and really until we arrive at a new viewpoint from which to get our whole vision of life and its meaning; a new table of values, a new standard of estimates for measuring all things. It must be the viewpoint from which our prophet got his vision; it must be the standard which Christ established. We must make a "man more precious than fine gold; even a man than the golden wedge of Ophir." We must recognize that "a man's life consisteth not in the abundance of the things that he possesseth," but in the wealth of his service unto God and fellow-men, and the richness of his personality. We must reorganize our industrial and social and educational world upon that basis. We have gotten it upside down. We must make wealth the servant of life rather than life the slave of wealth. We must put men above things, rather than things above men. Then, and only then, will the lives and souls of our toilers be worth more than the product of their industry, and the manhood of ourselves and our sons than the gains of our shrewdness and greed.

God help us all to stand stoutly, bravely, and unwaveringly for a true idealism against this flood of materialism, the idealism of the Kingdom of God as against the materialism of the kingdom of this world; until it shall come to pass even in the most commercial realms of our common life, even in the industrial and political world, that "a man shall be more precious than fine gold; even than the golden wedge of Ophir."

Charles D. Williams, *A Valid Christianity for Today* (New York: Macmillan Company, 1909), 70-84. (Excerpt)

79.

Report of Joint Commission on the Relations of Capital and Labor, 1910

The Joint Commission on the Relations of Capital and Labor was established by the fortieth General Convention at San Francisco, October 2-17, 1901. It studied the purposes of labor organizations and investigated the causes of industrial disturbances. The findings of the Joint Commission were expressed in this report.

So far as our commission is concerned, the most important single event since 1907 bearing upon social conditions is the meeting of the Lambeth Conference. The importance of this meeting lies in the fact that the keynote of the Encyclical issued by the Conference as of the various reports and resolutions appended was social service.

In relating the work of the church to the social movements of the time, the Encyclical points out that—"By the power of the truth which it carries and declares, the church is constantly serving the cause of true progress. But it has a further duty—to be watchfully responsive to the opportunities of service which the movements of civil society provide. The democratic movement of our century presents one of these opportunities. Underlying it are ideals of brotherhood, liberty and mutual justice and help. In these ideals we recognize the working of our Lord's teaching as to the inestimable value of every human being in the sight of God, and His special thought for the weak and the oppressed. These are practical truths proclaimed by the ancient prophets and enforced by our Lord with all the perfectness of His teaching and His life. We call upon the church to consider how far and wherein it has departed from these truths."

In such a spirit in the various reports and resolutions the Conference touches upon all the great social problems of the day. Its wise and clear words should be read by everyone whose interest is alive to those manifold terrible questions which press society for an answer. As especially related to the field of our work, we call attention to certain of the principles laid down concerning property:

> "48. The Church should teach that the Christian who is an owner of property should recognize the governing principle that, like all our gifts, our powers and our time, property is a trust held for the benefit of the community, and its right use should be insisted upon as a religious duty.

> "49. The Conference urges upon members of this Church practical recognition of the moral responsibility involved in their investments. This moral responsibility extends to—(a) the character and general social effect of any business or enterprise in which their money is invested; (b) the treatment of the persons employed in that business or enterprise; (c) the due observance of the requirements of the law relating thereto; (d) the payment of a just wage to those who are employed therein."

Significant of this same steadily increasing interest is the establishment of Diocesan Social Service Committees in twelve Dioceses and one Missionary District. Their growth has been fostered by the members of this Commission, as well as by the recommendation of the Lambeth Conference, that every Diocese should have some such body. The work of these Diocesan bodies, as revealed in their printed reports, has been comprehensive, careful and thorough. In most cases they have limited their activity to investigation and report; but in some instances the Committee, either through individual members or sub-committees, have assisted actively in the furtherance of legislation, and it is quite evident that the individual members have been constantly active and influential in all such matters.

The range of topics upon which reports have been made is very wide. All the Committees whose reports have been accessible to us have dealt with the problems of childhood, especially child labor, truancy and sex. All have investigated public health questions. Some have studied tenement house conditions, and one, at least, is responsible for the draft and passage of the Tenement House Ordinance of one of our great cities—San Francisco. The social evil amusements (theatres, gambling, slot machines, and the like) and temperance come next in interest. The New Jersey Committee studies marriage and divorce questions. Chicago contributes a very interesting study of the attitude of labor towards the church. Several Committees give lists of books to guide the clergy and others in their reading.

We have felt it worthwhile to mention these details in order to make clear to the Church the possibilities of this movement. Many Dioceses have been slow to take up such work. Some have been afraid. There is, however, nothing beyond occasional rashness to fear. There is everything to gain. Such a Committee gives to a Diocese a constantly growing number of active workers, a general diffusion of knowledge among the Clergy and the laity, and the formal pledge of the Church to play her part in the great work of social improvement.

We are impressed in reviewing these reports with the need of better co-ordination among the Dioceses in their work and of better general guidance of the movement. We regret that Bishop Potter's death put an end to plans which he had in mind for carrying out the instructions looking in such direction given to us at the last Convention. The work should be done. It cannot be done effectively by so small a Commission as at present established. We append, therefore, to this report, resolutions discharging the present Commission and establishing a larger one with title conforming more nearly to those in use by most of the Diocesan Committees.

This needed work of co-ordination has been undertaken unofficially with considerable success by the Christian Social Union of the C.A.I.L. At Trenton last May a conference of Diocesan Committees was held under the auspices of the union, as in New York two years ago under the auspices of the C.A.I.L., and its officers have kept in touch with the various Diocesan workers and endeavored to keep them in touch with each other. The Union has also vigorously prosecuted its other work of issuing literature bearing upon social questions, arranging for meetings, disseminating information and the like. The other chief organization of social workers, The Church Association for the Advancement of the Interests of Labor, of which Bishop Potter was long president, has also continued its special work. The New York Child Labor Law is, we believe, due to its activity. It rendered conspicuous aid in the strike of the shirt-waist makers in 1909. One of its Committees is now assisting the work of other bodies in the problem of Tenement House Congestion.

Such a brief review, which does not even touch upon the work of special societies, like The Church Temperance Society, indicates the alacrity with which this Church is responding to the present call. This is but our part of the general response of Christian America. The sentiment of American Protestant Christianity has been gathered up and expressed in the reports and recommendations of the Federal Council of the Churches of Christ. The reports on social questions are sane and forcible, and we trust that they may be widely read by members of this Church. We are glad to make our own recommendation for the observance of Labor Sunday, and to state our conviction that the three appeals made by the Council's Commission on Social Services in behalf of labor, constituting, as they do, a suggestion of the direction in which improvement of labor conditions may move, deserve the support of every Christian man. These are:

First : The gradual and reasonable reduction of the hours of labor to the lowest practicable point, and that degree of leisure for all which is a condition of the highest human life.

Second : A release from employment one day in seven.

Third : A living wage as a minimum in every industry, and the highest wage that each industry can afford.

We see no way by which any Christian man can escape responsibility for assisting such reforms. The most notable work in any one Communion continues to be that of the Department of Church and Labor of the Presbyterian Church, under the direction of the Rev. Mr. Stetzle. So deeply are we impressed by the possibilities of such an organization of the work that we commend the whole subject to the consideration of the new Commission.

This review of the work and prospects of the Church in the field of social service would not be complete without a reiteration of some of those general principles which must guide her action. Our previous reports have uttered them. They are commonplaces of every meeting of religious people in connection with this kind of work; yet we have the prophet's witness to the value of "line upon line, precept upon precept." It requires repetition to weariness in order that even such commonplaces may sink deep into the general mind and become springs of action.

The Church herself has concern not with any specific outward form of society, either political or industrial. Her concern is with the spirit which shall ultimately mould fit forms for its own expression. She cannot, therefore, stand officially for or against individualism or socialism, democracy or autocracy. But she must be hospitable towards every view which claims to utter her own spirit and realize her own ideals. She must give its proponents a free hearing and trust in God's working through humanity to establish permanently only that which is of value.

In the same way the Church represents all classes. Whatever she may be in certain places or at certain times, she is always in ideal the Church of all men. She must deal impartially with all. She cannot ally herself with capitalist or laborer, but must throw her influence fearlessly for every movement which means the upbuilding of humanity. She must fearlessly rebuke, warn or encourage rich and poor alike, as the need is.

In delivering such message today we are convinced that the Church must throw her chief emphasis upon the value of human life. This is but reiterating what we have already quoted from the Lambeth Encyclical. The property right is merely one conferred upon the individual by the community. Morally it exists only in return for social services. It must, in every case, yield to the needs of humanity. No business interests, no profit, however great, can warrant the deliberate deterioration of human life. Such a principle has clear implications. To illustrate in facts recently brought in a startling way to the public: No Christian employer can find valid ground for conducting an industry which requires, or even permits, the regular employment of men for twelve hours a day seven days in the week at a wage which necessitates the work of women and children that the family may live.

Christian society ought not to permit the existence of any industry which cannot succeed without the labor of women and children under unnatural conditions. "Inasmuch as ye have done it unto one of the least of these my brethren," is the final test of our Christianity. The first care of the Christian employer should be, not his profits, but his men. He should think not so much of getting work out of them as of helping to form those habits of industry which contribute to health and character.

The same principle governs the Church's message to the laborer. It is her business to help him to understand his own struggle and its meaning. He must learn that it is development of the whole man which gives his struggle dignity. The better physical conditions and the opportunity for recreation and education and family life which he seeks are not ends, but means to the end, of better men and women. His unions are justified through seeking such an end. When, therefore, he seems to stand for mediocrity, for the diminution of opportunity for individuals, for a purely class interest and spirit or for violence, the Church must equally reprove. When in ignorance that his whole present advance springs from the Life which the Church preserves for the world he attacks her or neglects her, she must reach out in tenderness to win him back. Only in sympathetic touch can the Church find the way to that hold upon the life of the laborer which she has so largely lost.

Once more: It is an ominous characteristic of our age that we encounter widely spread among both rich and poor a spirit which utterly loses sight of the value of man, not through seeking profit or material gain, but in the making of pleasure the end of life. Much that is said of the emancipation of labor, much that is urged in certain kinds of socialist writing and speaking proceeds upon the assumption that work is an evil to get through in order that abundance of time may be given to pleasure. It is a false ideal. Pleasure is right, but it must supplement faithful work and recreate body and mind for work. There is a mission for the Church in meeting such ideals by the setting forth of the Christian ideal of service as willing work, as that which gives life value. Here we touch rich as well as poor. The menace of the idle poor who must work but long to be idle is not more serious than the menace of the idle rich whose extravagant pleasures corrupt not only their own ideals, but set false ones for the poor. To inherit a fortune and give one's life up to pleasure is more respectable but no more Christian than to tramp the country in unconcealed idleness.

The final solution of all the problems which these remarks suggest lies, we believe, only in the steady increase of the power of Christianity in the community. The power of the Christian ideal of life and the supreme value of every human life, let the Church show forth the one and proclaim the other, and her work will be well done.

(Signed) Wm. Lawrence,
Chas. P. Anderson,
Randolph H. McKim,
Edward L. Parsons,
Samuel Mather,
Henry Lewis Morris.

Journal of General Convention, 1910, 534-538.

80.

George Hodges, The Church and the Labor Movement, 1914

George Hodges (October 6, 1856–May 27, 1919) was the fifth dean of the Episcopal Theological School in Cambridge, Massachusetts, 1894-1919, now the Episcopal Divinity School. The Episcopal Theological School was founded in 1867 and has been a center of liberal Evangelicalism. Hodges taught that the Church must be as much interested in politics and society as in religion. The Heresy of Cain, from which this selection is taken, was first published in 1890.

What can the church, as an organization do in the labor movement? At present very little; first, for lack of disposition.

Many members of the church are enthusiastically disposed toward the cause of the workingman, but not all; probably less than a majority. Some who hold back do so from interested motives, being themselves upon the other side. A portion of the employers, the operators, the owners, the capitalists, against whom the labor movement is directed, are members, or at least attend the services, of the church. Dives belongs to the vestry; Mammon passes the alms basin. It was natural and easy for St. James and some of the other writers of the New Testament to preach against the rich, because their audiences were made up almost entirely of the poor. Wealth in that day was all on the side of the devil. Such sermons are not common in our pulpits. The parable of the camel vainly essaying to pass the eye of the needle is not often taken as a text. Nor will you hear a well-dressed congregation exhorted either in words or in the spirit of this apostolic utterance, "Go too, now, ye rich men, weep and howl for your miseries which shall come upon you. Your riches are corrupted, and your garments are moth-eaten. Behold the hire of your laborers who have reaped down your fields, which is of you kept back by fraud, crieth; and the cries of them that have reaped are entered into the ears of the Lord of Sabbaoth."

Some, of course, will be prompt to say that we do not preach after this fashion because we fear that such a sermon would affect our salary. But, while I am not prepared to deny that the clerical mind works in some cases quite like the lay mind, I am altogether convinced that the chief reason why the clergy of the present day do not more often shake their rhetorical fists in the faces of the rich is because they do not feel that the rich deserve that sort of treatment. Most parsons are acquainted with a great many people of all conditions, rich and poor, employers and employed; and they know perfectly well that the figures of a man's income do not at all show where he stands upon the scale of sanctity. You cannot persuade them by any socialistic arguments that the poor are all saints, and that the rich are all sinners. They know better. They know that the bad and the good are closely intertangled in this queer world. They are personally acquainted with labor leaders who are wholly given over to selfishness, and with capitalists who are altogether devoted to the good of others.

Moreover, it ought to be kept in mind that in the present condition of things, when the capitalist goes to church and the workingman stays away, the parson naturally knows the employer better than the men whom he employs. And personal acquaintance counts for much in the formation of our judgments. I am surprised that there is so much disposition toward the cause of labor as there is in the church, where so many of the leading laymen are men of wealth, and where the clergy are so naturally turned for counsel toward their direction.

In addition to these members of the church, who are thus in the position of partisans in this matter, and who can hardly help looking at things from their own point of view, there are many others who are selfishly satisfied. Even in the church not all are Christians. The devil always gets in everywhere,—into the church, into the labor unions,—and hinders our progress toward the right.

Still others have a narrow notion of the purpose of the church. It is such a spiritual society, as they regard it, that it is quite in the air, barely touching this profane planet, looking ever into the sky. The church is organized not for interference in the labor movement or in any other mundane matter, but for the saying of litanies, for the offering of adoration, and for the saving of the soul. The clergy are to preach on sacrifices, but they may not mention that form of sacrifice which makes a man devote himself to the interests of the town he lives in. Jerusalem may be named in sermons, but not Boston. The preacher may praise the golden pavements of the celestial streets, but he is out of his province if he ventures to criticise the unclean thoroughfare beside his door.

This sharp and foolish distinction between the sacred and the secular, which cannot stand in the light of the life of Jesus Christ, and which is disappearing as we get closer to him and look into the world as he did, still holds among some, and hinders sympathy.

An organization is evidently made up only of the people who comprise it. The church, as an organization, contains these three kinds of people,—those who thus limit the functions of the church and stand aloft from any combination between religion and economics; those who are well off themselves and do not care, preferring the present conditions for selfish reasons; and those who are not prepared to go very far in the labor movement because they see the other side, men of wealth, careful and conservative, knowing their own business sometimes better than we do. What we want is the real truth; what we seek to know is not things as they ought to be, but as they are. The church as an organization can at present do little in the labor movement for lack of disposition.

Secondly, for lack of knowledge.

It is not unlikely that a unanimous church enthusiasm for the cause of labor would just now do more harm than good. For the great, good-hearted church, having its eyes open to the evils that beset the world of industry, and being vigorously disposed to do something, would probably do something rash, foolish, and mistaken. The conditions are exceedingly complicated. Those who imagine that they are simple, and may be remedied by the application of this or that economic nostrum, do not know what they are talking about. The truth is, that nobody knows what ought to be done. That is the most discouraging feature in the whole situation. The times are evidently out of joint, but the fracture is such a complicated one that our wisest surgeons do not know how to treat it.

In this condition of things we may well pray to be delivered from the parsons. It is within easy memory, for example, how the parsons dealt with the scientific difficulties that were involved in that great readjustment of ideas caused by the teaching of the doctrine of evolution. Again and again the whole matter was disposed of in a twenty minutes' sermon.

Darwin's epoch-making book, the "Origin of Species," begins with this significant paragraph: "When on board H.M.S. Beagle as naturalist, I was much struck with certain facts in the distribution of the organic beings inhabiting South America, and in the geological relations of the present to the past inhabitants of that continent. These facts, as will be seen in the latter chapter of this volume, seemed to throw some light on the origin of species—that mystery of mysteries, as it has been called by one of our greatest philosophers. On my return home, it occurred to me, in 1837, that something might perhaps be made out of this question by patiently accumulating and reflecting on all sorts of facts which could possibly have any bearing on it. After five years' work I allowed myself to speculate on the subject, and drew up some short notes; these I enlarged in 1844 into a sketch of the conclusions which then seemed to me probable; from that period to the present day I have steadily pursued the same object. I hope that I may be excused for these personal details, as I give them to show that I have not been hasty in coming to a conclusion. My work is now (1859) nearly finished; but as it will take me more years to complete it, and as my health is far from strong, I have been induced to publish this abstract."

The results of these twenty-two years of patient and painstaking research were completely disproved again and again to the complete satisfaction of the preacher, by the youngest graduates of the theological schools, and by other men also, who were old enough to know better. One dreads to have another problem, equally complicated, equally demanding time and study and knowledge of details, set forth for discussion in ecclesiastical conventions. Fortunately the disposition to discuss it is lacking, else there is no predicting the will-o'-the-wisp millenniums into which we might be persuaded. The sermons that are occasionally preached upon the labor movement, taking strikes for texts, are such as to fill all intelligent labor leaders and all intelligent employees alike with blank despair. The brethren speak unadvisedly with their lips.

Indeed, if the church will consult the example of its Founder, it will hesitate, even with a fair equipment of knowledge, to deal with the labor question in a detailed way. We wish to know what is the best service that the church can render; and that best service, judged by the example of Jesus Christ, is the setting forth, not of regulations, but of eternal principles. The instance is a familiar one, where the two brethren came to him and desired that he would decide a dispute in which they were engaged over their father's will. They were dividing the estate between them. And one said, "This much belongs to me;" and the other answered, "No, a part of that is mine; you take too much." And they asked Jesus to be their arbitrator. You remember that he immediately declined. He refused to look at the account books, to consult the will, or to inspect the ground. "Take heed," he said, "and beware of covetousness, for a man's life consisteth not in the abundance of the things which he possesseth." That is, he set forth this deep and abiding principle, which, taken into the hearts of the disputants, would settle the dispute forever. We can see evidently enough that no interference in the discussion would have finally settled the fraternal variance. These brethren would not agree by reason of any argument based on addition or subtraction, on measurements or valuations. The trouble lay deeper than these surface matters. And the trouble to-day lies deeper far than an adjustment of the scale of wages.

The church does not, indeed, know enough about the details of the situation to speak with intelligence; but if the church were ten times wiser, the best voice would be one, not of political economy, but of religion. What we ask of the church, speaking in her representative assemblies, or from her pulpits, is inspiration, uplift, eternal principles, guidance of motives, the strengthening of a right spirit. A church which is set against the workingman, arguing as a partisan advocate in refutation of his cause, lacking in sympathy with his needs and his purposes, is of the devil. It is a synagogue of Satan. But I do not know where such a church is to be found.

True there are occasional utterances and silences which are discouraging. That the parsons in a town where the street-car men were working seventeen hours a day without any clerical complaint should rise up in almost unanimous objection against the opening of a public conservatory of God's flowers on the Lord's Day is disheartening to one who wishes to be loyal to the church. That owners of unsanitary tenements should be able to sit comfortably cushioned in the house of God, and listen serenely and somnolently to the preacher's sermon, Sunday after Sunday, shows that the preacher is making a mistake as to the meaning and application of the Christian religion. That men and women should find it possible to carry their selfish and unbrotherly hearts to church and bring them away again untouched, is evidence of something wrong. But this wrong is not to be righted by sermons upon the details of sanitation, or upon the better regulation of industry, but by the declaring, and impressing, and emphasizing, and reiterating over and over, so that nobody can mistake it, that no man can possibly be a Christian without behaving like a Christian, and that he alone lives like a Christian who speaks and acts as Christ did; friendly as he was, brotherly as he was, loving as he was, wishing not to be ministered unto, but to minister, and to give even his life for others.

Principle, rather than details, are the province of the church. The clergy are of more use in the labor movement as inspirers than as instructors; partly because principles go deeper into the heart of things; partly because people are more likely to heed the applications which they are left to make for themselves; partly because no man can speak with wisdom unless he knows what he is talking about. Yet it is the duty of the church to bring heaven and earth into close contact; to speak not into the air, but into the individual ears of particular people; to make sure that its eternal principles are understood in their concrete relations by those whose lives they touch, and, wherever it has certain knowledge, there to speak with emphasis.

The principle that every man is his brother's keeper is one which falls quite within the limits of the responsibility of the teaching church. And the obvious inference from that principle—that no man has a right to profit by his neighbor's disadvantage—is an excellent theme for a Christian sermon. And the cases which that inference concerns,—the carrying on or encouraging of a business which depends upon the payment of starvation wages, or upon the doing of the work under unsanitary conditions; the taking of rent from a tenement house which is so constructed or so crowded as to make Christian living, not to say decent living, impossible; and, in general, the receiving of money without knowing how it was earned,—these are good things to preach about.

The kindred principle that every man who lives is a son of God, and the brother—not the slave or tool—of even his most prosperous neighbor, comes also into the proper scope of the Christian pulpit. And the preacher is fruitfully occupied who draws out the evident consequences of that principle, that every man has a right to that which tends toward his best life, and may not by any Christian be ground down to such short wages and long hours as to deprive him of a chance to be anything better than an animal—these inferences, which carry the necessity and the righteousness of trades' unionism along with them, ought to be preached by the Christian church. The church knows enough already for such teaching, and has no need to wait for further economic light.

It is in the application of these truths to individual misdemeanors that the church is in peril of error. The clergy, by the mere fact of their seclusion from the industrial world, are inevitably ignorant. Arguments based upon the statements of newspapers are liable to serious fallacy. Ideas gained by reading books rather than by knowing men are open to mistake. The parsons would best confine themselves to principles. The church, as an organization, is not prepared at present to do much in detail in the labor movement, for lack of knowledge.

You may remember against me the story of the herald who stood by the city gate when the king entered, and informed him that the mayor was unfortunately unable to meet him, for seventeen reasons, the first of them being that the mayor was dead. The king dispensed the herald from reciting the other sixteen. Now that I have said already that the church is detained by lack of disposition and by lack of knowledge from meeting the labor movement with extended hand of welcome, it may be thought unnecessary that I should add a third reason to the other two. I will venture, however, to suggest such a third reason in the church's lack of utterance. If the church, as an organization, had an ideal disposition toward the labor movement, and a sufficient knowledge, it would be still hindered by the fact that it has no voice. I meant that the church, except in a most imperfect and fragmentary way, is not able in these days to say anything. To this has our spirit of unhappy separation brought us.

There was a time when the church, gathered in a representative assembly, was able to express the great truths of the Christian faith, so that everybody could hear and understand. The time may come when a united church, meeting again in a convention which shall represent Christianity rather than partisanship, shall be able to utter forth the great truths of Christian morality, so that they shall be heard and heeded.

But at present there is a Roman Catholic Church and a Presbyterian Church and an Episcopal Church, each speaking for a certain number of Christians, for a fragment of the community, representing divisions, strife, weakness. And outside is the admirably disciplined army of the devil—the allied forces of intemperance, of impurity, of corrupt politics, of fraud and falsehood, of theft and murder. And the Christian church stands in the mist of these abominations, reads the morning newspaper sorrowfully and helplessly, and accomplishes—next to nothing. Here and there some good man makes an assault upon the satanic forces, running out alone in front of the Christian rank; but his brethren behind throws stones at him to bring him back, and the rest of us preach sermons upon interesting texts touching the remote sins of Israel, and meet in conventions to debate rubrics and pass canons.

Not because we are wholly deaf to the great and bitter cry of our brethren about us, but because we do not see what we can do. We are divided among ourselves. We are in no condition to go into a real battle.

One may easily dream of a united church, gathering into its one fold all the people in the community who are on the side of righteousness, and insisting that the right and not the wrong shall prevail among us. There is nothing which such an organization could not accomplish.

All the temperance societies, all the law and order leagues, all the white-cross guilds, all the city clubs and good-citizenship associations, all the labor unions, under one banner, Christ's banner, against the enemies of the country, of the city, and of the soul—who can doubt the outcome of such a combination? Certain it is that the church, united and converted, can overcome the world. Of old it stood on the side of the people against the tyranny of kings; it may again be the people's advocate against the tyranny of other corrupters and oppressors.

At present, however, partly from lack of disposition, partly from lack of knowledge, and partly from lack of utterance, the church as an organization can do little in the labor movement. And yet the church, possessed of disposition, of knowledge, and of utterance, could bring in the industrial millennium to-morrow. The church is beyond comparison the most powerful engine which can be brought into action in any cause. In no other way can a truth, a purpose, a reform, be brought so closely into contact with so many people. The ministry of a whole nation, teaching definite instead of vague and general religion, applying Christianity to the concrete lives of actual present people, enforcing particular and detailed betterment, and setting forth these matters two or three times every week everywhere, could do almost anything. The vantage ground of the pulpit and the parish is not adequately understood.

The question, then, may need reversal. Might we not cease to ask what the church, as an organization, can do in the labor movement, and consider what the trades' unions, as an organization, can do in the church? The church is open to capture; the leaders of the labor movement may take possession of it. What we lack in disposition, knowledge, and utterance, these, the men who have this cause at heart, can give us if they will. The church, as represented by its ministers, is hospitable to the truth, interested unusually at present in social and economic questions, honestly desirous to do right and to serve all righteous causes, and tender-hearted to a fault. We need better acquaintance with the men and with the ideas of the labor movement. So long as the representatives of this movement and their followers stand apart from the church, antagonistic to it, suspicious of it, just so long must the church be impeded in its progress toward right thinking and right acting.

The present duty is not of an organization, not of the individuals who compose it, or who ought to compose it. Every man and woman who desires to follow the life of Jesus Christ, and to work and speak in his spirit, must put the emphasis of action where he put it, not upon the church, not upon the creed, but upon character, and upon character not personal alone, but social. Jesus thought not of himself. His thought and care and effort were for the people about him, always.

Much which we value he utterly despised. To be brotherly he accounted the supreme virtue of a man—to care for those who were in trouble, to right those who suffered wrong, to lift up those who were down. Not to be ministered unto, but to minister—it was for this he came; and that these things and such as these might be done he established the church. Nobody is a Christian who looks with indifference upon the oppression, the robbery, the manifold and aggravated iniquity, against which the labor movement is a righteous revolt.

The Christian will inform himself, as best he can, regarding this most significant of all modern discontents. He will read and study, that he may be intelligent about it. He will account it of more consequence to be informed regarding the history of the rebellion of the workingmen against their modern bondage than to be learned in all the chapters and the verses which describe the escape of the Hebrew slaves out of the bondage of Egypt. God is in his world to-day as much as he ever was. The morning paper records his administration of this planet yesterday in as true a sense as the Old Testament tells us what he did three thousand years ago. He who believes in God and looks brotherly towards his neighbors, as Jesus did, will not be satisfied to remain in ignorance. He will both learn and teach.

And by and by, with the growth of disposition and of knowledge, must come utterance. The church is nothing more than all of us. When we all are sympathetically and intelligently interested in the labor movement the church will be. And then the church must speak. Christian unity is likely to come about not by agreement first in policy or creed, but by co-operation, by working side by side in the labor movement and in every other movement for the general good.

Whenever any man or woman anywhere enlists with enthusiasm and eagerness in any righteous cause, the millennium, the day of blessed freedom, the kingdom of God and his righteousness, comes a step nearer.

George Hodges, *The Heresy of Cain*, rev. ed. (New York: Macmillan Company, 1914), 58-77. (Excerpt)

81.

The Forced Resignation of
Bishop Paul Jones, October 17-18, 1917

Paul Jones (November 25, 1880–September 4, 1941) was consecrated the fourth Bishop of Utah on December 16, 1914. He was a pacifist and opposed American participation in World War I. He was one of the founders of the Episcopal Pacifist Fellowship on November 11, 1939. (On May 24, 1965, its name was changed to the Episcopal Peace Fellowship.) He was forced to resign as bishop in 1918 because of his pacifism. This statement was made by Bishop Jones to the House of Bishops concerning his pacifistic convictions.

Minutes of the House of Bishops, Wednesday, October 17, 1917

The presiding bishop also presented a memorial from the Council of Advice of the Missionary district of Utah, in reference to the pacifist attitude of the Bishop of Utah in relation to the present war, and petitioning that he be relieved of further Episcopal duty in that District; which, on motion, was referred to a special committee of three bishops; and the Chairman appointed as such Committee the Bishop of Southern Ohio, the Bishop of Newark, and Bishop Lloyd.

Statement by Bishop Paul Jones on October 18, 1917

. . . In the first place, let me say that I, as a loyal citizen, am whole-heartedly for this country of ours in which all my hopes and ideals and interests are bound up. I believe most sincerely that German brutality and aggression must be stopped, and I am willing, if need be, to give my life and what I possess, to bring that about. I want to see the extension of real democracy in the world, and am ready to help that cause to the utmost; and finally, I want to see a sound and lasting peace brought to the world as a close to the terrible convulsion in which the nations are involved.

But the question is that of method. It is not enough to say that the majority have decided on war as the only means of attaining those things and therefore we must all co-operate. I believe that it is not as easy as that, for the problem goes deeper.

We all feel that war is wrong, evil, and undesirable. Many even feel that war is unchristian but unavoidable as the world is now constituted, and that the present situation forces us to use it. Some contend that this is a righteous war, and that we must all fight the devil with fire, even at the danger of being scorched, or all the ideals which we hold dear will go by the board, and therefore we are solemnly, sadly, and earnestly taking that way.

In spite of my respect for the integrity of those who feel bound to take that course, and in spite of the knowledge that I am occupying an unpopular and decidedly minority point of view, I have been led to feel that war is entirely incompatible with the Christian profession. It is not on the basis of certain texts or a blind following of certain isolated words of Christ that I have been led to this, for I am not a literalist in any sense of the term; but because the deeper I study into it the more firmly I am convinced that the whole spirit of the gospel is not only opposed to all that is commonly understood by the word 'war,' but offers another method capable of transforming the world and applicable to every situation which the individual or the nation is called to face.

If we are to reconcile men to God, to build up the brotherhood of the kingdom, preach love, forbearance and forgiveness, teach the ideals that are worth more than all else, rebuke evil, and stand for the good even unto death, then I do not see how it can be the duty of the church or its representatives to aid or encourage the way of war, which so obviously breaks down brotherhood, replaces love and forbearance by bitterness and wrath, sacrifices ideals to expediency, and takes the way of fear instead of that of faith. I believe that it is always the Church's duty to hold up before men the way of the cross; the one way our Lord has given us for overcoming the world.

I know that some good people believe that in this present crisis we are following the way of the cross, but I think that it is a false analogy to say that the sacrifices we and the allies are making are analogous to our Lord's sacrifice. He did not die to save his mother or the apostles, or to punish evildoers, but rather died the just for the unjust. . . . Moreover, because Germany has ignored her solemn obligations, Christians are not justified in treating the sermon on the mount as a scrap of paper.

Prayer is, I believe, the best test of the whole matter. If it is right and our honest duty to fight the war to a finish, then we should use the Church's great weapon of prayer to that end; but the most ardent Christian supporter of the war, though he may use general terms, revolts against praying that our every bullet may find its mark, or that our embargoes may bring starvation to every German home. We know that those things would bring the war to a speedy, triumphant close, but the Church cannot pray that way. And a purpose that you cannot pray for is a poor one for Christians to be engaged in.

On another side we fault Germany, and rightly, for exalting the supremacy of the state over religion and morals and everything else. The state then relies on might alone and becomes the supreme cause for all its people. I believe that that is the path we are laying out for ourselves in exalting obedience to the state without regard to whether Christianity seems to stand in the way. If the Church's first duty is the kingdom of God and His righteousness, it is not only possible, but judging from history, rather to be expected that its duty will often lead it in antagonism to the policy of the state. . . . For the state, on either side of this struggle, has the support of organized Christianity within its borders, though it involves the sending forth of Christians to destroy each other, and that fact alone should cause serious questionings.

I would appeal to my own Church on the larger ground of our claims to Catholicity. How can we ever say again that we are the Church for men of all nations and ages, if we so abandon the world ideal and become the willing instrument of a national government? We must stand for the whole truth of God for the winning of men and society to His allegiance, and it savors too much of Mohammedanism with its policy of carrying religion by the sword for me to try to twist a justification for this war and a sanctification of its prosecution out of the apparent righteousness of the purpose for which it was begun. If the method is wrong, I believe that the Church should have nothing to do with it; for back of the things that may possibly be achieved by the war, stands the terrible indictment that will be made that the Church abandoned the way of the cross that she was teaching. . . .

I am not blind, however, to the difficulties involved, for the active expression of the point of view that I hold is believed by some to involve disloyalty to our country. But I think a distinction must be made between loyalty to country and loyalty to any particular course of action adopted by the officers of the government. It is often necessary for citizens who love their country, because they love their country, to oppose the policy of the government. The very existence of opposing political parties through all our history indicates the validity of this distinction. Sincere criticism of the authorities is sometimes the best evidence of a concern for the best welfare of the institution involved. Of the long list of distinguished men of this and other countries who felt it necessary to stand against governmental action with all the power at their command, only those who were insincere or who attacked the institution itself, have been adjudged disloyal.

History has not always vindicated the opinions of the majority. But I recognize that there is a time for all things, and while I may have used poor judgment as to the occasions and purpose to which I have spoken, yet I have been guided by what I believed to be my duty, and I feel sure that you would not have me refrain from speaking for the faith that is in me when I believe it to be my duty to do so. But these are matters involving judgment and discretion upon which I shall be glad to be guided by your advice and counsel.

As I believe, then, that the adoption of the way of Christ would be the best thing possible for this land we love and through it for all the world, I must, with all the wisdom God has given me, and with all the earnestness which I possess, try to reach men with that message in the terms which I can express it. If you believe that the church and the nation are better off without my message, I am quite ready to accede to your judgment, but as long as I represent the Church as I do now, it seems to me that I would be apostate to my high commission did I take any other course. And if I have misinterpreted the meaning of the Gospel, I shall be glad to be set right.

Nathaniel W. Pierce and Paul L. Ward, *The Voice of Conscience: A Loud and Unusual Noise? The Episcopal Peace Fellowship, 1939-1989* (Washington: Episcopal Peace Fellowship, 1989), 87-89.

82.

House of Bishops, Pastoral Letter, October 18, 1917

On April 6, 1917, the United States declared war on Germany. The Pastoral Letter of October 18, 1917, called for support of the war effort and the silencing of non-resistance and pacifism.

Brethren of the Clergy and Laity:

Our nation is at war on behalf of justice, liberty and humanity. When these are in danger, the Church's station is at the front.

When the nation has with solemn deliberation entered war, voices which have spoken for neutrality, non-resistance or pacifism are silenced. We hate war, and we shrink from its horrors, but we who enjoy the privileges of civil liberty won by the blood of our fathers must, when they are endangered, defend them at the cost of our blood. In the overthrow of injustice and inhumanity is the only hope of permanent peace. Loyalty demands of every citizen unconditional consecration to the service of the nation.

We thank God that from their homes and parish churches have gone the boys and men of the church, eager to do their duty whenever the nation sends them. We watch them with pride as they are mustered into the Army and Navy.

As the nation is preparing to enter the awful conflict, we, your bishops, remind you of certain definite duties and opportunities.

I. A nation fighting to keep the world safe for democracy must in character and action be true to democracy. Racial strife, class antagonism, impurity and intemperance wreck civil liberty. Before we can conquer injustice and inhumanity in others, we must first overcome them in ourselves. Our guilt in these respects we must acknowledge with shame. We expect of our soldiers and sailors concentration of thought and action, self-discipline, courage and serenity under stress. We can demand no less of ourselves. In humility and sincerity we must live by the principles for which we fight. National character gives thrust and force to the National army. The war with all its suffering and loss may prove a blessing if it rouses us from the indifference to religion, to spiritual concerns and moral issues, which threatens our very life.

At the source and foundation of the character of this people are Christ and his church. If the force of arms is necessary to put down wilful disregard of the rights and decencies of human life, it is only by the persistent teaching of Christian principles that these can be preserved for ourselves or for the world. We need plain teaching of the Christian religion, with its insistence on the claims of God and the claims of our fellowmen, and on God's present gifts of grace by His Spirit through His Church and Sacraments to enable us to live up to the examples and precepts of His incarnate Son, our Lord.

II. The president has well said that this is a war not of armies but of peoples. Every man, woman and child has a place and is enlisted in the cause, the Army and Navy at the front, we close beside and behind them; though they be in France and we in America, we are one with them, bound together in a common cause. Hence everything that we are and that we do will unite in their support. Every man on the fighting line, in hospital or on lonely guard duty, must feel behind and with him the heart, sympathy and action of the people. To express this, we must not only work for the Red Cross, and give generously in money and comforts; we must also be ready to pay heavy taxes cheerfully, and buy Liberty Bonds. It is upon the people's substance that the armies move.

Failures in efficiency there are and will be. Let us withhold until we are sure it is justified. Rivalry for position or fame has no place in war or in organized beneficence. Force depends on united action.

III. Next to the character and consecration of the people, the fighting power of a nation is in the possession of the staples of life in food and clothing. Upon the economy, simple habits of self-restraint of Christian people the nation has a right to call with confidence. Every housekeeper and child, every man, whether traveling or at home, has his duty to save food and clothing, money and everything so as to provide for our allies and for ourselves. Covetousness and the seeking of selfish gain in the country's time of need should be frowned upon as no less disgraceful than cowardice or rebellion.

IV. The War Department is working out a great, and we believe beneficent, experiment in warfare. Military discipline used to cut the armies off as much as possible from home and natural associations. Men in abnormal positions became abnormal. A soldier is still a man. Confident that the normal man is the best fighter, the government is doing everything in its power consistent with military efficiency to keep the soldiers and sailors in touch with society and home, to encourage right associations with the women and girls in the neighborhood of the camps, and to build up the men, physically and morally, through recreation and social and religious influences. While we trust the general high character and awakened moral sense of our soldiers, every officer of the church and every citizen should see to it that his town is clean enough for the soldiers to roam in, and the officials and people should do their part to protect the girls of the neighborhood as well as the men and boys who have come from distant homes.

Grateful for the action of the president and of congress in restricting the manufacture and sale of liquor, we urge all to support the authorities in enforcing the law; and to set a personal example of abstinence.

V. The War Commission of the Church has been created to marshall the forces of the church for efficient action.

We want the church to follow our boys and men with sympathetic interest and to offer them the sacraments and pastoral care. Reinforcing the commissioned chaplains, voluntary chaplains of our communion, welcomed by the authorities, will keep close to the camps and naval stations, both in this country and in France, and give guidance and spiritual leadership to the men.

Strong laymen also, members of the brotherhood of St. Andrew and others, engaged for that special work by the Commission, will, as Secretaries of the Y.M.C.A., keep in touch with the churchmen. Chaplains will be equipped; the names of churchmen in the National service will be listed; literature will be sent; duplication of work and of appeals for help will be avoided by coordination of local efforts and Church organizations with the War Commission.

Within a few weeks the Commission will ask of the church Five Hundred Thousand Dollars. The Bishops are confident that every local churchman and churchwoman will respond generously to this war call of the Church.

VI. Finally, brethren, let us be earnest and constant in prayer, at home and in church, for God's blessing on what we are confident is a righteous cause; for the president and his advisers; for our Army and Navy; and for our sons, brothers and husbands, first that they may, in camp and battle, on leave and in hospital, be faithful and unafraid; then, if God wills, that they may have a safe return.

Let our churches be open for private prayer, as well as for the regular services, and for others of a less formal character, with opportunities afforded for the mention of particular persons and needs.

Let the opportunity of these days of stress and anxiety be seized for the preaching of the deep truths of the living God, our Judge and our loving Father, and of His Son, who, in becoming man, assures us of His sympathy with the struggles and sorrows of His people.

After war will come peace; let us prepare for it by sustaining a worthy spirit. Christian people will throughout the war hold high the standard of chivalry and charity. Reparation and not revenge must be the object kept before us. We will control our feelings of resentment, and try to believe the best possible interpretation of the motives and ideals of the people who are fighting us and over whom we shall be victorious.

We will steadily press the education of the young, and prepare them for a better citizenship than ours of to-day.

We will support and advance the cause of Christian missions with greater and not diminished loyalty or generosity, knowing that it is the power of Christ alone that will inspire and enable the nations of the world to work together for peace and righteousness, for human brotherhood and the fulfillment of human life in the Kingdom of God.

Journal of General Convention, 1919, 503-505. (Excerpt)

83.

James O. S. Huntington, Bargainers and Beggars, 1919

James Otis Sargent Huntington (July 23, 1854–June 29, 1935) was a supporter of the social gospel. He was active in the Society of Christian Socialists. Huntington was a priest, and the founder of the Order of the Holy Cross, a religious community for men. In this writing he describes the biblical foundation for the social gospel.

The Parable

No one can doubt that work lies before us. It is the building of a new world, to take the place of that which has passed away in the flames of the Great War. That new world must be built out of individual men and women. What they are, their world will be. The foundation on which men build their own lives will be the foundation of the society which they form in their relations to one another. A horde of slaves cannot make a free state until they cease to be slaves. A hundred blind men cannot combine into a seeing fellowship. The edifice of a generous democracy cannot be raised on the basis of materialism and self-interest.

The first question for each of us, then, is: "On what ground must I build my life?" "What is my fundamental attitude?" "How can I so live and act as to contribute to a true and enduring social order?"

As a person I stand in various relations to other persons. But one relation is primary, and fundamental to all others. That is my relation to God. What I am to Him that I really am. Only if I am right with Him can I be right with my fellowmen. If I am wrong with God I shall sooner or later be wrong every way.

The parable of the laborers in the vineyard sets before us the relation between a householder and his workmen. That, in fact, is the very point of the parable. In other places of the Bible a vineyard is described in a highly symbolic way. In this parable there is no suggestion of that sort. It is not the kind of work that matters but the attitude of the mind of those who do it, the human relations between them, and their relation to the man who hires them. This is what gives the parable such a contemporary character. There are other parables that require an effort to adjust ourselves to them. The parable of the wise and foolish virgins, for example, refers to marriage customs utterly alien to those of which we have experience. But a parable which describes transactions between an employer and his employees,—in our modern jargon between "Capital and Labor,"—puts us on familiar ground.

Not that the parable of the laborers in the vineyard is a lesson in political economy. The Bible is not a text-book in "the dismal science" any more than in any other science. It does not settle out of hand the problems that arise in the gradual changes of society. It does not say that we must, or must not, be democrats, or socialists, or nationalists, or collectivists, or syndicalists. The Bible does tell us that we must all be Christians.

The Bibles takes the plain facts, of nature and of human life, and uses them to instruct us as to spiritual things. Our Lord pictures bread made with leaven, wine stored in skins, fish caught in nets drawn to shore, a wound treated with oil and wine,—not as though other ways of doing these things might not be better, but because these ways were in common use among those to whom He spoke. So He takes certain actual or possible, easily understood, relations between father and children, rulers and subjects, and employer and his employees, and uses them in showing what is the true and right relation between God and His people. When He describes the woman calling in her neighbors to rejoice with her over the recovery of the lost coin He does not imply that every woman should celebrate the discovery of a mislaid article by a social gathering, but under homely incidents He pictures the joy of the angels in Heaven as they respond to the joy of God over a soul restored to Him. So in the parable of the laborers in the vineyard we are not taught that an employer should pay as much for an hour's as for a whole day's work, or that workmen should not stipulate for a wage-scale, or that a corporation, which exists only by the permission of the community, can claim unlimited control of its property. But on the field of human action principles of the divine order are set forth. The Judge of all the earth will do right. The "Great Taskmaster" will be infinitely merciful as well as infinitely just. He who says, "Can I not do what I will with mine own?" is He who says, and who alone can say, "I am good."

This much seems necessary to say to forestall misgiving in some minds, although the use of the parable is but an instance of what is true of all human language, which is, after all, a system of most imperfect symbols, borrowed from our sense experience, even when we babble of heavenly and divine things.

Let us now go through the parable and try to emphasize the contrast between two classes of men therein portrayed. As we go on we shall see whether we are right in characterizing them as "the Bargainers" and "the Beggars."

There is a certain work to be done. It is work in a vineyard. It might be work at any season of the year, pruning or tying the vines, fertilizing or cultivating between the rows. But it seems natural to think of it as the crowning work, the work of the vintage, the gathering in of the grapes. We picture, then, the autumn sunlight, the purpling grapes hanging in the great clusters among the leaves that were lately so broad and green but are now withering and shriveling day by day. The harvest has come quickly at last. Time passes. The sun blazes down. The winds will soon be out. The crop must be gathered at once or it will be lost,— scorched by the heat, or scattered by the storms.

So the owner of the vineyard goes out to hire laborers. He goes forth in the brief and sudden dawn of an Eastern day. He takes his way to the market-place, the point where, in town or village, men naturally gather and converse, where people come from the country and offer their produce for sale, vendors set up their booths, purchasers, repressing their eagerness, come and bicker over the various wares. There, too, are men who are looking for a chance to use their strength to earn their living. The "householder" finds them there when he arrives. They have risen bright and early. They are in time to begin with the first hour of the working day. They are quick to recognize the well-to-do landowner as he comes toward them. They are not unprepared for his offer of employment. The interview which follows is of a purely business character. There is a mutual transaction, a contract. There are conditions, expressed or implied, on both sides. There is to be a full day's wage for a full day's work of a sort that requires no great skill or training. (The "penny" of the Authorized Version represents a coin which, at the purchasing power of money would be about two dollars of our currency.) The agreement concluded, the workmen move off towards the vineyard without more ado. Their intercourse with the owner of the vineyard has had no further significance. They take no interest in him as a man or a brother, as a fellow-townsman or a co-religionist. To them he is simply a payer of wages. Pay them he will; of that they make no doubt. He cannot afford to do otherwise. Were it known that he did not live up to his agreements he would soon find himself without workers. Self-interest, if not the social demand or the law of the land, will hold him to his word.

So much for the first group that takes its place in the vineyard. It is not invidious to call them "bargainers." Not, as has been said, that there is any hint that workmen should not make definite terms with those who engage them. Many of the conflicts between labor and capital might have been avoided if there had been fair and well-understood agreements faithfully carried out on both sides and mutually readjusted as occasion arose. But what is entirely legitimate between a man and his fellows may be neither reasonable nor right between a creature and his Creator, between a man and God. Of that anon.

After this transaction in the early morning there is a break of two or three hours. Then, at nine o'clock, three o'clock, and five o'clock, the householder again visits the market-place. He finds there faces that he has not seen before, faces that are wistful and downcast. Why these men were not on hand with their fellows at an earlier hour we do not know. They may have been looking for work in some other direction or their lateness in arriving may have been their own fault. What is of consequence is that a new situation presents itself. On the side of the employer we find a willingness to engage men for less than a full day's work. That is not customary with workers at unskilled labor. The natural inference would be that the need for a larger force in the vineyard is pressing and that the employer is anxious to bring in additional hands. Such a motive is not excluded, but, if we take as one group all the men set to work through the day, from nine o'clock on, (and, evidently, they are all in practically the same situation) another motive suggests itself. For the advantage to be had from bringing in fresh workers decreases rapidly as the day passes. It certainly seems as though the householder who so persistently seeks men is doing it not for his own sake but for theirs, not from self-interest and business enterprise but from sympathy and fellow-feeling for the unfortunate and neglected. To set the men to work when the day is almost over argues some rather unusual attitude of mind in the householder, something that does not at all appear in his interview with "the bargainers." As for those who go to work at nine o'clock, or at any of the later hours, their attitude is strikingly unlike that of those who made their stipulation at the beginning of the day. These men really want to work. They want it more, perhaps, than those who went to the vineyard at the beginning of the day. They are not like men of whom the boys on the East Side of New York, used to say that, "they went round looking for a job and praying they mightn't find it." No, they are not only miserable, but they know their misery and are ready to take the first chance offered them to escape from it. They belong to "the unemployed" but they are eager to regain their place in the ranks of labor. They feel, perhaps, what I have known many men in their condition to feel, that a terrible danger lurks in a state of enforced idleness arising from lack of opportunity of remunerative employment. When, as in our own day, in great cities and industrial centers, ten or fifty or a hundred men compete for one position, a certain proportion of them is bound to be unsuccessful for long stretches of time together. It is hard for those who have not been put to such a test to realize how ever repeated failure saps the courage and undermines self-respect. A young fellow in the slums of New York said to me once: "Father, you don't know how a fellow feels when he's out of work. He's just about crazy. He gets up at four o'clock in the morning, and looks through the 'Wanted' columns of the papers, and walks up and down both sides of the river to all the places he knows where he might find employment. And he does that for a week and a month and for three or four or five months may be. But if he's out of work for six months he never wants to do a stroke of work again. And that's the way I'm afraid it's going to be with me." "Hope deferred," said the wise man, "maketh the heart sick." In such cases it may well prove a fatal malady. I suppose that there is the way that many a man becomes a tramp. His ambitions, even his physical needs for food and shelter, have shrunk to a point at which they can be met by "pan-handling," "cadging," and the cheap lodging-house or the seat in the park. Why make any further effort? Why not drift with the stream?

So we may think of these heart-sick suppliants as haunted by grim fear. Their very manhood seems to be oozing out. They are sinking in the bitter waves of discouragement and despair. If even now, before it is too late, they could have a chance to get back into the field of industry! If they could only get their hands stained with the grape juice, if they could only be in the line when the men file out of the vineyard, then they may hope to regain their foothold in the social order, they will be, not loafers but laborers, not outcasts but men. And, further, they will have a vantage-ground for the morrow. During years of a city ministry it was my privilege to find situations for a good many men. Scarcely one of them kept the place I have found for them, but almost always he at once found a situation for himself. Why this was I do not know. The man might have been out of work for months. He might have been making persistent, yet quite ineffectual, efforts to find a chance for himself. Yet if I could only get him started in a shop, or a factory, or office, he seemed to have no difficulty in being taken on else-where. Perhaps the fact has a psychologic explanation. Perhaps some subtle change, the result of renewed hope and courage and self-respect, something in the lift of his head or the timbre of his voice, as he made his application, ren-dered those to whom he went more disposed to engage him. It is not unreason-able, then, to assume that these men, lingering, idle and irresolute, in the market-place, felt, as the hours slipped by, that they were at the crisis of their fate, that, in their being set to work at the vines before the sun went down depended all their future. And, yet, they could not bid for employment. The time for that had passed. With the sun well up towards the zenith, or already beginning to slope westward, they could not offer a day's work. They were not on common ground with the householder. They were in no position to chaffer about wages, or to stipulate as to the terms of a contract. One claim for employment alone remained. That was their desperate need. To bring forward that need would be to take the attitude of suppliants, craving a boon. Perhaps they had not the heart even to make a request. Yet, not the less, their abject looks, their hungry eyes, their drooping figures, made appeal for compassion and relief. And to them the householder draws near. He understands their plight. He knows how far they are from the smug self-confidence of the early morning bargainers. He lends himself to no pretence. He does not mock them by asking them what they will work for. He meets the situation frankly. "Go ye into the vineyard and whatsoever is right I will give you." The very tone of command implies that he recognizes a relation to them. But it is vastly different from a mere business partnership, from all that is involved in barter and exchange. There is a promise, indeed, "whatsoever is right I will give you," but it is a free encouragement to the despondent spirits of the men, not secured to them by any legal instrument or formal agreement. The relation is in a wider field than that of labor and capital, it is in the broad reaches of personal, that is of spiritual, appreciation and sympathy. The householder *feels* for his needy fellow-men,—shows it, we may be sure, in kindly glance and friendly accent. The men covertly study him who offers to befriend them, and then make an essentially human response, as they fling themselves, in self-abandoning trust, upon his word. They make their venture, leaving their case in the hands of their benefactor, and hurry to the vineyard. Happy and care-free who were but a moment ago wretched and anxious, they will not take umbrage if we call them "beggars." They will, perhaps, answer gaily, "Yes, indeed, we are even as fortunate as that. For, had we not been 'beggars' we should not have found our friend."

The Bargainers and the Beggars. In these two classes we see the two attitudes of man towards his Maker. No other attitude is possible, if God is taken into account at all. Either we are utterly dependent upon God, or we have a ground of our own on which we can stand. Either we owe everything to God or we have something in our own right, which we may, if we choose, render to God—on specified conditions. Either we receive from God blessings to which we have no claim, and for which our gratitude should know no bounds, or God is paying us what we have earned and we need not to be extravagant in our appreciation of His goodness. Here are two ways in religion. It is absurd to treat the difference as unimportant in our own character or in our influence upon the world about us. What we say we believe may be of small consequence, but what we actually do believe will, in the long run, determine what we are, and what we are will express itself in what we do. To be sure, all sorts of influences play their part in the moulding of our lives, and many a man is "better than his creed." The line that divides the Bargainer and the Beggar runs athwart all organizations. Splendid social work is done by men and women who have no conscious faith in God, or whose professed faith in regard to Him seems strangely imperfect or awry. And the profession of the Catholic Faith in the most exact terms, and even with a sincere purpose, may not enable a man to transcend his environment or to see the true line to follow in social and economic questions. The intransigents, if they are growing in humility and self-mistrust, are making their contribution to the cause of justice and liberty for all.

But the responsibility rests on each of us to learn the truth, as God has made it known, concerning Himself and our relation with Him. And, through union with God, to live out that truth in the sphere of human relations, those of our own immediate circle, and those of society at large.

James O. S. Huntington, *Bargainers and Beggars: A Study of the Parable of the Laborers in the Vineyard* (West Park, N.Y.: Holy Cross Press, 1919), 11-30. (Excerpt)

84.

The Church and World Peace, 1922

In the years following World War I there was strong support for world peace. The forty-seventh General Convention met at Portland, Oregon, September 6-23, 1922. In this statement on September 21, 1922, the House of Bishops called for a "warless" world and the reduction of armaments.

The world looks to the Christian Church for a clear and definite declaration of the principles of peace and an active participation in bringing those principles to bear in world relationships. One phase of Christian responsibility even from a military point of view is expressed by General Tasker H. Bliss: "If the clergy-men of the United States want to secure a limitation of armaments, they can do it now without further waste of time. The responsibility is entirely on the profess-ing Christians of the United States. If another war like the last one should come they will be responsible for every drop of blood that will be shed, and for every dollar wastefully expended."

"There is one way and one way only to outlaw war. We must first establish a peace system. Mere disarmament by itself will not stop war. Only the firm estab-lishment of the institutions and agencies of justice and of liberty under the law, maintained by effective sanctions at the hands of law-abiding and peace-loving nations, can possibly banish war from this war-cursed world. The most urgent need of mankind is the speedy establishment of international institutions to assure equal justice, full security and fair economic opportunity for all nations alike. These are essential pre-requisites to permanent peace."

It is highly important that the moral religious forces of the United States should speak with one voice. The Social Service Commission of the Federal Council of Churches, the Catholic Welfare Association and the Association of American Rabbis have accepted such a peace policy with the following statement of belief which your Committee recommends that this Convention adopt as their own.

I.

We believe that nations no less than individuals are subject to God's immutable moral laws.

II.

We believe that nations achieve true welfare, greatness and honor only through just dealing and unselfish service.

III.

We believe that nations that regard themselves as Christian have special international obligations.

IV.

We believe that the spirit of Christian brotherliness can remove every unjust barrier of trade, color, creed and race.

V.

We believe that Christian patriotism demands the practice of good will between nations.

VI.

We believe that international policies should secure equal justice for all races.

VII.

We believe that all nations should associate themselves permanently for world peace and good will.

IX.

We believe in a sweeping reduction of armaments by all nations.

X.

We believe in a warless world, and dedicate ourselves to its achievement.

Journal of General Convention, 1922, 379-380. (Mistake in numbering in the original text.)

85.

House of Bishops, Pastoral Letter, November 9, 1933

The Pastoral Letter of November 9, 1933, called for a new economic order, a spiritual recovery, and world peace.

DEAR BRETHREN OF THE CLERGY AND LAITY:

In this momentous period in the life of the Church and State, your Bishops, with a solemn sense of their responsibility, lay before you certain matters that they believe deserve your serious consideration. They do this in the hope that at this time of stress the Church may contribute its full share to the stabilization of those things that are indispensable to the happiness, peace and security of the nation.

A finer type of Christian faith and courage calls for service and sacrifice to meet the modern world chaos.

The rehabilitation of agriculture and of industry we recognize as urgently important, but causes deeper than those that have to do with economic dislocation, with its attendant privations, lie at the root of the world's ills. Spiritual recovery must be made coincident with economic recovery. Apostasy, the neglect of fundamental Christian principles as related to domestic, social and industrial conditions have contributed to the catastrophe of recent times. The reactions from the severe strain of the great war resulted in the lowering of moral standards that had been the security of our people, standards that had given them a place of commanding power and influence at home and aboard. The consuming passion for gain, disclosed in an era of wild speculation, with its accompanying excesses and indulgences that brooked no restraint; the untempered lust for varied and unwholesome forms of pleasure; recent disclosures of incompetence and mal-administration; the looseness of marital ties leading to the disintegration of the home; these and other moral lapses contributed to the breakup of our social and economic institutions, and made easy the way for our common disasters and misfortunes. Widespread suffering, hunger and distress in the face of unparalleled power, mechanical ingenuity and prodigal abundance present an appalling paradox such as our nation has never before witnessed.

In arrogance and conceit we had built our house upon insecure foundations, thinking the while that our cunning and skill could arm us to resist the blighting ills of panic and misfortune. Our pride and self-confidence have suffered a severe shock and our boasted capacity to weather all storms has brought us perilously close to a condition bordering on the overturn of our cherished institutions. A selfish and soulless individualism that was insular and arrogant impaired our security and wrought havoc in our social and economic life.

353

No appraisal of the events of recent years can we leave out of consideration of these factors. Unless they are frankly recognized and repented of there can be no salutary change effected in our economic and social order. Coincident with the lowering of moral standards we have witnessed a most malevolent and violent attack upon Christian institutions and the Christian faith. This attack is made on many fronts. In magnitude and persistence it is without parallel. It is insidious, cunning and determined. It pervades our literature, the drama, the screen, and touches with its blighting influence schoolhouse and university. It addresses itself particularly to the younger generation. As we survey the drifts and tendencies in our modern life it becomes increasingly evident that cleavage of division in our household of faith, stress upon individual conceits, over-emphasis upon practices unrelated to the supreme purpose of Christ's Church must contribute to inevitable failure and defeat. "A house divided against itself cannot stand." The Church's unity and solidarity are indispensable; never more so than now. To point more definitely the responsibility that is laid upon us as Christians and Churchmen we present certain matters we hold to be vitally important.

Economic and Social Order

Involved in an economic situation which has left millions confronted by the horrors of unemployment and dire want in the mist of plenty, the world abounds in many and, at times, conflicting experiments which seek to meet the needs of suffering humanity. There is no certainty in the minds of most men as to which of these experiments will surely solve our problems. It is, however, our conviction that Christians must assert without compromise that no experiment which falls short of the demand of Christ can permanently advance the welfare of all mankind. No standards short of the Christian standards can lead us out of our darkness into light. No ideal save that of the Kingdom of God can satisfy the minds and hearts of Christian people.

No experiment which seeks to bring recovery for any one group, industrial, agricultural, or any other, without considering the needs and welfare of all men, is in accord with the mind of Christ. If we would be saved we must be saved together, for in God's sight all human beings of whatever kindred or tongue are equally precious. The members of the Church must make it clear that, as followers of the Master, they cannot give their support to any program of reconstruction which does not recognize the fact that national recovery depends upon world recovery.

No mere reestablishment of an old economic order will suffice. Christ demands a new order in which there shall be a more equitable distribution of material wealth, more certain assurance of security for the unemployed and aged, and, above all else, an order which shall substitute the motive of service for the motive of gain. Christians should face the fact that this new order can succeed only as the followers of Christ sacrifice and suffer greatly. It is not enough for us to "do our part". The Master calls for us to consecrate our all. For us the cross stands as the symbol of a world recovery act. It demands that we become world recovery agents who dare to carry the Cross. It demands that through loyalty to our King we serve as leaders in bringing to pass a national and world recovery and redemption.

One vital issue faces us at this moment, the imminent repeal of the Prohibition Amendment. It calls for renewed emphasis upon the value of temperance. Such a period of change as that upon which we are entering will lay upon us the demand for self-control and the exercise of viligance that unrestricted traffic in liquor shall not become a menace to our people.

World Peace

Signs on the horizon give evidence of a growing suspicion among nations. Beneath the surface the world seethes with unrest. The horrors of the World War seem to be forgotten as nation rises against nation and competition in armament once again occupies a sinister place in the chancellories and parliaments of the world. Pacts and agreements, readily entered into, are regarded lightly, if not abandoned. The hopes of a peaceful and orderly world are shadowed by distrust and selfish ambition. Forbidding and terrible as the contemplation of a fresh outbreak may be, direful and disastrous as may be its consequences, unless America, as the most potential force to world peace, can play a part consistent with her high ideals, and do it with Christian fidelity, a situation may ensue beyond her power to restrict or restrain. It is our duty as disciples of the Prince of Peace to insist upon policies that are consistent with the maintenance of equity, fair dealing and the sanctity of pacts and agreements among races and peoples. We are bound by every solemn obligation to wage unremitting war against war. An excess of nationalism or an attitude of detached unconcern for the ills of other nations, together with the building up of an armed force beyond reasonable national needs, deprives us of any opportunity to be a conserver of the world's peace. Love of country must be qualified by love of all mankind; patriotism is subordinate to religion. The Cross is above the flag. In any issue between country and God, the clear duty of the Christian is to put obedience to God above every other loyalty.

No nation can live unto itself. We must cooperate or perish. War will be abolished finally only when Christ's spirit of forgiveness and reconciliation is in control of the world's international relations.

We make this appeal especially to the youth of America. Encouragement is found in the fundamental soundness of modern youth. We acknowledge that we, their leaders, have not always understood our young people. Their ways are different from our ways. Many of their standards were not those of our youth. We were born of the old world; they are the children of the new. We trust them, we thank God for the honesty of their approach to religion, and we confidently look to them, with the help of the Holy Spirit, to fashion a more enduring social structure than their fathers builded.

A Spiritual Opportunity

Days of material anxiety are days of spiritual opportunity. The present situation gives the Church one of the greatest opportunities in history, because the Church has spiritual gifts to impart, which were never needed more than now. Our power to help in a time of confusion and change lies in our grasp upon those things which are unchanging and eternal. Christian people must demonstrate spiritual values and share the world-wide vision of service given to us by Jesus Christ.

We urge upon you, the people of the Church, to dare to do some of the things Jesus Christ died to make real in a Christian's daily living. If it is a question of compromise between honesty and anything less, dare to do the honest thing. What if it is costly? Are we followers of Jesus Christ or not? That is the final question. Let us show the people around us that we care, that our Christian religion really works. If it is a decision between the pure and the impure, take the Christ way. We must dare to discourage any other way. Buy and sell on the basis of the Law of Love, "Thou shalt love thy neighbor as thyself." Let us not be misled by the false slogan, "My country, right or wrong." Dare to meet intolerance with good will. Christ's way is the only way for a Christian, and the only way for a world in need. Stand alone if we must. Be counted a fool if it is necessary. Let us dare to do the thing now that counts. Let us practice what our religion stands for.

The world is coming to a new birth, and the pains of travail are to be expected. They may well be wholesome, if unpleasant. The times call for a stiffening of our faith. Too much spiritual ease makes soft Christians. Therefore we are told that "We must through much tribulation enter into the Kingdom of God." We should be better prepared for it than our fathers of Apostolic days. They endured much hardness for Christ, because of the hope that was set before them. We still have that same indomitable hope, and in addition we have behind us the reassuring experience of twenty centuries of Christian fortitude. Confidence is our watchword, not confidence in ourselves, but in Christ, to whom our loyalty is pledged.

Though material values collapse, spiritual values remain unimpaired. We are the followers of those who faced lions without flinching, and who endured the perils of persecution without whine or whimper. In Him we find assurance of final victory. God has not abdicated. Christ is not dead. The power of the Holy

Spirit still prevails. The foundations of the Church remain secure. We cannot be dismayed, God reigns. We dare not be discouraged, Christ lives. We may not relax our Christian loyalty, the Holy Spirit moves again over a chaotic world. Let us prove our faith in practice, and nothing can withstand the spiritual momentum that must follow.

Lift up your hearts; a new Advent of the Son of Man is at hand.

House of Bishops, "Pastoral Letter," November 9, 1933, in *Journal of General Convention, 1934*, 78-81.

86.

Vida D. Scudder, Social Problems Facing the Church in 1934

Vida Dutton Scudder (December 15, 1861–October 9, 1954) was a writer, professor, and Christian socialist. She was devoted to St. Francis of Assisi, and she was committed to social activism. This article is the first in a series of articles on the Christian responsibility for social awareness and action.

WE ALL REMEMBER vividly our own Bishops' recent Pastoral Letter from Davenport, with its clear statement not only of our chaotic conditions but of the imperative need for a new economic order (see THE SPIRIT OF MISSIONS, December, 1933, page 627). Words as brave as theirs come from other Christian bodies. At the National Conference of Catholic Charities which met last October, a formal statement was made:

Catholic Charities can not be satisfied merely with the alleviation of human suffering and want—but must assume leadership in working for a new industrial order in which the rights of the wage-earner will be more fully protected.

Papal encyclicals have been saying this same thing for over forty years; but that great Church which acknowledges their authority listens as never before. Here again comes the most influential voice of the Russian Church in its sad exile—that of the philosopher and theologian, Nicholas Berdyaev:

The whole future of Christian societies depends on whether Christianity, or rather Christians, leave off supporting capitalism and social injustice; or whether the Christian world sets to work in the name of God and of Christ to put into practice that justice which the Communists are now introducing in the name of a godless collectivity.

357

Official statements to the like effect from various Protestant bodies might be cited.

The Church at large, through its leaders, is putting itself on record as solemnly repudiating our present economic system. "A New Order" is on its lips. Further than this, a phrase about "assuming leadership" is addressed now and again to Christians in their corporate capacity. It is an arresting and terrifying phrase.

For *we* are the Church; you, and you, and I. It is to us this phrase is addressed. Now to denunciation of social evils and to the yearning for a new age, many of us yield swift assent. But when the summons to action reaches us, most of us feel perfectly helpless. We could do something while the call was confined to charity. In "the alleviation of human suffering and want" every honorable Church member has probably played his part, at expense, now of money, now of time and effort. But by this more stirring and searching call we are baffled: as to this great task of building a new world, we do not know in concrete terms what is expected of us.

So many private citizens have no relations with corrupt bankers! All we know about banking is that it seems of late painfully insecure. We have never run or knowingly patronized sweat shops, or underpaid workers; the struggle between organized labor and company unions is wholly out of our picture. Indeed, we have really no direct contact with these great abuses and injustices which wise men are denouncing. We live within the capitalistic order, to be sure; and we are being taught not to approve of it; yet we can not run away. We could not escape the profit system for that matter, even if we wove cloth for our own garments on Gandhi's spinning wheels. There are always a few interesting idealists who are trying to run away but they are very partially successful. We can not escape; we do not feel responsible for the system; we agree with our spiritual guides that it is a very bad system. Then they tell us that "we" must change it, and we inevitably ask them, "how?" No answer comes.

The apathetic indifference toward social reconstruction or reform which undoubtedly still characterizes great numbers of nominal or even of genuine Christians, is due first and foremost to this sense of helplessness. They are apathetic because they have no notion what in the world they can do. Men do not get excited about a situation unless they are in some personal relation to it. It must either hurt them, or suggest some possible action on their part. A comet may any day send our earth spinning disintegrated into space; nobody is much disturbed by the prospect. In the presence of tragedy that does not touch us we usually remain calm.

We are not wholly calm today. One of the most hopeful things about the present state of affairs is that most of us are being hurt. Even if we are among the few exceptional folk who have escaped personal loss and anxiety, we are hurt surely enough if we are decent Christians and have any vestige of sympathy in us. Nobody can consign one S.O.S. call after another to the waste-basket, nobody can remember the millions of unemployed, and not suffer. Sympathy today grows agonized, it is strained to the breaking point; and this is well. We ought not to be happy while these things go on. Here is our Church calling us through its appointed spokesmen to put an end to them. But there comes the rub.

Doubtless, this rousing of social imagination by the crisis upon us is a good thing. For the imagination is a mighty and creative force. "I know of no other Christianity," wrote William Blake, "than the liberty both of body and mind to exercise the Divine Arts of Imagination." Often, alas, we degrade and misuse this liberty. "O Human Imagination! O Divine Body I Have crucified!" cries Blake again. But we are slowly learning to use imagination nobly, as a social force; witness contemporary fiction and poetry, charged bitterly and tragically often, as Victorian novels and poetry rarely were, with recognition of social issues as affecting human lives; charged often with revolutionary fervor. The imagination is waking up, is enlarging its scope; every modern novel proves it. Yet the imagination, while it extends our sympathies, is not telling us what to do. Nobody is telling us plain folk.

The purpose of the series of articles inaugurated herewith is to suggest ways of action to Christian people. Experts are preparing these studies of what the Church can do to further feasible reforms. It is to be hoped that nearly every one reading this article will discover some form of activity in which he can help; for the series drives at action. It drives, however, at conviction too; for we must know what we believe before we can go very far in deciding what we shall do. In journeying toward the far land of justice, brotherhood, and peace, the eyes of modern students are carried to more and more remote horizons. Let us gaze ahead with these keen-sighted men. Guides are many to that good country, and many are the paths proposed by which to travel thither, but we shall not take the next step until we choose among them, we shall stand still unless we decide on the direction in which we wish to go. The necessity for thought confronts us, and brave, forward-looking thinking, ready if need be to discard old conventions however comfortable, is the order of the day. If the imagination hurts us, it can refresh us too; no one can afford just now to let his mind be lazy or timid; the widening of social vision required merely to follow the plans of the Administration at Washington from week to week is amazing. This series should be rich in suggestion of ideas.

We Church people may be glad that religious minds today are making valuable contributions to social theory. Economics and religion are permeating each other in a remarkable fashion. The least that we of the rank and file can do is to read what these thinkers have to say; for thought governed by Christian assumption and inspired by Christian vision is, as we must all concede, especially likely to help us. Even if we can not share in any active enterprises, simple reading and studying about them will do much to remove that oppressive sense of helplessness which saddens and clogs us. To form an enlightened body of Christian opinion is a crying need of the hour, and every member of Christ's Church should share in that great task; first and foremost by enlightening himself, by familiarity with the work of outstanding Christian thinkers, like R. H. Tawney, like W. G. Peck, like Archbishop Temple or Maurice Reckitt; to mention only men of our communion.

There is one sure outlet for our sluggish inertia, one way of directly helping on the Kingdom of God. That way is prayer. Social intercession may be the mightiest force in the world. And here is something which the simple, the sick, those wholly removed from active life, can practise as effectively as any one else. The whole Church should be on her knees these days praying quite concretely for definite ends: for the peace of the world; for wise agricultural policies; for financial reform. If prayer is the deep secret operative force that Jesus tells us it is, we should be very busy with it. He meant us to pray for definite things; He pointed to a real mountain when He said that prayer could dislodge that mass and cast it into the sea. Now He did not want that foolish thing to be done; but He did and does mean that prayer is a force as real as electricity, and competent to overthrow all piled up evils which interrupt our vision of the heavens.

The responsibility for social intercession is not satisfied by vague aspiration, "Thy Kingdom Come." That petition, to be sure, covers all our desires; but if we pray specifically for the recovery to health of a beloved friend, for example, we should be equally specific in our prayers for the health of the body politic. Now we can not be specific unless we have some conviction and some intelligence. There is a type of purely formal prayer; not wholly useless, we hope. But most Christian people have some little experience at least of another kind of prayer, the prayer of power. That kind of a prayer must be enlightened; it must be lit at the torch of knowledge. The chief reason why all Christian people should be making themselves intelligent about the great issues of the day, is that they may learn to pray with fervor and to use the prayer of power.

To cultivate social imagination; to study; to pray; here even if no practical activity is possible to us, are outlets for that need of action native to men, here is sure release from bewildered and unworthy private-mindedness. The series now opening hopes to help us in these ways, as well as through suggestions for practical work. But let us not suppose that what lies before us will be easy. To evolve that "new economic order" which the Churches desire, will mean heavy cost to every single man. Let us rejoice; for tests of heroism and of readiness for sacrifice await us. The fate of our whole Western civilization hangs today in the balance; and on the Church, that is, on the body of her children, this fate may well depend.

No one can tell where his own test may come. Perhaps in tearing himself free from his natural group and inherited tradition. Perhaps in salvaging time from congenial and profitable pursuits, for cooperation with some of those causes to which this series will direct attention. It may be in relentless flight from mental laziness and in mastering a difficult subject like social credit. Just possibly it might be in the most difficult and perilous task of all—perilous because charged with such danger of self-deception—spiritual discipline in inward poverty, while outward circumstances beyond one's control remain unchanged. One thing is sure; for us all, the test will involve eagerness to welcome any cost to oneself or one's own class, if such appear to be the condition of an advance toward justice. It would seem equally certain that we must all summon the aid of sacramental faith to strengthen those forces within the Church which tend toward sacrificial policies on the part of privilege.

Do we face victory, or defeat? In one sense, no man can tell. We or our children may have to experience the overthrow of the social order as we know it; though we hope that if Christian forces rally, this order may be peacefully transformed through obedience to the law of love. But whichever prospect waits, whether our civilization be doomed or no, we can rest assured that the Church advances toward effective triumph only if we her children march with the Cross of Christ before us.

The Spirit of Missions 99 (January 1934): 6-9.

CHAPTER TEN

Christian Education (1826-1979)

Introduction

Christian education seeks to encourage a deeper relationship with God through teaching, sharing of wisdom and experience, and continuing formation of the whole person in Christ. The Episcopal Church has adopted a variety of initiatives to meet the changing educational needs of its members, and the changing opportunities to serve through education. The colonial church was involved in the founding of some of the most significant educational institutions in America, including schools such as Columbia and William and Mary. This commitment to education in America was later continued by the Episcopal Church through diocesan initiatives that led to the founding of schools such as Trinity College, Hartford, Hobart, and Kenyon. However, the denominational ties and the distinctive Episcopalian identity of these schools were often not maintained. Other schools, such as the University of the South, have continued a strong sense of identity and affiliation in the Episcopal Church. The Episcopal Church also sought better education for African-Americans through the founding of several colleges for blacks, including St. Augustine's in Raleigh, North Carolina, Voorhees in Denmark, South Carolina, and St. Paul's in Lawrenceville, Virginia. Seminaries for the education and formation of clergy became normative for those preparing for ordained ministry, generally displacing the practice of "reading for orders" under the supervision of a local member of the clergy. The General Theological Seminary was organized by direction of the General Convention of the Episcopal Church, but many other seminaries were founded by diocesan or regional initiative, or through the leadership of one of the parties in the church. Several Episcopal seminaries have merged in the twentieth century, while others have closed or struggled for survival. Other seminaries have thrived and grown stronger in the modern era. Many seminaries have expanded their mission to include training of the laity for ministry, and continuing education of clergy. In the early 1800s the Episcopal Church sought to provide religious instruction on a weekly basis for young people through parish Sunday schools. The Sunday school movement spread widely throughout the church, with Sunday schools continuing to be an expected part of congregational life and mission in many modern Episcopal parishes. Modern initiatives in Christian education have sought to help adults and young people to appreciate and experience their Christian identity through the stories of faith. Members of the Episcopal Church were also actively involved in the founding of boarding schools and other secondary schools with Episcopal ties. Many of these schools were founded and operated by Episcopal religious orders, dioceses, and parishes. These schools continue to provide both general education and religious instruction for many young people today. The Episcopal commitment to excellence in education and service through education has been demonstrated in many forms of education and contexts for instruction.

87.

General Protestant Episcopal Sunday School Union, 1826

The General Protestant Episcopal Sunday School Union was organized in 1826. The Bible, the Prayer Book, and the Catechism were used for instruction by the Sunday School Union. This statement urges that Sunday schools teach the beliefs of the Episcopal Church.

The object of the General Protestant Episcopal Sunday School Union is to combine the resources of Episcopalians into one great whole, which, by its concentration of power, may be enabled to give life and vigour to the multitude of branches which now pine in solitude and neglect. The talent and experience of the most active supporters of our Sunday Schools will be united in the invention of efficacious systems of instruction, and their combined wisdom exerted in the choice of proper books.

Without in the least interfering with the claims or pretensions of other religious societies, the Protestant Episcopal Church has always considered it her duty assiduously to instruct her younger members in the nature of her own peculiar character and claims, that they might at all times be ready to state the grounds of their attachment to her pale, and thus be armed against any temptations to dereliction from her faith and discipline. This can be done nowhere so well as in the Sunday School.

It is evidently desirable that Sunday Schools under the patronage of the Protestant Episcopal Church should be conducted on principles purely Protestant Episcopalian, and should afford a prominent place in their instruction to the doctrines and constitution of the church to which they belong...It is the duty of Protestant Episcopalians to associate among themselves for the purpose of providing the means of exhibiting to their youth the principles of Christianity in what they believe to be its purest form—a form derived from Christ and his apostles.

Clifton Hartwell Brewer, *A History of Religious Education in the Episcopal Church to 1835* (New Haven: Yale University Press, 1924), 184-185.

88.

James H. Otey, Christian Education: October 5, 1859

James Hervey Otey (January 27, 1800–April 23, 1863) was consecrated the first Bishop of Tennessee on January 14, 1834. Much of his ministry was devoted to education. This sermon was preached before the General Convention of the Protestant Episcopal Church in the United States of America at St. Paul's Church, Richmond, Virginia, on October 5, 1859.

Children have souls to be saved, as well as duties to perform to society. To those whose thoughts are exercised seriously about the things of another life, the chief and engrossing subject of anxiety is, not how children may be made respectable and prosperous during their abode on earth, but how they may become fellow-citizens of the saints, and fitted for the society of heaven. And however their right of baptism may be questioned, the ground is fearlessly assumed, that, if all the conditions of the covenant are faithfully met and discharged by those who have the care of them, we may as certainly and confidently look for a blessing on efforts for their spiritual improvement, as for the full development of their faculties and powers in other things. To the labor of Christian education in this highest view, we have the most animating encouragement. The conviction of success, it is true, is an exercise of our faith, and not a part of our knowledge; the responsibility for their own souls will ultimately devolve on the children themselves, and God only knows how they will sustain it. Our present efforts and prayers will not be alone effectual; but that intercessory prayer and Christian education are means through which the gifts of the

Spirit are very freely bestowed, and that the faithful use of these means affords the strongest encouragement for expecting it, is what no Christian can reasonably doubt. We must not forget, indeed, that the whole work of religion is not performed by the inculcation of truth and the culture of moral sensibility. We know and lament that there are too many to be found, whose minds have been enlightened by the truth, softened by the spirit, and embellished by the ornaments of Christianity, and who yet have never received the gospel as the principle of a new and holy life; and it will be found further, that this perilous and unhappy state is owing simply to an obstinate refusal of the means of grace, and the resistance they make to the Author of all grace. Still while we perform our duty in conveying religious instruction to the mind of the child, we know that his heart will be much better prepared hereafter to receive and profit by the influences of the Spirit of God.

Truths instilled in childhood live forever in the memory. They are interwoven with all the sensibilities of the soul. They are the fortress of the conscience, not impregnable, but indestructible. They furnish the mind with chords which never cease to vibrate to the touch of faithful expostulation. They are an inextinguishable spark, which, after being seemingly smothered under a mass of corruption, are often revived, by providential circumstances, to a pure flame of piety. We cannot pluck up the *roots* of evil, but we may prune and repress its developments. We may soften the soil in which heavenly seed must germinate, and make it pervious to the dews of Divine grace. The work is noble, the hopes are strong and scriptural, the duty is imperative, and the machinery to be employed is all of heavenly temper and Divine appointment.

From the days of the Apostles downward, the Church's care of little children has been assumed as an eminent duty. Timothy, from a child, was instructed in the Holy Scriptures. We read of certain persons called *helpers*,—as Priscilla, Aquila, and Urbane,—who are reasonably presumed to have held the office of *catechist*, which was universal in the early ages of the Church; and ever since the Reformation it has been the prescribed duty of the Ministers of the Church, "diligently on Sundays to instruct and examine the children" of the Parish in the *Catechism* prepared for that special purpose, and which contains in itself perhaps the most complete summary of Christian doctrines and duties ever brought together in the same compass. Bring before your minds the immense multitude of Ministers and Catechists and teachers employed in this work, wherever the seas thunder round the world, or winds sweep over the habitations of men,—the countless numbers of children collected weekly together to be taught. Think of the prayers, the admonitions, the lessons, in which this unnumbered mass of living and immortal beings are every Sunday engaged. Reflect on the pious impressions which these holy occupations must make on instructors and children,—

their accumulating knowledge of Divine things; their diligent investigation and explanation of religious truth; this employment of holy time, in holy things, when that time might be misemployed in the things of the world; the rebounding influence of pious children upon their parents and others; the amount of moral and religious sentiment thus communicated; the silent but sure operation of that sentiment imperceptibly finding its way to millions of accountable and rational living beings, and these in their turn influencing other millions to come after,— and can you conceive, by any effort of mind, a moral spectacle of more imposing grandeur and soul-stirring sublimity? Are we not justified in offering the prayer, and in indulging the hope, that the incense thus rising to the throne of God may, by His blessing, burst forth over the guilty millions of our world, without limit and without restraint, in heavenly benediction, its sanctifying influences be felt in human institutions, mingle itself with all social elements, regulate all the pulsations of feeling, consecrate all political movements, exalt all the productions of science and learning, purify every intellectual and moral enterprise, and communicate heaven's peace and gladness to every nation, every family, and every heart? Can we employ a more powerful consideration to move the Church, its Ministry, and its members, to undertake and vigorously prosecute this glorious work commanded by Christ, blessed of God, and indispensable to man?

William Mercer Green, *Memoir of the Rt. Rev. James Hervey Otey, D.D., LL.D., The First Bishop of Tennessee* (New York: James Pott and Company, 1885), 318-321. (Excerpt)

89.

Thomas F. Gailor, A Church University, August 1, 1897

Thomas Frank Gailor (September 17, 1856–October 3, 1935) was consecrated Assistant Bishop of Tennessee on July 25, 1893, and became the third Bishop of Tennessee on the death of Bishop Charles T. Quintard, February 15, 1898. He was Vice-Chancellor of the University of the South, August 6, 1890–July 27, 1893, and Chancellor, June 23, 1908, until his death. This baccalaureate sermon describes the mission of a Christian university.

A Church University, then, is first of all a Christian University. And this does not mean, as is so often understood, or misunderstood, even by our friends, an institution for the defense and maintenance of the Christian religion—not at all. It means that an institution for the furtherance of higher education and wider scholarship must make choice among many theories and many methods of education; and that therefore this institution has deliberately adopted that theory and that method of education, which has grown out of the Christian view of human life, as being the very best theory and method of education that has ever been proposed. It is not a question of choice between religions, but a choice between plans and theories of education.

A Christian University believes in Christian education, not because it is Christian but because, after eighteen centuries of trial, it has been found to be the best. Such a plan, of course, necessitates a recognition of the truth of distinctively Christian principles and ideas. It assumes that there is a God—the Creator and Lord of all; that he is not indifferent to human conduct and human suffering, who is ready to help, to guide, to redeem our life. It assumes that man is an immortal being, with sure hope of an eternal destiny; that he is free, personal, moral, responsible; that the work of self-development and self-culture which he accomplishes here shall have value and significance forever; that humility and not pride, forgiveness and not resentment, unselfishness and not selfishness is the true law of life; that faith—faith in himself and faith in God—is the abiding inspiration of his efforts to be educated; that he is not a brute adorned with reason, nor an athletic animal merely, but a being with moral and spiritual faculties that demands God for their satisfaction and eternity for their fulfillment; that finally, in his hopeful struggle for the perception of truth and the achievement of righteousness, he is not left to his own unaided efforts, but has promise of blessing and help from One, Who, "though He was rich, yet for our sakes became poor, that we through His poverty might be rich."

These are distinctively Christian principles, and these are the only sure and permanent foundations of hope and confidence in the efforts that we are making for the higher education of mankind. An education based upon these principles is, so far forth, a Christian education. An institution that builds upon these principles and refuses to recognize the source from which they emanate is untrue to itself and its students; and an institution of learning that denies or ignores these principles has simply narrowed and crippled and handicapped itself in its attempt to realize the high and sacred purpose for which it stands. This, then, is the first characteristic of a Church University: a firm confidence in the great principles of Christianity as the healthiest and broadest foundation of higher education; and the second characteristic is the careful provision that these principles shall not be narrowed, or enfeebled, or distorted by modern sectarian accretions and interpretations. This is the spiritual meaning of the Apostle's precept in the text, "Ye shall add to faith virtue; and to virtue, knowledge." For the

Christian faith and Christian virtue have this of the human in them, that without knowledge they may run into fanaticism; and fanaticism in any form is a deadly foe to education. What we need in the pursuit of learning more than anything else—after the conviction of the sacredness and moral value of human life which makes the pursuit of learning reasonable and possible—is breadth and freedom in its scope and aim. The best scholarship is broad and free; it disregards and depreciates no fact, no sentiment, no affection in the rich development of human life. Truth and beauty and goodness in every phase and form of human effort is the object of its patient and sympathetic investigation. It can tolerate nothing that dims and darkens the native brightness and healthfulness of human character, as it can encourage nothing that inculcates intellect without principle, beauty without conscience, and art without devotion. . . .

Thomas F. Gailor, "Baccalaureate Sermon," *The University of the South Papers*, Series B, Number 87 (1897), 14-17. (Excerpt)

90.

William Lawrence, Educational Organization in the Church, October 1916

William Lawrence (May 30, 1850–November 6, 1941) was consecrated the seventh Bishop of Massachusetts on October 5, 1893. He was the fourth dean of the Episcopal Theological School, 1889-1893, now the Episcopal Divinity School. This essay expresses his views concerning religious education.

. . . Religious education, as I understand it is the process by which the child develops in body, mind and spirit into the fullness of Christian life. We do not develop the child. The child develops through our aid and leadership under the power of God's spirit of truth. This involves development in all his faculties, physical, mental and religious. It is for us simply to give the opportunities, present the conditions, offer the leadership, and the child grows into the Christian life.

None of us is divided into water-tight compartments. Each child is a living thing. Every tissue, nerve, thought and inspiration is bound up with every other. Therefore the development of a child into the religious life must, like the growth of any living thing, rise from the breaking forth into the life upward. Through the prayer at the mother's knee and through education in the home the beginnings are made, and from year to year the growth goes on until the old man is laid to rest.

Religious education, therefore, involves unity, breadth and elasticity in the educational influences and work. As the little child reaches twelve or fourteen years of age, he is growing along the lines of broad educational interest and of service. Every person, place and hour have their influence in the growth, the home, the Sunday School, the playground, the day school. No one of us can confine religion to any one of these divisions of life in the effort to create compartments. Life, real life is stifled.

It is, therefore, a radical misconception of religious education to insist that unless the child is taught definite religion in the day school, he will become a godless child. He may or he may not gain the religious influences in the day school. The essential thing is that he gain them somewhere. If not there, then there falls upon the Church and home the greater responsibility and opportunity. We citizens of this country must keep this principle clearly in mind. We cannot expect the public schools of the United States to teach Christian religion. In the first place, with the conglomerate population that is now filling our cities, it is an impractical proposition, and to my mind those Church people who assume that there cannot be a full, fine and complete education of boyhood and manhood unless the Christian faith is definitely taught in the public schools are not only revealing a weakness of faith in religious education and undermining the efforts of the Church to do its best by its own children, but they are at the same time in danger of leading the community into such a relation of Church and State as is inconsistent with the traditions of this country and the relative independence of Church and State.

In taking the position that the Christian faith must be taught in the public schools, we are in danger, to my mind, of putting our Church before the people of this country in an unfavorable light, and we are at the same time forgetting the lessons of history. For surely the history during the past generation of Italy, France and Spain tell no uncertain story.

Any person who is to teach religion must be a disciple of the religion that he teaches. As surely as you incorporate definite religious teaching in the public schools, you have got to have religious tests of the teacher, and in this country that is impossible. Hence we Church men and Church women must keep this fact in mind. In our efforts to present to this Church the best system of religious education we, taking the conditions of this country as they are, cannot expect our children to receive definite religious instruction in the public schools. We must, therefore, turn all our forces to give them education through the home and in Church and in all the influences of life. I believe that if we can turn our thoughts and convictions directly along that channel, we will have created a spiritual force and we will have supported an educational organization which will carry the stream of spiritual refreshment into the great fields of human life and enrich the characters of the boys and girls as are the fields refreshed and enriched by the powers of irrigation.

William Lawrence, *Educational Organization in the Church* (New York: General Board of Religious Education, Protestant Episcopal Church, 1916), 2-3. (Excerpt)

91.

Hughell E. W. Fosbroke, The One Foundation: The Dean's Installation Sermon, February 5, 1917

Hughell Edgar Woodall Fosbroke (April 5, 1875–October 19, 1957) was the fifth dean of the General Theological Seminary, 1916-1947. General Seminary, the oldest of the Episcopal seminaries, was founded in 1817, and has been characterized throughout most of its history by a moderate high-churchmanship. This sermon discusses the challenge of ordained ministry in the context of theological education.

For other foundation can no man lay than that is laid, which is Jesus Christ.—I Cor. 3:11

These are the words that come often and instinctively to our lips as we of today take our part in the great and noble heritage that has come down to us. That is surely what they would have us say into whose labors we have entered. Into the fashioning of this Institution's hundred years of loyal service have gone the unremitting toil of faithful servants of God, the generous giving of large-hearted benefactors, the wise planning of devoted minds, the reverent thought of able scholars, the high aspirations of generation after generation of young hearts aglow with the enthusiasm of entrance upon holy service, the prayers of countless devout souls; and all these have been woven into a living unity in Christ. And in him they live who have given and planned and taught and learned and prayed, and of their life in him we partake. It is not simply that we reap the advantage of their toil, the residuum of their earthly existence now that they are removed from the scene. It is the glory of the Christian faith that for the Church of the living God there is no dead past. All glows and palpitates with life pressing eagerly and insistently upon the future, touching with the radiance of eternity the fleeting moment that we call the present and giving even to our brief years of troubled aspiration a worth that has no end. "To whom coming, as unto a living stone, disallowed indeed of men, but chosen of God, and precious," we "also, as lively stones, are built up a spiritual house, a holy priesthood, to offer up spiritual sacrifices acceptable to God by Jesus Christ."

This is not said merely because a reverent and grateful acknowledgment of the labors of others is the fitting mood at such a time as this. Herein lies the first and necessary premise for any consideration of the problem of theological education. Amid all the confused questionings and bewildering doubts and perplexities which beset our day this at least stands fast for those who believe in theology at all. God has revealed himself to human hearts and minds. It is his holy reality with which we begin, a reality given in the world of nature all about us, in history, in the discipline of a chosen people, in the life and death and rising again of Jesus Christ, in the work of the Holy Spirit uniting men in the fellowship of the Church; and all this is set forth for us concretely in the living tradition of this Seminary in which God has given us a part. We build upon a certainty. Our city hath foundations. We begin not with theory but with fact. "God has claimed us all in Christ as his sons." It is this givenness of basic fact in the acknowledgment of which we are faced with God's self-revealing that distinguishes theology from that religion which is today appropriately called comparative. In quite impartial ways the students of this latter-day science explore the darker recesses of psychology, gather their data from the remote and obscure regions of anthropology, hail with delight every survival of the primitive and barbarous. We are profoundly indebted to them, for the results of their investigations serve to throw new light on the hidden treasure of the Christian faith and reveal in unexpected ways the universality of the human need which that faith alone can meet. But in so far as they themselves disregard the great outstanding facts of revelation and pride themselves on their detachment from tradition they arrive only at a mysterious something, a nameless god, unknown and unknowable. But we have sure word of witness that enables us to "speak that we do know and testify that we have seen."

Our primary concern then is with a great tradition. It is to the deeper understanding and explication of this that our energies are first of all directed. We do not in the first place create or imagine or devise, we seek to interpret that which is given. We do not even begin by seeking evidence for its truth. We desire to understand it as it is. God has spoken, is speaking, and we listen eagerly that we may miss no syllable of his utterance. "Speak, Lord, for thy servant heareth" is the cry in our hearts. For it is an enterprise to challenge all our powers, this elucidation of a splendid tradition of life. It is easy enough to be a traditionalist and catch up phrases of the past and make their frequent repetition the badge of orthodoxy; but to grow into the larger life that has created these phrases, to learn to look out upon the world in all its manifold variety, its seemingly chaotic struggle, in the light thrown upon it by God's revelation of himself, to feel the thrill as well as hold the theory of the universe as God's universe and the Church as the body of our Lord, this would be impossible if it were a task for the brain alone. Study will do much, is of course indispensable, the kind of intensive concentrated study that theological students are singularly loath to give, but it must be study supported and sustained by prayer, enriched and made creative by worship. For the end that we seek is freedom, freedom of the domain of the spirit, the franchise of the Kingdom, the liberty of Catholic faith, the power to deal consistently with life in the terms of the great Christian truths, not simply by direct and conscious focusing of the mind so that in face of a crisis we are not worried and nervous about the correctness of our procedure but with an instinctive loyalty that can, as occasion demands, meet the emergency with that originality which shall reveal anew the astounding richness of the old truths. We tend in these days to alternate between two slaveries, the slavery of the letter and the slavery of our own moods. We seem shut up to a choice between a cold precision, void of life, and an intense sensationalism that has no meaning or value beyond itself, a mere surface play of emotion. Are not both the result of the shallowness of our thought, our failure to enter into the fullness of our heritage, to draw upon all the resources of faith? We may learn here surely from one who went not with us. "Deep minds," says Goethe, "are compelled to live in the past as well as in the future."

If, then, I plead for a more intensive attack upon the ancient disciplines of theology, for a devotional knowledge of the Bible which shall have entered through the gate of criticism into its life and spirit, for such an understanding of dogmatic theology and history as shall lead men anew to go behind phrases and events and feel the way in which, in and through them all, the living God has been teaching and disciplining children, let it not be supposed that I am oblivious of the urgent demands made upon the priesthood of today for service in many fields. The priest of the Church is to work in this modern world, and to win men for Christ he must be sensitive to the perplexities and the needs of this present age. Let us face the problem fairly in all its complexity. Here are social, economic, political questions upon which he must have a mind of his own, which yet must be in some way the mind of Christ. Or in another direction there is the appeal of the individual soul as expressed in the quest for healing of mind and body. Whether that is to take the form of psychotherapy or that weird psychoanalysis which Freud has brought to our attention, simple ignorance may mean forfeiting that opportunity to serve which the priest of God must always crave. Or again, child study clamors for attention. There is new ferment in the world of education. Can the priest hold aloof and refuse to heed the cry of the little ones? Some few there will be who feel themselves called to select one of these needs of our modern life as an especial field of endeavor, and it is altogether right that as ministers of Jesus Christ they should take their place among these self-sacrificing laborers for the sake of what they can give and the first-hand knowledge which they can thus gain for the Church. But if such men are to be more than, for example, social service experts, if they are actually to give to those with whom they work new understanding and broader vision, if they are to enable these devoted workers to derive their inspiration more directly from our Lord, if they are to be saved themselves from that narrowing of interest which waits upon the footsteps of the specialist in any department; if, in other words, they are to make the distinctive contribution that their priesthood should enable them to give, they must above all be possessed of that intensive living knowledge of the depth and meaning of the Christian faith of which I have been speaking, even though the time spent in winning it prolongs the period of their preparation. In these days there are many who think of religion as social morality touched with emotion and lose in well-meaning sympathy the power to see the greatness of men's souls and the look of eternity in their eyes. It is when the priest comes to them as an ambassador of Christ knowing what his Lord doeth that he makes his true contribution to their need and work.

Then for the great majority of the clergy who cannot and ought not to be experts in any one of these fields and yet should have some knowledge of them all and for this must be dependent in large measure on the results of others' investigations, what shall save them from falling prey to the latest theory, subservient followers of those with whom the last cry has become a shrill yell? There is in the loyal and faithful understanding of the Church's life, in the pervasion of soul and mind with the working of the Holy Spirit, such a contact with reality as gives discernment, the ability to distinguish between true and false even when they are so closely intermingled as in so many of the movements of our own day. It is not mere acquaintance with new theories with power to add to their number that we need. Sympathetic insight is the necessary thing. With this, we shall neither hold coldly aloof nor commit ourselves headlong to the latest program; but, quietly and simply, more by patient representation that by vehement assertion, we shall enable men to perceive the difference that Christ makes. The approach should doubtless be indicated in seminary days, lectures perhaps given, the right books pointed out, but in the brief time at our disposal it is principles upon which the emphasis must be laid and principles so wedded with life that they may be applied flexibly in many directions.

It is, in a word, character, the character of members of the Body of Christ that is all-important; and character as we know in this time of insistence upon the unity of personality is a matter of thinking as well as doing, of the instincts and the affections as well as of the will. It is the power to function freely and naturally in the common life of thought and action because that common life is given from above. What men are feeling after in secular education is but the feeble echo of that which the Church can surely give. "What is needed," says Professor Dewey in his recent book *Democracy and Education*, "is intelligent sympathy or good will. For sympathy as a desirable quality is something more that mere feeling, it is a cultivated imagination for what men have in common and a rebellion at whatever unnecessarily divides them"; and one notes the resemblance, while one feels the difference, in this utterance of a Belgian monk: "The unfailing criterion by which to judge of the value of a thing from the supernatural point of view consists chiefly in this, to examine if it helps or hinders the union of men with God and through God with one another." Here in this Seminary we make the discovery, the reasoned discovery that is to control heart and mind and will, of how rich and fruitful the life of fellowship in Christ may be.

And if this seems to center too much attention upon life as it is to be lived here with too little direct regard to the years of service that lie beyond, it may, I think, fairly be urged that so long as the great purpose is kept in view men will best prepare for it by devoted application to the full opportunity of the present. So much of what may be said of the future bears the aspect of theory, lies in the realm of hypothesis, while the present has a living actuality. When all is said the theological seminary cannot quite be classified with the professional schools. It is life itself with which the priest is to deal, and in living we shall find the way. At Harvard they have been trying to discover whether the study of economics is of greater value for good citizenship or for vocational efficiency. Even there it is only for the purpose of analysis that the distinction can be maintained. There can be no really good citizenship that does not include vocational efficiency, no true vocational efficiency that is not a part of good citizenship. For us certainly the one passes almost inevitably into the other. Good citizenship in the Kingdom of God, if the word "good" be not emptied of its meaning, should enable a man to give account of his stewardship. For true goodness recognizes responsibilities and is a quality of the mind as well as the heart. "What men call simple goodness," said Bishop Paget, "is under very complex conditions of work not so simple or obvious a matter as it sounds. The unembarrassed insight that goes straight to the real character of an action or suggestion, the just imagination which can enter into another's position, the kindly shrewdness which is never credulous and never cynical, the strength of mind that can resist the temptation to be clever, and, above all, that sense of things unseen which makes palpable the folly of ever fancying that there can be through evil a short cut to good."

Simple goodness, wise with the wisdom that is from above, understanding what the will of the Lord is—that has been sought and found here by the help of the Holy Spirit. Priests whose lips keep knowledge, true messengers of the Lord of Hosts, have gone forth from this Seminary. And in humble reliance upon the selfsame Spirit we go forward.

Hughell E. W. Fosbroke, *God in the Heart of Things* (Greenwich, Conn.: Seabury Press, 1962), 50-56.

92.

The Church Looks Ahead to the New Curriculum: Specifications, 1948

The Church Looks Ahead to the New Curriculum: Specifications was written to prepare the Church for the new Seabury Series curriculum. John Heuss (July 30, 1908–March 20, 1966) was director of the Department of Christian Education of the Episcopal Church at the time. This statement identifies the characteristics of a good religious education curriculum.

Teacher was the title by which Christ was commonly addressed through His earthly ministry. Following in His steps, His Church always has been a teaching Church. The eternal Gospel must be interpreted afresh for each age, and set forth in ways and with methods that are relevant to the times.

The Christian today is living in a world not dissimilar to that into which Christianity first came. Then the pagan faced life, sometimes with a noble stoicism, but more often with a cynical disillusionment, or a bewildered and reckless abandon. To him Christianity brought the Gospel, the glad tidings. The power it gave to overcome the world even while living in the midst of it, drew many to ardent discipleship. The Christian Gospel is equally needed, and can be equally Good News today.

But the Church's present influence falls far short of men's needs, or the magnitude and worth of what it has to give. One important failing is that its teaching ministry is no longer well geared to current urgencies, approaches, and opportunities. Christian education as judged by its prevailing results today seems generally deficient in at least three important respects:

Church members have little clear-cut knowledge of what they believe and why. Against a reasonably well-informed antagonist they would be unable to defend themselves adequately, let alone convince him of the error of his ways.

They lack the solid foundation of a conviction based on facts. They fail to grasp wherein guiding Christian beliefs differ markedly from outright secularism.

The daily conduct of Christians is apt to be governed by mere common-sense standards. The goals, the aims, and the ambitions which they have accepted for themselves consequently have distressingly little specifically Christian content. Heedless of requirements their allegiance lays upon them, their example supplies little to commend what they profess to believe.

Christians feel little obligation to the Church to which they belong. What each individual chooses to do about membership, attendance, and other observances is his business and his alone. By comparison, numerous voluntary groups seem to succeed in uniting their members by stronger and more compelling bonds. Consequently, Church members widely lack that contagious fervor and evangelistic zeal which must share with others the joy of a glad discovery, and which has always been a marked characteristic of the days of the Church's strength. . . .

There are numerous evidences that such a strengthening of religious education would be widely welcomed. Intimations of a reawakened interest in religion are unmistakable:

1. Many non-Churchgoers turn hopefully toward Christian ethics as the world's best way out of their troubles, even though they hold no particular brief for the Church.

2. The disillusioned intellectual has seen his enthusiastically-held hopes battered down by the times. As little gods go, the great God comes, and many such are now looking wistfully toward historic Christianity in the hope it may become for them that firm and challenging faith to which they can dedicate themselves.

3. Parents brought up without religious training are realizing in their maturity how much they have missed. So they want for their children the Christian faith and convictions and standards which they themselves did not possess. Feeling at a loss how to proceed, such parents are groping for help.

4. Within the Church, members exhibit a growing and active interest in its beliefs and teachings. Feeling ignorant, they are eager to be informed and directed.

True, excellent religious education programs are operative now here, now there. The Church today has faithful, loyal, energetic members. Individual Christians again and again are proving themselves shining lights in their community and nation, and so living as to commend their beliefs to the world at large. The Church's task is to bring the best of existing theory and practice to bear on present needs. But such outstanding products of Christian education are too few, and the present situation taken as a whole is far from satisfactory.

Life does not stand still; children and adults alike are constantly being educated.

To fail to make Christian influences effective is to assure that secular influences will be so. Along with the sense of urgency and of hope is a widespread conviction that the Church's present educational machinery is not adequate for its task. This is expressed in a spontaneous reaching out for something better. One tangible result is the action taken by the General Convention of the Protestant Episcopal Church in the fall of 1946, directing the preparation of a new curriculum for Christian education in the present day. . . .

CRITERIA OF A GOOD CURRICULUM

Before any material or presentation can be accepted for inclusion in the new curriculum, it must first pass a three-fold test:

1. It must be sound. Is it correct as far as it goes, and in accordance with the best understanding on the matter?

2. It must be adequate. Mere correctness as far as it goes is only a first step, for the treatment must also be sufficiently full and balanced to pass the test of adequacy. At times, expansion and explanation will be called for.

3. It must be relevant. Material however interesting in itself that is not really significant for the immediate purpose at hand, and does not contribute to it is to be eliminated. Drastic pruning will sometimes be the indicated course.

All parts of the curriculum, to say nothing of the curriculum as a whole, must meet the requirements of being accurate and sufficient for furthering a worthwhile purpose. . . .

Realistic

The average Church School curriculum is of course intended to give a well-rounded and balanced program to a child starting at the beginning and continuing to graduation at whatever level that may be set. But in practice contact with the complete program will seldom occur. With population changes, there is a constant shifting from one parish to another. Many children do not start at the beginning; most drop out long before the end. Further, attendance from Sunday to Sunday is generally spasmodic, far less regular than with the public school.

Realistic recognition of this means that not only the curriculum as a whole, but each year in the curriculum, each section of the year or project, almost each individual lesson must be arranged to make some contribution of its own apart from what went before or what is to follow. The total program will be in the nature of a spiral, again and again picking up each area of knowledge at a higher level than before. But of course this is to be done in such a way that children have a constant sense of progress, and the presentation must be sufficiently different to avoid being thought of as "old stuff."

The major areas of Christian knowledge are these:

1. God's self-revelation and mighty acts are recorded in the

Bible and especially in the life and teachings of Christ.

2. The historic life of the Church, including its present-day work.

3. The beliefs of the Church.

4. The Prayer Book, liturgy, and worship of the Church.

5. The world in which we live and the Christian's duties, problems, and opportunities in it.

No one will be studied to the exclusion of the others for as long as a year. They will not necessarily receive equal allotments of time, but in the course of any two or three successive years all will be given substantial attention.

Furthermore, an adequately realistic program must take account of the conditions under which much of the teaching will be done. It will not presuppose as to size of school, equipment, money available, educational background of children, and the like, conditions remote from those which actually exist. It will recognize the abilities and disabilities and potentialities of the average teacher. It will be realistic also as to how much can reasonably be expected of the clergy in connection with the religious education program. Yet at the same time it will recognize that in these and other respects there exists within the Church the widest sort of variety, and therefore the total program must have sufficient flexibility to render it reasonably adaptable to a wide variety of local conditions.

The Church Looks Ahead to the New Curriculum: Specifications (New York: National Council, Protestant Episcopal Church, 1948), 7-10, 40, 46-47. (Excerpts)

93.

Theodore O. Wedel, The Church's Teaching: An Introduction, 1949

Theodore Otto Wedel (February 19, 1892–July 20, 1970) was warden of the College of Preachers, 1943-1960. This pamphlet was written at the request of the authors' committee of the Church's Teaching Series, and it discusses the meaning of education in the context of faith. The Church's Teaching Series was a series of books on topics such as scripture, doctrine, church history, ethics, and worship to be used for adult education. A new series by the same name was published in the 1970s.

EDUCATION itself is taken very seriously in America. But the education that is considered important is secular education, that is, education in the things of this world. A secular school curriculum consists of courses in science, mathematics, art, and history, but with little or no reference to religion or to God.

This kind of education demands and receives disciplined study. It leads to success in business or a profession. Social prestige attaches to keeping up with the times in art, literature, and current events, or even the technical vocabulary of science. Americans probably know more about psychoanalysis or the working of an automobile than about the Hebrew prophets or the history of the Christian Church. Ignorance of Christian truth causes no social embarrassment. Even loyal Churchmen frequently have little time for the intellectual effort necessary for growth in Christian knowledge. We are tempted to label Christian truth *theology*, and to dismiss it as the business of the ministry, forgetting that theology means simply "knowledge of God," and far outranks in importance all earthly knowledge whatsoever.

A strange fate, indeed, has overtaken the once Christian culture of our grandfathers. Teachers who, themselves, are devout Christians are puzzled as to how to witness to their faith in an educational system in which Christian truth has been so largely ignored. An educational system, prevented from teaching Christian doctrine as such because of the separation of Church and State, might not be fatal, provided that it recognized its limitations and pointed beyond itself to the Church. Week day pilgrimage to school house could be preparation for pilgrimage to church on the Lord's day. It was this once in our more Christian past, and is still in some communities.

But great dangers threaten this once happy interdependence of church and school. Every child goes to a school. Only a fraction of the children of a community attends a church. The secular school, quite naturally, therefore, finds itself prior in importance and influence. The school is burdened with a more inclusive responsibility. Nor do leaders in secular education take this responsibility lightly. All serious educators are aware of the fact that youth dare not be cheated of at least a minimum training in the duties of citizenship and in the demands of the moral life. The question, accordingly, arises: Why cannot ethical ideals be taught apart from the religion of the Churches? Talk of God may not be proper in the classroom, but we can substitute for it talk about society and humanity and man, even ideal society and ideal humanity and ideal man.

No immediate blame can be laid upon leaders of secular education for accepting the limits within which they are compelled to work. But a moral education which begins by ignoring God, may end by denying Him altogether.

Secular Humanism Is Not Christianity

As a matter of fact, a God-ignoring, yet moral, philosophy of life exists in the modern world. The educator finds it lying ready to hand and can utilize it in place of the religion of the Churches. It even has a name: secular humanism. The words partly define themselves. Man and not God is made the center of interest and of moral authority. Secular humanism, in short, becomes a religion on its own. The term religion is used advisedly. A worship of man can replace a worship of God. Yet, since the name religion is not technically attached to it, this philosophy of life can find ready entrance into almost any classroom. It fills the vacuum created by the omission of Christian instruction from the secular school system. In large areas of the educational world it has become, in fact, an almost officially adopted substitute for the authentic Christian faith.

Decision as between the two religions may be the major issue of our age. But a word should be said first to modify harsh judgment. There are important connections between secular humanism and Christianity. It is only when these links are broken that it stands forth as something which Christianity must fully oppose. Secular humanism is, in final depth, worship of man in place of God. But man, as the secular world knows him, is still Christian man, the product of two thousand years of Christian nurture. He is man with the moral conscience of the Christian centuries still in his heart. Modern education, secular and this-worldly though it be, frequently continues to take this background for granted. And, so long as the Christian faith is still there to give meaning to man, humanism can be a handmaid of Christianity. Secular humanism, for example, believes in the social virtues of honesty and fair play, and many of its ideals of the good life run parallel with those of Christian morality. In other words, it shares with Christianity belief in the moral law. A morally earnest agnostic and a Christian have much in common. The Christian, too, needs to be instructed in the laws of right conduct on the human plane. Hence, if he learns love of neighbor in a secular school system, even though God may never be mentioned, this lesson can be utilized by the Church and by Christian teachers. The Bible, too, gives much instruction in the law. The Ten Commandments come early in the Old Testament story.

Yet allusion to the Ten Commandments already points to the gulf which separates secular humanism from Christianity. Humanist ideals for the good life for man do correspond to what God's law means in the Bible and to the Christian. Yet the difference between human ideals and divine commandments is profound. One rests upon the authority of human experience; the other has the sanction of the eternal and the divine. An unbridged chasm exists between even the morally most lofty faith in man and faith in God. Despite all reservations, secular humanism is, after all, a rival, and not merely a handmaid or diluted version, of the Christian faith. When it presumes to replace Christianity, it unveils itself as a dangerous enemy. It violates the first Commandment: *Thou shalt have none other gods but me*. It dethrones the God of the Bible, and enthrones Man in His stead.

Man, in the secular humanist faith, is good by nature. He is lord in creation and self-sufficient. If you educate him enough and free him from superstitions, he will be able to build a satisfactory life for himself and a happy world. The humanist admits, of course, that evil exists in the world. Often secular humanists are more shrewdly realistic about evil than sentimental Church folk. But they do not see that evil is deeply rooted in the will of man and, therefore, can be cured only by conversion and a new relationship with God. Instead, they see evil only as a result of social environment, ignorance, and the lag of undeveloped science. Salvation, therefore, results from man's own efforts. It must be achieved in this our one-story universe. Talk of eternity is often satirically labelled "pie in the sky by and by." Concern with eternal life, it is said, weakens man's moral effort here and now. So does Christianity's view of man as a fallen creature, helpless except God come to his rescue.

Faith In Man Is Not Enough

This secular religion is not without its substitute for God. But this God is no longer a personal Being dwelling apart from His universe, "high and lifted up." God is at best a picture word for man's own ideals. He does not exist outside these ideals. He can be found in man's own experience, in art, in imagination, in science, and, above all, in service to one's fellow man. This secular substitute for traditional Christian faith has a great appeal and frequently presents a noble moral challenge. But it sees no need for a supernatural God. Man is his own saviour.

This faith in man is, to be sure, running into difficulties. It is beginning to refute itself. During the closing decades of the nineteenth century, and the opening years of the twentieth, it was the reigning faith of educated Western man. Progress was the key word. Salvation, so it was thought, lay in man's hands within the historical process itself. Time and effort alone would be needed. World War I, however, jarred this optimistic creed. World War II dealt it a staggering blow. Scientific and technological progress, can this any longer be thought of as automatically creating a satisfactory life on this earth? It looks today as though mere scientific progress might lead instead to a cinder planet. Hence the opposite of optimism is beginning to be the mood of the younger generation. Its name is cynicism. It is a "What is the use?" philosophy of life. Close to a blind fatalism, it is a hard view of man's doom in a meaningless universe which has no answer to the problems of life except the pursuit of pleasure or courageous endurance. It may lead to a kind of despair in which man surrenders himself to new idolatrous religions.

The mood of disillusionment which is overtaking our generation presents a great opportunity for the Christian Gospel. But if the Christian faith is to save man, it must be known and understood. This is why religious illiteracy is so tragic. The only alternative to cynicism or despair which many a modern youth sees on his horizon is the faith in man which still rules in secular education. True Christianity has ceased to be an alternative, not because it has been tried and found wanting, but because it is not even known.

Nor has the Church in our day fully opened its eyes to what is happening. Christianity, as shown in the Bible, the creeds, the historic liturgies, is the very opposite of the secular faith in man. Man as his own saviour is plainly not the story of man in the Bible. Man in the Bible is not an undeveloped angel, but a creature who is lost unless rescued by a Redeemer. Yet to present boldly the contrast between faith in God and faith in Man is not easy. The temptation has been to soften down the contrast and to accommodate the Christian faith to the climate of the secular world. Faith in Man, accordingly, has found lodgment in Christian classrooms also. The Episcopal Church, perhaps, has been spared the more extreme forms of this error, thanks to the Book of Common Prayer. But even in the Episcopal Church that which is taught in the classroom often bears little relation to the compelling message of the Prayer Book. We, too, have not entirely escaped. . . .

Authentic Christianity

When God walks upon the scene we are ready for the Christianity of the Bible. Then we realize that all along we may have been like Adam and Eve, hiding ourselves *from the presence of the Lord God amongst the trees of the garden. And the Lord God called unto Adam, and said unto him, "Where art thou?"*

But to begin a dialogue with God, at least with the God of the Bible, will be a different experience from that of moral self-culture. Like Isaiah, when first he saw the Lord *high and lifted up* we, too, may cry, *Woe is me! for I am undone; because I am a man of unclean lips.* We begin our dialogue with the realization of the gulf between ourselves and the maker of heaven and earth. This may lead to coming into judgment, to confession and repentance, and the wonders of conversion, and to rebirth into a life of the redeemed people of God.

To explore these mysteries and wonders, however, is not the purpose of this introductory essay. Here it is proper merely to indicate how true Christianity, with its God of holiness and judgment, but also with its Saviour Christ on His redeeming Cross, alone can give meaning to the very religion of moral idealism which has become its secular rival. Like the son in the great parable of the

Gospel, our "prodigal-son culture" needs to return to the home whence it departed. The fulfillment which it vainly sought in the far country, it will meet in its parental household. All other search for it will prove bitter illusion.

Christianity has a faith in God, not Man, as the chief actor in the drama of salvation. The Gospel of God or the gospel of ideals, there lies the contrast. What, in fact, can ideals do for you? Yes, even the ideals of the Sermon on the Mount or the figure of the Christ as nothing more than a biographical model to be imitated by our puny strength? You cannot pray to ideals. You cannot repent before them and receive the grace of forgiveness. You are on your own. They may dazzle you in their isolated splendor. You may endow them with the aura of divinity, and even call them God, but they will not come down out of their empyrean heaven to rescue the fallen and the broken in heart.

But let the God of the Bible and of the majestic faith of the Church march upon the scene, and see what happens to ideals. They are transformed into commandments. They become the Law handed down amidst the thunders and lightnings of Mount Sinai. *Thou shalt*, and *Thou shalt not*. No ideals ever spoke in tones such as these. Divine commandments bear the sanctions of eternity. Obedience or disobedience now means life or death; life with God or exile from His presence. The Sermon on the Mount, too, ceases to be a mere blueprint of idealistic perfection. This, too, becomes law, the demand of holiness voiced by God Himself in the flesh.

Does this bring judgment upon the scene? Of course it does. It brings before us heaven or hell, eternal life or eternal lostness. What we called our shortcomings now we know as sin. And the wages of sin is death. But the very concepts of sin and judgment are already tokens of divine love, a love of which a religion of ideals has not even dreamed. The universe itself is mindful of our actions. God cares. He would not judge if He did not care. *Man that is born of a woman,* so Job addresses the judging God, *is of few days and full of trouble. He cometh forth like a flower, and is cut down; he fleeth also as a shadow, and continueth not. And dost thou open thine eyes upon such an one, and bringest me into judgment with thee?*

The commandments of this judging, holy God are but the setting for His love. They reveal to us our state as sinners. The Law is only the beginning of Christianity's good news. Against that setting there looms the drama of redemption, the mighty acts of the Incarnation and the Cross summarized in the Christian creeds. In that story the Christ is no longer a mere exemplar of ideals or of perfectionist humanity, but a Saviour. He is now Son of God Himself, God of God, Light of Light, Very God of Very God. He is One whom men nail on a cross, but who rises from a tomb, returns to heaven and now rules over the universe. Nor does the story end there. A redeemed people of God carry on the divine life upon earth. The Church becomes the colony of heaven. Christianity's Gospel becomes good news, not merely good advice.

And note what happens to the perfectionist ideals which secularized Christianity has made a substitute for God. Are they lost out of sight? Not at all. They first, as already indicated, become commandments of the Maker of heaven and earth. The whole power of the universe stands behind them. They are no longer mere dreams which we can alter at our will. But neither are they laws which we cannot possibly obey. If we repent, and experience the joy of God's forgiveness, we discover the miraculous fact that, because of our gratitude to God, we actually want to obey His laws. Prodigal sons, returned home, find joy in the life of obedience. The Christian Church is, in fact, a fellowship of forgiven prodigal sons. When we find ourselves forgiven, we find it possible to forgive our fellow men. Men and women begin to exhibit Christ-like love toward one another. Here is an imitation of Christ—yes, an imitation of God, which no religion of ideals, with all its noblest striving, can ever produce. Self-salvation has given place to God-salvation. . . .

A Hopeful Fact

Is our indictment of the religious illiteracy of our time too severe? Is there hope for us despite our neglect of Christian education? Yes, great hope. An analysis of our state will be incomplete without a reminder of our resources.

Above all, we have the Church herself. We are already members of the colony of heaven. And our membership in the Church did not depend upon educational requirements. Most of us were baptized as children, totally ignorant of the treasures of grace showered upon us. Most of us have been nurtured in Christian homes, and have participated in the common life of the people of God. We may not have realized what was happening to us. But we were being grafted into a fellowship possessing powers undreamt of in any other society on this earth. We have, however, taken the privilege of being Christians for granted.

Special privileges have been ours in the Episcopal Church. The Church has a peculiar treasure in the Book of Common Prayer. As this little volume has gradually become familiar to us, perhaps from earliest childhood onward, we have become heirs of an inexhaustible tradition of the Church's worship through the centuries, a tradition going back to the days of the Apostles. The prayers of the Book of Common Prayer have implanted themselves in our memory, as have the songs in our hymnals. Our subconscious grasp of Christian faith and life has been greater than we knew.

Why, then, if all this is true, should religious illiteracy be a serious concern? An honest reply could grant at once that if a choice is ever forced upon us, Church as against classroom, the classroom must take a subordinate rank. We do not become Christians by memorizing textbooks. Millions of Christians have lived and died as redeemed children of God who may have never even been taught to read and write. But we are not illiterate. We do not live our secular lives in a mental vacuum. Emptiness of mind is equally impossible for our life as Christians. We must acquire a conscious understanding of our faith or else a rival pagan religion will take its place.

Christian Education's Revival

The members of the Episcopal Church are not the only modern Christians who suffer from ignorance of their faith. The whole Christian world is awakening to a realization that it is today facing gigantic rivals and that it can no longer remain unarmed against them. In the Episcopal Church such an awakening, however, is going to prove costly, since our neglect of Christian education has been conspicuous.

A hopeful sign of revival is the fact that confessions of neglect are being heard on all sides in the Church today. These are not limited to the clergy. Lay people in large numbers are realizing their ignorance and that of their children and are asking the leaders of the Church for help in the recovery of Christian nurture. Nor has this cry gone unheeded. The National Council, through a reconstituted Department of Christian Education, has, within the past three years, formulated a statesmanlike plan for the rebuilding of the educational resources of the whole Church. This will touch every group in the Church, from the very youngest to the oldest.

The National Council's Department has called into conference many professional leaders in Christian education, and large projects are already launched. These include the preparation of educational material for use at home by parents of pre-school children; a plan for a carefully graded new curriculum for the growing child; study courses for the youth of the Church, and for mature adults. Fragments of this project are even now available in published form, though the comprehensive whole must be thought of as only in its infancy. Institutes for the training of the clergy in their difficult educational task are part of the larger plan.

The Church's Teaching

This pamphlet is an introduction to a series of books on the Church's faith and practice designed for lay people. The need for such a series arose in this wise. When the large educational project came to be seen in perspective, it was quickly realized that one of the first needs of the Church was a setting forth, in the form of simple textbooks, of the basic content of the Church's faith. Such a series of basic volumes will answer several needs. Those entrusted with writing new courses for Church School children require a guide to what the Christian faith, as the Episcopal Church holds it, really is. Church School teachers, in their turn, have long expressed a desire for help in securing background information for their weekly task in the classroom. Confirmation classes, particularly for adult candidates, could use such a series, as could students in college. Nor need dreams of a revived study of Christian truth be limited to the young. Adult education is making large strides in popularity today all over America. Why should the Church lag behind secular enthusiasts for the reading of great books?

Theodore O. Wedel, *The Church's Teaching: An Introduction* (New York: National Council, Protestant Episcopal Church, 1949), 5-10, 16-19, 21-23. (Excerpts)

94.

John M. Gessell, The Urgency of the Church's Educational Task: Prolegomena to Any Future Theology of Christian Education, 1961

John Maurice Gessell (June 17, 1920–   ) was associate rector of Grace Church, Salem, Massachusetts, when this document was written. He was editor of the St. Luke's Journal of Theology, *1976-1990, and a member of the faculty of the School of Theology of the University of the South, 1961-1984. In this writing he discusses education relative to living in Christian community.*

That our children may live or die depending on how we carry out our educational responsibility should be a matter of great urgency for us all. We are in principle dedicated to the care and nurture of our children and to teaching them all things which they as Christians need to know and believe to their soul's health. The health of their souls will determine whether they will live or die.

At the moment it appears as though the Church wished to ignore these facts of religious life. The result could be a generation of stillborn children growing up with little inner knowledge of the meaning of the Christian religion in their lives. The central fact which underlies all Christian education is that finite human existence is not self-authenticating. Its authentication comes only from the relationship we have to God as the unlimited ground and support of all life. How this may come to be known, not as an idea but as inner reality, is the central purpose of all Christian education.

There is a double edged quality to this urgency about the Church's educational task. It may well be that one of the crucial problems in the educational situation in the Church is its unwillingness to face the implications of the Gospel in its own life now. It would be better, however, to speak not of "the Church," but of "we" or "I" in this situation. To make Church the problem will make it possible to ignore the fact that the urgency about the task and its undertaking lies in the hands of concerned persons. The focus of this essay on Christian education must be perceived by people who are willing to assume their responsibility.

The focus itself lies in the problem concerned with how people learn. It is as simple as that, but the simplicity is deceptive. We have apparently been concerned about this issue now for some fifteen years and yet seem, as a Church, to have moved very little toward its resolution. Further, this is an educational issue in which the whole Church has a concern but will never know it unless it can enter into the issue realistically and with a sense of urgency. To be able to enter into it will mean to face up to the issues in our own lives and then to do something about it so that children may live and not die.

. . . .

VII The Dynamics of Christian Education

What should we be seeking to do as we teach? There are four things which go on in the educational process if we are truly able to enter into the task. These are:

> **1.** Living some real life together, coming into contact with ourselves and with each other at some specific point of concern.
>
> **2.** By reflecting upon it, recognising, identifying and describing the nature of this life lived together and the nature of the problem and the concern.
>
> **3.** Discovering the symbols that emerge which can interpret the meaning of this life and bear the power which will hold it together and relate it to the wider focus of our religious heritage.
>
> **4.** Ordering all that goes on by catching it up into the ongoing life of the Church where it comes into the deepest focus of meaning and expression.

In any educational process these four things all go on at the same time. The Church at its best has always carried on its educational task in this way. But we are at a point in the Church's life where we need to be able to do this with consciousness as well as within a known discipline and structure. We begin where life is, where it is being lived as indicated in (1) above. All the other levels of the process follow from this and take on meaning.

The chief disaster comes when the symbols of the Christian Church get talked about alone and abstractly without any apparent connection with the life and the concerns of the people involved, and without the benefit of the disciplined process of identifying and describing the life out of which the symbols emerged. So much of the Church's educational effort is perversely this kind of juggling the symbols as objects of teaching instead of helping people to discover them in their own lives. Yet this is precisely what we dare not do if we want the symbols to continue to speak and to be the bearers of the power and grace of God to our lives.

The task of problem recognition and identification as indicated in (2) above is an education discipline only within which we can discover for ourselves the symbolic forms which are our inheritance and which can speak to us, too.

Let's take a brief look into this. A woman comes out from Church following the service saying to herself, "That's the most unfriendly place I've ever been in. I won't go there again." An eighth grade girl refuses to sing with the choir because it means wearing nylons to Church school and the boys whistle after her. A man watches his co-workers go off together, and then heads for a nearby bar where he spends the evening before returning to his rooming house. A child becomes separated from his parents in the crowd leaving the circus tent and stands in terror until grasped by a familiar hand. Two small boys playing together get into a fist fight. One of them runs crying to their mother and the other just stands and watches her wondering what will happen to him.

Judy arrives as a baby, a little Miss Nobody who some people are concerned about because they know the necessity that she become a little Miss Someone. "Name this child." "Judith." "Judith, I baptize thee in the Name of the Father, and of the Son, and of the Holy Ghost. Amen." Now she is someone, a very important small person with her own place in the structure of the universe. Several years later on a Sunday morning as the rector was presenting the offering on behalf of the congregation and everyone was singing "All things come of thee, O Lord," Judith was seen very quietly moving up the aisle, up the chancel steps, and up to where the rector stood before the altar. Judy wanted something; some people felt they knew what it was; others probably didn't have any idea but smiled at the picture it presented; others probably thought the child should never have been there at all.

What is important is that Judy felt so much that she belonged there that she could go right up and tug on the rector's surplice in the middle of service. This was important to her. These were her people and it should be important to them, even though they did not understand what she wanted. The trumpet sounded as one small girl went forward to present her request. The congregation was changed, if only for a moment. "All things come of thee, O Lord, and of thine own have we given thee."

Is there a single common denominator running through all of this? It would be the common denominator of belonging to something or to someone. The first woman was sensitive to not being a part and felt an essential denial in her life. The eighth-grader would give up something she very much enjoyed rather than feel separated from her peers. The man spent his evening in a bar in his search for companions. The child felt the terror of separation from his own people. And the small boy wondered if he is still "at one" with his mother.

Judy knows she has a place that is rightfully hers because it was given to her at baptism. She is Judith who lives among people who support her in her travels up to the sanctuary. Judy has none of these thoughts in her mind. She simply knows that it was all right, that people might smile with her and for her, but not at her. It is up to the adults to recognise the religious implications of this and what sort of thing they are saying by their actions as they meet other people.

While it is obvious that all of these events can be seen on the surface level, they can also be seen as significant events in the lives of the people for whom they happen. Our task has this deeper implication. We are involved in the very stuff of which life is made—the whole meaning of our existence. This meaning is discovered in these simple situations.

There is danger for all these people, that they may never find their place and the meaning of their lives and the power to be themselves as God created them in the ongoing life of the holy fellowship. There is danger that the meaning of their experiences may never appear for them. There is danger that they may be so protected that they will never know the threat of the existence, of finitude and of freedom. There is danger that we will never learn that we must enter into our life and its destiny at the point of the Cross if we are to become new creatures in Christ and partakers with Him in His Resurrection.

The task of Christian education is further developed as we discover the symbols of the life which we are living as they arise in relation to that life as indicated in (3) above. These symbols emerge and focus our life together, reflecting it in its meaning, interpreting it, and knitting it together with the grace of God who is its author. Our task is to help our children see in the Bible and Prayer Book these reflections. If we have been able to do this for ourselves, we shall be able to do it for them and willing to live with them into their own experiences.

In this way the symbolic forms of the Church, our heritage and the common inheritance of the people of whom we are a part, are understood as the "kind of language in which a group of people understands itself." The Church's Creed is one of its primary symbols and this is a kind of language in which the fellowship of the Christian Church understands itself. (It is most definitely not the kind of language in which we understand God, for God is not thus to be measured by our understanding. Thus we do not ask children to learn the Creed and assume that thereby they know all about God. The Creed is man's understanding of his own experience of God.)

As the Church itself is discovered to be a holy fellowship and the guardian of our precious heritage as the sons of God by adoption and grace, it is seen in a broader sense in its history as the form of man's coming into touch with his own life's meaning both in time and in eternity. The life we lead together is caught up into this structure of the holy fellowship and given articulate form and meaning as indicated by (4) above. Thus we may be able to speak to others the wonderful works of God.

It is on this understanding that we say that the curriculum for Christian education is basically the life of the parish itself. It is there that we have our primary experience of Church. In this experience, as we face concrete situations, we are engaged in a learning process. This informal curriculum is always in need of formalisation through the conscious discipline of the educational process in itself. Let us examine this proposition.

The real curriculum of the Church is reflected in the total life of a given parish as an organism. It is always the parish, in connection with home, that does the real teaching of the rising generation. This process goes on all the time regardless of what we plan to do in a parish house class room. Religion happens wherever decisions are being made in the course of daily living. The decisions we make determine the shape and meaning of our lives.

Thus a primary issue in Christian education is the shape of the curriculum. This has to do with the dynamics of the parish and not necessarily with the materials which may be used in teaching. Educational materials may be created out of the dynamics of parish life. This is to say that we start with life, where it is being lived, at the points especially where people are under pressure, face problems, make decisions. The faith context within which this life gets lived is that offered by the parish church, be it good or bad.

True and dynamic Christian education must help people to interpret the meaning of their lives in the context of the actual experiences and decisions they are called upon to make in their daily lives. Obviously our children are interpreting the meaning of their lives on some basis or other and this basis is provided for Church people by their parish Church. We must carefully question what we are teaching our children here, for this is far more dynamic and vital learning than the often irrelevant learning going on in the classrooms.

The parish Church itself is therefore called upon to make a decision as to what kind of basis it proposes to present to its people for the interpretation of their lives. . . .

John M. Gessell, "The Urgency of the Church's Educational Task: Prolegomena to Any Future Theology of Christian Education" [unpublished], 1961, 1, 24-27. (Excerpts)

95.

John H. Westerhoff III,
Challenge to Church Educators, 1974

John Henry Westerhoff III (June 28, 1933–   ) was professor of religious education at Duke University Divinity School, Durham, North Carolina. He is a leading Christian educator. In this selection he challenges the church to an educational revival.

The church is required continually to judge and reorder its life so that its people can be captured by a vision of God's kingdom and inspired and supported in ways which enable them to join God in his history-making. That struggle for reformation is what I mean by adult resocialization. There may have been a time when persons could simply be brought up as Christians, never knowing themselves as anything else. There may have been a time when the church was naturally a community of Christian faith. That just isn't true today. A reformation that builds new faith communities is essential. The resocialization of adults into the Christian faith is also essential. The two go together, for without new faithful communities we will not be able to resocialize adults; without resocialized adults we will be without the necessary faithful communities. We cannot do one unless at the same time we do the other.

Adult resocialization in the Christian faith can only take place in a particular sort of community. It is a community which has conscious goals, aims, purposes, objectives, and conviction. It is a community of converted persons—those what have had their lives turned around—who, being aware of the life they were unconsciously socialized into as children and the required life of a disciple, have consciously chosen the latter and committed themselves to live and act in a supporting community which shares their understandings and commitment. It is a community with shared experiences, self-understanding, and vision. It is a community which has a faith it wants to tell and do and is thus willing to sacrifice all the world's praise and benefits on behalf of a life of faithfulness. The church has in moments of history been that sort of community, and men and women have left everything behind to give their individual lives to its corporate action in history as an agent of God's kingdom-building.

Only as we unite the inner and outer search of persons with the quest for self-knowledge and social justice will we be faithful to our Lord. Bound by a common vision and a commitment to a new future for personkind and nature, the Christian is liberated from the prison of what is and motivated by what yet can be. No longer can we Christians consider ourselves victims of history. Rather we are to know ourselves as molders of history. No longer can we perceive life as a matter of adaptation. Rather we are to understand life as transformation. Such perceptions are as possible as any other. It is simply a matter of deciding what communities we will join and commit our lives to. For it is within such chosen communities that we are socialized and reshaped.

If as adults we have come to realize the bankruptcy of our lives as we have been socialized to live them, then it is time for us to unite with others who share our desire for new life and so live together as to resocialize ourselves into new understandings and ways.

Socialization is not only for children. Today we are in a period when many aspects of enculturation which have been blessed by the church are recognized as corrupt. The times call for a new reformation, a reformation that will bring into being new communities of faith where the resocialization of adults can take place. Only then will the church be able once again to nurture the next generation in the faith.

We need a revival, not of the sort supported by some evangelical conservative or fundamentalistic movement but a revival in our liberal, socially concerned, and committed churches. We have lost our nerve in the quest for popularity, our motivation in the ignoring of our biblical-theological roots, and our commitment in the frustration of not achieving instant gratification. Our times require a revival and a reformation in the church. Only then will those new communities of faith which are necessary for the resocialization of adults into Christian faith and life be possible.

John H. Westerhoff III and Gwen Kennedy Neville, *Generation to Generation: Conversations on Religious Education and Culture* (Philadelphia: United Church Press, 1974), 157-159. (Excerpt)

96.

Education for Ministry, Theological Reflection, 1979

Education for Ministry (EFM) is a program of lay theological education administered by the School of Theology Extension Center, the University of the

South. Education for Ministry began in 1976 and is a four-year program based on specially prepared texts and theological reflection in a small group with a mentor. It is designed for lay persons who want a deeper knowledge of the Christian tradition and training for ministry. This section on theological reflection is from the Manual for Mentors, *a guide for those who will lead and facilitate the group learning process of EFM. The* Manual *has been revised frequently and this selection is from a later revision.*

Theological reflection is a task of the whole church. Biblical scholars and church historians dedicate their lives to ensuring that we have clear access to the light of the tradition, unclouded by the biases of our culture. Theologians look to tradition to illuminate issues and questions raised by our contemporary world. In our day these responsibilities are carried out chiefly by professional academics. Their work is vital for the task of theological reflection, but it is only a small part of the work of the church as a whole. The responsibility for the greater part of theological reflection lies with the *laos,* the people of God.

> *We receive you into the household of God. Confess the faith of Christ crucified,*
> *proclaim his resurrection, and share with us in his eternal priesthood.*

These words from *The Book of Common Prayer* (p. 308) greet each newly baptized person in the Episcopal Church. To whom do we confess Christ crucified? How do we proclaim his resurrection in our communities? What does it mean to share in his priesthood? To address these questions is to embark on the task of theological reflection.

Theological Reflection and EFM

Theological reflection is a major component of the Education for Ministry program, because it is a path the journeying Christian can take to reach the point where faith and daily life converge.

Christian doctrine asserts that the gospel is relevant to all persons; its truth is universal to all cultures; it offers each person meaning and purpose; and in it, there is comfort and strength. The church makes all these claims and more. Yet sometimes it is difficult to perceive and understand how these claims relate to our experience. There is often a tremendous gap between Christian teaching and an individual's personal experience of truth. Closing that gap is a vital concern for all committed Christians.

A major task facing the church, especially in the twentieth century, has been to demonstrate its relevance to personal experience, its claims to universal truth, its assertion that each person has a purpose, and its promise of God's comforting and strengthening power. EFM provides an opportunity for people to reflect on questions of life's basic meaning. How do Christian teachings connect with people's lives? How can Christians be bearers of truth in a pluralistic society? How can all persons have meaning and purpose when each is only one individual among billions? How can there be strength and comfort given when one feels so much pain and sorrow?

Bridging the gaps between life and Christian teaching presents a great challenge. The EFM program offers students a model and some methods of theological reflection to link their own experience with the story of the people of God so they may become more confident, effective, and faithful ministers of the gospel.

An Example of Theological Reflection

Theological reflection occurs naturally and spontaneously throughout the church as committed Christian people read the Bible, participate in worship, struggle to find meaning in the events of their lives, and discuss their beliefs, hopes, and fears. Here is one example from an adult class which met before the main worship service on Sundays. The theme of the class was the Trinity. The class had widely differing understandings of the place of the Holy Spirit in the doctrine of the Trinity. The leader drew on John Taylor's book on the Holy Spirit, the *Go-Between God,* for a contemporary explanation of the Holy Spirit. The following quotation from page 19 produced a strong reaction from some of the participants:

> *The Holy Spirit is that power which opens eyes that are closed, hearts that are unaware and minds that shrink from too much reality. If one is open towards God, one is open also to the beauty of the world, the truth of ideas, and the pain of disappointment and deformity. If one is closed up against being hurt, or blind towards one's fellow-men, one is inevitably shut off from God also. One cannot choose to be open in one direction and closed in another.*

"That's nonsense!" was one response. "There are a few people at work who are quite impossible. I have closed myself to them completely, and God is certainly the most important thing in my life. In fact, Jesus tells us to shake the dust off our feet when we are not treated with hospitality."

"I don't think Jesus meant us to shut out our neighbors though," said another member.

A third person chimed in, "I was at a stress reduction clinic last week, and the presenter emphasized the importance of letting go of the resentments and hostility we feel toward others. That seems to support what Taylor is saying."

The discussion continued until it was time for the service to begin. The leader wondered how many of those present had changed their positions in the slightest. On the way home after the worship service, she thought of some of the people in her own life against whom she felt quite closed. "What is the truth of the matter?" she wondered. "God does seem so close to me in the beauty I see all around me, but I know how little I really am able to open myself to others." That evening, as she always did, she said the Lord's prayer before going to sleep. As she came to the part "forgive us our sins as we forgive those who sin against us," she remembered someone she had been angry with for a long time. She felt her heart soften, and she became more willing to forgive him and, in turn, to receive God's forgiveness.

The leader had allowed herself to entertain a conversation which embraced material from a number of different sources: the quotation from John Taylor, the events in her own life, her experience of the Lord's prayer, and her own beliefs. What we mean by theological reflection is the kind of conversation that allows our understanding and our actions genuinely to change.

The EFM Four Source Model for Theological Reflection

Sources have long been important for theological learning. Richard Hooker, a 16th century Anglican theologian, used three sources: scripture, tradition, and reason. Paul Tillich, a 20th century theologian, indicated that the theologian's sources are the Bible, church history, history of religion, and culture (cf., *Systematic Theology*, I, 40). Contemporary theologian John Macquarrie, while disliking the term "sources," lists six "formative factors": experience, revelation, scripture, tradition, culture, and reason *(Principles of Christian Theology,* 1st ed., 4). Our experience with the program indicates that theological reflection is more likely to occur if we are careful to distinguish among four sources: *Action, Position, Culture,* and *Tradition.* In this discussion we have been alluding to these four sources. Now we will define them explicitly.

The *Action* source involves that which we do and experience. The specific actions we take, as well as the thoughts, feelings, and perspectives associated with the actions, come from this source. In constructing our spiritual autobiographies, we work principally with the *Action* source. We remember past events and weave them into a pattern that tells our life stories. We say, "I remember . . ." or "My thoughts were. . ." or "I felt. . ." And we say, "Then I walked to . . ." or "I did. . . ."

The *Position* source refers to that for which we consciously argue our attitudes, opinions, beliefs, and convictions. Phrases beginning, "I believe . . . ," "I know that . . . ," "That's the way it is . . . ," and "It's true that . . ." indicate that we are drawing from the *Position* source. Included here are tentative opinions as well as passionately held convictions.

The *Culture* source encompasses almost all the objective content available to us. The libraries of the world contain material that is in the *Culture* source. The attitudes and opinions generally held in a society also fall within this source. Phrases like, "They say . . . ," "Medical opinion is unanimous that . . . ," and "Carl Jung says . . ." indicate that a person is drawing from the *Culture* source.

The *Tradition* source refers to the content of the Christian heritage. It begins with the Bible and extends to the liturgies, stories, documents, music, artifacts, and history of Christianity. The *Tradition* source contains the literature that the Christian community has designated as authoritative. In addition to conveying truth and meaning, the contents of the *Tradition* source evoke awareness of the Holy, experiences of awe, or a sense of God's presence. Phrases like, "The Bible says . . ." and "According to the Prayer Book . . ." mark this source. The EFM program provides a four-year presentation of the *Tradition* through the students' reading material.

It is useful both to distinguish among these sources and to notice where they overlap. We draw on each source as we try to make sense of the world around us. Each source functions as a kind of framework within which we interpret our experience. Often we keep these frameworks separate from one another. For example, what happens to us at work may lead to quite cynical conclusions about human nature. We may keep these conclusions altogether apart from how we view life as a family member or as a member of the church. In theological reflection we bring together these different ways of looking at the world. We look at each of the four sources so that our entire understanding may be informed by the Christian Tradition.

Theological Reflection in a Group

A complete reflection moves naturally through four phases: identifying, exploring, connecting, and applying. The specific methods which EFM has developed for use in its seminars are all designed to facilitate this progression. Before describing any method in detail, we will give a broad overview of the four phases.

Identifying

During the first phase of reflection the subject is identified. This may be something that has happened to the student, a particular belief the student holds, something from our Christian tradition, or an aspect of contemporary culture. Before we can begin, we need to name the subject. What exactly are we going to talk about? Where does it begin? Where does it end? How are we involved?

The more theological reflection begins from a sharply defined focus, the more likely it is that the reflection will shape the understanding and the actions of the participants. Using the "theology of the Psalms" as a starting point for reflection is likely to lead to a very general discussion. However, using the first two verses of Psalm 37, for example, provides much finer focus:

Fret not yourself because of the wicked, be not envious of wrongdoers! For they will soon fade like the grass, and wither like the green herb.

Dealing with a particular passage makes it more likely that our partner in conversation will be the tradition itself and not merely our opinions about the tradition. Similarly, when the starting point for reflection is an experience from our life, it is important to describe that experience with specificity and clarity in order to avoid merely rehashing previously held positions. The focus that is chosen for reflection should not only be clearly identified, but it should also matter to the participants. Whether the reflection begins with *Action*, *Tradition*, *Culture*, or *Position*, the focus should engage the interest and attention of the group members. Unless this happens, the reflection is likely to lack energy.

Exploring

The second phase explores the subject which has been identified. What is it like? What language best describes it? What do we discover as we examine it from different vantage points? If the subject has been raised by some life event, what does this event say to us about our world? If we are reflecting on some belief that we hold, to what does this belief apply? What assumptions and values are implicit in the belief? If our starting point is a text from the Christian tradition or our contemporary culture, what do we find when we get inside the world of the text? What does the text say to us on its own terms?

As we explore the subject of our reflection, we will often find it useful to use the language of metaphor. Using an image or metaphor deliberately encourages the evocative, intuitive quality of exploration.

Connecting

The third phase makes connections between what has been discovered so far and the wider sources of meaning and truth. A reflection becomes theological by making deliberate connections between the Christian tradition and our own experience. Christian theological reflection links the Christian heritage with the personal and cultural dimensions of our lives. In this phase we are interested in the following general categories of questions:

• How does our exploration of this particular subject fit with our beliefs, with the scriptures, and with the creeds of the church?

• Does our exploration test out in everyday life? What would others in our family or work say about this?

The questions above are too broad to be of much practical help. More sharply defined questions help us connect and compare one source with another. A particularly helpful question is one which moves us right inside the subject of our exploration so that we can see what things look like from this perspective. We refer to questions like these as *perspective questions*. An example follows:

- *What kind of world* is depicted in the first two verses of Psalm 37? It is a world in which there are wrongdoers, and the wrongdoers sometimes flourish, but not for long. The question *"What kind of world?"* gives us a structure for developing a conversation with other sources of meaning. For example, we can think back to our own experiences with wrongdoers. Have they in fact "faded away like the grass?" What kind of world do we seem to inhabit when we look at what happens to us and at how we actually behave?

Then we can move from questioning the *Action* source in this way to questioning the *Culture* source. What is the wisdom about wrongdoers in the magazines we read? What kind of world do our newspapers' editorial pages assume? And what of our own *Position*? What do we really believe about the place of wrongdoers in the world we inhabit?

The above example illustrates *"What kind of world?"* as a question that allows us to explore the perspective associated with a particular source and then structure a conversation with elements from other sources by asking the same question of those other sources. A question focuses our attention on a particular aspect of a given source.

In the EFM program we frequently use perspective questions designed to investigate the doctrinal themes of *Creation, Sin, Judgment,* and *Redemption*. *"What kind of world?"* is a question which opens up our perspective on the doctrine of *Creation*. *(See also* "Specific Steps of the Microscope Method," pages 38-39.)

Applying

The final phase of theological reflection deals with the insights gleaned from conversation among the sources and with the implications for action decided by each individual on the basis of these insights. A desired outcome of theological reflection is a renewed understanding of what it means to be one of God's ministers in the world. To this end students take their insights and learnings from the reflection and apply them to their lives and ministries. Sometimes this involves a clear direction for action. More often the resulting application clarifies their questions, thereby preparing them to explore further their study of the Christian tradition. During this phase of reflection, questions fall into the following general categories:

- How can I apply my learnings and questions?
- What am I being called to do differently?
- What do I want to take into our time of prayer?

The more specific each student can be about the next small step necessary to apply the insights gained, the more likely it is that the reflection will be of lasting value.

Education for Ministry: Manual for Mentors (Sewanee, Tenn.: School of Theology Extension Center, The University of the South, 1991), 29-33. (Excerpt)

CHAPTER ELEVEN

Theological Shifts and Changes (1895-1934)

Introduction

The theological and intellectual world was blown open by the shifts and changes of the post-Civil War era. Charles Darwin's theory of evolution seemed to shake the very foundations of Biblical faith by challenging a literal understanding of creation. The scientific method brought discoveries and inventions, but the scientific method was also applied to scripture through "higher criticism." Reason seemed to be at odds with faith, and the foundations of religion seemed to be in question. Many faithful church members felt threatened and challenged. New concepts and ways of theology were needed to express the faith relative to the concerns and questions of the time. New theologies emerged, with different approaches to the life of faith. This openness to new ways of discovering religious truth was invigorating for the church. The church sought theology that was open to the future but rooted in the traditions of faith.

97.

Francis A. Shoup, Paper on Evolution, 1895

Francis Asbury Shoup (March 22, 1834–September 4, 1896) served a number of parishes in the South. At the time this paper was presented at the sixteenth Church Congress, Boston, he was rector of St. Peter's Church, Columbia, Tennessee. Also in Tennessee in this era was the sensational Scopes *trial, which was the focal point for the American controversy over evolution. In that case a public high school teacher was brought to trial for teaching evolution in a science class. Shoup's paper deals with evolution in the context of reason, history, and faith.*

400

The doctrine or principle of evolution is as old as speculative thought. There never was a time when an ordinary sequence and causal dependence of the phenomena of the world were not recognized, when it was not held that the higher and more complex forms of existence follow, and somehow result from, the lower and more simple. Not only in the material world, but in the domain of life and mind, there has always been the contention that there is a gradual unfolding from the inchoate and uniform to the special and varied, and that the progress of man, as an individual and as a race, has been conditioned by, and is dependent upon, the transitions in physical nature.

This sequence and correlation is too obvious in the history of the human race to admit of question; and it is especially marked in that most marvellous of all historical phenomena the Christian faith. The distinguishing characteristic of the Old Testament scriptures is their Messianic foreshadowing, and preparation for the stupendous fact of the Incarnation of the Son of God—a movement without which the Gospel of Jesus Christ would be incomprehensible to us; and the Catholic faith, in like way, shows the same unfolding of the definite and exact from the general and undefined. It is, therefore, far too late for the theologian to denounce evolution, at least in universal or unmeasured terms.

Space does not permit even a mention of the many phases of the theory of evolution, from Aristotle, not to go further back, through Descartes and Leibnitz, Harvey, Buffon, Lamarck, and a host of others, to Darwin and Wallace, including the speculations of Spencer and Haeckel. For our purpose all the theories may be thrown into two classes; first, those which deny, or at least declare that there is no need for, an original creative power; and, second, those which recognize, with greater or less distinctness, an ultimate source of all energy—an original cause of the cosmos.

With regard to the first class there is small room for an argument from design, or, as it seems to me, for an argument of any sort. I am free to confess that I do not understand the philosophy of the unconscious, and have no capacity for the apprehension of Hartmann and his school when they declare that creation is a mistake, and being, such as we know it, is not as good as non-being, and death better than life. Such words as "mistake," "good," "better," indeed, their whole vocabulary, have no meaning for me except in the domain of the conscious, and I cannot understand except through the understanding. If that school has a power through which they rise superior to ordinary thought processes, I am not so happy, and give it up at the start. If, however, we may be permitted to use our ordinary logical powers,—they seem to have no better,—this evolution of the conscious out of the unconscious leads to extraordinary results. For example, there was a time, as these men are fond of telling us, when there was no such being as man on the earth, but, as they themselves declare, the whole movement of the phenomenal world pointed on to, and prophesied of, his coming. There was no *human* consciousness in existence to read those signs; and if thought and personality did not exist somewhere or somehow, in the universe, they were unread and utterly meaningless for countless ages; that is to say, we have the most stupendous design, with an infinitude of details all working together in the most beautiful correlation toward a concerted end, without a designer or contriver in existence! Now, if the greatest of all possible designs was accomplished without thought or purpose, what is the use of thought, and how is effort better than non-effort? What is the use of the power to note the relation of things, and of purpose to order and control events to ends, if these powers and this correlation and the ends themselves could be produced without the comprehension of how one thing bears upon and effects another? But I suppose I am only showing that I do not understand—unhappy word!—the superior in sight of those philosophers. At any rate, the doctrine is not new. There were those in the days of the prophet Isaiah who claimed to be able to reach the same depths, for we hear him asking; "Shall the work say to him that made it, He made me not? or the thing framed to him that framed it, He is without understanding?"

Again, these men profess to recognize the laws of induction and analogy, but surely they set them at naught at every turn. In all the broad round of phenomena did any man ever see a "fortuitous concourse" of elements producing useful or admirable results of themselves? Did anyone ever see iron and steel and brass, fire and water, rush together, without the guidance of thought and purpose, to produce a steam engine or a printing press? Even granting that the things we call "elements" are ready furnished at hand, yet man never saw materials combining to make anything. Whenever he is in the secret of the making, he always discovers that there has been what we call a personal element behind the production. If it be answered that this is not true in the processes of nature, the obvious reply is that that is the very point at issue, that it is a pure assumption, contrary to all analogy, that there is no thought power by which its processes are directed.

It may be asked,—it often is,—if this thought power and intelligence, may not be material—may it not be a more subtle physical element, like iron and wood, only infinitely refined, and so be part of the machine, after all? No, certainly not, if we use the word machine in its accepted sense. A machine is an instrument merely, and the notion of an instrument carries with it necessarily a power which uses it. For example, a loom is a machine for weaving textile fabrics; but a loom does not make cloth. Cloth is made by means of it. Man makes cloth. A machine, no matter to what degree of perfection it might be carried, could do nothing of itself. If in the category of its perfections it be demanded that it shall have the power to go into the fields and gather its own materials, discriminate as to the quality, devise the pattern of the fabric, and enjoy the pleasure of its beauties when made, in a word, become self-conscious and self-determining, it ceases to be a mere machine and becomes just what we mean by person. Man is such a machine, and if the old contention that the world is a conscious, self-ordering animal be maintained, we may not agree, but the incompatibilities complained of will be in some sort avoided.

In the second of the two classes into which we have roughly divided all evolutionists we have difficulties enough. An original, ineffable First Cause is granted, and the demand of the heart for an ultimate explanation of the cosmos is met; but when one comes to grapple with the "how," the trouble looms up, and refuses to be laid over again, except in the embrace of faith. We are thrown upon the mysteries of "being" and "becoming," and we are simply urging our finite capacities upon the work of understanding the infinite. Anyone who has had even a smattering of metaphysical training knows that a beginning is utterly incomprehensible; and that if one be so senseless as to insist upon comprehending the ultimate in the becoming, either as absolute beginning or as absolute end, he simply shows himself to be ignorant of the problem. From the days of Parmenides and Heraclitus this mystery has stood out in thought, and the problem is no easier today than it was in the heyday of Greek philosophy. Aristotle has pointed out that in every movement of the incomplete to the complete the latter antedates in conception the movement and is its motive. That is, the end is always at the beginning. It is manifest at a glance that there can be no purposive action in which the purpose or design does not precede the movement from the potential toward the actual. The savage who puts two sticks together to construct a fire sees the fire in his imagination before he moves a finger toward accomplishing the end. This is the sort of problem which the evolutionist must encounter in attempting an explanation of how this world came into existence. The only consolation in it all is that the difficulties do not present themselves until all the actual needs of practical life are met; and if one is content to carry the experience and simple logic of daily life into the solution of these higher problems, the conclusions are still simple; but one finds one's self in the domain of that theological virtue called faith.

The effort has been made, over and over again, to construct a theory of the cosmos which shall dispense with a creator. The most notable of such efforts in our day is that of Mr. Herbert Spencer. When he was about to put forth the first volume of his philosophy, he found himself in considerable perplexity to hit upon a satisfactory name for the unintelligent somewhat which he felt himself bound to postulate as the beginning and cause of all things. He believed firmly in an Original and Ultimate Cause, but he was unwilling to recognize in it any intelligence and purposive power. He wanted to express an "unconditional reality, without beginning or end," but he could find no word or phrase which did not imply what he was so anxious to exclude. In his perplexity, as he tells us in a note to the sixth chapter of "First Principles," he went to Professor Huxley and unfolded to him his trouble, and asked him to help him out. He could not permit himself, he explained, to use the word "energy," "since it is impossible to think of energy without something possessing the energy." He was unwilling to adopt "conservation of force," a phrase then in current use among scientific men, "because, first, conservation implies a conserver and an act of conserving; and, second, it does not imply the existence of the force before the particular manifestation of it which is contemplated." He goes on to say: "I may now add, as a further fault, the tacit assumption that, without some act of conservation, force would disappear."

He tells us that in place of conservation Professor Huxley suggested *persistence*, and adds: "This meets most of the objections, and though it may be argued against it that it does not directly imply pre-existence of the force at any time manifested, yet no other word less faulty in this respect can be found. In the absence of a word specially coined for the purpose it seems the best, and as such I adopt it."

This is how "persistent force" came to be the ultimate in Herbert Spencer's system. But since that day science has turned its back upon the word force, except in a conventional and apologetical way! There is now, in the opinion of the leaders of scientific thought, no such thing as force. Just as the danger Mr. Spencer was so apprehensive of,—namely, that "without some act of conservation force would disappear,"—has come to pass; and force, as an objective reality, has disappeared. Force is a phenomenon, an effect, like velocity, and needs a somewhat behind it to serve as its subject. Now, the only reality we know of without doubt as an original source of power is the self. We know in consciousness that we put forth effort and exert energy; and so it has come to pass that the scientific world has substituted "energy" for "force," and the phrase "conservation of force" has been abandoned for "conservation of energy," and the old *vis viva* of mechanics has disappeared in "kinetic energy." In all departments of engineering and mechanics we now have "push" and "pull," "thrust" and "strain," and "energy" and "work" to designate the actions and reactions of material objects upon each other, distinctly implying an ultimate source of personal power to which they are the manifestations. The scientific mind has come to see that while there is everywhere a manifestation of power, we really have no capacity to conceive of an original cause or source of power except in personality. This original creative power we do know at first hand in consciousness when overcoming resistances; and so science, perhaps without foreseeing the end at which it was arriving, has opened the way for men to recognize once more the Infinite Effort-Maker in the Lord of All Power and Might.

Mr. Spencer now freely uses the word "energy," and it is to be presumed that he is less anxious than he was thirty or forty years ago to shut out the possibility of an ultimate thought power. He now holds that his Ultimate "Cause, which transcends our knowledge and conception," is an "infinite and eternal energy." He says: "I held at the outset, and continue to hold, that the inscrutable existence which science in the last resort is compelled to recognize as unreached by its deepest analysis of matter, motion, thought, and feelings, stands toward our general conception of things in substantially the same relation as does the creative power asserted by theology."

He still hesitates to admit personality in this "inscrutable existence," lest it should be thereby limited. He would not degrade this source of "infinite and eternal energy" below personality, but raise it above and beyond it. This, I take it, is just what the theologian would do, if he had the power. But does not Mr. Spencer, by his hesitation to grant personality to this original source of power do just what he is so anxious to avoid ? To withhold the unquestionably highest attribute we can conceive of, personality, from what he does not scruple to call the "All-Being" is certainly to limit it, in so far, by negation. If he should grant it personality and more beyond, then he and the theologians are at one.

Let us try this teleological question further in the light of the best scientific thought. It is agreed by the analytical physicists that all phenomena of nature are resolvable into mass and motion; and the one branch of science to which all others look submissively is mechanics. The leaders are fearless and perfectly candid: and while they declare mass and motion to be the elements of all phenomena, they do not hesitate to admit that they do not know what they are. Motion, *per se*, is incomprehensible, and so is mass. The best that can be done by way of definition with regard to motion is to say that it is a phenomenon which discovers itself in bodies not at rest, without in the least knowing what rest is; and the one characteristic which, in the last analysis, remains with respect to mass is resistance, or inertia. But this, too, is a phenomenon; so that the foundations of mechanics are seen to be at best but phenomena. Phenomena of what? Not of themselves, of course; so that a somewhat is absolutely demanded as their ground. Matter, then, cannot be ultimate; and Herbert Spencer is distinct in repudiating what he calls "gross" or "brute" matter, declaring matter to be "as absolutely incomprehensible as sensation, or the conscious something which perceives it." This is the general voice of scientific men; Professor Romanes expresses it clearly when he says: " We cannot think of any of the facts of external nature without presupposing the existence of the mind which thinks them; and therefore, so far at least as we are concerned, mind is prior to anything else."

Again, the fundamental principle upon which the whole fabric of mechanics, and so of all science, rests is Newton's first law. By virtue of this law an inert object would lie just where it is forever if not disturbed by some form of energy. Its molecular state or constitution would never change unless acted upon by some mode of energy, converting potential into kinetic or the reverse. So also if a body be in motion, it must move in a right line with uniform velocity. That is to say, if this is a mere material world, there is no possibility of any change whatsoever, and the Eleatics were right. All change is a delusion, thought is a delusion, obligation is a figment, and the world is not ! But who and what says it? It is I, and in saying it I postulate the ego—I reaffirm the dictum of Descartes: *Cogito, ergo sum.* If it be admitted that there is such a thing as change in the world, it cannot be due to matter. There must be self-movement, which is the very contradictory of the inert. This is the property of life, and in the consciousness we know ourselves to be the original sources of change. Thus we arrive once more at personality as the necessary *prius* of the universe.

From all this we conclude that the argument from design is in no wise touched by the theory of evolution. It is simply one phase of the doctrine of causation, and causation is but the empirical phase of the infinite *Causi Sui.* This world is a real world, but it is, in mystery, the absolute fiat of Jehovah.

Not many years ago, in the French Academy, there was a remarkable utterance from a man whose fame is in all the world. M. Pasteur, who had been elected to the place made vacant by the death of M. Littré, the Comtist, on taking his seat, was pronouncing a eulogy, according to custom, upon his illustrious predecessor. He had given him all praise for the admirable abilities he had shown and the excellent work he had done, but when he came to speak of his religious opinions, M. Pasteur unequivocally declared his dissent. In explanation of his inability to accept the teachings of positivism he broke forth in the following exalted strain: "Beyond the starry vault above us, what is there? Other starry skies. Well, and beyond those? The human mind, swayed by an invincible impulse, will never cease to inquire what there is beyond; and there is no point in time and space which can set at rest the implacable question. It is no use to reply that beyond any given point there is boundless space, time, or magnitude. Such words convey no tangible meaning to the human mind. The man who proclaims the existence of the infinite,—and there is no man who does not,—accumulates in that bare statement more supernatural elements than are to be found in the miracles of all religions; for the nature of the infinite has this double character— that it is at once self-evident, that it forces itself upon the mind, and yet is incomprehensible. This positive and primordial notion, with all its consequences in the life of societies, positivism sets at naught. The Greeks understood the power of the unseen world. They have left us the noblest world in our language, 'enthusiasm,' εν θεος, an inner God. The greatest of human deeds can be measured by the inspiration that gives them birth. Happy the man who has an inner

God, an ideal of beauty, and who obeys his behests. The ideal of art, the ideal of science, the ideal of country, the ideal of the verities of the Gospel—those are the living sources of great ideas and deeds; they are illuminated by a gleam from the infinite."

It may be a long way off, but the time is surely coming when the scientific world will be most forward to do homage to the Lord of All Power and Might. There are many signs of it, and the great men who now stand professedly in the ranks of agnosticism, cannot conceal, at times, the unsteadiness of their footing. The following words of the late, and deservedly great, Professor Tyndall are a precursor of what is sure to come; he said: "it is no departure from the scientific method to place behind natural phenomena a Universal Father who in answer to the prayers of his children changes the currents of phenomena. Thus far theology and science go hand in hand."

Francis A. Shoup, "Paper," *Protestant Episcopal Church: Papers, Addresses, and Discussions at the Sixteenth Church Congress in the United States Held in the City of Boston, November 13, 14, 15 and 16, 1894* (New York: Thomas Whittaker, 1895), 187-193.

98.

William Porcher DuBose, The Church, 1917

William Porcher DuBose (April 11, 1836–August 18, 1918) was the first chaplain of the University of the South, 1871-1893, and the second dean of its School of Theology, July 31, 1894–June 24, 1908. He used evolution as a theological theme in this writing.

What is the Church? The God of Christianity cannot stop short with Himself; He must be God in His world—in all the "not Himself" that proceeds from Him, and that He would fill with Himself. The Christ of Christianity cannot stop short with Himself in heaven. The Christ of our *faith* is there,—because faith must see Him in the consummation and perfection of His part in the world. The Christ of our *hope* must be there, because hope too is of the end of our human participation with Him and in Him. But the Christ of the *process*—of the *all between* us and our faith and our hope—must be infinitely and awfully in the world and in ourselves, if His part is ever to be actually accomplished. In our faith and our hope we want Christ *there*—i.e., crowned and seated; but, for that, we first need Christ *here*—in the present fact, the stress and the strain, of the battle.

And He *is* here: The Church is as much the sacrament of His Presence, as His human Body was of the Presence, the Incarnation, of God in Himself. He is in us, *as* God was in Him; there is no difference in the act and fact of His oneness with us from that of God's oneness with Him—*other* than that which we place there by our want of faith in it. Christ's human oneness with God was an act of perfect human faith under perfectly human conditions: an act of faith consummated in and by an act of perfect faithfulness. In other words He realized or actualized His faith in *fact*: the same faith that made Christ one with God will make us one with Christ; when the faith in oneness is complete, the fact of oneness will be complete.

For the present, and as a mere beginning of further applications which we should all make, let us take these truths more intimately into ourselves and our lives. Christ humanly made Himself one with God only as God divinely made Himself one with Him; it was of faith only as it was by grace. We make ourselves one with Christ only *as* Christ has made Himself one with us. *That* Christ has done in His Church, which is His Body, which is Himself. Until we take the Church for what it is—as *being* all that it means—oneness with Christ, and in Christ with God, and in God with one another and with *all*;—until we learn how to do that, and begin to *do* it, we shall not be either in truth or in earnest in the quest for the unity without which Christianity is a predestined failure.

The principle of the Church we see realized and revealed in the person of Christ as embodying humanity in Himself,—or as exhibiting in human life the conception, process, and completion of divine Incarnation. Christ is human redemption or salvation because He is human righteousness, human self-fulfillment through self-correspondence with reality. But the principle of the Church in Christ ought to be better understood as it comes home to us in its application to our common humanity. Our relation to the righteousness and life of Christ is our relation to the person of Christ: it is described simply as our "being *in* Christ." That can have no other meaning than our being in the Church, as the body of Christ, and as Christ Himself. And that is so far off from our conception only because we are so far beneath God's conception of our humanity as the subject and object and body of His Incarnation.

The first note (and, if we take it aright, the one all-sufficient note) of the Church is unity. The Church originated in Christ, and was fully realized and expressed by Him in the words, "I and my Father are one." That was, of course, true of Him primarily only in His deity. But He came into the world to extend it to, to make it equally true of, His humanity also: and it was in His humanity that He uttered the words. And He came not only to make Himself, as one of us, Son of God and one with God, but to make us all, as one with Him and one in Him, in like manner one with and one in God. He was to be only "the first-born among many brethren"—the leader, captain, author and finisher of a common salvation. It is not being holy that makes us one with God, one in ourselves, or one with one another: it is the being one that makes us holy, that is our holiness. Oneness is the essence and substance of holiness, of righteousness and of eternal life: and the only oneness is that of God—the inherent, essential, and completive oneness of Divine Love.

The Church was complete in principle in Christ alone; it will be complete in application only in humanity. If our Lord's conquest of the world, His accomplished righteousness, was first an achievement of faith, an attained oneness with God—it was, in the second place, an act and victory of *obedience*.

The tremendous fact of the oneness of God with all, and of the oneness of all—if ever—only in God, and with God, and through God: which is the reason, and meaning, and end of Christ,—that becomes the essence and substance of Christianity.

The point I wish to make is this: Our Christianity is too far off from us; we think of the Incarnation of God and the presence of Christ as too exclusively in heaven, and not sufficiently on earth and in ourselves. We do not know that in the mind and heart and will of God *we* are the body of Christ and the subject of the Incarnation.

The process of God in His world—or more definitely, in the mode or degree of His relation to the world—cannot but compel our attention and thought, however it may forever transcend our knowledge. In the first stages of the physical evolution in which we find ourselves to be—viewed now in the light of what it has become and is evermore becoming—we may discover the immanence of Somewhat which we may call Reason, Meaning, End or Purpose,—or God. We believe it to be indeed God, but a God Whom we can know, or know of, only by logical inference. The theory or postulate of God comes to us to account for a somewhat in the movement or direction in things which, we think, the mere things of themselves cannot account for. If this be God, then God so far is apparent to us, not in Himself, but only in the working of the things,—and so far as we know, may *be* only in and of the things.

But we have long since passed out of that world of the mere becoming of things into a higher world of knowing and controlling them. We are not any longer only inside and of, but outside and over the movement and direction of things,—and what is more, of ourselves. What has come in (we know not how) to make the great change, is not the mere appearance in phenomenon of self-consciousness and freedom, but the birth amid things of the *self* as subject of consciousness and freedom.

As ourselves no longer only immanent in but transcendent above the world of things in which we are—God no longer appears to us as only immanent in things but as infinitely and supremely without and above them: He meets us in the plane of our own transcendence or objectivity—that is, of our reason and freedom. However we may infer or postulate Him, and even worship Him, in the elements, forces, or operations of physical nature, we cannot see or know Him there as separate from these. To worship God in nature is simply to worship nature as God; and that is as far as nature-worship can go. But when we pass out of the world of mere natural and necessary sequence into that of the higher and wholly different calls and claims of reason and freedom, of holiness, righteousness and life, God is ready to come to us—or we are ready that God should come to us—not as mere force or movement, operation or law, no matter how majestic or divine, but as Himself, Person as we are persons, and transcending, as we transcend ours, even all His own presence and part in the world that comes from Him. When we know God not alone as Reason and Will and Purpose, but as Love and Grace and Fellowship, as the Life and Soul and Substance of our own righteousness or personal and social perfection,—then indeed we know Himself, and not some inference or predication about Him.

What we know of God in physical nature is expressed in the terms universality, uniformity, and unity. We know Him only *in* these and not in exceptions, violations, or contradictions of them. So in human nature we know God in the totality of His relations with us, only *in, with* and *through* what He is in ourselves—that is, in the integrity of what *we* become in Him. We know God as Person because we are persons,—as Spirit because we are ourselves finite spirit. If God is anything more than Spirit or Person we are agnostic of it because we do not share it with Him; but we are not agnostic of God in so far as He makes us partakers with, and partakers of, Himself in actual experience. Only we must not expect God to interfere with His own wisdom and love in making us persons, in putting us upon a reason and freedom of our own, any more than to violate the necessary laws and uniformities which He imposes upon nature. Not only nature but human nature must work to its end, in accordance with, and in the integrity of, itself.

It might be said with reverence that if the term, along with the thing, Incarnation, had not been given us, the human instinct of it would not only have created the want but have found the expression. But indeed God could not have given it if men had not so wanted it. When we say that God could not, we mean only that He could not act outside of or counter to His own wisdom and working in the matter. He is as much in the instincts and wants, the purely natural impulses, of His world, as He is in their answer or supply—natural or supernatural. He feeds the raven which He caused to hunger and to seek its food; and He comes in person to meet the soul that hungers and thirsts for nothing less than Himself.

It is amazing how immediately, how definitely, and how perfectly

Christianity, or the Incarnation, assumed its cosmic, as well as human aspect. It was the crisis, the turning point, of God's eternal relation with His world. The completion of nature in human nature, of mere sequence and necessity in reason and freedom and personality, is contingent upon and leads up to the further process of the perfection of human nature, the sanctification and glorification of man in God.

If we are seeking the emphasis, or the emphases, which will restore reality and power to our Christianity, we must begin with that upon the personality, what we might call the objectivity, of God Himself. We must lift God above nature and above ourselves, and learn to enter into personal relations with Him: we must be able to say and to mean—"Our Father Who art in heaven." And the heaven we mean must be not one in which God is, but one which is in God— which only God Himself is: the heaven of love and grace and fellowship of God, of holiness and righteousness and life in God. If we seek *that* first, all other things that belong to heaven will add themselves.

The Gospel as a mode or process of human salvation—i.e, redemption and completion—is best understood in contrast with law. Law means the fulfilling of nature, the realizing of self, the discharge of obligation and perfection of relation with God and man,—in a word, law means that spiritual as well as natural "correspondence with environment," which is the definition of life and blessedness. It *means* all that, but how far can it go towards effecting or enabling it? Nature by itself, or without *us,* will not do for us what it does for the bee or the beaver; the fact or the knowledge that righteousness *is* life and transgression *is* death will not make us righteous or give us life of ourselves. For that nature and law and self have all to be transcended, and it is wholly with that transcendence that the Gospel has to do: it is not so much the *What* as the *How* of salvation.

"The law," says St. John, "was given by Moses; grace and truth came by Jesus Christ." Grace from God, and truth (realization and reality) in us,—are the Gospel. Is the law then older than the Gospel by so many years as Moses was before Christ? The idea is universally repudiated in the Scriptures. All the Gospel in the New Testament was implicitly contained in the growing promise of the Old Testament. Going backward, in David was the promise of a universal and everlasting Kingdom of God or of Heaven upon earth. In Abraham was promised what was to be the principle and substance of that Kingdom—a righteousness of grace or of God through the human answer and acceptance of faith. Our Lord asked how He could be merely Son of David, Whom David himself had called Lord, and affirmed, "Before Abraham was I am." In Adam there was the primitive promise that though the serpent had wounded the heel of his seed, yet that seed should in the end crush the serpent's head. Humanity had fallen under the power of sin and death, but would in time turn by the grace of God

411

and put those enemies under its feet. But the Gospel of Christ, or Christ Who is the Gospel, was older even than Adam or man. He was before the world—the whole process of creation which (here at least) culminates, finds its reason, meaning, and end in man. "Thou lovedst me," our Lord says to the Father, "before the foundation of the world"; and St. Paul adds to this that "God chose us in Him before the foundation of the world . . . having foreordained us unto adoption (rather, unto realization or attainment) of sons through Jesus Christ unto Himself." The Gospel then is as old as the eternal divine thought or purpose of man: it is what God had in mind in his creation, in the planning of his nature and the predetermining of his destiny. Christ was then predestined humanity: man in, not only the mind, but the heart, wish and will, the forethought, provision, and prepared actual inheritance of sonship to God. As thus "Man from (and for) heaven"—Son of God by both origin and destination, Christ is carried back into yet prior and higher identification with God, is seen to be one with the reason, meaning and end or final cause of all creation—the Logos by Whom all things are, and Who eternally is with God, and *is* God.

The essence or substance of the Gospel is thus seen to be: humanity or *we* eternally and infinitely *in God,* and God through Christ, progressively (we might say evolutionally and eventually) *to be* in us. The Church is literally and exactly in *Ecclesia:* "Whom God foreknew He predestined to be conformed to the image of His Son (to the attainment of sonship through participation in the attained or accomplished human sonship of Jesus Christ); whom He predestined He called, whom He called He justified, whom He justified He glorified." The process of glorification or of becoming *de facto* sons is told on God's part, which is unfailing and invariable. Nothing is said of the multitudes who are called and do not hear or answer, and are therefore not justified or glorified,—not that it is not theirs to be, but that they "will not" be. The gospel of human redemption and fulfillment is essentially and necessarily a "call," or an invitation: it has no message or meaning save to human freedom, to personal, spiritual, moral distinction, choice and self-determination. Apart from these *we* are not in it, and can in no wise be qualified or characterized by it. To make human quality or character or destiny any other than a "call" to our own faith, faithfulness and achievement or attainment is to annul and abolish the "us" or "we" in the matter, and destroy all image or likeness of God in us. God's parts in the process follow with something more than mere natural infallibility. He cannot contradict Himself: He cannot be anything less than the all-loving Self, the all-sufficient Grace, or the perfect divine Fellowship or Oneness with us—which are the factors on His part in our glorification or accomplished sonship. But even all that can be defeated by our non-concurrence: the human factors of faith—acceptance and reception of "God with us"; of hope, which sees and means *us* in the matter as well as God; of love, which is the only actualized "God with us";—these human factors are as essential as the divine in the result of a human salvation. The Church, therefore, may be defined (as in I Cor. 1, 2) to be "The sanctified in Christ Jesus, called to be saints." That is to say,—it is humanity—on God's part already and always included in the love, grace, and fellowship which alone and perfectly can make it son of God, partaker of His nature and of Himself: but on man's part, "called" and waiting "to be," to become by its own act of acceptance and appropriation, son of God and partaker of His holiness, righteousness and eternal life. The eternal Word become flesh, sonship incarnate—the Love and Grace and Fellowship of God, the Kingdom of Heaven, placed at our disposal and made "ours to command"—can only give us the right and the power, it cannot force upon us, or dispense with in us, the *will* to become sons of God. There is forever in the heart of God,—would that it could sound ever in our ears—the divine lament, "How would I—and ye would not!"

"One cannot but admire the unhesitating and unqualified manner in which the Church, in all its offices, utters the simple and straightforward language of faith. The trumpet gives forth no uncertain sound. By baptism we are dead with Christ and risen with Christ, and therefore *regenerate*. The only non-regeneration of one whom God has baptized is his own ignorance, or unbelief, or rejection of the fact that he *is* regenerate. But the Church assumes, or suggests, no such doubt or denial, but puts into his mouth only the language of faith, assurance, and fulfillment. As Christ died and rose, so the baptized person is to call and account himself dead to sin and alive to God. He is to *be* regenerate by believing himself regenerate. God has *made* him so; therefore he must account himself, and *be* so. And he will only not be so in fact through not being so in faith, i.e., through not believing that by God's grace and act he is so."

"The Church as a living Church should bring up her children in a living faith to realize their baptism, i.e., to make it real by accepting and treating it as real; to *be* children of God by believing that they *are* children of God, and not that they have to make themselves so by any act of theirs. And if we were born of and into such a living Church, our faith would be such a living faith, and our baptism would be, both to us and in us, such a living fact. At any rate, if it were not, the fault and failure would be, not in it, but in us: not in its not regenerating, but in our rejecting and making naught our regeneration. It would no more make baptism not a divine and a divinely efficacious act, than the fact of our Lord's inability to do His mighty works, on account of man's unbelief, made Him not a divine person."[1]

---

[1] See Soteriology of the New Testament, pp. 374, 375. [by William Porcher DuBose]

If we are to follow the transcendent, prehuman Christ in His Incarnation, Resurrection, Ascension, Descent in the Spirit—the next step must follow co-equally and of necessity. If Christ is not as really and as actually present in His Church as in all His previous manifestations, energies, and activities—then Christianity has lapsed. If baptism into Christ does not mean, *is* not, for us, all that it meant and was for Him in His humanity—then by so much has it ceased to be what God made it and gave it. I do not say, as much *in* us as *in* Christ, for there is this immeasurable distance if not difference between Him and us: In Christ God has shown us the completeness of His love, grace, and fellowship working in the perfection of our human faith, hope, and answering love: He has shown us what we would be if we were in perfect response to Himself as Christ was. But even in Christ, however foreshortened, it was a process that required time: Christ, in a few years, *longam expositionem hominis in se recapitulat,* sums up all man's evolution or destiny in Himself. Because our faith, realization, reproduction of Christ in ourselves is a thing of endless growth, or of growth that ends not here,—therefore Christ here cannot be *in us* as God was in Him. But Christ *for* us, as an end, a goal, a destiny, to which we must always be looking and moving, Christ as our faith, our hope and love—is as real, as present and as complete in our baptism as He was in His own. What I mean is that the "given" in my baptism is the same as that in Christ's—however infinitely different the "received": it is my everlasting task, and privilege, and glory to make up that difference. All the love, grace, fellowship was there, and was there, on God's part, made mine; it is for me now, by never-ending growth in faith, hope, and love, to appropriate, assimilate, and convert unto myself all that is eternally mine in God. We are wholly in Christ by God's grace, it remains for Christ to be wholly in us through our faith. What we need to see is that God's gift to us of eternal life, through His Word to us and by His Spirit in us, is absolute, unlimited, and unconditioned. Baptism receives us into the Kingdom of Heaven and makes it "ours." There is no limitation or condition about it— save the one of our own creation and interposition: viz., the question whether we will take it, and how much we will make it. Whatever of penalty, of death or of hell, of loss or torture to ourselves, there must of necessity be in the rejection, contradiction and consequent opposite of life, blessedness and heaven, is not of God's will or ordaining; it is the result of logical, natural, human consequence. If God says, "Be blessed," and we say "No," the curse of non-blessedness is not of His but of our own infliction. I am speaking only of or to those who have real opportunity and consequent responsibility, or accountability. The Gospel is of course only for those who have it: those who have it not we may safely leave to a God Who is all of love and mercy.

The "in me" of Christ—in Him as eternal Word, Promise and Fullfilment of us, in His Incarnation, Death, Resurrection, and Eternal Life—is as present and patent in the New Testament as the responsive "in Christ" which became at once the all-inclusive expression of Christianity's relation to Him. "To be in Christ and Christ in us"—as integral parts, continuation and extension, universality, and perpetuity of the Incarnation,—how was this to be effectuated and established as a permanent fact in the world? Was it to be left in the air, or written and left in a book? The Book or Bible was no part of the original institution of Christianity. It arose out of the actual and conscious life of the Church, and was the inspired means of recording and perpetuating that original consciousness for all time. The actual institution of Christianity might be said to have been in the two sacraments—of the new birth and the new life in Christ. But what were those two sacraments? Divinely given signs and seals or pledges of a deeper fact, parts of a fuller whole than themselves. The fact or whole was achieved, accomplished, realized and fulfilled oneness of humanity with God—its now actually "determined" or effected "sonship in power according to the spirit of holiness, out of or through resurrection from the dead." But of this fact or whole Christ was only the beginning, the first fruits, the first-born from the dead. God's predestination was of humanity, of us, unto fulfilment and inheritance of "sonship to Himself through Jesus Christ." "Whom He foreknew He foreordained to be conformed to the image of His Son (the end or goal of our creation)—that He might be the first-born among many brethren." The whole process of Incarnation therefore was not terminated, it was only begun, in the Ascension of our Lord. The body of His individual, natural humanity was to grow through all space and time into the all-inclusive body of His corporate, spiritual humanity.

To say that Christ did not institute a Church is on a par with saying that He did not take our flesh, or rise from the dead, or ascend into heaven. It is a break or a halt in the process of His human task and activity just where it begins to apply itself to its real end and purpose. The Church is Christ's one real and whole sacrament to us of Himself—of our being "in Him" and "He in us." Any other sacraments are only acts and parts of that one—"outward and visible signs of the inward and spiritual grace" which is ours only as we are in Him and He in us. It is not our faith, or our conversion, or anything whatever on our part, that places us in Christ or makes us sons of God. It is absolutely and altogether an act of God long before and wholly without us—in our creation, our predestination, and the incarnation in us of His Word and Spirit through our union with Christ. The function of faith is simply to accept, to appropriate, to make our own; true conversion is what will take place in us as the necessary result or fruit of a true faith. Just as in the human Christ the fact and reality of His saying "I and my Father are one," was the legitimate utterance and expression of His perfect acceptance and realization of the baptismal word "Thou art my Son,"—so with us the essence and matter of true conversion is the reality with which we appropriate our baptismal oneness with Him and His with us. To be born anew in the Risen Christ, and to live in Him the ever new life of death to sin and resurrection to God and eternal life is the one simple and all containing truth of the sacraments.

It is not adding a new truth, it is only unfolding the most vital content of the one truth, to say that the Church as the Sacrament of Christ (as Christ Himself is to us the Sacrament of God) is not the medium of relation between "God and the soul, the soul and its God,"—if the soul be taken individually, as though religion were a matter solely between each man and his God. Christianity is distinctly a corporate and social act and life. As Christ, so God says: He that hath done it unto the least of mine hath done it unto Me—and there is no doing unto Me that is not unto all mine. I am willing to extend this so far as to say: There is no whole relation of correspondence and co-operation with God that is not in sympathy and unity with creation, with nature, with humanity, with all things and pre-eminently all persons. In Christ must be the ultimate unity of all these—of science, philosophy, business, politics, personal, social, national and international intercourse and relations—if He is to be unity with God. The divorce and disunity of the various parts of truth, which is one with God, must be overcome before we can be all-one with Him: to be alien from any is to be so far alien from Him Who is All-in-all.

The Church then is in the highest sense the sacrament of unity. Its one mark of unity includes and covers all the others, of holiness, universality and perpetuity. The Church may be defined as organized unity, or as unity incarnate: its earliest expression was, "I believe in the Holy Catholic Church, the Communion of Saints": i.e., the one Holy and Universal Church, the Unity and Community, the Fellowship or Oneness of all Christians. Now what, again, was that oneness? It was primarily the oneness of each and all with Christ, or with God in Christ. But God in Christ recognizes no oneness with Him that is not oneness of all in Him with one another. There is no common or universal oneness with God that does not abolish between those who share it, I will not say all differences among themselves, but at any rate all differences that deny, contradict, defeat or hinder their oneness together in Him. "As many of us as were baptized into Christ did put on Christ. There is neither Jew nor Greek, there is neither bond nor free, there is neither male nor female,—for we are all one in Christ Jesus." These natural differences and many others, did not actually cease in Christ, but they ceased in so far as anything in them constituted a bar, a hindrance, or a contradiction to their oneness with Christ or with one another in their relation to Christ.

There is no question in any of our minds that the one thing needed, the one condition of all life, is unity—unity in itself and unity with all else, oneness in inward constitution and with outward environment. Nature as such will never of itself bring about that unity. In the wisdom that underlies nature we are passing out of an immeasurable stage of strife and competition in to a yet distant future one of unity, co-operation and order: order among ourselves, though slowly acquired, because rational and free, cooperation with God. Nature of itself will not give us that unity,—nor selfish prudence and experience, nor legislation, nor law, nor outward compulsion of any sort. Only the Spirit of God as new-creative power can accomplish it: "new" only in the sense of ever anew coming into demonstration and action as it can awaken the reason of man to wisdom, and the will of man to true freedom. The Spirit of God has moved upon the waters from the beginning; it begins to move in the sphere and realm of finite created and responsive spirit only as "life becomes light" (attains to consciousness of God and itself) in man. Christ is the incarnation and manifestation of that Spirit not so much in its origin or potential existence in man, as in its historic coming to itself and its complete realization and revelation of itself in His person. And as Christ needed to come in the objective and concrete visibility of a human body at the first, so He needs to come again not in the abstract and suppositious conception of an invisible unity (which if it were true would manifest itself)—but in a visible body as before, the body of all in Him, in which in its unity man may see Him, even as in Himself man could see God.

That the Church, as herein understood, could come into the world only in some concrete and organic form is, I suppose, self-evident. That the Apostolate which Christ invested with His authority was the foundation and source of its future order is, I suppose, equally so. But to the apostles the Church founded through them was the Body of the Risen Christ within it: *It* was the organ of His "returned," universal and perpetual presence and activity upon earth,—and they were but the members, the parts, to whom were committed the several functions. A permanent ministry to continue these functions after them I assume to have been the first condition of the organized permanent presence of Christ in our humanity. As a matter of fact the constituent elements of a visible Church as the Body of Christ have been and are among all—the faith, the sacraments, the ministry and the worship.

It may be assumed that if unity were—not only of the essence, but the very and sole essence itself of the Incarnation and the Church—one of the earliest provisions that would have to appear and establish itself would be the provision for world-wide and time-long unity.

The question, How to restore and conserve Unity—must go back to a prior one,—What is the Unity in Question? Let us recall and repeat it in our Lord's own words: "I will not leave you orphans; yet a little while and the world seeth me no more, but ye see me: because I live, ye shall live also. In that day ye shall know that I am in my Father, and ye in me, and I in you." And in His last prayer: "Father, the glory Thou hast given me, I have given unto them: that they may be one, even as We are one; I in them and Thou in me, that they may be perfected into one; that the world may know that Thou didst send me, and lovedst them, even as Thou lovedst me."

The Church, as we have seen, is the Body, Incarnation, or Sacrament of that Unity. In such a Union or Unity of two, there is the inevitable danger of holding one, either one, at the cost—even to the extreme of the denial—of the other. In the transcendent person of Jesus Christ Himself there have been from the beginning those who have held His divinity to the practical annihilation of any real humanity in Him; and on the other hand, those who have seen Him only human, to the practical exclusion of any real divinity. It is not surprising that in what we might call the corporate personality of our Lord—that which He shares with and in which He includes *us*—there should be similar extremes of contradiction, some denying and others exaggerating and distorting the real divinity of the Church. But all the way between these widest and even outside extremes there are few who call themselves Christians that would not resent the thought of being "out of Christ," that would not acknowledge the necessity of being "in Christ" and "one with Him" in all that "Unity" means or involves. And also,—all the way between these widest extremes there is no one point at which we can say that Christ is all *there*—to the exclusion of every, or of any, other point.

If then, in all our differences we are thus able to concentrate and agree upon the one necessity of being in Christ and of being one in Him, we must not despair of some ultimate Way to it. If we will cultivate and prepare the disposition, the will, and the purpose—God will make the Way. The curse of the present state of Christendom is that our differences have erected such barriers and entrenchments that intercommunication, exchange, and mutual understanding are well-nigh impossible. Let us once begin in very reality to reverse this spirit, attitude, and policy—to bring together, compare, and contribute to the common good of the One End, the End of Oneness;—let us, I say, once begin on that line, and the differences that do not eliminate themselves will be turned into the higher service of deepening, broadening, and heightening the resultant Unity.

William Porcher DuBose, "The Church," *The Constructive Quarterly* 5 (March 1917): 1-18.

99.

Edward Lambe Parsons, The Liberal Evangelicals' Message in Our Church Today, 1934

Edward Lambe Parsons (May 18, 1868–July 18, 1960) was consecrated Bishop Coadjutor of California on November 5, 1919. He became the third Bishop of California on the death of Bishop William Ford Nichols, June 5, 1924. He had a great influence on the Prayer Book of 1928, and co-authored The American Prayer Book: Its Origins and Principles *(1937). In this selection he describes the genius of the liberal evangelicals.*

The Liberal Evangelicals bring no new Gospel to the Church of today. They believe with all the followers of Christ through all the ages that the old Gospel is for the present and the future the hope of the world. Nor when they speak of adjustment to the modern world do they mean an old Gospel either watered down and become that kindly respectable teaching which Henry Adams found had taken all the power from religion, or broadened until the difference between Christian and non-Christian, is altogether blurred. Nor yet again do they come after the manner of certain well-known groups in Church as well as state, warning us of perilous tendencies, fearful of the future and living in a dream-past which corresponds to no present that ever was or ever will be.

The Liberal Evangelicals seek no party ends, no ecclesiastical offices, no control of conventions. They seek only by insistent teaching, by the devotion of small groups growing into larger groups, by preaching if they are clergy, and by personal touch of clergy and laity alike, to help the Church to meet the cry of the new day. Like all Christians in a machine age they call men to reverence personality; in a materialistic age to get values right in the supremacy of the spiritual. But not like all Christians in an age swinging perilously toward authoritarian theories in Church and state alike, they proclaim the freedom of the Gospel. In an age in which many religious leaders take refuge in obscurantism they stress the unity of all truth and the revelation in scientific and historical discovery of the wider meanings of the Personality of God.

To be specific, Christ is always being lost in dogmas, in institutions and in things. His followers do not escape the same fate. They too are perpetually lost in dogmas, in institutions and in things. True to its evangelical tradition, the Liberal Evangelical movement would persuade us to get behind these "things," to discover that they are but the clothing of a deep and essential personal relationship. True to its "liberal" profession the movement would guide us to see the God with whom we enter into this personal relationship revealing himself in the wide sweep of human history and the "whole labor house vast of being" as well

419

as in the pages of Scripture and the Person of Christ. The liberal too would persuade us to get behind the things of the world, its institutions and its dogmas, to the personal living God. All the liberal stands for is involved in that personal relationship, if we understand God aright. Liberal and Evangelical in exploring deeply enough the meaning of God in the field of personal relationship discover each the other. Their unity in a phrase is not an artificial patching, such as I take it many have thought, but a real synthesis. Liberal and Evangelical have often thought themselves poles apart. The Liberal Evangelical movement proclaims that they are essentially parts of one experience. Indeed for myself I feel sure that it is in the full exploration of the meaning of God that those three traditional ways of approach to God which have in our Communion called themselves by various names,—Catholic, Evangelical and Liberal—that these three are one in God.

It is in that field of personal relationships also that we discover the unity of those principles which constitute a kind of platform for the Liberal Evangelicals of today. They are all expressions of faith that God is Father in a definite personal way and that in our personal relationship to Him and to the members of His great human family is the key to life. No legal theory keeps the Prodigal from his father's arms. The direct approach to God is that of person to Person. The Church is primarily not an institution but a fellowship of persons. The Sabbath is made for man, not man for the Sabbath. Truth is the apprehension of reality by persons and must have something of the fluidity of personal relationships. "He shall guide you into all truth." Fellowship is between persons and must be limited only by the capacity to share in common experience. "Where two or three are gathered together in my name, there am I."

Or to put it another way, freedom and love are the supreme expressions of personality and within the network of personal relations with God and man which constitutes our religion the tests of truth and action lie not in dogma and law but in freedom and love.

Let me try now to point out the bearing of all this upon some of the matters which concern us so deeply in the Church today.

And as if I were developing a theological treatise, first of God. I recall that in his illuminating comment upon the last Lambeth Conference Canon Raven suggested that the bishops, after proclaiming their acceptance of a most adequate statement concerning the doctrine of God, failed to see its application to some of the problems they had to discuss. What he evidently had in mind was the contrast between the inclusive and catholic love of God and the exclusive and sectarian emphasis which he conceived the report laid upon ecclesiastical order. That has always been one of the tragic failures of Christianity. There is undoubtedly genuine acceptance by all Christians of Peter's word that "in every nation he that feareth Him and worketh righteousness is acceptable to God." The acceptance is sincerely meant, but it does not include for every Christian the corollary that what God has cleansed man is not to make unclean. God's love as we know it in Christ is comprehensive and absolutely personal. The question with Him is not of a man's inheritance or his acceptance of a certain code, ecclesiastical or ethical. Because He is the Eternal Person His one question is how far any one of those other persons, His children, weak, frail, ignorant, willful, have sought even blindly to find friendship with Him. The whole message of the Gospel as embodied in our Lord's ministry is but that. Children of Abraham! Sons of the Kingdom! Keepers of the law! In His vision of the Kingdom there is no place for such claims. They crowd from the East and the West and the North and the South, all kinds of people, long bearded Scribes and beardless boys, devoted widows and reclaimed harlots, Jews and Greeks and Scythians. I see them now within the field of our wider world, yellow and brown and red and black and white. Yes, and Methodists and Baptists and Presbyterians are there, and Roman Catholics and long-haired priests from the East.

But one must not grow rhetorical. Truth is a sacred thing and must not be sullied by words; and this truth is a simple truth. These are all God's children. He loves them all as Jesus loved them all. He accepts them for what they are because he is no respecter of persons but a lover of souls. The environment in which these people have been brought up and the inheritance which has started them in life can make no difference in His love, in His readiness to give them the best He has and the yearning of His Father's heart for companionship with them. He is concerned with what they are and not with what they have, with the use of privilege, not with its nature.

This great company constitutes the invisible Church of the Reformers or that soul of the Church which even the most rigid of Christians has been compelled to recognize. It is an assembly of persons and because it is built upon love and not upon power, freedom is of its very essence. A regimented Kingdom of love is a contradiction in terms. The free development of personality through the response of one to another and to God is the condition of its existence.

I shall speak later of this matter of freedom in relation to truth. The point I am making now is that this free fellowship of the spirit, this "general assembly" of persons who have entered into relationship with God lies in the background of any conception of the visible Church which we can frame. It keeps reminding us that we are dealing primarily with persons and not with institutions, and that the boundaries of an institution like the Church are perforce inadequate and unsatisfactory. It forbids any too rigid conception of the visible Church. It excludes altogether any claim of infallibility whether it be linked to Pope or Council or to tradition.

But it does not usurp the function of the visible Church. Too often in history the evangelical movement has developed into individualism. It has conceived of the Gospel as something quite independent of the Church and prior to it. But Church and Gospel cannot be separated other than in abstract thinking. Many of you will remember the striking contribution to this question made by that group of German theologians who four years ago met in the historic Wartburg to consider what the New Testament had to say concerning it. With practical unanimity they accepted at the beginning of their study the view that the Gospel was prior and the Church grew out of it. With equal unanimity during their study they discovered that to New Testament thinking there is no distinction. The Church, to paraphrase Loisy, is as much part of the Gospel as the Gospel is of the Church. Indeed when one stops a moment to think it is clear that it must be so.

St. Paul's superb insight reveals it. If the Church is the Body of Christ it means that the moment two or three are walking with Christ, trying however imperfectly to reveal to men his reconciling love, the Church is there. The mystical Body becomes visible, tangible. The often asked question as to whether Christ founded a Church is really quite irrelevant. Where is Christ, there is the Church. Christianity is a fellowship in Christ. The very nature of the Gospel message requires the personal relationship of those who have found God in Christ. They belong together. They cannot stay apart. When their love burns strong it burns away all barriers. The Evangelical of the past, as I have said, has often been an individualist. He has thought of his religion as a solitary walking with his God. He has not seen that the very depth of his personal devotion which practically has bound him in closest relationship with his fellow Christians carries with it the essential Catholic position. Certainly the Liberal Evangelical of our day is Catholic through and through. He believes in the Church, in the fellowship of believers, in the orderly processes of corporate life. History and personal experience alike reveal to him that the Church is the great sacrament and that in its sacramental life alone can the fulness and richness of Christ be his.

What he cannot forget however, is that this is a fellowship of *persons* in Christ. It must, of human necessity, take on some kind of organization. Its life must flow in orderly channels. In the field of history it must be an institution. Indeed as the Theologia Germanica reminds us "God will have all these things to be . . . for fitness and order are better and nobler than their contraries." "One who is poor in spirit and of a humble mind doth not despise or make light of law, order, precepts and holy customs." The mystic puts the thing in the right order. But he like the Evangelical will remind us that "law, order, precepts and holy customs" are but the way in which the free man exercises his freedom in the fellowship of his brethren. The first and most fundamental matter is his personality. The purpose of the institution is not institutional but personal. The glory of the

Church makes men forget this. They see the Church as an end. They exaggerate its characteristic notes, assuming them to be not ideals but realities which sometimes give warrant for crushing the tender life of the soul, sometimes lead to ruthless or totally unloving exclusion. We will have none such.

But if the institution is the expression of personal relationships and its end is not the institution but the individual, the Church has its meaning because of what it does for the souls of men. Its business is not to be saved but to save. The loss from our Christian thought of the beauty and power of the Platonic idealism would be a sad impoverishment. We need to think and speak of the Mystical Body of Christ, of the Bride of Christ, the One Holy Catholic and Apostolic Church. In a very real sense the Church is our Mother. But we must never forget that those lovely phrases are ideals. They have their immediate contact with reality in that invisible Church of which we have already thought. The Christian religion being a matter of personal relationship is a desperately pragmatic affair,—as witness Our Lord's constant insistence upon the test of fruit-bearing. God's love never goes seeking in the wilderness a lost Church but rather the lost souls that constitute it.

It follows that for the Evangelical all those characteristics of the Church which develop in the course of the centuries,—ministry, creeds, liturgies, the New Testament itself, must yield to the primacy of persons. They have their necessary functions but those are properly exercised only within the field of personal relationships. If like that system known of old the Church visible, powerful "shuts the Kingdom of heaven against men," starves and defrauds men's souls, then the refuge for the starved soul is that other Church, the vast invisible host of the faithful. Therein I take it lies one of the chief distinctions between what for lack of a better name we may call the typical Catholic and the typical Protestant conscience. The former will suffer spiritual deprivations rather than risk separation. The latter like our spiritual ancestors of the sixteenth century, will risk separation rather than endure poverty of soul.

It is for the same reason that in approaching the problems of unity the first thought of the Evangelical turns to the common experience of Christian people. He cannot see himself privileged and others left to that unworthy evasion, the uncovenanted mercies of God. He will not see sectarianism prevail though it call itself by the great name of Catholic. The common experience, the shared love of God in Christ, seems to him to transcend all the boundaries fixed by canons or doctrines or liturgical usages. Nothing can be so important as making visible the essential spiritual fellowship. Where kindred cultures, racial and national, give a kindred outlook upon life that importance grows; and with it the purpose to take advantage of every freedom which the Church permits in moving towards the perfect unity in Christ. I choose my words carefully for I am not suggesting the propriety of lawless action. The Evangelicals know very well (I quote the Theologia Germanica again) "that order and fitness are better than disorder and therefore they choose to walk orderly, yet know at the same time that their salvation hangeth not thereon." I am only insisting that to the Evangelical there is a certain indifference concerning those traditional regulations. He will use his utmost liberty. Indeed in that vexed matter of inter-communion one sees so clearly the difference of judgment. The fruit of good living, the obvious presence of Our Lord, the intimate fabric of personal relationships built up with God through Christ seem to the Evangelical to make considerations of order and regularity, vastly important though they be, nevertheless of secondary importance. He is ready to sit at the Lord's Table wherever the Lord himself may be found. He will not be less Catholic than Christ. Where God seems to find joy, he too will rejoice.

It is out of the great Sacrament of the Church that the lesser Sacraments grow. They are ways in which the fellowship feels after and expresses the common life of its members and brings them larger measure of God's grace, which is but another way of saying more intimate fellowship with God.

It would be altogether inappropriate for me to attempt any discussion of sacramental doctrine. But it is appropriate to point out that the constantly recurring controversy over it rests back upon precisely the same difference of approach which we have noted in relation to the Church itself; this different approach is perhaps quite as correctly described as a difference in standard of values. The Evangelical insists upon emphasizing the personal element in the Sacrament. He ought not to be afraid of anything; but sometimes he is afraid that that may be lost. He reads in all history the story of man's attempt to tie God into certain physical happenings and thus ensure the action desired from Him regardless of the moral condition of the worshipper. Superstition is nothing but this imprisoning of the divine action in impersonal agents. It has been and is everywhere. The Church and Christian people (Catholic and Protestant alike) have been perpetually falling into it. The safeguard is in no Quaker principles such as would release the spiritual from all connection with the physical. That cannot be done. It should not be done, for all life is eloquent of the essential unity of the two. Indeed as has been said a myriad times, the Incarnation means precisely this thing. The sacramental principle is altogether true. The safeguard lies not in shutting one's eyes to an obvious truth; but rather in emphasizing the continued and essential presence of the personal element. No one doubts that in all the best sacramental doctrine, however high it may be, this recognition of the personal is present. Indeed Catholic and Protestant are not so far apart in this matter as they sometimes think.

But the Liberal Evangelical will avoid the danger of superstition by continually going back to the personal relationship involved. He sees baptism as incorporation into the fellowship of the Church and regeneration as the molding of life within that fellowship. In confirmation he is concerned with the affirmations of the confirmed and the new opportunities which shall be channels of the grace of God. The Eucharistic feast is to him a feast indeed. He rejoices in the phrase, "The Lord's Table." He finds the culmination of the offering and reoffering of the memorial of the sacrifice of Calvary in the moment when for the faithful the priest cries "And here we offer and present unto thee, O Lord, ourselves, our souls and bodies." But whatever the detail of his theory, the Sacrament itself is always a closer intimacy with God through Jesus Christ. It is a transaction of persons. It foreshadows the feast in the messianic Kingdom at which already sit those of the general assembly of the first born.

In all that I have said, if I have said it with even tolerable clearness, there has been made apparent that element of fluidity, of freedom, of wide sympathy and forward look which because no personality has achieved growth without it, brings Liberal and Evangelical together. But it is really in the consideration of those expressions of the Christian experience which touch upon doctrinal truth that this essential unity becomes most apparent. What, I ask then, does this primacy of the person mean in relation to the creeds, confessions and liturgies of Christian people?

Truth, which I take it we may roughly define as our apprehension of reality, always has a personal element in it. We do not create truth, some of our modern philosophies to the contrary notwithstanding; yet we do carry into it something personal. We establish a new relationship in every apprehension of reality. An Eddington working over electrons and protons or a Poincare over intricate mathematical problems, objective as he may strive to make his work, is bringing a certain creative element to the relationship. To use modern philosophic jargon, he creates an occasion; he forms a new center of reference. The world of reality instead of being a solid affair of hard atoms or on the other hand an eternally frozen picture gallery of ideas has a fluidity, a mobility, an indefiniteness. Its bed rock is not bed rock at all. It is a vast and moving network of relations; and that from the Christian approach means that the ultimate reality is personal, is God. The ancient Greek had a glimpse of it when he rested the world upon the shoulders of Atlas.

The modern Christian, taking his start from his faith that in Christ he finds God, cannot see the universe as other than this extraordinary, intricate, puzzling network of personal relationships sustained and tied together in God. In such a world it is not strange that there should be vast varieties of view, of creed and confession, among those who profess the name of Christian. We are not dealing with a closed system of truth. There is no such thing. Do not mistake me. I do

425

not mean that truth is an individualistic vagary and that *any* man is the measure of all things. Christian truth is the apprehension of right relationship to God through Christ. God like Christ is the same yesterday, today and forever. But men are cast in different molds. Each from race and culture and immediate inheritance will bring some personal creative element into his relationship with God and his devotion to Christ. Great fundamental elements in that relationship will be shared in common, but approaches, emphases, culminations must vary. George Fox and Bossuet will both discover in Christ the same truth; but it is impossible to picture them portraying that discovery in any system which would satisfy both. Think of Mercier and Kagawa and Schweitzer. Christ lays hold upon them all; but how different the frame of truth into which they set their personal relationship.

This is a dangerous doctrine, but as long as we must fashion our doctrine out of the raw material of personal experience it is a true one, and today it is vital. It protests against regimentation. It exalts freedom. It protests against mass emotion. It exalts personal responsibility. In the Church it protests against drill-master methods and ideals of uniformity, and the exaltation of even age-long customs into tests of Christian life. External objective systems have their value; but they are only schoolmasters to bring us to Christ.

So likewise we see that the whole forward movement of Christian thought and life is inevitable. Friendship, if it is a real friendship of two real persons, is never a static thing. Each friend is discovering new realities in the life of the other. So it is inevitably with the Christian life in God. This personal relationship is an experience of amazing and ever new discoveries. Christ is not the same to a man at sixty as in his adventurous youth. His creed, which symbolizes his relation to Christ, changes. And as to the individual, so to that 'blessed company of faithful people' who are still learning of God in Christ. It is this certainty that new truth must grow out of personal relationship that, as I have before indicated, binds together Liberal and Evangelical. Each if he knows his own position thoroughly, finds himself going hand in hand with the other. He is the other.

The creeds of the Church are not locked gates. They are signposts pointing down the wide highways of the future. The liturgies of the Church are rich embodiments of past experience of God; but they point us forward, not back. The old creeds and the later confessions were but trying to express in the terms of their own day the fulness of their experience of Christ; but each newer day finds new insights, new revelations of what that personal experience means. In our day the greatest change has been in discoveries which have come to us from outside the direct experience. We have learned of the long and slow working out of the purposes of God.

We talk of progressive revelation, of emergent evolution, of the continued guidance of the Holy Spirit. They are but phrases to describe a growing intimacy with God; the signs of a friendship which is constantly exploring new fields. We do not repudiate a creed or a confession; we try to fulfill the promise crystallized in it. In worship too our liturgies must carry the wealth of earlier experience; but they must steadily incorporate the newer tokens of the Divine companionship. No revised Prayer Book however successful for 1928, can set a limit to the inpouring and the outgoing of God's relationship to man.

That I take it is especially true of all that touches upon our social order. Dr. Morrison's recent book on the Christian Cultus and the Social Gospel strikes a fine note in his insistence that the social ideals of Christianity must be incorporated into its worship. The prophet of social righteousness now needs the priest, he says, and, I add, the striking fact to one who has watched this growth of the social consciousness of the Church from the start is that the Church is ready for it. Our Church is ready for it. No Church Congress, no Catholic Congress, no Liberal Evangelical Conference would any longer evade the issues raised by and in the social order.

The Catholic point of view has almost always assumed the Church's responsibility in social conditions. The Evangelical has been individually oftentimes the very soul of social reform; but in spite of St. Francis and Wesley and Shaftesbury he has tended to an individualistic theory. There is vast truth in the cry that if we are going to change the world we must change men; but it is only half truth. The sacramental principle insists that we cannot altogether save men unless we save the physical conditions of their lives. All this is implicit in our faith that the Gospel means a personal relationship with God. Their right relationship is a family relationship. Every social order must ultimately stand the test of the family relationship. In its poor way the great Church is the herald and prophecy of this family order. The ethics of the Kingdom are family ethics. The cooperative commonwealth is the commonwealth of love.

It is the business of the Church to do what it can to reveal this commonwealth of love to the pagan world in which we live; and to strive mightily to change the social order so that the primacy of personality may be secured. In the light of the Christian ideal the systems of Fascism and Communism which deny freedom to the individual and exalt the corporate life as an end must wither and dry up. We stand for freedom; we exalt personality. We know that no social order can last except as it trains and develops the free life of its members. The Church is the conservator of freedom because God cares for each individual soul. But we ask for no Church which shall dominate society; for no authority other than that which asks free acceptance of the truth in Christ Jesus. We preach and teach a social Gospel because the Gospel means just the relationship of men together within the great family of God. We must have a new social order. We must proclaim it as God's will with the tense devotion of an Amos. But it must be a commonwealth of love, a family not of slaves but of free men. We must be radicals because the roots of our troubles lie in the human soul and especially in the corporate sin of human society today. But it is a constructive radicalism, not forgetting the high and noble contributions of the past, desiring to build on all that is great in the past and all that is fine in society and the human soul today. It attacks the systems which mislead or distort or abuse the personalities of the children of God. Against such the Church declares eternal war. In that war there are no party names, no partisan ends. The Kingdom of God is our end. We are to free the slaves of society. But we must release them into the glorious liberty of the children of God.

With what better phrase can I close than that even though it be a misquotation! The glorious liberty of children of God!

It is indeed that which we seek for ourselves and for our Church today! Freedom of thought, of research and of expression, freedom in worship and in action, freedom to utter the prophetic word in the chaos of our social order. But it is an ordered, a sane and responsible freedom. We are part of the great Church of the ages. Our experience is part of the accumulated experience of Christian people. And back of this Church of history, the visible tangible frail delinquent and splendid Church there is that invisible Church known only to God, always reminding us that the supreme end of life is our personal relationship with God in the family of his children and in the closer fellowship of those who know Him through Christ. This freedom of ours is a serious, yes even a terrifying thing; for in exercising it we are responsible to the Church of history, to the mystical Body of Christ, to the whole family of God and to Him, the Eternal King and our heavenly Father.

Edward Lambe Parsons, *The Liberal Evangelicals' Message in Our Church Today*, Liberal Evangelical Pamphlets, no. 2 (Cambridge, Mass.: Cosmos Press, 1934).

CHAPTER TWELVE

Missions in the Twentieth Century (1916-1982)

Introduction

The mission field is the whole world. Mission work in the modern era has needed to adapt to the demands of a global community. Mission workers have also faced the realization that the cities and suburbs of America can be as much in need of the Gospel and as much lacking the Gospel as anywhere in the world. The Episcopal Church in the modern era came to recognize the need for indigenous ministry in the overseas mission field. This understanding developed into a commitment by the Episcopal Church to Mutual Responsibility and Interdependence with overseas mission partners. The Episcopal Church responded to the call of the 1988 Lambeth Conference for a decade of evangelism, although some have suggested that the Episcopal Church might need a decade to get ready for evangelism. Some members of the Episcopal Church seem to consider their faith a private matter which they hesitate to share. The Episcopal Church continues to seek ways to reach out in faith and service, inviting and welcoming others to share in the life of the church.

100.

Julia Chester Emery, Forty-Fifth Annual Report of the Woman's Auxiliary to the Board of Missions, 1915-1916

Julia Chester Emery (September 24, 1852–January 9, 1922) was General Secretary of the Woman's Auxiliary to the Board of Missions for forty years, 1876-1916. The General Convention of 1871 authorized the women of the church to organize the Auxiliary, and it began work on January 2, 1872, with Mary Abbott Emery, Julia's sister, as General Secretary. Under the leadership of Julia Emery, the Auxiliary had offices in every diocese, and branches throughout the Episcopal Church. Julia Emery traveled extensively for the church's mission work. She attended the first Pan-Anglican Congress in London, June 15-24, 1908, the fifth Lambeth Conference, July 6–August 6, 1908, and visited missionary districts in the Philippines, Hawaii, China, and Japan. The following excerpt from her Report to the Board of Missions discusses the work of the Woman's Auxiliary and calls for an expanded role for women in the church. She is commemorated on January 9 in the Episcopal Calendar of the Church year.

The Woman's Auxiliary to the Board of Missions as it is known to-day, with its provincial organization and officers in five of the provinces, with diocesan officers in all its dioceses and missionary districts, with its parish branches and officers in over 5,500 of the 8,500 parishes and missions, and an individual membership which has never been numbered; with its yearly gifts of more than $100,000 towards the Board's appropriations, and specials in money and boxes of $260,000 more; with its Triennial United Offering, now reaching $300,000 and beyond; with its ever increasing intelligence through meetings, conferences, summer schools, institutes, mission study through reading, and its ever rising tide of prayer; with its reiterated efforts to reach all women and to train and enlist the children and young people of the Church—this Woman's Auxiliary is the development of that "Woman's Society, Auxiliary to the Board of Missions," which "the Reverend Secretaries of the Board" were empowered to organize in 1871.

To this Woman's Auxiliary the Board has always been most kind and generous. It has housed it freely, has met its central expenses, has received and disbursed its funds, it has relieved it of numberless responsibilities and cares. Its officers have been more than friends, always ready to give counsel and personal help, placing at the service of the Auxiliary not only the equipment with which the Board has furnished them—including the invaluable aid of the Missionary from the field—but themselves also.

The Auxiliary gratefully acknowledges this unstinted kindness and the friendly appreciation shown it through all these years. And it records with grateful thanks, as well, that approval and personal interest and help on their part of the Bishops of the Church and the parochial clergy and of our missionaries, which have made the establishment of the Auxiliary in diocese and missionary district, in parish and mission, a possibility.

But it is not satisfied with itself nor content to feel that the women of the Church have compassed their capacity for helpfulness. The gain of $29,000 towards the Board's appropriations, largely in response to the Emergency appeal, the suggestions that led to the day of unbroken intercession, now twice kept at the Church Missions House, are by no means a sufficient answer to the Board's latest call. We feel that Board and Bishops and parochial clergy may gain much more from this company of women who stand so ready to co-operate with the men of the Church under their leadership in the widest plans that may be made for the spread of Christ's Kingdom throughout the world.

Therefore, at this time we ask the Board if, in reviewing the Auxiliary's work, it will not hold back its praise, and, instead, give a judicial and constructive help; tell us what it sees not of strength only, but of weakness; not of success, but failure; and set before us some call which shall exercise the very best that not only the women of to-day's Auxiliary, but all the women of the Church, can give.

. . . .

The principle of the Woman's Auxiliary has been that it should be true to the authorities under which it is constituted—as a whole, to the Board of Missions which instituted it to be its helper; in diocesan and parochial branches, to the Bishops and parish clergy who have organized them.

Its purpose has been to help the Board of Missions bring to the realization of the Church that the *Field* is the *World*.

Its method: Under each Bishop to procure the establishment of a diocesan branch, under each parish priest the formation of one or more parochial branches, and along with this organization of the women, to enlist in its Junior Department the children and young people of the Church.

To these organizations the Auxiliary has constantly presented three ways in which the work entrusted to it should be advanced—through gifts, through study and through prayer.

It has pressed among its branches and individual members the *duty* of helping the board make up the sum of its appropriations. It has emphasized its *privilege* of giving, that those appropriations might be supplemented by missionary boxes, for domestic missionaries, the insurance of foreign missionaries, the erection and furnishing of buildings, the numberless specials that have marked its years. It has gladly made its gift of *thanks* in its Triennial United Offering.

And since the days when Mrs. Tuttle, wife of our beloved Presiding Bishop, and Miss Upfold of Indianapolis and others long ago began to set the Auxiliary to study the conditions of the Mission field, and since we first welcomed the help of the Misses Beach of Hartford, and others of the Church Missions Publishing Company—faithful through difficult years before the Board established its Educational Department, and faithful still—here and there in the

Woman's Auxiliary have been always those who believed one chief part of the member's duty was *to know*.

To that end numberless journeys have been undertaken, visits of officers and missionaries planned, addresses made, the SPIRIT OF MISSIONS has been introduced to new subscribers, books have been lent and read, program meetings conducted, institutes held, normal and other study classes led, and summer schools and conferences attended.

And, as to prayer, we turn back to the leaflet of Auxiliary Collects furnished to members through all the years; we recall the earliest days of Auxiliary work for Foreign Missions, and see Miss Cornelia Jay gathering the tiny band of courageous women about her and leading them in Bible reading and prayer; it is many years that Quiet Hours and Corporate Communions have been known, and this year for the twelfth Triennial the entire representative body of the Auxiliary will assemble for the Service to which for three years it has been looking forward.

Such ways as these, in gifts, in study and in prayer, have become the familiar ways of the Woman's Auxiliary to the Board of Missions, pursued in the almost untrammeled freedom to which the Board with such kindly confidence has left its helper. For forty-five years it has been practising them, and now it stands on the threshold of its forty-sixth year and looks out, all unsatisfied with its past and eager for its future. It would ask the Board of Missions to give it serious thought, and to consider if there are not means through which what has been tried may be made the starting-point for a new and larger conception of what woman's work in the Church shall be.

The Woman's Auxiliary enlists far from all our women in Missionary activity. In Connecticut, on the day preceding the annual convention of the diocese, there is a meeting of the clergy and laity—men and women—and the work of the Woman's Auxiliary, in whole or in part, is presented among other subjects. In New York and Newark at their last conventions an officer of the Auxiliary was introduced, and addressed the convention.

In California and Eastern Oregon a House of Churchwomen is convened at the time and place of meeting of the Diocesan Council; from East Carolina, Atlanta, North Dakota and elsewhere comes to us the report of Auxiliary work, linked with that of work—friendly, philanthropic, reform, diocesan, parochial; the Synod of the Province of the Mid-West has appointed a committee "to consider the subject of the co-operation of women in the work of the Provincial Synod."

Can the Woman's Auxiliary to the Board of Missions, introduced into the Church in 1871 and developing as we have pictured here, be further used by the Church through its Board of Missions in helping to meet the peculiar calls of the present time? Is it possible for the Board of Missions to bring to the councils of the Church a proposition to consider some fresh departure which shall gather in and conserve to the Church the force of the Church's womanhood, as yet so inadequately utilized? Cannot some call be sent to the Bishops in their dioceses and to the parish clergy in their parishes, urging them to review this entire subject of woman's work for the extension of Christ's Kingdom through all the world, and asking them how they can best gain the co-operation of the women, already interested and intelligent, in carrying out the Church's plans for making diocese and parish the working Missionary unit?

The Woman's Auxiliary has suffered from having been left so largely to its own devisings, which have presented to it tasks entirely incommensurate with its strength. Women whose intelligence is good and cultivated, whose outlook is broad, whose ability is excellent, whose power has never been tried for the Church's service, women who love the Church and devote themselves gladly to her works of love and mercy in their parish lives and rejoice in the beauty of her holiness, would be won to it in increasing numbers, were the limitless possibilities for the winning of this world for Christ set before them in a large and commanding and persuasive way.

Is there no farther work suitable in which they may be enlisted and in the doing of which, under their rectors and Bishops and the organized authorities of the Church, they may realize more fully than they yet have done that they have a valued and valuable contribution to make?

We would ask both the Board and the Auxiliary to consider whether a real gain might be made if we should emphasize the Auxiliary less as an organization but rather as a reminder, a co-operator, and a vehicle by and through which the general missionary interests of the Church might be strengthened in any and every department of parish life.

JULIA C. EMERY, Secretary.
Church Missions House, October, 1916.

Julia C. Emery, "Forty-Fifth Annual Report of the Woman's Auxiliary to the Board of Missions, 1915-1916," in *Annual Report of the Board of Missions for the Fiscal Year September 1, 1915, to September 30, 1916* (New York: Domestic and Foreign Missionary Society of the Protestant Episcopal Church in the United States of America, 1916), 232-234. (Excerpt)

101.

Henry Y. Satterlee, The Idea of an American Cathedral, 1916

Henry Yates Satterlee (January 11, 1843–February 22, 1908) was consecrated the Bishop of Washington on March 25, 1896. He was an advocate of the cathedral system, and he describes the mission of a cathedral in this essay. Not all dioceses have cathedrals, and most cathedrals are parish churches used for diocesan purposes. The Cathedral of Our Merciful Saviour in Faribault, Minnesota, was one of the earliest, and the Cathedral of Saints Peter and Paul (the National Cathedral), Washington, the Cathedral of St. John the Divine, New York, and Grace Cathedral, San Francisco, are three of the more significant in the Episcopal Church.

The Cathedral (except as a building) is new in the American Church, and if properly organized it will supply a great want, that is, a sphere for episcopal work. Hitherto the American Church, while technically Episcopal, is in effect parochial, for the Bishop is little more than (1) a parish visitor; (2) an ordinary; (3) a president of the diocesan convention. Missionary bishops fill a larger sphere than diocesan bishops and have consequently more freedom as chief pastors of the flock. The consequence is that the pastoral office of the diocesan bishop is shorn of great possibilities in diocesan work. On the other hand, there are these considerations: (1) the present supra-parochial activities of the Church are sporadic and in some cases individualistic. They suffer because they are isolated from one another; (2) the supra-parochial *potentialities* of the Church are a great unutilized opportunity. No one can forecast the extended sphere of usefulness that would be created if this mine of wealth in Church effort were explored. New York parishes are now trying to do a Cathedral work at the expense of their pastoral work. A prominent Southern bishop said to me: "New York parishes are no longer spiritual homes for the people; they are great eleemosynary institutions." Now, the Cathedral, as the bishop's church, gives him a sphere for the exercise of his pastoral office, with spiritual opportunities that he cannot have in any parish, where he would either be interfering with some rector, or else be awakening the jealousy of the other parishes; and it is, at the same time, the mother church of the diocese, where all parishes are welcomed on equal terms, and where diocesan efforts both converge and radiate, and where missionary and educational efforts originate. This is an ideal which belongs to the primitive, not the mediæval Church. . . .

Charles H. Brent. *A Master Builder, Being the Life and Letters of Henry Yates Satterlee, First Bishop of Washington* (New York: Longman, Green and Co., 1916), 457-458. (Excerpt)

102

Amy M. Burt, U.T.O. Worker at Appalachian School, 1929

At the thirty-sixth General Convention in New York, October 2-24, 1889, the United Offering (now the United Thank Offering, U.T.O.) was established. It was the project of the Woman's Auxiliary to the Board of Missions of the Episcopal Church which was established in 1872. The U.T.O. provided funding for female missionaries. In this article Amy M. Burt describes her work at a U.T.O.-funded Appalachian school.

At a point three thousand feet above the sea level, in the heart of the Blue Ridge Mountains, stands a school where those in charge of the U. T. O. have chosen to place a memorial to the devotion of the women of the Church, in the form of a much needed building.

This is the Appalachian School at Penland, Diocese of Western North Carolina. It is in the midst of a superior class of mountain people. They are by nature sincerely religious. They frequently meet in groups in different cabin homes for a service of prayer and praise and study.

Were this the end of the story one might be content, but a great change has come over the country. Five years ago there were only mountain trails with rocks and deep mud to connect one little settlement with another. Now the highways are everywhere bringing their opportunity for betterment, and their temptations. Mountain youths are quick to learn the mechanics of motor cars. The world beckons and they ride often as upon the whirlwind to their destruction. The sterling Anglo-Saxon ideals of their ancestors may give place as readily and as completely as does the slow pace over the old mountain trails give place to modern speed.

There is no place in the world where the Church has a greater opportunity than where too rapid a transition is made from one civilization to another, and the people of the Appalachian Highlands are being shuttled from the civilization of the sixteenth to that of the twentieth century. All the older generation represent life of an earlier and sterner time, when the question, "What shall we eat and where withal shall we be clothed," had to be answered at the opening of every day and answered by ceaseless toil, the man wresting the raw materials from the soil while the labor of the woman completed the cycle of feeding and clothing the family.

The Appalachian School through its community work and its day and boarding school has developed in the minds of sons and daughters of the community a respect for the older generation and its standards that helps in meeting this problem.

The department of weaving, under the direction of Miss Lucy C. Morgan, has created an economic independence, a self-respect, and a recognition for the women over a radius of about seven miles around the school. There are over seventy women who have some part in this work. Once a week, through all the best part of the year, in larger or smaller groups they meet at the weaving cabin which was built coöperatively, the logs and part of the labor being given by the people. These meetings contribute much to lives that had been isolated, inhibited, starved.

The work is an outlet for their native artistic ability. A spirit of neighborliness has grown up so that every one is ready to help a neighbor even at a good deal of inconvenience.

All the weavers are dependent upon the school for all contacts with the outside world, such as marketing. All weaving sold brings varied advantages to the community. Families are not only enabled to have the services of dentist and physician, and other assistance requiring money in hand, but they even send their children to college with their earnings. Some girls in their later teens earn their own school money.

Until this revival of colonial art began there had been no remunerative work for women and often very little for men. Now the old spinning wheels and reels are busy again, old drafts are brought to light. Over all this region a new life is born with an artistic channel for self expression, a life of coöperation.

The rugs, the scarves, coverlets, table linens, cloth by the yard for dresses, coats, etc., done by these weavers whose ancestors helped to "subdue the dangers of the mountain wilderness" in colonial days compare favorably in artistic coloring, in excellence of workmanship, and in charm of design with the displays of foreign handwork that are greeted so enthusiastically over these United States of ours.

The Appalachian School is a day and boarding school for children through the period of elementary education. Here all children within reach are prepared for high school if their interest goes that far.

The boarding school furnishes a home for little children who are orphaned or homeless for some reason. The majority of these children are from the Appalachian highland with a smaller number from families that had moved into factory towns and there met with misfortune.

It takes but a limited knowledge of the psychology of childhood and of the leading social problems of the day for one to understand that work of this kind in early childhood is the only real opportunity that offers for making a real contribution in human character to our Church and our country for the age that awaits at our doors.

Experts in criminal psychology tell us that four-fifths of all the crime and insanity and that most of the social, moral, and intellectual irregularity of the world could be prevented by proper care during the first seven years of child life.

The Appalachian School serves as nurse, home, parent, teacher, for over seventy boys and girls between the ages of two and fourteen who by day and by night receive from Miss Katherine Califf and her co-workers a sympathy, an understanding care and devotion that no money could ever buy.

Long hours of sleep, pure mountain air and water, simple food carefully prepared, much life in the great out of doors where birds and flowers are their friends, hikes, swimming, the joy of work, for every child has his duties, happy hours in the day school, are conditions of life which invite prayer and praise.

Our children delight in religious services. The Rev. Frederick D. Lobdell comes often to give the services of the Church and to prepare children for Confirmation. He is loved by every child.

The children who join in our daily prayers, read the children's literature in our library, who learn to be honest, to be industrious, to be thoughtful for others, to love and respect their elders, who exercise fair play in their games, who learn to meet God in the life of every day, are engaged in the art of building a character which will go with them into the responsibilities of manhood and womanhood.

Amy M. Burt, *The Spirit of Missions* 94 (March 1929): 162-163.

103.

Lyman C. Ogilby, The Church's Mission II, 1959

Lyman Cunningham Ogilby (January 25, 1922–) was consecrated Suffragan Bishop of the Philippines on February 2, 1953. He was Bishop of the Philippines, 1957-1967, Bishop Coadjutor of South Dakota, 1967-1970, Assistant Bishop, 1971-1973, Bishop Coadjutor, 1973, and Bishop, 1974-1987, of Pennsylvania. As noted in the following excerpt, the shift toward empowerment of indigenous leadership for younger churches reflects a shift in missionary strategy with the end of the colonial era after World War II.

The apostolic Church is the Church on mission, sent into the world; and this historic Christ-commissioned community on a mission is not safely at home but risks her very life in service to those outside her life. The Church has broken through the walls of Jerusalem and has shaken the dust of Antioch and Ephesus from her feet in response to the Macedonian cry; and, except for brief times in the Church's history when martyrdom or retreat into the catacombs was the sole witness possible, the Church has obeyed and will proudly obey God's orders, and has never halted and will never halt her march for the purpose of self-culture and self-nurture.

Many of the younger churches of Southeast Asia, Africa, and India—once and even now in part considered missionary jurisdictions and "receiving churches"—are courageously rising to God's mandate, and are sending their own missionaries beyond their national boundaries. The Philippine Episcopal Church, needful of all its forty national priests at home, is about to send two Filipino priests to North Borneo; and the Philippine Independent Church, our sister communion with whom we have close family relationships, has sent a priest to Honolulu. The church not on the missionary march is not true to her Lord and Saviour.

The *status quo*, "leave-well-enough-alone" voices have been heard wherever and whenever the people of God have dared to rise to his command to go, with his power and might, heralding and establishing his Kingdom and in this obedience, upsetting and overthrowing the familiar, estranging father and child, delivering brother to brother, and shattering golden calves for the sake of God's laws. . . .

Mission as well as government schools do play their part to bring enlightenment to the back-water societies of the world, where the waters are still muddied by pagan beliefs. Mission as well as government hospitals and clinics and dispensaries do play a significant role amidst primitive cultures in combatting disease and saving or prolonging human life. Agricultural and industrial endeavors, both mission and government sponsored, have made great and progressive strides in bringing about constructive social and economic changes in backward communities. But education and medicine and economics do not, by and in themselves, change the wills of men. The Church has surely known and lived under the Pauline injunction that the right knowledge, correct methods or techniques, and good intentions do not save souls. The gospel of Christ Crucified, the creating and redeeming and sanctifying life of God, is the only power that changes, overcomes, and wins the wills and allegiances of men; and the Church has lived gloriously and triumphantly under the truth that only through the passion of Christ may men know a peace and joy which the world has failed to give. This is the saving message that the Body of Christ must bring to man and society, near and far, though sheep will be separated from goats, new wine will shatter the old bottles, and the last will come first as this Person draws the hearts and wills of men into his love. . . .

The Younger Church

The Church is the Church on mission; and her essential character is missionary. The purpose of the Church's missionary outreach to men and society outside her present life and work is to initiate Christianity where it is unknown; to plan its future and development in a new land or in a new area of society; and to provide guidance and education, care and nurture until Christianity has taken firm root. In brief, the mission of the Church is first to proclaim and herald the redeeming gospel of Christ Crucified, and second to naturalize and acclimatize Christianity in each land and area by building up a native, national, and indigenous Church. This story of the outward expansion of the Christian community from Jerusalem two thousand years ago over the face of the world is filled with triumphs as well as tragedies, with glories as well as disgraces; but the missionary record of the Church can be clearly seen by the foot-prints of Christians living today on every continent. For our purposes, we will assume this history and consider the object of the Church's mission as the foundation of a self-extending, self-supporting, and self-governing Christian community, part of the Body of Christ. These three aspects of a younger church of the twentieth century are obviously interrelated and interdependent, but in this brief examination and evaluation we will treat them as three entities or characteristics marking the life-growth of the younger churches.

The self-extending and self-perpetuating character of a younger church, which has been founded and fostered and favored by an older sending-church, must be nurtured and nourished, encouraged and maintained from the moment the cross is first planted on new soil or in a new area. Yet the planting of the church in new ground can never be the transplanting of the fully matured plant taken from other soil, for roots must grow down just as branches must grow up. The older church plants the seeds, and local conditions will supply whatever necessary and natural transmutations will take place in the process of growth. But the beginnings of a local priesthood, the development of local lay leadership, the initiation of all the groups, agencies, and activities that will encourage the spontaneous growth and expansion of the younger church must be fostered and favored, for the Church—young or old—is missionary. If the extension and perpetuation of the younger church is the sole responsibility of the older sending-church, this younger Christian community is less than a church and will never grow beyond its infant, dependent, and parasitical stage, and will continue to be a foreign mission doing little more than carrying on various Christian or charitable acts of service, commendable though many of these services may be, for the local society. Foreign and professional missionaries, charged with the initial responsibility of leadership, must so order their lives, attitudes, and outlook that they increasingly move from doing things for the younger church or the members of the young church to doing things with and in the young church; and eventually, by God's grace, work themselves out of their positions.

From the very start, the seed of self-extension and self-perpetuation must be planted.

As with self-extension, the seeds for the self-supporting and self-sufficient character of the younger church must be in the luggage of the first foreign missionary to arrive on new soil. And the problem of nurturing this self-supporting aspect of the younger church's life and work is often complicated when this foreign missionary arrives from one of the rich and powerful western nations with a higher standard of living and a greater political influence than the land in which he will serve as Christ's ambassador. But this is a modern complication. Saint Paul, going in the opposite direction, never had to face this problem. Surely, the level at which the self-support is set or the standard by which the self-sufficiency is judged and evaluated must be determined for the local scene and by the local church.

When one uses this phrase, self-support, one is tempted to limit its connotation to finances, but certainly the self-sufficient character of the Church encompasses the whole canvas of Christian stewardship—of time, talents, and treasures; of faith, order, and worship; of holy mysteries and redeeming truths. As Anglicans with a glorious Christian heritage, the best and the perfect and the complete is ours: creeds, sacraments, Bible, and apostolic order—apostles, prophets, and saints—the Book of Common Prayer revealing and manifesting and nurturing this catholic and apostolic and reformed tradition. This sacred trust has been given to us by the High Priest and Saviour Lord himself. This is the faith given to us, God's unworthy stewards; and these are the divine gifts we are called and commanded to use as his stewards, and these are the sacred treasures we are ordered to carry to the ends of the world as his messengers.

The younger church, to be worthy of Christ's name, must from its very beginnings be built on the foundations of Christian stewardship; and though at first she may not be able to carry heavy burdens and care for great treasures, if she is found faithful with the few talents she will be charged with great trusts.

And finally, the self-governing and self-ordering life of the younger church must likewise be fostered and favored from the moment of the birth of the young church. The local structuring of society, the peculiar and particular currents of nationalism in the land, local culture or cultures, the role of women, the agriculturization or urbanization or industrialization of the scene—all will play a part in determining how these initial seeds will mature and later stand as trees ordering, directing, and governing the younger church.

Here, in the Philippine Episcopal Church, after sixty years of history in this land, we have just consecrated our first Filipino bishop, who will serve as suffragan to the ordinary. Although it is never easy to signify the point in life and development of a younger church when this positive and progressive step in self-government should be made, certainly we can say that if foreigners are charged with the responsibility of making such a decision, as they are in Anglican polity, it is better to anticipate this move rather than to delay it so long that it is demanded by a spirit of rising nationalism or unfriendly independence or anti-foreignism on the part of the younger church.

And the older church's evaluation of and judgement upon the degree to which the younger church can support and sustain its local leaders, such as a national bishop, should not be a "pass-mark" to be attained by a younger church before she can be granted the privilege and responsibility of elements of self-government.

If these seeds of self-extension, self-support, and self-government are aboard the ship with the first arriving foreign missionary, and are carefully planted and nourished in the infant church, she will surely grow in stature and in favour with God, worthy to be called his Body and sent on his mission.

Lyman C. Ogilby, "The Church's Mission II," in *Viewpoint: Some Aspects of Anglican Thinking*, ed. John B. Coburn and W. Norman Pittenger (Greenwich, Conn.: Seabury Press, 1959), 246-248, 250-253. (Excerpts)

104.

Report of Committee of Conference on Overseas Missions to the Presiding Bishop and the National Council, Protestant Episcopal Church in the U.S.A., 1961

The Committee of Conference on Overseas Missions was appointed in 1958 to make recommendations for leading the Church into greater understanding, support, and service for world-wide mission. This report provides principles for world mission.

Mission—The Church's Essential Nature

The mission of the Church is rooted in her very being. It is not an adjunct or subsidiary activity to be set alongside other Christian pursuits, but is integral to the Church's given nature.

The mission of the Church is in its deepest sense God's, not ours. The Church is the chosen instrument used by the Holy Spirit to continue what God initiated in Jesus Christ. At the Incarnation He broke into the finite world of alienated men, that through the ministry of Jesus in proclaiming the Good News and through His Cross and Resurrection they might be reconciled to God and their lives transformed. God's almighty act opened to all men the possibility of new life in Christ, infused with God's forgiving and healing power. God continues this saving work in the world through us, who are His Body.

To history the mission of the Church imparts direction and unity, disclosing to anxious man the meaning of his destiny as the new being in Christ. This is its reconciling work. Yet on the stage of history demonic forces still rage, tempting the faithful and corrupting the world. Here must stand God's judgment, upon Church and world alike.

The calling of the Church is to be the agent of the continuation of the mission of Christ Himself. His mission knows no distinction of geographical area, age, sex, culture, or race. The Church deals with these historical differences in her administrative structure, but does not recognize them as creating differences in the divine dispensation. For the Church there can be no basic difference between her mission at home and her mission abroad. In both spheres, "the whole of life has a missionary dimension," and is therefore one.

1. Everyone is a Missionary

If the Church "exists by mission as fire exists by burning,"[1] then one who is baptized and confirmed into her fellowship is thereby a missionary. A member of the Church "cannot have fellowship with Christ without being committed to partnership in His mission to the world."

Responsibility for witness to the transforming power of God, therefore, rests with each member as he shares the life of the Church. He bears that witness at whatever station he occupies: at home, in his recreation, and through his labor.

It follows from this that, as the Bishops said at Lambeth in 1958, the Church's mission can never be left to a professional cadre of clergy or other trained evangelists, but inheres in the life of the whole Christian community. By means of the diversity of gifts within its fellowship, God calls his people to share His work in healing the world, and reconciling man to Himself.

Our Church recognizes this in Canon 3, Article 1, which states: "This organization shall be called The Domestic and Foreign Missionary Society of the Protestant Episcopal Church in the United States of America, and shall be considered as comprehending all persons who are members of the Church." This

---

[1] Emil Brunner.

canon is perhaps the basic utterance of the Episcopal church in defining a missionary: it commissions all members as missionaries.

2. The Word and the Sacraments

God has given His Church the Word and the Sacraments as the principal means for fulfilling its mission.

The Holy Bible is indispensable to the mission of the Church, in the first place, because Christians universally recognize in its total record an account of the saving acts of God toward man. In the sense that it records what God has done, not man, it is God's Word, not ours. Being, then, the first and basic witness of the faith in which we have been nurtured, it remains the common standard by which all faith is tested, redefined, refreshed and renewed. The Bible guards against the vagaries of interpretation which will characterize any given time or place, and thus proclaims the essence of God's love for each new people or age in terms of its own life.

Secondly, since God's Word is expressed through the words of men and God's action on the stage of human history, the Bible constitutes the bridge by which the Church's mission may advance to meet the thoughts and lives of men, wherever they are in the world. God has already established a beachhead in the understanding and experience of people so that in their hidden longing for the holy, they are prepared to receive the Good News we are commissioned to proclaim.

As instruments of her mission the Church provides the Sacraments. Through these means of grace Christians are nourished and renewed by Christ himself, and the world beholds the image of how God sanctifies and redeems the common things of the earth.

Here lies the special role of the clergy in the Church's mission, for they are ordained to administer the Sacraments. It is the priest's vocation to be "a faithful Dispenser of the Word of God, and of His holy Sacraments."

3. One God, One World

The mission of the Church lies in the world, a world created by God and destined by Him for salvation. Even in rebellion, man is still in the embrace of God's care; he is still the bearer of God's "image." As one theologian has written:

"The manifest Church opens up what is potentially given in the different religions and cultures outside Christianity. In some way and on some level, every human being is longing for a new reality in contrast to the distorted reality in which he is living. People are not *outside* of God; they are *grasped* by God, on the level in which they can be grasped,—in their experience of the Divine, in the realm of holiness in which they are living, in which they are educated, in which they have performed acts of faith and adoration and prayer and cult, even if the symbols in which the Holy was expressed seem to us extremely primitive and idolatrous. It was distorted religion, but it was not non-religion. It was the reality of the Divine, preparing in paganism for the coming of the manifest Church, and through the manifest Church the coming of the Kingdom of God."[2]

St. Paul often refers to what we might call the "latent Church," which exists by virtue of God's creation in all times, places, and cultures, including our own. Thus the Apostle reminded the pagan crowd at Lystra that since the world began God "left not Himself without witness" (Acts 14:17).

The mission of the Christian Church, therefore, is to transform that which is latent into the manifest fulfillment of man's common life in Christ. In Biblical language, this is to prepare for the coming of the Kingdom of God.

As in the days of the Old Testament prophets, so in our own time there is a desperate need to acknowledge *one God for one World* as the basic fact of human existence. God in His Unity has the almighty power to lead His people in the task of reuniting a critically dismembered world. At the same time, it is our urgent duty to proclaim this monotheistic faith, which is the religious dimension of the same truth recognized in the fields of economics and politics—that this is one world, and that it must act as such before it is too late.

Because God is Creator, there is no area of human activity that is not susceptible of salvation. Because God is Redeemer in Jesus Christ, the Church must not be a refuge where holiness may dwell separate and undisturbed. Its task is to bring together the sacred and the secular, not to divide them. The Church must not identify Christianity with any particular cultural expression of it, nor may it stand apart from culture; rather its task is to be God's agent in the transformation of culture.

This will properly result in a reciprocal communication between the Church and the world which is vital to the Church's life. When the Church pursues her mission among men, God uses their resistance and criticism to cleanse the Church of those tendencies within her fellowship which, through self-righteousness, and shallowness, betray her work. Missionary activity, therefore, is an exchange: a listening on both sides, a mutual cleansing. The propensity toward arrogance of which some accuse the Christian mission can be avoided by the honesty of this two-way communication.

4. Communication

Too often the Church has tended to oversimplify its commission to "be witnesses unto me . . . unto the uttermost past of the earth."

---

[2]Paul Tillich, in an unpublished lecture.

That which it proclaims, being unique, has no analogy. As Paul said it is "unto the Jews a stumbling block, and unto the Greeks foolishness." Christian communication cannot escape misunderstanding. Logic and willpower are not sufficient to insure that the Gospel will be received; the grace of God is indispensable. It is God who speaks through us, and no word of ours is ever adequate or worthy.

The Christian mission is set in a world of such cultural disparities as to make its task always dangerous and difficult.

Christians, because of their natural concern for the whole of man's life, have often looked toward social service, particularly medical and educational missions, are effective channels of Christian communication. We recognize thankfully the increasing support given to these endeavors. This method of witness by example is proper and legitimate, but it should not be divorced from the Word and the Sacraments or be made a substitute for them, nor should it be allowed to promote the institutionalization of the Church in such a way as to hinder conversion by the Holy Spirit.

While Christianity is historically rooted in a particular culture, yet it must be expressed and embodied in every culture, and this responsibility must never be evaded. And since man is both body and spirit, word and deed must be married in the Church's mission in such a way that men whose ways and thoughts may be very different from our own may appropriate to themselves the grace that Christ so royally offers for the fulfillment of the will of God in their lives.

Journal of General Convention, 1961, 768-771. (Excerpt)

105.

Wesley Frensdorff, Holy Orders and Ministry: Some Reflections, 1977

Wesley Frensdorff (July 22, 1926–May 17, 1988) was consecrated Bishop of Nevada on March 4, 1972. Later he was Interim Bishop of the Navajoland Area Mission and Assistant Bishop of Arizona. He was a leader in the development of the Church's total ministry, which he describes in this reflection.

[T]oday, as always, the Church yearns for empowerment in mission through the revitalization of ministry, all ministry, that of every member. However, the fullness of ministry, so clearly envisioned in Scripture and tradition, remains thwarted *in actual practice*. We can speak easily of the ministry of the laity, but we find it so very difficult to effect, at least on any significant scale. That is not to say that there are not many of the nonordained who exercise much ministry. There are. In fact, they continue to hold before us the potential: what the Church could become if the fullness of her potential in ministry could be realized. There are also those who are "doing" ministry, but do not know it, because the concept has been so much limited to the "professionals." These need to become aware of their ministry. But, even with all that, the laity who are actively engaged in ministry are the exception rather than the rule. What most Church members understand as ministry is the performance of those tasks which either the clergy have largely shunned, do not do very well, or which are auxillary to the more important functions.

The implementation of the New Testament vision of the fullness of ministry has always been elusive, at least so it appears. One of the primary causes seems to have been that what developed gradually as the "ordered" or "ordained" ministry of the Church has frequently been a block to the ministry of each member, rather than being the vehicle and enabling force for the royal priesthood in which we all share.

As we examine the state of ministry in the Church today, this appears to be the case once again. "Ordained ministry" important, or even essential, as it is to the life and mission of the Church, has for a long time been the plug or the cork in the bottle of ministry. This was also one of the central issues of the Reformation. Robert Capon puts it this way: "The best theological insight of the Reformation, the priesthood of all believers, went whistling out the window because no practical provisions were made to insure that the orders of the ministry would sacramentalize them. We are about to recover that insight again. Let's not make the same mistake twice."

We must have a clearer understanding of the relationship of "ordained" ministries to the other ministries, an understanding based on the New Testament, the early Church experience, and consistent with the essence of the tradition. These concepts must be such as to serve as a theological base for an operative model of ministry which will enlist, facilitate, and engage the full membership of the Church in meaningful and significant ministry. Contrary to most theories of ministry, the majority of the Churches' membership conceives of ministry as something done *to* and *for* them, rather than *by* them, and as something sent *to* them, rather than something sent *from* them to the world.

If the Church is to become truly alive for mission in our time, then we must discover the way in which the power for ministry of the whole Body can be more effectively released than in the past. Can we make the exercise of the priesthood of all believers a reality? Can we develop a model or models for ministry in which all share and yet in which the traditional "Orders" have a place?

Wesley Frensdorff, "Holy Orders and Ministry: Some Reflections," *Anglican Theological Review* 59 (July 1977): 281-282. (Excerpt)

106.

James C. Fenhagen,
The Many Faces of Ministry, 1978

James Corner Fenhagen II (November 4, 1929–) was dean of the General Theological Seminary, 1978-1992. He has written extensively on the ministry of the whole Church. In this selection he discusses the importance of identifying gifts for ministry.

In his autobiography, *Report to Greco*, Nikos Kazantzakis tells of a visit to a monastery in Crete which he made during a period of intense spiritual searching. "It was the wise Father Joachim who, clapping his hands as though I was a pullet, shooed me away. 'Return to the world,' he cried. 'In this day and age the world is the true monastery; that is where you will become a saint.'"

Kazantzakis' words echo a call to ministry, a call to open our lives in such a way that they may be used in the healing of the world's pain. The ministry of the Christian Church is the ministry of Jesus Christ. It is a ministry to the isolation and the brokenness and the injustice that fragments the human family. "The spirit of the Lord is upon me," Jesus proclaimed to the synagogue in Nazareth. "He has sent me to announce good news to the poor, to proclaim release for prisoners and recovery of sight for the blind" (Luke 4:18-19). We are called to share in this ministry. It is a call to be more than concerned citizens, more even than regular contributing members of a local congregation. It is a call to open our lives to the claim of Jesus Christ so that everything we do, we do in his name, as a part of His ministry to the world. "Though many are invited," Jesus said, "but few are chosen" (Matthew 22:14). I understand this to mean that the call is to all of us who "profess and call ourselves Christians," but that choice comes only after we freely respond. We are chosen for ministry when we are willing to take the next step.

The Desire for Something More

Not long ago I happened to pick up the parish bulletin of a church in

Washington, D.C., where a particular effort had been made to give support to the ministry of laity. The leadership of this congregation had worked hard to develop an innovative program for the education of their adult membership, borrowing ideas from every source possible and, of course, creating some of their own. As I read the first line of this bulletin, I found myself especially intrigued. "Now that we have incorporated most of the best programs we heard about," it stated, "and now that so many people are ready to grow in new directions, the challenge is one of coming up with new and promising directions. Let me tell you my thoughts on this subject. For a long time I have had a day dream of a secular religious community at St. Columba's. I don't know exactly what it would look like, but it would allow lay people to have a discipline of spiritual growth, a small community of support, and multiple avenues of mission outreach. There are just so many people who are coming alive in the Faith and who deeply desire 'something more.' I do not know what the 'something more' is, but my intuition is that if we could investigate other models of religious communities, we might be able to develop a healthy model of our own."

And so, for this particular church, the search began. What struck me about this bulletin, however, was the recognition that there are people in our churches who are searching for "something more." They may not be the people that you would automatically think of. Indeed, they may be people whose Christian commitment is exercised primarily outside the life of the congregation, yet whose faith has brought them closer and closer to an awareness of those things that give life meaning and purpose. They are people who in a variety of ways have been claimed by the Lord Jesus Christ, and who know it. For them the question of "something more" has a particular intensity.

It is when we are ready to ask the "something more" question that we are most open to the call to ministry. Ministry is more than doing good. It means to serve in the Lord's name in ways—often small and unnoticed—that enable Jesus Christ to act through us for the healing of the world. Ministry, therefore, is not something we do on our own. It is rather the response to those "gifts" that each of us has been given, but which in most cases lie buried within us still waiting to be called forth.

Claiming Our Gifts

"In each of us," writes Paul to the church at Corinth, "the Spirit is manifested in one particular way, for some useful purpose" (I Corinthians 12:7). The way in which the Spirit manifests itself within us is what we call "gift." Gift is the action of God which calls forth those special qualities that are needed for the Lord's work. The New Testament speaks of gifts of healing and wisdom and teaching, to name but a few. But there are also gifts of listening, caring, problem

448

solving and personal witness. It is the work of the Spirit to activate these gifts for ministry. In one of his better known parables, Jesus tells of the three servants who invested the gold they had been given in different ways. One servant was given five bags of gold, another two, another one, "each according to his capacity." The servant with five bags put it immediately to use and doubled his investment. So did the servant with two bags. The man with one bag, however, took his gold and buried it in the ground because of his fear of risking what he had (Matthew 25:14-30).

Our concern here is with the servant whose gift was buried—the fearful one. It is a truth that, when we allow the gifts we have been given to be called forth in ministry, they are expanded often beyond our wildest dreams. But it is also a truth that for most of us fear gets in the way. Buried within each of us lie gifts that we have not used, gifts that are often lodged in that part of us that we most avoid. For the cerebral, thinking types, it might be the intuitive, imaginative side of ourselves that needs to be exposed to the activating power of God. For the ecstatics among us, the opposite might well be true. "It is inevitable," John Sanford writes, "that in the growth of our personalities, much that potentially is part of us will not be developed . . . All this undeveloped self is the unlived life which for the Kingdom to be realized, must get into our life in a legitimate way." It is no accident, therefore, that there is so much attention paid in the New Testament to the recovery of that which is lost. The Kingdom of God is like finding a coin that had disappeared or discovering a pearl of special value or the treasure that had been buried in the field. The point is, the gifts necessary for sharing in the ministry of Christ are available to us all, but without the willingness to risk opening the unused, guarded parts of ourselves to the action of the Spirit they will lie within—dormant and untapped.

The primary task of the local congregation is to enable persons to discover their gifts for ministry so that these gifts may be celebrated and developed. One way to go about this is to provide settings in which persons can share with one another those aspects of their spiritual journeys that reflect their exercise of ministry. In doing this, four questions seem to me to be particularly helpful.

1. What are the gifts that lie buried within us?

2. Where are we already doing ministry?

3. What are the theological dimensions of what we do?

4. How can we covenant with others for mutual accountability and support?

The first question is a deeply person one. It cannot be approached superficially or with haste. Its aim is to help us uncover those unique gifts or talents that we have possessed for a long time, yet which never have been developed. No one else can identify these gifts for us. The discovery is a personal one, coming out of the discipline of reflective prayer. To ask this question of ourselves involves time for solitude and the courage to respond to the Spirit's deep probing. It requires that we give our imaginative and intuitive self free reign, so that those gifts that we do not see may surface freely and without restraint.

Urban Holmes, in his book *Ministry and Imagination,* makes the persuasive claim that the primary agenda of the ministry today is to enable people to rediscover or relearn their capacity for intuition and wonder. "The fact that religious experience is considered so rare a thing among us," he writes, "does not mean that God is no longer present, but that in our Western culture we have made so little of the imagination, intuition and wonder to discern within our culture the presence of God." The discernment of our deepest gifts is an experience of encounter with God. When these gifts emerge, even tentatively, our task is to address them, to determine how they may be actualized, and then begin the process of putting them to use.

The second question—Where are we already doing ministry?—is aimed at helping us reflect on those gifts that have already been called forth, yet are still unknown and undeveloped. It is based on the assumption that we are already engaged in Christian ministry in a number of ways that reflect those gifts that are uniquely ours. To look at the things that we are already doing for others, things that stretch us or call forth the best in us, is but another way of identifying those inner resources that have been brought into play by the action of the Spirit.

One of the most effective ways of examining the nature of our ministries is through the use of a "critical incident." There are many ways of doing this, most of which involve writing out a description of an experience where we are called upon to make a decision that was difficult and about which we were uncertain or felt particularly vulnerable. As we follow this decision through, with the help of others, we are better able to see that gifts were being called forth and what was either enhancing or blocking their use. When a group of persons helps one of its members to identify his or her gifts of ministry, they are not only exercising ministry themselves, but embodying the very essence of Christian community. There is no more important work that a church can do than to enable persons to share their gifts for ministry and confirm what is offerd by others.

The third question opens us up to the theological dimensions of the decisions we make. In approaching this question we might look first at the values and perspectives reflected in the various poles of our decisions. Then we can more accurately examine how the Christian understanding of creation or personhood or redemption are present in what we see. In one group that worked with critical incidents, a mother shared her pain in trying to relate to her daughter who was living with a man to whom she was not married. The daughter's worldview was quite different from her mother's, yet not without value and integrity. As the

450

group explored these two different worlds, not only new understandings, but new dimensions of ministry emerged.

"Christianity," says Hans Küng, "consists of the activation of the memory of Jesus Christ in thought and practice." Jesus brought sight to all aspects of human blindness. He unmasked the powers, both internal and external, that hold us in bondage so that we may be free. He brought forgiveness to those ravaged by guilt, and new life to those without meaning and hope. It is this precise ministry that continues both in us and through us. It is the ministry for which our gifts have been given.

The final question has to do with building covenants of accountability and support. Like our Jewish brothers and sisters, Christians are people of the Covenant. We are the heirs of the New Covenant given to us in the death and resurrection of Jesus Christ. Covenant is a symbolic word. It signifies an agreement that has deep spiritual roots. To make a "ministry covenant" with another person is to say that you want to be held accountable for what you intend to do. With accountability comes also support. We need people who will stand with us so that we might remain faithful.

Covenant groups usually range in size from eight to twelve persons, meeting regularly for set periods of time. The aim is to provide a setting in which members can explore how their gifts might be best put to use with enough specificity as to determine whether or not what they are doing is actually worthwhile. One man I know developed a ministry which began one evening at a dinner party when a troubled father poured out his anguish to my friend, who, in turn, found he was able to respond in a healing way. By sharing this with his covenant group my friend not only received suggestions about how his ability to listen reflectively might be developed, including, of course, further exploration into the meaning of family trauma and adolescent rebellion, but also help in how he might go about exercising his ministry in a more disciplined way. By stating beforehand what he intended to do, he was able to ask the group to hold him accountable. They not only agreed to do this, but also took the responsibility of praying regularly for the success of his ministry.

Eventually, all members of this particular group were relating to each other in the same way. One member developed a ministry within his business; another was concerned with a particular political issue; another with persons confined to nursing homes; another member of the group developed a ministry to single-parent families. In each case the area of ministry was spelled out, intentions were clarified and a covenant developed which provided accountability, support and regular prayer for the persons involved.

Ministry has many faces. It begins to happen when we discover that Christ lives in us. It is the direct result of an inner transformation that causes us to see the world with new eyes. Ministry is the fruit of the Gospel promise, but for it to deepen, it must be sustained both from within and without. The purpose of the four questions just discussed is to help this sustenance to take place in a regular and disciplined way. We are called to serve others in the name of Christ. Finding "something more" involves taking this ministry seriously and building an inner discipline that gives what we do both substance and depth. . . .

James C. Fenhagen, *More Than Wanderers: Spiritual Disciplines For Christian Ministry* (New York: Seabury Press, 1978), 16-25.

107.

A Theology and Policy of Mission
in Global Perspective, 1982

"A Theology and Policy of Mission in Global Perspective" was produced by the Standing Commission on World Mission. The commission chairman was Bishop Edmond L. Browning (March 11, 1929–) of Hawaii. This statement discusses the theology and role of church mission in a global context.

Theological Affirmations

The Sovereignty of God

Despite changing times and circumstances, is there anything constant about the mission God has given the church? There is. In all times, places and circumstances it is the mission of the church to attest in word and act to what God has made known and accomplished in the life, death and resurrection of Jesus and to pray that, through the Holy Spirit, all people will come to know and love God as he in truth is.

The worship of the church, its holy scriptures and sacraments, creeds and preaching, the pattern of its common life and practice, all attest to a fundamental belief. God and no other is the creator, redeemer and sanctifier of the world. God is the source of all things and only in God will both nature and history find their fulfillment. Nature and history comprise a great drama in which all things have their origin and end in God and in which God himself is the principal actor. The central event in the drama is what God has said and done in the life, death and resurrection of Jesus.

It is the mission of the church to testify in word and act to its belief that it is God in and through Christ who speaks the first and last word in the great drama of history of which the present age is a part, and that it is God's presence, his speaking and acting, that move the course of events toward their fulfillment. In a real sense, all mission is God's.

To put the matter another way, it is the mission of the church to proclaim that no earthly power, no person, people, government, economic force, social movement or church can be the world's providence. Only God is sufficiently loving, powerful and just to utter the world into being and to bring it to its appointed destiny.

It is, therefore, the mission of the church to make a proclamation about the sovereignty of God. The church is sent to give testimony to all who will hear that God is the world's creator, redeemer and sanctifier and that in this work he never speaks or acts in a way contrary to the way in which he has spoken and acted in the life, death and resurrection of Jesus. In Christ, God has spoken the definitive word about himself and about human destiny and in so doing he has also made known who he is. God has at the same time overcome the forces which separate us from himself and which place us in conflict with him and with one another. In Christ, therefore, God is manifest as one who can be trusted, followed and obeyed. He has made himself known as one whose love, power and justice are such that no matter what the circumstances may be, we may give our lives over to his care and guidance. It is this self-revelation in Christ that makes known God's way to himself, which points the way to our fulfillment and so gives birth to faith, hope, love, joy and peace. God's way to himself and so to the destiny appointed for all people is through Christ and it is this way which leads in fact to the health and fulfillment for which all people seek.

The Uniqueness of Christ

In all that it says and does, the church is called to make a statement about what God in Christ has made known and accomplished. In making this statement the church will bring into view through its witness the truth about human nature and destiny. In his mercy, God in Christ holds before the peoples of the earth a mirror in which they may see themselves as in truth they are. Because God has appeared in a life like our own, we can see ourselves both as we are and as we are meant to be. Through the life of Jesus we can at last come to understand our own nature.

In Christ, we know that nature to be glorious. Each and every person is created in the image of God. We know, therefore, that all people are made to share in God's life and to live with him and one another in a community of knowledge, love and peace. By revealing to us the image in which we are made, Christ makes plain also the law of life—that we are created to know and love God and, through God, to know and love each other. Christ thus points the way that leads out of our hopeless divisions and confusions.

Particularly because we see in Christ that we are created for life in community with God and one another, it is possible to view all people in a way quite different from the world's normal pattern. It is the way of the world to make distinctions between rich and poor, developed and underdeveloped, friend and foe, weak and powerful, male and female, black, brown, yellow and white. These distinctions inevitably become perceptions not simply of difference but of value.

In Christ, however, we know that God loves and values all persons equally and that, because this is so, no life is more or less valuable than any other. Each life is surrounded by God's love and care. Each life, therefore, has sanctity. To see ourselves mirrored in the love of God manifest in Christ is not only to know but also to delight in this fact.

Furthermore, in Christ we know the glory and value of each life. We know also, however, that as an image of God, we are not gods but the creatures of God. In Christ, we come to understand both our glory and our limitation. Although made to share God's life, we are nonetheless weak and dependent beings.

Strange as it may seem, it is this very perception of glory and limitation that serves to confirm one of the deepest hopes of the human spirit. In Christ, we learn that in our limited and dependent state we may nonetheless rely on God to sustain and preserve us, and that, as his dependent creatures, we may act on his behalf in both confidence and hope as guardians and keepers of a world made for our delight and enjoyment. As the manifestation of God's image, Christ's life confirms also the hope of all people that the ability and freedom we have to form, order and enjoy human society and so express the rich potential of our being in the works of human culture are from God, and intended for our benefit and not for our enslavement or corruption.

In Christ, we are privileged to see what we are created to be—the image of God our creator. The church exists to point out again and again this manifestation of what human nature under God truly is and to call all people to themselves by calling them to God through Christ. In its attestation to Christ, the church necessarily reminds the world of both the glories and the limitations of its creatureliness.

In its witness to Christ, the church confronts people with the fact that they repeatedly deny and distort their own nature. When Christ is proclaimed, it becomes apparent that all people are irresistibly given to denying their dependence on God and, in consequence, each takes upon himself powers and projects which in fact belong to God alone. There is no one who does not try to sustain and fulfill his life by his own wisdom and strength. There is no one who does not fail to trust God.

God in Christ has made clear what in fact life's central problem is. It is not human limitation. It is not ignorance, error or desire. It is not weakness of will, a poor upbringing or faulty social institutions. It is not the evil intentions of those who for one reason or another we consider to be our enemies. The central problem is sin—the irresistible tendency of each person and all peoples to reject God and, in consequence, both to reject their creaturely status and to make the assumption that they can sustain and fulfill life through their own wisdom and power. It is this rejection that separates us from God and divides us from one another.

The tendency to doubt God, reject creatureliness and take hold of life without reference to God is universal and it has many expressions. Some are personal, some are social or political and some are religious. A god can be made of anything.

It is the mission of the church to point to Christ who, in his faithfulness, makes apparent the faithlessness of the world. In doing so, all people may see themselves in comparison and so come to understand that the forces which so distort and injure our lives have their origin within our own minds and wills. It follows that in every age Christians are to struggle to understand how our fallen nature is manifest in the particular circumstances of our own time and place. It is an aspect of the church's calling to name the world's idols and expose them for what they are.

More central, however, is the mission given to all Christians to bear witness to Christ who, as the manifestation of God's judgment and mercy upon human sin, offers redemption from a state of bondage which human will and intelligence cannot remedy. Having rejected God and fallen under the spell of self-love, we neither know nor love God, ourselves or others as God wills. Furthermore, it lies beyond our powers to restore the sort of relationship with God, with others or ourselves which is the purpose of our life and upon which our lives depend.

Christ then brings to light the sickness of the human heart, but even more, he is the source of healing for the sickness he makes plain. Central to the mission of the church is its attestation to the power of God in Christ to bring about reconciliation and healing which lie beyond human ability.

The church in its witness reminds the world of what human nature is created to be, of what in fact it is like and it points the way God has appointed for healing the human spirit of its fatal sickness. The witness of the church to God's judgment and mercy in the life, death and resurrection of Jesus also brings to light what each person is destined to become. In Christ, each person and all people may see life's fulfillment. Jesus opens up for the world its destiny.

The limited but essential role of the church

It is the mission of the church to attest to what God has made known and accomplished in the life, death and resurrection of Jesus. What God has made known in Christ implies certain other things about mission which the church forgets only at great harm to itself and to the world. The first is that the church's mission is of a provisional and temporary nature. It takes place between the beginning of all things and their fulfillment in God. As in the beginning, so at the end, there will be no church because all things will exist in God.

The mission of the church is only for the time being. Nevertheless, for the time being that mission is essential. God has called the church to himself and sent it into the world so that through its witness and through the power of the Holy Spirit, God may be known and loved as he truly is.

Though the task assigned the church is essential, if it does not keep in mind the limited and temporary nature of that task, the church will inevitably fall victim to the temptation to claim for itself the role of God in human history. Only the most realistic humility about its mission will prevent the church from seeking to make itself into the power that brings the world to its appointed destiny. Only by holding fast to the provisional character of its service will the church avoid becoming the very idol it is called upon to expose.

A second implication is that in carrying out its mission, the church will share not only in the victory but also in the sufferings of Christ. Witness to the truth about God and the human heart are means whereby God makes life new, but they cannot be separated from rejection, suffering and, on occasion, martyrdom. Witness to the truth inevitably calls forth resistance to the truth.

There have been more martyrs in this century than in any other. The witness of these thousands of men and women remind us of God's victory over sin and death. They remind us also, however, that the victory of God does not come separated from combat.

As God struggles to reconcile a defiant world to himself, so the church shares in that struggle. As Christ's witness to God sheds light upon the very heart of human darkness so also does the witness of the church to the truth of God revealed in Christ. Witness to Christ also exposes the inequity that lies hidden under the world's glittering surface and it brings to light the shame that hides the world's glory.

To the extent that the church is faithful to its mission, it will share in Christ's battle and in his sufferings. Attestation to the truth revealed in Christ calls forth repeatedly the very forces which crucified him. If the church is faithful in its witness to Christ, it will suffer with him. It will share in his battle with all the forces that oppose God. It is the belief of the church, however, that through sharing in this combat and in these sufferings, God's love, power and justice are made known through the Spirit. Suffering for Christ's sake is for this reason the church's joy and its crown.

Since God and no other can create and bring the world to fulfillment, the church carries out its mission with a particular attitude. The church is a body of people who in their witness to God persevere while waiting in faith and patience for God's appearance. The mission of the church cannot be separated from perseverance and patient waiting. Faith teaches the church to continue on its way and to await God who, through the power of the Holy Spirit, transforms life in the present and who, in glory at the end of time, will bring the great drama of nature and history to its close and fulfillment.

Because God is the primary actor in history, the life of the church is defined more by what it awaits than by what it does. The church is a community that lives by God's power and not its own. In carrying out its mission the church is utterly dependent upon God. Thus, although the church in its witness is constantly active in love, its most fundamental attitude is that of a patient servant that waits for the command and favor of his master. Waiting is basic to the life of the church as it carries out its mission. That is why the basic missionary prayers are "Thy Kingdom Come" and "Come, Lord Jesus."

Because its mission is carried out always in a time of waiting upon God and suffering for his sake, because prayer for the establishment of God's rule and the fulfillment of his purposes express its deepest longing, the church repeatedly learns in faith to practice perseverance and patience. Because the church waits for God as revealed in Christ's life, death and resurrection, it can trust God and so with perseverance and patience wait even in the midst of trial. In these trials, the church is sustained and strengthened by the Holy Spirit which preserves its life with God and gives power to the witness it makes.

Perseverance and the patience of faith are characteristic of the life and mission of the church. Its patience is never, however, to be equated with the sort of resignation that is born of despair. Perseverance and patience born of faith produce hope and are manifest in works of love. Perseverance and patience sustained by the spirit of God, do not imply a refusal to act. They do not mean that Christians are called to do nothing. On the contrary, the church is called to be urgent in its witness, to speak and act both in season and out of season. The church knows, however, that the fruit of all that it says and does depends upon the power of God who is present through his spirit. Thus, through the entire course of history, the faith, hope and love present in the speaking and acting of the church and in its persevering, patient waiting and suffering become, by grace, signs of the rule of God. Consequently, the attitude in which the church carries out its mission cannot be separated from the witness it is its mission to make.

The Episcopal Church as a missionary community

These beliefs about the mission of the church are rooted in holy scripture and in Christian tradition. They are meant to inform the thought and action of the church in any time or circumstance in which it may find itself. The immediate question before the Episcopal Church is, therefore, what implications these beliefs may have for the present thought, policy, action and organization of this church as it involves itself in world mission.

There are several points that must be made. The first is certainly that *the Episcopal Church itself exists in a missionary situation.* Just as Christians in Uganda or Shanghai are called to proclaim what God has made known in Christ, so are Episcopalians. It will be difficult for this shift in consciousness to come about but come about it must. The Episcopal Church has long thought of itself as "established." Its origins in England hardly make such a view surprising and it is probably because of this historical heritage that the Episcopal Church has for so many years thought of itself as in some way appointed or destined to be *the* "national church."

These hopes and aspirations were held with the greatest sincerity. They were probably never very realistic. As other Christians in North America, Episcopalians live in a culture whose dominant vision and values are less and less Christian. Episcopalians, whether they realize it or not, live as did the faithful in Collosae or as do those now in Tokyo—as ambassadors of Christ to a people whose vision of God and human destiny is in many ways different from what has been made known in the life, death and resurrection of Jesus.

There are jurisdictions within the Episcopal Church where these matters have been grasped with greater clarity. Episcopalians from Latin America, for example, see more clearly than do those in the United States how essential it is for the church to understand that mission is fundamental to its nature.

If the participation of the Episcopal Church in world mission is to have any degree of seriousness American Episcopalians must first wake up to facts others have already grasped and see that the situation of this church is like all others—a missionary one. Episcopalians also need to recognize that evangelism, like service and worship, is an integral part of the church's life. To speak of mission apart from the sort of testimony which is intended to bring others to faith in Christ, is to speak without an adequate understanding of what the mission of the church really is. Episcopalians, with all other Christians, are called to represent God revealed in Christ to those who do not believe. Once again, the implication of God's act in Christ and of his calling of the church will come as a shock to many Episcopalians, but it is essential for the health of the church that the shock come.

Mutual responsibility and interdependence, renewed

Everywhere and always, mission involves the same testimony, the same perseverance, the same waiting and patience, the same faith, hope and love and, indeed, may involve the same sort of suffering. *All churches are part of one body in such a way that if one is blessed, all are blessed, or if one suffers, all suffer.* In consequence, it is the joy of each church to share in the common life of all others and it is the duty of each church to offer others support and encouragement during the time of waiting and trial which is common to all.

All Christians and all churches are mutually responsible and interdependent in the body of Christ. It was, no doubt, his desire to make this point as firmly as possible that led Paul to insist on the importance of the collection taken up in the churches of the Gentile world for the support of the Jewish Christians in Jerusalem. In living a common life and carrying out a common mission, no Christian and no church can stand alone. For its own health and the health of the church throughout the world, each must call for and be able to rely upon the support and encouragement of the others.

The Episcopal Church should therefore do all in its power to overcome a particularly destructive form of thinking. We are speaking of that attitude which characterizes some churches as older or younger, or which speaks of the historic churches of Europe or North America as if they were in some way fundamentally different from or in opposition to the churches in the developing world. All churches exist in a missionary situation and each has the same mission to carry out. Each shares with all others one Lord and one baptism. All eat from one loaf and share one cup. Each shares both the joys and sufferings of the others. The situation is the same today as it was when Paul wrote to the churches of the Gentile world on behalf of the church in Jerusalem.

Mutual responsibility and interdependence have characterized the life of the church from the beginning. Now, as always, these principles imply a continuous reformation and spiritual renewal as well as profound changes in the way each church conceives of itself, orders its common life and allocates its resources. For the Episcopal Church, we believe mutual responsibility and interdependence imply that we continue to do all in our power to eliminate the vestiges of a colonial era which left some churches under the domination and control of others. The Churches of the Anglican Communion and, indeed, all Christian communities, are partners in mission. Each is to aid and assist the other. Each is to share its common life and resources and thus encourage the others, as all wait for the coming of the Lord of all.

The Standing Commission on World Mission of the General Convention of the Episcopal Church, *A Theology and Policy of Mission in Global Perspective* (Cincinnati: Forward Movement Publications, 1982), 14-25. (Excerpt)

CHAPTER THIRTEEN

The Modern Ecumenical Movement

Introduction

The Episcopal Church has shared actively in the modern ecumenical age. Bishop Charles Henry Brent provided leadership for the Faith and Order Movement which led to the World Council of Churches. The Consultation on Church Union (COCU) was launched by a sermon preached by Eugene Carson Blake, a Presbyterian leader, at Grace Cathedral, San Francisco, in 1960. The Episcopal Church participated in COCU for years, although the Episcopal Church's commitment to an apostolic ministry has limited the possibilities for organic union with many Protestant denominations. During the years after Vatican II, members of the Episcopal Church participated in bilateral dialogues with the Roman Catholics, the Orthodox, and the Lutherans. After warnings about the ecumenical impact of the ordination of women, the Roman Catholic Church responded negatively to the Anglican-Roman Catholic dialogue. Some Episcopalians feel that future dialogue with Roman Catholics will be limited until there is a changed understanding of the ministry of women in the Roman Catholic Church. Despite the lack of progress at the denominational level, some Roman Catholic and Episcopal parishes continue in covenant relationships of mutual support. The Lutheran-Episcopal Dialogue (LED) resulted in a limited interim sharing of the Eucharist, beginning with a joint Eucharistic service at the Cathedral of St. Peter and St. Paul in Washington, D.C., on January 16, 1983, led by Presiding Bishop John M. Allin and Lutheran Church leaders. The understanding of apostolicity has been broadened in recent discussions (especially the Lutheran-Episcopal Dialogue) to include doctrine and mission as well as ministry. The focus of ecumenical attention has likewise moved to understand the unity of churches in terms of a "communion of communions" instead of one "superchurch."

108.

Charles Henry Brent,
That They All May Be One, 1949

Charles Henry Brent (April 9, 1862–March 27, 1929) was consecrated the first Missionary Bishop of the Philippines on December 19, 1901. He became the fourth Bishop of Western New York on January 19, 1918. Brent was a leader in the Faith and Order Movement, which led to the World Council of Churches. This selection is made up of quotations from the Bishop's diaries, addresses, and sermon notes which were posthumously published. His ecumenical leadership is commemorated in the Episcopal Calendar of the Church Year on March 27. In this selection he explains the need for Christian unity to precede church unity.

It is the purpose of Jesus Christ to unify the church. Unity, visible and invisible, is not an accident of the Gospel. It is the Gospel. A fragment can suggest the whole. It cannot reveal it.

The unity of Christendom is not a luxury but a necessity. The world will go limping until Christ's prayer that all may be one is answered. We must have unity, not at all costs, but at all risks. A unified church is the only offering we dare present to the coming of Christ, for in it alone will He find room to dwell.

Do not be deceived; without unity the conversion of great nations is well-nigh hopeless. The success of missions is inextricably bound up with unity. It would seem that missionary progress in the future will depend mainly upon the Church's unity, and that national conversions can be brought about by no other influence.

God has used, beyond anything we had a right to expect, our divided Christendom. But now that we know the sin and disaster of sectarianism, we cannot hope that he will use it much longer. Sectarianism, in spirit and in form, is *par excellence* the cult of the incomplete. It is a refusal to consider truth and life in terms of the whole, not merely the whole of now but the whole of yesterday. It pins its trust to the dicta of a group or the findings of a fixed period. It is content to worship and to defend a conception of God instead of God. It lacks the shape of the Cross which rises vertically as high as God, and stretches right and left to the outermost bounds of humanity. In its extremist form it not only refuses to recognize as acceptable to Christ any group-culture save its own, but it also questions others' rights to continue to be. It is precisely this spirit, not in one special Church but in many, which has disrupted Christendom.

It may be that up to the present a divided Church has been used by God for the extension of His Kingdom among men, but we have no guarantee that He will continue to do so. Indeed there are indications that the divided Church has passed the zenith of such power as it has had, and is declining toward desolation. Divided Christendom has had fair trial—it is a failure.

Division is the Achilles' heel of the Christian enterprise. Much of the anguish of soul, of the doubt, of the alienation of men from the Kingdom of God and His righteousness, lies at the door of the broken condition of the Church, her uncatholic temper, and her apathetic acceptance of the divisions which rend her as though they were not her own fault.

If it is a prophecy that the gates of hell shall not prevail against the Church, it is also prophecy that the Church divided against herself will fall. Disorder in the Church is more terrible than feuds in the family or civil war in the State. If war is an evil in national life, it is a thousand fold greater evil in Church life.

If unity has slipped from our grasp, it is the common fault of the Christian world. If it is to be regained it must be by the concerted action of all Christians. Every section has shared in shattering unity. Every section must share in the effort to restore it. To me, the most important movement of the day is that in the direction of unity from whatever angle. There is no room for impatience. It is absurd to expect definite results in so brief a time.

Is the Church to lead in unity? If so, she must begin by unifying herself. It is laughable to think of a warring Church preaching about a world at peace. There is no lesson which the Churches are learning of greater importance than the importance of our divided Christianity. It is absurd to aim at a united mankind, or even a united Christian civilization, and to be content with a divided Church. A confused Church will be a potent factor in maintaining a confused world. I see no glimmer of hope for permanent and fraternal peace among the Churches. Unity of heart and hands among the Churches is the sole hope for the Great Peace. As it is with the family of the nations, so must it be with the family of the churches.

There are four main obstacles in the way of promoting unity: first, acquiescence in the broken order; secondly, the sense of security among the great dominating Churches like the Church of England, the Roman Catholic Church, and the Orthodox Churches of the East; thirdly, the misuse of the word "Church"; fourthly, substitutes for unity, of which there are two principal ones called respectively Interdenominationalism and Uniformity.

Humbled and awakened the Churches must renew their search for peace and unity according to God's will. But how? (1) Not by slurring over honest differences or by slighting convictions. There is one thing worse than war—saying peace, peace, where there is no peace. (2) Not for economic reasons. (3) Not for the sake of ease and convenience.

Labor for unity must lay its claim on every Christian soul. It will come when it does come, not with observation, but through the slow process of the mills of God. The Churches will become the Church when there is in them all mutual horizontal as well as unified vertical self-giving. The way to recover unity is to practice fellowship.

Experience has taught me that what is needed for a long time to come is unsuspicious, friendly, personal touch between Christian leaders of every opinion, not in order that they may have joint services or force outward ecclesiastical unity, but that they may come to understand one another by the only process that can create mutual understanding. I mean by human fellowship an interchange of living thought for which even friendly books are no substitute. Christian Unity, which is a thing of the Spirit and is founded on Christ's twofold law of love, comes first, antedating ecclesiastical unity, in which unity of worship is a necessary climax. It is dangerous to confuse the manufacture of joint services for the sake of their being joint, with unity.

Must we not do two things—first, train the hearts of all professing Christians to the recognition of every professing Christian of whatever denomination or race as a brother beloved without distinction or difference, and secondly, in frequent and frank conference, deliberate on the things pertaining to the Kingdom, sitting loosely to our opinions and sectarian tenets? Nothing but a united Church will be adequate for that which is fast becoming a united world. Today no man is true to Christ who ignores or thinks lightly of the unity of His church. The call comes not from beneath but from above. A split Church can present only a split Christ.

Church Unity will come after Christian Unity. It would not be gain to aim at oneness as an end in itself. Mere oneness would be a sort of saccharine monotony in which differences would not have been reconciled but rather smothered and hidden under a thick coat of sentimentality. Unity, as I understand it, will come as the result of a whole-hearted devotion to a common vision, and a common purpose. We do not seek for unity in order to come to Christ, but in coming to Christ we are thereby committed to unity according to His mind, and if we fail to find unity we have missed the way.

Frederick Ward Kates, ed., *Things That Matter: The Best of the Writings of Bishop Brent* (New York: Harper and Brothers, Publishers, 1949), 38-42. (Excerpt)

109.

Statement of Faith and Order, 1949

The following statement on Faith and Order was part of the report of the Joint Commission on Approaches to Unity presented at the fifty-sixth General Convention, San Francisco, September 26–October 7, 1949. In this document the Episcopal Church adopts sacramental language for rites other than Baptism and the Eucharist. This position received official status in the 1979 catechism. It is significant as a movement beyond the Thirty-Nine Articles and the Quadrilateral.

The Joint Commission on Approaches to Unity presents this statement of Faith and Order as a basis for intercommunion, looking toward organic federation with other Christian bodies.

Intercommunion between two churches is understood as meaning that members of either church shall be permitted to receive Holy Communion in the other, and that ministers of either church shall be competent to celebrate the Holy Communion in the other.

One example of intercommunion now actually in effect is that between the Anglican and Old Catholic churches in Europe and America. The Bonn Agreement, which is the basis of this intercommunion though not necessarily normative for all future agreements, reads:

"1. Each communion recognizes the Catholicity and independence of the other, and maintains its own.

"2. Each communion agrees to admit members of the other communion to participate in the sacraments.

"3. Intercommunion does not require from either communion the acceptance of all doctrinal opinion, sacramental devotion, or liturgical practice characteristic of the other, but implies that each believes the other to hold all the essentials of the Christian faith."

Organic federation, which presupposes intercommunion, may take any one of several forms. It may be: (1) a federation, such as now exists among the churches of the Anglican Communion, with a council whose functions are purely advisory; (2) a federation which has an advisory council as in (1), and in addition merges administrative and missionary agencies, the autonomy of the uniting churches being not affected; (3) a federation which merges administrative and missionary agencies as in (2), and in addition has an overall legislative body with limited delegatory powers.

The Quadrilateral has had a long and interesting history. Its four points originally appeared in a reply from the American bishops to a memorial on the subject of Christian unity. The reply was set forth by the House of Bishops meeting in Chicago in 1886, and was later ratified by the House of Clerical and Lay Deputies. We make our own the following words from this statement:

"We . . . do hereby solemnly declare to all whom it may concern, and especially to our fellow Christians of the different Communions in this land, who, in their several spheres, have contended for the religion of Christ:

"Our earnest desire that the Saviour's prayer, 'That they all may be one,' may, in its deepest and truest sense, be speedily fulfilled;

"That we believe that all who have been duly baptized with water, in the name of the Father, and of the Son, and of the Holy Ghost, are members of the Holy Catholic Church;

"That this Church does not seek to absorb other Communions, but rather, co-operating with them on the basis of a common Faith and Order, to discountenance schism, to heal the wounds of the Body of Christ, and to promote the charity which is the chief of Christian graces and the visible manifestation of Christ to the world;

"We do hereby affirm that the Christian unity now so earnestly desired can be restored only by the return of all Christian communions to the principles of unity exemplified by the undivided Catholic Church during the first ages of its existence; which principles we believe to be the substantial deposit of Christian Faith and Order committed by Christ and His Apostles to the Church unto the end of the world, and therefore incapable of compromise or surrender by those who have been ordained to be its stewards and trustees for the common and equal benefit of all men."

In the statement of the bishops there followed four points which have since become familiar to the entire Anglican world and beyond. Originally known as the Chicago Quadrilateral, they were adopted by the Lambeth Conference of 1888 as follows:

"1. The Holy Scriptures of the Old and New Testaments as 'containing all things necessary to salvation,' and as being the rule and ultimate standard of faith.

"2. The Apostles' Creed, as the Baptismal Symbol; and the Nicene Creed, as the sufficient statement of the Christian faith.

"3. The two Sacraments ordained by Christ Himself— Baptism and the Supper of the Lord—ministered with unfailing use of Christ's words of Institution, and of the elements ordained by him.

"4. The Historic Episcopate, locally adapted in the methods of its administration to the varying needs of the nations and peoples called of God into the Unity of His Church."

Reaffirmed in slightly different forms by subsequent Lambeth Conferences, these points were incorporated in 1920 into *An Appeal to All Christian People*.

II. The Quadrilateral

A. *The Holy Scriptures*

The Holy Scriptures are the inspired record of God's self-revelation to man and of man's response to that revelation. This is the primary ground of the authority of the Scriptures.

The fact that the Church under the guidance of the Holy Spirit has accepted the Bible as canonical invests it as a whole with an authoritative character for all Christians. Its authority is further validated by the continuing experience of Christian people.

The Bible has an inner unity as the record of the special preparation for Christ, and of His redemption of man through His Life, Death, Resurrection, and Ascension, and through the gift of the Holy Ghost. Both in the Old and in the New Testaments the Kingdom of God is proclaimed and everlasting life is offered to mankind in Christ, the only Mediator between God and Man.

The Bible has been and is for the Christian Church the ultimate criterion of its teaching and the chief source of guidance for its life. It contains all doctrine required for salvation through faith in Jesus Christ.

The reading and preaching of the Word of God are indispensable for the life and worship of the Church.

B. *The Creeds*

The Apostles' Creed rehearses the mighty acts of God in creation, redemption, and sanctification as recorded in the Holy Scriptures. Upon these, the life of the Church is based. As a declaration of allegiance to the Triune God the Apostles' Creed is a profession of faith appropriate to Holy Baptism.

The Nicene Creed likewise witnesses to the faith of the historic Church in its assertion of fundamental Christian truths and its denial of fundamental errors and is appropriate to Holy Communion.

While liberty of interpretation may be allowed, the Christian faith as set forth in these two creeds ought to be received and believed by all Christian people.

The recitation of the Creeds in public worship is to be commended, though their invariable use in such fashion is not essential to the unity or the life of the Church.

C. *The Sacraments*

Baptism with water and with the Spirit, in the Name of the Father and of the Son and of the Holy Ghost, is a divinely instituted sacrament whereby we are made children of grace and incorporated into the Church, and receive forgiveness of sin and a new birth unto righteousness. The requirements for baptism are repentance and faith, declared by the recipient or on his behalf by his sponsors.

The Supper of the Lord, ministered with unfailing use of Christ's words of institution and the elements ordained by Him, is the supreme act of sacramental worship in the Christian Church. This Sacrament is a corporate act of the Church towards God, wherein it is united with its Lord, victorious and triumphant, Himself both Priest and Victim in the sacrifice of the Cross. In it the faithful continue a perpetual memory of the precious death of Christ who is their Advocate with the Father and the propitiation for their sins, according to His precept, until His coming again. For first they offer the sacrifice of praise and thanksgiving; then next they plead and represent before the Father the sacrifice of the Cross, and by it they confidently entreat remission of sins and all other benefits of the Lord's passion for all the whole Church; and lastly they offer the sacrifice of themselves to the Creator of all things which they have already signified by the oblations of the bread and wine which are His creatures. In the Supper of the Lord the faithful receive and partake, spiritually, of the Body and Blood of Christ; and thus enter into communion with Christ Himself and with one another in His Life.

In addition to the sacraments of Baptism and the Supper of the Lord, the Church recognizes sacramental rites or mysteries, namely, Confirmation, Absolution, the Marriage Blessing, Holy Orders, and the Unction of the Sick.

D. *The Historic Episcopate*
1. The Ministry

The fundamental Christian ministry is the ministry of Christ. There is no Christian priesthood or ministry apart from His. His priestly and ministerial function is to reconcile the world to God in and through Himself, by His Incarnation and by His "one sacrifice once offered" and by the gift of the Holy Spirit, delivering men from the power of sin and death.

The Church as the Body of Christ, sharing His Life, has a ministerial function derived from that of Christ. In this function every member has his place and share according to his different capabilities and calling. The Church is set before us in the New Testament as a body of believers having within it, as its recognized focus of unity, of teaching and of authority, the Apostolate, which owed its origin to the action of the Lord Himself. There was not first an Apostolate which gathered a body of believers about itself; nor was there a completely structureless collection of believers which gave authority to the Apostles to speak and act on its behalf. From the first there was a fellowship of believers finding its unity in the Twelve. Thus the New Testament bears witness to the principle of a distinctive ministry, as an original element, but not the sole constitutive element, in the life of the Church.

2. The Episcopate

Anglican formularies deal with the episcopate as a fact rather than a doctrine. It is, however, a fact deeply rooted in history. The Lambeth Quadrilateral is, accordingly, employing a defining phrase when it speaks of the "historic episcopate." Acceptance of episcopacy as a basis of reunion necessarily means acceptance of it not as a bare fact, but a fact accompanied by its historical meaning.

The maintenance of a ministerial succession, by way of ordination with the laying on of hands, is a familiar fact in the life of most Christian communions. All such ministerial successions are in some sense historic, differing from one another, however, in form and in the degree to which succession is continuous in history. Anglican formularies pronounce no judgments on other ministerial successions. They do claim, however, for the churches of the Anglican Communion for which they speak, that these churches have preserved both the form and the succession which traces back to the "Apostles' time," and they make the preservation of this succession a matter of scrupulous discipline. They define ministers within this historic stream as "Ministers of Apostolic Succession."

It should be clear, therefore, that while acceptance of the "historic episcopate" may not involve acceptance of any one formulation of the doctrine of the ministry, it does involve acceptance, in the form of a fact, of the three-fold ministry of bishops, priests, and deacons, and the acceptance of it also as accompanied by the claim that it is a ministerial succession tracing back to the "Apostles' time."

The Lambeth Conference Report of 1930 enlarges upon this claim as follows:

"When we speak of the Historic Episcopate, we mean the Episcopate as it emerged in the clear light of history from the time when definite evidence begins to be available. . . . Without entering into the discussion of theories which divide scholars, we may affirm shortly that we see no reason to doubt the statement made in the Preface of our Ordinal that 'from the Apostles' time there have been those Orders of Ministers in Christ's Church: Bishops, Priests and Deacons.' Whatever variety of system may have existed in addition in the earlier age, it is universally agreed that by the end of the second century episcopacy had no effective rival. Among all the controversies of the fourth and fifth centuries the episcopal ministry was never a subject of dispute. . . . If the Episcopate, as we find it established universally by the end of the second century, was the result of a process of adaptation and growth in the organism of the Church, that would be no evidence that it lacked divine authority, but rather that the life of the Spirit within the Church had found it to be the most appropriate organ for the functions which it discharged. In the course of time the Episcopate was greatly affected by secular forces, which bent it to many purposes alien to its true character and went far to obscure its spiritual purpose. . . . The Historic Episcopate as we understand it goes behind the perversions of history to the original conception of the Apostolic Ministry."

The concept of the episcopate can, accordingly, receive definition as an historical fact. It can also receive clarification from a description of its functions.

To quote from the Lambeth Report of 1930: "When we say that we must insist on the Historic Episcopate but not upon any theory or interpretation of it, we are not to be understood as insisting on the office apart from the functions. What we uphold is the Episcopate, maintained in successive generations by continuity of succession and consecration, as it has been throughout the history of the Church from the earliest times, and discharging those functions which from the earliest times it has discharged."

When we refer to the historic episcopate we are concerned with the essentials and purposes of the office of bishop and not with the incidental attributes of the office or the details of the administration of the Church, which have changed from time to time and may continue to change.

The most obvious function of the "historic episcopate"—the one which in the course of its varied history, has been most scrupulously guarded—is its vocation of transmitting the ministerial succession. The bishop is thus the organ of ministerial continuity. He is also the personal organ of the Church's unity. The very name bishop (episcopos) implies the function of pastoral care, of oversight. He is addressed in the Church's traditional liturgies as Father-in-God. He is also addressed as the Church's Shepherd. He represents the Church catholic to his flock, as the localized minister cannot do. Expressive of the Bishop's function of ministering the Word and of pastoral oversight is the opening prayer of the Anglican *Form of Ordaining or Consecrating a Bishop*.

"Almighty God, who by thy Son Jesus Christ didst give to thy holy Apostles many excellent gifts, and didst charge them to feed thy flock; Give grace, we beseech thee, to all Bishops, the Pastors of thy Church, that they may diligently preach thy Word, and duly administer the godly Discipline thereof."

The fourth point of the Lambeth Quadrilateral was rephrased by the Lambeth Conference of 1920, in its *Appeal to All Christian People*, as follows:

"A ministry acknowledged by every part of the Church as possessing not only the inward call of the Spirit, but also the commission of Christ and the authority of the whole Body."

We close this section by further quoting from this *Appeal*:

"May we not reasonably claim that the Episcopate is the one means of providing such a ministry? It is not that we call in question for a moment the spiritual reality of the ministries of those Communions which do not possess the Episcopate. On the contrary, we thankfully acknowledge that these ministries have been manifestly blessed and owned by the Holy Spirit as effective means of grace. But we submit that considerations alike of history and of present experience justify the claim which we make on behalf of the Episcopate. Moreover, we would urge that it is now and will prove to be in the future the best instrument for maintaining the unity and continuity of the Church. But we greatly desire that the office of a Bishop should be everywhere exercised in a representative and constitutional manner, and more truly express all that ought to be involved for the life of the Christian Family in the title of Father-in-God. Nay more, we eagerly look forward to the day when through its acceptance in a united Church we may all share in that grace which is pledged to the members of the whole body in the apostolic rite of the laying-on of hands, and the joy and fellowship of a Eucharist in which as one Family we may together, without any doubtfulness of mind, offer to the one Lord our worship and service."

3. The Priesthood and the Diaconate.

The office of a priest (presbyter) is to minister to the people committed to his care; to preach the Word of God; to baptize; to celebrate the Holy Communion; to pronounce absolution, or remission of sins, and blessing in God's name. Thus he exercises part of the Apostolic office, and it is significant that in the Anglican Ordinals, as in the general practice of the Western Church, which is itself based on very early usage, priests are associated with the Bishop in laying on of hands at the ordination of priests.

The office of a deacon is to assist the priest in divine service, and in his other ministrations, under the direction of the bishop. In the early Church the diaconate represented the ministry of the Church to men's bodily needs, but not as though these were separable from their spiritual states. Though this function is still emphasized in Anglican Ordinals, the deacon today exercises his office almost entirely in spiritual activities.

4. Laity.

To the whole Church of God and to every member of it belongs the duty and privilege of spreading the good news of the Kingdom of God and the message of salvation through Jesus Christ and of interceding for the brethren. All, according to their measure, share in the priesthood which the Church derives from Him. This is the meaning of the doctrine of the priesthood of all believers.

III. The Quadrilateral and the Church

We have confined our exposition to the Quadrilateral; its interpretation must be seen in the context of the scriptural doctrine of the Church. This involves more extended consideration than can be given in this statement. We can, however, join with other Christian bodies in the affirmation in the Edinburgh report on *Faith and Order*:

"We are at one in confessing belief in the Holy Catholic Church. We acknowledge that through Jesus Christ, particularly through the fact of His resurrection, of the gathering of His disciples round their crucified, risen, and victorious Lord, and of the coming of the Holy Spirit, God's Almighty will constituted the Church on earth.

"The Church is the people of the new covenant, fulfilling and transcending all that Israel under the old covenant foreshadowed. It is the household of God, the family in which the fatherhood of God and the brotherhood of man is to be realized in the children of His adoption. It is the body of Christ, whose members derive their life and oneness from their one living Head; and thus it is nothing apart from Him, but is in all things dependent upon the power of salvation which God has committed to His Son.

"The presence of the ascended Lord in the Church, His Body, is effected by the power of the one Spirit, who conveys to the whole fellowship the gifts of the ascended Lord, dividing to every man severally as He will, guides it into all the truth and fills it unto all the fullness of God.

"We all agree that Christ is present in His Church through the Holy Spirit as Prophet, Priest, and King. As Prophet He reveals the divine will and purpose to the Church; as Priest He ever liveth to make intercession for us, and through the eternal sacrifice once offered for us on Calvary He continually draws His people to the Most High; and as King He rules His Church and is ever establishing and extending His Kingdom.

"Christ's presence in the Church has been perpetual from its foundation, and this presence He makes effective and evident in the preaching of the Word, in the faithful administration of the Sacraments, in prayer offered in His name, and through the newness of life whereby He enables the faithful to bear witness to Himself. Even though men often prove faithless, Christ will remain faithful to the promise of His presence, and will so continue till the consummation of all things."

IV. Conclusion

The foregoing statement is not a complete formulation of the faith and order of the Church. It is an exposition of the background and chief implications of the Chicago-Lambeth Quadrilateral. It has been formulated, not as a final pronouncement to which literal subscription should be asked, but as a means of assuring a substantial agreement upon the basis of which formal schemes for Church Union with any other Church may later be drawn up. We hope that the document will form a useful instrument of further negotiation with those Christian bodies which may be willing to join with us in seeking a way into that unity to which our Lord is calling all Christian people.

"Report of the Joint Commission on Approaches to Unity," *Journal of General Convention*, 1949, 662-669.

110.

Peter Day, Episcopalians and Ecumenicity, 1964

Peter Morton Day (August 1, 1914–May 5, 1984) was editor of The Living Church, *1952-1964, and the first ecumenical officer of the Episcopal Church. He was active in the Consultation on Church Union, the major American Protestant ecumenical effort of the 1960s. While COCU has flagged, the consultation is still in existence. In this article he discusses the ecumenical mission of the Episcopal Church.*

Part I

It has been remarked that a history of Christianity could well be written with Church unity as its central theme. This was the problem of the Council at Jerusalem that is recorded in the Book of Acts. It has certainly been a central concern of Anglicanism from the beginning of its separate existence, and the Thirty-nine Articles owe their peculiar characteristics to the fact that they were an effort at a unity platform.

But, in spite of the agelong concern for Christian unity, there is something different about the ecumenical movement of our time. With Bishop Brent's speech at the Edinburgh missionary conference of 1910 it burst forth with a new proclamation, a new voice comparable to the "Comfort ye, comfort ye my people, saith your God" of the 40th chapter of Isaiah.

The ecumenical movement grew out of the world missionary movement. And perhaps one of the powerful motivations of the world missionary movement had been the disunity of the Churches. There was an effort on the part of each Church to prove how good and true its interpretation of Christianity was by competition in evangelizing the non-Christian world.

For long centuries before, the life of Europe and European man had been such that people could very easily conceive of their religion in terms of getting on the best possible terms with God in a world that was already Christian as far as the eye could see. But with the great missionary expansion, and later with the break-up of old cultural patterns in Europe, they began to see that the mission of the Church was opposed by vast and powerful forces.

Further, they began to understand more deeply, and with growing intensity in the two world wars which occurred in this century, that the Gospel preached by Jesus Christ is itself a call to unity. He came and preached peace to those that were far off and those that were nigh. He broke down the wall of partition between Jew and Gentile. The gospel is about human unity. Christian disunity is a living denial of the central message of the Gospel.

Thus we may see in the ecumenical movement a call to renewed faithfulness to the Lord of the Church, a call to return to truth, and to Him who is the truth. For the word "truth" as it is used in the New Testament does not convey the connotations of our modern use of the word for an abstract proposition, a generalization about nature or man or God, or a mathematical equation, such as two plus two equals four. When our Lord told Pontius Pilot that He came into the world to bear witness to the truth, He was not declaring Himself to be a philosopher or a mathematician. He did not come to bear witness to truths but to the Truth. He came to bear witness to God, to the faithfulness and steadfastness of God in His dealings with men. The Hebrew word for truth, the word from which our "amen" is derived, has such connotations. In the battle with the Amalekites, where the Israelites prevailed as long as Moses held up his arms, the literal rendering would be, not "Moses' arms were steady," but "Moses' arms were *truth* until the going down of the sun."

Jesus walking on the water and stilling the tempest is the word of truth made visible. Jesus on the Cross is truth in action. This concrete, personal, active truth, the kind of truth to which men bear witness rather than the kind men argue about, is what truth means in the Bible. And it is this that was restored in part to the Church when it began to proclaim the Gospel in the missionary field, it is this truth, this fidelity to the God whose word is His deed, that will be more fully restored when Christ's servants and witnesses come together.

To those who say that the ecumenical movement seeks unity at the expense of truth, we can answer that it is not unity but disunity that denies the truth as it was proclaimed by our Lord and His apostles.

As we all know, the Episcopal Church is engaged and involved in the ecumenical movement at many levels, and has been from the first. It was our General Convention of 1910 that, in a resolution proposed by Bishop Manning, first invited the Churches of the world to join in a World Conference on Faith and Order. Our Church was much less enthusiastic in its official relationships with the Federal Council of Churches in its early days, but became a fully participating member in 1940, and from the time that the National Council of Churches was formed we have been full participants in its life and work.

The World Council of Churches, combining the coöperative movement of life and work, the missionary movement, and the faith and order movement, has had the Episcopal Church as a participant, along with the other Churches of the Anglican Communion, at every stage of its development.

The ecumenical involvements of the Episcopal Church have become so complex and interrelated that a growing need was felt for the appointment of an ecumenical officer to serve as the Presiding Bishop's assistant in this field and as a coördinator of ecumenical efforts. This was provided for by the General Convention of 1961 and an empty office for him with a nice carpet on the floor has been waiting for the arrival of the officer-to-be in the new Episcopal Center.

I will be taking up this position next February 1st. As a matter of fact, my personal ecumenical involvements had already become so numerous and time-consuming that THE LIVING CHURCH office was not seeing as much of the editor as it should. I hope the new editor gets in a few years of being an editor before he becomes overly encumbered with outside activities.

The ecumenical officer will be responsible for keeping in touch with three Commissions of General Convention that are working in the ecumenical field: the Commission on Ecumenical Relations; the Commission on Approaches to Unity; and the Commission on the Eastern Orthodox and Old Catholic Churches.

The Commission on Ecumenical Relations has a proud history, for it maintains historical continuity with the Commission on a World Conference on Faith and Order created by the General Convention of 1910. Under the chairmanship of Bishop Mosley of Delaware, it is concerned with our relationships with the World and National Councils of Churches. With the aid of its wonderfully energetic secretary, the Rev. James Kennedy, it publishes the *Ecumenical Bulletin* and maintains contact with diocesan ecumenical chairmen, women's chairmen, and others in the ecumenical field.

The Ecumenical Commission also has responsibility for our relations with other branches of the Anglican Communion, and as such has been the body to make recommendations about our relations with Anglican Churches that have entered or are thinking of entering into united Churches in other parts of the world—South India, Lanka, North India-Pakistan, etc. In this work, its subject matter overlaps that of the Commission on Approaches to Unity, which conducts our own negotiations with other Churches.

Proposals for united Churches involving Anglicans are under discussion all over the world. In England, the convocations of Canterbury and York are negotiating with the Methodists. More comprehensive unions are under consideration in Nigeria, Ghana, and other African areas. The Canadians are reopening negotiations with the United Church of Canada.

Meanwhile, our own Commission on Approaches to Unity, under the chairmanship of Bishop Gibson of Virginia, is at work in the Consultation on Church

Union with the United Presbyterian Church, the Methodist Church, the United Church of Christ (formed by the recent union of the Congregational-Christian and Evangelical and Reformed Churches), the Disciples of Christ, and the Evangelical United Brethren Church. We wish to have the Polish National Catholic Church beside us in these negotiations, but so far they are not ready to come in. The only result of our invitation to them so far has been the addition of Disciples and the EUB to the negotiations in addition to the original four proposed by Eugene Carson Blake in his famous San Francisco sermon in Bishop Pike's Cathedral with Bishop Pike's hearty support. When we invited the PNCC, other Churches had to be granted the right to include Churches with which they were negotiating.

From the experience of the first session with these two additional Churches, I feel that they are a most useful addition—the Disciples with their great emphasis on Baptism and Holy Communion and their even more amazing self-criticism of the radical congregationalism and radical biblicalism on which they came into being; the EUB with a more clearly articulated and vigorously held theology than the Methodists with whom they are negotiating.

The Consultation on Church Union has met twice, and will hold its third meeting in Princeton, N.J., next April. The second meeting adopted a statement of great importance on the subject of the relation between the Scriptures and Tradition —a statement anticipating the finding of the Montreal Conference on Faith and Order and of the Second Vatican Council. To put the subject in capsule form, one of the great issues of divided Christendom has been the question of Scripture vs. Tradition. Protestant Churches took the position of sola Scriptura—the Scriptures alone; the Roman Catholic Church took the position of Scripture and tradition. Some elements of Christian truth were conveyed by the Scriptures, and some by unwritten tradition. But current theological scholarship has recognized a vital relationship between Scripture and tradition. Protestant Churches have found it necessary to develop traditions of scriptural interpretation. Catholic Churches have had to face the normative, critical and reconstitutive character of Scripture as the norm by which later traditions are evaluated. Scripture is the repository of the apostolic tradition in a way in which no other traditions or writings can be. And both sides have had to recognize that to oppose Scripture and tradition is a false opposition. The New Testament itself was produced by a process that included oral tradition. Each needs, each absolutely requires the other; both proclaim the same Christ, are witnesses to the same mighty acts of God, and both are the arena of the Holy Spirit's operation. Neither can exist, nor be rightly understood, without the other.

The importance of this development to the Episcopal Church in its relationships with other Churches hardly needs underlining. It is as exciting a development in opening up lines of discussion toward future agreement as Dr. Blake's original call for a Church which would be both Catholic and Reformed—and, as the final form of the invitation, under the influence of the Methodists put it, truly Catholic, truly Reformed, and truly Evangelical. If a Church which meets these specifications should be the result of the consultation on Church union, the Episcopal Church would be happy to be a part of it. . . .

Part II

But what is the ecumenical commitment of the Episcopal Church? It is fortunately my task not to answer the question, but merely to raise it. The most decisive answer, I think, is not to be found in past resolutions of General Convention, nor in the statements with which our representatives have associated themselves in meetings of the World and National Council of Churches. Rather, it is to be found in the prayer of our Lord for the unity of His followers, in the unremitting prayer for unity in the Prayer Book services of Morning and Evening Prayer and Holy Communion, in the degree to which we discern the operation of the Holy Ghost in other Churches in spite of their unfamiliar folkways.

How serious are we about the unity of the Church and the mission of the Church to unite mankind in the Body of Christ? To what extent do we dare to disassociate ourselves from the saving acts of God in other Churches? Can we fail to see that God has given to the world in general a thirst for human solidarity, a revolution against barriers of race, class, and economic isolation which is determined to make men one, whether or not they are made one in Christ? We can, of course, sit back and wait for the world to discover that it is following a false Messiah, if we think that this is what the true Messiah requires of us. But Jesus said, "I, if I be lifted up will draw all men unto me."

Our ecumenical commitment must be neither more nor less than our dedication to carrying out the will of the Lord of the Church. And after we have made up our minds about that, we should look at the councils of Churches, world, national and local, which are collectively called the "conciliar movement," to see what they are doing and what we can do through and in them to carry out His will. We Episcopalians are not bound to agree on anything the conciliar movement says or does. Rather, we are bound to consider whether the councils are useful instruments for manifesting the unity that already exists and moving toward the unity to which God calls us. If our role must be partly or even mostly negative or critical, we do not need to be embarrassed in the least. Our commitment is not to agree, but to testify to the Way and the Truth and the Life as we have known Him, and to listen with open minds and hearts to those who also have something to tell us about Him.

Instinct tells me that the place to begin is with the laity. Ecumenicity has to become something they understand in relationship to their personal religious concerns, in relation to their parish life, before we can expect the clergy to take up the task of guiding their laypeople and parishes into this new territory. We expect too much of the clergy, I think, when we try to make them the agents of propaganda from the diocesan and national headquarters for each new enthusiasm of the Church outside the parish. Many of our national program divisions of the Christian enterprise simply do not fit the parish. For example, my experience with the parish social relations committee is that it dies within three years. We have learned that the special pledge for "missions" is a much less effective way of raising money for support of the Church outside the parish than a soundly based campaign of Christian stewardship. Similarly, ecumenicity probably has no important place in the formal parish structure, but it has a real place in the hearts and minds of Christian people.

So after some time has been spent in communicating the ecumenical imperative to the Church in general, I would look forward to a series of meetings with the clergy to consult with them about our ecumenical commitment in the parish and the diocese.

The Church's participation in state and local councils of Churches has been spotty. Many of the concerns of such councils seem peripheral and some even seem regrettable to Episcopalians. Perhaps it has not occurred to us that we have a right to ask the local council to take into account our interests and concerns, to record our dissent when we cannot agree, to deal with subjects in which we are more interested than some others. Perhaps the Church as a whole can learn from the successful experience of those dioceses and parishes who have a vital relationship to local councils.

The 1963 General Assembly of the NCC has spent much time on the local aspects of Faith and Order. Perhaps this, following out the New Delhi statement of the WCC on local unity, gives hope for real ecumenical encounter in the faith and order area in state and city councils. It would seem that room must be made for facing our differences in these councils before they can genuinely serve the cause of composing differences. But we must also be sympathetic about the reluctance of local leaders to delve into these "divisive" areas when their entire past program has been to emphasize the things on which the Churches were agreed.

The great new ecumenical fact of our time, of course, is the emergence of the ecumenical movement in the Roman Catholic Church. The first thing that this tells us, perhaps, is that ecumenicity is no monopoly of the conciliar movement of the Churches. (Nobody understands this better than the people professionally engaged in the conciliar movement.) Fundamentalists are holding serious

477

theological conversation with Liberals in the Lake Forest Consultations, in which the Rev. Charles Long, Jr., a priest of our Church, is a participant. A small committee appointed by the Presiding Bishop of our church has been having quiet conversations with the leadership of the Assemblies of God. The National Association of Evangelicals has welcomed the Seventh-Day Adventists into its anti-ecumenical ecumenical fellowship, having surmounted the difficult problems of special revelation that once kept the Adventists apart. The Missouri Synod Lutherans have emerged from their isolation to a truly remarkable degree. All these significant ecumenical developments have taken place outside the organized ecumenical movement.

But the new look in Roman Catholicism is an earth-shaking development. For the first time we can hope to escape from the concept of Church unity which Anglicanism has always disliked—the concept of the two big Churches, one Catholic and one Protestant—and think of the one Church of Christ as a dream to be seriously entertained.

We may thank God that this development is not happening so fast as to overwhelm us with confusion. If Roman Catholicism were to seek to enter the World Council or the National Council today, the upheaval involved might be more than these organizations could encompass. More things have to happen, and will happen, before we can even begin to guess at the shape of the future formal relationships.

At this point I might note that Roman Catholic ecumenists are on the whole more impressed by Anglicanism when it is adventurous in its dealings with Protestantism than when it is making distinctions between "Catholic unity" and "pan-Protestantism." For example, Fr. Maurice Villain, in his book, *Unity*, recently translated into English comments that the Church of South India "rises appreciably above the original level of each of the four constituent bodies," one of which, of course, was Anglican. He rejoices that the Lambeth Conference "tolerated" the departures from Anglican ordination practice involved in that Church, instead of exerting its influence to keep the united Church from coming into being.

Fr. Gregory Baum, a member of the Vatican Secretariat for Christian Unity, remarked to me that he is disappointed with Anglicans who are preoccupied with the idea that the Vatican Council might reopen the question of Anglican orders. Roman ecumenists are interested in the unity of all Christians, Catholic and Protestant, and interested in us when we maintain both traditions in balance.

It is up to us, of course, to assure ourselves that any united Church into which the Episcopal Church may enter will be "truly Catholic" as well as truly Reformed and truly Evangelical. Thank God, no Church is a Church of ecumenists and all must listen to the wisdom of their upholders of tradition as well as to their prophets and enthusiasts. . . .

Peter Day, "Episcopalians and Ecumenicity," *The Living Church* (January 5, 1964), 12-13; (January 12, 1964), 13-14. (Excerpts)

111.

Declaration on Unity, 1979

This Declaration on Unity was adopted by the sixty-sixth General Convention at Denver, September 6-20, 1979. It expresses the Episcopal Church's commitment to the visible unity of the church, and stresses a "communion of communions" as the goal of the ecumenical movement.

Resolved. . . . That this 66th General Convention declares:

The visible unity we seek will be one eucharistic fellowship. As an expression of and a means toward this goal, the uniting Church will recognize itself as a Communion of Communions, based upon the acknowledgement of catholicity and apostolicity. In this organic relationship all will recognize each other's members and ministries. All will share the bread and the cup of the Lord. All will acknowledge each other as belonging to the Body of Christ at all places and at all times. All will proclaim the Gospel to the world with one mind and purpose. All will serve the needs of humankind with mutual trust and dedication. And for these ends all will plan and decide together in assemblies constituted by authorized representatives whenever and wherever there is need.

We do not yet see the shape of that collegiality, conciliarity, authority and primacy which need to be present and active in the Diocese with its Parishes as well as nationally, regionally, universally; but we recognize that some ecclesial structure will be necessary to bring about the expressions of our unity in the Body of Christ described above.

We do not yet know how the particular traditions of each of the Communions will be maintained and developed for the enrichment of the whole Church. We do not see how the Church will be shaped by the particular histories and cultures within which she is called to fulfill her mission.

All Christians are challenged to express more fully among themselves the Biblical call to mutual responsibility and interdependence. We believe ways can now be found to express this call to a Communion of the Churches in the Body of Christ. As the Churches become partners in mission they will move from present interrelatedness to interdependence. . . .

Journal of General Convention, 1979, B-40.

112.

Commentary on Eucharistic Sharing, 1979

This Commentary on Eucharistic Sharing is part of the Report of the Standing Commission on Ecumenical Relations presented to the General Convention at Denver, September 6-20, 1979. It provides guidelines for receiving the Eucharist in an ecumenical setting.

A. Fundamental Understandings

The Holy Communion is a sacramental event in the life of God's people. It is a special offering of thanksgiving by those who are united by a common faith, responsive to the Word proclaimed in their midst and recalling in Eucharistic Liturgy the sacrifice of Jesus Christ, their common Lord. It is a sacrament of unity for God's people, as it is the divine presence of the one and undivided Lord, and serves to bind into a common body those whose differences He has reconciled.

There is a very special relationship between the Holy Communion and the *koinonia*, or community in which it is celebrated. That community is in some way always related to a larger community of the Holy Catholic Church. Yet each Eucharistic community must have a life of its own as well—faith, fellowship, and response to the Word of God. Since each individual Eucharistic *koinonia* is an expression of a larger community, it is subject to the regulation and direction expressed, however imperfectly, by that larger community.

B. The Present Reality

1. Normative Practice

We are constantly faced with the anomaly of celebrating the Sacrament of unity within the pain of incompleteness caused by divisions within the Body of Christ. This is less apparent when the gathered community is united in faith and order, as is the case when only Episcopalians are in attendance at a celebration presided over by an Episcopal priest or bishop. Eucharistic sacrifice is but a single offering. But at least the norms, standards, and disciplines of the Episcopal church apply equally to all who are present. (Where there is a concordat of intercommunion with another church, freedom of access to the Holy Communion of both bodies is generally offered to all members in good standing in their own church.) Increasingly this church must face the reality of exceptional cases and special circumstances wherein these conditions do not all prevail and for which some consistent standards are necessary as a basis for Eucharistic sharing.

2. Exceptional Cases
The exceptional case of an individual under circumstances of *emergency needs,* spiritual and pastoral, is widely recognized within the catholic church. Emergency needs of this kind are so exceptional that there is no way to regulate the occasional act of shared communion by a Christian of another church who requests the Sacrament of Our Lord's Body and Blood, out of a deep need for grace.

3. Special Circumstances
By far the greater concern for communion involving persons of other churches is presented by those special cases where some but not all of the elements normally required for the church's Holy Communion are present. It is the bishop of each diocese who shall be ultimately responsible for interpreting the extent of participation by non-Episcopalians in such cases, according to the criteria of this commentary.

4. Respect for Church Discipline
Whatever provision is made for Eucharistic sharing under these *special circumstances needs to be done in such a way that the receiving of communion strengthens and sustains the responsible participation of a Christian in the ecclesial body to which he belongs.* Certainly his own conscience must always be respected as must the right of his own church to determine the sacramental discipline of those who, by their own choice, make that their spiritual home.

C. Receiving Communion in a Church Other Than That of Membership
When non-Anglicans attend a Holy Communion Service where an Episcopal bishop or priest is presiding, their reception of the elements of the Communion is appropriate when these four conditions are applicable:

> **a.** They shall have been baptized with water in the name of the Father, Son, and Holy Ghost, and have been admitted to the Holy Communion within the Church to which they belong.
> **b.** They shall "examine (their) lives, repent of (their) sins, and be in love and charity with all people," as this church in its

catechism, (PBCP, p. 860), says is required of all those who come to the Eucharist.

c. They shall approach the Holy Communion as an expression of the Real Presence of Jesus Christ whose sacrifice once upon the cross was sufficient for all mankind.

d. They shall find in this Communion the means to strengthen their life within the Christian family through the forgiveness of (their) sins, the strengthening of (their) union with Christ and one another and the foretaste of the heavenly banquet . . . (PBCP p. 859-60).

If local circumstances present a pastoral need for a public invitation, it should not in any way be coercive, nor should it be in terms of an "open Communion" applied indiscriminately to anyone desiring to receive Communion.

Serious attention needs to be given to the repeated practice of communicating in an Episcopal Church on the part of someone who holds nominal membership in another church even to the exclusion of worship in his own communion. It is no service to the unity of Christ's Church when one group contributes to the weakening of loyalty and undermining of discipline of another. Dealing honestly with the problems raised in such a case is a pastoral responsibility of the church and frequently becomes the occasion for a renewed Christian commitment and a more responsive decision about church membership within the Body of Christ.

All of these considerations naturally raise the question which faces a member of the Episcopal Church who is present when the Holy Communion is celebrated in another Christian Church. In general the same standards which should apply for those who intend to receive Communion at Episcopal altars should be present. It is important that church members respect the teaching and discipline of the church by whose authorization the Sacrament is celebrated as well as those of their own church. In cases of doubt the counsel and direction of the ordinary and/or the parish priest should be sought to give guidance. Once again the ultimate guide of conscience informed by the teachings of the Church will be expected to determine the individual decision. The action of receiving the Holy Communion in a church other than one's own should be the consequence of an intentional decision for the unity of Christ's Body as well as a response to personal spiritual need. It should not be an avoidance of coming to terms with difficulties, an act of convenience, a cover for embarrassment at being different, or the avoidance of coming to terms with difficulties in one's own church. To communicate at the altar of another church is a solemn act of faith and unity within a divided church, and can only be justified if it builds for the unity of God's people.

D. Pain of Broken Communion

What about those times when Christians cannot communicate at the same altar because of church doctrine, discipline or reasons of conscience? One of the realities of life within a divided Church is this very brokenness at the Table of the Lord. There is great temptation to pretend that this is not true or to believe that we as individuals can do what denominations still feel should not be done. This is an experience of the Cross in a sinful world. Often it is more appropriate to bear the pain and give testimony to the integrity of faith and discipline in one's church than to act as though full unity existed where it does not. For centuries individual Christians have found both blessing and pain in a kind of spiritual communion which is possible on occasions when it is inappropriate to participate in the Breaking of Bread with other Christians. The spiritual communion is in itself a participation in the presence of Him who died upon the Cross to the end that full unity might one day be restored. Both the blessing and the pain to those who have such spiritual communion together, when Eucharistic sharing is not possible, give added incentive to work for a full and complete unity within the Body of Christ.

Journal of General Convention, 1979, AA-80–AA-82.

113.

Principles of Unity, 1982

At the sixty-seventh General Convention, New Orleans, September 5-15, 1982, the Chicago–Lambeth Quadrilateral was reaffirmed. This statement is called "Principles of Unity." It is a commentary on the Quadrilateral and speaks of the church as a sacrament, which provides a new starting point for speaking of the sacramentality of its rites. Continuity in teaching is emphasized, with apostolicity placed in a larger context than the older one of apostolic order.

Resolved, the House of Deputies concurring, That the 67th General Convention of the Episcopal Church re-affirm the Chicago-Lambeth Quadrilateral as found on pages of 876-878 of the Book of Common Prayer as a statement of basic principles which express our own unity, and as a statement of essential principles for organic unity with other churches, and affirm the following as an explication of that basic document without denying anything contained therein: that

1. The Holy Scriptures of the Old and New Testament are the word of God as they are witness to God's action in Jesus Christ and the continuing presence of his Holy Spirit in the Church, that they are the authoritative norm for catholic faith in Jesus Christ and for the doctrinal and moral tradition of the Gospel, and that they contain all things necessary for salvation.

2. The Apostles' and Nicene Creeds are the forms through which the Christian Church, early in its history under the guidance of the Holy Spirit, understood, interpreted and expressed its faith in the Triune God. The continuing doctrinal tradition is the form through which the Church seeks to understand, interpret and express its faith in continuity with these ancient creeds and in its awareness of the world to which the Word of God must be preached.

3. The Church is the sacrament of God's presence to the world and the sign of the Kingdom for which we hope. That presence and hope are made active and real in the Church and in the individual lives of Christian men and women through the preaching of the Word of God, through the Gospel sacraments of Baptism and Eucharist, as well as other sacramental rites, and through our apostolate to the world in order that it may become the Kingdom of our God and of his Christ.

4. Apostolicity is evidenced in continuity with the teaching, the ministry, and the mission of the apostles. Apostolic teaching must, under the guidance of the Holy Spirit, be founded upon the Holy Scriptures and the ancient fathers and creeds, making its proclamation of Jesus Christ and his Gospel for each new age consistent with those sources, not merely reproducing them in a transmission of verbal identity. Apostolic ministry exists to promote, safeguard and serve apostolic teaching. All Christians are called to this ministry by their Baptism. In order to serve, lead and enable this ministry, some are set apart and ordained in the historic orders of Bishop, Presbyter, and Deacon. We understand the historic episcopate as central to this apostolic ministry and essential to the reunion of the Church, even as we acknowledge "the spiritual reality of the ministries of those Communions which do not possess the Episcopate" (Lambeth Appeal 1920, Section 7). Apostolic mission is itself a succession of apostolic teaching and ministry inherited from the past and carried into the present and future. Bishops in apostolic succession are, therefore, the focus and personal symbols of this inheritance and mission as they preach and teach the Gospel and summon the people of God to their mission of worship and service. And be it further

Resolved, the House of Deputies concurring, That this 67th General Convention commend to the Anglican Consultative Council this commentary as an explication of the Chicago-Lambeth Quadrilateral to guide this Church in its ecumenical dialogues.

Journal of General Convention, 1982, C58-C59.

114.

The Final Report: Anglican-Roman Catholic International Commission, 1982

The Anglican-Roman Catholic International Commission began meeting in 1970. It is one of several bilateral conversations in which the Episcopal Church is involved. It has issued four major statements: 1971, Windsor Statement on Eucharistic Doctrine; 1973, Canterbury Statement on Ministry and Ordination; 1976, Venice Statement on Authority in the Church I, and Windsor Statement on Authority in the Church II. On December 5, 1991, the Vatican responded and stated: "There still remain between Anglicans and Catholics important differences regarding essential matters of Catholic doctrine."

Introduction

1 Our two communions have been separated for over 400 years. This separation, involving serious doctrinal differences, has been aggravated by theological polemics and mutual intolerance, which have reached into and affected many departments of life. Nevertheless, although our unity has been impaired through separation, it has not been destroyed. Many bonds still unite us: we confess the same faith in the one true God; we have received the same Spirit; we have been baptized with the same baptism; and we preach the same Christ.

2 Controversy between our two communions has centred on the eucharist, on the meaning and function of ordained ministry, and on the nature and exercise of authority in the Church. Although we are not yet in full communion, what the Commission has done has convinced us that substantial agreement on these divisive issues is now possible.

3 In producing these Statements, we have been concerned, not to evade the difficulties, but rather to avoid the controversial language in which they have often been discussed. We have taken seriously the issues that have divided us, and have sought solutions by re-examining our common inheritance, particularly the Scriptures.

4 The subjects which we were required to consider as a result of the Report of the Joint Preparatory Commission all relate to the true nature of the Church. Fundamental to all our Statements is the concept of *koinonia* (communion). In the early Christian tradition, reflection on the experience of *koinonia* opened the way to the understanding of the mystery of the Church. Although '*koinonia*' is never equated with 'Church' in the New Testament, it is the term that most aptly expresses the mystery underlying the various New Testament images of the Church. When, for example, the Church is called the people of the new covenant or the bride of Christ, the context is primarily that of communion. Although

485

such images as the Temple, the new Jerusalem, or the royal priesthood may carry institutional overtones, their primary purpose is to depict the Church's experience as a partaking in the salvation of Christ. When the Church is described as the body of Christ, the household of God, or the holy nation, the emphasis is upon the relationships among its members as well as upon their relationship with Christ the Head.

5 Union with God in Christ Jesus through the Spirit is the heart of Christian *koinonia*. Among the various ways in which the term *koinonia* is used in different New Testament contexts, we concentrate on that which signifies a relation between persons resulting from their participation in one and the same reality (cf. 1 John 1.3). The Son of God has taken to himself our human nature, and he has sent upon us his Spirit, who makes us so truly members of the body of Christ that we too are able to call God 'Abba, Father' (Rom. 8.15; Gal. 4.6). Moreover, sharing in the same Holy Spirit, whereby we become members of the same body of Christ and adopted children of the same Father, we are also bound to one another in a completely new relationship. *Koinonia* with one another is entailed by our *koinonia* with God in Christ. This is the mystery of the Church.

6 This theme of *koinonia* runs through our Statements. In them we present the eucharist as the effectual sign of *koinonia, episcope* as serving the *koinonia*, and primacy as a visible link and focus of *koinonia*.

In the Statement *Eucharistic Doctrine* the eucharist is seen as the sacrament of Christ, by which he builds up and nurtures his people in the *koinonia* of his body. By the eucharist all the baptized are brought into communion with the source of *koinonia*. He is the one who destroyed the walls dividing humanity (Eph. 2.14); he is the one who died to gather into unity all the children of God his Father (cf. John 11.52; 17.20ff).

In the Statement *Ministry and Ordination* it is made clear that *episcope* exists only to serve *koinonia*. The ordained minister presiding at the eucharist is a sign of Christ gathering his people and giving them his body and blood. The Gospel he preaches is the Gospel of unity. Through the ministry of word and sacrament the Holy Spirit is given for the building up of the body of Christ. It is the responsibility of those exercising *episcope* to enable all the people to use the gifts of the Spirit which they have received for the enrichment of the Church's common life. It is also their responsibility to keep the community under the law of Christ in mutual love and in concern for others; for the reconciled community of the Church has been given the ministry of reconciliation (2 Cor. 5.18).

In both Statements on authority the Commission, discussing primacy, sees it as a necessary link between all those exercising *episcope* within the *koinonia*. All ministers of the Gospel need to be in communion with one another, for the one Church is a communion of local churches. They also need to be united in the apostolic faith. Primacy, as a focus within the *koinonia*, is an assurance that what they teach and do is in accord with the faith of the apostles.

7 The Church as *koinonia* requires visible expression because it is intended to be the 'sacrament' of God's saving work. A sacrament is both sign and instrument. The *koinonia* is a sign that God's purpose in Christ is being realized in the world by grace. It is also an instrument for the accomplishment of this purpose, inasmuch as it proclaims the truth of the Gospel and witnesses to it by its life, thus entering more deeply into the mystery of the Kingdom. The community thus announces what it is called to become.

8 The *koinonia* is grounded in the word of God preached, believed and obeyed. Through this word the saving work of God is proclaimed. In the fullness of time this salvation was realized in the person of Jesus, the Word of God incarnate. Jesus prepared his followers to receive through the Holy Spirit the fruit of his death and resurrection, the culmination of his life of obedience, and to become the heralds of salvation. In the New Testament it is clear that the community is established by a baptism inseparable from faith and conversion, that its mission is to proclaim the Gospel of God, and that its common life is sustained by the eucharist. This remains the pattern for the Christian Church. The Church is the community of those reconciled with God and with each other because it is the community of those who believe in Jesus Christ and are justified through God's grace. It is also the reconciling community, because it has been called to bring to all mankind, through the preaching of the Gospel, God's gracious offer of redemption.

9 Christ's will and prayer are that his disciples should be one. Those who have received the same word of God and have been baptized in the same Spirit cannot, without disobedience, acquiesce in a state of separation. Unity is of the essence of the Church, and since the Church is visible its unity also must be visible. Full visible communion between our two Churches cannot be achieved without mutual recognition of sacraments and ministry, together with the common acceptance of a universal primacy, at one with the episcopal college in the service of the *koinonia*.

The Final Report: Anglican-Roman Catholic International Commission (Cincinnati, Ohio: Forward Movement Publications, 1982), 5-8. (Excerpt)

115.

Lutheran-Episcopal Dialogue, September 1982

The Lutheran-Episcopal dialogue in the United States began in 1969 under the auspices of the Joint Commission on Ecumenical Relations of the Episcopal Church and the Division of Theological Studies of the Lutheran Council in the U.S.A. This series of dialogues, known as LED I, concluded in 1972. The second series of U.S. Lutheran-Episcopal dialogues met from 1976 to 1980, and is known as LED II. This second series of dialogues approved the following recommendations: (1) the mutual recognition of the respective church bodies as true churches, (2) a call for interim eucharistic hospitality, (3) a request for joint worship under certain circumstances, (4) a recommendation of cooperation in the publication and circulation of dialogue material, (5) a suggestion of local covenants between Lutheran and Episcopal congregations, and (6) an encouragement for a third series of national dialogues. In September 1982 the American Lutheran Church, the Association of Lutheran Churches and the Lutheran Church in America approved the following recommendations. These three Lutheran groups merged effective January 1, 1988, as the Evangelical Lutheran Church in America. These recommendations were approved by the General Convention in New Orleans in September 1982. The first Interim Sharing of the Eucharist was celebrated on January 16, 1983, at the Cathedral of Saints Peter and Paul, Washington, D.C.

Resolved, the House of Deputies concurring, **That this 67th General Convention of the Episcopal Church:**

1) Welcome and rejoice in the substantial progress of the Lutheran-Episcopal Dialogues (LED) I and II and of the Anglican-Lutheran International Conversations, looking forward to the day when full communion is established between the Anglican and Lutheran Churches;

2) Recognize now the Lutheran Church in America, the Association of Evangelical Lutheran Churches, and the American Lutheran Church as Churches in which the Gospel is preached and taught;

3) Encourage the development of common Christian life throughout the respective Churches by such means as the following:

a) Mutual prayer and mutual support, including parochial/congregational and diocesan/synodical covenants or agreements,

b) Common study of the Holy Scriptures, the histories and theological traditions of each Church, and the material of LED I and II.

c) Joint programs of religious education, theological discussion, mission, evangelism, and social action.

d) Joint use of facilities;

4) Affirm now on the basis of studies of LED I and LED II and of the Anglican/Lutheran International Conversations that the basic teaching of each respective Church is consonant with the Gospel and is sufficiently compatible with the teaching of this Church that a relationship of Interim Sharing of the Eucharist is hereby established between these Churches in the U.S.A. under the following guideline:

a) The Episcopal Church extends a special welcome to members of these three Lutheran Churches to receive Holy Communion in it under the Standard for Occasional Eucharist Sharing of its 1979 General Convention. This welcome constitutes a mutual recognition of Eucharistic teaching sufficient for Interim Sharing of the Eucharist, although this does not intend to signify that final recognition of each other's Eucharists or ministries has yet been achieved.

b) Bishops or Dioceses of the Episcopal Church and Bishops/Presidents of the Lutheran Districts and Synods may by mutual agreement extend the regulations of Church discipline to permit common, joint celebration of the Eucharist within their jurisdictions. This is appropriate in particular situations where the said authorities deem that local conditions are appropriate for the sharing of worship jointly by congregations of the respective Churches. The presence of an ordained minister of each participating Church at the altar in this way reflects the presence of two or more Churches expressing unity in faith and baptism as well as the remaining divisions which they seek to overcome; however, this does not imply rejection or final recognition of either Church's Eucharist or ministry. In such circumstances the eucharistic prayer will be one from the Lutheran Book of Worship or the Book of Common Prayer as authorized jointly by the Bishop of the Episcopal Diocese and the Bishops/Presidents of the corresponding Lutheran Districts/Synods.

c) This resolution and experience of Interim Sharing of the Eucharist will be communicated at regular intervals to other Churches of the Lutheran and Anglican Communions throughout the world, as well as to the various ecumenical dialogues in which Anglicans and Lutherans are engaged, in order that consultation may be fostered, similar experiences encouraged elsewhere, and already existing relationships of full communion respected;

5) Authorize and establish now a third series of Lutheran-Episcopal Dialogues for the discussion of any other outstanding questions that must be resolved before full communion (communio in sacris/altar and pulpit fellowship) can be resolved between the respective Churches, e.g., implications of the Gospel, historic episcopate, and the ordering of ministry (Bishops, Priests, and Deacons) in the total context of apostolicity; ...

. . . .

Commentary

In a general way we trust that the text for the foregoing resolution is self-explanatory and self-authenticating, but for the sake of subsidiary questions that might be raised we offer the following comments on paragraphs 2-5.

Para. 2. For the Lutherans, recognition as "a Church in which the Gospel is preached and taught" is of paramount importance. Episcopalians, although they would perhaps attach less weight than the Lutherans to such a description, have never before officially accorded such recognition to any other Church save for those already in full communion.

Para. 3. It has been well said that "Ecumenism is not real if it is not local," and we hope that both Episcopalians and Lutherans will concur and act accordingly.

Para. 4. This, we believe, is the major ecumenical advance proposed in the resolution. It is a proposal for "interim sharing of the Eucharist" (a new term used to describe a new relationship) based upon a mutual recognition of eucharistic teaching sufficient for this purpose, "although this does not intend to signify that final recognition of each other's Eucharists or ministries has yet been achieved." At first this wording may sound slightly negative, but the Episcopal and Lutheran ecumenical commissions think it best to be clear as to what the proposal is and is not. In effect, for Episcopalians this (Para. 4a) will mean an extension of our 1979 General Convention's Standard for Occasional Eucharistic Sharing (Journal C-49) (which was intended for individuals, "guests," who are baptized and previously admitted to communion in their own Churches, repentant of their sins, and approach the Holy Communion as an expression of the real presence of Jesus Christ) to one entire group, the members of these three Lutheran Churches, on the basis of a recognition of their eucharistic teaching as consonant with the Gospel and sufficiently compatible with our own eucharistic teaching. If approved by Lutherans, the proposal will mean a corresponding welcome to ourselves on the basis of their 1978 Statement on Communion Practices. For neither Episcopalians nor Lutherans is this necessarily a complete recognition of every point of the other's eucharistic teaching, but a recognition deemed to be sufficient for the purpose intended.

Because final recognition of each other's Eucharists or ministries has not yet been achieved, however, the proposed text does not constitute what otherwise might be called "reciprocal intercommunion." Individual members of each Church are left to make their own decisions about whether to accept the invitation from the other. Neither Episcopalians nor Lutherans as *Churches* declare here that they reciprocally *accept* on behalf of their members this invitation. It should also be noted that both the Anglican and the Lutheran traditions have consistently refused to legislate in such a way as to *exclude* their members categorically from the Eucharists of other Churches.

Many hope, of course, that further steps can be taken so that further states of unity (such as reciprocal intercommunion itself, final recognition of each other's Eucharists and ministries, even full communion) will be reached in the not too distant future. For the present, however, we are convinced that mutual recognition of each other's *teaching* to the extent proposed can and now should be made, and if done it will constitute the first time that the Episcopal Church or these Lutheran Churches have mutually recognized the eucharistic teaching of another Church in this way. This, we believe, will be a significant and responsible step towards unity. It will also be unique, a new relationship described by a new term, and not the same as other previous arrangements such as with the Consultation on Church Union. We dare to hope (Para. 4c) that this may serve also as a model for other ecumenical relationships in the future.

The resolution also proposes that this new relationship, "interim sharing of the Eucharist," can be realized and actualized in another way, which is described in Para. 4b as "common, joint celebration of the Eucharist." When done in the way prescribed, subject to the bishop's regulation, with an ordained minister of each participating Church at the altar, with the use of a eucharistic prayer authorized jointly, many Episcopalians will recognize this as a "concelebration" in which ordained clergy of both churches appropriately join together "in the consecration of the gifts, in breaking the bread, and in distributing Communion" (BCP, pp. 322, 354). Such a "common, joint celebration of the Eucharist" should not be taken to imply either rejection or final recognition of either Church's Eucharist or ministry, however, since it simply does in fact "reflect the presence of two or more Churches expressing unity in faith and baptism as well as the remaining divisions which they seek to overcome." Clearly, then, neither Church's ministry is here rejected, but neither is it yet finally recognized. Final recognition itself could only follow upon resolution of the subjects proposed for further discussion in Para. 5. Nonetheless, it may be said, if the proposed resolution is approved, that the Episcopal Church and these Lutheran Churches are now within these limits willing for their ordained clergy symbolically to *stand together* at the altar, although not yet *in place of each other* there. This too, we believe, will be a significant and responsible step on the way.

It should be added that the Standing Commission has asked the Theology Committee of the House of Bishops whether it can confirm the Standing Commission's own positive evaluation as to the suitability of the Lutheran eucharistic prayers of consecration for use in this way. Also, this provision for "common, joint celebration of the Eucharist," if approved, would come under the general regulations for priests and bishops participating as celebrants or concelebrants in all such ecumenical events with all other churches in the future being proposed in Resolution #A-44.

The provision of Para. 4c safeguards a concern expressed at the 1981 meeting of the Anglican Consultative Council, that before any one part of the Anglican Communion moves to its own full recognition of the Lutheran (and, by implication, of any other Church's) ministry, broad consultation should be taken.

Para. 5. Obviously, the questions here noted (as well as others suggested by the LED II participants) must be resolved before the stage of full communion can be reached. but the ecumenical commissions of the Episcopal and Lutheran Churches are convinced that by God's grace this is possible.

"Lutheran-Episcopal Dialogue, Resolution A-37A," *Journal of General Convention*, 1982, C-47–C-48. "Commentary," *The Blue Book: Reports of the Committees, Commissions, Boards, and Agencies of the General Convention of the Episcopal Church, New Orleans, Louisiana, September*, 1982, 46-47.

CHAPTER FOURTEEN

Modern Social Issues

Introduction

In the modern era the Episcopal Church has given attention to a variety of issues that threaten the life and well-being of society. Poverty, injustice, disease, prejudice, threats to the environment, war—these issues cause the church to reconsider its values and practices. The church faces the question how it may best proclaim the Christian faith to the people and concerns of this day. What responsibility does the church have to be actively seeking and participating in solutions for the social problems of its time? Does the church consciously or unconsciously encourage the exploitation of the environment, or militarism, or the maintenance of dehumanizing stereotypes based on race or gender? As the church faces these questions, it also faces the challenge of articulating the faith in response to the concerns of people who live in a world where traditional assumptions and values are called into question. Even when the questions of modern social issues are not easily answered, the church's response to these questions can help clarify the meaning of faith and new possibilities for ministry.

116.

Integration Crisis at Sewanee, 1952

In 1878 the trustees of Virginia Theological Seminary founded the Bishop Payne Divinity School at Petersburg, Virginia, to train Negro clergy. It closed in 1949, and the Synod of the Fourth Province on October 24, 1951, urged that Episcopal seminaries in the South be opened to students of all races. The Synod passed a resolution on Negro education and sent it to the trustees of the

University of the South. The trustees considered the resolution on June 6, 1952, and responded with their own resolution. On June 9, 1952, six faculty members of the School of Theology and two faculty members of the College sent a letter of protest to the trustees. In June 1953 all eight of these faculty members resigned.

Report and Resolution Regarding Negro Theological Education

The 23rd Synod referred to the Department of Christian Social Relations the following resolution, to be considered and studied, report to be made to the 24th Synod:

Whereas work among Negroes is an important phase of the work of our Church, and

Whereas the shortage of Negro clergy poses a considerable problem in every Diocese in this Province, and

Whereas there is at present no theological seminary for Negro candidates for the ministry in this Province;

Therefore, Be it resolved: That the desirability and advisability of establishing such a seminary in this Province be considered by a committee of this Synod to report to the next Synod.

The Bishop of Lexington, chairman, reported:

The Department of Christian Social Relations sums up its thinking that it would not be desirable or advisable to establish a segregated seminary for theological education in our Province; but it thinks it desirable and advisable that we should open the existing seminaries in the South to students of all races.

The Department, as special committee, recommends to the Synod that:

1. It accept with approval the report of the Department of Christian Social Relations on the question of seminary training of Negro candidates for the ministry.

2. That the Secretary of the Synod refer this information to the Board of Trustees of the University of the South with the request that the Synod be informed of action taken.

Proceedings of the Board of Trustees of the University of the South, 1952, 13.

Trustees' Resolution

Resolved, that the Trustees of the University of the South inform the Synod of the Fourth Province that there is nothing in the ordinances of the University to prevent the admission of Negroes, or men of any other race, to the School of Theology, but that the Trustees are of the opinion that the encouragement of the enrollment of such students now is inadvisable for the following reasons:

494

1. We are informed by several legal authorities that such action would be in violation of statutes of the State of Tennessee.

2. The School of Theology at Sewanee, unlike most of our theological schools, is not a separate and self-controlled institution, but is part of the University both in administration and in social life; and therefore most consider the whole life of the University community which is located on an isolated domain.

Therefore, we are of the opinion that furtherance of the Church's work and the happiness and mutual good will of both races will not now be served by the action requested by the Synod.

Proceedings of the Board of Trustees of the University of the South, 1952, 14.

Letter of the Faculty

Gentlemen:

We, the Dean and Members of the Faculty of the School of Theology, the Chaplain of the University, and the Department of Religion of the College of Arts and Sciences, of the University of the South, are deeply disturbed by the statement in the public press reporting the negative action taken by the Board of Trustees on the resolution from the Synod of the Province of Sewanee, asking for the admission of Negro students to the School of Theology.

We therefore wish to put on record our convictions on this matter.

First, we deplore the Trustees' failure to state any Christian principle involved, with the consequent reduction of the whole issue to the level of expediency only.

Second, the position taken seems to us untenable in the light of Christian ethics and of the teaching of the Anglican Communion:

> "God has given man responsibility. To exercise it, he must have freedom. The Christian Church therefore demands essential human rights for all, irrespective of race or colour. There are unhappily countries in the world where such rights are denied. We are grateful for the work which is being done by the Commission of the United Nations on Human Rights. We pledge ourselves to work for the removal of the injustice and oppression, and, in particular, to stand by those whose right to religious liberty is threatened." (The Encyclical Letter, the Lambeth Conference, 1948).

Third, the statement that there are ten other Episcopal seminaries which do accept Negro students, together with the implication in the Chancellor's remark that the Sewanee Trustees' refusal to admit Negroes now is in "the furtherance of the Church's work and the happiness and mutual good will of both races", can only mean that the ministry to the Negro members of the twenty-two owning Dioceses and the training of clergy for their needs is no concern of the University.

Fourth, we believe that the statement of the Trustees, as reported, if not re-examined and revised will do irreparable harm to the reputation of Sewanee as a center of Christian education.

Fifth, the actions of the Trustees undermines our effectiveness as teachers of the Christian faith and way of life. It compromises us as priests and teachers in this University, which is owned and operated by the Episcopal Church.

We therefore request a reconsideration of this question by the Trustees. We request that the public be informed that the issue is being considered. We request a statement from the Trustees, not later than their next regular meeting, that they approve in principle the relevant resolutions of the Lambeth Conference and that they are prepared to allow admission of qualified Negro students to the School of Theology. Meanwhile, we shall do our best to serve the Church in training men for the Ministry, though under adverse circumstances which we protest.

If our request is ignored or if the assurance sought is refused, we are without exception prepared to resign our positions and terminate our connection with the University in June 1953.

F. CRAIGHILL BROWN
The Very Reverend F. Craighill Brown, D.D., Dean
ROBERT M. GRANT
The Reverend Robert M. Grant, Th.D.,
Professor of New Testament
R. LANSING HICKS
The Reverend R. Lansing Hicks, B.D.,
Associate Professor of Old Testament
ROBERT M. MCNAIR
The Reverend Robert M. McNair, Ph.D.,
Assistant Professor of Christian Ethics and Moral Theology
J. ALLEN REDDICK
J. Allen Reddick, Ph.D.,
Assistant Professor of Church History
CLAUDE E. GUTHRIE
The Reverend Claude E. Guthrie, B.D.,
Instructor in Practical Theology
RICHARD H. WILMER, JR.
The Reverend Richard H. Wilmer, Jr., D.Phil.,
Chaplain of the University and Professor of English Bible

117.

W. Norman Pittenger, Controlled Sex, 1954

*William Norman Pittenger (July 23, 1905–   ) was professor of apologetics at
the General Theological Seminary, New York, 1935-1966, and the author of
numerous books. He discusses issues of sexuality in this theological writing.*

We have seen that man was made for God and that he is therefore constituted
a sexual being who generally seeks and requires fulfillment in another, as a
sacrament of his only complete fulfillment in the Other who is God. But since
this is so, there can be no area of human experience in which concupiscence, as
we have defined it, expresses itself so readily as in sexual life. Sin and sex are
not coterminous. But sexuality is so central and important in man's life that it
can be used most easily for self-gratification and self-satisfaction, for the pre-
tense and pride which are in man. Not that the sheer physical act is the sinful
thing about this perversion of man's sexuality. The act in itself is *good.* It can
never be altogether *evil,* since it is a part of God's good creation, but it can be so
distorted in its functioning that it becomes *instrumentally* evil. What is sinful in
the distortion of human sexuality is man's arrogance, his self-assertion against
the right order of things, his *hubris* or pride. He can and does use this particular
instrumentality of sexual life to disrupt and disarrange the given pattern. It is
precisely because man's sexuality may be the means to highest fulfillment that it
can also be the means to lowest degradation: "the higher we can rise, the lower
we may fall." The perverted sexuality of sinful man is our best illustration of the
truth *corruptio optimi pessima.* The best, when it is corrupted, becomes the
worst.

This is why man's sexuality is at once the symbol for the union between God
and man, "the marriage of the soul with God," as the old mystics described it,
and also the symbol for the worst fall of man into self-centeredness and utter
depravity. Dean Church once stated this in these words: ". . . the relation of the

497

sexes, the passion of love: how strange, how extravagant, how irrationally powerful over all the world, how at the root of the best things in life, how at the root of the very worst . . . Strange, ambiguous, perplexing lot for creatures made in the image of God."[1]

There is, then, nothing automatic about the splendor of sexuality in man; it is given to him, but at the same time it must be achieved by him. While it is eternally true that we "fall in love," and can in a way do nothing about it—it is "of grace, not of works"—yet, it is also necessary to remember that grace is *manifested* in works, and that in this respect sexuality is no different from, but is a part of, that total experience to which St. Paul referred: "Work out your salvation with fear and trembling, for it is God that worketh in you, both to will and to do of his good pleasure."

When man's sexual life is distorted, we witness both a symptom and a reacting cause of human evil. Not always is this crude and blatant; sometimes it can be very subtle and deceiving. The use of another personality to procure one's own ends in utter disregard of the good of the other, is as evil, even if not as obvious, a thing as the crudest rape. Soames Forsyte in John Galsworthy's *Forsyte Saga* is a "man of property" who considers his wife a possession for his own employment as he desires. It is only when he comes to see that the consequences of such misuse are disastrous to himself that he recognizes the situation for what it is; and then it is too late to do anything for himself, while on the other hand he has infected a succeeding generation with the virus of his own possessive and disproportionate sexuality.

In the vulgarity of so much sexual expression in the modern world, we see another illustration of the same principle. The sexual consciousness can be reduced to its lowest terms, with no penumbra of sacramental meaning, no self-giving and tenderness; then it takes on the quality of sheer ugliness. The advertisements in subways and magazines, the cartoons and comic strips, the blatant distortion of sexuality in popular writing and conversation, are all of them reflections of this vulgarization.

Dr. William Temple once remarked that the reason vulgar jokes about sex are so distasteful is not that there is anything nasty in sex, but that sex is a holy thing; the reduction of it to the level of nastiness, Dr. Temple said, is like making jokes about the Holy Communion.

In order to bring sexuality to its rightful place, it must be controlled. Since man possesses the capacity to govern his choices and to act responsibly, he denies the *differentia* of his human nature and reduces himself to the level of the

---

[1]R. W. Church, *Life and Letters* (London: Macmillan, 1897), p. 329.

beasts when he forgets or denies this control. The moral life of man must be under control, ordered aright. It is the dissipation of man's life by uncontrolled self-assertion which produces the deterioration of personality and the destruction of community that can only end in what classical theology has called hell. Yet, as we have already pointed out, it is precisely this control, in the sense of right ordering, which man cannot of himself provide.

Once again, the greatest need of man is for restoration. The whole Christian faith has its bearing upon this point. It is quite impossible to discuss the sexual nature of man, if we are Christians, without placing him in the Christian context and seeing him as a potential or actual member of the redeemed and redeeming fellowship which is the mystical Body of Christ.

The way to recovery, therefore, is not through human effort, struggling to reach wholeness (holiness) by moral earnestness and moral energy alone. The way of recovery is through community, through relationship. Now of all social groups, societies, peoples, and nations on earth, the only true community that exists—not to assert itself as the center of its life, but to relate itself to the true center of life—is the Church. The Church in principle—although, tragically enough, not always in practice—exists solely to relate itself, its members, and all men to God who *alone* is the Center of things.

There is the striving of the Church from the human side; but on the divine side it is God Himself, fully personal, who has called this community into being. In it and through it He wills to come to man. This is the meaning of the Gospel and of all church life. It is for this reason that original sin is said to be overcome by Holy Baptism—not that one is magically saved from the chances of falling into evil, or that the self-defeating tendencies in one's self are removed, but that by baptism one is initiated into the one community on earth where self-centered-ness is offset by attention focused upon God.

This meaning is also clear in Holy Confirmation, where in full self-response and self-responsibility one commits one's life to God and where God more fully relates one in the whole range of one's being to God Himself, through the bless-ing of the bishop. This meaning is clear in confession of sins and forgiveness, where one is re-established in right relationship with Him who brings order out of all things, even sin and its results.

The redeeming action of relating man's self-bound life to its true center in God is pre-eminently the meaning of the Holy Communion where man through Christ offers himself to God and where God gives Himself through Christ that we may dwell in Him and He in us in true Holy Communion—communion which includes the whole company of faithful people and which would incorpo-rate all our fellow men. The "mystical" union betwixt Christ and His Church redeems man by overcoming his false centrality, and relating him to the true

Center of his life. It is through true community, true relationship, that help comes to man. The "expulsive power of a new affection" alone can release man from his bondage to claims lower than the best, re-directing him in the path which God has set before him to his blessed destiny of life in love.

W. Norman Pittenger, *The Christian View of Sexual Behavior* (Greenwich, Conn.: Seabury Press, 1954), 61-65. (Excerpt)

118.

Racial Cooperation, 1955

On May 17, 1954, in Brown v. Board of Education of Topeka, *the U.S. Supreme Court ruled that segregation in public education was a denial of equal protection of the laws. In this resolution at the fifty-eighth General Convention, September 4-15, 1955, the Episcopal Church called for racial cooperation.*

WHEREAS, Almighty God, through His Son Our Lord Jesus Christ, has offered salvation to all the races of mankind; and

WHEREAS, Our Church has declared through the General Convention, the Lambeth Conference, the Anglican Congress, the National Council of Churches of Christ in the United States of America and the World Council of Churches, that unjust social discrimination and segregation are contrary to the mind of Christ and the will of God as plainly recorded in Holy Scripture; and

WHEREAS, This Church in thanksgiving can proclaim now in every diocese and missionary district, every race has full representation in its Councils; and

WHEREAS, The Supreme Court of these United States has ruled that every citizen shall have open access to the public schools and colleges of the entire nation; therefore be it

Resolved, The House of Bishops concurring, that the 58th General Convention of the Protestant Episcopal Church in the United States of America now commends to all the clergy and people of this Church that they accept and support this ruling of the Supreme Court, and, that by opening channels of Christian conference and communication between the races concerned in each diocese and community, they anticipate constructively the local implementation of this ruling as the law of the land; and be it further

Resolved, The House of Bishops concurring, that we make our own the statement of the Anglican Congress that "in the work of the Church we should welcome people of any race at any service conducted by a priest or layman of any ethnic origin, and bring them into the full fellowship of the congregation and its organizations."

Journal of General Convention, 1955, 258-259.

119.

War and Peace, 1964

This statement was adopted by the House of Bishops on October 31, 1962, at its meeting in Columbia, South Carolina. It was part of the Report of the Joint Commission on the Church in Human Affairs presented to the sixty-first General Convention at St. Louis, October 11-23, 1964. It presents the Gospel mandate for peace-making in the modern era.

Because of the nature of the Christian faith, Christians have an imperative obligation to pray and to work for peace among men and nations. Questions of war and peace are not remote and peripheral concerns for the committed Christian; they grow out of basic understandings of man and his destiny which are inherent in the Christian revelation.

The Church through its official bodies must seek to define the obligations of the Christian as a peace-maker for every age, and to fit them to the situation of man at every juncture of history. In earlier periods of Christian history, the "just war" doctrine represented such an effort to define the conditions of Christian support for and participation in war.

Since the early decades of this century there has been much less clarity about what constituted a "Christian" view of war and peace. Some in the Church have taken a pacifist position, and many of the Resolutions of General Convention and other bodies have reflected this position; and with the emergence of "total war" concepts and technologies, there has been greater confusion about the Christian's approach to the waging of war. The increase of nuclear weapons, missile systems, and new ideological, military, and economic challenges have made the situation at once more difficult and more deeply critical for the Christian conscience.

In the midst of all this, we believe it is possible to affirm an approach of Christian realism which is grounded in the basic truths of the Christian Gospel. Such an approach must be specific in its interpretation of the theological basis of

Christian concern for all issues of war and peace, and must speak concretely to the frustrations of individual citizens faced by bewildering questions of nuclear testing, military services, the threats of aggression, and the seemingly insoluble tensions of international affairs.

This Report consists of a brief summary of the theological basis of our concern and specific suggestions for Christian action.

I. The Theological Basis

Basic elements of the Christian faith lay a demand upon all Christians to come to grips with issues of war and peace.

Among them are the following:

A. There is one God who is sovereign over all men. For a Christian, there is no loyalty which transcends his loyalty to the will of God. No earthly state is omnipotent. Before God, all men and all nations stand under judgment. God alone commands our ultimate obedience on all issues, including those of war and peace.

B. As there is but one God, so in Him there is one family of men. Christians are, by virtue of their membership in the Church, already a part of a world-wide community which transcends the purposes and policies of any national government. We are citizens of our own nation and fulfill its civic obligations; yet we are part of a universal brotherhood which God wills for his people, and under a demand to make this evident in all that we do. Our Lord died for Russians, East Indians, and Chinese, as well as for Americans.

C. In the Gospel, the worth of each individual person is central. Respect for persons does not arise from humanistic logic, but stems from our faith that God has endowed all people with great worth, and that in His sight they must be treated as His creatures, not as things. The concern of the Christian in foreign policy, as in political affairs generally, must embody a sense of the individual dignity and rights of men, rather than partisan causes in support of secular goals of a particular nation.

D. We live in a sinful and fallen world, yet a world blessed by the grace of God and divine Providence at work in human history. There is place neither for unbridled optimism nor unlimited pessimism about man's situation, nor for national complacency. We are all fallen creatures, standing equally with our enemies in need of God's forgiveness. We cannot escape the sin of the world, the agony of our international tensions, nor the guilt for our human sinfulness which lies at the root of the threat of disaster.

E. We partake of a fellowship of redemption created by our Lord. The Church is called to be an extension in time and history of the saving ministry of His life, called to bear witness to an eternal kingdom beyond time and to His death until

His coming again. Even though we live in a world in which it is often impossible to do what is absolutely right, yet nothing can separate us from the love of God which is in Christ Jesus our Lord. Death is not the ultimate threat. No catastrophe in this world, not even the destruction of our world by a nuclear war, can threaten our redemption in Jesus Christ.

F. The knowledge of God's love compels a vertical return of this love and a horizontal out-reach to our fellow men. We cannot say that we love God and hate our neighbor. The gentle, compassionate, understanding, forgiving love of a Christian for all men lies at the very heart of the Gospel. Therefore, we must not fail to respond to that part of God's image which is in every man.

G. The Church is, through hope, free to witness in daily life to the power of Christ for healing. Because of our faith, the Church and Christians can take upon ourselves the special burdens of reconciliation in this world. Claiming the divine mercy and the power of the Holy Spirit, we have hope. It is the calling of the Church to make available to our own selves and to all men the accumulated Christian experience of the past, always realizing the danger of doing violence to the complexity of this human situation by a too-easy application of abstractions to the needs of the present. In Christ, we discern an eternal pattern to history, glimpsing an ultimate meaning beyond time and space, living with courageous faith in the world as we meet it, and accepting the hard choices without self-deception. Our witness is to an eternal Lord; but it must be exercised amid the particularities of life. It must therefore be specific and concrete, expressed within the choices open to us at our particular moment in human history.

II. Specific Christian Action
(individual and corporate)

There are issues concerning war and peace which divide Christians in our own country and elsewhere: the question of nuclear testing; the extent to which national policy must rely upon military deterrence; the concept of a "just war" over against other interpretations of Christian ethics, including the pacifist position. To some extent, our attitudes reflect the nature of our present responsibilities, our access to information, and the like. But we are unanimous in believing that there are specific courses of action on which the whole Church can give witness.

A. The Church corporate, and individual Christians, must meet all the issues of war and peace, including the menace of nuclear weapons. At all levels of its life, the Church must charge its people with the insistent duty of working with all their strength for the prevention and elimination of war.

Several suggestions for concrete action are listed below. The Church cannot fail to minister to those people who are working with the weapons of war under existing world conditions, as well as those people who are working to meet the economic and social conditions that will exist when peace is finally achieved and total disarmament comes. The Church's ministry cannot dissociate itself from any of its people and in fact should have a pastoral longing to share their frustrations. We can recognize the work of those of our people in military and military-related activities. To the men at the missile bases, scientific centers, and diplomatic posts, as well as to the people as a whole, united in their determination to remain free, we must not hesitate to offer a full ministry, realizing the political and military complexity of our national situation, and the fact that the situation for all of us, military and civilian alike, is not totally of our own making. With equal—in some cases even greater—poignancy, we recognize the validity of the calling of the conscientious objector and the pacifist and the duty of the Church fully to minister to him, and its obligation to see that we live in a society in which the dictates of his conscience are respected.

B. The Church calls upon all people, especially the leaders of nations, to exercise the strongest discipline of conscience to prevent total war. Under modern conditions, such war cannot serve any moral or even useful purpose. Every possible moral force must be summoned to prevent its occurrence. It is becoming increasingly evident that all-out modern war cannot protect the world's people, that an atomic holocaust cannot serve the purpose that war may once have served as an instrument of political or police action to secure justice and peace, that total war under modern conditions is self-defeating, and that it will utterly fail to secure peace with the enemy or even peace within the borders of the countries waging it. When world disarmament is feasible, the weapons of war, including all nuclear weapons, must be abolished. Christians can and should exert every influence to insure that any war which breaks out anywhere in the world is limited. In any armed conflict, we must set clearly defined objectives and cease to wage war when they are achieved.

C. Realizing the social sin inherent in the world, the Church recognizes that the United States must remain strong militarily as long as the threat of military attack from without remains. The Church recognizes that a strong military posture does serve as a deterrent to an aggressor nation intent upon military conflict. To this end, the Church further recognizes that the government must keep itself abreast of all developments in warfare. However, the Church declares that the concept of massive retaliation marked by obliteration bombing of large areas and masses of people should be repudiated.

D. Christians are called to be peace-makers. Such responsibility exists not solely in relation to the larger issues of our society. Indeed, the Christian should be distinguished by the irenic quality of life which he brings to family, work, and community life. The ministry of reconciliation is not a special calling, but an understanding of the Christian life as one which seeks to remove the barriers which separate the children of God from each other both at home and among nations.

Journal of General Convention, 1964, 658-662.

120.

American Martyr: The Jon Daniels Story, 1965

In 1965 Jonathan Myrick Daniels (March 20, 1939–August 20, 1965) was a student at the Episcopal Theological School, Cambridge, Massachusetts, and a member of the Episcopal Society for Cultural and Racial Unity (ESCRU). He spent the summer of 1965 in Alabama teaching remedial reading to black children. On August 20, 1965, he and a white Roman Catholic priest were shot as they approached a country store. Daniels died, and the accused killer was later acquitted by an all-white jury. Daniels' life and martyrdom are commemorated in the Episcopal Calendar of the Church Year on August 14. These selections from Daniels' writings reveal his commitment to integration and human equality.

The following letter was written to the Rt. Rev. C. J. Carpenter by Jon Daniels and Judy Upham protesting the treatment they and their friends received at St. Paul's Church, Selma, Alabama.

April 21, 1965

Right Reverend and Dear Sir:

Shortly after your visit on April 15 with the rector and vestry of St. Paul's Church, Selma, we were advised by the rector, the Rev. T. Franklin Mathews, that you had directed that our racially mixed group of worshippers could not be excluded from the Eucharist, but that the ushers might seat us at their own discretion. Mr. Mathews indicated that this policy would subsequently be followed.

At the early service of Holy Communion on Easter Sunday we were seated in the left rear pew, six pews behind the nearest communicants in front of us, and without access to the central aisle. Not only were we thus the last to be communicated, but were were furthermore forced to remain in our seats until after the rest of the congregation had communicated and returned to their seats. Only when the altar rail and the several aisles were empty were we finally allowed to approach the altar.

As we had approached the church before the service we were met by an usher, who insisted that we not bring any Negroes to the festal celebration at eleven. When we left the church at the conclusion of the service, though we were among the first to approach the rector, we were nearly the last to whom he gave his attention. We made several quiet attempts to gain his attention, and each time he rather studiously ignored us until at last he could presumably do so no longer. Thus we were forced to wait for five minutes or more to wish him a good morning and a blessed Easter.

We and the Negro children worshipping with us have repeatedly been the objects of obscene remarks and insults by some of the congregation as we have entered and left the church and the recipients of hostile glares by others, though a small minority have been extremely gracious. Though Mr. Mathews has been most cordial during most of our conversations with him, he requested on Holy Saturday that, as our ecumenical interest ought to indicate that the Episcopal Church was not a necessity for us, we cease worshipping at St. Paul's and worship instead at a local Negro church of another denomination.

Though the policy attributed to you and the attitude displayed by the parish may indeed approximate the letter of the canon, they scarcely fulfill its spirit. We are distressed at what appears to be a deliberate breach of the conditions cited in the Invitation to Holy Communion—and a compromise of the gospel, as well.

Surely the gospel, as it is delivered to this Church and proclaimed at her altars and pulpits, calls for a charity, a witness, and a living reconciliation that the racial policy of St. Paul's Church currently negates. As Episcopalians, as representatives of ESCRU, as seminarians, as members of the Holy Catholic Church we must lament the policy you are represented as having enunciated and urge you to use your considerable influence to correct the situation. This we cordially and respectfully ask you to do.

With every good wish for you and the prayer that the Risen Lord will bless you now and always as you go about the difficult task of reconciling the children of God to the purposes of God, we have the honor to remain

Yours obediently in Him,
Jonathan Myrick Daniels
E.T.S., Class of 1966, New Hampshire
Judith Elizabeth Upham
E.T.S., Class of 1967, Missouri

. . . .

To Mary Elizabeth Macnaughtan:

. . . Technically, I haven't made my own decision—but the chances are about a thousand to one that I'll decide to come back. ESCRU wants me to come back, and I'm so well acclimated by now that it seems a shame to throw it all away. We would definitely be involved in the following: keeping St. Paul's integrated, talking informally with members of the white power structure whom I've encountered at or through St. Paul's (doctors, lawyers, judges, the rector, etc.), relating with kids and adults here in the Negro community (for instance, I have been working some with my family, specifically on their marital difficulties, the father's alcoholism, etc.), and just constituting the presence of the Church in the social revolution which is gathering strength here. Other potential activities might include tutoring both kids and adults in basic reading and writing skills, demonstrating (that's almost inevitable once in awhile: and you should have prepared in advance, *both physically and spiritually*, for the possibility of tear gas, arrest, and I suppose even for death, though that's a bit unlikely). It is true abstractly (as I see it) that no white outsider here is entirely safe—and I feel very strongly that one should make a realistic estimate of what that means. I say this because I decided a long time ago that the Holy Spirit had brought me here, that I believe very firmly in the gospel and its faith, that my life is not my own but His—which means that before anything else I am a servant of Christ, however sinful I may also be—and that consequently the possibility of death, whether immediate or remote, cannot be a deciding factor for me. I can't decide all that for you—only you, on your own knees and out of the context of your own commitment to the Lord and His Kingdom, can make the "estimate" for yourself. You will find people here who are not Christians or even theists, who have dealt with the question of danger on other grounds. I have no other grounds, so can recommend only these. . . You will surely find things, situations, decisions, and people here that you wouldn't like anywhere. That has been very true for me. You will also find wonderful work to be done and a situation in which (I assume from my own experience) you will grow in holiness and devotion to His service, in social consciousness, and in your own vision of what life will be for you. Offhand, I can't think of a more productive way for you or for any college student (or any Christian!) to spend a summer. . . Also: rustling up people who haven't registered to vote yet. Perhaps also helping to administer food and clothing sent from the North. There are any number of programs that will be available (recreation, etc.) and you might want to work independently some of the time—for instance if you don't feel like picketing! . . .

Selma, Alabama
May 1, 1965

. . . .

It was high noon as we walked into the Selma Post Office to sign for a registered letter, and the lines at the windows were long. In the line next to me a redneck turned and stared: at my seminarian's collar, at my ESCRU button, at my face. He turned to a friend. "Know what he is?" The friend shouted "No." Resuming, the speaker whinnied, "Why, he's a white niggah." I was not happy thus to become the object of every gaze. And yet deep within me rose an affirmation and a tenderness and a joy that wanted to shout. Yes! If pride were appropriate in the ambiguities of my presence in Selma, I should be unspeakably proud of my title. For it is the highest honor, the most precious distinction I have every received. It is one that I do not deserve—and cannot ever earn. As I type now, my hands are hopelessly white. "But my *heart* is black . . ." Oh, the drolleries one could spin! I *was* proud, for the redneck's contempt was the obverse of an identity and an acceptance that were very real, if still ambiguous, in another part of town. Hear, O Israel: given an irony or two in the holy mystery of His economy, I am indeed a "white nigger." I wouldn't swap the blessings He has given me. But *black* would be a very wonderful, a very beautiful color to be.

William J. Schneider, *American Martyr: The Jon Daniels Story. Commemorative Edition* (Harrisburg, Pennsylvania: Morehouse Publishing, 1992), 73-75, 79-80, 85-86. (Excerpts)

121.

John Hines, Sermon, 1967

John Elbridge Hines (October 30, 1920–   ) was the twenty-second Presiding Bishop of the Episcopal Church, January 1, 1965–May 31, 1974. At the sixty-seventh General Convention at Seattle, September 17-27, 1967, in the midst of the riots and racial disturbances of the time, Hines called for a commitment by the Episcopal Church to social justice. His plea for social justice was expressed in this sermon, which was the genesis of the General Convention Special Program.

As Presiding Bishop of this Church, by God's help I trust, and with the help of others—some not of this Church—I have tried to hear what God may be saying to the Churches in the crisis in American cities.

Extreme actions on the part of a dispossessed people bespeaks a conviction that white man's justice is no justice for the black man, particularly those trapped in the ghettos of this land. And many of them have despaired of attaining that justice through structures and institutions which they see as channels of the white man's power. The grim consequences of the rioting indicates a tenaciously held conviction that any relief that comes will have to come by acquisition of, or seizure of, sufficient power on their part to enable them to shape their own destiny, taking their place equally alongside other men. This they are prepared to do—even if they have to die in the attempt. Further, and this touches us at a sensitive point, these unfortunate people—many of them—have written off the Churches as possible allies in their quest for justice, for they have seen little concrete evidence that Church people are concerned about their plight or will take the necessary risk to help redeem it.

In trying to hear what is being said in the confusion of our time, I have walked—a little bit—in the ghetto-areas of two of our cities. I can only tell you what I know—know from an unrehearsed face-to-face confrontation with black people, some militant leftists, others solidly moderate—most of them bearing in their soul (and some on their bodies) the indignities and brutality which have erupted in anger and rebellion. I recruited a task-force of our own staff, together with competent outside advisers. I requested the counsel of a group of ghetto leaders in exploring the question: "How can the resources of this Church, resources human and financial, be enlisted intelligently and humbly in the service of the people of the cities; and by what criterion can this Church enter into partnership with the indigenous community-groups in impoverished slum-areas which have been organized by the residents themselves, are run by them, and are seeking to alleviate the conditions which are destroying them?"

I believe that people in all walks of life, Churchmen in our own land and abroad, the people from whom hope is being squeezed out, want to know where we, as Christians, stand—and whether our position is manifested in deeds that cannot be misunderstood.

As at least the beginning of this Church's response to the deep human need dramatized by the conflict in the cities, I am recommending the development of a program, to be extended over the next triennium, by which this Church can take its place, humbly and boldly, alongside of, and in support of, the dispossessed and oppressed peoples of this country, for the healing of our national life. Among its aims will be the bringing of people in ghettos into areas of decision-making by which their destiny is influenced. It will encourage the use of political and economic power to support justice and self-determination for all men. It will make available skilled personnel-assistance, and request the appropriation of substantial sums of money to community-organizations involved in the betterment of depressed urban areas, and under the control of those who are largely both black and poor, that their power for self-determination may be increased and their dignity restored. It is suggested that these efforts be administered through coalitions with other Churches and agencies such as the Inter-Religious Foundation for Community Organization, that we may be joined with and by other groups in similar efforts directed toward the same goals.

I am requesting the funding of such a program in the amount of approximately $3 million annually; such funds to be secured from various sources, principally from the General Church Program.

Finally, a re-ordering of primary emphases and priority-ratings in the proposed General Church Program will be required, in order to support the programmatic response outlined here.

I am requesting the General Convention and the Triennial of the Women of the Church to create appropriate committees to review this call to action by your Presiding Bishop and the Executive Council and charging them to make such recommendations as may seem wise to them in the light of the critical nature of the need. I am sure that means for mutual discussion and co-operation between these committees can be found by such ingenious and creative personnel.

But I would heavily underline a word of caution: no matter what this Church at the national level may decide we can do, both in human and financial terms, it will be only a token, a symbol, if, perhaps happily, a sacrament. What we do here can never be more than an "earnest," pointing to the necessity for, and the effectiveness of, a sensitive and sacrificial response on the part of the people of the Church. For, unless our men, women, and young people enlist in patterns of diocesan, parish, and mission engagement, which involves them personally as well as financially, even the best effort at this level will prove fruitless.

What is before us is not primarily a matter of money. Money can help if we take our hands off its control, giving it because we realize that it is God's and not ours. But if we attempt to use money to "buy our way" out of responsibility, the less credible we will appear to men and women struggling with their misery, and the less likely we are to build our part of a bridge between our alienations. Perhaps we can understand a little that it is only through our sharing in the pain and agonized frustration of the dispossessed that our own renewal can come to be.

I hope that this plea for a corporate response of Episcopalians will not have to stand alone. We are too small a group, and our resources—even if given freely— are far too limited to cope successfully with the crisis in our city streets. I hope I am not presumptuous in appealing to the nation-wide community of faith—to our Jewish brethren, to our Christian brethren—Roman Catholic, Orthodox and Protestant—to join together with us in a bold, full-scale, mobilization of our resources that can be dedicated to the righting of a great wrong and the healing of a bleeding wound in the body of our nation's life. For it may be that we are in "a moment of passing grace" given to us by God, that may never again re-occur—and in which we are given together the opportunity to act.

Journal of General Convention, 1967, 1-3.

122.

Jenny Moore,
The People on Second Steet, 1968

In 1949 Jenny and Paul Moore and two other Episcopal priests moved into the rectory of Grace Church on Second Street in Jersey City, New Jersey. For eight years the Moores lived among the poor, the hungry, the rejected, and the exploited of the city. In her book, Jenny Moore gives a picture of life as it is lived in the inner cities of America. She describes the community and ministry they shared with the people of Jersey City. Paul Moore later became the Bishop of New York.

Recognition

A community is a group of people who band together for mutual support because they are stronger together than alone. A Christian community is an open community, offering its warmth to any who wish to come in. As Kim said in his sermon that first Sunday at Grace Church, it is an exchange of love, and the bearing of one another's burdens. In its simplest—and deepest—sense, it is the touch of a hand, laughter, the exchange of names in conversation, the listening to hurts of childhood and age, the sharing of petty worries, the mutual binding, however tenuous, of one another's wounds; it is sheltering, feeding, sharing. It is a joyful place, and it continues because God exists within it, sustaining it.

After our first year in Jersey City, we thought we knew something about community. At that point, we could still use the word without embarrassment, and we spent many hours discussing its meaning for us and for the people who were gathering under the shelter of Grace Church. We also began to accept the fact that things couldn't be changed overnight, and in some cases ever. We had already found that an open-arms approach in the parish would not solve every problem; it was sometimes an invitation to theft instead of trust.

With these thoughts working in our minds, we exported the children, persuaded a friend from the seminary to take over church and rectory duties, and, tight-lipped and worthy, the four of us charged off for a stock-taking session at a vacation lodge a few hours distant. As we walked in the sunshine and talked, we realized that the problems we had at Grace Church, Jersey City, would be with us as long as we were there. We stepped around them, examining them. We clung to our belief that the difference between a non-Christian and a Christian is that the former may work to alleviate suffering but that the latter attempts to share in it as well. Suffering was part of life, and it had profound meaning for us. We believed that it could be creative, if accepted yet not masochistically sought out, and that sharing it lessened it. We shared insofar as we lived in the midst of it. We laughed, talked, listened, ate, drank, and prayed together with our neighbors. We swept the same dirt, saw the rats, smelled the smells, were antagonistic toward and depended on the same, very human policeman—yet not in the same way. We knew we could afford to eat better than our new friends, take vacations away from the grime, and, finally, enjoy the galling luxury of intellectualizing about life.

We talked of the church building, whose vaulted grandeur had become a symbol of hope to some, but remained alien to others. We talked of church worship—how despite its beauty it seemed so often unrevealing of God's love for all creatures, how by its very inflections it was more comprehensible, as Dennis's brother James once told me, "to white secretaries than to Negro teenagers." This church—"the gift of the dead rich to the living poor," Bob always said—was where men trained in the intricacies of theological dialectic, men who wore cassocks and cottas and brocade chasubles from the religious closets of other centuries and other lands, led prayers in language like "propitiation," "made flesh" and "lamb of God." This building, where for more than a hundred years men and women had come, to kneel thankfully or to sit stonily with nothing about which they could feel grateful, to doze, to search for comforts that life had refused, to rest, to whisper, to be happy, to weep—was it a kind of home for Dennis and others? Was it a source of strength for Dennis's big brother, James, a "good" boy, lonely because he was unwilling to join the neighborhood gang, sitting stiffly in a dark suit and tie in the back pew? Or for Mrs. Hogan, arrogantly prepared to defend until death the legacy of refinement she felt her deceased Episcopalian relatives and friends had bequeathed to these very walls? Did it strengthen the heart of Sally, Mrs. Hogan's niece, whose secretarial job was a fearsome eight-hour journey into a world that scared her?

We asked ourselves what made Grace Church different from a settlement house? Surely we weren't brimming over with professional casework skills, but the relationships in the "cases" we had did not terminate; technically there were no good-byes. There was enduring emotional involvement. We believed that with all its crashing ineptitude, the church made the "we" who lived in the Victorian rectory and the "they," our tenement friends, all "we"; at my kitchen table and at God's altar we broke bread together.

Our talk grew less abstract. Imperfect, vulnerable to satire, a very fragile community did exist. In our very early Jersey City days, it described the coming together of people on the front walk of the rectory, the talking around the kitchen table, the working together at the craft evenings, the applauding at television Westerns, the uniting on Sunday mornings. This was different from the fiercely loyal little parish of individuals who had clung together for protection against the assaults of the city outside. This was different because the edges of exclusivity were crumbling. The Dennises, the men who came for coffee or clothes, the gypsies, the Mrs. O'Briens were as much a part of the church as the Mrs. Hogans and Mrs. Powells, whose sanctuary it had been for so long. Implicitly, the amount of money in the collection envelope, the primacy of Elizabethan prayers, the hymns of milk and honey were far secondary to what the Church could be: a place of welcome, of mutual support, of talk and laughter. Exclusiveness may breed a narrow unity that is a mockery of love, but a community that encompasses everyone enlarges us all.

This huge church, with its mahogany pews and frayed cushions, its black-and-white octagonal-tiled floor dulled and cracked by heat, cold, and the steps of generations, was becoming, however falteringly, a kind of home, perhaps not for the first time, but again. Might Paul and I, newly mindful of the inequalities of chance, opportunity, love, find in it a place of hope? The church was an arena where community was being acted out. For all of us it was an offering of all our brokenness together; it was forgiving and being forgiven; and it made us all, in our separate yearnings and despite all our differences, one.

Jenny Moore, *The People on Second Street* (New York: William Morrow & Company, Inc., 1968), 135-138. (Excerpt)

123.

Euthanasia and Abortion, 1973

The Joint Commission on the Church in Human Affairs made this report to the sixty-fourth General Convention at Louisville, September 26–October 22, 1973. It deals with the beginning and the ending of life.

Philosophy of Total Life Existence

Recognizing the impurity of our motives and the limited information available to us at times, the fulfillment of the worldly humanness of man comes as he assumes the responsibility for the conditions of his own situation and accepts or transcends these conditions. He comes most nearly to God who recognizes limitations and works towards ways of pushing them back, who accepts the inevitable and transcends it, and who sees in the life process opportunity rather than defeat.

It is, therefore, the responsibility of society to provide for all men, of whatever situation, economic level, ability, or talent, those opportunities for proper growth and development that will allow each man to exercise and celebrate his individuality within the community of man, to his and its corporate good. From a medical point of view, as well as from others, this imperative implies, and we vigorously support, provision of high-quality medical care to all persons and the assurance of each individual's right to claim it; the provision of a high nutritional level for all men and the assurance of their inalienable right to call for it; and the highest possible degree of freedom in the exercise of individual conscience, in company with others, in the determination of a life style, functional identity, and participation in the fullest expression of individual life, including the choices surrounding his own death.

The common threads running through all of the material discussed above, and connecting them together, are the following:

1. Human life begins with the genetic determination of the new individual, and continues throughout its development through the entire process of its death.

2. Human life is influenced by its surroundings and by participation in the decisions that affect it.

3. The free exercise of choice by every individual, with the knowledge of the alternatives open to him, and if possible the consequences of each of the alternatives, is necessary for the full development of the potentialities of each person.

4. There is a moral imperative to be actively, rather than passively, involved in the decisions that affect one's own life and death.

5. Death, regarded as a part of the living process, is not to be avoided or denied, but rather to be participated in.

6. Man must have the right to define himself validly in functional terms, as well as in terms of normally accepted or imposed titles.

7. In order to do this, each man must be guaranteed the right of survival (the provision of adequate nutritional levels) and the right of protection from attack by others (high-quality medical care for protection against disease or disability; and the protection of one man against unwarranted or constraining action of his neighbors). Since man is affected adversely as well as advantageously by his total environment, this environment should be as "freeing" as possible.

8. In order that all individual men may have the rights described above, groups of men, with informed conscience and willing to be aware of and to bear the responsibility for their actions, must participate together in the decision-making processes affecting not only their own lives but also the lives of those who will follow.

9. In particular, no one may be used as an object, either in research or outside of it, without his informed consent and knowledge of the consequences of his decision.

CONTRACEPTION AND FAMILY PLANNING

The most pressing problem in this area is the concept of family. The traditional concept is undergoing profound change in the secular society, with the appearance of temporary families or family styles that are never seen as long-term arrangements. Persons enter and leave more or less on their own volition, and the supporting function of the family ties does not exist long enough to be of profound help in determining life style or in the establishment of deep personal inter-relationships. There is no question but that the Church must take seriously the meaning of this new style of existence, but at this time the question is outside the scope of this discussion.

The Lambeth Conference of Bishops and the General Convention have both gone on record as approving the concept of family planning, and have urged the dissemination and use of contraceptive information and technique in aiding the planning. In this regard, it should be emphasized that mere size of the family is not sufficient criterion of the health, both physical and spiritual, of that family. Both large and small families may be right and good, all other factors being considered. What is important is the consideration of the welfare of all members of the family, including the parents (and by extension, the society), so that deprivation of any member of the family does not occur, or is held to a minimum, and that all members of the family can participate in the warmth, love, and support of all other members. Limiting family size is a legitimate method of assuring, at least, that physical facilities and means are not unduly strained.

Limitation of family size may be seen as a matter of conscience by the husband and wife and should be so treated. Similarly, the choice of the method of contraception should be handled in such a way that the free exercise of conscience is permitted. For some, the choice of the intra-uterine device or an abortifacient drug will be contrary to their understanding of their moral responsibility to the unborn conceptus. They should be given all possible help in obtaining other, morally acceptable, methods such as the pill, tubal ligation, or vasectomy. Since the last two involve, in some cases, the individual's concept of himself as real male or female, full knowledge of the consequences or lack of them should be made clear and available.

ARTIFICIAL INSEMINATION AND OVUM TRANSPLANT

We believe that employment of artificial insemination by husband and wife is morally licit and proper, understanding that only the sperm derived from the husband and the ova derived from the wife are used. This includes external fertilization and intra-uterine implantation of ova. There is serious question of the propriety of the use of semen derived from a donor in situations where the concept of the family is in question to begin with or where it might be raised later.

515

Similarly, the use of a host uterus to obtain the gestation of a child outside the family almost necessarily involves the treatment of the second woman as a mere object.

Since the object of artificial insemination is the increase in the size of a family by circumventing blocks to normal conception and gestation, care should be given that the adoption of children now without the chance of normal family life be considered as one of the options available to such couples and families.

ABORTION

The Commission must reject the concept of abortion as a legitimate method of birth control. By definition, it is not birth control and has serious implications for those who accept the concept of the sacredness of all human life outlined in the paragraph on Biological Information. The Commission does recognize, however, the needs inherent in the safety of the mother when medical or psychological problems make the birth of a child an event antithetic to her safety. In addition, it recognizes that the safety of the family unit may be at stake in the birth of unwanted or unplanned-for children, and considers this an important consideration in the decision to terminate a pregnancy. Again, it is urged that the greatest possible support and counseling be made available to the prospective parents facing this decision, and that once the decision has been made and implemented the Church accept the persons involved as fully and completely as their relationship to God indicates they must be.

At the base of the issue, is the knowledge that the decision to employ abortion or not to must be a matter of conscience on the part of the woman. . . .

It should be made clear at this point that the Church should be vigorous in its encouragement and teaching among its own people of the values implicit in the family and the sacredness of life, but it should also acknowledge the right of those outside the Church family to make decisions according to their own consciences within a pluralistic society.

AGING

The Commission recognizes the rapid increase in the population of those over the age of 60 years. It joins the President's Commission on the Aging in deploring the tendency to isolate these people from the rest of society and the deprivation, both physical and mental, that such isolation has produced. In keeping with the concepts of "*continuum* of life" and "family life," the productive maintenance necessary to allow functional rather than subsistence existence of senior citizens should and must be provided for. Their isolation deprives society at large, and every individual in particular, from the experience and wisdom they have acquired, and makes even more difficult the acquisition of the understanding of aging so necessary to every person who will ultimately grow old himself.

More than this is the implicit abrogation of the right to participation in the decisions that affect the life of the aging person. In isolation, he has no control over the course of his life, what he has to give no one takes or accepts, and what he needs to receive few people are ready to give.

EUTHANASIA

There are two meanings of this word, as commonly used, which need clarification. One is the deliberate use of means for the termination of life decided upon and prescribed by the physician in charge. This practice we reject. Moreover, we believe that in actual practice it is not an appreciable problem in our society at the present time.

The other meaning of euthanasia (sometimes called Dysthanasia) is the deliberate withholding or withdrawal of available clinical means for the prolongation of life of a patient for whom there is little or no hope of recovery or survival. With this restricted meaning, euthanasia is a genuine and pressing moral problem in today's world. We believe that the physicians in charge of each patient must reach such clinical decisions in consultation with the patient (where possible), his family and relatives, his minister, and others closely related to him. Such decisions must be made, under God, with deep concern for the value of each human life in this world, but without the morbid concern to deny mortality and the ultimate facing of death. A full appreciation of the extent of the possibility of unforeseeable turns toward recovery and healing beyond the scope of medical practice must always be included in such decisions.

Our emphasis would be on the treatment of death as a normal event in the whole of life, in contrast to the regarding of it as an unintended catastrophe, and on the right of every person to prepare for and experience his own death. It is natural for some to insist on the use of heroic methods for prolonging life when there is essentially no clinical value indicated in their use. Against this, it must be admitted, also, that others might give up too easily. In the tension between these two poles, the ultimate decision must be left to the corporate conscience of all parties under God, including the patient himself, and the guidance of the Christian principles set forth in the foregoing.

Journal of General Convention, 1973, 593-597.

124.

The Church and Homosexual Persons, 1976

This statement affirms the personhood of homosexuals and recognizes their contributions to Church and society. It was drawn from the report of the Joint Commission on the Church in Human Affairs, which was presented at the General Convention of 1976 in Minneapolis.

1. Homosexual persons are children of God, who have a full and equal claim with all other persons upon the love, acceptance, and pastoral concern and care of the Church.

2. We make grateful recognition of the substantial contributions which homosexual persons have made and are making to the life of our Church and society.

3. The question of the causes of sexual orientation, the personal meaning of that orientation, and the ethical implications of homosexual acts are shrouded in great obscurity. This is clearly but one aspect of a confusion and tension which exists in the consciousness of the Church and in many individual Christians concerning the relationship between the traditional Christian ethic and current developments and concepts of pastoral ministry, understanding of human psychosexual development, and the sexual practices of contemporary society. Our awareness and concern in these areas arises from within our own experience as a Christian community in ministry and dialogue with one another. We are conscious of the personal suffering experienced by many homosexual persons and the various unnecessary ways in which society contributes to that suffering.

Journal of General Convention, 1976, AA153.

125.

Journey Toward Justice, 1979

John McGill Krumm (March 15, 1913–   ) was the sixth Bishop of Southern Ohio, March 20, 1971–April 1, 1980. During his episcopate the Institutional Racism Project was conducted. Journey Toward Justice *was a report on the Institutional Racism Project in the Diocese of Southern Ohio.*

The problems of racism—both individual and institutional—are difficult and enduring. They gained our attention during the Sixties, a decade of demonstrations, riots, and civil rights legislation. In spite of much effort by concerned Christians, the Kerner Commission reported in 1968 that "our nation is moving toward two societies, one Black, one white—separate and unequal." The Commission said that whites are primarily responsible for this division. "What white Americans have never fully understood, but what the Negro can never forget, is that white society is deeply implicated in the ghetto...White institutions created it, white institutions maintain it, and white society condones it."

The Seventies have been more "peaceful" for whites but no less problematic for Blacks. In 1978, a survey of institutional racism (conducted by the New York *Times* and the CBS News Bureau) headlined that "The Black-White Split Persists." Whites believed that progress had been made; Blacks saw it differently. For example,

- In 1968, 49% of Blacks thought that there was real hope of ending racial discrimination in this country; in 1978, only 37% expressed that hope.
- In public schools, the actual concentration of Black and Latino children is *greater* than in 1968.
- The unemployment rate for Black people has *doubled* in the past ten years.

The study concludes, "The division between white and Black Americans still exists, and prospects of healing the rift may be more dismal today than they were ten years ago." It is evident that although the problems of racism may be out of the spotlight today, they are not out of existence.

The Diocese of Southern Ohio adopted the Kerner Commission's definition of institutional racism as the basis for its work: institutional racism is *any policy or practice of an organization which benefits one race at the expense of other races.* We focused on institutional behavior because institutions shape the attitudes and behavior of the people within them; therefore, institutions can take significant leadership in bringing about changes in their members. Furthermore, *one* change in institutional policy or practice can affect many more lives than *one* change in any individual's attitudes and actions. . . .

We know that institutional racism can be conscious or unconscious. *It is not the motivation of the institution or its members that counts. It is what results from the policy and/or practice that counts and determines whether the institution is racist.* For example, we learned that the Christian education materials we used in our diocesan and parish programs did not include Black Christian experience and contributions to our Church. This was a practice that was not intentional; nevertheless, it prevented Black Episcopalians from seeing their experience and contributions to the life of the Church and the nation affirmed by their Church. At the same time, it led the white majority of Episcopalians to assume that there was nothing of special significance to learn from or about Black Christians. Our remedy was to develop eighteen Christian education units for children, youth, and adults to compensate for that lack of inclusiveness. Black contributions to Church and nation are now available in our educational curriculum. This has become our new policy and practice. . . .

Hurdles

Institutional change is hard work. There are impediments everywhere. Some are obvious and some are subtle; all recur. Some that we face regularly are the reluctance to admit that skin color *does* make a difference, the perception that racism is passé as a critical issue in the life of the Church and the nation, and the desire for the Church, particularly the local parish, to be the final and secure retreat from the ever-changing world.

Karen E. Steanson, *Journey Toward Justice: A Report on the Institutional Racism Project in the Diocese of Southern Ohio*, September 1979, 4-6, 12, 18. (Excerpts)

126.

Biblical Views of Human Sexuality, 1979

Issues concerning sexuality proved controversial for the Episcopal Church during the 1970s, 1980s, and 1990s. The Commission on Human Affairs and Health has been the official agency studying these issues and reporting to General Convention. The following report was made to sixty-sixth General Convention that met at Denver, Colorado, September 6-20, 1979.

1. A Variety of Views

A careful reading of the whole Bible provides no immutable ethical rules about human sexuality. Of course, in various parts of the Bible one can find specific moral judgments about certain particular actions such as fornication, adultery, prostitution, etc. But such instances must be seen in the full historical and cultural context in which they occurred and were recorded. Thus, one can see many changing verdicts about the same action. An unfaithful wife could be stoned to death lawfully, yet Hosea was ready to forgive his adulterous wife. By the law, a man could divorce his wife for all manner of reasons—some pretty capricious. But Jesus elevated the previous low status of women by asserting that only in an obvious case of adultery could a man divorce his wife. And there are many,

many other accounts of various specific deeds—sexual and non-sexual. "Rules are the cultural clothes worn by a principle." Therefore part of our task is to find the basic principle(s) underneath the historical fashions.

2. Sex Basically Good

The major point to be made, however, is that the biblical view of sexuality is that it is a basic part of life, a force that is essentially good—like creation. The problem, as with all gifts, is the use and misuse of sexuality. The Bible provides examples of the good use of sex—as an expression of love, family and friendship; and examples of the misuse of sex—as in infidelity, breaking up family love, regarding people as things as in the case of prostitution, etc. The basic problem of sex, therefore, is not sexual, but ethical and religious.

While the Bible clearly regards sex as basic in human nature, yet sexuality is not of primary concern. Its importance lies in how it is used. In the teachings of Jesus, there is little concern about "a sexual ethic" *per se*. In contrast to some of the later fathers of the Church, we find no major concern by Jesus about sexual problems, no emphatic rules against this or that sexual behavior, no calls for celibacy and abstinence. He was unmarried, yet it is clear that women were attracted to him, and he was criticized for associating with some, as well for "wine-bibbing and feasting" with people of both sexes.

In the letters of St. Paul, there are more specific references to sexuality. Like his Judaic predecessors, he was against promiscuity (*porneia* or *pornos* in the Greek New Testament Text). He lashed out at other obvious forms of sexual misbehavior, heterosexual and homosexual. Paul recognized the validity of sex and marriage.

Again, taking the Bible as a whole, most scholars agree that the Bible views sexuality and other aspects of personhood as essentially good but in need of control and direction in the interests of the abundant life. But again it must be stressed that "abundant life" does not mean just the individual's happiness or even a family's pleasure and growth. Abundant life is at least partly a gift from God and his love is for us all. Therefore, be it sex, reason, morals—all must be directed toward a better life for society, nations, tomorrow's children—the whole structure of life. From the New Testament Gospel perspective, then, the issue of sexuality is how can it contribute to greater human well-being? In contrast to much of our modern culture which emphasizes only individual good or satisfaction, the Gospel-love ethic requires us to expand love to include family, friends, and society as a whole. Our criterion is not does my ego like it and do I feel happy, but rather, do my actions, in relation to others, to my faith, and God enhance or hinder the quality of life? This is why we say the problem of sex is not sexual, but love. The purpose of sex is love in individual lives, not sexual sensations. The purpose of sex for the human race is to enhance the well-being of mankind.

3. Some Changing Rules and Customs

While there are specific condemnations of homosexuality in the Bible (as noted in the Sodom and Gomorrah story, in Leviticus 18:22, and elsewhere), there is none in the teachings of Jesus, nor in the formal announcements of the Church Councils. It is hard to take specific condemnations of homosexuality found in the Old Testament as authoritative when we do not accord other such specific examples of moral teaching in the Old Testament such dignity. There is a progression in the development of morality through the course of the Old Testament. The low status of women, for example, who were regarded as mere property in Exodus 20:17 is certainly not the view of Jesus or later Old Testament writings.

Similarly, many moral rules were made in order to meet immediate cultural or local conditions. The injunctions against "unclean sex" did not mean that all sex was dirty. Rather, in most cases, it referred to ritual impurity either of men or women related to sexual functions.

4. More Established Positions

On the other hand, this does not mean that all sexual practices are purely relative and culturally changeable. Adultery, prostitution, and homosexual acts are regarded in the Bible as immoral. But note why such actions are so regarded. They are immoral, often in the Old Testament but especially in the New Testament, not because they are sexual but because such acts violate personhood, family love, and the social quality of life. Likewise, some homosexual persons are regarded as immoral not because of their homosexuality but because some of their actions reflect an idolatrous obsession with sex, or violate another person's freedom, or are seen as deleterious to the family and/or to the structure and quality of society.

The doctrine of Creation is often cited as bearing on this issue. In order to create humankind in his image, God found it appropriate to create both male and female. Also noteworthy is the fact that throughout both the Old and New Testaments the heterosexual covenant is used as a metaphor for the relation of God to his people. Not everyone believes those doctrines have any bearing on contemporary thinking about homosexuality.

5. Wider Social Effects

There is no formal biblical injunction against premarital sex nor exclusive approval of a nuclear family life-style. This does not mean that there is no guidance in Scripture. As we have noted, the Bible is everywhere against promiscuity (*porneia*). And the Bible is positive in asserting the desirability of fidelity, loyalty in friendships, commitment to social justice, concern for society. Jesus wept over the coming fate of Jerusalem. The family is seen in the Bible as a basic reality to be nourished, but there is no one form or specific style that is supreme. Yet there are cautions against defying the family or tribe when they interfere with larger social justice issues, or communal welfare. Here the two basic points need to be stressed. When the Bible proclaims a clear moral position, it is almost always because the specific act violates a basic character. Actions are good or bad not because they are sexual or spiritual, male or female, "gay" or "straight", etc.; actions are good or bad in terms of human well-being and the quality of existence for all.

Therefore, opponents or proponents of particular types of sexual orientation or action cannot use the Bible to sanctify or condemn persons by classifying certain deeds under general labels. All heterosexuals are not more moral than homosexuals or vice versa. General labels applied to specific external actions are not warranted for moral condemnation of persons by the New Testament Gospel. "Hate the deed. Love the sinner!"

Even though we may agree in defining certain obvious deeds as morally wrong (such as sadism, torture, exploitation, etc.) the New Testament reminds us that we must also include in our consideration the motives, health or illness and the condition of the doer of the deed. We cannot fairly judge solely by motives and intentions, neither can we evaluate solely by the external deed. It was this internal and external, humanly personal and lawfully moral, combination which Jesus so uniquely demonstrated.

Journal of General Convention, 1979, AA129-AA131.

127.

M. Fletcher Davis, Of Foxes and Birds and the Son of Man: Ministry to Refugees and Other Strangers, 1982

On May 7, 1992, the Episcopal Church celebrated the fiftieth anniversary of the Presiding Bishop's Fund for World Relief. This Fund was established to help displaced refugees of World War II relocate. Since its founding it has helped millions of persons throughout the world. The selection that follows by M. Fletcher

Davis (September 20, 1935–), a priest and former staff person of the Fund, while written in 1982, illustrates the ministry of this program.

To help the stranger and the sojourner, especially the refugee, victims of social, political, economic, cultural and racial movements which impinge upon people without their consent, is a divine imperative from scripture and from the tradition of the Church. The plight of the dispossessed needs to concern every faithful Christian, both on the level of seeking relief of the pain and suffering of dislocation, and on the level of giving a cup of water to the thirsty and welcome to the stranger in our midst. The problems of refugees are the basic religious problems: they raise the central questions of the meaning of human life.

Xenophobia—the fear, suspicion and hatred of foreigners—is likely to increase as America's place on the world stage is adjusted by changing international fortunes and as the realities of oil supplies and human hunger make themselves increasingly apparent. Philoxenia—love of the foreigner—is often translated from the Greek of the New Testament as "hospitality," a theme we have seen is central to the biblical tradition. As followers of Christ we must not only open our hands to support the sojourners in our midst, but we must open our hearts to be touched and torn by their stories and to become their friends and advocates of their causes—for their story is our story. We are all sojourners here.

Among the many models of the Church emerging today, one of the most useful for us in analyzing the response of the Church to strangers, sojourners, refugees and immigrants in our midst is the insistence of Second Isaiah that the people of God should be a saving rather than a saved remnant. It is an important idea.

Two dominant modes of parish orientation exist today in uneasy dichotomy: the pastoral and the missionary. In the pastoral model, the shepherd takes care of his flock, a thoroughly biblical image that cannot be faulted—unless it takes the form of paternalistic clergy looking after the spiritual needs of a passive, helpless flock of recipients. The danger here is that the Church may become ingrown and self-absorbed, with a goal of serving only its own welfare.

To avoid the danger, another model of ministry emerges which sees the ministry of the Church as ministry to the world through the Church. The clergy, in this missionary model, help the laity minister to their own society to transform its life through the light of Christ. The faithful become the leaven of the loaf. This runs contrary to most models of ministry in which the majority of Church members conceive of ministry as something done *to* and *for* them rather than *by* them; as something sent to them rather than something sent from them to the world.

The difference between these two models is vividly shown in their approach to the ministry among strangers and sojourners. In the pastoral model, the goal of ministry outside the Church is to win converts and so increase the household of faith. This work is seen primarily as the work of the clergy who may or may not enlist the laity to help build church membership. In the missionary model, by contrast, the goal of ministry is more broadly to enable all people to come into life-transforming encounter with the living Christ. This task belongs to all the faithful working together, laity and clergy, sharing the responsibility of opening people to the possibilities of new life in Christ.

M. Fletcher Davis, *Of Foxes and Birds and the Son of Man: Ministry to Refugees and Other Strangers* (Cincinnati, Ohio: Forward Movement Publications, 1982), 9-11. (Excerpt)

128.

Nathan Wright, Jr., Self-Development and Self-Respect

Nathan Wright, Jr. (August 5, 1923–), is a priest, an activist and a scholar. He has served as a parish rector, and as chaplain of several institutions in the Boston area. As executive director of the department of urban work in the Diocese of Newark, he was chair of the 1967 National Conference on Black Power and of the International Conference on Black Power in Philadelphia in 1968. His main area of research and teaching has been urban affairs. This address was delivered in the Abyssinian Baptist Church, New York, and is a statement of his philosophy of self-help approaches to empowerment and economic development.

Self-Development and Self-Respect

When I was a child, I spake as a child, I understood as a child, I thought as a child: but when I became a man, I put away childish things. (1 Cor. 13:11)

The central concern of the current issue of Black Power—for the good of the Negro and for the larger good of this whole nation and of our world today—is the self-development and the growth into maturity of the black people of America. Black people have been the sleeping giants of this land. Among all Americans, their power, insights and experience, potentially ready to enrich this nation, have been least developed. In words of cosmic import which speak to black people in uniquely immediate terms, "we have not yet become what we shall be."

The black people of America are this nation's most rich and ready asset—its greatest raw material—as once the unmined earth and its untouched forests, fields and rivers were. In former years this nation built its greatness upon the utilization, not unmixed with wastefulness, of the vast physical resources which had lain untapped. Today, the new frontier of this nation's destiny lies in the development and utilization to the full of its infinitely greater human resources. What greater and potentially more useful reservoir of undeveloped and unutilized human resources does this nation have than in the black people of this land?

The great difficulty which we have had in coming into our own in America has only, in these recent days of impetus toward Black Power, begun to be made plain. We have operated, for at least the last crucial period of thirty years, on the assumption that Negroes needed to be led into their wanted place of maturity in American life. This assumption should perhaps have been seen to be fictitious on its face. It is simply naive to believe that any person or any group of people may grow into maturity save in terms of their own self-development. As Dr. Adam Clayton Powell has repeatedly emphasized from this pulpit and elsewhere, human growth cannot be produced from without: it must always be developed from within. Thus, to the undoubtedly divine accident of the current focus on Black Power, black boys and girls, and black men and women—long lulled into a feeling of functionlessness and little worth—are awaking to realize that only through self-development can they become the people of power and of majesty and of might which their bearing the image of their Creator has destined them to be.

There is, on the part of the Negro, a manifest need for self-development. Yet, of recent years, we as black people have assumed that a slave mentality of dependence upon others, as we had in former years, was appropriate for the twentieth-century destiny to which we are called. This crippling dependence upon others has hung like an albatross on our necks. It has led us to the state of stagnation which we find, with a few notable exceptions, pervading the life of the black people of America today.

The experience of all rising ethnic groups in this our beloved land has been that each rising group in American life must do for itself that which no other group may do for it. Each rising group has had to devise, to engineer, and to control in its own way its own plan, however crude or inept it may seem to have been, for its own particular growth into freedom, into self-development, into self-sufficiency and into self-respect.

This path of self-development has been—since the well-known rejection by the American people in 1776 of the King George Plan for Colonial Development—the one and only truly American way. There has never been in the American experience a German-American plan for Jewish development. Nor has there been in the American experience a Polish plan for Italian development. Yet the black people of America have been led to believe that their due fulfillment and their appropriation of their due inheritance in America could come best, or even only, from a white American plan for black freedom. This is incongruous on its very face. The issue of Black Power for black people—and for the good of American people as a whole—speaks to the need for black people to move from the stance of humble and dependent and impotent beggars to the stature of men who will take again into their own hands, as all men must, the fashioning of their own destiny for their own growth into self-development and self-respect. Now herein lies precisely the singular difference between the impetus toward Black Power on the one hand and what we have known as the civil rights movement on the other.

While the civil rights movement has emphasized what black people have been due, the emphasis of black self-development is on what black people may give to America. The thrust of Black Power is toward national fulfillment through the utilization of the potentialities and latent gifts of all. Both Black Power and the civil rights movement must have their vital and necessary places. The civil rights movement has in its own invaluable way emphasized what the American Negro has been due as an American from the day of each black man's birth. Without the efforts of the civil rights movement, particularly over these past thirty and more years, it would be difficult to speculate on where we, and this nation as a whole, might be. The civil rights movement, with its interracial dialogue, needs to grow and to flourish. We must never indulge in the vain luxury of criticizing what our leaders—with the aid of others—have done for us in the past.

In the past we have needed help; and we have received it. But we lacked even more the fundamental necessity of self-help, and self-initiative. It is by this alone we as a people may grow into that self-direction and self-sufficiency which is incumbent upon all who would claim respect due to responsible and mature men. It is by black self-development that this nation may come most fully into its own. The absence of black self-development has taxed the resources of the nation and limited the national destiny. Black Power means black development into self-sufficiency for the good of Negroes and for the good of the whole nation. We want—as others must want—to replace the helping hand which now aids us with our *own* hand—to sustain ourselves and not be burdens on all others.

Black self-development means something more, as well. It means that we want to put into glorious use the latent resources that we have for devising new ways of bringing fulfillment to all life. From our position of powerlessness we have learned that only through an immediate and equitable extension of power can the white and black poor of our land be transformed from crippling liabilities into tangible assets. Poverty will begin to be abated most effectively when the particular and precious insights of black people are used in devising antipoverty efforts.

Black self-development also means that we as black people must take the initiative—using the brainpower and the other resources of all, under our own leadership—in building black unity, black pride and black self-confidence for the larger good of this whole nation. A strong, independent press oriented to the needs of black people will help us to achieve this. Black people have much to give to America. But it is only as black people first have confidence, pride and self-respect that they can give to America the rich gifts which it needs and must demand of us.

Undoubtedly, the most crucial part of black self-development is the building of our self-respect. We must see in ourselves nothing less than the image of God. Of all Americans, the black people of this land are by far the most intensely loyal. No one has ever questioned this. We are the unique products of our native land; and in every respect—for good *and* for ill—we have sought to emulate and to fulfill all that is American. In this endeavor, we have even gone so far as to adopt the white disdain for all that pertains to blackness. The sad fact is that in America black people have been taught that to be like other Americans they must come to hate themselves. Negroes are culturally conditioned to see themselves as childlike, immature and powerless. But the Scriptures tell us that we must love God with all our hearts and our neighbors *as ourselves*. How can we love our neighbors when we do not love and respect ourselves?

No one can instill pride and self-respect in another person. The same is true with ethnic groups. Every ethnic group, like every family, devises means of instilling group pride. Each idealizes its past and glorifies its ventures. So must the black people of America do. Instead of hating ourselves—as any group which dwells on its weaknesses does—we must accentuate the positive aspects of who and what we are. Every Negro in America must come to grow each day in self-esteem and self-respect. We need to have pride in ourselves. No one may give this to us. It is a matter of self-development. This task is our burden and ours alone as the central task, as the main business which is before us. This we must accept and aggressively and forthrightly implement not only for our needed self-respect, but also for the respect and acceptance of others, which must inevitably follow upon our growth into self-esteem and into self-respect.

This nation needs us, as does our world. We must take our hats from our hands, and we must stand on our feet. The old, if we but open our eyes to see it, has passed away. The new day is at hand. We must put away childish things, and assume the proud demeanor of men. So again the subject of our text: "When I was a child, I spake as a child, I understood as a child, I thought as a child: but when I became a man, I put away childish things" (1 Cor. 13:11). Amen.

Nathan Wright, Jr., "Self-Development and Self-Respect," in John M. Burgess, *Black Gospel/White Church* (New York: Seabury Press, 1982), 52-56.

CHAPTER FIFTEEN

Spirituality

Introduction

Spirituality is the whole of life in Christ. Spirituality can be understood in terms of the many ways of experiencing and being available to God's active presence. Spirituality is concerned with loving God more completely, and sharing that love in the world. The Episcopal Church includes many spiritualities that lead to the holy and reflect the diversity of traditions and styles in the church. Spirituality is lived in many ways.

129.

Phillips Brooks, Lectures on Preaching, 1877

Phillips Brooks (December 13, 1835–January 23, 1893) was rector of Trinity Church, Boston, 1869-1891. His Lyman Beecher Lectures on Preaching, delivered at Yale University, 1876-1877, were later published as Lectures on Preaching. *On October 14, 1891, he was consecrated the sixth Bishop of Massachusetts. Brooks defines preaching in this selection.*

What, then, is preaching, of which we are to speak? It is not hard to find a definition. Preaching is the communication of truth by man to men. It has in it two essential elements, truth and personality. Neither of those can it spare and still be preaching. The truest truth, the most authoritative statement of God's will, communicated in any other way than through the personality of brother man to men is not preached truth. Suppose it written on the sky, suppose it embodied in a book which has been so long held in reverence as the direct utterance of God that the vivid personality of the men who wrote its pages has well-nigh faded out of it; in neither of these cases is there any preaching. And on the other hand, if men speak to other men that which they do not claim for truth, if they use their powers of persuasion or of entertainment to make other men listen to their speculations, or do their will, or applaud their cleverness, that is not preaching either. The first lacks personality. The second lacks truth. And preaching is the bringing of truth through personality. It must have both elements. It is in the different proportion in which the two are mingled that the difference between two great classes of sermons and preaching lies. It is in the defect of one or the other element that every sermon and preacher falls short of the perfect standard. It is in the absence of one or the other element that a discourse ceases to be a sermon, and a man ceases to be a preacher altogether.

If we go back to the beginning of the Christian ministry we can see how distinctly and deliberately Jesus chose this method of extending the knowledge of Himself throughout the world. Other methods no doubt were open to Him, but He deliberately selected this. He taught His truth to a few men and then He said, "Now go and tell that truth to other men." Both elements were there, in John the Baptist who prepared the way for Him, in the seventy whom He sent out before His face, and in the little company who started from the chamber of the Pentecost to proclaim the new salvation to the world. If He gave them the power of working miracles, the miracles themselves were not the final purpose for which He gave it. The power of miracle was, as it were, a divine fire pervading the Apostle's being and opening his individuality on either side; making it more open God-wards by the sense of awful privilege, making it more open man-wards by the impressiveness and the helpfulness with which it was clothed. Everything that was peculiar in Christ's treatment of those men was merely part of the process by which the Master prepared their personality to be a fit medium for the communication of His Word. When His treatment of them was complete, they stood fused like glass, and able to take God's truth in perfectly on one side and send it out perfectly on the other side of their transparent natures.

This was the method by which Christ chose that His Gospel should be spread through the world. It was a method that might have been applied to the dissemination of any truth, but we can see why it was especially adapted to the truth of Christianity. For that truth is preeminently personal. However the Gospel may be capable of statement in dogmatic form, its truest statement we know is not in dogma but in personal life. Christianity is Christ; and we can easily understand how a truth which is of such peculiar character that a person can stand forth and say of it, "I am the Truth," must always be best conveyed through, must indeed be almost incapable of being perfectly conveyed except through personality. And so some form of preaching must be essential to the prevalence and spread of the knowledge of Christ among men. There seems to be some such meaning as this in the words of Jesus when He said to His disciple, "As my Father has sent me into the world even so have I sent you into the world." It was the continuation, out to the minutest ramifications of the new system of influence, of that personal method which the Incarnation itself had involved.

If this be true, then, it establishes the first of all principles concerning the ministry and preparation for the ministry. Truth through Personality is our description of real preaching. The truth must come really through the person, not merely over his lips, not merely into his understanding and out through his pen. It must come through his character, his affections, his whole intellectual and moral being. It must come genuinely through him. I think that granting equal intelligence and study, here is the great difference which we feel between two preachers of the Word. The Gospel has come *over* one of them and reaches us tinged and flavored with his superficial characteristics, belittled with his littleness. The Gospel has come *through* the other, and we receive it impressed and winged with all the earnestness and strength that there is in him. In the first case the man has been but a printing machine or a trumpet. In the other case he has been a true man and a real messenger of God. We know how the views which theologians have taken of the agency of the Bible writers in their work differ just here. There have been those who would make them mere passive instruments. The thought of our own time has more and more tended to consider them the active messengers of the Word of God. This is the higher thought of inspiration. And this is the only true thought of the Christian preachership. I think that one of the most perplexing points in a man's ministry is in a certain variation of this power of transmission. Sometimes you are all open on both sides, open to God and to fellow-man. At other times something clogs and clouds your transparency. You will know the differences of the sermons which you preach in those two conditions, and, however little they describe it to themselves or know its causes, your congregation will feel the difference full well.

But this, as I began to say, decrees for us in general what the preparation of the ministry is. It must be nothing less than the making of a man. It cannot be the mere training to certain tricks. It cannot be even the furnishing with abundant knowledge. It must be nothing less than the kneading and tempering of a man's whole nature till it becomes of such a consistency and quality as to be capable of transmission.

Phillips Brooks, *Lectures on Preaching* (New York: E. P. Dutton & Company, 1877), 5-9. (Excerpt)

130.

Thomas C. Darst, He Loved Me, and He Gave Himself for Me, 1931

Thomas Campbell Darst (November 10, 1875–September 1, 1948) was consecrated the third Bishop of East Carolina on January 6, 1915. Here he describes a spirituality for facing adversity. This was written during the Great Depression in America.

We have seen the crashing of financial institutions in which we trusted. We have heard the tramp of thousands of our unemployed brothers seeking a chance to live. We have seen the toil of the farmer come to naught, and we have sensed the deep silence of our closed factories and mills. We have had to face stark realities, and some of us will, I believe, have made a fresh discovery of God.

It has been a time to try men's souls. I believe we have needed such a time, a testing time, when men, shaken from false security and transient content, fall back upon God and find peace.

The easy days, so sadly abused, so wantonly squandered, are gone, and the very salvation of America may depend upon the length of time they remain away.

The hard days are here, the days of planning and thinking and giving up, the days of readjustment of living and restoration of values and discovery of self. These days are here. May we have the courage to thank God for them; may we have the wisdom to use them, not as valleys of depression through which we toil in bitterness and defeat, but as God's own highways, over which we march in confidence and faith to that larger life of service, that wider field of usefulness that we could have never known if we had not learned the lesson of the hard high road.

At such a time as this, we should pause and take stock of our resources. We should ask ourselves: Have I been living in a fool's paradise? Have I been depending upon temporary, transient resources? Have I anything left upon which to build my life?

Such an examination, honestly made, should lead us to a realization of the truth that we have lost nothing that is permanent, nothing that makes for character, nothing that could possibly endure for one moment after the breath leaves our body; and that we still have the possibility of possessing all things that make for the splendor of our manhood and the winning of our souls.

We still have God. We have our Master, Christ. We have membership in His Body, the Church. We have our task, and we have the certainty of victory, through faith.

In a recent issue of a financial pamphlet, I read these words:

> "These times test men's courage, and they test faith more than courage. There is such a thing as being foolhardy and calling it courage; but experience shows that our peril is the lack of faith. It would seem as though some social leaders have no faith in America, and some church leaders have no faith in

God. A defeatist attitude dominates most enterprises for the well-being of society and the advancement of the Kingdom of God. We are in retreat. The challenge of the sacrificial has been lost in coping with emergencies.

"Reductions, curtailments, cuts, discarded programs, abandoned fields, surrender, retreat! These are the prevailing attitudes. Faith has crumpled. Men charged with great programs are panic-stricken. They have lost their nerve.

"Courage, love, spiritual passion, sacrifice, religious fervor, service, generosity! The sense of immediacy, the sense of opportunity, Faith. These are the qualifications for a time like this."

God send us faith. God send us courage to thank Him for permitting us to live and labor in such a time as this.

At such a time as this, we take notice of our foundations, we dwell on the glory of our heritage; our minds swing back to the beginnings of this mighty organism, of which we are living members, the Church of the Living God.

We see a little band of men and women gathered in an upper room in Jerusalem. We wait with them as they wait for the Promised Power. We see them going out from that little corner of the world in response to the marching orders of their Master. We see them go without material equipment, without influence or earthly power. We see them in complete and glad surrender to the will of God, in absolute loyalty to Christ, in utter self-forgetfulness, going forth against kingdoms of selfishness and lust and greed and sin, and we see them winning those kingdoms and transforming them into the Kingdom of our Lord and of His Christ.

We speak of our sufferings, our little self-denials, our inability to maintain our luxuries. God pity us for our pettiness. They thanked God that they were permitted to suffer for His sake, and even in awful flame of martyrdom they lifted their radiant faces to the throne of God and cried out their triumphant death song—"Thy kingdom come. Thy will be done, On earth".

At such a time as this, God is leading His Church back to the meaning of the Cross, so that it may learn again the glory of its mission; so that from the lesson of that Cross, it may march forward with fresh faith and passionate devotion to join forces with that lonely leader, Christ, Who has been waiting so long for us to come.

At such a time as this we must take stock of our environment and make a survey of the conditions of our day. It does not require the skill of a keen student of human affairs to realize that conditions of our world are far from normal. Unrest and rebellion characterize a large section of the world; hate and fear permeate human society. China has her revolutions. Russia and her radical experiments are no longer distant disturbing movements to which we give casual, curious attention from time to time. Industrial revolution lifts its head in our Nation, and radical influences find their way more and more into the very life of our working people.

We must realize that our house is not in order. With far more than half of the people in this great Nation outside of any form of organized religion; with an increasing disregard of law on the part of respectable citizens; with the appalling increase of crime among youth; with the breaking down of the standard of decency in human relations; we must know that our house is not in order, and that the Kingdom of God on earth is still an elusive hope.

From the ignorant and the sinning, from the forgotten and the neglected, from the tenant farmer and the pale children of the mill village, the call is coming for our leadership, our loving sympathy, our Christ-like devotion to those for whom He died.

"He loved me, and He gave Himself for me," cried St. Paul out of the fullness of his grateful heart as, in absolute surrender, He gave himself to the mighty work to which he had been divinely called. The same blessed assurance should send us out today, determined, at whatever cost, to play our full joyful part in carrying that blessed message to the heart of a weary, waiting world.

In the days of our prosperity, we gave without joy and without sacrifice, to the support of the Church and spread of the Kingdom of Christ, and because so many of us gave without this sense of privilege, the act was not sacramental, and, therefore, easily abandoned when prosperity ceased. Because our meat was not to do the will of God, we were hungry, even in our prosperity and miserable in our poverty.

Admitting our failures, we will not admit defeat; conscious of our poverty of soul, we will not refuse to be fed; unworthy of our sonship, we will not give up our heritage. We will, please God, go on from this place with courage and with faith to accomplish the work committed to our hands. We will clear from our souls those barriers that have blocked the way of Jesus. We will offer and present ourselves to His service. Out of our plenty, we have given with indifference; out of our poverty, we will offer with joy. We will face the problems of our day with understanding hearts, and give to a perplexed and distressed people that leadership which will enable them to find God, and in finding Him, to find peace.

Surely we can say with a measure of confidence and joy that we have come to the Kingdom for such a time as this, a time of danger and opportunity and high privilege, a time for the testing of souls. It is no time for superficialities, no time for surface contacts, but it is a time when clergy and laity alike must so deepen their faith and renew their courage that they may be enabled to show men and women that the only way out is the way of the Cross. It is not the easy way, but it is the only way; it is not the way of the weakling, but it is the way to victory.

"Whatsoever is born of God overcometh the world, and this is the victory that overcometh the world, even our faith."

Thomas C. Darst, "He Loved Me, and He Gave Himself for Me," *The Spirit of Missions* 96 (March 1931): 141-143.

131.

James O.S. Huntington, Beginnings of the Religious Life for Men in the American Church, 1933

James Otis Sargent Huntington (July 23, 1854–June 29, 1935) took the vows of poverty, chastity, and obedience before Assistant Bishop Henry Codman Potter of New York at the Chapel of the Sisters of St. John the Baptist, New York City, November 25, 1884. This was the beginning of the Order of the Holy Cross, the first religious order for men in the Episcopal Church that was founded in America. In this writing he describes the religious life.

Has what is known as "The Religious Life" a legitimate place in the Church?

As to that, there are different opinions. To some persons such a life seems to be the fairest burgeoning of Christian discipleship. By others it has been regarded as a perversion of the Christian ideal in a morbid asceticism, and a false, because self-centered, spirituality.

Whatever view may be taken, there is no question but that the Religious Life, as organized in communities, has been found in the historic Church from shortly after the apostolic age. The course of the Christian fellowship has been deeply affected by it, and without it would have had a very different history, in many ages and lands. The Religious Life is a fact to be reckoned with in any comprehensive account of the Church and of civilization.

This article does not attempt to deal with the question as to whether the Religious Life has been a help or a hindrance to Christian Faith and morals, or whether, if it has served some good purpose in the past, it is now outmoded and has become an anachronism. All that will be aimed at is to describe the first efforts to establish the Religious Life for men in the Protestant Episcopal Church in the United States of America.

Two things may, however, be said, in the way of preface, to remove misunderstanding.

Prejudice against the monastic state has arisen from the use of the very phrase "The Religious Life." This has been taken to mean that the upholders of this state mean to assert that those who associate themselves in Religious Communities surpass other Christians in piety and moral excellence. That would, of course, be shocking Phariseeism, subversive of all true humility. But the term "Religious" is not used with any such implication. It simply indicates that the duties and obligations of the monk or nun are of a religious character,—worship, prayer, meditation, intercession, etc. That is their business or *métier*. If they sincerely fulfil their vocation they are doing that which will unite the soul with God. That is not true of many useful professions. A man may be a skillful physician and yet live apart from God. A man may be an honest and upright merchant and yet never say a prayer or exercise faith in God. But a "Religious" cannot discharge the duties of his calling without entering into converse with his Maker. That is why he is said to be in the "Religious State," although, alas, he may have the outward marks of a "Religious" and be secretly unfaithful to all that it should involve of loyalty and devotion; he may "have a name to live and be dead."

The other thing to be said is that the Religious Life is not, in its essentials, alien to the life of the faithful Christian whatever his status and work may be. The virtues of the Religious State are none other than the virtues which all followers of Christ should seek to exercise. Every Christian is called to discipline his body, his mind, and his spirit, that he may advance in the way of holiness. The "Religious" disciplines his body by a life of strictest purity in the celibate state; he disciplines his mind by embracing the condition of poverty, calling nothing his own; he disciplines his spirit by placing himself under the Rule of his Community, and acting in accordance with the will of his superior. In this he is seeking to carry out, under special conditions, the programme incumbent on all Christians. All souls are commanded to seek perfection: the "Religious" vows to use certain means which, he believes, have been indicated by divine instruction and witnessed to through centuries of experience as conducive to that adventure.

James O. S. Huntington, "Beginnings of the Religious Life for Men in the American Church," *Historical Magazine of the Protestant Episcopal Church* 2 (March 1933): 35-36. (Excerpt)

132.

Angus Dun, The Church: A Community, 1946

Angus Dun (May 4, 1892–August 12, 1971) was consecrated the fourth Bishop of Washington on April 19, 1944. This essay discusses the spirituality of the Church community.

WHAT is the Church to which is given this task of rebuilding the deep, hidden foundations of man's life?

It is itself a community, a communion, a shared life. That lies at the heart of it. The buildings, the priesthoods and ministries, the furnishings and organization, are all instruments of the community of lives, necessary and of high value, but instruments.

THE COMMUNITY OF FAITH

THE Church is a community of faith. No man and no community of men can live, let alone live vigorously, without a faith. The most powerful forces in history are believing men and believing communities of men. We cannot hold or regain the precious values of anything we could call Christian civilization without supporting beliefs. The values we hold dear, freedom and the worth of individual men, need a reality to climb on.

The Church is the community of Christian faith. It is the faith that our lives and the total scheme of things in which they are set are rooted in and dependent for their existence on a spiritual reality to which the highest in our own beings is akin and answerable; that the minds of men and the loves of men and the moral purposes which stir in men are not homeless, orphaned things; that the basic moral claims of life descend upon man from the source of his existence; that there is a Holy One who inhabiteth eternity, who dwells in the high and holy place with him that is of a humble and contrite spirit.

The Christian faith is the faith that in One who bears the human name of Jesus of Nazareth, there was given to us from heaven to be the leader of our common humanity, with rightful claim on our devotion; that in Him the character of God is unveiled, the very life of God brought near; that His commandments are indeed the commandments of God; that the forgiving, rescuing love He manifested is indeed the very love of God; that His broken life passed beyond tragedy and triumphed in heavenly places.

This faith, when truly alive, reinvigorates the dreams of brotherhood; it makes men ill at ease with injustice; and because it exalts the meaning and potentialities of common human lives, it gives energy to the passion for freedom, and even makes believers sensitive to the bondage of others.

The Church is the community of Faith. It is also the community of worship. Worship is an act of faith. It is bringing one's life in the presence of the object of one's faith; it is the renewal of one's vow of allegiance and the confession of one's imperfect service; it is giving honor where honor is due.

The Christian faith leads into and renews its strength in Christian worship. Christian worship is the act in which believers and the community of believers bring their lives into the presence of God and His Christ in the fellowship of His Spirit. In worship, the Christian and the community of Christians expose themselves to the word that comes to them from God through His prophets. They listen again to the words of Christ, asking what he has to say to them. They receive into their hands consecrated gifts of bread and wine, in terms of which Christ pledges and gives His own life to those who put their trust in Him. In worship, believers lift up their hearts. They give praise and thanks for the heroic charity of Christ. They declare their contrition for their failures and disloyalties. They offer up their hopes and gifts and affections to be taken up and used and refined by the Will to whose obedience they have pledged themselves. And from this worship they draw the strength to build.

THE COMMUNITY OF CHARITY

FINALLY, the Church is the community of charity. There is no escape from membership in communities, and we seek none. Our individual existence ties us to one man and to one woman. Our inescapable needs bind us to those who grow our food or make our clothes or tend us in our sickness. The State claims us, whether we will or no. It may draft us or our husbands or our sons, when its own existence is at stake. The family and the State claim our service, but unless they have been leavened by something far beyond themselves, they claim our service for themselves and that service can be a kind of slavery.

The Church, because it is a community of faith, is a community of free service, for compelled faith is no faith at all. And because the central object of its faith is the free, unearned love of God in Christ, the Church is the community of charity. It exists as its Lord lived, for the service of the world. Its task is to nurture men in the spirit of unpurchased and uncompelled servanthood. As someone has said, "Every human occupation is either a racket or a vocation." And they can only be saved from becoming a racket by becoming a vocation.

The Mission of the Church is at bottom Christ's mission, carried on through the community of lives He has claimed for His service.

Yet the Church is not the saviour of the world. Think honestly: is your parish the saviour of the community in which it is set? I hope your parish is a leaven and a light in your neighborhood, but it is not the saviour. God is the Saviour of the world, and the Church is a leaven and a light and an instrument of rebuilding just in the measure that it points beyond itself to Him and draws men to faith and contrition and self-devotion towards Him.

What we call missions are simply the farthest outreach, the most heroic, daring, foolish expressions of the mission of Christ to His Church. This mission of Christ has built hospitals and schools and churches; founded leper colonies, trained nurses; above all, sent and sustained men and women who were laid hold of by the love of Christ and the needs of men.

ONE LORD: ONE FAITH: ONE CHURCH

It is the glory of Christ that He has set the imagination and the love of men to look beyond the needs of their own race and time to the needs of outcasts in India, of Chinese farmers in remote villages, and of brown men in the hills of the Philippines. It is the glory of the Church that with all its failure, it has had the vitality to be a light to the Gentiles and to those who sit in darkness, and that it discovered One World before that was a popular discovery.

To apologize for missions is like apologizing for the wideness of God's mercy. Let us always be mindful that Christ is no beggar crying for our alms, but a royal and heroic king, inviting us to share in the largeness of his mission and offering us His strength to build.

Christ, who gives to the Church its worldwide mission, summons it to seek for unity in its own life in the furtherance of that mission. Behind the manifold drawing together of Christian people in recent years, our faith discerns the hand of God. Within all the variety of human motives, we discover the workings of His Holy Spirit. As always, He has guided us by the stern Must of outer circumstance and by the inspired wisdom of prophetic leaders. By the necessities of impoverished congregations, by the harsh disclosure of the feebleness and scandal of our competitive and divided witness, by the scorn of common men for what appear to them meaningless differences, by the prophetic judgment "the world is too strong for a divided Church," God has shaken us out of our complacent acceptance of disunity, and led us to where we stand. He has driven us together and called us together. And through all this working together and talking together and praying together, there has been coming to us from our One Father and our One Lord a growing vision of the One Church. Our ears have been unstopped, and we have heard again the Word of God speaking to us of the Lord's unalterable will that we should be one as He and the Father are One; of the one body with many members; of the diversity of gifts but the one Spirit.

In simple honesty, we must acknowledge that the rank and file of our Christian ministers and Christian people in this and in other lands have as yet little share in this fresh vision. As always, God grants His saving vision to His chosen servants and bids them bear witness to His whole people.

God has been teaching us that His Church is in its deepest nature a community, a shared life of faith and worship and charity. The One Lord loved the Church and gave Himself to call it into being. To this community of discipleship He entrusted His truth, His prayer, and the witness by word and sacrament to His offered life and victorious resurrection. Since His life is its life, its calling, like His, is not to be ministered unto but to minister, and to reconcile men to God and to one another.

Angus Dun, "The Church: A Community," *Behold the City of God* (New York: Woman's Auxiliary to the National Council, 1946), 40-45. (Excerpt)

133.

Anglican Fellowship of Prayer,
A Rule of Life and a Prayer, 1958

The Anglican Fellowship of Prayer was founded in 1958 at Calvary Church, Pittsburgh. It encourages the individual and corporate prayer life of the Church. Helen Smith Shoemaker was the wife of Sam Shoemaker, rector of Calvary Church and one of the founders of Alcoholics Anonymous. The following are the statement of purpose and rule of life for the Anglican Fellowship of Prayer.

The Purpose of the Anglican Fellowship of Prayer

At the last Lambeth Conference, the 440 Bishops of the Anglican Communion who were gathered issued a Call to Prayer. "Since prayer, both corporate and personal, is central to the Christian life, and therefore essential in the renewal of the Church, the fulfilling of the Christian mission, and the search for justice and peace, the Conference gives thanks for all who are endeavoring to increase and strengthen the companionship of prayer throughout the world, and joins in calling the whole Christian community to share personal prayer daily and corporate services of prayer on regular and special occasions."

As the only worldwide prayer organization in the Anglican Communion, the Anglican Fellowship of Prayer seeks to answer that Call to Prayer by increasing and strengthening the companionship of prayer throughout the world.

The essence of the life of the Church is the relationship between the Christian and his Lord. That relationship is, first of all, a prayer relationship. Prayer is the hub of the wheel that moves the Church in its work and worship.

Prayer is essential to the vitality and the ongoing life of the Church.

The Story of the Anglican Fellowship of Prayer

The Anglican Fellowship of Prayer became an official association of the Anglican Communion in 1958. It has pioneered in the fostering of the prayer group movement; schools of prayer; retreats, workshops and conferences; and tying together the prayer concerns of the Anglican Communion.

In the spirit of "Prayer Unites" the Anglican Fellowship of Prayer is inclusive of all forms and expressions of Church life whether lay or clerical, Catholic or Evangelical, monastic or secular, formal or informal. Its services are available to all people of the Church in all places.

RULE OF LIFE
A Discipline of Christian Ideals of Piety, Study, and Action

What follows is a rule of life which you may use as a guide. It allows for flexibility according to your own personal needs and therefore is not intended to be a rigid format.

1. Regularity in Piety

Set a regular time each day for quiet prayer and study. Let it be as essential to you as your pattern of eating. If we did not eat we would sicken and die. Spiritual nutrition is no less vital. Have your time with God whether you particularly feel like it or not. This kind of determination spells the difference between the soldier of Christ and the dilettante. Though prayers are essential throughout the day and into the evening, it is good to begin each day with these devotions. This "sets us up" for the whole day. We invoke God into our daily pursuits at its outset. It makes all the difference as we work, meet people, relate to our families, encounter temptation.

2. Quiet

Spend the first part of your devotions in quiet, "Be still and know." Too often we approach God in an attitude of impatience, with a form of spiritual activism. We need to practice the joy of simply being in His presence, seeking nothing except just to be with Him. Try to find a quiet place. Noise and confusion are obvious enemies of inner peace. There still may be noise within our spirits and we need to offer that up to the Lord. Do not begrudge time spent in quiet. It is productive, for God is beginning to arrange the disarray of your day as He comes into your being.

3. Prayer

It is artificial to distinguish between quiet and prayer but for the sake of progression in our devotions we need to understand that God, whom we know as the compassionate Christ, is ready to hear us. He is the one who said, "Ask and you shall receive, seek and you will find, knock and it shall be opened to you."

Therefore, take time to speak to Him, even to cry out from the depths of some need. In a productive rule of life it is good to have a pattern of prayer that allows for breadth. Narrowness of prayer such as the practice of only petitioning God, often stifles our prayer life. Many use daily offices as a discipline.

One helpful pattern is that of the Cross of Prayer. The vision of the cross is kept before your eyes to remind you of God's love for you, which alone makes prayer possible. As you think of the top of the cross you are led to Adoration. Spend time in simply telling the Triune God of your love for Him and your joy in being of the redeemed in His holy presence. Then think of the left transept of the cross and offer God your Confession of sins. This naturally follows as we come into His holy presence. Sin is not simply what we have done or left undone; it is our lapse of trust in God in the totality of our lives. Think, then, of the right transept of the cross and enter into the prayer of Thanksgiving. Again, how appropriate this follows as you consider the Lord's gracious forgiveness. Ask for a spirit of gratitude so that all that you do in the ensuing day will be done not for duty's sake but as a joyful act of thanksgiving.

Move to the center of the cross, the "crossing", where the two shafts of the cross meet and begin the prayer of Intercession. This reminds us that our lives cross others' lives and in love we lift them up before Him. Pray for all the members of you family. If you don't, who will? Certainly people outside your family wouldn't care as much on a daily basis. Then pray for needs of those whom Christ places before your vision who are your neighbors (whether near or far). Each day pray for your larger family, which is the Church, remembering always your clergy. So often we leave these prayers to formal liturgical acts on Sundays. Now, move to the foot of the cross and pray the prayer of Petition. Here you are bringing your own needs before Him. To have this at the last, after adoring, repenting, thanking and interceding puts our requests in the proper perspective. Yet, do not hesitate to lay before your Lord your every thought of yourself. If it is unworthy He will deal with you in love and patient correction. Then remember that personal piety always leads us to corporate prayer (see No. 7).

4. Study and Meditation

Spend some time in prayerful study, preferably with the Holy Scriptures. St. Paul said, "Have this mind in you which is in Christ Jesus." To have the mind of Christ is to come to know Him more and more intimately in the Gospel narratives. This is so essential in coming to have more assurance about doing everything according to His will. We need to be able to ask ourselves in all that we think or do, "Is this the way of Christ?" By studying the Bible with openness to the illumination of the Holy Spirit we will come more and more into an awareness of His loving and righteous response to all things. Read systematically not sporadically. Progress slowly, meditatively, through portions of scripture on a day to day basis. Don't skip difficult passages. These will prove to be the most helpful of all if you will pray them through. Let the practice of meditation lead you to Godly contemplation, affirmation and resolution.

5. All through the Day

"This is the day which the Lord has made, we will rejoice and be glad in it." As we leave our devotions and launch into another day we need to go forth with a strong sense of the companionship of Christ. In our rule of life we do not leave this to a chance encounter. We make conscious recognition of Him throughout the day. We might adopt the process of the late Dr. Frank Laubach, the Apostle to the Illiterate, who began to have a growing consciousness of Christ by thinking of Him once each hour. When he could do this he trained himself to think of Him every half hour. Later it was every 15 minutes. Finally he got to the point where he could think of Christ every minute. There was nothing so great or trivial in his life that he could not constantly refer to Christ. In our rule of life we are taking seriously the promise of Christ, "Lo, I am with you always."

6. Apostolic Groups or Reunions

Small group fellowships for prayer or study are important in a rule of life for those who have shared some experience of renewal in Christ. Form a prayer group if there is not one already available. It only takes two or three people to begin. There should be no more than twelve in a group. Remember also that the most basic prayer group would be your own family. To grow in piety, study and action, let Christ be the leader. "Where two or three are gathered in my name there I am in the midst of them."

7. Worship

Remembering that the spiritual life of a Christian always leads into the whole experience of the Body of Christ, a rule of life always includes the corporate worship of the Church. The person who exercises daily prayer comes to the liturgical acts of the Church with the fervor that makes them alive to himself and also ignites the faith of others. What a difference there is in the hymning, praying, and communing of the daily Christ-bearer from those who come perfunctorily with no great expectation! Though it would be almost unthinkable that weekly worship would become a difficult effort, yet the same discipline applies here as in daily prayer; worship Him whether you feel like it or not. In all our discipleship we are called to live above the level of feeling; i.e., on the level of responsive obedience. Holy Communion is a command of Christ. "Do this," He said. Sacramental means of grace become power for action.

8. Apostolic Action

Action is always a part of a Rule of Life. You are led from what could be sentimentality to a life of service. It obviously reaches into your stewardship. The tithe is a simple response to the Lord who has given you everything. Action has to do with your willingness to work in the parish as well. The church should be able to see a direct relationship between a new life in Christ and a life of offering.

Remember also that giving includes sharing with others what Christ means to you. Witnessing for Christ is, indeed, a reflection of what you are becoming as Christ walks with you daily. Beyond that it includes the unaffected speaking forth to others concerning the goodness of God. You are not asked to "buttonhole" people but simply to be willing to express your faith to those whom God puts in your path. Usually they will reach out to those whose life has a certain power and serenity for which they hunger so deeply.

. . . .

Prayer is the mightiest force in God's universe.
When we pray, we align ourselves with Jesus' eternal prayer for us.
When we pray, we throw our love with His like a lariat around the world.
Our prayers go where we cannot and speak whole spiritual continents into being.

—*Helen Smith Shoemaker*

Brochures of the Anglican Fellowship of Prayer.

134.

Sam Shoemaker, Extraordinary Living for Ordinary Men, 1965

Samuel Moor Shoemaker (December 27, 1893–January 31, 1963) was a leading Episcopal priest of the twentieth century. He was influential in the founding of Alcoholics Anonymous, Faith at Work, and the Anglican Fellowship of Prayer. His work with business people in the Pittsburgh area developed into the Pittsburgh Experiment, which encouraged groups of lay people to discuss how to bring Christianity into their daily lives and their business relationships. This selection describes the power of faith.

Spiritual Power: The Force Which Makes Life Different

The religion of Jesus, when it comes to us authentically, is always characterized by power. We see power in the very bad people made good. We see power as the moderately good and bad people come to realize that neither is good enough. We see power in the life held from an old defeat by a new charge of spiritual conviction. We see power when the sick are made well, not only by medicine, but by prayer, and any convinced Christian ought to be able to lead you into touch with persons in whose lives something like this has taken place.

We see power when the tensions which grip men's minds and bodies in this stressful time are released into quiet functioning and health. We see power when a light is lighted in a darkened mind that could not believe, but suddenly begins to believe because of the contagion of another's witness and faith.

The church is meant to be the channel and organ by which that spiritual power which is in Jesus is made available to man. Is your church like that? Are you yourself such a believer in power, that it flows constantly into you and through you? If not, you ought to be, for it is part of your birthright as a Christian. Let us not beg off, and offer substitutes. The church is dropping down to a lower level and offering people "ersatz" and synthetic spiritual power—but nobody is fooled.

Power is *not just taking responsibility for the Church's work*. That is a very good thing, and we depend greatly on people who will do it. But it is not necessarily power. You can do a great stint of church work very much on your own steam, by self-effort, without any power needed from God and without any power being transmitted to other people.

Power is *not just efficiency*. It is a good thing to be as efficient as we can in Christ's work. But I can take you to churches that run with the utmost smoothness—the program is full and swift and runs like a clock—but it is all much more like a railroad station than it is like a real church of Christ. True power will usually manage to be efficient, but efficiency does not of itself constitute spiritual power.

Power is *not common sense*. The church is full of people with a lot of common sense. We abound in common sense. I would not say we always abound in spiritual power. The two are not in necessary conflict, and true spiritual power will be full of super common sense. but common sense by itself can cut the thread of spiritual power. I have seen it happen more times than one.

Power is *not intellectual smartness*. If it were, our modern universities and seminaries would be turning out better men than they did in the past, but it is doubtful if they are. A certain kind of spiritual power is very alert intellectually, and as smart as you can find men to be—witness the swift answers which Bryan Green gives his questioners concerning the intellectual matters of religion. Our Lord Himself was not above a witticism now and then. But one feels this came from power and did not constitute it.

Power is *not personal gifts and charm*. Those who have them are blessed and, if they are rightly used, I think none of us will deny that they can be one channel of power. But they do not constitute power. How many men have I known, even in Christ's ministry, whose personal gifts and charm have led them astray from the Gospel, so they like to be set apart from the great body and common run of Christians, and to be something special and unique! This is not power—this is simple dramatics, and ought to be labelled so.

Power is *not points of view*. When our religion has been a long time with us, without the grace of renewal, when it has got stale and gone to seed, it continues on in viewpoints. It was born in power; it lives on in mere attitudes. A person is truly converted to Jesus Christ, and brought into the church; but time goes on, and this person becomes just an Evangelical or just an Anglo-Catholic, just a Liberal or just a Fundamentalist. The power is gone, but its corpse and echo remain in points of view. True evangelistic power is firsthand and original.

Many of us hold points of view within the faith, because they represent our intellectual convictions. But they are always dangerous, because pride, divisiveness, and even hostility often lie just beneath their surface. Seldom do they constitute power, and often they negate and undercut it.

True spiritual power of the Christian order is a kind of possessedness. It arises in and flows through a life hid with Christ in God. Its source is the grace of our Lord Jesus Christ, and the potency of the Holy Spirit. True spiritual power is the child of two parents: the truth as it is revealed in Jesus and our own experience resulting upon our acceptance of Him and His truth. The objective factor is that the whole set of facts and truths, of historic events, and of interpretation of them, which is held by the church and set forth in the Bible. The subjective factor is what happens in the crucible of your life and mine when we accept that set of facts and truths and interpretations, and it begins to work in us. We have then a two-edged witness.

We witness to the truth as it is in Jesus, and we witness to the Christian experience as this transforms our own lives. If you take only the truth, and leave out the experience, you will probably become dogmatic and hard. If you take only the experience and leave out the truth, you will probably become woolly and amorphous and sentimental. But when you take both, and both are watered by the streams of grace, you have authentic spiritual power. . . .

Sam Shoemaker, *Extraordinary Living for Ordinary Men: Excerpts selected from the writings of Sam Shoemaker by his daughter, Helen Shoemaker Rea, and the Staff of Faith at Work* (Grand Rapids, Mich.: Zondervan Publishing House, 1965), 136-139. (Excerpt)

135.

William Stringfellow, The Liturgy as Political Event, The Political Authority of Baptism, 1966

William Stringfellow (April 26, 1928–March 2, 1985) was a layman and a leading theologian of the Episcopal Church. He was an author, lawyer, and activist whose spirituality had a political dimension, as seen in the following selection.

Our gratitude for the contemporary friendly disposition among the multiplicity of people who call themselves Christians and among the several churches should tempt none to minimize either the profundity or the pathology of the estrangement to which all men who are baptized are heirs. These experiences of renewed contact, genuine humility, and mutual respect should not quiet the conscience of Christians but, rather, provoke greater awareness of continuing divisions.

At no point in the witness of the Church to the world is its integrity as a reconciled society more radical and more cogent than in the liturgy, the precedent and consummation of that service which the Church of Christ and the members of this Body render to the world. Of course, there are many Protestants who regard the liturgy as peripheral to the Christian life. Some even boast that *they* have no liturgical life, but this is a betrayal of ignorance, since liturgy means nothing more than style of life. In the broadest sense, all of life is liturgical. The conventions and ceremonies of courtship are a liturgy, articulating and dramatizing the love between a man and a woman. Or, to take a less attractive example— Joe Valachi, in the Senate hearing in which the chief witness expounded at great length upon the peculiar actions and symbols and rituals which constitute the extraordinarily sophisticated liturgical fabric of the Cosa Nostra.

As for the Church, all forms of its corporate life—from the Quakers sitting in silence in a circle, to the exuberance and patience of a Negro congregation, and the majesty and richness of the venerable Orthodox service—are liturgical. The only serious question is whether or not a given liturgical practice has integrity in the Gospel. There are both laymen and clergy who regard liturgy as an essentially religious exercise—separate, disjoined, self-contained, unrelated—confined to the sanctuary and having nothing to do with this world. Some even regard liturgy superstitiously, as something having an intrinsic efficacy, as a means of procuring indulgences, as if God were so absurd—and so ungodly—as to be appeased by the redundant incantations of men.

There is, however, nothing so spooky or lucky about the liturgy, and nothing magical or mechanistic about its performance. The liturgy of the Gospel is, on the contrary, a dramatic form of the ethical witness of Christians in this world. In this sense, though there may be much variety in different times and cultures in regard to language, music, action, and movement, the liturgy is always characterized by certain definitive marks:

1) *Scriptural Integrity*—The liturgy of the Gospel is the theatricalization of the biblical saga of God's action in this world, thus relating the ubiquity of the Word of God in history to the consummation of the Word of God in Jesus Christ. A biblically authentic and historically relevant liturgy is always the celebration of the death and Resurrection of the Lord; the most decisive event in all history is remembered and memorialized in a context in which God's every action in this world since creation is recalled and rehearsed, and the hope of the world for the final reconciliation is recited and represented in the liturgical portrait.

The scriptural integrity of the liturgy requires that the laity not be spectators but participants—not as a matter of piety, not merely for their own sake but because they gather, as a congregation, as delegates and, indeed, advocates of the world.

That is why the traditional Protestant "preaching service"—even when the preaching is an exposition of the Word of God, and not some religious diatribe—is an impoverished and inadequate liturgy for the Church; by the same token, that is why the Mass recited in the absence of a congregation, or celebrated in a language not familiar to the people, is a compromise of the scriptural integrity of the liturgy.

2) *The Historicity of the Liturgy*—The liturgy of the Gospel is both a transcendent event and a present event. It shatters the categories of time and space and location because it both recalls and dramatizes the estate of Creation in the Word of God, and beseeches and foretells the end of this history. As a transcendent event, the liturgy recollects *all* that has already happened in this world from the beginning of time, and prophesies *all* that is to come until the end of time.

But the liturgy is also a contemporary event, involving these particular persons gathered in this specific place in this peculiar way. The reconciliation celebrated in the liturgy is not only a reconciliation remembered from Creation or expected eschatologically but also in actual event the reconciliation here and now of those gathered as a congregation and society within and among themselves, and between each and all of them and the rest of the world.

That is precisely why the confessions and the intercessions of the people of the congregation within the context of the liturgy are so indispensable to its integrity. *This* is the time and *this* is the place and *this* is the way, in a most immediate sense, in which the whole, manifold, existential involvement of the members of Christ's Body in the everyday life of the world—both all that seems good and which men are tempted to honor or praise, and all that seems evil and which men are fond of rationalizing or denying—is offered and consecrated for the discretion of Christ Himself, the Redeemer of all men and all things.

Thus the liturgy is the normative and conclusive ethical commitment of the Christian people to the world. The liturgy is the epitome of the service which the Christian renders the world. All authentic witness in the name of Christ, exemplifying in the world the virtue of Christ, which Christians undertake in their dispersion in the practical life of the world, is portrayed in the liturgy celebrated in the gathered congregation.

3) *The Sacramental Authenticity of the Liturgy*—It is both this transcendence of time in time and the scriptural integrity of the liturgy of the Gospel which constitutes the sacramental essence of the liturgy. The actual, visible, present event retains all its own originality and contemporary significance as a particular reconciled community, and at the same time is transfigured to embody to the world the cosmic enormity of the reconciling accomplishment of Jesus Christ.

Thus the liturgy as sacrament is inherently different from religious ritualism, in which the propriety of the ritual practice itself is all that matters. (Such may be sufficient for initiation or elevation in the Masons or the Knights of Columbus, but ritualistic piety is radically inappropriate to the Eucharist.) Notice, too, that the liturgy as sacrament appropriates as its ingredient symbols, among others, the ordinary things of the common existence of the world—bread, wine, water, money, cloth, color, music, words, or whatever else is readily at hand. Sacramentally, we have in the liturgy a meal which is basically a real meal and which nourishes those who partake of it as a meal. At the same time, this meal portrays for the rest of the world an image of the Last Supper, of which Christ Himself was Host, and is also a foretaste of the eschatological banquet in which Christ is finally recognized as the Host of all men.

The liturgy, therefore, wherever it has substance in the Gospel, is a living, political event. The very example of salvation, it is the festival of life which foretells the fulfillment and maturity of all of life for all of time in this time. The liturgy is social action because it is the characteristic style of life for human beings in this world.

The Political Authority of Baptism

A particular confusion has arisen in the American churches, especially in this last decade, because of the clergy's involvement in direct social action. Although several Roman Catholic priests have lately been disciplined for speaking out on specific issues, this is a confusion which particularly afflicts Protestants, because they have far less certainty about the office of the clergy in relation to the ministry of the laity dispersed in the world.

What must never be lost sight of in the relations of clergy and laity is Baptism. All baptized people, whatever their work or rank, location or function, charismatic gifts or personal talents, share in the one ministry of the Body of Christ for the world *in* the world. Indeed, according to I Corinthians, every baptized person is beneficiary of the charismatic gift of faith. Baptism bestows the power to live in Christ as a servant of the world.

This gift and office of service to the world is vouchsafed for all baptized people, and is not superseded or minimized by ordination. A clergyman remains, in a sense, a layman, and retains the same authority and responsibility as every other layman. Ordination gives him the office of priest and charges him with the functions of that office to serve the laity in the administration of the sacraments, the preaching of the Word of God in the congregation, and the nurture of the members of the congregation, both as individuals and as a body.

It is, of course, often the practice to commission clergymen to perform other services in addition to those for which they are ordained, particularly in relation to the maintenance of the institution of the Church or the administration of a parish. These tasks are not essentially related to the peculiar work of the priesthood, though they may be essential to, or convenient for, the existence of the Church or of a particular parish. These are functions that a layman, however, might undertake, which means that priests, even in this parish, are sometimes engaged in work as laymen.

Ordination does not remove the clergy from the world, though that which characterizes their specific office in ordination is an esoteric and internal servanthood within the Church. Thus, clergy who become publicly involved in antiwar protests or in support of "my country, right or wrong," in the civil rights demonstrations and school boycotts, or as Kloods (chaplains) for the Ku Klux Klan and apologists for racism, or in public issues of any sort, do so as laity. There is nothing specific or peculiar pertaining to the functions for which they are ordained that authorizes such involvement. As with any Christian, what authorizes their political involvement is Baptism; what informs and disciplines their commitment must not be any personal whim or prejudice or any allegiance to worldly interests or factions but what it means to be a baptized person.

All Christians act politically and socially under the peril of dishonoring—and even, at times, disowning—the estate of reconciliation with all men vouchsafed to them in Baptism. Indeed, this fact is the Christian's only recourse against making political decisions according to the discriminations of other men.

For the man who is baptized, the world as it is, is precious. It is the recipient of love because God made it; as the Apostle James reminds us, His Word is to be beheld in all things and in all men. Christians are called to enjoy God's presence in the world for the sake of those in the world who cannot yet do so. While involved in this world, the Christian is characteristically, profoundly, and constantly immersed in the Bible, because it is the testimonial evidence of God's care for, and activity in, this world. From the Bible, we discern the manner of God's presence and vitality in the world's common life. Christians see the ministry of Jesus Christ as the example of what it is to be reconciled within one's self, with all men and all things in the mercy and judgment of God.

William Stringfellow, *Dissenter in a Great Society: A Christian View of America in Crisis* (New York: Holt, Rinehart and Winston, 1966), 150-156. (Excerpt)

136.

John B. Coburn, Don't Waste Pain, 1975

John Bowen Coburn (September 27, 1914–) was dean of the Episcopal Theological School, 1957-1969, president of the House of Deputies, September 23, 1967–September 23, 1976, and the thirteenth Bishop of Massachusetts, October 2, 1976–December 27, 1986. In this writing he engages the spirituality of suffering.

"My child, I pray that this pain will not be wasted on you," he wrote her after the death of her daughter.

What did he mean by that, Lord? Don't waste pain! Don't let it slide off into nothingness. Don't drug yourself so the pain is numbed. Then *you* become numbed. What's a numbed person worth?

The pain is so great I can't bear it? Not true. You can bear it. Open yourself to it. *Become* the pain. Then it won't be wasted. Then it will make a difference because *you* will be different.

How not waste pain, Lord?

Well, you don't waste it if you take it, agonize over it, wrestle with it, acknowledge it, see that reason cannot explain it. It's there. Let it come.

Then go about your business. Wake up in the morning and brush your teeth. Go to bed at night with your companion. And in between, go be yourself.

Don't flaunt it. Don't fly it. Don't boast about it. Don't be noble. Don't talk about it except when you must.

Pain is at the heart of the mystery. It is embedded deep in the heart of man and God.

The other side of it is joy.

And with that comes a zest for living.

So live.
> Live your pain,
>> and joy will
> come to live you.
>> Then it's never wasted.

John B. Coburn, *A Diary of Prayers: Personal and Public* (Philadelphia: Westminster Press, 1975), 43.

137.

Massey H. Shepherd, Prayers, 1976

Massey Hamilton Shepherd, Jr. (March 14, 1913–February 18, 1990) was one of the great liturgical scholars of the Episcopal Church. He was chaplain to the House of Deputies at the sixty-fifth General Convention, September 11-22, 1976, at Minneapolis, where these prayers were delivered.

Tuesday, September 14

Almighty and merciful God,

In the great love with which you have loved us,
> your beloved and only-begotten Son,
> who shares with you eternally
> the oneness of your divine Being,
> humbly and of his own free will
> took upon himself our human nature,
> and suffered the agony, shame, and derision of the Cross,

to be the expiation for our sins,
and not for ours only,
but for the sins of the whole world.

On his Cross you exhibited the full measure of your love,
and the glory of your almighty power chiefly
in showing mercy.

By his Cross the whole of humanity was given the earnest
of our reconciliation with you and with one another,
thereby breaking down the wall of hostility.
From his Cross you entrusted to all who follow in faith
the way of his obedience,
to complete what is lacking in his sufferings
for the sake of his Body, the Church,
by making your world fully known,
and the riches of that mystery,
which is Christ in us, the hope of glory.

O God, heavenly Father,
In our baptism you marked us with the invisible sign
of the Cross and gave us his Name.
We have no altar but his—outside the camp,
in the place of defilement,
where our sacrifice of praise bears the abuse he endured.

Yet that sign and that altar are the destruction
of every principality and power of oppression and injustice,
that sets itself up against you as god.

Give us, we pray, the grace
to see the image of his face in everyone we meet,
especially in those,
whether they know and believe in him or not,
who reflect his poverty, his homelessness,
his afflictions, and his disgrace.
Let their sorrow reveal his sorrow,
and their hope become his hope.

This we ask for the sake of him,
    who bore our griefs and carried our sorrows,
    and made intercession for the transgressors,
    our Lord Jesus Christ, who taught us to pray:
    "Our Father. . . ."

Wednesday, September 15

Almighty and most merciful God,
Your Son our Savior came among us
not to condemn the world,
but that the world through him might be saved.
He did not come to be served, but to serve,
and gave his life as a ransom for many.
He was a scandal to the self-righteous,
to those who trusted in their position,
their reputation and their pious credentials,
who thanked you because they were not like others,
who kept all the commandments except that of love.
He was not ashamed to consort with sinners and outcasts,
nor even to search them out,
to eat and drink with them,
and offer them faith and loving forgiveness,
and so draw them into newness of life.
He did not despise the rich and privileged,
nor did he ask for their contributions,
but only for their discipleship.
To those who would follow him,
he offered no special rewards,
but to be baptized with his baptism
and to drink his cup,
that by serving others, as he served us,
we might become his friends
and share the joy of his humility and patience.
O God, pour out upon his Church
the full grace and power of his ministry.
Let not our pride, nor any fear or anxiety

for our safety and reputation,
stand in the way of following in his footsteps;
for only if we have him are we secure.
He will not abandon us,
nor will he let the gates of hell prevail against us.
So when he comes again to take account of us,
may he find us good and faithful servants,
and receive us at his right hand, saying,
"Come, O blessed of my Father,
inherit the Kingdom prepared for you
from the foundation of the world.
As you did it to one of the least of these my brethren,
you did it to me."

Thursday, September 16

O eternal God,
In whom there is no beginning nor end,
for you are the sovereign of all that is created,
and by your will all things exist and have their being.

We praise and magnify your holy Name
for the mysteries and marvels of your world:
for the heavens, the stars and planets in their courses,
which by day and by night
unceasingly declare the glory of your works;
the earth and the seas that give life and refreshment
to all living creatures,
both great and small.

We praise you for making us in your image and likeness
to share your joy and care for all creation.
You gave us mind and reason
to explore the secrets of your marvelous works,
to search for truth and find your wisdom in it.

You gave us imagination and skill
to create from the things you made
things beautiful and useful for our life.
You set us not in solitude, but in companionship
of families, friends, and fellow workers,
for common enterprise and mutual love.
You recognize our frailty,
and love us even in our sinful rebellion
against your will and purpose for our lives.
By the mystery of the Word made flesh,
your Son our Saviour Jesus Christ,
you have offered liberation
from the powers of evil and death and the fear of them;
and you have opened to us new life,
the earnest of resurrection and eternal glory
with you, with him, and with all the holy and humble of heart.

You are ever at work
to restore all your creation,
and bring it again to the perfection of its origin,
by the reconciliation wrought for us
and the whole cosmos by our Lord Jesus Christ,
who, when he ascended on high,
poured forth upon us the Holy Spirit of promise
with his manifold gifts of grace;
The Spirit of wisdom and discernment, for right judgments;
The Spirit of strength and compassion,
for courage to do what is just and right;
The Spirit of joy and inner peace,
to overcome all tribulation;
The Spirit of reverence, for everything you have made.

Give us, gracious God, this day
and throughout the days to come,
the light of your wisdom and the strength of your love,
to discern how to worship you aright,
and offer you continually that praise
which is your due and which is acceptable in your sight.

This we ask through him who ever intercedes for us,
Christ Jesus our Lord, who gave us the pattern
of all prayer, all praise, and all sacrifice.

Malcolm C. Burson, ed., *Worship Points the Way: A Celebration of the Life and Work of Massey Hamilton Shepherd, Jr.* (New York: Seabury Press, 1981), 49-53. (Excerpt)

CHAPTER SIXTEEN

Renewal

Introduction

God promises to "make all things new." The believer in response may experience new understandings, sing new songs, and find new ways of expressing God's love. Renewal of the members and ministries of the church may take many forms. Renewal transforms the heart as well as the head. Renewal is rooted in the experience that God's love makes a difference. Renewal can mean greater spontaneity and participation in the life of the church. In this regard, renewal may be threatening for some Episcopalians. Renewal can mean the reclaiming of the biblical roots of faith, and a willingness to share the Good News with others. Renewal can mean a more dynamic life of Christian community. The renewal movement has roots in enthusiastic expressions of faith in other denominations, including pentecostal and charismatic churches. Episcopalians involved in renewal developed close ties with similar movements in both Evangelical churches and the Roman Catholic Church. The modern renewal movement in the Episcopal Church is focused on revitalization of the church's mission and ministry, with an emphasis on evangelism.

138.

Fellowship of Witness Doctrinal Basis, 1964

The Fellowship of Witness was organized in 1964. Its doctrinal basis is the Statement of Faith for Trinity Episcopal School for Ministry, in Ambridge, Pennsylvania, which opened on September 25, 1976.

It is important to remember the essentials of our faith. From time to time, persons curious about the F.O.W. wish to know what the group believes. The following are the articles which form our doctrinal basis:

ARTICLE I—The Holy Trinity

The mystery of the Holy Trinity, namely, that the one God exists eternally in three persons: Father, Son and Holy Spirit; and has so revealed himself to us in the Gospel.

ARTICLE II—The Lord Jesus Christ

The full diety and full humanity of our Lord Jesus Christ, God incarnate, who by reason of his birth of the Virgin Mary, sinless life, atoning death, bodily resurrection, glorious ascension and triumphant reign, is the only Mediator between God and man.

ARTICLE III—The Holy Scriptures

The trustworthiness of the canonical books of the Old and New Testments as "God's Word written," which contain all things necessary for salvation, teach God's will for his world, and have supreme authority for faith, life and the continuous renewal and reform of the Church.

ARTICLE IV—Justification and Sanctification

The justification of the repenting and believing sinner as God's gracious act of declaring him righteous on the ground of the reconciling death of Christ, who suffered in our place and rose again for us; and sanctification as the gracious continuing activity of the Holy Spirit in the justified believer, perfecting his repentance, nurturing the new life implanted within him, transforming him into Christ's image, enabling him to do good works in the world.

ARTICLE V—The Christian Church

The Church as the Body of Christ, whose members belong to the new humanity and are called to live in the world in the power of the Spirit, worshipping God, confessing the truth, proclaiming Christ, supporting one another in love and giving themselves in sacrificing service to those in need.

ARTICLE VI—Spiritual Gifts and Ministry

The calling of all Christians to exercise their God-given gifts in ministry, and to work, witness and suffer for Christ; together with the particular calling of ordained ministers, who, by preaching, teaching and pastoral care, are to equip God's people for his service, and to present them mature in Christ.

ARTICLE VII—The Gospel Sacraments

The sacraments of Baptism and Holy Communion as "visible words" which proclaim the Gospel and are means of grace by which faith is quickened and strengthened; in particular, the significance of the Lord's Supper as a communion in the Body and Blood of Christ, who offers himself to us in the action of this sacrament, so that by faith we may feed on him in our hearts and offer ourselves to him in gratitude for our salvation through his cross; Also, the openness of the Lord's Table as the place where all baptized believers, being one in Christ, are free to celebrate their common salvation in the Lord, and to express their common devotion to his person and service.

ARTICLE VIII—The Return of Christ

The personal return in glory of our Lord Jesus Christ at the end of this age for the resurrection of the dead (some to life, some to condemnation), for the glorification of his Church, and for the renewal of the whole creation.

Fellowship of Witness Newsletter I:1 (July 1991): 2.

139.

Dennis and Rita Bennett, The Overflow, 1971

Dennis Joseph Bennett (October 28, 1917–November 1, 1991) was prominently identified with the charismatic renewal in the Episcopal Church. This movement is usually dated from the Sunday in 1959 when he announced to his congregation in Van Nuys, California, that he had been baptized with the Holy Spirit and had spoken in tongues. He and his wife, Rita, conducted charismatic seminars and co-authored several books. In this selection the Bennetts describe the power of receiving the Holy Spirit.

When you received Jesus as your Savior, your *spirit* came alive, began to assert its new life and take its rightful place as head over your *soul*—your psychological part (intellect, will, and emotions)—and your *body*, your physical part. Your body and soul, however, were accustomed to "running the show," and it wasn't long before they had pretty much overwhelmed your new life in the spirit, and resumed the driver's seat. When you pray in the morning, the busyness of your soul and body is quieted; your spirit has a chance to let you know he is there; and at this, and other times, you get an inkling that, deep inside you, the new life is very real. But as soon as the clamor of existence begins again, you automatically start to trust your soul and body rather than your spirit. You were so accustomed to living by your thoughts, feelings, and desires—by your soul, your psychological being—and by the demands of your body, that you soon lost track of the voice of the newly living spirit deep within you. It would seem that something needs to happen to your *soul* and *body* before your *spirit* can gain stronger control.

This "something" that needs to happen is that the Holy Spirit Who is living in your spirit needs to *flow out* to fill your soul and body. This is described in the Scripture in a variety of ways. Just as the experience of accepting Jesus is spoken of throughout the Bible in different ways, so a number of descriptions are given of the next experience: "baptism in (or with)[1] the Holy Spirit," "receiving the Holy Spirit," "Pentecost," "receiving power," the Holy Spirit to "come upon" or "fall upon" a person. All these are expressions of the same truth, viewed from different sides.

There is much difference of opinion over what terminology to use. We don't want to erect any verbal barriers for anyone, so, if using any one of these titles to refer to this second experience disturbs you, why not call it "experience X-2," or something like that? However, we feel on especially safe scriptural grounds using the term "baptism in the Holy Spirit," since quite an impressive list of biblical Persons so used it: God the Father (John 1:33); God the Son (Acts 1:5); and God the Holy Spirit, Who is, of course, the Inspirer of the Scriptures in which these expressions are found. There are also John the Baptist (Matt. 3:11, Mark 1:8, Luke 3:16, John 1:33); the four evangelists, Matthew, Mark, Luke, and John, in the places just cited; and the Apostle Peter (Acts 11:16). If you will read these references carefully, and compare them, you will see in each case it is not salvation that is spoken of, but a second experience.

This is called in the Scripture, "the baptism in the Holy Spirit," because it *is* a baptism, meaning a drenching, an overflowing, a saturating of your soul and body with the Holy Spirit. When the Bible speaks of Jesus "baptizing" in the Holy Spirit, we immediately visualize something external, somebody being *put into* something. However, the word *baptize* in Greek means to "completely suffuse"—it is used in classical Greek of a sunken, water-logged ship—so it does not really make any difference whether Jesus immerses us in the Holy Spirit in an external sense of the word; whether He inundates us from outside; or whether Jesus causes the Spirit to rise and overflow from where He is living *inside* us, to suffuse our souls and bodies. Probably both pictures are true—He "comes upon us" both from outside and inside, but it is important to remember that the Holy Spirit is living *in* you, and that therefore it is from within that He can flood your soul and body. Jesus says:

"He that believeth on me . . . *out of* his belly shall flow rivers of living water [the Holy Spirit]" (John 7:38),[2] and the Amplified Bible says: "*Out of* his inner-

---

[1] The Greek preposition en, used in this phrase, may be translated "in," or "with."
[2] Italics ours

most being shall flow . . . ." When we receive Jesus as Savior, the Holy Spirit *comes in,* but as we continue to trust and believe Jesus, the Indwelling Spirit can *pour out* to inundate, or baptize, our soul and body, and refresh the world around.

This, too, is why again and again in Scripture the first normative evidence of this Pentecost experience is an *out*pouring:

"They were all filled with the Holy Ghost, and began to speak in other languages . . ."(Acts 2:4).

Some are puzzled by the term "receiving the Holy Spirit." A Christian may ask the question: "How can I *receive* the Holy Spirit when I already have Him living in me?" This expression can be understood easily if we remember that we are talking about a Person, not a thing or a quantity of something. Some have talked about the Holy Spirit in a quantitative way—as if you could receive *some* of the Holy Spirit at salvation, and some *more* at a later date. But if the Holy Spirit is a Person, which He is, then He is either living in you or He isn't.

We all know what it means to "receive" a person. Let us imagine the Brown household. It is 5:40 p.m., and Mr. Brown has just come home from work, and is taking a shower before supper. Mrs. Brown is putting the finishing touches on an especially nice meal, for the Browns have invited the Joneses over for dinner. Their guests are scheduled to arrive at 6:00 p.m., but alas, at 5:45 comes a ring at the doorbell. Mrs. Brown flutters a little—she isn't through with the gravy; she has flour on the end of her nose; and her hair is a mess!

"Susie!" she calls to her daughter, "for goodness' sake will you go and let the Joneses in; give them the evening paper, or visit with them—I'm not ready for them yet!"

Just then the phone rings in the kitchen, and Mrs. Brown answers.

"Hello! Marie?" says the voice on the line. "This is Helen. Do you have the Joneses over there?"

"Yes," replies Mrs. Brown, "we do."

"Well, how are they?" says the voice of the caller.

"I really don't know," says Mrs. Brown, patiently. "I haven't *received* them yet. I'm still out here working in the kitchen."

"You'd better hurry and receive them," says Helen. "I happen to know they have some wonderful news, and that they have brought you some beautiful gifts!"

So Mrs. Brown hangs up the phone, quickly finishes her cooking, straightens her hair and powders her face, and then, together with her husband, receives her friends, hears the news they have, and accepts the gifts they have brought. The Person of the Holy Spirit has been living in your "house" ever since your new birth, but now you fully acknowledge His Presence and receive His gifts.

Let us sum up, then, by saying that the first experience of the Christian life, salvation, is the *incoming* of the Holy Spirit, through Jesus Christ, to give us new life, God's life, eternal life. The second experience, is the *receiving,* or making welcome of the Holy Spirit, so that Jesus can cause Him to pour out this new life from our spirits, to baptize our souls and bodies, and then the world around, with His refreshing and renewing power. "Out of his belly shall flow rivers of living water!" The word used here is *koilia* which means quite literally the "physical body"; it is by means of the physical body and its speech and actions that we contact our environment and the people around us. The world is not going to be helped or challenged until it sees and hears and experiences Jesus' life flowing from us.

Imagine an irrigation canal in Southern California, or some other area that is normally arid most of the year. The canal is dry, and so are the fields around. All the vegetation is dried up and dead. Then the gates from the reservoir are opened, and the canal begins to fill with water. First of all the *canal* itself is refreshed! The cool flow of water carries away debris and slakes the dust. Next, grass and flowers begin to spring up along the banks, and the trees on either side of the canal become fresh and green. But it doesn't stop there; all the way along the canal, farmers open the gates and the life-giving water pours out into the fields to make the "desert blossom as the rose."

So with you and me. The reservoir, the well, is in us when we become Christians. Then, when we allow the indwelling living water of the Spirit to flow out into our souls and bodies, *we* are refreshed first. Our minds come alive in a new way to God's reality. We begin to think of Him, even dream of Him, with a new frequency and joy. Our emotions respond, and we begin to be happy in Him. Our will responds, and we begin to want to do what He wants. Our bodies respond, not only by feelings of well-being, but by actual renewed strength and health and youth. Then the living water begins to pour out to others, and they see the power and love of Jesus in His people. He is now able to use us to refresh the world around us.

Dennis and Rita Bennett, "The Overflow," in *The Holy Spirit and You: A Study-Guide to the Spirit-Filled Life* (Plainfield, N.J.: Logos International, 1971), 16-21. (Excerpt)

140.

Bob Slosser, Miracle in Darien, 1979

Bob Slosser (March 23, 1929–   ) has written for the New York Times *and is the author of several books.* Miracle in Darien *is the story of charismatic renewal at St. Paul's Episcopal Church, Darien, Connecticut, and the leadership of its rector, Everett Leslie (Terry) Fullam (July 9, 1930–   ). Fullam is now a non-parochial priest.*

My first Sunday service under Fullam's ministry also revealed the importance of music in additional aspects of worship. The processional had occurred, we had been welcomed in the name of the Lord, and all two hundred twenty-five of us—maybe two hundred fifty, for it was tight—were settling down for a happy time.

"I have another song for you."

Everyone smiled, and a few chuckled audibly as Terry stood full-robed and spread-armed before us. The remembrance evokes a line by one of the more out-going parishioners some years later when a visiting minister, Dennis Bennett, commended the church for its singing.

"We sing under duress," remarked Lee Buck from the back of the room. Perhaps "happy coercion" was more accurate.

"It goes like this," Terry said that Sunday morning, moving his right hand in accompaniment, almost as though it held a conductor's baton:

> Let all that is within me cry holy!
> Let all that is within me cry holy!
> Holy! Holy!
> Holy is the Lamb that was slain.

We sang well. Indeed, we sang very well. If we hadn't, he would have stopped us, rehearsed us, and had us start over gain, which he often did. There were many accomplished singers who were able to provide harmony and a proper rising and falling in volume. We actually worshiped the Lord.

But it was nearly forty-five minutes later when that worship took on an extra dimension. Terry was celebrating Communion, assisted by two lay readers. The people began to file forward to be served and he started to sing *a cappella* the song we had learned earlier. Gradually the choir and then the congregation joined in. This was not an Episcopal custom in that spring of 1973. The singing swelled as verse after verse was added. First it was "Let all that is within me cry *holy*." Then "Let all that is within me cry *worthy*." Then "glory," then "Jesus." The Communion was very sweet.

As the scores continued to file forward, and then return ever so prayerfully, the song shifted to "Alleluia," over and over, verse after verse, "My redeemer . . . Jesus is Lord . . . If you love Him, why not serve Him? . . . alleluia. . . ."

Many of those Episcopalians—and those Presbyterians, and those Lutherans, and those whatever—had never worshiped in song at that point in the service. They had never lifted their voices or their hands to the Lord in such adoration.

From the middle of the sanctuary, a sweet soprano voice lifted to great, delicate heights, and then blended in with the others. I knew it was Diane Kelley. Once a fine singer, she had stopped, seemingly having lost her voice. But in deep worship, it was there—bell-like, then whispery, holy.

Internal and External

Free worship was difficult for many of the people at St. Paul's, as it was among Episcopalians generally and other sacramental, liturgical groups. And affluence, advanced education, and the urbanity of New York suburban life did not promote freedom of expression in worship either. Patience and understanding were required, along with teaching.

The latter came persistently. The parishioners were led, for example, into an examination of Romans 1:21: "For although they knew God they did not honor him as God or give thanks to him, but they became futile in their thinking and their senseless minds were darkened."

Those the apostle was writing about knew God, but they did not honor Him as God; they did not glorify Him; they did not give Him the worship that was due Him. Not worshiping the Lord, they did not, as Terry had taught, *give themselves* to Him. They gave Him other things perhaps—their goods, their sacrifices. But they did not give themselves as living sacrifices, which was their *spiritual worship*.

So it seemed that it was not enough to *know about* God, or even to *know* God, if one didn't *worship* God. Eventually, it seemed, there came a drying up, a futility, a darkening, and a collapse.

The drying up, the darkening, was inevitable because, according to Psalm 22:3, God, who is holy, inhabits the praises of Israel, His people—He is "enthroned" on their praises. He lives in the praises, the worship and adoration, of His people; He assumes His proper place, on the throne. Reality is achieved. Without the worship, the components of reality are not in order; God is not seen as on His throne. To our senses, reality evaporates. Darkness threatens.

Undergirding this is an old chestnut in Scripture, part of which is spoken Sunday after Sunday by participants in Episcopal services. It is found in Psalm 51:15-17:

> O Lord, open thou my lips,
> and my mouth shall show forth thy praise

For thou hast no delight in sacrifice;
    were I to give a burnt offering, thou wouldst
    not be pleased.
The sacrifice acceptable to God is a broken spirit;
    a broken and contrite heart, O God, thou wilt not
    despise.

In that declaration, we suggest an understanding of our duty to praise and worship God and we acknowledge that the pathway for that praise is through the giving of ourselves, the humbling and breaking of our proud spirits and hearts. We indicate a belief that we must give ourselves fully to the Lord in worship of Him, or it will be as nothing.

The people of St. Pual's ever so gradually found themselves giving themselves inwardly in their worship. They drew closer and closer to the Lord, especially individually. But, as they did so and let the reasons for their worship, as found in Scripture, sink into their hearts, they found themselves giving quiet *external* expression to their worship also.

I recall vividly seeing this overt expression for the first time at St. Paul's, following an absence of several months. I noticed it first during the singing of a simple song that line by line elevated personal and collective worship to the highest form.

We have come into His house and called
    upon His name to worship Him;
We have come into His house and called
    upon His name to worship Him;
We have come into His house and called
    upon His name to worship Christ the Lord;
Worship Him, worship Christ the Lord.

It proceeded through numerous verses, including one in which the key line was:

We have come into His house *to lift up holy hands* and
    worship Him. . . .

Many pairs of hands were already raised toward heaven, but virtually all in the congregation reached upward, yearning, as the song reached that point.

I knew they were by that time well acquainted with the verses in the Bible calling for that expression of worship and yearning, that turning of the face heavenward and reaching with the hands toward the Creator. I knew they had read, in a little-discussed portion of the Scripture called The Lamentations of Jeremiah, of the people of God and their fall to utter ruin. They had read how Jerusalem had fallen to Nebuchadnezzar of Babylon, how the Temple had been destroyed, how glory had turned to tragedy. And they knew in the depths of despair, the people of Israel had been exhorted to turn back to God.

> Let us test and examine our ways,
> And return to the Lord!
> Let us *lift up our hearts and hands*
> *to God in heaven.*[2]

In the midst of their degradation and suffering, in the throes of hopeless humiliation, God's people had been told to lift not only their hearts, but also their hands toward Him. They reached toward the Lord internally and externally. They worshiped Him inwardly, and they worshiped Him outwardly.

The people of St. Paul's were being taught that this yielding of self to their God, this worship with the whole being, was for good times as well as bad, for happy circumstances and for unhappy circumstances. If they wanted God to live in their midst, they must enthrone Him upon their praises and their worship. They were to *know* that He was the head of the church and to *glorify* Him as such.

Bob Slosser, *Miracle in Darien* (Plainfield, N.J.: Logos International, 1979), 98-
   103. (Excerpt)

141.

Betty Pulkingham and Mimi Farra, Cry Hosanna, 1980.

Betty Pulkingham and Mimi Farra are members of the Community of Celebration, also known as the Fisherfolk. The Community of Celebration is a religious community known for its worship which blends the contemporary and traditional. This selection discusses the role of music in praise of God.

All over the world Christians are discovering new freedom in praise as they draw together to worship the living God.

> From the fears that long have bound us
> Free our hearts to faith and praise.
> *Harry Emerson Fosdick*

Most of us have been bound at some point to the particular tradition out of which we come, and have needed the Spirit's driving wind to dislodge us from

---

[2]Lamentations 3:40-41.

568

the place where we were 'stuck' and blow us into a larger place—a place of exposure to different cultures, different theologies, different ways of honouring God. Once we have been blown upon and into this larger place, we find an adventure of faith awaiting us, with ever-broadening horizons. The same Spirit who drove Jesus into the wilderness will drive us—his contemporary brothers and sisters—into similar places of exposure, challenge and blessing. It is there that we will learn to cry 'Hosanna'. We will neither croon, nor drone, nor chirp (the world's ways of romanticizing, deadening, or making frivolous the songs of God). But we will sing his praises with a pure heart, fervently, as we have been taught by him to love. From our innermost beings, out of experiences of costly obedience and purifying pain, will well up the Spirit's songs. We will learn to sing them with strong, clear voices, and only such praise as this, plumbed from the depths of God's people, will be able to sustain them through suffering, through persecution, through martyrdom, through the challenges of the last decades of this century.

Betty Pulkingham and Mimi Farra, eds. *Cry Hosanna* (Carol Stream, Ill.: Hope Publishing Company, 1980), 9. (Excerpt)

142.

Michael T. Malone,
Traditionalist–Renewalist Tensions, 1983

Michael Taylor Malone (February 5, 1937–   ) is Canon to the Ordinary, Diocese of South Carolina. He was rector of St. Batholomew Church, Hartsville, South Carolina, when this article was published. He discusses the need for charity and openness to diversity among traditionalists and renewalists.

In recent years the Episcopal Church along with other mainline churches has experienced a new surge of personalist piety, "turned on" if not actually "born again." The growing popularity of, and Episcopalians' participation in, such movements as Faith Alive, Cursillo, Marriage Encounter, among others, have resulted in an infusion into long-established (and establishment) parishes of persons caught up in a new fervor of commitment and devotion. As interdenominational lay movements devoted to prayer, Bible study, and lay witnessing widely flourish, hardly an Episcopal parish has been unaffected as participants often seek by word and deed to commend these evangelical particularisms.

Considerable though often underacknowledged tension often results then within parishes between those I shall designate as "traditionalists" and "renewalists."

By traditionalist I mean those Episcopalians who feel that the church's historical ethos, whether high church or low, pro-1928 or pro-1979 Prayer Book, provides the healthiest setting wherein the individual churchman can be encouraged and equipped to grow spiritually. These traditionalists often are the pillars of their parishes and serve with distinction in leadership positions, though they are often reticent about talking about their personal religion and/or problems. Taken as a group the traditionalists resemble their caricatures of being shallow Christians; they are apt to speak in terms of "the church says" rather than "Jesus says." The traditionalist tries unsuccessfully to enter into praise services but is secretly embarrassed in the company of arm raisers; he wonders to himself, "why join the Episcopal Church and then want to act like a Baptist?" Taken as a whole, traditionalists run the gamut from bishops to inactive laity, but what they all have in common is the often uncritical thought that an infusion of evangelical particularisms would be more disruptive of than helpful to parish life.

The renewalist sees the issue from quite the other perspective. Typical Episcopal parish life seems to him dull, devoted to the status quo, and captive to the leadership of Sunday-only Christians. As he may remember his own former church involvement—best described as premeditatedly indifferent—and as he reflects upon those influences which subsequently have made his personal faith a consuming passion, he alternately experiences exhilaration within a circle of renewalist companions and frustration with the parish as a whole.

While often polite to one another, both traditionalists and renewalists when gathered among their own kind share misgivings, resentments, and fears of the opposite group. Traditionalists knowingly confide to one another that the renewalists are balmy nuisances and meddlers, and renewalists sadly reflect that the Great Commission requires them to get to work upon their own parish. Balance of power within the parish becomes a touchy but critical issue. One parish of my acquaintance is made up of perhaps 50% traditionalists, 25% renewalists, and 25% puzzled conciliators; needless to say, a recent search process for a rector was cagey in the extreme. Many if not most Episcopal parishes are experiencing such tensions among their communicants. The tension may be minimal with conciliatory leadership, or fiercely triumphalist when leaders say, "Extremism in the pursuit of tradition (or renewal) is no vice."

. . . .

My modest conciliatory proposal then is, let both traditionalists and renewalists consider whether their personal histories and emotional constitutions do not leave them with blind spots. For all the avoidance of ontology William James'

570

liberal pragmatism may be guilty of, that pragmatism is constructive as it stresses that varieties of people experience life and God variously. Intensity is not obviously more godly than is serenity, or vice versa.

People who are forever "once born" do become saints and some do not. People who are "twice born" do become saints and some do not. Secular psychological analysis may be sufficient unto itself adequately to explain the structure of religious experience but it cannot thereby preclude ascription of divine causation to times of ecstasy; failure to observe this rule results in the traditionalist's attribution of balminess to the renewalist. Ascription of divine causation of religious ecstasy does not warrant exempting that experience from subsequently humbling psychological analysis, which analysis may be crucial for keeping the particularity of the experience in perspective; failure to observe this rule results in the renewalist's attribution of shallowness to the traditionalist.

Historians have documented that Christians have come in all shapes and sizes, all races and color, with all varieties of temperament. To St. Paul's insistence that in Christ we are neither Jew nor Greek, male nor female, slave nor free, we might boldly add "neither traditionalist nor renewalist." We traditionalists need to be challenged to look at life more deeply and more seriously and to enter more fully into the joy of the Lord—this the renewalists in our midst beckon us toward. We renewalists need to be challenged to live life more rationally and critically and to see God's grace in the lives of the beautifully "once born"—this the traditionalists in our midst beckon us toward. In his final prayer with his disciples our Lord prayed for them, not that they would be broad and hazy, nor hot and crazy, but that they might be one in him.

Michael T. Malone, "Traditionalist–Renewalist Tensions: William James and a Modest Conciliatory Proposal," *Anglican Theological Review* 65 (April 1983), 167-168, 175-176. (Excerpts)

143.

What is Cursillo?, 1987

The Cursillo movement came into the Episcopal Church from the Roman Catholic Church by way of Spain. Cursillo means "short course" in Spanish, and the three-day weekends are intended as a short course in Christianity. Cursillo participants are called "Cursillistas," and their "Fourth Day" means continuing the weekend by prayer and fellowship groups. In 1979 the National

Episcopal Cursillo was formed. "Happenings" for youth and "Marriage Encounter" are some of the off-shoots of Cursillo. This statement discusses the principles of Cursillo.

. . . Cursillos were not designed to be "put on," as if they were a form of entertainment—a three-day spectacular. Rather, they were designed to be "lived." In many places, the Cursillo has suffered from over-zealous proponents who want to cram as much into a weekend as it is possible to do. "The more, the better" seems to be their motto. But the weekend is only a piece of the Cursillo strategy, and a very small piece at that. It is meant to be the catalyst for Christian action; a crucible into which the various elements of our faith are mixed and from which emerges effective Christian witnesses. It can, of course, be an exciting adventure for people who have never heard that they are called to be apostles, or for those who have not the slightest idea what being an apostle could be like. Nevertheless, very simple weekend experiences offer as much to their participants as more elaborately designed ones do. And in any case, the weekend is like a launching pad more than it is a destination. The mission of Cursillo is NOT to put on weekends, but to put apostles into action-orbits.

. . . .

What did Jesus do when he wanted to bring his Gospel to the world? He went out to look for certain types of individuals. He was not, in that way, being exclusivist. Instead, he was being practical. He chose leaders—or potential leaders: people who had the potential to influence others.

Cursillo works in the same way. Since the goal is to penetrate everyday living situations with Christian witness, it makes sense to try to find those individuals—already active members of their churches—who have the potential to be effective witnesses.

Of course, such individuals will be found in every walk of life, from every rung of the socio-economic ladder, of varying educational and cultural backgrounds. The important keys are a willingness to struggle with the Christian faith, ability to engage in active Christian witness in community, and openness to God's leading through the Spirit.

Once such persons are identified, they are invited to "make a Cursillo." The purpose of doing so is to provide these persons a common ground with others like them—to provide them a laboratory, as we have said, for plumbing the depths of their faith.

What is Cursillo? (Cedar Falls, Iowa: National Episcopal Cursillo, 1987), 4-5.
     (Excerpt)

CHAPTER SEVENTEEN

Modern Controversies in the Church

Introduction

The modern era has been a time of conflict and rapid change for the Episcopal Church. The church's unity has been strained by disagreements with respect to the most basic issues of ministry and faith. The Episcopal Church has been particularly susceptible to controversy during this period because of its diversity. It has struggled to maintain comprehensiveness and unity. Shortly after his election as Presiding Bishop, Edmond Browning promised that there would be "no outcasts" from the Episcopal Church. This goal and ideal has been difficult to fulfill. Modern controversies have forced the church to face a variety of hard questions about how to respond to disagreement and change: Can the church value different perspectives while listening and seeking consensus? Can the church include a host of views while maintaining a distinctive witness? Can the church face modern controversies in ways that serve mission and strengthen witness? Through all the controversies, the church seeks to express the faith in ways that respond to the needs and questions of today's world. Faith can be strengthened and renewed as the church rediscovers the meaning of tradition in the face of controversy.

144.

Progress Report to the House of Bishops from the Committee to Study the Proper Place of Women in the Ministry of the Church, 1966

The creation of the Committee to Study the Proper Place of Women in the Ministry of the Church was authorized by the House of Bishops on September 9, 1965. The report was presented to the House of Bishops on October 27, 1966, at Wheeling, West Virginia. It considers arguments for and against the ordination of women and states that opponents of women's ordination must bear the burden of proof for their position.

573

Scope and Urgency

The Committee presents this preliminary Report, indicating that the place of women in the Church's Ministry demands the facing of the question of whether or not women should be considered eligible for ordination to any and all Orders of that Ministry. No one would deny that women are part of the lay ministry of the Church, and the Committee does not think that another examination of the status of Deaconesses alone would do justice to the matter.

The Committee is convinced that a number of factors give the question a new urgency, require a fresh and unprejudiced look at the whole issue, and warn against uncritical acceptance of beliefs, attitudes, and assumptions that have been inherited from the past and strongly persist at the present time. Three such factors seem especially important:

a. *The growing place of women in professional, business, and public life,* in medicine, in teaching, in politics and government, in the Armed Forces, even high executive positions within this Church.

b. *The development of new forms of ministry* that permit greater flexibility and call for many more specialized skills than is the case when the ministry is limited largely to one priest in charge of one parish, generalist rather than a specialist. As one member of the Committee put it, "We need to stop talking or thinking of the ministry as though it were a single unitary vocation. Rather, we need to think of the many functions of ministry which are needed today—the sacramental ministry, preaching, theological and Biblical research, teaching, pastoral work and counseling, social services, etc. In an age of specialization and of a tremendous explosion of knowledge we must face the fact that no one person can possibly be adequate in all these areas. . . . We need to encourage specialization according to a person's gifts and interests and organize our corporate life to use specialists." This fact requires consideration of how women may be used in a changing and increasingly specialized ministry.

c. *The growing importance of the issue in ecumenical relationships.* The question is being discussed in many parts of the Anglican Communion. . . . The initiation of a study of the experiences of ordained women was urged by the World Conference on Church and Society, meeting at Geneva in the Summer of 1966. In this country, the Consultation on Church Union has reached the point of considering the drafting of a plan of union, involving this Church and a number of others that now admit women to the ordained ministry, and the question of the ordination of women in such a united Church obviously must be faced as the negotiations proceed.

Nor does it seem that the question of the ordination of women in the Orthodox and Roman Churches can be regarded as finally and forever decided in the negative, particularly in view of other changes that have occurred, especially in the Roman Church.

There is a sentence in one of the official documents of Vatican II that reads, "Since in our times women have an ever more active share in the whole life of society, it is very important that they participate more widely also in the various fields of the church's apostolate." (*The Documents of Vatican II*, Walter M. Abbott, S.J., General Editor, Guild Press, New York. 1966, page 500.) The Archbishop of Durban, South Africa, Dr. Dennis Hurley, recently predicted that "there are going to be some fantastic developments" in the role of women in the Church. (See *Christian Century*, September 15, 1966.) And in an interview with the Secretary of this Committee, given on October 11, 1966, the Rev. Dr. Hans Küng, Professor in the University of Tübingen (Germany) stated, "There are two factors to consider regarding the ordination of women to the Sacred Ministry of the Church. The first is that there are no dogmatic or biblical reasons against it. The second is that there are psychological and sociological factors to be considered. The solution to the problem depends on the sociological conditions of the time and place. It is entirely a matter of cultural circumstances."

BURDEN OF PROOF

The Committee has become increasingly convinced that the burden of proof is on the negative in this matter.

For, to oppose the ordination of women is either to hold that the whole trend of modern culture is wrong in its attitude toward the place of women in society, or to maintain that the unique character of the ordained ministry makes that ministry a special case and justifies the exclusion of women from it.

REASONS GIVEN AGAINST THE ORDINATION OF WOMEN
Mental and Emotional

The alleged mental and emotional characteristics of women are said to make them unsuitable to serve as clergymen. Such arguments are never very clear, consistent, or precise. Sometimes, the weakness of women is stressed, despite the fact that women are healthier and live longer than men. Or, it is claimed that women think emotionally rather than rationally and that they over-personalize problems or decisions.

The same sort of arguments could be used to show that women are unfit for almost any business, professional, or public responsibility. They were used against the admission of women to higher education, to the practice of medicine and law, and against women suffrage. They are still being used against the admission of women to the House of Deputies of the General Convention.

None of these negative arguments has been borne out of any other walk of life. Women have proved to be capable, often brilliant, lawyers, statesmen, scientists, and teachers. They have enriched the practice of medicine, and politics have neither been redeemed nor debased by their participation.

As experience has demonstrated, only experience can show the extent to which women might fulfill a useful role in the ordained ministry, as well as ways in which their role might be different from the role of men. Here, as in other callings, women would need to be better than men in order to compete with them.

Emil Brunner states, "It is absolutely impossible to put down in black and white, as a universal rule, which spheres of activity 'belong' to women and which do not. This can only become clear through experience; and for this experience, first of all the field must be thrown open."

Because the field has not been thrown open, any judgment based on the Church's experience with professional women workers is limited and inadequate. With the highest respect for the contributions these women are now making the Committee is convinced that an absolute bar at the level of ordination has a deterring effect upon the number of women of high quality who enter professional Church work or undertake theological study, and that this same bar places theologically trained women in a highly uncomfortable and anomalous position.

Marriage *versus* Ministry

There is alleged the impossibility or impracticality of combining the vocation of a clergyman with domestic responsibilities, with marriage, as well as the bearing and care of children. Would it be possible for a wife and mother of a family to bring to the priesthood the required degree of commitment, concentration, and availability?

First, it must be said that many women choose careers and never marry, others combine marriage and careers. The Church recognizes that the latter is an entirely legitimate vocation, both in the secular world and in the Church itself.

Secondly, the question of married women is partly answered by the fact that married men are permitted to serve as Bishops, priests, and deacons in the Anglican Communion. Such permission implies an acknowledgment of the strong claims that the wife and family of a married clergyman rightfully have upon his time, his money, and the conduct of his vocation. All would grant that a clergyman has a duty, as well as a right, to take into account his wife's health, or his children's education, in considering a call, in negotiating about his salary, in determining his standard of living and the amount of money he will give away. While other, and perhaps more serious, problems might exist for a woman who wished to combine ordination with marriage, the Commission is by no means convinced that such a combination would not prove practical in many instances. Even such demanding professions as teaching and medicine are finding ways of using skilled and trained married women with children, both on a part-time and a full-time basis. Many intelligent women find that they are better wives and mothers by combining an outside calling with the care of a family. Many also can look forward to years of full-time professional work after their children are grown.

The Commission would ask whether the leadership of the church does not possess resourcefulness and imagination similar to that displayed by other institutions in using married women, if not often as ministers in charge of parishes, yet as assistants, or for the specialized types of ministry that are sure to develop much more rapidly in the future. It is thought unlikely that any great number of women would seek ordination, considering the very real difficulties involved. But difficulty is not impossibility, and at the least there need be no fear that women will "take over" the Church.

Theological Arguments

Then there are certain theological objections which seem to the Committee to present a strange mixture of tradition and superstition.

Biblical

Some of the objections rest on a rather literal approach to the Bible and fail to take into account the degree to which the Bible is conditioned by the circumstances of its time. It is not necessary to dwell upon the Creation Story, in which woman is created after man and taken from him, nor be influenced by the fact that women were excluded from the covenant-relation of God with Israel, any more than one would support polygamy or slavery because both have clear sanction in the Old Testament. Nor is one moved by the familiar argument that our Lord chose only men to be his apostles. Any sound doctrine of the incarnation must take full account of the extent to which Jesus lived and thought within the circumstances and environment of his own time. To deny such facts is to deny the full humanity of Jesus and to subscribe to a grotesque Docetism. Our Lord did choose women as close associates, even if he did choose men as the transitional leaders of the new Israel. The Committee also believes that St. Paul, as well as the authors of *Ephesians* and the Pastoral Epistles, were sharing in the passing assumptions of their own time, as well as advising wise strategy for the First Century Church, in recommending that women keep silent at services, cover their heads, and be subordinate to their husbands; just as St. Paul thought it wise to send a run-away slave back to his master. Much more permanent and basic are St. Paul's words, "There is neither Jew nor Greek . . . slave nor free . . . male nor female; for you all are one in Christ Jesus."

577

Image of God

Then, there is a cluster of theological objections based on the assumption that the female is a less true or complete image of God than the male; and that, therefore, woman is less capable, or is quite incapable, of representing God to man and man to God in the priesthood, and of receiving the indelible grace of Holy Orders.

This line of reasoning has a number of curious sources. In the Bible, God is thought and spoken of as "he", for the most part, as would be entirely natural in a culture first militant and warlike, always patriarchal, and with a developing monotheism. Even so, God can be compared with a mother who comforts her child.

Jesus Christ was born a man. Obviously, God's unique child would need to be born either a man or woman; and, again, in a patriarchal culture, only a man could fulfill the role of Messiah, Lord, or Son of God. When one calls God personal, one can mean no more than that human personality is the best clue we have to the nature of God. Perhaps male personality is a better clue than female personality in a masculine-dominated society, but who would presume to project such sexual differentiation upon the very nature of God? The first of the Anglican Articles of Religion states that God is "without body, parts, or passions". To call God "he", implies no more than to call the entire human race "man" or "mankind".

The view that the female is a less true or complete image of God than the male is sometimes still supported by a tradition coming from Aristotle and St. Thomas Aquinas, which holds that woman is an incomplete human being, "a defective and/or misbegotten male". This tradition was based upon the pre-scientific biology which held that woman was an entirely passive partner in reproduction. On this subject, the Rev. Dr. Leonard Hodgson has commented, "We should be unwise to base our theological conclusions on notions of a pre-scientific biology which has never heard of genes or chromosomes."

Emotional and Psychological Pressures

The Commission is also aware that all the intellectual arguments against the ordination of women are connected with and reflect strong emotional and psychological pressures. These pressures *may* point to profound truth about men and women and their relationship to each other. Or, they *may* reflect magical notions of priesthood and Sacraments that linger on in the most sophisticated minds. Or, they *may* reflect the fact that our deepest emotional experiences in the life of the Church, experiences often associated with the birth and baptism of children, maturity and Confirmation, worship and Sacraments, the pastoral ministry in times of crisis, joy and sorrow, are all closely associated with an episcopate and a priesthood that is exclusively male. Or, they *may* illustrate the sad fact that historical and psychological circumstances frequently make the church the last refuge of the fearful and the timid in a changing world and that, the more rapidly the world changes, the stronger become the pressures to keep the Church safe and unchanged. Or, they *may* represent a threat to the present ordained ministers, to their wives, to lay men or lay women. The Commission is disturbed by the scorn, the indifference, the humorless levity, that is occasioned by the question of seating women in the House of Deputies, let alone their admission to ordination.

Finally, one cannot place much weight upon the common opinion that women themselves do not wish to be ordained. Who knows? Most women obviously do not, just as most men do not, wish to become clergymen. But some women do. Kathleen Bliss has written, "This is not a woman's question, it is a Church question." The Church's answer must be determined, not primarily by what is good for woman, but what is good for the Church.

Journal of General Convention, 1970, 533-537.

145.

Theological Freedom and Social Responsibility, 1967

On January 23, 1967, Presiding Bishop John E. Hines appointed a committee to advise him concerning the theological situation of the Episcopal Church, especially the possibility of a presentment of charges against the resigned Bishop of California, James Albert Pike. Pike (February 14, 1913–September 3-7?, 1969) was rector of Christ Church, Poughkeepsie, New York, dean of the Cathedral of St. John the Divine, and Bishop of California, September 20, 1958–September 15, 1966. He was a contributor to the Church's Teaching Series, a social activist, an advocate of women's ordination, a liturgical reformer, a popular writer on ethics, the person who invited Eugene Carson Blake to deliver the sermon that initiated the Consultation on Church Union, and a popularizer of the theological trends of the 1960s. Bishop Henry Irving Louttit (January 1, 1903–July 24, 1984) of South Florida and other bishops charged Pike with incorrect teaching about the Trinity, the Holy Spirit, the centrality of Christ for salvation, the Incarnation, and the atonement. The House of Bishops refused to charge Pike with heresy but did censure him for "cheap vulgarizations of great expressions of the faith." Stephen Fielding

Bayne, Jr. (May 21, 1908–January 18, 1974) was chairman of the committee appointed by Hines, and the report is known as the Bayne Report. Bayne was the fifth Bishop of Olympia, June 11, 1947–December 31, 1959, and the first executive officer of the Anglican Communion. This statement concerns the role of the Church relative to social criticism and theological inquiry.

I. *What obligations does the Church have for encouraging theological discussion and social criticism? What procedures should it provide to fulfill those obligations?*

We take "the Church" to mean not merely certain officers or instrumentalities but the whole body of those united in Christ. We would subscribe to Dr. Knox's description of it as "a real and identifiable community in human history and . . . as something given by God—created in love, for us men and for our salvation, in and through an actual historical development culminating in Christ, and kept in being by him through the centuries since. I believe that we would further agree in finding its essential inner being to consist in a shared memory of the Lord Jesus and in a shared experience of the Spirit apprehended not only as God's Spirit but also as the actual living Presence of Christ crucified; and that we should agree also in recognizing that, despite its failure and infidelities, this community of memory and the Spirit is, and has always been, characterized by a distinctive way of life—of thinking, feeling, acting—which is appropriate to, and consequent upon, its nature as the community it is and which is, therefore, recognizably and inseparably its own."

As this continuing community, the Church owes it to its own nature, first of all, to be related to, in constant communication with, the world. The obligation to such steady, informed dialogue, in terms of both thought and action, is not an option; it is the Church's breath of life. Without the constant restatement of its teachings there could be no continuity to its life—it would be no more than a memorial society. Equally, without the constant reassessment of its public actions, its witness within society, there would be no way to maintain its distinctive way of life, arising from its nature.

The Church also has an obligation to its Creator, who is not only the source of the Church's life and tradition but of all truth, wherever and however discerned. Faithfulness to him therefore plainly requires of the community the ceaseless, restless, arduous work of relating his saving acts in the gospel and the Church to all else that he does—that the gospel may be heard in the terms which any given world understands, that the teachings of the community may be held in the same frame of reference as that in which all truth is held, that the community itself, generation by generation, may fully understand its own nature and remember aright the fullness of its tradition.

Again, the Church's obligation to minister in Christ's name to men and women requires that it enter fully into the world's always new, always agonizing search for truth and justice. This search goes on in all that men think and do. If the Church is to be an instrument of God's love for mankind, then it is imperative that it be wholeheartedly engaged in the world's arenas of reflection and action, not for the sake of its own image or popularity but because of the love which is its commanding duty as it is its sole treasure.

These are general statements, and not likely to be controversial. The painful issues arise when the question shifts to the procedures appropriate to the obligations. In our society, the question of what is appropriate is perhaps uniquely difficult to answer. It is not easy at any time to define the ordered magisterium of the Church or reconcile it with free and creative interpretations of Christian teaching. In the contemporary world, this definition and reconciliation is almost impossibly difficult. Suspicious of all authorities, with only fragmentary communications, skeptical of all precedent and structure, sometimes skeptical even of the possibility of rational thought itself, with only a shadowy sense of continuity with the past, with its generations crowding on the heels of generations and yet separated by frightening gaps in understanding, our world lacks many of the assumptions which served the theological processes of the Christian community in time past. Yet it is precisely this world, with its unprecedented problems of communication and self-understanding, which has unparalleled political and social decisions to make—decisions from which the Church cannot withdraw.

Our situation is not merely one more example of rebellious youth or disenchanted and secularized unbelief. Christians may recognize many familiar dynamics; but the contemporary pattern of those dynamics is radically and explosively different from any the Christian community has had to face in the past. Where there is an appeal to authority, especially institutional authority, in our time, it is likely to be made for the wrong reason, to establish a refuge from the bewildering uncertainties of our life. Such retreat from encounter is an enemy to true theological or social inquiry.

This is not to say that the Church has lost all ability to communicate intelligibly with the world or to maintain its own integrity within the world. Rejecting corporate authority, the world is all the more attracted to the charismatic, the unconventional, the individual. Much of this respect may indeed be of little depth and little consequence; but it illustrates what we feel to be profoundly important, that the ability of the Church to communicate, to enter intelligently into the intellectual and social debate of our time, depends on the degree to which the Church seeks solidarity with all men in this present critical confrontation. Where it is clear, as in the life and ministry of a sensitive teacher, that Christians share the world's pain and uncertainties and mean to join in the world's search for honest answers, fruitful engagement in theological and social inquiry becomes a reality.

Therefore the first requirement for the Church, in meeting its obligations, is that it sincerely mean to share the world's pain, and face with the world the frightening enigmas of its life. Along with this, a second characteristic is required, that of devotion to freedom of conscience. By itself, this principle is little more than a platitude. And it is equally a platitude to say that freedom can be and is abused—thrown as a cloak over individualism, eccentricity, even irresponsibility. This is no new thing. Nevertheless, to espouse freedom as a ruling principle entails a risk which the Church of all human associations must be the first to be willing to run. Why do we say this? Because the Church realizes that a faith which does not liberate cannot claim to be the authentic saving faith of Christ.

That the Church be truly one with humanity and at humanity's side, and that it be seen fully to respect man's freedom, are the two indispensable characteristics of any responsible engagement on the theological and social frontiers. Those characteristics grow out of the Church's nature. In turn, they must control the Church's response.

We are led, now, to make certain proposals to the Episcopal Church. In making them, we recognize that neither the problems nor the answers are peculiarly Episcopalian; and wherever it may be appropriate, we would share our suggestions with our companions in Christ's Body.

First, the Church must now provide new and carefully planned opportunities for dialogue, experience and experiment in these matters. These opportunities should be planned to include not only our own lay people and clergy but also those of other churches and non-Christians as well. Such seminars or institutions, whether sponsored nationally or otherwise, for mutual discussion of, and reflection upon, theological and social problems, in settings which will encourage encounter with the world, are essential to the Church's renewal. We do not envisage them as occasional, top-level episodes, but rather as continuing opportunities at every level, for engagement in a process of corporate renewal.

Second, the Church must provide for the preparation of its lay members to engage more responsibly in this encounter, including their preparation for ecumenical dialogue, and the Church must undertake this task with a depth and seriousness not always true of "lay training programs." In a phrase of Bishop Pike's, "theological inquiry and social criticism come naturally to responsible thinking persons." If such inquiry and criticism is to be informed, stimulated, and representative of the Christian community at its best, more will be needed than an encouraging climate of freedom alone.

Even such a climate cannot always be taken for granted in the Church, for there is an uneasiness among some churchmen—a fear lest the laity be not sturdy enough or sensible enough to withstand the shock of radical encounter with inquiry or criticism. We share no such uneasiness ourselves; but we know it exists; and we can suggest no better response to it than Mrs. Sorg's powerful admonition:

"The obligation of those in the Church who participate in social criticism and theological inquiry is not to retreat, or to shield the people by a conspiratorial silence. Their obligation is to help people to understand doctrine, dogma, and new concepts alike in relationship to life, so that faith may have reality and depth. Belief built upon a rock is not shaken by passing winds. But the sands of shallow understanding, prejudice, and fearful withdrawal, are unstable indeed."

Every member of the Church shares in its work and witness—well or poorly— and speaks for it. To say that is no subversion of the special responsibilities of bishops and priests. But if laymen are to fulfill their responsible ministry of speaking and acting for the Church, they have the right to the mature theological preparation they increasingly seek. This means, in our view, an immediate and massive expansion of resources for the laity, such as funds to permit interested and qualified laymen to pursue special courses of study, books and other teaching aids for individuals and groups, opportunities and training for encounter with other Christians and non-Christians, in settings designed to stimulate engagement and dialogue and to lead to clearer and more informed witness.

Third, the Church should establish a coordinated, adequately financed, and generally understood program for the continuing education of the clergy following ordination. Such a plan would require, among other things, a system of study leaves as well as a reorganization of seminary faculties and their duties; and it would be senseless to undertake it without the will to make a major investment of energy and time in it. This training should provide more than "refreshment"; it should give the clergy first-hand contact with the most threatening conflicts; it should qualify them to participate more effectively in doctrinal restatement; it should equip them to guide their parishes into more responsible action in urban and national affairs; it should provide new competence in ecumenical understanding and action. This might well increase tensions within the Church; but we do not doubt that such tensions can become the source of greater vitality.

Fourth, we suggest that the corporate activities of the bishops be redesigned so as to make possible a greater degree of theological discourse, and more informed collegial participation in the Church's encounter with the world. In our Church's understanding, the bishops have a special responsibility for guarding and interpreting the Church's tradition and for teaching its faith. This does not imply any oracular authority on their part or unique theological gifts conferred by ordination and consecration. Corporately—even individually—they have working responsibility for the Church's teaching which we believe God has called them to fulfill. But those responsibilities can be met only as the bishops are supported by regular communication with the Church's theologians and with others, lay or clerical, with competence in the decisive fields of contemporary society. A pattern in this direction was set at the Second Vatican Council in the attendance of selected theological consultants; and we understand that a somewhat wider experiment of this nature will be made at the 1968 Lambeth Conference. This kind of corporate study and reflection, we believe, should be a major element in the meetings of the House of Bishops, and at other occasions as well, to assist in giving the Church the strongest and most clearly corporate leadership in the great issues of faith and life. We would urge also that this collaboration of bishops, theologians and other skilled and thoughtful people be carried out on a regional basis, at frequent intervals.

Fifth, we strongly recommend that the General Convention establish a standing commission on the Church's teaching, of the kind that now exists, for example, in the Church of England and the Church of Scotland. This commission should not be in any sense a censoring body, nor should it claim for itself the teaching responsibility that belongs to the whole Church. But it could perform useful advisory functions. It could undertake studies of questions referred to it by other organs of the Church. It could initiate studies relevant to the issues confronting the Church today. Such a commission could also initiate and encourage programs of theological discussion and social criticism, as outlined above.

II. *What obligations should participants in such discussion assume?*
This question often excites oversimplified answers. One may say, "I have no obligation except to truth as I personally see it" even though his views may contradict the central traditions of the Christian community. Another may say, "Whatever my personal doubts, my primary obligation must be to the deposit of faith at the heart of the Church's life." We feel that such diametrically opposed answers, each reflecting an element of truth, demonstrate the complex character of the question, and the discriminating answer it requries.

No one of us, any more than any conscientious man or woman, would reject the obligation of fidelity to the truth. No one of us would disregard the obligation all churchmen have to the community which has given them their Christian freedom and identity. But to say only this is to fail to recognize either the agonizing conflict of loyalties which theological or social inquiry arouses or the equally complicated question of what role each person has, with respect to the community, and the many duties which spring from that.

Any discussion of obligation requires one to identify and evaluate the role in life which the participant plays. Every churchman, ordained or unordained, in a sense speaks and acts for the Church, in every situation. But the responsibility of a child in a confirmation class is quite different from that of a bishop in his diocese. Both have responsibilities. Both are members of the Christian community and must accept the obligations that membership establishes—obligations to the community itself, to the Father who gave us the community, to the world which he loves. But their accountability and responsibility vary.

Accountability and responsibility—essential elements in the word "obligation"—are not merely a matter of order. The promises made by men at ordination and consecration establish certain degrees of responsibility; and the Church's Constitution and Canons prescribe certain degrees of and procedures for accountability. But these distinctions alone are inconclusive. One of our members has drawn our attention to the considerable difference between the Christian theologian and the independent philosopher of religion. The latter is an individual investigator in a relatively detached position from his subject matter, and it may be said that his commanding obligation is that which belongs to any scholar—to work with scholarly integrity. The theologian indeed shares this obligation (and we include every Christian teacher and preacher in this); but he is also, by definition, within the Church and speaks from the standpoint of the faith of that community. His sources are the Christian revelation, the Bible, and the traditional interpretations these have received in the community of faith. He cannot turn his back on them without ceasing to be a Christian theologian. Yet he is also addressing the culture of his day and his society, and must use its thought forms; and he is therefore always engaged in the work of reinterpretation; and sometimes it may not be clear to him just what is reinterpretation and what is a complete departure from the faith transmitted by the Church.

Again, a discussion of obligation requires that men understand and allow for the personal limitations inherent in our human situation. Human opinions are of value according to the competence of the person concerned to have an opinion about a particular matter. Human opinions differ, inescapably, according to the interests which may be served by holding a given opinion. Most deeply, human opinions reflect the personal needs, gifts, hopes, fears of the person holding them. Many of these matters are not susceptible to human judgment in any way; and certainly, while each of us must be loyal to his opinions, he must also, as a Christian, guard himself against too readily equating his opinions with divine revelation.

We do not attempt any further discussion of these matters. Our thoughts rather turn to three general areas of obligation, which seem to us to affect every member of the Church in his vocation and ministry.

First, there is an obligation to respect one's own personal integrity and the claims of truth—truth as clearly as it can be seen. We cannot see that any member of the Church is exempted from this, in any particular; and in an age of unparalleled restlessness and ferment, this obligation seems to us of paramount importance. Precisely because of the ferment, most of those within the Church are aware of the impulse, nourished by troubled times, to reject all experiments and all innovation. Nor is it possible to avoid, in our sinful condition, another equally seductive invitation in a contrary direction. One man's stake in explosive innovation and anomaly can be just as doctrinaire and inflexible as another man's stake in the "faith once delivered to the saints." Times like ours require all churchmen, of whatever temperament, to commit themselves to steady search for that disciplined self-judgment which respect for integrity and truth require.

One of our advisers had wise counsel for us in this. Bishop Moore said, "In an age of transition like our own, the need for freedom of theological experimentation is necessary. The clergy and the laity as well as the professional theologians should be invited to enter in, at whatever level they are capable, this exciting work of the Spirit, so that they can learn to live with experimental formulations while depending with even increased assurance upon the core of certainties." In this connection, he adds a significant comment, in our opinion, about the role of the bishop in all this. "The bishop's role is the calm enabling of the theological dialogue. They themselves need not phrase experimental formulations, though if they are theologically competent and phrase them in an expressedly experimental fashion, they need not refrain. However, the bishop's principal role would be to encourage inquiry."

We would identify ourselves with both these comments (although recalling periods in the Church's history when bishops generally were called to play a more central part in the experiments themselves). Certainly the encouragement of theological inquiry is a necessary condition of the framing of sound doctrine; and if sound doctrine is to be given us, there must be encouragement and support of freedom of theological experimentation. This freedom is impossible without both respect for integrity and truth, and humble recognition that no man's motives are pure and no man's understanding is complete.

Dr. Vogel wrote movingly of this: ". . . life in Christ, since it embraces the crucifixion and Christ's death to self, should enable the Christian inquirer to be completely open to the truth. If the Christian has died to himself to the degree necessitated by the cross of Christ, he is by that fact completely open to the truth of God's love and of man's perversion of that love because of Christ's cross, the Christian should be the paradigm of nondefensive inquiry."

Second, there is an obligation to the fundamental purposes of the Church itself. When churchmen speak of engagement in the theological and social debate of our time, they cannot speak as men who are neutral in the struggle of human existence. Whatever his station or duties, every Christian speaks from within commitments as to the fundamental purposes the Church was established to serve. It is not a debating society. It is not an academic exercise. The Church is the community of those who have, to some degree, recognized and accepted the love of God who for us men and for our salvation undertook the amazing intervention described in the Gospel. The Church, as we understand it, is the community of those who accept his purposes and mean to be obedient to them. It follows that churchmen may not enter the field of theological and social debate merely as inquirers. They are not neutral about Christ; they are men who have taken sides for him already. Therefore, in any aspect of the Church's engagement in the universal struggle for justice and truth—including the struggle for justice and truth within the institutional Church itself—it is bound to the fundamental purposes of God in sending his Son and in establishing the Christian community.

The end to be served by theological debate within that community is not to prove one's self "right"; it is not to make Christianity respectable or more palatable; it is not to mitigate or minimize the central and shocking decision of faith. The controlling motive in theological debate is obedience to the Church's mission—the urgent mandate that through whatever language Christians use, and whatever actions they take, the love of God may be made clear to men who do not yet know him—indeed even to those who claim they do. Any restatement of the Church's teaching, any expression of the Church's social witness, must be measured by its adequacy to express the love of God made known in Christ.

This obligation includes responsibility for the identity and the continuity of the community itself, for the sake of its mission. That identity is given in the living tradition of the Church; and that tradition, from the beginning, has developed in continual ferment and unrest. Every generation, we suppose, looks back on its predecessors with envy, coveting for itself the supposed certainty which the earlier people enjoyed. But there are few more deceptive reflections on history than this. The tradition of the Church, its continuity, is always, in every generation, a matter of constant disturbance. One need only recall the vehement debate as to Christ's nature, which issued finally in the Nicene Creed, or reflect on the contemporary controversy about "just" or "limited" war, to be aware of the ceaseless anguish through which the Church's tradition is received and transmitted.

Yet there is continuity to the Christian community, given by the successive formulations which find their place in the Church's worship and teaching. Anglicans do not believe that the Church is inexorably bound to any previous formulation of the Church's tradition. There is no infallible propositional statement of the Christian faith, as we understand it. Yet the fact of the Church's continuity, and the successive instruments which have been ministers of that continuity, are matters of great consequence to us. True reinterpretation is given only to those who have first accepted and then respected the continuity of the community from the beginning. No surer witness to this can be cited than the Old Testament prophets who so often led Israel to new obedience and understanding through a renewed allegiance to her ancient faith.

There is no reason why a particular man or woman should not disclaim any responsibility for the community's identity, and leave it. Indeed, even in this rejection of it, he is showing respect for its identity. But if he stays within it, he accepts an obligation to speak and act so as to maintain the identity and the recognized historic continuity of the community. The community, no doubt, is ultimately responsible for determining what constitute the marks of "recognizable continuity" at any given time. But to say that requires that it also be stressed that the community—to assure its own authenticity—must be prepared to learn even from its severest critics to discern new marks and adopt them, leaving with the critics, as long as is humanly possible, the decision to maintain or sever the relationship.

We repeat that in our society, inclined to be skeptical of constituted authority and impatient of tradition, there is likely to be a corresponding enhancement of the personal, the individual, the vivid, even the eccentric. It would be idle to find fault with this; it is a fact. But it is a fact—and this affects all we say about the community and its continuity—that takes for granted precisely the existence of the community without which the individual would lose much of his significance. The rebel against the tradition of the community is still linked to it. This is more than merely a vexing necessity. It is an illumination of the peculiar position of the Christian teacher or apologist. We need hardly add that the community shares this vexation. The community cannot disclaim its own responsibility; it is called to recognize teachers of unpopular doctrine as potential embodiments of its own authentic tradition of protest—to recognize their ministry and to minister to them.

Third, there is an obligation to the Church's unity as discovered and expressed in its worship. This obligation may indeed have a peculiar force in the Anglican tradition. One of the characteristics of that tradition is that it holds unity—at least its own interior unity—to depend not so much on people thinking alike about the "how" of God's action as it does on people doing the Christian things, including the liturgical acts, together. This conviction about unity naturally welcomes the way in which the liturgy, the Prayer Book, serves us as teacher, expresser, transmitter of the Christian tradition. Certainly the Book of Common Prayer has a unique place in our whole system of allegiance. Therefore we would say that, in our opinion, one of the primary obligations of Anglicans is that of respect for the integrity of the Book of Common Prayer itself.

When Episcopalians are questioned about the supposed orthodoxy or heterodoxy of one of their number, their most likely response is to ask whether or not he wishes—sincerely and responsibly—to join them in the celebration of God's being and goodness in the prayers and worship of the Prayer Book. Assuming his integrity, they would not be likely to press the question beyond that point.

No doubt this attitude is often an excuse for sentimentality and vaporous thinking, even for the postponement of fundamental spiritual decisions. No doubt it opens Anglican practice to the risk of mere conformism. Nonetheless, we would still say that the willingness of a person to share in the worship of the Prayer Book with a consenting mind is, for most purposes, an adequate test of his right to claim the privileges of the community.

Such a test implies two responsibilities. One is that of the individual, who must himself decide that he can and should identify himself with the Book of Common Prayer. If he feels he cannot, then he should acknowledge that he can no longer function as an authorized officer or teacher of the Church. But the decision is not one which should be forced on any individual (save in the rare cases of canonical excommunication) but one only to be freely taken by him.

The other responsibility is that of the Church, to recognize and provide for the constant review of its liturgies as central instruments of its renewal. In our Anglican tradition, the Prayer Book is far more than a manual of public worship. It is a principal agent and effective means of maintaining our corporate identity, of our continuity with the whole Body, of our ministry of the tradition of the Church. Therefore it must be a principal frontier of the Church's constant encounter and dialogue with the world. Liturgies rightly are conservative, in that they play so central a part as guardians and transmitters of the tradition. But for exactly those reasons, liturgies are inescapably in the forefront of reformation and renewal. In them the continuing reinterpretation of the tradition is best found; in them is expressed the passionate partisanship of the Church with the world's pain; in them the Christian is confronted by the wholeness of the Faith and its glorious gifts and radical demands, spelled out in terms of his daily concerns. There can be no escape, then, from the Church's corporate obligation to liturgical experiment and change, if it is to keep faith with its Lord.

III. *What is heresy? How should the Church define, detect, and deal with it?*
We are of the opinion that the word "heresy" should be abandoned except in the context of the radical, creative theological controversies in the early formative years of Christian doctrine. In that historical sense, the word serves a useful purpose, describing one side of the controversies which led to the formulation of the great symbols of our tradition. As Dr. Casserley says, "Heretical formulations were not at first intended to be heretical, but were proposed as serious definitions of apostolic faith. It was something almost akin to theological intuition, or the instinct of the Church for Christian truth, that led to the condemnation of the

heresies as dangerous and misleading perversions of truth which would prove in the long run fatal to what we may call Christian existence, to the characteristic faith, hope, life, and worship of the Christian man."

But the word has now accumulated a multitude of pejorative overtones. It too often conjures up a picture of a static fortress of propositional theology that requires to be, and can be, defended by appeal to the letter of a theological statement. It presumes to a measure of theological prejudgment which is inappropriate to the mature Christian community. It too often implies a set of theological categories unconditioned by their historical and cultural period. It presupposes, by appeal to literal statements, a form of the Church which no longer exists. It takes for granted that there is a clear limitation on the permissible area of theological experimentation. It is a weapon far too easily found in the hands of those fearful of any change.

If the word and concept of "heresy" is to fall into disuse, what should take its place? Is any alternative needed? If it is, what kind of process should it refer to?

Our reflection as a committee, as we consider it, seems to have led us toward two poles of thought about this. One is the necessity of a living community to guard its own *wholeness* of life—its balanced integrity, its ability to maintain its own nature. The other is its parallel need to be a *living* community—to show, by its supportive attitude toward experiment and reformulation, the unmistakable signs of growth and health.

We recall, for example, how Dr. Knox led us to understand the Church's need to reject certain kinds of teaching, not because they were "wrong," in verbal comparison with some written formula, but because they clearly threatened the life of the community itself. He began by speaking of "teaching which strikes at the existential reality of the Church's distinctive life." He continued: "Since this reality can be expressed only in the terms in which it has been expressed from the beginning—the rich, concrete terms of the New Testament and of the Church's devotional literature—terms like the love of God, his truth and grace; his self-revealing action in the history to which the Church belongs and of which its own creation is the center; the redemption in Christ, human and divine, crucified and risen, a redemption from both the guilt of sin and its power; the new life in the Spirit, rich in joy and peace and hope, the earnest of an everlasting inheritance—since these are the Church's characteristic and indispensable terms, any teaching which denies the objective truth being expressed in them, empties them of their precious and perennial existential meaning, and leaves them, not rich, inexhaustible symbols of a transcendent and very present reality, but mere shells reminding men of an earlier faith—such teaching is, I should say, heretical. It strikes not at the opinions of churchmen, whether singly or in council assembled, but at the very existence of the Church itself. It should be recognized, perhaps, not as heresy at all but as unacknowledged apostasy; it is not a deviant way of understanding an 'article of faith'; it is a denial of faith itself and a betrayal of the Church as the community of faith."

On the other side we were impressed by Bishop Robinson's vigorous charge: "The task of the Church is to encourage the movement of prophetic inquiry and criticism, to listen to it, to test, acknowledge, and act upon whatever in it is of God. And the primary way in which the Church encourages is by giving the maximum possible freedom—both in the conditions and security which it affords to its thinkers and agents and in its refusal to suppress voices however uncomfortable or embarrassing. These may indeed be genuinely embarrassing (as, equally, may be the voices of those who are theologically or socially reactionary). Moreover, there must be the fullest opportunity for those who think them inadequate or wrong to state the contrary opinion.

"All exploration, whether in the theological or the social field, involves the risk, indeed the certainty, of mistakes. But it is at least arguable, from the study of church history, that more damage has almost always been done in the long run by the suppression of opinion than by any error given rein by freedom. At any rate the Church must act on the assumption, till proved otherwise, that freedom will in any instance be less harmful than the attempt to curb it."

Those two statements, from two of our advisers, suggest the polarity to which we refer. On the surface, this polarity could be described as simply one more example of the timeless conflict of authority and freedom. But this does not seem to us to be an adequate conclusion. The tension is not between two principles or two logical systems or two sets of values. The Church is a living community—an organism rather than an organization, to use a familiar distinction. Its problems are those of such a community, not merely of abstractions. The choices it must make, and the alternatives among which it must choose, are those of men and women whose very life as persons is involved in their choices.

Therefore we feel all the more strongly that the response of the Church to the novel and the unconventional cannot be the static process suggested by "heresy" but, rather, one which speaks clearly of the living, personal choices involved. At this point another of our advisers, Father Murray, reinforced our feelings by writing of "a distinction I like to make . . . between adventurous answers, which may well be mistaken, and hardened positions which deserve to be called errors. The former are an affair of deficient intelligence; the latter, of deficiency in what can only be called good will. Errors in faith are a matter of will."

This distinction emphasizes exactly what we feel needs emphasis, that the problem we are wrestling with cannot be reduced to a mere contest of words, but must be seen and approached in terms of the choices men find they must make.

Father Murray then continued in this vein, leading us one more step along the way: "Today there are abroad all sorts of tendencies, currents of thought, climates of opinion. And many uncertainties attend the necessary business of a renewal of the personal structures of conscience and the further business of a reform of the objective expressions of the Christian faith. We all live in an unbelieving world. And a 'credibility gap' has opened between the doctrines and structures of the Church and the sheer experience of the world as it is. The truths of the Church and the forms of her life are supposed to interpret the experience of human life and to give it some saving structure. But is this happening? Many say no, and not without reason. This answer seems to have lain behind John XXIII's distinction between the 'substance' of Christian faith and the 'forms' of its expression. The distinction could be given a too-simplistic meaning, as if only words were at stake. But it points in the right direction, toward a task we must take firmly in hand. We shall do the task badly, of course. There will be lots of 'mistakes,' but they are readily dealt with, since they involve no will to error. This latter thing is the danger. How to avoid it? I think the corrective is a will to community—of thought and love. The Christian community is not in error, whatever mistakes it may make."

We would agree with Father Murray's warning against an oversimple distinction between "substance" and "form"; but we also agree that the direction is right, pointing not to barren verbal quarrels but "to community—of thought and love." It is only within that community, acting as such a community should act, fulfilling in its relationships the promise implicit in its own being, that the answer to the aching tensions of Christian liberty and unity can be found.

The proposals we are about to make reflect this dynamic, organic view of the Church. The Church's concern is neither to find some blander word to substitute for "heresy" nor to devise some less disruptive methods of detecting and trying "heretics." Its concern must rather be to give new respect and vitality to every reconciling, healing impulse of a body determined to maintain its own wholeness. When Christians are moved to turn to judicial remedies, to trials and punishment, they must do so only when there is, clearly and finally, no alternative left except the death of the community itself. We shall underline this point in a moment. But let it now speak of the prime characteristic of the Church as of any living organism, that it must fight to the end to hold in its own balanced life every element, every person, which belongs to its fullness. Where the organic unity of the Church is broken, the first search must be not for the legal remedy but for that failure within the community itself which permitted the breach to happen. Until every possible step in reconciling love has been taken, we have no right to admit defeat and adopt defeat's harsh weapons.

Our intent will be clear, we hope, in our proposals. We think that only rarely is it appropriate to deal with matters of theological or social teaching in the same terms as those with which the Church may properly deal with what the canon describes as "crime or immorality." There may be such instances. We are not unmindful that, in Father Murray's words, "There is a distinction between adventurous answers . . . and hardened positions which deserve to be called errors"; and we would agree with him that the latter are instances of a "deficiency in what can only be called good will. Errors in faith are a matter of will."

"Will" may not be a fashionable word or a completely satisfactory one. But it suggests what we feel needs to be said, in this matter—that the Church should not be, and does not want to be, easily betrayed into dealing with honest exploration and experiment as if they were sins. They may be sinful. It may be that a given man or woman deliberately chooses to wreck the Church which has given him identity and foul the nest where he was born. In dealing with such pathology, the extreme measures of the law may be justified. But it should be most difficult to reach the point of such measures; and it should be practically impossible to apply them, except where the responsible choice of the offender is clear.

What does the Church need, where must it change, if this primary ministry of love is to have room and time to work for the saving of the living community? We do not know all the answers to this question. We have suggested some we feel of real significance, in the first section of our report. But we are still convinced that the Church needs to study its processes and structures of reconciliation quite as intently as it now studies its systems of law and administration.

When all the strategies of reconciliation seem to have been exhausted, and the Church finds itself finally bound to take official legal action, we suggest that there are still unexplored alternatives to the procedure which deals with controversial views by providing for the trial of a man for "holding and teaching publicly or privately and advisedly, any doctrine contrary to that held by this Church."

The first alternative which should be explored is that of a procedure for clarifying the relationship between the disputed views and Christian truth as understood by the Church. Such a procedure might lead to a statement of the "disassociation" of the Church from particular teachings or actions, without judgment of the motivations or characters of the persons who said or did them.

In the case of a bishop, the House of Bishops would doubtless be the appropriate body to make such a statement; in the case of a priest or deacon, it would appropriately lie in the discretion of the diocesan authority. In either case, the procedure would need to be guarded by the applicable safeguards of due process. Notice should be given of the intention to consider issuing such a statement, to those whose views or actions are concerned as well as to those involved in the process. Time should be allowed to those whose views are questioned for the preparation and presentation of any reasons why such a statement should not be adopted. Provision should be made for appropriate and informed discussion of the issues. Certainly the canonical legislation required to permit such a procedure must clearly establish the equitable grounds on which alone such a statement should be made. The intent of this proposal is to give the Church an alternative method of dealing with doctrine—spoken or acted out—which is clearly irreconcilable with the Church's teaching, without rejection of the person himself. In our eyes, this procedure commends itself as an expression of pastoral responsibility and love far more characteristic of the Church, and more appropriate to the living community which it is, than the more drastic procedure of trial.

Such a statement of disassociation clearly depends for its effectiveness on its acceptance as a legitimate exercise of collegial pastoral concern. Where such a statement were to fail of its purpose, then alternative procedures may well be necessary.

One such, often mentioned in this connection, is that of "censure." The word is not now in the Church's official vocabulary and we do not argue for it. But we are agreed that if "censure" (as the word is commonly used) were to enter into the Church's procedures in dealing with recalcitrant problems, two things must be unequivocally clear. First, a judgment of "censure" ought never be applied to statements of theological or moral opinion or teaching, but only to acts—perhaps specifically only to acts which openly and notoriously violate essential elements of order and decency, or subvert the essential processes of the community. Second, no such judgment should ever be made except after every safeguard of due process has been provided. Canonical provision would include protections parallel to those specified in the proposal of "disassociation."

We speak of "censure" in this report not because we think well of it as a way of dealing with doctrinal matters but because we don't, and yet are aware that some do consider it a remedy for bad doctrine, and that there may be a danger of allowing an undefined, unofficial and unguarded practice to creep into the Church's life. If this is a danger, then the protection against it is to make it unmistakably plain that the Church does not "censure" people for their opinions but only for deliberate acts which violate the customary standards of Christian and civilized behavior; and that even such elementary rebukes may not be given save after due process.

Somewhat oblique to this is still another procedure which may call for exploration—that of the dissolution of the tie of a bishop with his diocese. An appropriate procedure is established by Canon 45 for the dissolution of the relationship of a rector with his parish. It is not inconceivable that the provision of a comparable procedure for bishops and dioceses might call for exploration. If the Church were to provide for such a procedure we feel that the initiative should lie with the Standing Committee of the diocese concerned. They should bring their concern to the Presiding Bishop, who then should act only with the advice and consent of a group of ten bishops designated either by him or by the House of Bishops. Again, appropriate canonical and perhaps constitutional provision would be required; and it would be of special importance that every safeguard be given the bishop in question, as well as the Standing Committee, to avoid the clear dangers inherent in this process.

Only as a last resort, we feel, should recourse be had to the procedures of a trial for "holding and teaching publicly or privately and advisedly, any doctrine contrary to that held by this Church." In this connection we feel bound to say that the present canonical provisions—as they relate to a bishop at any rate—are ill-conceived and irresponsible. For one thing, they put into the hands of three bishops the power to invoke the whole portentous machinery of the Church's law. For another, they take away from the people most concerned—the bishops—an opportunity even to say whether the trial itself is justified. In both instances, they encourage the abdication of the reconciling processes of pastoral responsibility long before the possibilities of those processes have even been explored.

We feel that it is probably inescapable that provision be made for such final and definitive action. We also feel it should be made as difficult as possible. Specifically we would propose that the present canons be amended to require that at least ten bishops must join in the presentation; that a supporting brief be filed concurrently with the Presiding Bishop; that ample notice be given the bishop charged, and adequate time be allowed for him to prepare an answer to the presentment; and that the consent of at least two-thirds of the bishops qualified to vote in the House of Bishops be given before the proceedings may go forward to trial. This vote should not replace the present requirement of Canon 58, Sec. 5 as to the approval required before sentence is imposed.

IV. *In summary, we say:*

God makes men free. It does not behoove His Church to try to hobble their minds or inhibit their search for new insights into truth. The Church not only should tolerate but should actively encourage free and vigorous theological debate, application of the Gospel to social wrongs, restatement of Christian doctrines to make them more intelligible to contemporary minds, and experimentation with new forms of worship and service. Any risks the Church may run by fostering a climate of genuine freedom are minor compared to the dangers it surely will encounter from any attempts at suppression, censorship or thought control. The Church can command the respect of modern man only if it has the confidence, courage and honesty to test its faith in the free marketplace of ideas. We believe that the historic Christian faith can stand that test, and are not afraid to have it subjected to the most searching scrutiny. To that end, we recommend the establishment of institutes and seminars and provisions for new training which will enable laymen and clergymen to participate more positively in theological discourse. We recommend a new design for meetings of the bishops to give more opportunity for theological discussion. We recommend the formation of a standing commission on the teaching of the Church.

While we affirm the right of every man to choose what he will believe without any kind of coercion whatever, we also assert the right of the Church to maintain its distinctive identity and continuity as a community of faith centered around the historic revelation of God in Christ. Although we certainly do not uphold a narrow verbal orthodoxy which requires a person to give literal assent to some particular formulation of doctrine, we do believe that if an individual finds himself unable, in good conscience, to identify with the living tradition of the Church, reflected in the Bible, the Creeds and, especially for Anglicans, in the liturgy of the Book of Common Prayer, he should as a matter of personal integrity voluntarily remove himself from any position in which he may be taken to be an official spokesman for the whole community.

Without censuring or condemning any individual for his ideas, the Church may find it necessary on occasion to disassociate itself publicly from theological views which it considers to be seriously subversive of essential Christian truths. But this should be done in a positive and constructive way, and with scrupulous fairness to those concerned, by explaining what the Church does believe. The best answer to bad doctrine is good doctrine. "Heresy trials" are anachronistic. Although the Church may feel that it must maintain a last-resort power to deal juridically with bishops or priests who publicly engage in persistent and flagrant contradiction of its essential witness, we strongly recommend that initiation of this process be made extremely difficult. To that end we propose a drastic revision of canon law, to insure that no charge of deviant teaching may be put forward by only three bishops, and that no such charge may proceed to the stage of a formal trial without the advance concurrence of two-thirds of the House of Bishops.

We do not believe that there are many who willfully set out to destroy the Christian community. We are prepared to say that there are many ideas and speculations which fail to do justice to the acts by which God gave us the Church in the beginning. We agree that it is essential that the Church make its own judgments as to those ideas and speculations. But in all this, we pray that the Church may not act as less than what it is—the community of those who know, have accepted, and mean to show the love of God and His supporting grace for all who mean to bear honest witness for Him.

Journal of General Convention, 1967, Appendix, 6, 6.5-6.24. (Excerpt)

146.

Coalition for the Apostolic Ministry: A Declaration of Principle, 1975

The Coalition for the Apostolic Ministry (CAM) was organized in late 1972. It dissolved after the General Convention of 1976 voted to ordain women to the priesthood and the episcopate. There were irregular ordinations of women to the priesthood prior to the approval for such ordinations by General Convention. On July 29, 1975, eleven women deacons were irregularly ordained to the priesthood at the Church of the Advocate, Philadelphia, by Daniel Corrigan, retired Suffragan Bishop of Colorado, Robert DeWitt, retired Bishop of Pennsylvania, Edward Welles, retired Bishop of West Missouri, and Antonio Ramos, Bishop of Costa Rica. On September 7, 1975, George Barrett, retired Bishop of Rochester, irregularly ordained four women to the priesthood at the Church of St. Stephen and the Incarnation, Washington, D.C. The following is a basic statement of CAM's beliefs.

The Coalition for the Apostolic Ministry Believes That
1. The Episcopal Church Has No Ministry Of Its Own.
    The faith and order of the Anglican Communion are the faith and order of the Catholic Church. We have no authority to change that order by admitting women to the episcopate and priesthood without a consensus of historic Christendom.
2. The Word Of God In Holy Scripture Speaks Only Of A Male Priesthood.
    The sexuality of Jesus is no accident; it is the flesh of his incarnation by God's own act. This male image is continued by Christ's choice of male apostles and their choice of apostolic men to succeed them. This cannot be dismissed as "cultural conditioning" without denying that God prepared a chosen— without disparaging the Jewishness of Jesus.
3. The Holy Spirit In Christian Tradition Reveals Only A Male Priesthood.
    The persisting tradition of 2000 years in Church order

reveals the mind of the Spirit for the future of the ministry of the Church. Christian priesthood has consistently been male through cultures with varying sexual patterns. To obey the Spirit we must be faithful to this history.

4. Jesus Christ The One And Only Priest.

The priests of the church have no priesthood of their own; they participate in Jesus' priesthood. Ordination is a gift of the Holy Spirit which bestows this participation. It is not the creation of the Church to do with as it will. It is to be given only to those congruous with the example of Jesus Christ, the authority of Holy Scripture, and the witness of Christian tradition. There is no right to ordination.

The Living Church (September 14, 1975), 7.

147.

Carter Heyward, A Priest Forever, 1976

Carter Isabel Heyward (August 22, 1945–   ) was one of the eleven women ordained to the priesthood on July 29, 1974, at the Church of the Advocate, Philadelphia, prior to General Convention's authorization for the ordination of women to the priesthood and the episcopate in 1976. She is now professor of theology at the Episcopal Theological School, Cambridge. In this selection she discusses her identity as a woman priest and the gifts that women offer the Church through ordained ministry.

In a society and a Church in which woman has been put into a place out of which she cannot move, any effort on her part to burst out of this place will be considered strange or abnormal. Those invested with institutional authority are likely to get their backs up and balk defensively at her efforts. For such a woman is a threat to both men and women who have heavy investment in maintaining the present order.

And the threat is not imaginary. It is real. As women enter into new ecclesiastical roles, with responsibilities not only for decision making and leadership in heretofore male arenas of activity, but also for new *symbol-building*, the present order *will* change. All roles, those of both men and women, will change. Nothing will remain the same. We are agents of transformation.

Our transforming power is not inherent to our gender, for we are simply human, like our brothers. Our power lies in our having been born, nurtured, and acculturated into a corporate symbol: a symbol not necessarily of "femininity," but rather a symbol of *difference*. Together, we offer a difference to the Church, a difference that includes the corporate experience of exclusion, and the particular experiences of being daughter, wife, mother, lover, and the various other roles we have played.

I do not offer any peculiar brand of "softness" or "sweetness," "seductiveness" or "saintliness" to the Episcopal Church. I offer myself—my softness, my toughness, my sweetness, my bitterness, my seductiveness, my honesty, my saintliness, and my sinfulness to the Church. As a woman, together with my sisters, I offer a difference—a different ethic, derived from collective exclusion, which I will help build on behalf of other "outsiders"; a different visual, audible, sensory image I will help create; a different theology I will help shape; a different priesthood into which I have been ordained; indeed, a different Episcopal Church, as one manifestation of catholic Christendom.

People seem amazed that so much turmoil has spun off the Philadelphia ordinations. But why? The Church is in throes of rebirth. An old order is passing away. The process of renewal is always denied by a few, resisted by many, unwelcomed by most, and chaotic to all.

The wisest among us will move with the currents of the chaos, not resisting them, but rather letting ourselves be washed in time onto new shores. We will not recognize the shores, but they will be our home. We can be then amazed appropriately by God's capacity for recreation and offering of new life to us, God's confused people.

Carter Heyward, *A Priest Forever* (New York: Harper & Row, 1976), 32-33.
    (Excerpt)

148.

Statement of Conscience, 1977

"A Statement of Conscience" was adopted by the House of Bishops on October 3, 1977, at it meeting at Port St. Lucie, Florida. This statement affirms freedom of conscience for those who support and for those who oppose the ordination of women to the priesthood and episcopate. The ideals of this statement were questioned in later years.

The decision of General Convention to authorize the ordination of women to the priesthood and episcopate has raised anew problems of the Christian's obligations in cases of conscience.

(1) For those earlier opposed to this decision, unable genuinely to affirm it or unable to accept it, the problems arise in a special form. Are such persons to regard themselves as disloyal Episcopalians or to be regarded by others as disloyal if they do not implement or participate in implementing that decision?

(a) It may be claimed that they are bound by the canon (III.9.1) because the suggestions of a conscience clause was by many felt unnecessary at Minneapolis. Yet much of the discussion at that time centered around protecting a bishop's conscience, and it was asserted that a bishop cannot be forced to ordain anyone. Now, however, it has become more clear that the issues involve clergy and lay persons, not just bishops. Furthermore, the bishop's possible involvement includes more than only the matter of ordaining or not ordaining. Those who are opposed to such ordinations or are uneasy about their rightness require greater assurance of respect for conscience.

(b) It is oversimplifying to demand obedience to the canon just as one does for every other canon. This particular issue involves judgment on matters of deepest theological import, such as one's interpretation of Scripture and the authority of Scripture, the nature and force of Tradition, as well as the nature of the Church and of the Anglican Communion. The issue is much more clearly subject to problems of conscience than, for example, a canon on the Church Pension Fund or the number of joint commissions.

(c) The meaning of a law involves not only the wording of the legislation, but also the intent of the legislation. Did General Convention intend (1) to make certain that dioceses prepared to ordain women were assured that they had the approval of the Episcopal Church in going ahead or (2) to require such action even by dioceses not yet prepared to act nor persuaded that they could rightly do so? By the nature of the case absolute proof is impossible, but majority opinion would seem to support the first understanding. At any rate there are adequate grounds for seeing at least sufficient doubt about the intent of the legislation, so as to inhibit insistence that women priests be accepted by all and at once.

(d) The basic Anglican position has been to insist upon that which is clearly discerned from Scripture interpreted by the Tradition of the undivided Church, and enlightened by Spirit-guided reason, while refraining from the imposition of that which cannot be so demonstrated. Some would claim that Scripture and Tradition forbid the ordination of women, but General Convention did not accept that assertion. Yet many believe the rightness of such ordinations has not from these basic sources been clearly demonstrated. One is not a disloyal Anglican if he or she abstains from implementing the decision or continues to be convinced it was in error.

(2) Those convinced of the rightness of the ordination of women are spared the particular problem of conscience just sketched. They may, however, when they find themselves in the minority in a diocese or parish, be made to feel much the same way. The action of General Convention and even some of the points listed above can reassure them. Yet they are faced, as are those of opposing views, with the burden of living in this Communion at a time when Episcopalians disagree on matters of great importance. How as Christians do we deal with such circumstances?

(3) For all persons wrestling with the implications of these decisions, the following observations may be helpful:

(a) We respect the conscience of others, neither despising nor condemning those whose convictions differ from our own. St. Paul was sensitive to a grave matter of conscience when he said, concerning meats offered to idols, "The man who eats must not hold in contempt the man who does not, and he who does not eat must not pass judgment on the man who does; for God has accepted him" (Rom. 14:3).

(b) We avoid any kind of pressure which might lead a fellow Christian to contravene his or her conscience; for it is evil for anyone to do what is believed to be wrong, whether that belief be right or mistaken (Rom. 14:20). Every Christian has a charge to perceive and prevent any wrong pressure, but since episcopacy serves as the principal ministerial symbol and means of unity in the Church, a bishop has a special responsibility. Such pressures as social ostracism, black-listing for diocesan positions, threats of denying consideration for another post, the displeasure of superiors, and so on may lead to an offense against conscience which is an offense against Christ (I Cor. 8:12).

(c) We see an informed conscience for ourselves and for others. The gift of true discrimination in moral decisions is an object of prayer for the Christian (Phil 1:10), and we dare not assume that our first opinion is the final answer. A vital part of this desire for an informed conscience is a willingness to seek that corporate understanding of the Faith which is possible only for the Church as a whole (Eph. 3:18).

(d) We hold fast to the Anglican tradition which seeks to distinguish between what is required or not required of believers. Anglican comprehensiveness is not just trying to be gentlemen, not weak so-called "tolerance," and certainly not numbers-seeking. Rather it is this distinction between what must be believed by a Christian and what cannot be clearly demonstrated from basic Christian sources, together with the awareness that the Spirit leads the Church into further penetration of the Truth (John 14:26, 16:13). Since Jesus Christ is the Truth, there can be no adding to the Truth, but there is a promise of deepened understanding of that Truth as the Spirit guides the Church. It is tempting to cry to others as to ourselves, "The Church—love it or leave it." Yet to say it hastily assumes that we already know fully what it is, much less what the Church will be like when brought at last to "nothing less than the full stature of Christ" (Eph. 4:13). Leaving this Communion or forcing others to leave interferes with the process of searching together for that fuller penetration of the truth.

(e) We need the precious gift of patience. St. Paul was rather confident of his theological insight and was not a very permissive man by nature. He could write, however, "Let us then keep to this way of thinking, those of us who are mature. If there is any point on which you think differently, this also God will make plain to you." (Phil. 3:15).

(f) We need to trust that our fellow Christians are indeed seeking the truth, even if we feel they could find it faster by just asking us. Yet even when it is hard to trust in their seeking, we still may trust in the power of the Spirit to enlighten us all. For we do have our Lord's promise that "the Holy Spirit will guide us into all Truth."

. . . .

(4) In the light of all this and in keeping with our intention at Minneapolis, we affirm that no Bishop, Priest, Deacon or Lay Person should be coerced or penalized in any manner, nor suffer any canonical disabilities as a result of his or her conscientious objection to or support of the 65th General Convention's action with regard to the ordination of women to the priesthood or episcopate.

Journal of General Convention, 1979, B193-B195. Adopted at Special Meeting of the House of Bishops, Port St. Lucie, Florida, October 3, 1977.

149.

Edmond Browning, Address to General Convention, 1985

Edmond Lee Browning (March 11, 1929–   ) was the sixth Bishop of Hawaii, July 8, 1976–January 11, 1986. He became the twenty-fourth Presiding Bishop on January 1, 1986. This statement was made shortly after his election as Presiding Bishop. It identifies key themes for his ministry as Presiding Bishop and for the Episcopal Church.

Dear Friends, our membership through Baptism gives us as diverse a family as any in Christendom. I believe that diversity is our strength as each of us is challenged never to fall into the complacency of partisanship.

We Episcopalians know how to stir the pot when things begin to get somewhat dull. In this ability to sometimes, oft times, stir one another up, we find our faith re-vitalized and challenged and the Gospel of Christ more truly alive.

I have today invited you, all of you, to share the diversity of views, of hopes, of expectations for the mission of this Church. I want to be very clear—this Church of ours is open to all—there will be no outcasts—the convictions and the hopes of all will be honored.

Let me change the pace for a moment. In the several interviews I've had during the past 48 hours, one of the subjects that has been constant was the relationship between the pastoral and the prophetic — as though they were mutually exclusive. For me there could be nothing further from the truth. There is no question in my mind — however uncomfortable at times it becomes — the Gospel of Jesus Christ requires a pastoral ministry which leads to prophetic witness and action. And I will pledge to you the exercise of both!

This leads me to say that for you I seek to be a listener, an enabler of the ministry of the whole Church, to be pastorally sensitive *and* to speak out unequivocally on the issues of justice and peace.

Edmond Browning, "Address to General Convention," 1985. (Excerpt)

CHAPTER EIGHTEEN

The Evolution of the Episcopal Identity

Introduction

The Episcopal identity can be elusive because Episcopalians resist over-defining things. They tend not to be dogmatic, and seldom use rigid categories or definitions of faith. They include catholic, protestant, evangelical, charismatic, traditional, liberal, conservative, and renewed members of the church. All the labels and categories apply truly to the Episcopal Church, but no single label or descriptive word can tell the whole story. The church is diverse and changing, but still rooted in tradition. Members of the church are secure enough to claim the truth where it is found. They are open to the future and what it may bring. They can be trendy, but only up to a point. They will not finally accept anything just because it is new. The church balances a variety of tendencies and styles in a way that can be very open to discovery. Sometimes diversity can be confusing. There may be no simple answer for people who ask, "What does the Episcopal Church really believe?" There is room for a variety of perspectives. Episcopalians do not require belief in a party line or denominational creed. They can disagree and still pray together. Church members are learning to listen to each other and work for consensus. They respect authority enough to share it. The Episcopal Church is not always efficient. In practice, the church relies more on the test of time than official pronouncements by the leadership. The church gives attention to the issues of today without being possessed by them. Episcopalians remember the lessons of their tradition, but know that there are more lessons to learn.

150.

Thomas H. Vail, Further Suggestions on Church Comprehensiveness, 1871

Thomas Hubbard Vail (October 21, 1812–October 6, 1889) was consecrated the first Bishop of Kansas on December 15, 1864. His book, The Comprehensive Church *(1841), anticipated the Chicago-Lambeth Quadrilateral.*

The ground assumed and defended is, that as the visible church is, in the scriptural representations, and in the nature of things, one, so her entire outward system of Ritual, including Formularies, and also her Canonical Legislation, should be so arranged as to embody, and make it possible to embody, in one communion and fellowship, all the sincere disciples of Christ, who, by the one baptism, are members of the one Holy Catholic Church visible. In other words, the basis of Church Comprehensiveness should be only that which is essential to be believed and to be done, as touching faith and morals, while in regard to all things non-essential, large liberty and toleration should be permitted, both as to matters of opinion and as to matters of ceremonial order, within the unity of this grand comprehension. The nature of the church, abstractly considered with reference to its component parts, and the ends for which it is constituted, demands this. And the history of its primitive construction and outgrowth, as developed under the guidance of Apostolic inspiration, and as still perpetuated in a few of its important principles and fundamental precedents, is in accordance with the same position. An illustration of such a system, as requiring only essentials, is given in the form of the Apostles' Creed, and in the Vows of Baptism, which are the only conditions of admission to church membership, both of which substantially are historically traceable to the times of the New Testament inspiration, and thus show us the mind of God in this matter. The question arises: If, in any particular, our present church system is not in harmony with this example, are we prepared so to modify it that it shall correspond with such a Divine model? Or, are we yet too narrow, and too little in sympathy with God's forbearance?

Thomas H. Vail, "Further Suggestions on Church Comprehensiveness," in *Papers on the Proposition of "the Nine Bishops"* (Philadelphia: Claxton, Remsen & Haffelfinger, 1871), 79-80. (Excerpt)

605

151.

H. Boone Porter, Then Cometh the End, 1960

Harry Boone Porter (January 10, 1923–) was Associate Professor of Ecclesiastical History at Nashotah House when this selection was written. He was editor of The Living Church, *1977-1990, and has published a number of books on liturgics. In this selection, Porter summarizes the results of his study of the Christian experience of Sunday.*

ALL things in the Christian life are carried out in faith, hope, and charity, looking forward to the glory that is yet to be revealed. This is pre-eminently true of the Sunday gathering of the faithful. On the Eighth Day, the perpetual First Day of a new age, this view of eternity comes into focus. Then, in a particular sense, our heavenly citizenship is clearly and unequivocally affirmed. This of course is why attendance at the Eucharist has been a crime both in ancient Rome and in modern concentration camps. Here we renew our allegiance each week to the Jerusalem that is above, here we are given some vision of the hope of our calling.

On Sunday this is given to us not merely in homiletic exhortations to belief or catechetical declarations of the faith, but in the actual living experience of a full and comprehensive worship. The Scripture readings come to us, as St. Augustine somewhere says, 'as letters from home'. The preacher speaks as one who has discovered, in living a life consecrated to God, the certainty of the truth that is in Jesus. In corporate intercessory prayer, we share in the actual working of that power whereby Jesus is able even to subdue all things unto himself. In the offertory Christians, as a priestly people, present to the Creator tokens of his creation that is being renewed in Christ. In the eucharistic Thanksgiving, all of these things are summed up in the recounting of the victory of the Son of God, who even now deigns to invite his people to eat and drink with him. At the same time the faithful perform that sharing with the poor which is the promised work of those for whom the Kingdom has been prepared. In doing all of these things we learn the reality of the Holy Ghost who is the pledge of our inheritance, the Spirit of the new age inaugurated in Christ, and our foretaste of the glory to come.

The experience of these acts makes heaven meaningful to the believer; it makes the Christian hope a significant and positive force in the ordering of life. The heavenly citizenship becomes something that can be seriously practised; the Christian goal becomes something toward which daily existence may in fact be oriented. The worshipper can go home to say grace over his Sunday dinner with the knowledge that earthly life and all that sustains it has become holy in Christ.

He can enjoy the company of his relatives and neighbours for the rest of the day with the assurance that such fellowship has a meaning in God's eternal plan. He can endeavour to cheer the ungrateful, the ailing, and the forlorn, for he has the perception of what is infinitely precious behind the dull eye or unsmiling mouth. He can drive through the countryside on Sunday afternoon, or survey the spires and bridges of the city, and be certain that in his good time God will gather an unperishing harvest from the field and vineyard of this earth.

It is in the knowledge of these things that the Christian life is lived; that Christian work is accomplished; and that the Christian death is died. For this God has given us his Day: unto this Day there is no night.

H. B. Porter, *The Day of Light: The Biblical and Liturgical Meaning of Sunday* (Greenwich, Conn.: Seabury Press, 1960), 81-82. (Excerpt)

152.

Virginia Hudson, Etiquette at Church, 1962

Virginia Cary Hudson was ten years old in 1904 when she wrote down some reflections of the world and the Church for her teacher in an Episcopal boarding school. O Ye Jigs & Juleps!, which provides a whimsical view of the liturgy through the eyes of a child, was assembled by her daughter, Virginia Cleveland Mayne.

Before I go into the house of the Lord with praise and thanksgiving, I lift up mine eyes unto the town clock from whence cometh the time to see if I am late. It is not etiquette to be late.

Do not hop, skip, jump or slide in the church vestibule. Tip. Tip all the way to your seat. Be sure and do not sit in other people's pews. Jesus wouldn't care, but other people would. Paying money makes it yours to sit in. The first thing you do is kneel down and thank the Lord for your mother and your father and your breakfast and your lunch and your dinner and your lovely wallpaper and your new pink garter belt. Then you can sit and look around just a little bit. Don't turn around and look. That is not etiquette.

Kneel when you pray, stand when you sing, and sit when you listen. On communion Sunday take off your right glove and leave it in your pew. Don't wait until you get to the rail and the Body and the Blood comes around. Don't try to drink up all of the wine. That is not etiquette. Leave some for the other people.

Never punch people in church, or giggle or cross your legs. Crossing your legs is as bad as scratching or walking in front of people or chewing gum or saying damn. Don't lose your place in the prayer book. Bow for the cross and for the Father, Son and Holy Ghost. When the choir marches back to the Vestry room and the minister calls out goodbye to the Lord until next Sunday, then you can speak to people.

. . . .

Etiquette is what you are doing and saying when people are looking and listening. What you are thinking is your business. Thinking is not etiquette. Hallelujah, thine the glory. Revive us again.

P.S. If you want to stay awake in church, go to bed early Saturday night. You can't go the Altar rail until you are 12. That is God's etiquette. You can't put on perfume until you are 16. That is Leesville etiquette. After you are confirmed your sponsors in Baptism can't be blamed for what you do. You are on your own then and if the devil gets you, it is your own fault and serves you just right.

Amen and the Lord have mercy.

Virginia Cary Hudson, *O Ye Jigs & Juleps!* (New York: Macmillan Company, 1962), 6-7. (Excerpt)

153.

House of Bishops, Pastoral Letter, 1964

This Pastoral Letter was issued by the House of Bishops on October 23, 1964. It stresses the balance of internal life and external ministry. The reference to Mutual Responsibility and Interdependence shows a new perspective on the Church's mission. MRI emerged at the Anglican Congress held in 1963 at Toronto.

I

First, the church, by its nature, is a worshipping body, living to God and not to itself. We are not self-contained, but a body open to God's Word in Scripture, singing his praises, confessing sins to him, and living by his Grace. This living to God is what makes us "a royal priesthood, a holy nation, a peculiar people." This is the source of our inspiration and renewal. If we have not joy, hope, and power from God; if we are not freed by him from earth's fears, hatreds, divisions, and hopelessness, how can we truly serve? If we are not put to rights by worship, how can God use us to put the world to rights?

We live, then, not to ourselves, but to Christ; praying that the Holy Spirit may give to us wisdom, unity, zeal, and love; praying that we may be what we are, a body living by God and for God, and never, never, a self-contained club, complacent in success, or filled with worldly despair over adversity. In the brave words of Bishop Lichtenberger, we are "joyful now," serving God with "a quiet mind, a ready will, and a merry heart." "With a joyful heart," said he, "we live hopefully in the world." Without God, we cannot please God; living to ourselves, we perish spiritually by ourselves.

II

Secondly, when we face God in worship, he faces us back to the world he created and loves. There are two conversions: one as we turn from self to God; the other as he turns us back to the world. The Creator has a will for his world, and poured forth his love for it in Christ, who taught that the second commandment is like the first. And so the Prayer Book prays in the world, for the world; it prays for the whole state of Christ's Church, for education, for justice, for government, for the home, for peace, for all sorts and conditions of men.

It is this turning to the world which saves Church life from being trivial; for, be it remembered, whenever we do not act in our communities as we pray, men come to believe that we are not related to life, that faith has no important consequences, and that the Church is not relevant to the world's joys and pain. Once again, "the Church that lives to itself, will die by itself."

The Church, as it lives for God and his world, must consider the new nature of the world, and read aright the signs of the times. Of the many marks of the new age, perhaps the most all-embracing is the massive fact of rapid change, leading us to say that an old person living today has seen more changes in man's daily life than occurred in all previous history. This means, not only that the Church, like all institutions, must change in order to preserve itself; but that it is called by God to change in order that it may serve.

If men can travel by jet to the ends of the earth, or within dioceses by superhighway, it is clear that, reading aright the signs of the times, God calls us to a new *Mutual Responsibility and Interdependence in the Body of Christ.* Let no man say that this curtails our freedom; for freedom, properly understood, is always social and responsible. The speed of communication of the modern world, then, liberates us to be true members of the Church universal, to "bear one another's burdens," to die to old and false isolations, and to lose ourselves that we may find ourselves. The Church is not, by its nature, a series of parishes or dioceses—like marbles on a tray; it is, rather, a world body, brotherhood, fellowship, through which there moves a common divine life. Let us see, then, as a great opportunity, that the hand of God in modern history is pushing us together,

609

and calling us to become what we are. To fail to adapt to new facts, the life, forms, and structures of the Church at all levels (national, diocesan, and parochial) is a form of disobedience, a living to oneself, which receives an observable judgment.

All of us are sometimes numbed by the massiveness of the world's problems and needs. In addition to racial tensions, the problems of urbanism, and the threat of nuclear war, we know that half the world goes to bed hungry. But God does not call his creatures to an impossible task; nor, since our circumstances vary, does he ask of us primarily to "succeed." He asks of us, rather, loyalty in the station in which we are placed. God has placed us all in subdivisions, in platoons, of the one human race, and it is in these, and through these, that we are called to learn, grow, and act. Our own spiritual home, subdivision, platoon—call it what you will—is the great inclusive Anglican Communion. We are not disembodied creatures, vaguely looking at an impossible task; we are members of this branch of Christ's Church, with God calling us at our different levels to quite definite local responsibility, Anglican fellowship, and ever widening ecumenical encounter within the whole company of Christ's people.

III

Because theology should end in action, and great facts should appeal to the will, we ask all the dioceses and congregations of the Church, without exception, to do the following:

1. Since what we do with our money is significant as a symbol of what we are doing with our lives, join, as your circumstances dictate, in greater support in money and manpower, through old and new channels, to be developed by our Overseas Department and The Executive Council, in cooperation with other churches of the Anglican Communion. As we ask our people to be responsible stewards of their possessions, let the leaders of the local congregation, the diocese, and the general Church never for a moment forget they, too, are stewards responsible to God for the world mission of the whole body.

2. Let us study and evaluate the structure and organization of the church at the level for which we are responsible, and test every activity at every level by the test of mission and service to others. Do our organizations and activities conform to the great purpose of the Church? Are our structures appropriate?

"The Church exists to witness, to obey, and to serve," said the leaders of our world Church; and that means that organizational structure must follow purpose. Every department of the national Church and diocese, every vestry and local organization, must ask itself whether its structure and activities show forth what is really important to God and men. Why, for example, if we have borrowed money for ourselves, do we never think of borrowing for others? And why,

610

when a thousand dollars will build a church in Zululand, and eight thousand dollars double the salaries of twenty-eight priests in Malawi, do we not wrestle with the problem of priorities as we spend so much on ourselves at every level of the Church's life?

3. Let us learn humbly the way to receive, as well as to give, when we enter into deep relationship with other cultures and other Churches. It is always a peculiar arrogance to believe that we do not need to receive; that, spiritually, we possess all we need. Surely, if others increase our vision, warm our hearts, and teach us the glory of Christ, that is receiving. If our values are straight, we know that fellowship in Christ is an end in itself, and that what we give materially from our relative abundance is a little thing compared to the fellowship, faith, and new meaning that can light our altars as we truly work and pray for the whole state of Christ's Church. "I long to see you," says St. Paul to the Church in Rome; "I want to bring you some spiritual gift to make you strong—rather, that we may be mutually encouraged by each other's faith, both yours and mine."

4. Let us develop every possible channel for communication with our distant brethren in the Anglican Communion, as well, of course, with our brethren in other parishes in our own diocese. We can do this generally through *The Anglican World, The Episcopalian*, and other magazines, and through the guided and specific prayers of the booklet, *Make His Name Glorious,* published by The Forward Movement. We can write to the committee or department in our own diocese concerned with world mission, and ask for advice on a particular relationship we can build with far-off people.

Already this great movement has begun. Seventeen dioceses and 191 parishes have established companion relationships with missionaries and dioceses in other parts of our Communion. Sixty-five parishes are in a partnership program with parishes of the Philippine Independent Church. Twelve dioceses have established Departments of World Mission or Committees on Mutual Responsibility. Already the gifts of the United Thank Offering have gone to the ends of the earth. This letter requests that, without exception, we begin these new relationships, opening our hearts that new life may flow in.

It is true that a Church, living to itself, will die by itself. But it is also true that, if we live for others, we will be blessed in both obvious and subtle ways by the Servant Lord of the Church.

Stir up, we beseech thee, O Lord, the wills of thy faithful people; that they, plenteously bringing forth the fruit of good works, may by thee be plenteously rewarded; through Jesus Christ our Lord. Amen.

House of Bishops' Pastoral Letter, 1964, 3-8.

154.

Some Reflections on the Office of a Bishop, 1966

The Committee on the Office of a Bishop made the following statement on October 26, 1966, at Wheeling, West Virginia. George Leslie Cadigan (April 12, 1910–   ), the eighth Bishop of Missouri, May 15, 1959–April 16, 1975, was chairman of the committee. This statement about the ministry and office of a bishop was made at the time of the controversy over alleged heresy and misconduct by Bishop James A. Pike (February 14, 1913–September 3-7?, 1969), who served as Bishop of California from September 20, 1958 until September 15, 1966.

The contemporary Church is caught up in a monumental ecumenical involvement, the rediscovery of the Bible, liturgical reform, and theological creativity, which few institutions have ever before countenanced; strong dissent from the culture which embraces us, with anguishing divisions among the ranks; and with the swelling demand that the laity—not the clergy—be the Church. This theological revolution co-incides with an urbanized culture, the death knell of a white minority's untoward and cruel dominion, vast technological changes, the explosions of populations and the Bomb, and with the management of life not by the Church but by a tangled interlocking of public and private bureaucracies.

What is the role of a Bishop in all of this? Can the Bishops lead the People of God to bring the Gospel to God's People? Can Bishops assist in the discovery of new life in God's new world? Can God's world discover new life in the Church? What is God asking Bishops to do? A Bishop of modern Romanism, Anglicanism, or South India cannot have the same functions as a Bishop of the Second Century, or of the Fifth Century West, or of the Eighth Century East, or of Eighteenth Century England.

It is the considered opinion of your Committee on the Office of a Bishop that the Office of the Bishop must provide a viable and radical leadership in every area of diocesan policy. The opportunity and need are in the area of those "public ministries" outside the scope or principal purpose of the normally private and personal parish ministry. The priority policy of diocesan structure is development of ministry with "public impact". A Diocese will work with its parishes so that the primary thrust of Diocese and Parish is Mission. Provision of land and buildings, while sometimes essential, is not the high priority goal.

The commitment to public ministry means that a Diocese, through and with the Bishop, seeks to be the agent and enabler of social change in community policy affecting basic issues of community life. Change must be sought in the areas of education, housing, public welfare, poverty, race, etc., etc., etc. A

Diocese must accept its responsibility, along with other institutions, for shaping the community as well as for acting remedially within it. A Diocese has a particular responsibility to exercise theological reflection in the developing community and to insert such reflection and critique into the public processes of its area. Such commitment to "public" ministry includes recognition that lone-wolf denominational action in these sectors is not desirable, is easily neutralized, and is probably ineffective. A diocesan policy should be to work with existing ecumenical structures and to work for new ones where necessary. This implies that diocesan policy is to develop major sources of non-parochial revenue for non-parochial ministries and to do this ecumenically wherever and whenever possible.

The policy of ecumenical co-operation is pervasive but flexible. In any given area (geographical or topical), a Diocese must work with those who are available and willing, through ecumenical task forces and ecumenical structures created *ad hoc* for the work to be achieved. Similarly, a diocesan policy must promote and encourage co-operation and communication in the local parish units. In all of this, and much more, the concern, commitment, and action of the diocesan unit will be the reflection of the Bishop's attitude.

Structure in National Church and diocesan units will require radical change to meet the crises and emergencies of these times. Metropolitan regions span diocesan and provincial lines and require thought, consultation and co-operation involving jurisdictional boundaries. Co-operation between the Dioceses of Maryland and Washington, Missouri and Springfield, Quincy and Chicago, and other areas, is a hopeful sign. There are still larger groupings concerned with Cuban re-settlement, the American Indians, and Appalachia. The proposals of the Committee on Diocesan Boundaries and the Joint Commission on the Structure of General Convention and Provinces are exciting and need encouragement.

Finally, the relation of a Bishop to a jurisdiction should be seen in the context of a more flexible use of the episcopate. Translation of Bishops was approved by the 1964 General Convention and will come before the 1967 General Convention for a second reading. This is a step that should be most useful in the life of the Church. Further, the possibility that a Bishop, after a due period of service in the episcopate, might accept a call to parochial ministry or to other responsibilities, either within or without the structures of the Church, should be recognized as a valid Christian ministry. Question as to the right of such Bishops to vote in the House of Bishops must be raised. This issue is also posed by the increasing and alarming demand for more Suffragan Bishops. Action, therefore, should be initiated to relate the vote of a Bishop in the House of Bishops to jurisdiction.

The expression of the pastoral responsibility of Bishops one to another, both individually and corporately, needs strengthening. The status and work of Suffragan Bishops must be debated and clarified. Guidance should be offered to newly-consecrated Bishops. Retired Bishops should feel the continuing concern of the fellowship for them. Those who face special problems should be enfolded by pastoral care. To achieve this, more frequent, small informal gatherings of Bishops are to be preferred to larger meetings of the whole House. Such meetings, however, should not be wholly regional.

Organization is a responsibility which contemporary Bishops cannot avoid. Good procedures must therefore be learned and be implemented in diocesan structure. Administration can be seen as a pastoral opportunity to "minister to" many people, some of whose lives are touched by a Bishop only within these patterns of organizational life.

In all of these matters, the life of a Bishop is bound to the clergy of the Diocese and their life to his. For this relationship is a two-way street. As a Bishop is chief pastor to his clergy, so the clergy have a pastoral responsibility to the Bishop. Yet, as a Bishop seeks to implement his pastoral concern for the clergy, he discovers that he has responsibility without authority, especially in the critical area of the placement and use of the clergy. A Bishop does not long for autocratic power, but rather, for the ability, working with the Priesthood and with responsible parish authorities, to minister effectively in this all important realm and to serve the good of the Church. There is need for the House of Bishops to face the chaos of the present methods of deployment of clergy and to offer creative leadership through appropriate canonical legislation. Until this can be accomplished, Bishops should welcome personal approaches of the clergy relating to placement problems. The House of Bishops might well share specific individual situations, seeking together such solutions as are possible at the moment. There is also need of a Canon that will permit withdrawal from the normative ministry in order to serve in new ways in community, economic, or political life. Appropriate episcopal care should be provided for such experimental ministries.

The inescapable dilemma of a Bishop in these affairs is that he is both judge and pastor of the clergy. Under God's Grace, this can be resolved if both Priests and Bishops recognize that "Father in God" represents not sentimentality but strong love. Discipline can then be seen as an aspect of a pastoral and paternal relationship.

These are matters of great concern, for a Bishop is involved in lifelong responsibility for the clergy. At the very beginning of postulancy, help is needed in appraising men who offer themselves for the ministry. Regional arrangements akin to the conferences held in the Church of England for men anticipating the ministry should be considered. After ordination, in-service training of Deacons is imperative. Continuous post-ordination education of the clergy in a Diocese not only breathes vitality into the ministry of that Diocese, but builds understanding between the Bishop and the clergy and strengthens the fellowship within which both the clergy and the Bishop work.

A Bishop is consecrated in the Church of God to provide humble and courageous leadership for all the people of God. By what he does, but more essentially by what he is, will the evidences of reform and renewal emerge from the cloudy multiplicities and perplexities of our times.

Journal of General Convention, 1967, 35-37.

155.

John H. MacNaughton, The Day Your Dollar Became a Christian, 1975

John Herbert MacNaughton (November 19, 1929–   ) was consecrated Bishop Coadjutor of West Texas on February 6, 1986. He became the seventh Bishop of West Texas on February 12, 1987. This writing concerns the principles of Christian stewardship.

The fact is that no stated percentage gift adequately expresses our stewardship before God. Indeed, the fundamental relationship of God and man is not that of a master to a steward. The New Testament clearly related God and man, not as a master and steward, but as Father and Son. In the Gospels God is not pictured so much as someone who entrusts his property to a steward but as someone who gives his love to a son. And this is not merely a play on words. Try, for example, to expand the word stewardship so that it may include the concept of our sonship. We would put it in this way: "You are God's steward but you must exercise your stewardship as a son." But that puts the cart before the horse. It gives priority in the Christian life to the steward's qualities of faithfulness, responsibility, and integrity. But reverse the relationship. Say instead, "You are God's son and you are called to exercise your sonship as a faithful steward." Here it is the qualities of the son that come to the fore, the qualities of thankfulness, love, joy, and intimate relationship. And from this second view, another truth steps out for us. It is not a portion of what we have that belongs to God and therefore must be returned—all of what we have is God's, is the Father's. And far from returning that portion which is God's because it is his due from faithful stewards, we are called upon to return all of what we are given. And we return all of it, some in service, some in prayer, some in the quality of our relationship, some in talent developed and used, some in a life consecrated to Him, and some in specific material gifts, gifts of money thankfully calculated out of that part of God's bounty to us.

To be sure, both sets of qualities, those of the steward and those of the son, are part of our Christian response to God. But it is in the qualities of our sonship that the concept of proportionate giving has its resting place. The connection between the two can be stated this way: As sons of God, we have the relationship that speaks to the "why" of our giving; as proportionate givers, we have the discipline that speaks to the "how" of our giving.

John H. MacNaughton, *Stewardship: Myth and Methods. A Program Guide for Ministers and Lay Leaders* (New York: Seabury Press, 1975), 42-43. (Excerpt)

156.

Episcopalians — Profile 1979

The profile of Episcopalians, 1979, was part of the report of the Committee on the State of the Church presented to the sixty-sixth General Convention at Denver, September 6-20, 1979. Market Facts, Inc., of Chicago collected the data.

Preliminary Summary Of The Results

There is no such thing as an "average" Episcopalian. As with most groups, we tend to cluster above or below midpoints. And we are only beginning to study the co-variances—the instances of people in the majority in one category who may be equal to or opposite from the majority in other categories. But we still can get an overall picture from the early printouts. Here, instead of repeating the phrase, "Most Episcopalians are such and such . . .", we postulate entirely hypothetical persons, whom we might call

"Typical Episcopalians—first draft"

A typical Episcopalian is a woman over 49. She is probably not working. But if she is, either she or her husband is engaged in professional work or business rather than in manual labor or farming. She lives in a town of from 2,500 to 50,000 population, in the Northeast. Her husband is four years older than she is;

their two children are grown and living elsewhere. Both husband and wife are college graduates; their family income is over $20,000. Still, there are more than 300,000 Episcopalians whose family income is below $10,000!

Religion plays a *very* important part in their lives. They go to church almost once a week. They usually pray at least once a day. Grace is said at home at meals. They firmly believe in life after death. They think of Scripture as the inspired Word of God, although not to be taken entirely literally. They think of Jesus as God (or Son of God) rather than as a great leader or divinely-inspired man.

Either the wife or her husband came to the Episcopal Church from some other group—rather than from a non-religious background—probably from the Methodists, Baptists, Presbyterians, or Roman Catholics—in that order.

The family makes a regular pledge of financial support. They feel responsibility toward the diocese and national Church. But, in December, 1978, they had not yet heard of Venture in Mission.

When asked to tell us what they consider the most important issues facing the Church today, without any prompting, they listed items we might have expected: "women in the priesthood," "prayer book revision," and "need to increase membership, especially among youth." But they expressed far greater interest in the "ministry within the congregation," "responding to social issues," (although they thought us sufficiently involved in such issues), "the family," and an overwhelming concern for "evangelism and spreading the Gospel." They gave us these replies entirely gratuitously, in their own words.

The "Typical Episcopalian—first draft" became a member of a local parish and continues there because of its particular type of liturgical worship, and the way the faith is presented. But a major factor is preference for the rector and his sermons. The most-wanted parish programs are adult bible study or doctrinal study, more opportunities for weekday worship, and family-oriented activities.

Our typical member went to Sunday school as a child but has had little religious instruction as an adult. He or she thinks that both the elderly and youth receive enough attention from the Church, that we are sufficiently involved in the community, and have placed sufficient emphasis on social justice.

Most agree that the Proposed Book of Common Prayer provides excellent services of worship. A substantial minority—nearly 25%—disagree. Almost all feel there is poor communication between the national Church and the people. They are not sure our goals are understood.

The Untypical Episcopalian

An even less likely person is the "untypical Episcopalian." Even so, in the Church there are more than 100,000 Episcopalians—classified as "active" by their rector who—

—have not attended church in the past six months
—don't know whether they believe in life after death
—think the Bible is a book of fables
—but still pray
—disclaim any responsibility for the diocese and national Church
—became affiliated with a local parish primarily because of its location
—never had any confirmation instruction
—completely disagree with any approaches to Rome or Protestantism.

Comparison of Episcopalians With
The General Churched Population

One of the opportunities afforded by our survey is the ability to compare the ways in which Episcopalians are similar to the general churched population of the United States, or differ from it. We asked some questions which were worded so as to be comparable to those of other national surveys undertaken recently.

As with most churched people, Episcopalians are more likely to be women, older, married, and with a higher income than others in the population. Episcopalians, however, are even less likely than other churched people to live in a large city (over 1 million), or to be engaged in work that can be classified as non-business or non-professional. Levels of faith in God, Jesus Christ, eternal life, and prayer are similarly high among all religious people.

There are some ways, however, in which Episcopalians differ from other churched people. First, despite adverse publicity to the contrary, they appear to attend church more frequently. While 84% of all churched groups attend at least once a month, 91.9% of active Episcopalians attend at least once a month. Their habits of worship extend into their personal prayer life, for they pray more frequently in private, with family members at meals, and as a regular part of a prayer group.

Religious training and an intellectual attitude toward their faith also differentiate Episcopalians from other Christians. A surprising number—94%—of Episcopalians have attended Sunday school as compared with 88% of the general churched group. Even more surprising is the fact that 75% have received special confirmation training while only 54% of the general churched group had any special training for full membership in the Church. It is possible that this training is partly responsible for the fact that only 15% of Episcopalians believe in a literal interpretation of the Scripture, while 46% of the general churched population accept a fundamentalist viewpoint.

When asked what are the most important issues facing the church today, almost 30% point to a combination of membership loss, evangelism, outreach, and attendance. No other issue approaches this level of concern. But their assumption of responsibility to face such problems is another matter. Here is a comparison of replies to the question, "Have you, yourself, invited someone to become active in a church in your area in the last 12 months?"

	YES	NO
Churched people in general	58%	41%
Inactive members in general	52%	48%
Active Episcopalians	43%	57%

Journal of General Convention, 1979, AA275-AA277.

157.

John H. Westerhoff III, Living the Faith Community, 1985

John Henry Westerhoff III (June 28, 1933–   ) is a leading Christian educator and a popular writer. This passage describes the place of story in Christian formation.

We all need a story. Stories are reality. Stories provide us with both a memory linking us meaningfully to the past and a vision calling us to a purposeful future. That memory and that vision make life in the present possible. Without a story we would live in an unreal world, life would make no sense. Without a story we could not live, we could not have community. The story that is foundational to our life provides us with the basis for our perceptions or faith, as well as for our character and moral life. The story that forms Christian community is comprised of a common memory and a common vision.

A common memory: It is essential that we share a common sacred story to explain the meaning and purpose of life and that we transmit it to the next generation. Unless this shared story is alive and shared, the gift of community will elude us.

Jews (in contrast to Christians) put five commandments on each of the two tablets representing the Ten Commandments. One side lists those concerning humankind's relationship with God and the other side those regarding relationships with human neighbors. The one commandment that Jews put on the "God side" and we Christians put on the "neighbor side" is, "Honor your father and mother" (Exodus 20:12). Christians commonly interpret this commandment solely in terms of human relationships. Jews understand it as indicating that honor, deference, and respect should be given to all the elderly, because they have the memory of who we are; without their memory we cannot know or relate to the God who is God, who loves us and saves us.

A common vision: We need to share not only an understanding of the past but also a desired and anticipated future. We need visions, and wherever a vision is shared, the gift of community is made possible.

Harmon Smith, an Episcopal priest, tells of visiting Dachau, Germany, and becoming sick from the experience of seeing what Christians did to Jews. Reflecting on the Holocaust with Pastor Reiger, a member of the Lutheran Confessing Church and one who himself had been a prisoner at Dachau, Smith asked, "How could this have happened in the land of Luther and Bach?"

"That is easy to understand," the old man responded. "The Christian church had become concerned with the here and now, a very practical institution; it had lost its visions and forgotten what the Bible teaches—'without a vision the people perish.' But," he continued, "Hitler remembered, and he gave our people a vision."

Christians are a people on a pilgrimage through seasons of profane time made holy by the eternal cycle of sacred time. The church needs to find a way to live God's re-creative story so that it touches, illumines, transforms, and forms personal and corporate lives to serve God's purposes day by day.

John H. Westerhoff III, *Living the Faith Community: The Church Makes a Difference* (Minneapolis: Winston Press, 1985), 28-29. (Excerpt)

158.

Milbrew Davis,
Conclusions and Implications, 1986

Milbrew Davis (November 4, 1930–) is a priest in the Diocese of West Texas. Davis' conclusions are based on his history of St. Philip's Episcopal Church in San Antonio, Texas.

Freedom, in Christ, is not just some eschatological hope, rather it is a constant challenge here and now to resist all the forces that tend to create or perpetuate the sin of oppression and dehumanization, or encourage the sin of submission. Therefore, a significant learning from this study for the Episcopal Church, if the Church is to be most effective in its ministry to the Black community, is that the Church must be in the vanguard in recognizing and seeking more clearly to analyze those forces, both within the Church and without—racism, paternalism, cultural subjugation, economic exploitation, institutionalized dehumanization—which wreak havoc upon families, personal lives and communities. The Episcopal Church must bear true witness and bring the Gospel of the Lord to bear upon any and all forces that seek to reduce, destroy or make Black people other than children and heirs to God. To the extent that the Episcopal Church seeks to actualize the Body of Christ and all its members to the fullest potential—persons of varying ethnic cultures and backgrounds—to that extent will the Church be fully actualized and free.

Milbrew Davis, *History of St. Philip's Episcopal Church, San Antonio, Texas, 1895-1985: Implications for the Episcopal Church's Ministry to the Black Community* (San Antonio: Trader Publications, 1986), 139-140. (Excerpt)

159.

Girault M. Jones,
Member in Particular, 1987

Girault McArthur Jones (June 30, 1904–   ) was the seventh Bishop of Louisiana, March 9, 1949–August 31, 1969. He was also the sixteenth Chancellor of the University of the South, June 5, 1967–May 28, 1973. In this statement he recalls the early years of his life in the Church.

In those early years when no one else in the family could possibly go, Pap frequently took me to church with him. Our family pew was up front, and I still have visions of an elderly priest standing at the altar and, as I thought, looking directly at me as he said, "God spake these words and said . . . ." St. Paul's, Woodville, Mississippi, had no Church School at that time. My earliest impressions came as an observer, if not as a participant, in public worship.

I still sense the atmosphere (what today we would call the *ambience*) which pervaded those simple services. I say simple advisedly, for we had no choir, no acolytes, no crucifer, no candles, and all too often, no organist. Consider: An elderly priest, a congregation of perhaps thirty, a limited selection of hymns plaintively sung. Despite the *Venite*'s eager "O come let us sing," we muttered it. When we recited the *Jubilate*, there was little joy in it. It was, in all honesty, dull. Much of it would have long since faded from memory but for one thing, the silence. People would nod smilingly to one another but not a word was spoken until everyone was outside. Coming as I did from a very boisterous household of (ultimately) eight brothers, such silence was awesomely impressive. More than anything else, it told me that God was somehow present, that going to church was something special.

By the time I was eight or nine a small Church School had been initiated. Four age groups met in the four corners of the nave. We heard Bible stories and memorized the catechism regardless of what corner we occupied. Most of that memory work was largely meaningless to me. Our teachers could hear us recite but no one attempted to explain anything. I could understand that God had "made me and all the world," but what God the Son did when He "redeemed me and all mankind" was a mystery. God the Holy Ghost "who sanctifieth me and all the people of God" meant nothing at all. Today's children simply refuse to do that kind of memory work. Perhaps modern educators know better, but after seventy years I am still quoting that catechism, and I am grateful to those who required it of me.

I now recognize two strong aspects of that parish's life which had bearing on my subsequent growth. The first was the conviction (not then realized) that it was the fellowship of that congregation which created for me a sense of God's presence. I did not have the slightest inkling of any "real presence," nor had I ever heard of sacramental grace. God seemed simply closer in that small congregation than at my bedside. For all their simplicity there was a presence and a power residing in those services which was very real to me. I grew up understanding what Jacob meant when he said, "Surely the Lord is in this place." Looking back, it is not the church building that I remember. It is the people, their strict silence, their reverence, their friendliness. Like all children, I had seen my elders lock their fingers and say, "This is the church, this is the steeple; open the door and see all the people!" That symbolism told me that the steepled church was the people, that the living God was not simply in a building made with hands, but in them. . . .

As I was in the days of my youth . . .

In 1915 the Rev. Holly Wilberforce Wells became the rector of St. Paul's, Woodville. In a few months two older girls and I were going regularly to the rectory for confirmation instruction. I doubt if many eleven-year-olds remember much of such training after seventy years, but I do. Mr. Wells was a mystic, a poet, and a very perceptive teacher. He had heard us recite the catechism in Sunday School, and he did not ask it of us. Instead, he began in his own way to explain what it meant to be "a member of Christ, the child of God, and an inheritor of the kingdom of heaven." I soon knew that he was giving meaning to many empty phrases long familiar to me. I was fascinated, for he was answering questions which I had never voiced. It was as though I had been reciting verses in a foreign language and someone finally began to translate them for me.

I caught my first glimpse of the larger Church; I saw myself for the first time a member of something larger than the local congregation. The great Mississippi River flowed only a few miles west of us, and we knew it well. Mr. Wells used that river to illustrate his point. The Church is like a river, starting with very small beginnings and flowing through space and time, growing larger as it went. He stressed the oneness of that river, how the waters flowing past the western edge of our county were part of the same unbroken body all the way back to Minnesota. He insisted that nothing about the Mississippi was more important than its oneness, its continuity; it was that unbroken unity which gave it power. In the same way, the Christian Church runs unbroken all the way back to Christ. The power of the Church, like the power of the river, is *within itself.* If that power were not in the river, it would not be a river. If the power of God's Spirit were not in the Church, it would not be Christ's Church. To be a member of the Church is to be a living member of a body reaching back to its living source. Members of the Church today are as much a part of that unbroken stream as were Peter, James and John.

That illustration set me afire. I had sensed a stability rooted in some kind of antiquity, but I had seen it only in local terms. Suddenly, the apostolic church began to come into focus. To be a member of that kind of divine community was an awesome discovery. His concept of membership in Christ was so illuminating that it has been a cornerstone of my teaching ministry.

Mr. Wells did not limit himself to such sweeping illustration; he could easily shift to things more immediate and personal. He took us to the window to point out four or five pairs of oxen hauling a huge load of firewood to fuel our local power plant. He said, "Look at those oxen. Look at that heavy yoke across their shoulders. I doubt if all four of us could lift one." Then he added, "They have to carry a heavy yoke in order to pull a much heavier load. That yoke is like the Church. Without the Church no one could carry the burden of a Christian life. As a Church member, you have Our Lord holding up the other end of the yoke." Even a small child can remember that kind of teaching.

Girault M. Jones, *Member in Particular* (Sewanee, Tenn.: The University of the South, 1987), 4-5, 9-10. (Excerpts)

160.

Garrison Keillor, Episcopal, 1989

Garrison Keillor (August 7, 1942–   ) became a leading American humorist with his radio show, "A Prairie Home Companion." He had recently become active in the Episcopal Church at the time of this writing. He describes a newcomer's impressions of a liturgy in the Episcopal Church.

I don't have the manual dexterity to be a true Episcopalian, who must juggle the prayer book, hymnal, and the order of service, and sometimes a special mimeographed Kyrie or Sanctus; the music sounds thin and sharp to someone brought up on the Wesleys; the bowing and kneeling are odd—in the Brethren we just clomped in and sat down, and there was no incense in the air, just cologne, and no statuary (though some of our members were less lively than others); and then if, on top of that, the sermon is about revolutionizing our awareness of homeless gay handicapped Nicaraguans, the Episcopal church is more exotic to me than anything in Scandinavia.

> There's white folks and black, and gay and morose,
> Some male Anglo Saxons but we watch them pretty close.
> Episcopalian, saving my love for you.

Back in Minnesota, where words like "tuna hotdish," or "chicken," or "Lutheran" always got a laugh and a great joke might be one about Lutherans eating tuna hotdish and feeding the rest to their chickens, "Episcopalian" was also mighty funny, especially if a Lutheran became one. To me and to my little radio congregation, a Lake Wobegonian moving to Minneapolis and turning Episcopalian was a case of social climbing straight up the hill, no doubt about it. Our clear picture of Episcopalians was of wealthy people, Yale graduates, worshipping God in extremely good taste. Episcopalian was the church in wingtips, the church of the Scotch and soda. So, when I moved to New York and walked into Holy Apostles, I was surprised to see no suits. Nobody was well dressed. A congregation of a hundred souls on lower Ninth Avenue, a church with no parking lot, which was in need of paint and the sanctuary ceiling showed water damage, but which managed (I learned the next week) to support and operate a soup kitchen that fed a thousand New Yorkers every day, more than a million to date. Black faces in the sanctuary, old people, exiles from the Midwest, the lame and the halt, divorced ladies, gay couples: a real good anthology of the faith. I felt glad to be there. When we stood for prayers, bringing slowly to mind the goodness and the poverty of our lives, the lives of others, the life to come, it brought tears to your eyes, the simple way the Episcopalians pray.

A woman stood in the aisle, to the rear, and led us in prayers, stopping after each call to leave a long silence where anybody could breathe a word or two in response—a prayer in which the people fill in the blanks. She called us to *pray for the Church* (help this church, God) . . . *for peace and justice in the world* (stop the drugs, the corruption of government) . . . *for all those in need or trouble* (for the sick and the dying) . . . *for all who seek God* (for my family and all the Plymouth Brethren) . . . *for those who have died* (Corinne, the people on the Iranian airliner) . . . *and offer our thanks.* Thanks for bringing me here. Thank you.

Garrison Keillor, *We Are Still Married: Stories and Letters* (New York: Viking, 1989), 179-181. (Excerpt)

161.

Robert M. Cooper,
The Fantasy of Control, 1990

Robert March Cooper (May 19, 1935–   ) was professor of ethics and moral theology at Nashotah House, 1971-1980, and professor of ethics at the Episcopal Theological Seminary of the Southwest, 1980-1989. He discusses the role of surprise in the Christian life.

God is not capricious. This is easier to assert than it is to demonstrate. We may want to argue that in forming the world and continuing to form the world, God reveals an element of control to us. That is, we do not so much impose control on the world as we discover that the material of the world is already controlled. There are many issues raised in the earlier parts of this essay concerning the relationship between human freedom, individual and societal, with regard to control. We are concerned in Christian believing and thinking for the freedom of God. It may be frequently that we are not about to find the freedom of God because of the increasing routinization of our lives. That is, in our preoccupation with control and with our fantasy of control, we do not see often what, in fact, is there because we do not know how to look at the world in which we live. We easily mistake our ideas—especially if they work well for us—for the world itself. Put another way, our ideology overwhelms reality.

Our contemporary life abounds in a variety of bumper stickers that indicate that the drivers of the automobiles on which they appear would almost rather be doing anything other than what they are, in fact, doing. This attitude is also reflected in looking forward to weekends, in saying "Thank God! It's Friday." This can be read in the following way: Five days of the week, especially the hours nine to five, are under someone else's control. The hours of the weekend are under our control. This is an obvious way to read our own misery within our routinization. The weekend then becomes something other than the rest of the world for us. It may be for us "the most real" part of our week. We fantasize about it and plan for it in order to control it. Recreation has become work for us, time over which we have to exercise control toward our own pleasure, our own ends. Jacques Ellul has been helpful in enabling us to see that the ideology of technique has come to dominate most facets of the Western world. The domination of technique or method can be found not only in the ways in which we attempt to pray, meditate, and contemplate but in a more corporeal fashion when we proliferate books about how "to make love," to become better lovers, when what we mean actually is to become better technicians at arousal and at achieving or giving orgasms.

If we so structure our lives toward total control of them, it is more and more difficult to think about what God may be doing with regard to God's own control of the world. God, indeed, is surprise. This could be shown from a myriad of texts and themes in the biblical literature. Let it be sufficient simply to cite one crucial theme or event. The New Testament bears strong witness that God in Jesus is a colossal surprise. It is not expected that God will act the way God acts. God acts beyond our expectations and in spite of them. Ritual and schools of interpretation are never competent finally to control our life with God.

God as surprise appears among us and acts among us as One who puts life out of human control. Grace always is an indication that we are out of control. Every time we attempt to control grace we begin to replace the real world with our ideas of the world (ideology replaces and overwhelms reality) and we render frozen what God evidently intends to be still in the process of creation. Nearly everywhere we turn we try to change what is passing away into something fixed. This is idolatry. Idolatry will always be the enemy of surprise. If I were asked what this means, I could give a simple—beguilingly simple—reply. It means at least that there is before us (as there always has been) the task of becoming contemplative even while we are at the necessary work that the world in all of its exigencies lays upon us. What is before us is the task of learning again what reverence is like, what care is like, and what wonder is like. Not to be able to be surprised is to be dead, or, if it is not yet at that extremity, to be unable to be surprised is to be in hell, is to be in total fixity, and is to be without hope.

Robert M. Cooper, "The Fantasy of Control," *Saint Luke's Journal of Theology* 33 (September 1990): 268-269. (Excerpt)

162

Verna J. Dozier, Saying "Yes" in a "No" World, 1990

Verna J. Dozier (October 9, 1917–   ) is a lay person and a leading theologian of the Episcopal Church. She is an adjunct faculty member in New Testament at the Virginia Theological Seminary. She reflects on her identity as a black woman who has grown old.

I'm me
I'm good
'Cuz God made me
And God don't make junk.

I see that motto every day of my life. It hangs in my bedroom beside a small chest of drawers. It is spelled in different colored letters on burlap.

I grew up black in a world in which white was right. I am female in a world in which male is the currency of power. I am old in a culture that idolizes youth.

I'm me
I'm good
'Cuz God made me
And God don't make junk.

This is a faith statement.

For all who believe it, it is the Judeo-Christian declaration of independence from every tyranny of the demeaning estimates of the world.

But it is a faith statement. Faith is something I live by. It is a decision to risk that this is the way God meant the world to be.

In a world that exalts whiteness, maleness, youth, I live by the faith that whiteness, maleness, youth is not the best part of reality—nor the worst either—but only part of reality and indeed, without blackness, femaleness, age, a very incomplete part.

In strange ways that only the faithful know—and I cannot articulate—faith is not only the decision to risk; it is also the power to make that decision.

It is the courage to be, to affirm yourself in the face of all that denies you.

To be able to say YES to yourself when all the environment is shouting NO, but to be able to listen to that NO and hear what message it is sending from which you can profit—in my experience, that is certainly beyond the possibility of fragile human beings. That takes a leap of faith. That takes a religious dimension.

I was taken on a tour of Ethiopian museums a few years ago by a bitter, hostile youth. He said to me as he proudly showed off the figures of Ethiopian kings in all their splendid regalia, "I do not see why they always picture us as naked savages. We have always worn clothes." I wondered why wearing clothes was to him such a sign of worth. In the Genesis story nakedness was a sign of innocence. Human beings only felt the need for clothing when they felt the need to hide. But obviously my young dude was taking his signals from another drummer, and not necessarily the drummer of his fathers.

With sublime arrogance, Sir Kenneth Clark writes a book about a small part of the world and calls it *Civilization*, and even proud blacks who would protest it most fall unwitting prey to the stance.

Out of scores of definitions for "black" in the Oxford English Dictionary, only a few are not pejorative. Black hearse, black days, black moods. Black is bad. White is good. Howard Thurman noted that *Moby Dick* is the only instance in American literature where white is a sign of evil.

So blacks follow that example. If blacks have been condemned by whites, blacks will condemn whites. You hate me, I will hate you more.

The response was inevitable, since we all, I believe, participate in fallenness, but there is no redemption in the response. If I have to say a death-dealing NO to you in order to say YES to myself, you still have power over me. I am still bound by the model you set. There is no freedom for me in that. I cannot point the way to a new reign of God that way.

Living by the death of the other, however, not only characterizes the relationships between the races; it characterizes the relationships between the sexes.

Women the world over are struggling to find a new definition of themselves, and their big handicap in the struggle, as I see it, is we have no model but the male one. Kill or be killed, win or lose, YES to me, NO to you.

Western civilization said NO to the black. East and West said NO to women. But the United States has written its own unique chapter in human history in its disparagement of the aging.

Dourness about growing old is not, of course, unique in America. Ecclesiastes warns, "Remember now thy creator in the days of youth, while the evil days come not nor the years draw nigh when thou shall say, I have no pleasure in them." Then the old preacher goes on to paint as grim and realistic a picture of aging as you will find anywhere:

> . . . *and the keepers of the house shall tremble, and the strong men shall bow themselves, and the grinders cease because they are few, and those that look out of the windows be darkened . . . And also they shall be afraid of that which is high, and fears shall be in the way . . .*

In our country the picture is grim. This is a young country, and we have always worshipped at the shrine of youth. Old and ugly companion each other in our thoughts like apple pie and cheese.

"What's new?" is the classic American greeting, and growing old is a fate worse than death. Our folk heroes are those who lived hard and fast and died young. The specter of turning 40 traumatizes the nation. Mid-life is a crisis. Robert Butler aptly titles his book about growing old in America, *Why Survive?* And the question is not lightly asked. Our culture writes the aging off. We can look forward to victimization by young hoodlums in the decaying neighborhoods to which our lowered earning power condemns us, and victimization by our government because we are increasingly powerless and dependent.

Our wrinkled skin and slowed movements are too-vivid reminders to the young of the fate that awaits us all, and they would just as soon forget it.

The good news for me in growing old is that the old have the possibility of breaking that vicious human history of living by the death of the other. Older people have an invaluable gift to bring to the world— the gift of reconciliation. I have always been responsive to the Native American saying about not passing judgement on another human being until you have walked a mile in his/her moccasins. It occurs to me that therein lies the possibility for a holy gift the old can offer our increasingly polarized society. Blacks have never been white—a white reporter tried to be black once, but the catch was that he could never really understand what it was like to be black with no escape hatch. Women have never been men. Men have never been women.

Older people can model a kingdom-of-God way for the opposing camps in our society. We have known what it is to be young and angry. In our time we have raged against the tyranny of *our* elders. We have walked that mile in another's moccasins. We have another life to remember. We have another word to say.

How often the NO is said to those who look different. You can't be the same as I. You look so different. From there it is a short step to, "You can't be as good as I. You are inferior."

In the face of that NO, I, for my soul's sake must do two things. I must first affirm myself, affirm the very realities the other denies.

Yes, I am black and blackness is good.

Yes, I am a woman, and womanhood is good.

Yes, I am old, and age is good.

Ultimately, I can only do that by the power of a Creator who is for me. "If God be for us," says St. Paul, "who can be against us?"

And that trust brings me to the second thing I affirm in the face of the NO against me.

You are white or brown or copper, and any color is good.

You are male, and maleness is good.

You are young, and youth is good.

The Creator is for all creation. "And God saw everything that God had made, and behold, it was very good. And the evening and the morning were the sixth day."

That is my faith. And that, to me, is the possibility for a new humanity, every man, woman and child saying YES to themselves and YES to every other human being.

We're us
We're good
'Cuz God made us
And God don't make junk!

Verna J. Dozier, "Saying 'Yes' in a 'No' World," *The Witness* 73 (May 1990): 8-9.

163.

James E. Griffiss,
The Sacrament of Names, 1990

James Edward Griffiss (November 22, 1928–   ) was professor of systematic theology at Nashotah House, 1971-1990. He is now editor of the Anglican Theological Review. *He considers the use of names for God in theological language.*

Jesus directs us to God. His name—the name at which every knee must bow, as Paul says—is a sign or sacrament of God's presence with us. It is a name that calls us into silence before the mystery of God. When we reflect upon this dimension of the name of Jesus, we can perhaps see more deeply the significance of all our names for God. The two great names from Scripture—I Am and Father—are sacramental names, because they call us into silence before the mystery. So, too, are any other names we may use in prayer and worship. They can enable us to speak to or about God, while at the same time calling us to see that God utterly transcends every name. What is revealed to us in those names is that, at the heart of all that is—Being itself, reality, call it what we will—there exists a benevolence, a caring, what we attempt to express by the word Love. As all lovers know, there are times, even in this life, when the lover cannot any longer be named, when there can only be silence before so great a mystery.

In this book I have not argued for the validity of one name for God over another. But as Christian people engage in the sometimes painful, but also joyous, exploration of the names we use for God, my hope is that we shall remember the dangers implicit in our contemporary idolatries. Idolatry is making God in our own image. It is a temptation especially real for Christian people, because we believe in a God who took our human nature and entered the history of our createdness. We cannot flee to an unknown and nameless God, nor can we worship a God who is simply the kind of God we want the Holy One to be—a God made in our own image.

All of our categories, images, and concepts tell us something about God, but they do not limit the reality of the one to whom we pray, whom we worship, and about whom we speak. Paul Tillich once remarked that the Old Testament is the history of God's battle with our idolatries. God is the one who is always recalling us to the God who is to be worshipped with reverence and awe, for God is a "devouring fire" who will cleanse us from all our idolatries.

James E. Griffiss, *Naming the Mystery: How Our Words Shape Prayer and Belief* (Cambridge, Mass.: Cowley Publications, 1990), 177-178. (Excerpt)

164.

Thomas Shaw,
A Letter from the Superior, 1991

Marvil Thomas Shaw III (August 28, 1945–) served as Superior of the American province of the Society of St. John the Evangelist, known as the Cowley Fathers. The Society was founded in England in 1866 by Richard Meux Benson (1824-1915). The Society was established in the United States in 1872, and the mother house is in Cambridge, Massachusetts. In this passage he describes a transformative moment for his community.

Had it not been for a guest in our refectory, an important event in the contemporary history of the Society of St. John the Evangelist might have passed unnoticed by our Community. "When was your apocalyptic moment?" he asked as we settled down to luncheon. I questioned what he meant. "When you asked me to come and do this workshop for all of you today," he went on, "I had never heard of your Society. So I asked around. Almost always the response was the same. People told me there had been many moribund years in your Society's history but five or six years ago there had been a burst of creative energy in your Community life and apostolate that continues to affect the life of the Church.

Something dramatic must have happened. So what was the apocalyptic moment that changed it all?" he asked again.

Instantly all of us at the table knew the answer to our guest's question. The apocalyptic moment wasn't very flattering, actually. Paul Wessinger had been our Superior at the time and he asked the life-professed members of the Community if the five of us who were in first vows might be given the right to vote in Chapter meetings. The request was denied. Paul challenged the decision of the life-professed by resigning as Superior on the spot; the five of us who were in first vows left the Chapter room with Paul. After some discussion the life-professed members reconsidered their decision and invited us back to the Chapter and reinstated Paul as the Superior. We all knew that event was the answer to our guest's question: that was the apocalyptic moment which seemed to let loose the power of the Spirit in our Community.

Thomas Shaw, "A Letter from the Superior," *Cowley* 17 (Summer 1991): 2.

165.

Garret Keizer, A Dresser of Sycamore Trees, 1991

Garret Keizer was born in Paterson, New Jersey, in 1953 and is a high school teacher. In June 1992 he was ordained a deacon. He describes the risks and rewards of Christian ministry.

Then Amos answered Amaziah, "I am no prophet, nor a prophet's son; but I am a herdsman, and a dresser of sycamore trees, and the Lord took me . . ."

—Amos 7:14-15

I remember that my palms were sweaty, and my wife was pregnant, and that at one point during the sermon the stained-glass windows were suddenly flooded with sunlight. After two years of lay ministry in Island Pond, the bishop had decided that he wanted to give "formal recognition" to my work there. So he had come in mitre and cope, with a silver crozier and a "Letter of Institution" affixed with his red wax seal, to install me as Lay Vicar of Christ Episcopal Church.

It was a glorious day, and because I did not have to preach or lead any part of the service, I was relatively free to take it all in. My parts in the liturgy were to receive the tokens of my office—a prayer book, copies of the canons, a church key—from representatives of my parish, and to kneel once in the aisle, in the midst of the congregation, and say this prayer:

O Lord my God, I am not worthy to have you come under my roof; yet you have called your servant to stand in your house. To you and to your service I devote myself, body, soul, and spirit. Fill my memory with the record of your mighty works; enlighten my understanding with the light of your Holy Spirit; and may all the desires of my heart and will center in what you would have me do. Make me an instrument of your salvation for the people entrusted to my care, and grant that I may by my life and teaching set forth your true and living Word. Be always with me in carrying out the duties of my ministry. In prayer, quicken my devotion; in praises, heighten my love and gratitude; in preaching, give me readiness of thought and expression; and grant that, by the clearness and brightness of your holy Word, all the world may be drawn into your blessed kingdom. All this I ask for the sake of your Son our Savior Jesus Christ. Amen.

In my case the prayer had had to be modified slightly. I did not pray to "faithfully administer your holy Sacraments" because as a lay person I could not do so. Once a month a priest from a neighboring parish would come and celebrate Communion, consecrating enough bread and wine for me to take to the sick until she returned again.

That difference notwithstanding, I felt myself a very special person that day and thereafter. I was to my knowledge the only lay vicar in the state, and I know of none elsewhere. I thought of the prophet Amos, "a herdsman and dresser of sycamore trees," seized unaccountably by the call of the Lord and sent to prophesy to Israel. Like him, I had been raised to an important task. And like him, in spite of the ceremony and its insignia, I was completely without credentials. "I am no prophet, nor a prophet's son . . ." I had never been to seminary. I was trained to be a high school English teacher. I had been confirmed in the church only several years before. I felt exalted, yes, but also at sea.

Yet, as I look back on the service of my institution, as "special" as it seemed and truly was, it bears a striking resemblance to nearly every other service in the prayer book. It was like a wedding in which a couple vows to love and honor each other for a lifetime; like a baptism in which parents and godparents vow to raise another human being, as yet a stranger to them, in the image of Christ; like a Eucharist in which we say "amen" to the announcement that the flimsy wafer we are about to eat is the Body of Christ. In short, it was like every other service in which we are sent out to sea in a frail little craft with a few provisions and a few stars to guide us.

Irish monks in the Dark Ages would sometimes be set adrift, literally, in just this way, hoping to land somewhere as missionaries, but realizing they might just as likely drown. They were only a little braver than the average bride and groom. Their mission was only a little more desperate than that of a conscientious parent. They looked only a little more precarious bobbing over the horizon than I did rising from my solemn prayer that day. They required only a little more faith.

So, when people have asked me what this book I am writing is about, after I tell them it is about my ministry in Island Pond, and after I tell them that the title comes from Amos, I say that the book is about doing any work for which one has had very little formal preparation. I tell them it is, essentially, a book about what almost everybody I know is doing almost every day of his or her life.

Garret Keizer, *A Dresser of Sycamore Trees* (New York: Viking, 1991), 46-48. (Excerpt)

APPENDIX

Chronology of Episcopal Church History

August 6, 1782   Publication of William White's *The Case of the Episcopal Churches in the United States Considered.*

August 13, 1783   Maryland clergy met at Annapolis and officially adopted the name "Protestant Episcopal Church." This name was first used on November 9, 1780, by a conference of clergy at Chestertown, Maryland.

November 14, 1784   Samuel Seabury consecrated Bishop of Connecticut by Bishops of the Scottish Episcopal Church at Aberdeen. First American Episcopal Bishop.

November 15, 1784   Concordat of Bishop Seabury and the Nonjuring Scottish Bishops, His Consecrators.

August 15, 1785   Letter of Samuel Seabury to William Smith.

September 27–October 7, 1785   First General Convention at Christ Church, Philadelphia.

October 5, 1785   Letter to the Most Reverend and Right Reverend, the Archbishops of Canterbury and York, and the Bishops of the Church of England.

April 1, 1786   "Proposed Book" of Common Prayer published. It contained a "Preface" by William Smith.

June 20–26, October 10-11, 1786	Second General Convention at Christ Church, Philadelphia, and Wilmington, Delaware.
July 28–August 8, September 30–October 16, 1789	Third General Convention at Christ Church, Philadelphia. On October 16 it adopted the Constitution of the Protestant Episcopal Church in the United States of America.
1793	Samuel Seabury, "On Christian Unity."
August 23, 1795	Absalom Jones (November 6, 1746-February 13, 1818) ordained deacon by Bishop William White at St. Thomas Church, Philadelphia. First Black Episcopal deacon in the United States.
1803	Vestry minutes of St. Michael's Church, Charleston, South Carolina.
1806	The Life of the Reverend Devereux Jarratt.
January 1, 1808	Absalom Jones, A Thanksgiving Sermon.
May 18, 1814	John Henry Hobart, *The Origin, the General Character, and the Present Situation of the Protestant Episcopal Church in the United States of America—A Sermon, Preached in St. James's Church in the City of Philadelphia, on Wednesday, May 18th, A.D. 1814, On the Occasion of the Opening of the General Convention of the said Church, and of the Consecration of the Right Rev. Bishop Moore of Virginia.*
May 27, 1817	Twelfth General Convention at New York, May 20-27, adopted resolutions approving the establishment of the General Theological Seminary in New York.
June 7, 1820	Philander Chase, Sermon.
October 30–November 3, 1821	First Special General Convention at Philadelphia amended and adopted the Constitution of the Domestic and Foreign

	Missionary Society of the Protestant Episcopal Church.
October 23, 1823	Protestant Episcopal Theological Seminary in Virginia opened at Alexandria.
November 3, 1824	Bexley Hall Theological Seminary founded at Worthington, Ohio. In 1828 it moved to Gambier, Ohio.
1826	Organization of the General Protestant Episcopal Sunday School Union.
May 20-22, 1834	Fiftieth Convention of the Diocese of Pennsylvania. William White presented "The Past and the Future, A Charge, on Events Connected With the Organization of the Protestant Episcopal Church in the United States of America, and the Lessons They Inculcate."
August 19–September 1, 1835	Eighteenth General Convention at Philadelphia created the office of missionary bishop.
September 25, 1835	Jackson Kemper consecrated Missionary Bishop of Missouri and Indiana. First missionary bishop of the Episcopal Church. George Washington Doane preached on "The Missionary Bishop."
January 1836	*The Spirit of Missions* began publication. It was published until December 1939.
November 27, 1836	George Washington Freeman delivered two discourses at Christ Church, Raleigh, North Carolina, on "The Rights and Duties of Slave Holders."
October 7, 1841	Jackson Kemper, "The Duty of the Church With Respect to Missions."
1841	Charles P. McIlvaine, *Oxford Divinity: Compared with the Romish and Anglican Churches.*

August 30, 1842	Nashotah House Seminary and semi-monastic community established at Nashotah, Wisconsin.
1847	Evangelical Knowledge Society founded.
1851	William Meade, *The True Churchman*.
October 5-26, 1853	Twenty-fourth General Convention at New York. Muhlenberg Memorial presented to House of Bishops.
May 5, 1854	Berkeley Divinity School founded by Bishop John Williams at Middletown, Connecticut.
1854	James Lloyd Breck, "Indian Mission—Minnesota."
October 1-21, 1856	Twenty-fifth General Convention at Philadelphia. "Preliminary Report on the Memorial" presented.
July 4, 1857	The University of the South, Sewanee, Tennessee, founded.
1857	Philadelphia Divinity School founded by Bishop Alonzo Potter.
1858	Seabury Theological Seminary founded by James Lloyd Breck at Faribault, Minnesota.
October 5-22, 1859	Twenty-sixth General Convention at Richmond. "Address to Their Brethren of the Laity of the Protestant Episcopal Church, By the Committee Appointed by the Session of the General Convention." James H. Otey, "Christian Education."
January 30, 1861	Pastoral Letter of Bishop Leonidas Polk.
January 1861	John Henry Hopkins, *Bible View of Slavery*.
1862	Pastoral Letter of House of Bishops, Protestant Episcopal Church.
November 3, 1862	Evangelical Education Society founded.

November 12-22, 1862	First General Council of the Protestant Episcopal Church in the Confederate States of America at Augusta, Georgia. Pastoral Letter of the House of Bishops.
1862	William Porcher DuBose, "War Experiences."
February 2, 1865	Sisterhood of St. Mary founded at St. Michael's Church, New York.
April 23, 1865	Phillips Brooks, "Abraham Lincoln."
October 29, 1865	Morgan Dix, "A Sermon Preached at St. Paul's Chapel, Trinity Parish, New York."
1867	Episcopal Theological School founded at Cambridge, Massachusetts.
1868	Thomas C. Brownell, "Of the Advantages of Forms of Prayer for Public Worship."
1869	Henry Champlin Lay, "The Missionary in the Field."
1871	Pastoral Letter on Baptismal Regeneration and Eucharistic Adoration.
1871	Thomas H. Vail, "Further Reflections on Church Comprehensiveness."
1872	Cowley Fathers established in Boston.
December 2, 1873	Reformed Episcopal Church organized in New York City.
February 2, 1874	Reply of Bishop Johns to Rev. J. A. Latané's Letter of Withdrawal.
October 6-7, 1874	First Church Congress at New York. William D. Wilson, "The Mutual Obligations of Capital and Labor."
October 26, 1874	James DeKoven, "The Canon on Ritual."
August 31, 1875	James DeKoven, "A Letter to the Clergy and Laity of the Diocese of Illinois in Convention Assembled."

1877	Phillips Brooks, *Lectures on Preaching*.
1877	Samuel Isaac Joseph Schereschewsky, Appeal for Funds to Establish a Missionary College in China.
1878	School of Theology, The University of the South, formally opened.
August 31, 1879	Letter of Sister Constance of the Sisterhood of St. Mary.
April 1881	William Reed Huntington, "Revision of the American Common Prayer."
1881	Thomas Gallaudet, "Church Work Among Deaf Mutes, Past, Present and Future."
July 25-28, 1883	Sewanee Conference on the Relation of the Church to the Coloured People.
1883	Richard Hooker Wilmer, "Contrary to the Mind of Christ."
October 3, 1883	Thomas March Clark, "The Mission of the Church."
December 1883	Western Theological Seminary established by Bishop William E. McLaren at Chicago.
November 25, 1884	Order of the Holy Cross (first American religious order for men) founded.
1884	Morgan Dix, "The Oxford Movement."
October 6-28, 1886	Thirty-fifth General Convention at Chicago. "Chicago Quadrilateral."
1886	Fred S. Jewell, "The Special Beliefs and Objects of Catholic Churchmen: A Statement."
1887	Constitution of the Church Association for the Advancement of the Interest of Labor.
July 3-27, 1888	Third Lambeth Conference adopted the Chicago-Lambeth Quadrilateral.

1889	Channing Moore Williams, "Annual Report of the Missionary Bishop of Yedo."
1890	George Hodges, *The Heresy of Cain.*
1891	William Reed Huntington, "Popular Misconceptions of the Episcopal Church, That It Is Given Over to Worldliness."
October 5-25, 1892	Thirty-seventh General Convention at Baltimore. Authorized a new *Book of Common Prayer.*
1893	Church Divinity School of the Pacific founded by Bishop William Ford Nichols at Berkeley, California.
1894	William J. Gold, "The Continuity of the Principles of Divine Worship, Contained in the Book of Common Prayer."
November 13-16, 1894	Sixteenth Church Congress at Boston. Francis A. Shoup, "Paper on Evolution."
1895	Francis J. Hall, "The Historic Episcopate."
August 1, 1897	Thomas F. Gailor, "A Church University."
1897	J. A. Ingle, "The Work at Hankow, China."
1897	Alexander Crummell, "Modifications of Methods of Work Among the Colored People."
October 2-19, 1907	Forty-second General Convention at Richmond. "Report of Joint Committee on Memorial from Conference of Workers Among the Colored People."
1909	Charles D. Williams, "The Value of a Man."
October 5-21, 1910	Forty-third General Convention at Cincinnati. "Report of Joint Commission on the Relations of Capital and Labor."
1914	George Hodges, "The Church and the Labor Movement."

1914	Charles C. Grafton, "The Catholic Movement."
1915-1916	Julia Chester Emery, "Forty-Fifth Annual Report of the Woman's Auxiliary to the Board of Missions."
October 1916	William Lawrence, "Educational Organization in the Church."
1916	Henry Y. Satterlee, "The Idea of an American Cathedral."
February 5, 1917	Hughell E. W. Fosbroke, "The One Foundation: The Dean's Installation Sermon."
October 17-18, 1917	The Forced Resignation of Bishop Paul Jones. Pastoral Letter of the House of Bishops.
1917	William Porcher DuBose, "The Church."
October 8-24, 1919	Forty-sixth General Convention at Detroit. Created the National Council (at first called the "Presiding Bishop and Council," now called the Executive Council). Presiding Bishop would be elected by the House of Bishops and confirmed by the house of Deputies. Launched "The Nation-wide Campaign."
1919	James O. S. Huntington, "Bargainers and Beggars."
September 6-23, 1922	Forty-seventh General Convention at Portland, Oregon. "The Church and World Peace."
October 10-25, 1928	Forty-ninth General Convention at Washington, D.C. Authorized a new *Book of Common Prayer*.
1929	Amy M. Burt, "U.T.O. Worker at Appalachian School."
1931	Thomas C. Darst, "He Loved Me, and He Gave Himself for Me."

July 1, 1933	Western Theological Seminary and Seabury Divinity School merged as Seabury-Western Theological Seminary at Evanston, Illinois.
November 9, 1933	Pastoral Letter of the House of Bishops.
1933	James O. S. Huntington, "Beginnings of the Religious Life for Men in the American Church."
1934	Vida D. Scudder, "Social Problems Facing the Church in 1934."
1934	Edward Lambe Parsons, *The Liberal Evangelicals' Message in Our Church Today*.
1935	Winfred Douglas, *Music Expresses Human Life*.
February 16, 1937	American Church Union organized.
November 11, 1939	Episcopal Pacifist Fellowship founded at the Church of the Incarnation, New York.
May 7, 1942	The Presiding Bishop's Fund for World Relief established.
1943	Walden Pell and Powell M. Dawley, *The Worship of the Church*.
1946	Angus Dun, "The Church: A Community."
1948	*The Church Looks Ahead to the New Curriculum: Specifications*.
September 26–October 7, 1949	Fifty-sixth General Convention at San Francisco. "Statement of Faith and Order."
1949	Theodore O. Wedel, *The Church's Teaching: An Introduction*.
1949	Charles Henry Brent, "That They All May Be One."
1950	*Prayer Book Studies I*.
September 1951	Episcopal Theological Seminary of the Southwest established at Austin, Texas.

1952	Massey H. Shepherd, Jr., "The Christian Year."
1952	"Integration Crisis at Sewanee."
1954	W. Norman Pittenger, "Controlled Sex."
September 4-15, 1955	Fifty-eighth General Convention at Honolulu. Statement on Racial Cooperation.
1958	Anglican Fellowship of Prayer, A Rule of Life and a Prayer.
1959	Lyman C. Ogilby, "The Church's Mission II."
1960	H. Boone Porter, "Then Cometh the End."
September 17-29, 1961	Sixtieth General Convention at Detroit. "Report of the Joint Commission on Church Music." "Report of Committee of Conference on Overseas Missions to the Presiding Bishop and the National Council."
1961	"The Problem and Method of Prayer Book Revision."
1961	John M. Gessell, "The Urgency of the Church's Educational Task: Prolegomena to Any Future Theology of Christian Education."
1962	Virginia Cary Hudson, "Etiquette at Church."
October 11-23, 1964	Sixty-first General Convention at St. Louis. House of Bishops, Pastoral Letter. Statement on War and Peace.
1964	Peter Day, "Episcopalians and Ecumenicity."
1964	Fellowship of Witness Doctrinal Basis.
1965	*American Martyr: The Jon Daniels Story.*
1965	Sam Shoemaker, *Extraordinary Living for Ordinary Men.*
1966	"Progress Report to the House of Bishops from the Committee to Study the Proper Place of Women in the Ministry of the Church."

1966	William Stringfellow, "The Liturgy as Political Event, The Political Authority of Baptism."
1966	"Some Reflections on the Office of a Bishop."
September 17-27, 1967	Sixty-second General Convention at Seattle. John Hines, "Sermon." General Convention Special Program (GCSP) approved. Women authorized to serve as deputies to the General Convention. "Theological Freedom and Social Responsibility."
1968	Jenny Moore, *The People on Second Street*.
August 31–September 5, 1969	Second Special General Convention at South Bend, Indiana. Granted $200,000 to the Black Economic Development Conference.
1970	Standing Liturgical Commission, *Prayer Book Studies* 26: "On Baptism and Confirmation."
1971	Dennis and Rita Bennett, "The Overflow."
June 30, 1971	Berkely Divinity School, New Haven, Connecticut, merged with Yale Divinity School.
September 26–October 22, 1973	Sixty-fourth General Convention at Louisville. Statement on "Euthanasia and Abortion."
June 6, 1974	Philadelphia Divinity School merged with Episcopal Theological School at Cambridge, Massachusetts. Named Episcopal Divinity School.
July 29, 1974	Irregular ordination of eleven women to the priesthood at Church of the Advocate, Philadelphia.
1974	John H. Westerhoff III, "Challenge to Church Educators."
1975	John B. Coburn, "Don't Waste Pain."

1975	John H. MacNaughton, "The Day Your Dollar Became a Christian."
1975	Coalition for the Apostolic Ministry: A Declaration of Principle.
September 11-22, 1976	Sixty-fifth General Convention at Minneapolis. Approved ordination of women to the priesthood and the episcopate. Statement on "The Church and Homosexual Persons." Massey Shepherd, "Prayers."
September 25, 1976	Trinity Episcopal School for Ministry opened at Ambridge, Pennsylvania.
1976	Marion J. Hatchett, "Sanctifying Life, Time and Space."
1976	Carter Heyward, *A Priest Forever*.
1977	Wesley Frensdorff, "Holy Orders and Ministry: Some Reflections."
1977	*Parish Eucharist*.
October 3, 1977	House of Bishops' "Statement of Conscience."
1978	James C. Fenhagen, "The Many Faces of Ministry."
September 6-20, 1979	Sixty-sixth General Convention at Denver. Authorized a new *Book of Common Prayer*. "The Episcopal Church" officially became an alternative name for "The Protestant Episcopal Church in the United States of America." "Declaration on Unity." "Commentary on Eucharistic Sharing." "Episcopalians—Profile 1979."
1979	Bob Slosser, *Miracle in Darien*.
1979	"Journey Toward Justice."
1979	Charles P. Price and Louis Weil, *Liturgy for Living*.

1979	Education for Ministry, "Theological Reflection."
1980	Betty Pulkingham and Mimi Farra, "Cry Hosanna."
1980	Marion J. Hatchett, "The Musical Ministry of the People."
1981	Urban T. Holmes, "Education for Liturgy."
September 5-15, 1982	Sixty-seventh General Convention at New Orleans. Approved *Hymnal 1982*. "Principles of Unity." "A Theology and Policy of Mission in Global Perspective." "Lutheran-Episcopal Dialogue."
1982	"Introducing the Hymnal."
1982	*The Final Report: Anglican-Roman Catholic International Commission.*
1982	M. Fletcher Davis, *Of Foxes and Birds and the Son of Man: Ministry to Refugees and Other Strangers.*
1983	Michael T. Malone, "Traditionalist–Renewalist Tensions."
1984	Robert A. Bennett, "The Power and Promise of Language in Worship: Inclusive Language Guidelines for the Church."
September 7-14, 1985	Sixty-eighth General Convention at Anaheim, California. Edmond Browning, "Address to General Convention."
1985	Marion J. Hatchett, "Architectural Implications of *The Book of Common Prayer*."
1985	Leonel L. Mitchell, *Praying Shapes Believing.*
1985	John H. Westerhoff III, *Living the Faith Community: The Church Makes a Difference.*

1986	Milbrew Davis, "Conclusions and Implications."
1987	"What is Cursillo?"
1987	Girault M. Jones, *Member in Particular*.
February 11, 1989	Barbara Clementine Harris consecrated Suffragan Bishop of Massachusetts. First woman bishop.
1989	Garrison Keillor, "Episcopal."
1990	Robert M. Cooper, "The Fantasy of Control."
1990	Verna J. Dozier, "Saying 'Yes' in a 'No' World."
1990	James E. Griffiss, "The Sacrament of Names."
1991	Thomas Shaw, "A Letter from the Superior."
1991	Garret Keizer, *A Dresser of Sycamore Trees*.

Biographical Information

Don S. Armentrout has taught church history at the School of Theology, the University of the South, since 1967. He is a graduate of Roanoke College, and received his Master of Divinity degree from the Lutheran Theological Seminary, Gettysburg. His Ph.D. is from Vanderbilt University. He is Professor of Church History and Historical Theology and Associate Dean of Academic Affairs at the School of Theology.

Robert Boak Slocum, an Episcopal priest, has served parishes in the dioceses of Louisiana and Milwaukee. He is a graduate of the College of Arts & Sciences and the Law School of Vanderbilt University. He received a Master of Divinity from Nashotah House Seminary, and a Doctor of Ministry from the School of Theology of the University of the South. He is currently Rector of the Church of the Holy Communion, Lake Geneva, Wisconsin, and a doctoral theology student at Marquette University.

INDEX

A

Abortion, 513
Allin, John M., 460
American Church Union, 98
Anglican Fellowship of Prayer, 541, 545
Anglican-Roman Catholic International
  Commission ("dialogue"), 485
Anglo-Catholics, 39, 73, 77, 82, 88
Architecture, 236, 298
Associated Parishes, 283

B

Baptismal regeneration, 39, 66
Bayne, Stephen Fielding, Jr., 579-580
Bennett, Dennis Joseph, 561
Bennett, Rita, 561
Bennett, Robert Avon, 296
Blake, Eugene Carson, 460, 579
Bliss, William Dwight Porter, 310
Book of Common Prayer, 40, 212, 236, 237, 243,
  246, 250, 251, 261, 266, 274, 280, 288, 289,
  298, 300, 312, 419
Breck, James Lloyd, 126
Brent, Charles Henry, 460, 461
Brooks, Phillips, 181, 193, 530
Brownell, Thomas Church, 246
Browning, Edmond Lee, 452, 573, 603
Burt, Amy M., 435

C

Cadigan, George Leslie, 612
Cannon, Harriett Starr, 146
Chase, Philander, 99
Chicago-Lambeth Quadrilateral, 208, 224, 227,
  228, 250, 464, 483, 605
Church Association for the Advancement of the
  Interest of Labor, 302, 310
Church Constitution, 2
Church Idea, The, 208, 224
Claggett, Thomas, 1
Clark, Thomas March, 142
Coalition for the Apostolic Ministry, 597
Coburn, John Bowen, 552
Community of Celebration, 568
Comprehensive Church, The, 605
Concordat of Agreement, 14
Constance, Sister, 146
Constitution of the Protestant Episcopal Church
  in the United States of America, 24
Consultation on Church Union, 460, 472

Cooper, Robert Marsh, 625
Cowley Fathers, 631
Crummell, Alexander, 152
Cry Hosanna, 568
Cursillo, 571

D

Daniels, Jonathan Myrick, 505
Darst, Thomas Campbell, 532
Darwin, Charles, 400
Davis, M. Fletcher, 523
Davis, Milbrew, 620
Dawley, Powell Mills, 257
Day, Peter Morton, 472
Decade of Evangelism, 429
DeKoven, James, 39, 73, 77
Dix, Morgan, 79, 176
Doane, George Washington, 108
Douglas, Charles Winfred, 254
Dozier, Verna J., 627
Dresser of Sycamore Trees, A, 632
DuBose, William Porcher, 173, 407
Dun, Angus, 538

E

Education for Ministry, 392
Emery, Julia Chester, 429
Enmegahbowh, 127
Episcopal Peace Fellowship, 338
Eucharistic adoration, 39, 66
Eucharistic controversy, 77
Eucharistic sharing, 480
Euthanasia, 513
Evangelical Knowledge Society, 58
Evangelical Lutheran Church, 460, 488
Evangelicals, 39, 58, 62, 419
Evolution, 400, 407

F

Farra, Mimi, 568
Fellowship of Witness, 559
Fenhagen, James Corner, II, 447
Fisherfolk, 568
Fosbroke, Hughell Edgar Woodall, 370
Francis, Sister, 146
Freeman, George Washington, 187
Frensdorff, Wesley, 445
Fullam, Everett Leslie (Terry), 565

G

Gailor, Thomas Frank, 366
Gallaudet, Thomas, 139

Pike, James Albert, 579, 612
Pittenger, William Norman, 497
Polk, Leonidas, 156
Porter, Harry Boone, 606
Potter, Henry Codman, 536
Prayer Book (see *Book of Common Prayer*)
Presiding Bishop's Fund for World Relief, 523
Price, Charles Philip, 285
Protestant Episcopal Church in the Confederate
    States of America, 156, 164, 200
Provoost, Samuel, 1
Pulkingham, Betty, 568

Q

Quadrilateral (see Chicago-Lambeth
    Quadrilateral)
Quintard, Charles Todd, 146, 156, 176

R

Reformed Episcopal Church, 68
Ruth, Sister, 146

S

Satterlee, Henry Yates, 434
Schereschewsky, Samuel Isaac Joseph, 137
Scudder, Vida Dutton, 357
Seabury, Samuel, 1, 14, 17, 27, 40, 236
Shaw, Marvil Thomas, III, 631
Shepherd, Massey Hamilton, Jr., 262, 553
Shoemaker, Helen Smith, 541
Shoemaker, Samuel Moor, 541, 545
Shoup, Francis Asbury, 400
Slosser, Bob, 565
Smith, William, 17, 237
Society of St. John the Evangelist, 631
Standing Commission on Church Music, 288, 293

Standing Commission on Ecumenical Relations,
    480
Standing Commission on Human Affairs and
    Health, 520
Standing Commission on World Misson, 452
Standing Liturgical Commission, 261, 266, 274,
    296
Stewardship, 615
Stringfellow, William, 548
Syle, Henry Winter, 139

T

Thecla, Sister, 146

U

United Thank Offering, 435

V

Vail, Thomas Hubbard, 605

W

War, 338, 342, 351, 353, 501
Wedel, Theodore Otto, 378
Weil, Louis, 285
Westerhoff, John Henry, III, 391, 619
White, William, 1, 2, 30, 181, 243
Williams, Channing Moore, 148
Williams, Charles David, 318
Wilmer, Richard Hooker, 156, 176, 200
Wilson, William DeLancey, 302
Woman's Auxiliary to the Board of Missions of
    the Episcopal Church, 429, 435
Women and Ministry, 429, 435, 573, 597, 598,
    599, 627
World Council of Churches, 460, 461
Wright, Nathan, Jr., 525